TAKING SIDES

Clashing Views in

Special Education

FOURTH EDITION

TAKING SIDES

Clashing Views in
Special Education

FOURTH EDITION

Selected, Edited, and with Introductions by

MaryAnn Byrnes
University of Massachusetts–Boston

McGraw-Hill
Higher Education

Boston   Burr Ridge, IL   Dubuque, IA   New York   San Francisco   St. Louis
Bangkok   Bogotá   Caracas   Kuala Lumpur   Lisbon   London   Madrid   Mexico City
Milan   Montreal   New Delhi   Santiago   Seoul   Singapore   Sydney   Taipei   Toronto

McGraw-Hill
Higher Education

TAKING SIDES: CLASHING VIEWS IN SPECIAL EDUCATION, FOURTH EDITION

Published by McGraw-Hill, a business unit of The McGraw-Hill Companies, Inc., 1221 Avenue of the Americas, New York, NY 10020. Copyright © 2009 by The McGraw-Hill Companies, Inc. All rights reserved. Previous edition(s) 2002–2008. No part of this publication may be reproduced or distributed in any form or by any means, or stored in a database or retrieval system, without the prior written consent of The McGraw-Hill Companies, Inc., including, but not limited to, in any network or other electronic storage or transmission, or broadcast for distance learning.

Some ancillaries, including electronic and print components, may not be available to customers outside the United States.

Taking Sides® is a registered trademark of the McGraw-Hill Companies, Inc.
Taking Sides is published by the **Contemporary Learning Series** group within the McGraw-Hill Higher Education division.

1 2 3 4 5 6 7 8 9 0 DOC/DOC 0 9 8

MHID: 0-07-351539-6
ISBN: 978-0-07-351539-7
ISSN: 1537-0739

Managing Editor: *Larry Loeppke*
Senior Managing Editor: *Faye Schilling*
Developmental Editor: *Jade Benedict*
Editorial Assistant: *Nancy Meissner*
Production Service Assistant: *Rita Hingtgen*
Permissions Coordinator: *Shirley Lanners*
Senior Marketing Manager: *Julie Keck*
Marketing Communications Specialist: *Mary Klein*
Marketing Coordinator: *Alice Link*
Senior Project Manager: *Jane Mohr*
Design Specialist: *Tara McDermott*
Cover Graphics: *Kristine Jubeck*

Compositor: ICC Macmillan Inc.
Cover Image: © Greatstock Photographic Library/Alamy (top left); © GeoStock/Getty Images (bottom left); © Digital Vision/Getty Images/Punchstock (right)

Library of Congress Cataloging-in-Publication Data

Main entry under title:
　Taking sides: clashing views in special education/selected, edited, and with introductions by MaryAnn Byrnes.—4th ed.

　Includes bibliographical references and index.
　1. Special education, I. Byrnes, Maryann, *ed.* II. Series.
　　　　　　　　　371.9

www.mhhe.com

Clashing Views in

Special Education

FOURTH EDITION

MaryAnn Byrnes
University of Massachusetts–Boston

Advisory Board

Mary Bay
University of Illinois—Chicago

Todd Fletcher
University of Arizona

Lusa Lo
University of Massachusetts—Boston

Maria Reyes
University of Central Florida

Preface

Special education is full of questions, emotions, and opinions. Public responsibility for the education of children with disabilities is a relatively new endeavor that is still exploring its identity and boundaries. Sometimes it seems that just as one set of issues is resolved (such as the creation of a range of services in public schools), a host of new challenges (such as leaving no child behind) arises. Other issues, including appropriate funding and inclusion, all but defy resolution. Through *Taking Sides: Clashing Views in Special Education,* I invite you to consider several current issues in this volatile and rewarding field.

Some basic principles guided the choice of selections for this book. Each reading needed to represent a widely held point of view on the question at hand. Other opinions surely exist, but the ones presented needed to be broadly held. Each had to employ solid reasoning; its position could not be easily refuted because of faulty logic. Finally, each selection needed to be interesting to read. If an article did not captivate my attention—and that of my students—I did not want it included.

Taking Sides: Clashing Views in Special Education has two major goals. First, to introduce key questions in special education, so readers can learn from authors who have thought extensively about educational policy and practice. Second, to encourage thinking and discussion, so readers can explore possibilities and debate the consequences of positions and actions. I hope you will find yourselves engaged and enlivened by the conversations these topics begin. Most of all, I trust your deliberations will contribute to constructive solutions to puzzles that demand careful thinking and dedication to all our children.

This book includes 20 issues, addressing active debates in the field. There are three units. Unit 1, Special Education and Society, introduces questions of social policy and practice. Unit 2, Access and Accountability, highlights perspectives on educational expectations and outcomes. Unit 3, Exceptionalities, presents critical considerations about atypical learners and the treatments suggested for their benefit.

Each issue is framed as a question and begins with an introduction, designed to set the stage. Two readings presenting contrasting points of view come next. Each issue closes with a postscript, summarizing the expressed points of view, suggesting others, and presenting additional readings on the topic. The introductions and postscripts also feature questions to stimulate your thinking as you weigh the topic at hand and its relationship to schools. Each question represents challenges to be resolved in the policy and practice of educating children with disabilities.

Due to space constraints, most selections have been edited. Use the heading citations to locate the entire article, along with its bibliography.

To further expand your thinking, you may want to look at the Internet References pages that precede each section. These contain a sampling of Internet site addresses (URLs) that represent varied points of view and offer resources as well as links to related sites and bibliographies.

The YES and NO positions on every issue express strongly held opinions. You may agree or disagree with the authors, or you may find your own view lies somewhere in between. Perhaps you will identify additional perspectives as you study the issues more thoroughly. You will certainly find connections between issues. Class discussions may lead you to formulate a fresh response to the issue question. Doubtless, as you continue in your professional and personal life, your thinking will change and develop. What is critical as you read this book is that you reflect on positions, possibilities, and emotions, so you can form opinions to guide your actions and decisions.

A word to the instructor *The Instructor's Resource Guide with Test Questions* (multiple choice and essay) is available through The McGraw-Hill Contemporary Learning Series for the instructor using *Taking Sides* in the classroom. Also available is *Using Taking Sides in the Classroom,* a general guidebook that presents strategies and examples of using the pro-con method in classroom settings. Faculty members using this text also have access to an online version of *Using Taking Sides in the Classroom* and a correspondence service, located at http://www.mhcls.com/usingts/.

Taking Sides: Clashing Views in Special Education is only one title in the Taking Sides series. The table of contents for any of the other titles can be found at the Taking Sides Web site at http://www.mhcls.com/takingsides/.

Changes to this edition The Fourth edition includes five completely new issues: *Can Whole School Reform Reduce Discipline Problems?* (Issue 4); *Is Response to Intervention (RTI) Ready for Implementation?* (Issue 7); *Can RTI Reduce the Numbers of Children Identified with Specific Learning Disability (SLD)?* (Issue 16); *Is Mental Health Screening an Unwarranted Intrusion?* (Issue 19); *Do Gifted and Talented Students Need Special Schools?* (Issue 20). Two issues contain one new selection apiece: *Has the ADA Accomplished Its Goals?* (Issue 1); *Does School Choice Open Doors for Students with Disabilities?* (Issue 5). In all, there are 12 new selections. The *Introduction,* as well as several issue introductions and postscripts have been revised with updated research references. Finally, this edition begins with a unique section entitled *What's Ahead for No Child Left Behind?* This section introduces readers to controversies surrounding the reauthorization of the No Child Left Behind Act.

Acknowledgements Spirited debate about "the right thing to do" has been part of my life since I became a teacher. So long as we keep children in mind, debating possibilities is exhilarating. First, and most importantly, I thank the children, educators, and parents who frame the questions and continually teach me that almost anything is possible—not always easy, but possible. Many thanks to my graduate assistant, Latanya Moore, whose detective skills uncovered many controversial ideas. Additionally, I have appreciated the helpfulness of Jade Benedict, new to *Taking Sides: Special Education,* and all the efforts of supporting staff at McGraw-Hill. And, of course, Joe.

MaryAnn Byrnes
University of Massachusetts Boston

Contents in Brief

Contents

John Hockenberry, an award-winning television commentator, radio host, and a foreign correspondent, who happens to use a wheelchair, celebrates the increased access brought about by implementation of the Americans with Disabilities Act (ADA). Lynda A. Price, Paul J. Gerber (university faculty members and researchers), and Robert Mulligan (a district special education administrator) contend that the opportunities for ADA-mandated access are underused by individuals with learning disabilities.

H. Rutherford Turnbull III, co-founder and co-director of the Beach Center on Disability at the University of Kansas, sees major changes in IDEA 2004. In line with the Bush administration's priorities, Turnbull identifies a shift toward requiring parents and students to take more responsibility for their own behavior and for relationships with schools. Tom E. C. Smith, professor at the University of Arkansas, focuses his research on disability law and inclusion. Reflecting on IDEA 2004, Smith believes that although some changes seem significant, they will make little difference in the daily practice of special education teachers.

M. Suzanne Donovan and Christopher T. Cross, researchers representing the findings of a National Research Council (NRC) study on minority students in special and gifted education, believe overrepresentation issues are complex and not easily resolvable. While teachers can make a difference, environmental factors and poverty have a large impact and require interventions beyond schools. Daniel J. Losen and Gary Orfield, both policy experts, present the results of research commissioned by the Civil Rights Project (CRP) of Harvard University. While agreeing with some of the NRC recommendations, these findings suggest that patterns will change with stricter enforcement of federal and state regulations.

Issue 4.   Can Whole School Reform Reduce Discipline Problems?   70

Howard S. Adelman and Linda Taylor, co-directors of the UCLA School Mental Health Project, based in the Center for Mental Health in Schools, believe that many discipline problems could be eliminated by whole school initiatives that create and sustain an environment that addresses positive social and emotional development as well as academics. William C. Frick and Susan C. Faircloth, assistant professors at the University of Oklahoma and The Pennsylvania State University, respectively, present dilemmas faced by principals torn between balancing the needs of one particular student who exhibits disruptive behavior with those of the rest of the student body, whose learning is affected by the single student's actions.

Issue 5.   Does School Choice Open Doors for Students with Disabilities?   91

Marcus A. Winters and Jay P. Greene are both senior fellows of the Manhattan Institute; Jay Greene is also a department head at the University of Arkansas. Winters and Greene found that Florida's McKay voucher program for special education students has improved education for those who remain in public schools. Barbara Miner, a freelance writer and former managing editor of *Rethinking Schools*, shares frustrating experiences with the pioneering Milwaukee voucher system. Her interviewees claim that exclusionary policies and practices limit access for students with disabilities who seek entry into voucher schools.

Jay P. Greene, senior fellow, and Greg Forster, senior research associate, both with The Manhattan Institute for Policy Research, assert that the number of students identified as disabled is increasing at an excessive rate, especially in states where funding systems provide a "perverse incentive" in favor of placement. Kanya Mahitivanichcha, research analyst, and Tom Parrish, managing director for the Education and Human Development Program, both at the American Institutes for Research, maintain that funding formulas are only one reason behind increases in special education placement.

UNIT 2 ACCESS AND ACCOUNTABILITY 133

Rachel Brown-Chidsey and Mark W. Steege, faculty members at the University of Southern Maine, who have conducted extensive research in the area of student assessment, describe Response to Intervention (RTI) as a systematic way for educators to help all children experience appropriate educational practices. Douglas Fuchs and Donald D. Deshler, professors at Vanderbilt University and the University of Kansas, respectively, prolific scholars, and co-directors of the National Research Center on Learning Disabilities, urge educators to identify and explore unresolved aspects of RTI before wholesale implementation.

Jennifer Booher-Jennings, a doctoral candidate at Columbia University, finds the accountability pressures of No Child Left Behind (NCLB) are leading some administrators to advise teachers to focus only on those children who will improve their school's scores; other students don't count much. The U.S. Department of Education FAQ Sheet on IDEA and NCLB advises readers that the link between these two statutes is sound, emphasizing how they work together to ensure that every student's performance and needs receive appropriate attention.

Issue 9.   Will NCLB Requirements Produce Highly Qualified Special Education Teachers?   179

YES: **Rod Paige,** from "Remarks at the Education Department's First Annual Teacher Quality Evaluation Conference" (June 11, 2002)   *181*

NO: **James McLeskey and Dorene D. Ross,** from "The Politics of Teacher Education in the New Millennium: Implications for Special Education Teacher Educators," *Teacher Education and Special Education* (Fall 2004)   *188*

Rod Paige, then-Secretary of the U.S. Department of Education, and former Houston, Texas superintendent, believes the promise of No Child Left Behind can be realized by mandating that every teacher be highly qualified, by increasing their focus in the content areas they teach and decreasing time spent on pedagogical skills. James McLeskey and Dorene D. Ross, teacher education faculty at the University of Florida, present competing views of what constitutes "highly qualified" special education teachers, one based on deregulation and one based on professionalization; they encourage ongoing consideration to determine the value and impact of each.

Issue 10.   Can Scientifically Based Research Guide Instructional Practice?   197

YES: **Samuel L. Odom, Ellen Brantlinger, Russell Gersten, Robert H. Horner, Bruce Thompson, and Karen R. Harris,** from "Research in Special Education: Scientific Methods and Evidence-Based Practices," *Exceptional Children* (Winter 2005)   *199*

NO: **Frederick J. Brigham, William E. Gustashaw III, Andrew L. Wiley, and Michele St. Peter Brigham,** from "Research in the Wake of the No Child Left Behind Act: Why the Controversies Will Continue and Some Suggestions for Controversial Research," *Behavioral Disorders* (May 2004)   *209*

Samuel L. Odom, Ellen Brantlinger, Russell Gersten, Robert H. Horner, Bruce Thompson, and Karen R. Harris, all college faculty members and educational researchers, begin their article with definitive support for research-based methodology. They herald proposals for quality indicators, to establish rigor in an array of research methods that can identify effective educational practices. Frederick J. Brigham, associate professor at the University of Virginia, Charlottesville; William E. Gustashaw III and Andrew L. Wiley, both doctoral candidates at the University of Virginia, Charlottesville; and Michele St. Peter Brigham, a special education practitioner, believe that disagreement, mistrust, and the shifting general education environment preclude the usefulness of scientifically based research to guide daily instruction.

Kevin S. McGrew, educational researcher and director of the Institute for Applied Psychometrics (IAP), and Jeffrey Evans, consultant and educational researcher for IAP, are wary that stereotypes of individuals with cognitive disabilities are used to form limited (and limiting) expectations and self-fulfilling prophecies. James M. Kauffman, professor emeritus of education at the University of Virginia, Charlottesville, and special education philosopher-researcher, believes that educators and parents must acknowledge that some students with cognitive disabilities cannot reach high academic standards and are best served by programs that develop other skills.

James M. Kauffman, a faculty member at the University of Virginia, along with Kathleen McGee and Michele Brigham, both special education teachers, maintain that special education has pursued its goal of normalization to an extreme. The emphasis has shifted from increasing competence to perpetuating disabilities through the unwise use of accommodations. MaryAnn Byrnes, a University of Massachusetts–Boston faculty member, former special education administrator, and editor of this *Taking Sides*, argues that relevant accommodations are necessary to ensure that people with disabilities have a fair chance to demonstrate what they know and can do.

Wayne Sailor, professor of education and associate director of the Beach Center on Disability at the University of Kansas–Lawrence, and Blair Roger, an educational consultant based in Oakland, California, believe that a school-based model of support services for all students would successfully increase inclusionary practices. Naomi Zigmond, professor of education at the University of Pittsburgh, maintains that promoting one model of services over another is the wrong approach and advocates that educators and researchers need to focus attention on individual students.

Issue 14. Is Full Inclusion the Least Restrictive Environment? 293

YES: **Rosalind Vargo and Joe Vargo,** from "Voice of Inclusion: From My Friend Ro Vargo," in Richard A. Villa and Jacqueline S. Thousand, eds., *Creating an Inclusive School*, 2nd ed. (Association for Supervision and Curriculum Development, 2005) *295*

NO: **Amy Dockser Marcus,** from "Eli's Choice," *The Wall Street Journal* (December 31, 2005) *302*

Rosalind and Joe Vargo, parents of Ro, use their voices to tell a powerful story of their daughter's success in fully inclusive educational programs, from kindergarten through college. Amy Dockser Marcus, staff reporter at *The Wall Street Journal*, records the voices of Eli's parents and teachers as they react to his message to leave a fully inclusive program in favor of a separate special education class.

UNIT 3 EXCEPTIONALITIES 311

Issue 15. Can Brain Scans Unravel the Mystery of Learning Disabilities? 312

YES: **Sally E. Shaywitz and Bennett A. Shaywitz,** from "Reading Disability and the Brain," *Educational Leadership* (March 2004) *314*

NO: **Gerald Coles,** from "Danger in the Classroom: 'Brain Glitch' Research and Learning to Read," *Phi Delta Kappan* (January 2004) *320*

Sally E. and Bennett A. Shaywitz, codirectors of the National Institute of Child Health and Human Development—Yale Center for the Study of Learning and Attention, and Yale University professors, summarize their recent research findings suggesting that advances in medicine, together with reading research, can virtually eliminate reading disabilities. Gerald Coles, an educational psychologist and former member of the Robert Wood Johnson Medical School, University of Medicine and Dentistry of New Jersey, contests the claim that neurological procedures can identify reading disabilities and identify the methods to help children read.

Issue 16. Can RTI Reduce the Numbers of Children Identified with Specific Learning Disability (SLD)? 330

YES: **Lynn S. Fuchs,** from *NRCLD Update on Responsiveness to Intervention: Research to Practice* (National Research Center on Learning Disabilities, 2007) *332*

NO: **Cathy G. Litty and J. Amos Hatch,** from "Hurry Up and Wait: Rethinking Special Education Identification in Kindergarten," *Early Childhood Education Journal* (February 2006) *340*

Lynn S. Fuchs, a prolific scholar in the area of learning disabilities and one of several researchers in the National Research Center for Learning Disabilities, explains how Research to Intervention (RTI) strategies can separate a struggling learner from one with specific learning disability (SLD). Cathy G. Litty (Western Carolina University) and J. Amos Hatch (University of Tennessee) discuss the increasing academic pressures for kindergarten children; they believe special education services should be provided as soon as possible to students who will eventually be found eligible.

Arthur Allen, reporter for *The Washington Post*, believes that ADHD exists, but thinks too many children are given this diagnosis, masking other conditions (or simply normal behavior), and resulting in the prescription of drugs which do more harm than good. Russell A. Barkley, director of psychology and a professor at the University of Massachusetts Medical Center, addresses several current beliefs about ADHD and maintains that ADHD is underdiagnosed and undertreated in today's children.

James B. Adams (Arizona State University), Stephen Edelson (Center for the Study of Autism), Temple Grandin (Colorado State University) and Bernard Rimland (Director of the Autism Research Institute) recommend to parents of young children with autism an array of effective treatment options, many of them biomedical-based. The Committee on Educational Interventions, chaired by Catherine Lord, director of the University of Michigan's Autism and Communication Disorders Center, summarizing their examination of research studies of educational treatments for children with autism, found little consistent evidence to support the efficacy claims made by their proponents.

Nathaniel S. Lehrman, clinical director (retired) of the Kingsboro (NY) Psychiatric Center warns that new mental health screening requirements, heralded as a way to increase the health of the nation, will intrude on basic freedoms, lead to inappropriate labels, and increase revenue for pharmaceutical companies. Mark D. Weist, Marcia Rubin, Elizabeth Moore, Steven Adelshiem, and Gordon Wrobel, consultants and researchers in mental health, see this screening as a way to identify those who need early intervention in order to prevent the development of debilitating mental illnesses.

Issue 20.   Do Gifted and Talented Students Need Special Schools?   412

John Cloud, a staff writer for *Time Magazine* since 1997, profiles a number of extraordinarily gifted young people challenged for the first time in a specialized school that pushes them to reach their potential in a way that public schools could not. Susan Winebrenner and Dina Brulles work with educators to design and deliver cluster-based programs that address the needs of the gifted within their neighborhood school and provide options for a range of students to reach their potential.

Correlation Guide

The *Taking Sides* series presents current issues in a debate-style format designed to stimulate student interest and develop critical thinking skills. Each issue is thoughtfully framed with an issue summary, an issue introduction, and a postscript. The pro and con essays—selected for their liveliness and substance—represent the arguments of leading scholars and commentators in their fields.

Taking Sides: Clashing Views in Special Education, 4/e is an easy-to-use reader that presents issues on important topics such as *social interaction, stratification, inequality* and *deviance*. For more information on *Taking Sides* and other *McGraw-Hill Contemporary Learning Series* titles, visit www.mhcls.com.

This convenient guide matches the issues in **Taking Sides: Special Education, 4/e** with the corresponding chapters in our best-selling McGraw-Hill Special Education textbook by Taylor et al.

Taking Sides: Special Education, 4/e	Exceptional Students: Preparing Teachers for the 21st Century by Taylor et al.
Issue 1: Has the ADA Accomplished Its Goals?	**Chapter 1:** An Overview of Special Education
Issue 2: Does IDEA 2004 Contain Substantial Changes?	**Chapter 1:** An Overview of Special Education
Issue 3: Is Eliminating Minority Overrepresentation Beyond the Scope of Public Schools?	**Chapter 1:** An Overview of Special Education
Issue 4: Can Whole School Reform Reduce Discipline Problems?	**Chapter 3:** School, Family, and Community Collaboration **Chapter 4:** Students with Learning Disabilities
Issue 5: Does School Choice Open Doors for Students with Disabilities?	**Chapter 4:** Students with Learning Disabilities
Issue 6: Do Funding Systems Create a Perverse Incentive to Place Students in Special Education?	**Chapter 2:** The Special Education Process: From Initial Identification to the Delivery of Services
Issue 7: Is Response to Intervention (RTI) Ready for Implementation?	**Chapter 2:** The Special Education Process: From Initial Identification to the Delivery of Services
Issue 8: Does NCLB Leave Some Students Behind?	**Chapter 2:** The Special Education Process: From Initial Identification to the Delivery of Services **Chapter 4:** Students with Learning Disabilities
Issue 9: Will NCLB Requirements Produce Highly Qualified Special Education Teachers?	**Chapter 1:** An Overview of Special Education **Chapter 3:** School, Family, and Community Collaboration
Issue 10: Can Scientifically Based Research Guide Instructional Practice?	**Chapter 2:** The Special Education Process: From Initial Identification to the Delivery of Services

Taking Sides: Special Education, 4/e	Exceptional Students: Preparing Teachers for the 21st Century by Taylor et al.
Issue 11: Should Students With Cognitive Disabilities Be Expected to Demonstrate Academic Proficiency?	**Chapter 11:** Students with Autism Spectrum Disorders
Issue 12: Have Schools Gone Too Far in Using Accommodations?	**Chapter 4:** Students with Learning Disabilities
Issue 13: Can One Model of Special Education Serve All Students?	**Chapter 3:** School, Family, and Community Collaboration
Issue 14: Is Full Inclusion the Least Restrictive Environment?	**Chapter 3:** School, Family, and Community Collaboration
Issue 15: Can Brain Scans Unravel the Mystery of Learning Disabilities?	**Chapter 7:** Students with Communication Disorders
Issue 16: Can RTI Reduce the Numbers of Children Identified with Specific Learning Disability (SLD)?	**Chapter 13:** Students Who Are At Risk: Early Identification and Intervention
Issue 17: Is Attention Deficit (Hyperactivity) Disorder Overdiagnosed?	**Chapter 14:** Students with Attention Deficit/Hyperactivity Disorder
Issue 18: Are There Scientifically Effective Treatments for Autism?	**Chapter 11:** Students with Autism Spectrum Disorders
Issue 19: Is Mental Health Screening an Unwarranted Intrusion?	**Chapter 6:** Students with Emotional or Behavioral Disorders
Issue 20: Do Gifted & Talented Students Need Special Schools?	**Chapter 15:** Students Who Are Gifted and Talented

Introduction

"I introduce . . . a bill . . . to insure equal opportunities for the handicapped by prohibiting needless discrimination in programs receiving federal financial assistance. . . . The time has come when we can no longer tolerate the invisibility of the handicapped in America. . . . These people have the right to live, to work to the best of their ability—to know the dignity to which every human being is entitled. But too often we keep children whom we regard as 'different' or a 'disturbing influence' out of our schools and community altogether. . . . Where is the cost-effectiveness in consigning them to . . . 'terminal' care in an institution?"

—Senator Hubert H. Humphrey (D-Minnesota), January 20, 1972, on introducing to Congress a bill mandating education for children with disabilities (as quoted in *Back to School on Civil Rights*, National Council on Disability, 2000).

"Unfortunately, this bill promises more than the federal government can deliver, and its good intentions could be thwarted by the many unwise provisions it contains. . . . Even the strongest supporters of this measure know as well as I that they are falsely raising the expectations of the groups affected by claiming authorization levels which are excessive and unrealistic. . . . [This bill also contains a] vast array of detailed, complex and costly administrative requirements, which would unnecessarily assert federal control over traditional state and local government functions."

—President Gerald Ford, November 29, 1975, upon signing federal legislation to mandate education for children with disabilities (as quoted in *Congress and the Nation IV, CQ Press, 1977*)

Special education was born of controversy about who belongs in schools and how far schools need to stretch to meet student needs. The debate continues.

Think hard about your school experience. When was the first time you saw someone with a disability? What do you remember? Compare your recollections with those of someone one generation older—and one younger. The differences will be startling.

Some of you might remember "The Room." Usually it was in the basement of the school. Hardly anyone went into The Room. Hardly anyone came out. The kids in The Room never seemed to be part of recess or assemblies, or lunch, or gym. The teachers too were invisible. Sometimes the windows of The Room were covered with paper. Usually the shades were drawn. Kids whispered about The Room, but no one really knew what happened "in there."

Likely, the students who went to school in The Room seemed older, bigger, and not as smart as most of the other kids in the school. They had few books to learn from and rarely studied any but the most basic academic subjects. No one really knew what happened to the kids in The Room once they left elementary school. There never seemed to be a Room at high school. Difficult as it is to believe, those who made it inside The Room may have been the lucky ones.

Thirty-five years ago, if you were the parent of a child with a disability, your local school had the option to tell you that your child was not welcome—that there was no place in the school for your child. Choices were limited—you could teach your child at home (or just have him spend his days there); you could try to find a space in a school run by dedicated religious people; or you send your child to live in a faceless institution. Try looking at Burton Blatt's *Christmas in Purgatory: A Photographic Essay on Mental Retardation* (Human Policy Press, 1974) for a view of some of the worst options.

I remember The Room in the elementary schools I attended, but I never knew much about its students. I also remember the Catholic school for girls with Down syndrome, where I volunteered as a Girl Scout. The residents learned cooking and sewing while I was getting ready for high school and college. I never saw the girls outside the school and didn't know what they did when they grew into adults.

I also remember the boys who sat in the back row of my classes and tried to avoid the teachers' attention. The teachers hoped these boys would just be quiet and behave. The boys dropped out of school as soon as they could.

Years later, in the early 1970s, I moved from being a fourth-grade teacher to a special education teacher because I was intrigued with unlocking the puzzles that made learning so hard for some of my students. One of my early jobs was as a teacher in an updated version of The Room. It was my first experience in a small district. The day before school began, all the teachers and their students were listed in the local newspaper, along with their bus routes. I eagerly looked for my name, but instead of Mrs. Byrnes, I read "Emotionally Disturbed Classroom." For the entire time I worked at that school, I was the "emotionally disturbed teacher."

Times had changed a little since I attended school. My classroom was on the main floor, next door to the third grade; we had some academic books and we had lunch and recess with everyone else. But we were still different. Each day, my students and I needed to leave our room from 11:30 to 1:30 so it could be used by the gym teacher, while the gym was used as a cafeteria. Since there were only 10 of us, taking our classroom space seemed an easy solution. No one appeared to care where we went or what we did during that time. Plenty of people were surprised to see us camp out in the library, tackling "real" school work.

In contrast, I think about the schools of today. Children with learning problems significant enough to be disabilities are the focus of concentrated attention. Skilled professionals and researchers strive to understand disabilities and address them with specific teaching methods and approaches. Parents and teachers actively consider ways to adapt instruction. Program options seem limitless. Many children with disabilities grow into adults who hold jobs and contribute to society instead of spending their lives in isolation at home, in institutions, or on the streets.

Despite this progress, I still know schools in which students with disabilities are separated into sections of the school where no one else ever goes. There are still districts where people must be reminded to include students with disabilities when counting up the number of new math books that need to be ordered. And once formal schooling ends, there are still many young adults who sit at home without jobs because there is no guaranteed support.

Has the promise of special education been met, fallen short, or been exceeded? Has society done too much or not enough? Despite what feels like progress, arguments about special education continue. Many of them are included in this book.

As you consider the issues in this volume, think about the first people with disabilities *you* remember. How did today's special education shape their lives? What about the young adults with visible disabilities working in your community? Where might they have been without special education? How have the dreams of Hubert Humphrey and the cautions of Gerald Ford been realized?

Recent History and Legal Foundations

The history of special education in American public schools is brief and defined by legislation. Private or religious schools have long offered specialized options for students who were blind or deaf, or who had mental retardation. Until the last quarter of the twentieth century, public options were largely limited to residential institutions and a few "opportunity classes" in public schools.

After the civil rights struggles of the 1960s came the realization that another significant group of children—those with disabilities—were not being offered a quality education. Although a few states instituted their own policies and regulations regarding the education of children with disabilities, districts could still refuse to admit these students.

Successful state court cases established that children with disabilities had the right to an education. This led in 1975 to the passage of federal Public Law 94-142, renamed the Individuals with Disabilities Education Act (IDEA) in subsequent reauthorizations. IDEA offered federal funds to every public school district delivering a free and appropriate public education to all children with disabilities. The regulations connected to these statutes form the foundation of special education. Individual states constructed legislation to clarify federal language or to extend commitments beyond the federal standard.

Elements of the No Child Left Behind Act of 2001 (NCLB) are reflected in the 2004 IDEA reauthorization. The 2004 IDEA holds schools accountable which holds schools accountable for student performance, sets exacting standards for teacher qualifications, and requires that educators implement research-based instructional practices. NCLB includes accountability provisions for students with disabilities; IDEA includes requirements for intervention strategies that must take place in general education classrooms.

There is much discussion about the interconnectedness of NCLB (a general education-based law) and IDEA (with its focus on special education). Some wonder if the two will eventually merge—and ponder the impact that would have on children and teachers.

Additional legislation affects the lives of individuals with disabilities: Section 504 and the ADA. Section 504 of the Rehabilitation Act of 1973 is a civil rights statute prohibiting organizations that receive federal funds from discriminating against any individual based on a disability that substantially limits a major life activity. Reasonable accommodations must be implemented so that individuals with disabilities have equal access to the activities of such organizations. Curb cuts, lowered water fountains, and signs in Braille all came to be in response to Section 504. Since all school districts receive federal funds, Section 504 forbids the exclusion of students with disabilities, although it does not address education at the level of detail that IDEA does. You may encounter students on 504 plans. These students do not require specially designed instruction, but they might need accommodations or related services to have access to education.

The Americans with Disabilities Act (ADA), which was passed in 1990, extended the protections of Section 504 to the private sector. The ADA forbids businesses, governmental agencies, or public accommodations (other than churches or private clubs) from discriminating against any individual who has a disability that substantially limits a major life activity. The ADA requires the same responsibility for accommodations as Section 504, impacting the practices of almost every employer.

Aspects of these laws are sometimes vague and undefined. Terms are interpreted differently across the states, and businesses struggle with the range of accommodations, the meaning of "reasonable," and conflicting research results. Clarity is often achieved through the resolution of legal challenges, some of which have reached the Supreme Court. Because of the continually changing natures of disabilities and society, a single court decision can radically alter the obligations of an employer.

Court decisions can cause the ground to shift for schools as well. For example, as you proceed through the readings, you will encounter the debate between "least restrictive environment" and "free and appropriate public education." Each term is critical to the development of a school's special education program, but each is also fluid in meaning. Federal law does not provide definitions that can be used with precision. Schools do their best to apply these terms to individual children with widely varying needs. As with businesses and the ADA, court cases about individual children continue to define what is "restrictive" and what is "appropriate." Medical advancements refine the meaning of "education."

Essential Terms and Concepts

Special education has its own unique vocabulary and terms, just as any other field. Being familiar with the concepts discussed below will increase your understanding of the issues ahead.

Disabilities

IDEA 2004 lists the following disabilities: autism, deaf-blindness, deafness, developmental delay, emotional disturbance, hearing impairment, mental retardation, orthopedic impairment, other health impairment, specific learning disability, speech or language impairment, traumatic brain injury, visual impairment. Autism and traumatic brain injury were added to this list relatively recently, as a result of lobbying and research developments. State laws frequently augment the federal definitions of each disability with particular diagnostic criteria, satisfied through the administration of appropriate assessment tools in the "language and form most likely to yield accurate information about what the child knows and can do academically and functionally" (IDEA 2004).

Children may show variations in learning, and even struggle with learning, without qualifying for special education. Note that the list of disabilities does not include children who need instructional assistance solely because of language differences, cultural differences, or lack of instruction. In order for a child to be considered eligible for special education, the school's educational team must determine that a disability exists.

Federal Definition of a Child Eligible for Special Education

According to IDEA, this is a child with a disability who is not making effective progress in school because of that disability and who requires specially designed instruction and/or related services in order to make progress in school. Federal legislation applies to individuals from birth to the receipt of a high school diploma or age 22. In most states, public schools are charged with educational responsibility beginning on a child's third birthday.

Individualized Education Program

IDEA requires each child's educational team, including parents, to meet at least annually to formulate this agreement, which describes the education of a child with a disability. The Individualized Education Program (IEP) outlines the impact of the student's disability, current educational status, necessary accommodations, the nature and amount of services to be provided to the child, and target goals for each year. All educators are bound to abide by the terms of an approved IEP. Services cannot be delivered—nor can they be ended—without signed parental approval. Parents who disagree with evaluations or services have the right to seek redress through an administrative hearing and/or legal suit.

Related Services

These supportive, noneducational services enable a child with a disability to access the general curriculum. Related services can include, but are not limited to the following: transportation, various therapies, mobility instruction, social work and medical services for diagnostic or evaluation purposes.

Free Appropriate Public Education

This cornerstone of IDEA guarantees that special education and related services are provided at no cost to parents. The word "appropriate," never clearly defined, has been the source of much controversy and litigation. The impact of the word "free" has strained many a town budget.

Continuum of Services

Special education services take many forms and are delivered in varied settings. Inside classrooms, these can range from consulting with a teacher on the format of a test, to team teaching between a special educator and an English teacher, to an individual aide. Outside the general education class, specialized instruction might be delivered to small groups of children with disabilities. A few children are taught in separate classes or schools (day, residential, or hospital) that enroll only children with disabilities. The entire spectrum of options, known as the continuum of services, must be considered when designing individualized special education programs.

Least Restrictive Environment

Another key element of IDEA, "least restrictive environment" refers to each school's responsibility to ensure that "to the maximum extent appropriate, children with disabilities . . . are educated with children who are nondisabled; and that . . . removal from the regular educational environment occurs only if the nature or severity of the disability is such that education in regular classes with the use of supplementary aids and services cannot be achieved satisfactorily." Here, too, differing interpretations of undefined terms can lead to disagreement and litigation.

Inclusion

This word may be one of the first that comes to mind when special education is mentioned. Surprisingly, the word "inclusion" does not appear in any federal legislation. Its meaning differs across states, districts, and even within schools, and can change from year to year. Defining and applying this term has resulted in inspiration as well as confusion, opportunity, as well as frustration creativity as well as litigation. The common element in all definitions involves increasing the participation of children with disabilities in general education classes.

Differing Orientations

Underlying the controversies in this *Taking Sides: Clashing Views in Special Education* are four distinct perspectives, each of which affects the way people envision a solid special education program. Although disagreements cannot always be reduced to one of these, it is likely that people who support differing sides of an issue question will also be on opposite sides of the following dynamics.

Medical or Educational Model?

The medical model of special education views disabilities as conditions that can be improved, remedied, remediated, and perhaps prevented. Medical model adherents seek a specific treatment or therapy to address the physical, psychological, or cognitive issues that result in school problems. Those who follow an educational model aim to address the impact of a disability on school performance directly. Proponents focus on improving educational success through teaching skills or particular strategies that compensate for areas of difficulty. Is it wiser to deliver occupational therapy to improve the penmanship of a child with cerebral palsy or to teach the child how to use voice-activated software to enable his or her words to become print?

Special Need or Disability?

Children can have a special need, but not a disability. Laws about special education specifically exclude children whose learning difficulties are solely due to language differences, cultural differences, poverty, or lack of instruction. Neither do they include students who are gifted and talented. In addition, almost everyone can remember struggling with learning at one point in life. Children in each of these groups may not have their needs met without extra attention.

Special education is about the education of children who have a disability rather than those who struggle. This delineation causes controversy. If we know children whose lives place them at risk for failure, should we wait till that failure occurs before we give help or should we expand special education to include them? If we expand special education by including these children, are we helping them or burdening them with a stigmatizing label?

General Education or Special Education Responsibilities?

In the early 1970s, millions of children with disabilities were excluded from school. Federal laws mandated their education, which initially occurred mostly in secluded locations by specialized teachers. Seeing these students grow, teachers and parents began to seek out special education services. In many districts, special education ceased being a stigma and became a desired and protected resource, particularly when budget stress increased class sizes and reduced overall supports.

As the number of children receiving services increased, resistance rose to the expansion and costs of special education and to its separation from the overall school curriculum. This backlash resulted in tighter definitions, restricting services to those who are truly disabled and increasing expectations that classroom teachers assume responsibility for a wider range of children.

NCLB takes these deliberations one step further, introducing the idea that students should not be considered for special education if it can be determined that they have not experienced research-based classroom instruction. Interventions by the general education teacher are required as part of the evaluation process. Will schools initiate and sustain general education supports for all children, lessening the pressure for special education?

Academics or Functional Skills?

The accountability provisions of NCLB are redefining the connection between general and special education personnel. Since schools must be answerable for the academic achievement of students in special education, "where" students learn is less important than the knowledge they acquire.

Learning priorities must be considered. The majority of students with disabilities can make good academic progress, with appropriate support. Sometimes teams determine that functional skills to support success in daily living are a higher priority. In the past, students with both emphases could receive a high-school diploma. With the advent of high-stakes testing, this is often no longer possible. Will heightened standards result in better outcomes for students with disabilities? Will students be equally prepared for adulthood?

Understanding Controversy

Precisely because the issues surrounding special education are so powerful, and the stakes for children so high, it is vital that we engage actively in their resolution. To achieve this end, it is essential to recognize differences and collaborate to reach common ground.

Disagreements About Applying the Law

Parents and teachers must come to agreement about the best way to meet the needs of a child with a disability. Honorable people may be equally committed to the goal of a free and appropriate public education in the least restrictive environment but differ on the definition and application of these terms. Although few would argue about the meaning of "free," some parents and teachers prefer focused instruction in small groups of children with similar learning needs, while other parents and educators feel the letter and spirit of the law can only be met when all children (regardless of individual need) are taught solely within the general education classroom. Two children may be very similar, but have dramatically different special education programs because the preferences and reasoning of their educational teams differ. Since each child is unique and can experience only one option at a time, it is impossible to guarantee which choice will lead to the best outcome. In fact, the "best" option may change as the child grows and develops.

Sometimes the differing interpretations of parents and teachers result in heated arguments. The keys to coming to consensus involve listening, learning, and being open to new information and different perspectives. Equally important is evaluating each source of information and each course of action, in a measured, careful way, even if it differs substantially from what you feel is right. Often, putting yourself in the other person's place helps. What would I do if this were my child? What would I do if I were the teacher?

It helps to focus on the child in the middle of this discussion. As with most issues regarding children, the best solution is achieved when the adults involved put aside attitudes, emotions, and pride, and strive to understand what the other person wants and why they want it. This can be very difficult to do.

Disagreements About Interpreting Facts and Figures

While some of the questions in this *Taking Sides* address decision making about individual children, others require the interpretation of objective facts. Analyzing these controversies requires a different approach.

For example, educators and legislators often argue about the significant increase in special education numbers and costs. While this is a debate that deserves examination, it is also one that highlights the importance of evaluating information carefully. The meaning of seemingly objective facts often depends on the context used for interpretation.

Consider the following statement, "Student enrollment in special education programs increased from 3.6 million in 1976–77 to 6 million in 1996–97. During that same time, the total student population increased by only 4.4%" (Center for Special Education Finance (CSEF) *Resource,* Winter, 1999–2000). A truly alarming increase.

This is a system run amok! The number of children in special education doubled at a time when the number of children in schools barely increased. There must be a way to slow this trend. At this rate there won't be any money to buy books. Perhaps the law is poorly written. Perhaps districts are not evaluated closely enough. Perhaps parents are too unreasonable or administrators too ready to provide any service requested. Which is it?

Additional information might change the interpretation. The cited enrollment statistics begin with 1976, the first year after federal law called for free and appropriate public education for all children with disabilities. In 1973, the Senate Labor and Public Welfare Committee documented that, of "more than seven million deaf, blind, retarded, speech-impaired, emotionally disturbed, or otherwise handicapped children in the United States . . . only 40 percent were receiving an adequate education, and many were not in school at all" (*Congress and the Nation, IV,* 1973).

Millions of children with disabilities were not *in* school in 1976, so their addition to the rolls made a big impact. Many children were in institutions, which declined in size and scope as school doors opened. Many children became identified as having a disability and entered the special education count—do the statistics subtract them from the "total student population"?

Background information about statistics or seemingly objective facts can affect your understanding of their meaning and, with it, your position on the issue. Bringing to light the assumptions made by others may do the same.

Some believe that special education enrollments have risen due to the creation of "invisible disabilities" invented by those looking for a cause, an excuse for poor performance, or any way to get extra help for their children. Others contend that science is becoming more adept at understanding learning and behavior. Research continues to discover evidence that explains why some students struggle, and it suggests productive strategies to facilitate learning.

Some maintain that society has become looser and more permissive. Drugs and alcohol are more available. Children are not supervised the way they used to be and are influenced heavily by exposure to media representations of violent behavior. Others point to statistics on poverty, one-parent homes, three-job parents, and the disintegration of family and community supports to explain increasing numbers of students who push the limits of courtesy, tolerance, and the law.

Some are proud that medicine is making remarkable strides, sustaining one-pound babies and victims of tragic accidents or chronic illnesses who survive, returning to school ready to learn. Others are concerned that these miracles of life require extensive support and extraordinary methods beyond the scope of schools.

Each perspective puts a different spin on the analysis of enrollment figures in special education. The interpretation you choose to accept depends on the argument you find most compelling. Careful deliberation of all information helps you formulate your own opinion.

Being Aware of Bias

Each of us brings to every discussion our own background and inclinations. We cannot help but apply these to the issues in this book. In fact, those individual experiences may very well lead to creative options that change the course of a debate. As you begin to tackle your first issue, I offer the following reflections, gathered from students, parents, and colleagues.

Acknowledge and Be Mindful of Your Own Experiences

If you, or a family member, encountered special education (or the lack of it), you will have formed strong opinions about its worth. If you have not had direct experience, your community's media coverage of special education may have shaped your thoughts. Recognize the impact of your experience and consider its influence as you debate the issues.

Be Cautious of Solutions That Claim to Apply Equally to Every Situation

Two children with Down syndrome can be as different from each other as two "typical" seventh-grade children. Urban and suburban elementary schools pose very different sets of possibilities and limitations. Appropriate strategies in kindergarten transfer poorly to tenth grade. Ideas can usually be adapted, but rarely duplicated.

Think of Possibilities Rather Than Limitations

It is easy to say, "That can't be done," and be constrained by what you have already observed. Creative solutions emerge from asking, "How could we do this?"

Consider the Impact of Roles, Motivations, and Perspectives

Teachers come to their work because they want to help children grow and learn. Special education professionals believe children can be helped to conquer the limitations of their disabilities and become productive learners and adults. Parents seek educators who are dedicated to helping children reach their potential. District administrators serve two masters. First, they believe in the power of education and want to clear financial and legal hurdles so teachers can focus on children as much as possible. Second, they understand that they are entrusted with the finite resources of a community and must be answerable for their decisions in a way that will sustain the confidence of the citizens. Finally, legislators are committed to ensuring equal treatment and benefit to constituents whose lives span a wide range of circumstances.

All of these roles demand responsibility and accountability. The tasks of each role shape opinions and decisions. The outlook of people holding each role can lead to distinctly different perspectives, powerful arguments, and creative solutions. Consider the background of each of the authors you read as you evaluate their viewpoint. What in their backgrounds led them to their respective conclusions?

Final Words

As you read the selections in this book and discuss them with your colleagues, your challenge is to sort through competing arguments and information, and form your own opinions about the education of children with disabilities. Perhaps you will have the opportunity to apply your point of view to an issue within your community or school. Perhaps you will discover practices in those schools that will change your opinion on an issue.

Controversies in special education will likely endure. The topics will change, but there will always be arguments about the right thing to do for children who seem to need so much. You might be tempted to search for global answers. You might find yourself frustrated by limited options. You might come to a unique solution that works perfectly for your district and your school.

As a special education administrator, especially in the spring, I often woke up in the middle of the night with a seemingly irresolvable problem running and running and running through my brain. Usually it involved balancing competing views of how to help a child. None of the options seemed totally satisfactory. A wise friend suggested I let go of the feeling that I needed to solve the problem alone and, instead, ask others to discuss together the pros and cons of each avenue. This suggestion has always served me well as I struggle over issues of doing the right thing for children; I have been comforted by knowing my colleagues too were awake. I hope the issues in this *Taking Sides* keep you thinking at night and that my friend's suggestion helps you come to your own conclusions about educating children with disabilities.

What's Ahead for No Child Left Behind?

No Child Left Behind (NCLB) was signed into legislation in 2001 by President George W. Bush. Educators may be familiar with the more pedestrian name of this latest reauthorization of the Elementary and Secondary Education: Title I. This statute provides funds for supplemental instruction to students characterized as disadvantaged. A bipartisan effort, NCLB focused on improving achievement for all students and reducing the achievement gap between disadvantaged students and those with more advantages.

NCLB was due for reauthorization in 2007. This section outlines the status of NCLB and some of the controversies that will be addressed by the 44th president. In keeping with the focus of this *Taking Sides,* elements affecting students with disabilities are emphasized. Several of these are treated in more depth in the issues that follow: *Is Response to Intervention Ready for Implementation?* (Issue 7); *Does NCLB Leave Some Students Behind?* (Issue 8); *Will NCLB Produce Highly Qualified Special Education Teachers?* (Issue 9); *Can Scientifically Based Research Guide Instructional Practice?* (Issue 10): *Should Students with Cognitive Disabilities Be Expected to Demonstrate Academic Proficiency?* (Issue 11); and *Can RTI Reduce the Numbers of Children Identified with Specific Learning Disabilities?* (Issue 16).

Reauthorization

Every five years, federal statutes undergo a lengthy reauthorization process. Constituent groups identify areas of satisfaction and irritation. Policy analysts reflect on how the statute aligns with the current administration's goals and priorities. Legislators pore over data, searching for patterns of performance, achievement, and financial expenditure to determine whether the intent of the legislation is being realized.

After all the input has been considered, the House and Senate create separate reauthorization bills, which are debated and amended. When these are passed, a joint conference committee undertakes the daunting task of combining the two versions into one document acceptable to both houses. The approved bill proceeds to the president for signature. Regulations are promulgated and sent out for comment. Finally, the new version moves to the states for implementation.

Legislators in both the House and Senate tackled the 2007 reauthorization with vigor. Many criticisms have been leveled at NCLB, which is sometimes called one of the most intrusive federal laws to have been visited on school districts. Representative George Miller (D-California) and Senator Edward Kennedy (D-Massachusetts) signaled that they envisioned major changes. President Bush vowed not to compromise on commitments for all children to be proficient beyond the basics by 2013–2014.

The year ended without a reauthorization. The 44th president will be selected before this task is completed.

Perspectives on NCLB's Impact on Students with Disabilities

The Commission on No Child Left Behind was established "to move beyond the often heated and uninformed rhetoric about the No Child Left Behind Act and examine the evidence about the law's effects through a dispassionate bipartisan process" (*Beyond NCLB,* http://www.aspeninstitute.org, 2008). After gathering information "from those all over the country who live with the law every day," the commission reported that the changes wrought by NCLB "have not been enough" to prepare students for college and work. As to students with disabilities, the commission recommended improvements in the quality of assessments and increased emphasis on teacher effectiveness and supports.

In its second report on the link between NCLB and IDEA, the National Council on Disability (*No Child Left Behind Act and the Individuals with Disabilities Education Act: A Progress Report,* http://www.ncd.gov, 2008) presented mixed findings. They expressed caution "Because of the relative lack of decent academic trend data since the passage of the No Child Left Behind Act, there is no credible way to connect academic trends and NCLB." But they also expressed optimism: "The most important result of NCLB and IDEA appears to be that students with disabilities are no longer ignored. To that end, NCLB and IDEA have had a significant positive impact. Teachers, administrators, and the community are becoming aware of what students with disabilities are capable of achieving if they are held to high standards and expectations." There is concern that NCLB's focus on academics shuts out emphasis on other necessary skills.

Richard Rothstein, a vocal critic, sees NCLB as "dead" because it was "flawed from the start" (http://www.prospect.org, 2008). The coalition supporting NCLB has "hopelessly splintered." Rothstein thinks it is admirable to hold students with disabilities (and other struggling learners) to high standards, but the one-standard-fits-all approach is inappropriate. Every child should be held to challenging standards, but "challenging" is different for the child with an IQ of 65 than it is for one with an IQ of 115. A single standard suits almost no one; a single test is misleading.

Targeted NCLB Elements

Hallmark elements of NCLB have included its goals of proficiency for all by 2013–2014, highly qualified teachers, and accountability for results. Details and positions for each broad area are debated by professional organizations, government officials, educators, and parents.

Proficiency for All by 2013–2014

The target is that every child in America will be academically proficient by 2013–2014. Is one standard appropriate for every child? Will growth models, which document the changes in individual students, be a better reflection of what each learns or a retreat that allows lower standards for some?

Highly Qualified Teachers

Special education teachers are harder to find than mathematics and science teachers. The pedagogy of teaching students with disabilities is key to the individualized nature of IDEA. NCLB puts a greater emphasis on content knowledge than on pedagogy. What will this mean for specially designed instruction? Will stringent content expectations create a more able teacher corps or a more acute shortage?

Accountability for Results

Under NCLB, schools are accountable for the Adequate Yearly Progress (AYP) of all students, including those with disabilities. Some states dodge accountability by identifying large subgroup sizes, others by using separate standards for students with disabilities. The accountability mechanism is affected by the fluid nature of this subgroup. Students exit special education when their skills improve; students who have just been found eligible enter the subgroup. Will a standardized subgroup size increase accountability? Can the calculation of AYP reflect the successes of those who leave special education, as it does for students who have become proficient in English?

In Closing

As you absorb the complexities of NCLB's reauthorization, weigh their influence. Which elements of NCLB are doing the most to help students with disabilities? Which elements are creating unintended barriers and problems for students with disabilities? What kind of differences will come from the reauthorization changes? How will they impact your life as an educator? How will they impact the futures of your students?

Internet References . . .

Individuals with Disabilities Education Improvement Act of 2004

The final Individuals with Disabilities Education Act (IDEA) regulations are over 1700 pages long. Should you want to consult them as a primary source, they can be found at this site:

http://www.ed.gov/policy/speced/guid/idea/idea2004.html

Job Accommodations Network

The Job Accommodations Network, operated through the Office of Disability Employment Policy of the U.S. Department of Labor, has as its mission facilitating the employment and retention of workers with disabilities by providing employers, people with disabilities, their family members, and other interested parties with information on job accommodations, self-employment and small business opportunities, and related subjects.

http://www.jan.wvu.edu

The School Mental Health Project

Based at the University of California Los Angeles, The School Mental Health Project (SMPH) was created in 1986 to pursue theory, research, practice, and training addressing mental health and psychosocial concerns through school-based interventions. SMHP works closely with districts, agencies, and organizations across the country to develop and disseminate effective resources and practices. The Web site contains an array of resources about controversial topics, positive programs, and research-based recommendations.

http://smhp.psych.ucla.edu

OSEP Technical Assistance Center on Positive Behavioral Interventions and Supports

This federally funded technical assistance center maintains an extensive Web site dedicated to informing educators and school systems about an array of school-wide behavioral interventions. Examples of positive practice are available for use with families, entire schools, classrooms, and individuals. The Web site includes links to practicing schools, a newsletter, and online information and supports.

http://www.pbis.org

Thomas B. Fordham Foundation

Affiliated with the Manhattan Institute for Policy Research, the Thomas B. Fordham Foundation supports research, publications, and action projects, with a special interest in education reform. This site contains a link to Rethinking Education for a New Century, a compilation of thought provoking essays about the status of special education in today's schools.

http://www.eexcellence.net/foundation/global/index.cfm

Special Education and Society

*I*t seems simple enough. Individuals with disabilities should have access to our environment. All students have a right to education. Unfortunately, society needs to be compelled by force of law to provide access and education. The boundaries of required services are interpreted as frequently by the words of litigation as by the decisions of educators. Opportunities for some are interpreted as limitations for others. As budgets strain, costs of the commitment to include everyone become increasingly contentious. As society changes, the definition of acceptability evolves. The spirit and the letter of the law are not always clear, but remain the source of heated discussion.

- Has the ADA Accomplished Its Goals?

- Does IDEA 2004 Contain Substantial Changes?

- Is Eliminating Minority Overrepresentation Beyond the Scope of Public Schools?

- Can Whole School Reform Reduce Discipline Problems?

- Does School Choice Open Doors for Students with Disabilities?

- Do Funding Systems Create a Perverse Incentive to Place Students in Special Education?

ISSUE 1

Has the ADA Accomplished Its Goals?

YES: John Hockenberry, from "Yes, You Can," *Parade Magazine* (July 24, 2005)

NO: Lynda A. Price, Paul J. Gerber, and Robert Mulligan, from "Adults with Learning Disabilities and the Underutilization of the Americans with Disabilities Act," *Remedial and Special Education* (November/December 2007)

ISSUE SUMMARY

YES: John Hockenberry, an award-winning television commentator, a radio host, and a foreign correspondent, who happens to use a wheelchair, celebrates the increased access brought about by implementation of the Americans with Disabilities Act (ADA).

NO: Lynda A. Price, Paul J. Gerber (university faculty members and researchers), and Robert Mulligan (a district special education administrator) contend that the opportunities for ADA-mandated access are underused by individuals with learning disabilities.

As discussed in the "Introduction," three basic federal laws govern the lives of individuals with disabilities: Section 504 of the Rehabilitation Act of 1973, the Individuals with Disabilities Education Act (IDEA), and the ADA.

Section 504 is a civil rights statute prohibiting organizations that receive federal funds from discriminating against any individual based on a disability that substantially limits a major life activity. Reasonable accommodations must be implemented so that individuals with disabilities have equal access to the activities of the organization. Since all school districts receive federal funds, Section 504 covers two groups: students and employees.

Regulations of IDEA form the foundation of special education, upon which individual states base the local legislation to clarify federal language, establish practices, and/or extend commitments beyond the federal standard. Students served under IDEA are automatically covered by Section 504.

2

Students with disabilities who do not require the specially designed instruction of IDEA are eligible to receive 504 Plans. These outline any accommodations necessary to ensure equal access to educational experience. Holler and Zirkel (*NASSP Bulletin,* 2008) found that the number of students covered by 504 Plans peaked in middle/secondary schools, perhaps as parents sought accommodations for SAT tests.

Finally, the ADA, passed in 1990 by the first President Bush, extends the protections of Section 504, prohibiting businesses, governmental agencies, or public accommodations (other than churches or private clubs) from discriminating against any individual who has a disability that substantially limits a major life activity. The ADA carries the same responsibility for reasonable accommodations as Section 504, impacting the practices of almost every employer.

John Hockenberry is a prominent journalist and foreign correspondent. At the age of 19, he became a paraplegic in a car accident. He now uses a wheelchair in his daily travel and in his overseas assignments. Reflecting on his experiences under ADA, Hockenberry reminds readers of the increased access that we now take as commonplace. Citing several examples, he observes that ADA-based accommodations have made life more accessible for those who do not have disabilities.

Lynda Price and Paul Gerber are university professors, whose research focuses on the employment of adults with learning disabilities. Robert Mulligan directs district special education services. These three authors present evidence that adults with specific learning disabilities do not tap into ADA-mandated benefits once they leave public schools. Their findings are a cause for concern, since half the students served by special education are categorized with this disability.

Writing in *Psychology Today*, Hara Marano (2004) thinks disability-related laws may actually have done their job too well. Marano maintains that parents seeking to ensure success for their children embrace "cleverly devised defects" to secure advantages like untimed SATs. This relentless hunt has created a group of fragile children, unable to resolve their own difficulties.

As you read these articles, consider the doors that IDEA has opened for children with disabilities. Access and expectations have greatly increased. Federally, eligible students are covered until they reach the age of 22 or receive their high school diploma. What happens when individuals covered by IDEA leave the schoolhouse and enter adult society—the ultimate inclusionary environment? Does ADA-mandated access depend on disability? Is the subway more accessible than a college classroom?

John Hockenberry

Yes, You Can

Careful! You might miss the light show. If you surrender to any nervousness or caution and avoid looking at me when I roll by in my wheelchair, you'll miss the fireworks in my front wheels: tiny, colored electric lights that blaze out red, blue and green when they turn. That's right. I have electric scooter wheels on my wheelchair, and the greatest thing about them is how they grab the nervous eyes of some folks and pull them in. "Awesome!" people will say to me as I race across the Brooklyn Bridge. "Hey, that's cool!" I'll hear at an airport as I race to catch a plane. *"Really cool."*

It was two 6-year-old girls who convinced me that high-profile, sparkly wheels were a big improvement over my quiet, in-the-shadows approach to being disabled in public. Those two girls are my oldest twin daughters, Zoe and Olivia. They are almost 7 now, and all of their lives they have ridden on their daddy's lap. Doctors may call me a paraplegic. Strangers might say I am "wheelchair bound." But to my daughters, I have always been a daddy who comes with his own playground apparatus. In their short lives, oblivious of the fears and anxieties of adults, they have known a wheelchair only to represent a warm, safe place.

Going Public

These days, Zoe and Olivia are nearly too big to ride comfortably on my lap anymore, and I will miss them terribly when they stop climbing up altogether. (At least I still have 4-year-old Zach and Regan, our second set of twins!) But I look into the faces of my children and see a sunrise of hope that people with disabilities are experiencing 15 years after the passage of the Americans With Disabilities Act (ADA).

Almost two decades into this landmark civil rights law, people determined to share their distinct talents have begun to take their places in the American mainstream. The signs of their presence go far beyond handicapped parking spaces and wheelchair ramps. Thanks to their persistence, today you are as likely to see a person with a disability on the ski slopes as you are in your workplace. And the momentum is picking up. All across the U.S., people with and without disabilities are bringing about lasting changes in their communities: There are city and state building codes, such as Michigan's, that go beyond federal law by mandating that doors, passageways and bathrooms be unobstructed. There is the unique federal and civic partnership that designed and built wheelchair access into Boston's venerated Fenway Park, which for decades was off-limits to the disabled. And there is the Center for Creative Play, a universally accessible indoor playspace in Pittsburgh, Pa., for children of all abilities, which projects such a powerful "Welcome, all!" message that families drive hours just to play there. Taken one at a time, these are small changes you might miss unless you modify old assumptions and look at the world with new eyes.

Strength in Numbers

Even the battles today are different. Fifteen years ago, there might have been a debate over whether someone like Tony Sylvester, a young man born with spina bifida, could even go to a public school. Recently, Tony, 19 and a graduate of Wauwatosa West High School in suburban Milwaukee, Wis., waged a tough campaign for his varsity letter. Tony's a forward for the highly ranked Wheelin' Wizards—a wheelchair basketball team that competes with other disabled athletes, independent of their high schools. To appeal the school superintendent's decision to deny the letter, Tony and his mother, Tish, got advice from a powerful ally—IndependenceFirst, a Milwaukee-based organization that helped them pack a school-board meeting with disabled athletes, coaches, parents and the media. As a result, Tony was awarded his letter—a big W, which he wears proudly.

No doubt, there is strength in numbers—and the numbers are growing. IndependenceFirst, the group that helped Tony and Tish, is just one of about 500 Independent Living Centers across the U.S. that have grown up with the ADA. Typically nonresidential, private and nonprofit (though many are state-supported), these community-based centers provide services and act as advocates for people with disabilities. . . . There also are 10 federally funded ADA & Information Technology centers in the U.S. to help businesses, architects and schools comply with the law by providing information, training and technical assistance. . . .

Clearly, there are fewer excuses today for being inaccessible and indifferent to the disabled. But, in the end, a truly inclusive world will depend on the efforts and courage of those who are not disabled—in a word, society at large. After all, the Civil Rights Act of 1964—which had the backing of the courts, the police and the National Guard—still has not wiped out racism.

It's Up to You, Too

Meanwhile, local victories like Tony Sylvester's boost morale for the bigger struggles that lie ahead. For instance, employment for people with disabilities has not improved significantly since the passage of the ADA. Disabled unemployment has stood near 70% for the past two decades. The ADA itself has suffered setbacks in court decisions and by its own limitations.

Businesses can be exempted from the ADA by claiming that compliance is an "undue burden." And houses of worship do not have to comply at all, even though thousands have because it is the right thing to do. Enforcement of the ADA is left to the courts, where the vast majority of lawsuits are thrown out before they ever reach trial.

Perhaps the most significant accomplishment of the Americans With Disabilities Act is that it has widened the expectation that there ought to be some way in for people with disabilities. One telling example is an incident that occurred a few years ago when I was riding on the New York City subway. The train was declared "out of service" and pulled into a station without an elevator—one of many. The conductor ordered all passengers off the train. With the exception of me and a few women with strollers, everyone got off and trudged up the steps to the sidewalk.

When the conductor offered me no help, my only option was to hop out of my wheelchair and lug myself up the filthy subway stairs on my keister. But then one of the stroller women laid into the conductor: "What's your plan for this man? Is he just supposed to stay down here forever? Is that your plan?" She was riled up on my behalf. "We're not stupid people," she continued. "There's a law that says you have to have a plan. Everybody knows that."

We All Benefit

The conductor went from ignoring a solitary man in a wheelchair to being intimidated by a volunteer SWAT team of Brooklyn moms. He told all of us to stay on the train, then drove us to the next elevator station. The stroller mom looked at me and said with a smile, "You're the guy on TV, right? I love your work." I thanked her and left the train in awe of the anonymous outraged lady who had saved the powerless TV star. Her outrage represented something deeper: an expectation that has grown up with the ADA that disabled people have certain rights that cannot be denied. That's what saved me: her expectation—*our shared expectation*—that there is a place for all in America.

It's not like only the disabled benefit from this. Those ladies with their strollers have me to thank for the sidewalk ramps they love. And do you think that young office workers in the gym realize that it is the deaf they have to thank for the captions on the TV screens that allow them to follow their stocks while they huff and puff? Having a place for all is both the American dream and the engine of our success. We've been working on this freedom thing for the past 229 years. As my daughters might say: It's high time for some awesome, sparkly wheels.

What You Should Know

On July 26, 1990, the Americans With Disabilities Act was signed into law, eliminating discrimination in employment, transportation and public accommodations for the nation's 50 million disabled adults and children.

Still, to this day, many with physical and mental disabilities do not get their due. To learn more or for technical-assistance materials, . . . call the ADA Information Line at 1-800-514-0301. (During business hours, specialists help you apply the law to your own situation.) For TTY, call 1-800-514-0383.

- Employers interested in hiring the disabled can consult the Employer Assistance and Recruiting Network (EARN), a free service of the Department of Labor. . . .
- Several states are marking the ADA's 15th anniversary this week with parades and other events. . . .

Lynda A. Price, Paul J. Gerber, and Robert Mulligan

➡ **NO**

Adults with Learning Disabilities and the Underutilization of the Americans with Disabilities Act

At its signing in 1990, then U.S. President George H. W. Bush commented that the Americans with Disabilities Act (ADA) had moved people with disabilities from an era of paternalism to one of empowerment. In essence, the ADA was constructed to markedly change the way that people with disabilities would participate in society. In the ensuing years, the ADA has had a positive effect on people with disabilities, but, when examined more closely, there are questions about whether the ADA has met its potential with all populations of people with disabilities, one of them being learning disabilities (LD).

The part of the ADA that has the most impact on people with learning disabilities is Title 1, which governs practices in the area of competitive employment. Provisions of law are carefully articulated, with precise concepts such as *disability*, *qualified*, *essential functions*, and *reasonable accommodation*. In order for a person with LD to effectively use the ADA, these concepts must be understood. Likewise, some other things need to be mastered pertaining to the learning disability itself. Knowledge of one's challenges, the process of self-disclosure, and monitoring performance under the auspices of the ADA via self-advocacy procedures are most important.

A review of the extant research literature on LD and the ADA is one avenue of discovery. Another is a review of commonly used ADA materials to

1. teach and prepare students with LD during their last years of high school,
2. train professionals about LD and the ADA, and
3. inform consumers (adults with LD and parents) about their rights and prerogatives under the ADA.

. . . This article seeks to uncover the state of the art regarding people with LD and the ADA, especially in terms of preparing for transition.

From *Remedial and Special Education*, 28(6), November/December 2007, pp. 340–344 (excerpted).

Review of ADA Research

Business and Industry and the ADA

At the beginning of the ADA era, Gerber probed the knowledge and under-standing of the ADA from executive officers, human resource directors, and personnel managers of nine Virginia companies, some Fortune 500 companies, national companies, and regional companies. It was apparent that the focus of business and industry was on compliance with the ADA, primarily for people with physical and sensory disabilities. At that time, LD were thought of as an enigma or not considered at all. There was even confusion about the true meaning of learning disabilities, which were sometimes equated with mental retardation. Gerber's conclusion indi-cated a shift in the role and responsibility for people with LD beyond their K–12 school experience:

> It must be remembered that business and industry are not expert when it comes to issues of disability, including learning disabilities. There-fore, the successes of people with learning disabilities will not be con-tingent upon law and the efforts of business alone. It will be linked to the capabilities and performance of individuals with learning disabilities themselves.

The onus of responsibility had clearly shifted as the expectations of the beyond-school culture set in. People with LD had to be able to effec-tively advocate for themselves. As adults, they had to be knowledgeable about their "LD profile," know how to self-disclose, and know how to use the provisions of the ADA to their benefit.

In a follow-up study to Gerber's work, Price and Gerber gauged the impact of the ADA. Nine employers . . . were studied to see how people with LD were faring with the ADA in 1998. . . . As in the 1992 study, man-agers, supervisors, and human resource administrators were interviewed. The results of the study were essentially the same. Moreover, it was very clear that employers were most willing to "work with" employees with LD under the provisions of the ADA. Also, they saw the effectiveness of the ADA being predicated on a partnership with the employees with LD themselves. In the absence of guidance and expertise in their workplace, employees with LD had to be "experts" in their own right when it came to LD and the ADA.

People With LD and the ADA

A series of investigations were made to discover the realities of the work-place for people with LD in the ADA era. Price, Gerber, and Mulligan stud-ied 25 adults with LD. . . . Five of the 25 respondents mentioned their learning disability while pursuing their job, but they never mentioned the ADA. The remaining 20 adults mentioned neither. None of the adults asked for pre-employment testing accommodations that were allowable under the ADA. Moreover, 19 respondents had no knowledge of the ADA, with many saying that they had never heard of it. Specifically, these adults did not understand how the ADA applied to them or how to use it for their own self-advocacy.

In a pilot study for a larger national study, Gerber, Price, Mulligan, and Williams found that very little was known about the ADA, and thus the ADA was underused. Some of the participants believed that the ADA was solely for people with physical disabilities. Of the 18 adults in the pilot, only 3 participants had learned about the ADA before leaving high school or in a postsecondary setting, with only one receiving any type of secondary transition assistance. . . . Furthermore, this study revealed the importance of a new element within the issue of underutilization—the issue of self-disclosure.

This set of findings foreshadowed what was seen in the national study of 80 adults with LD. . . . The majority of adults with LD in this larger study did not know of the existence of the ADA. If the adults had heard about the ADA, they knew very few details about it. Moreover, they did not see how it applied to them or to their disability.

Interesting enough, the findings of this study paralleled research done on 24 Canadian adults with LD. . . . Canadians have the Charter of Rights and Freedoms that protects individuals with disabilities (including LD) in all facets of society. Even though the Charter is not as focused as the ADA, it guarantees against discrimination in the workplace, including people with disabilities. Despite its existence, it was underused by adults with LD and just played a minor role in employment settings. Many participants in the study did not know how the Charter specifically applied to the workplace. In a comparative study of the American and Canadian data sets, the overall conclusion was that disability laws, whether American or Canadian, were not readily being used by adults with LD. This might be to the disadvantage of employees with LD not only at job entry, but also in job advancement.

Reasons for ADA Underutilization

Transition-Oriented Materials

Ever since transition became an important initiative of the federal government in the 1980s, special educators have implemented curricula to prepare students with disabilities for their beyond-school years. Such has been the case for students with LD, although they have generally been grouped in a high-incidence, generic-like category. Curricula have been delivered to students with LD who were going from school to work as well as school to school to work. Granted, when the transition initiative was first proffered to the field, the ADA had not yet become law. It was during the decade of the 1990s that the ADA became part of the conversation regarding transition. Indeed, the ADA was enthusiastically received by the LD community because approximately 85% of people with LD go straight to work in competitive employment settings.

Perhaps one of the reasons for the underutilization of the ADA can be explained by a lack of relevant information on the ADA and LD currently available for the transition planning process. This hypothesis was addressed in a preliminary manner through an examination of widely known transition materials used in secondary schools, taught in personnel preparation courses, and developed for adults with LD. . . .

The 10 transition materials selected were subjectively chosen by the authors as representative of what is currently available in terms of transition ideology and methodology. . . .

[Despite] the best efforts to develop relevant materials for the transition process—some pertaining to students with LD and some not—little or no information is available on the ADA in these materials. Of equal importance, virtually no information is presented on how the ADA and transition specifically apply to individuals with LD. . . .

[The] professional transition literature has not kept up with the challenges of individuals with LD in this critical and frequently neglected area.

The reason for this glaring omission is not entirely certain at this time, but it begs the question: If students do not receive information about the ADA and how to use it effectively in their latter years of school, then when do they ever learn it? Moreover, if the vast majority of students with LD go straight to work, then when will they ever learn about the ADA?

Self-Disclosure in the Workplace

Another issue interwoven with the connections of LD, transition planning, and adulthood is *self-disclosure*. Unlike the school-age special education laws (e.g., IDEA and Section 504), the ADA is predicated on self-disclosure. If people with LD do not self-disclose, then the protections laid out in the ADA are moot. Sadly, this seems to be the case for the vast majority of people with LD in employment settings, as noted in the preceding discussion. . . .

It should be noted that recent work by Gerber et al. has underscored self-disclosure as a significant and complex process in the lives of adults with LD. One component of this process, which is directly relevant to transition and ITPs is the notion of personal choice. Currently, more than 120 adults with documented LD have reported to the authors that they make new decisions everyday about revealing—and not revealing— their disability. However, such critical decisions are often based on adult-oriented environments (e.g., family, employment, college classroom, church). These choices mirror exactly the five consistent areas of transition planning anticipated by IDEA: postsecondary education, integrated employment, independent living, community participation, and recreation/ leisure. Preliminary studies in this area have revealed that most adults with LD are much more comfortable discussing their LD at home with parents or immediate family members, where legislation is not an issue. However, these same individuals are often very reluctant to self-disclose at work—the exact location where the ADA could be a valuable asset for job performance. . . .

Discussion

The underutilization of the ADA is an example of a missed opportunity for individuals with LD. The ADA can make a profound difference in competitive employment settings in job entry, in performance evaluation, and in job advancement. What is highlighted in the examination of the issue of the ADA vis-à-vis LD is that there is a disconnection between the school-age and beyond-school years. If preparation for the beyond-school years is not sufficient or effective, it has lifelong consequences. In effect, insufficient preparation largely discounts the possibility of accessing the ADA throughout the adult years. Preparation for the adult years is multifaceted. Transition curricula and materials need to be specifically focused on understanding and using the ADA in the most authentic, research-based manner possible. As a result, materials need to be more in-depth, comprehensive, and LD-specific.

This article also suggests the need for greater examination of the ramifications of LD on transition preparation and effective use of the ADA. Clearly, many questions remain to be answered, including the following:

- How do we provide authentic transition training about the ADA for individuals with LD, their parents, teachers, and other related professionals?
- How do we integrate knowledge about the ADA and its consequences in the workplace for individuals with LD into local ITPs?
- How do we provide the most effective preservice and inservice training possible for secondary and postsecondary professionals (high school teachers and counselors, special needs college faculty, etc.) who, in turn, teach others about the transition, LD, and the ADA?

POSTSCRIPT

Has the ADA Accomplished Its Goals?

John Hockenberry illustrates the successes of the ADA. Twenty years ago, the idea that a human being in a wheelchair could use the subway (much less reported from a faraway country) was an unlikely dream. Today, a woman pushing a stroller castigates the subway operator for not considering Hockenberry's needs. The curb cut that makes Hockenberry's travels possible makes life easier for every stroller-pushing adult.

The 2004 National Organization on Disability/Harris Survey of Americans with Disabilities studied changes in quality-of-life indicators. Shockingly, only 35 percent of people with disabilities are employed, compared with 78 percent of typical adults. Still, two-thirds of respondents said the ADA has improved their lives, increasing opportunities in education, income, and employment.

David Morris (*Wall Street Journal*, 2005), CEO of a global company, has hired large numbers of people with disabilities for 20 years. Morris' experience tells him equal employment is sound business practice. Referencing a number of national studies, Morris finds employees with disabilities to be resilient, dedicated, and high performing. Noting that most required accommodations are inexpensive, Morris thinks attitudes are larger barriers to overcome.

Morris' concerns seem on-target. Price, Gerber, and Mulligan note that adults with learning disabilities were uncomfortable with the self-disclosure necessary to gain workplace accommodations. Although these young adults had heard about accomplishments of individuals with disabilities as they attended school fully covered by IDEA's plans and accommodations, they are reticent at work.

The consequences of this silence can be far reaching. Mellard and Lancaster (*Remedial and Special Education*, 2003) observe that while students with less significant disabilities initially work a large number of hours, their overall pay eventually declines because their peers earn more as a result of postsecondary education and training.

Students with disabilities are increasingly enrolling in postsecondary education programs. Most colleges and universities have centers to assist students in obtaining accommodations and communicating with faculty members. As with employment, individuals must self-disclose their disability and request support. Despite the assistance from support centers, colleges can be more isolating than high schools. College faculty are unfamiliar with disabilities or the policies related to student rights and accommodations (Hong, Gonzalez, & Ehrensberger, *Teaching Exceptional Children*, 2007). Frustrated students give up and drop out.

Commissioned by the second President Bush, the President's Committee for People with Intellectual Disabilities (2003) acknowledged that many strides have been made through IDEA, including the development of self-advocacy skills. However, the committee expressed grave concerns that "faulty attitudes" held by the general public, especially employers, combined with well-intentioned federal policies, have led to a form of "enforced poverty" for individuals with intellectual disabilities (mental retardation). Finding that approximately 90 percent of adults with intellectual disabilities were unemployed, the committee recommended that schools increase transition services. It also advocated for more flexible federal policies among agencies, to ease the way into employment.

IDEA 2004 increased emphasis on transition planning. Beginning with the IEP in place when the student turns 16, educational teams must consider postsecondary goals related to training, education, employment, and independent living. An action plan must be created for securing postsecondary services to reach these goals. This emphasis may increase attention to the development of self-advocacy skills necessary for successful postsecondary experiences.

What will it take to facilitate access in the workplace or on the campus for those who have experienced it in their earlier education? Does society find it more acceptable to provide equal access to those with physical disabilities and to those whose disabilities are invisible?

ISSUE 2

Does IDEA 2004 Contain Substantial Changes?

YES: H. Rutherford Turnbull III, from "Individuals with Disabilities Education Act Reauthorization: Accountability and Personal Responsibility," *Remedial and Special Education* (November/December 2005)

NO: Tom E. C. Smith, from "IDEA 2004: Another Round in the Reauthorization Process," *Remedial and Special Education* (November/December 2005)

ISSUE SUMMARY

YES: H. Rutherford Turnbull III, co-founder and co-director of the Beach Center on Disability at the University of Kansas, sees major changes in IDEA 2004. In line with the Bush administration's priorities, Turnbull identifies a shift toward requiring parents and students to take more responsibility for their own behavior and for relationships with schools.

NO: Tom E. C. Smith, professor at the University of Arkansas, focuses his research on disability law and inclusion. Reflecting on IDEA 2004, Smith believes that although some changes seem significant, they will make little difference in the daily practice of special education teachers.

$\mathbf{T}$he first federal special education statute (The Education of All Handicapped Children Act) was passed in 1975. It opened school doors for millions of excluded children with disabilities.

IDEA 97 made some landmark changes to special education law. Perhaps the most earthshaking was the requirement that all students with disabilities participate in state and local assessment systems. Not only were students with disabilities into schools, but also they now must have access to the general curriculum.

The fifth reauthorization of IDEA began in 2001. It was expected to move quickly. Despite good intentions, the new Individuals with Disabilities Education Improvement Act (still called IDEA) was not signed by President Bush until 2004.

The process to formalize regulations was also expected to move quickly. However, these were not posted in *The Federal Register* until mid-August 2006, after the Education Department considered more than 5500 comments. Regulations became official 60 days after posting. Final regulations, over 1700 pages in length, can be found at http://www.ed.gov/policy/speced/guid/idea/idea2004.html.

Next, state governments aligned federal regulations with their unique state laws. The latter can exceed, but not fall below, federal standards. Not until state regulations are formulated do educators and parents know what they must do to comply with any reauthorization. Current IDEA information is available through your state department of education and/or the federal Web site: http://www.ed.gov/policy/speced/guid/idea/idea2004.html.

This reauthorization was conducted in a highly charged atmosphere. No Child Left Behind (NCLB), holding districts accountable for the progress of all children (including those with disabilities), was impacting schools. The Fordham Foundation had just released a comprehensive analysis of the accomplishments and shortcomings of IDEA (*Rethinking Special Education for a New Century,* 2001) as had the President's Commission on Excellence in Special Education (PCESE) (2002). Both called for substantial changes to increase accountability, reduce paperwork, and reign in what each perceived as rampant litigation.

The major changes in IDEA 2004 addressed many of the criticisms that had been levied. Substantial differences can be found in the following areas:

- Increased alignment with NCLB, including the definition of highly qualified teachers and the requirement to use research-based instruction
- Use of Response to Intervention, as a general education process and as an alternative means of identifying students with specific learning disabilities
- Flexibility of team practices, including the "excusal" of some participants
- Elimination of short-term objectives, except for students with significant cognitive needs
- Heightened emphasis on transition
- More administrative latitude in disciplinary proceedings, including manifestation determination

The two articles in this issue consider the changes in IDEA 2004. They differ dramatically in their interpretation of the significance of these elements.

H. Rutherford Turnbull III believes IDEA 2004 is substantially altered. He finds the new provisions substantially increase the responsibilities of parents and students, echoing the Welfare Reform Act of 1996.

Tom Smith predicts that although a number of new elements of IDEA 2004 appear substantial, they will have little real impact on the daily practices of schools. He sees that the core element of IDEA—providing free and appropriate public education—remains unchanged.

As you read these articles, consider the impact of IDEA 2004 on several constituencies. How has IDEA 2004 affected your life as an educator? As a parent? An administrator?

YES ↵   H. Rutherford Turnbull III

Individuals with Disabilities Education Act Reauthorization: Accountability and Personal Responsibility

It is important at the outset to recognize that law is a form of behavior modification. It regulates the behaviors between the government and the governed, and it shapes the behavior of both. In this respect, the law plays its traditional role of social engineering—shaping the ways that society operates.

Seen in this light, the reauthorized Individuals with Disabilities Education Act (IDEA; 2004) engineers society and shapes behavior in three basic ways. First, it authorizes the expenditure of federal funds and shapes how those funds and the complementary state and local educational agencies' funds are spent, and it aligns those funds and their expenditure patterns with the earlier IDEA (1997) and with the No Child Left Behind Act of 2001 [NCLB]. It continues to be—but becomes more like—a *school reform* law. Second, IDEA grants rights to students and their parents: It continues to be a *civil rights* law. Third, IDEA particularizes the relationships that students and their parents have with local and state educational agencies. It partakes of social reform on a large scale—more like a *"welfare state"* reform law than a civil rights or school reform law.

Taking these three approaches to social engineering as a whole, and based on a close analysis of IDEA's text, it becomes clear that IDEA is more consistent than ever with other federal policies that impose accountability standards and procedures on the beneficiaries of federal largesse. The accountability that IDEA (1997) and NCLB imposed on the schools is now imposed on the students and their parents as well. To support this argument, it is appropriate to begin with analyzing IDEA as an education law, then showing how IDEA retains its basic nature as a civil rights statute, and finally discussing its new accountability and responsibilities provisions, their origins, their relationships to other disability laws, and their implications as welfare law reform.

From *Remedial and Special Education*, vol. 26, no. 6, November/December 2005, pp. 320–326.

IDEA as Education Law

When Congress reauthorized IDEA in 2004, it aligned IDEA with the Elementary and Secondary Education Act (ESEA; 1965), as amended by the . . . NCLB. To understand how this is so, it is helpful to describe the six principles that underlie NCLB (Erwin & Soodak, 2005) and show how IDEA connects to them.

The most obvious and, therefore, the first to be mentioned principle of NCLB is *accountability* for the outcomes (results) of education. NCLB's provisions for the mandatory assessment of student proficiency during the elementary school years are its principal means for ensuring accountability. In 1997, IDEA provided that students with disabilities will have a right to participate in state and district assessments. In 2004, IDEA provides that students will participate, with accommodations and sometimes by alternate assessments, in the NCLB assessments. . . . The significant change is not that the students will engage in the state and district assessments, but that IDEA now references and therefore aligns with NCLB.

To support its accountability principle, NCLB adopts a second principle, the *highly qualified teacher* principle. Without a qualified teacher corps, improved student outcomes will be elusive, and accountability for those outcomes difficult to achieve. Accordingly, IDEA (2004) requires special education staff to be highly qualified. . . . The second principle is a means to achieve the first.

NCLB's third principle is also a means to achieve its ends: The highly qualified teachers will use *scientifically based instruction* (SBI; sometimes called *evidence-based instruction*). IDEA reiterates the SBI requirement through several different provisions:

1. It disqualifies a student from IDEA benefits if the student's educational needs or deficiencies result from "a lack of appropriate instruction in reading, including the essential components of reading instruction," as defined in . . . the Elementary and Secondary Education Act of 1965, as amended by NCLB. . . .
2. It restricts a student from being classified as having a specific learning disability by authorizing an LEA to "use a process that determines if the child responds to scientific, research-based intervention as part of the evaluation procedures.". . .
3. It requires a student's special education, related services, and supplementary aids and services (as set out in the student's . . . IEP) to be "based on peer-reviewed research to the extent practicable." . . .
4. It authorizes the SEA and LEAs to support preservice and professional development (inservice) activities that train educators to use "scientifically based instructional practices.". . .
5. It authorizes "whole-school approaches, scientifically based early reading programs, positive behavioral interventions and supports, and early intervening services" that can prevent students from being classified into special education. . . .
6. It defines "highly qualified" teachers in terms that originate in NCLB. . . .

7. It authorizes the SEA and LEAs to expend Part B money for "early intervening services" that are coordinated with their NCLB activities. . . .
8. It sponsors research, training, demonstration, and other programs that align with NCLB. . . .

NCLB's fourth principle is *local flexibility,* the theory being that too many restrictions are imposed on SEAs and LEAs by too many federal laws and that if the SEAs and LEAs have more flexibility to use their federal funds as suitable to meet their particular needs, they will achieve more acceptable outcomes. Thus, fiscal and programmatic flexibility advances agency accountability, and site-based management is sanctioned. Similarly, IDEA recognizes that SEAs and LEAs have the primary responsibility for educating students with disabilities and that there is a limited role for the federal government (Sec. 601)(c)(6). It is appropriate, then, for IDEA to seek to reduce federal paperwork requirements . . . and to grant SEAs and LEAs more discretion in how they use Part B funds. . . .

NCLB's fifth principle relates to *safe schools,* the theory being that agency accountability and student proficiency are unlikely to be realized when the teaching and learning environment is unsafe. To advance the safe school and acceptable outcome approach, IDEA retains the 1997 provision that allows an LEA to put a student into an interim alternative educational setting for a maximum of 45 days if the student carries weapons or drugs to school or injures others, but it now allows the LEA to take into account any "unique circumstances" relative to that student and his or her conduct. This vague provision is consistent with the flexibility principle, but it targets the discipline issue, not the expenditure issue: The LEA needs to be able to exercise its discretion to carry out the safety principle and thereby advance the accountability principle.

Moreover, IDEA (2004) also makes it more difficult for a student to prove that his or her behavior and disability are causally connected. . . . Under the 1997 law, the student's IEP team had discretion (the statute used the word "may") to conclude that the student's behavior was not a manifestation of his or her disability if (a) the student's IEP and placement were "appropriate," and special education services, supplementary aids and services, and behavior intervention strategies "were provided consistent with" the student's IEP; (b) the student's disability did not "impair" the student's ability to understand "the impact and consequences" of his or her behavior; and (c) the student's disability did not "impair" his or her ability "to control the behavior" for which the school would be disciplining the student.

Under the 2004 reauthorization, however, the discretionary "may" has been deleted. In its place, IDEA (2004) provides that the student's "conduct shall be determined to be a manifestation" of his or her disability under certain conditions. Furthermore, those conditions are more stringent. Instead of the original three conditions, there are now only two, and each is itself more exacting. One is that the student's conduct "was caused by, or had a direct and substantial relationship to" the student's disability. Note the change; "caused" and "direct and substantial relationship" are more immediately connected to the conduct than the two 1997 standards of "did not know" and "could not control." The other condition is that the student's conduct was "the direct result" of the LEA's "failure to implement" the student's IEP. Note again the change: Gone is the 1997 language about services not being provided "consistent with" the student's IEP and placement. "Causation" and "direct relationships" are now clearly more connected to conduct than "consistency" or fidelity of implementation.

NCLB's sixth principle is *parent participation and choice*. This has always been one of IDEA's six principles: the right to be involved in a nondiscriminatory evaluation, to be on the IEP team, to have access to and control over the release of records, and to be eligible for membership on various SEA or LEA advisory boards.

The new IDEA (2004) retains these provisions but clarifies that parents have responsibilities as well. Section 612(a)(10) limits tuition reimbursement and conditions it on the parents' giving an LEA notice and opportunity to cure alleged violations of the student's right to FAPE. Section 614(a)(1)(D) imposes duties on parents with respect to the initial evaluation, and Section 614(c)(3) does the same with respect to reevaluations. Sections 615(b)(5) and (e) make mediation available and create premediation meetings. Section 615(b)(6) creates a 2-year statute of limitations and thus requires parents to complain in a timely way. Section 615(a)(7) obligates parents to notify the LEA concerning "the nature of the problem of the child" and the "proposed resolution" of the problem of the child (not "of the school") and thus imposes on them the duty to specify what is wrong with their child and what the LEA should do for their child. Section 615(c)(E) restricts the parents' (and LEA's) right to amend their due process hearing complaint: The parents have to get their complaint right the first time around, or else the school cannot respond, because it would always be subject to being caught off guard by another and different complaint. Section 615(d)(1)(A) provides that parents may receive the procedural safeguards notice only once a year (with some exceptions), rather than on demand as often as they want it. Section 615(f)(1) requires parents and the LEA to hold a prehearing "resolution session" and to provide sufficient final notice so that the parents' complaint might be resolved before the hearing. Section 615(f)(2) requires the parents to disclose all evaluations and recommendations that they intend to use in the hearing. Section 615(f)(3)(C) creates a 2-year statute of limitations, counting from the time when a parent knew or reasonably should have known that a local educational agency violated IDEA, thus putting the parents to the task of regularly monitoring their child's education. Section 615(i)(3) regulates that award of parents' attorneys' fees and allows a court to charge the LEA's fees to the parents' attorneys if the parents' complaint is frivolous or if the parents do not proceed in good faith during the pendency of any hearing, trial, or appeal.

In summary, the reauthorized IDEA (2004) imposes many new duties on students and their parents, giving them the message that they are personally responsible for their conduct—a point that the following discussion expands.

IDEA as Civil Rights Law

IDEA is still a civil rights law. Section 612(c) parrots the Americans with Disabilities Act (1990; the disability community's civil rights law) by proclaiming that the nation's disability policy consists of ensuring equal opportunity, full participation, independent living, and economic self-sufficiency. The very term *equal opportunity* derives from the equal protection clause of the 14th Amendment (prohibiting a state from denying anyone in its jurisdiction the "equal protection" of the law), and the 14th Amendment itself was the basis on which students with disabilities first gained access to the schools as a matter of constitutional right. More than this, however, IDEA retains the original six principles that endow it as a civil rights law.

Section 612 codifies the *zero rejection* principle by continuing to require that the state plan to provide for the education of *all* students with disabilities and by retaining the "no cessation" provision. Moreover, the Section 615 discipline provisions ensure that students with disabilities will have procedural and substantive protection against discipline that might terminate their right to an education or alter the nature of FAPE for them.

Sections 614(a)–(c) continue the *nondiscriminatory evaluation* principle by retaining the safeguards for nondiscriminatory evaluation. The requirement that the evaluation now must attend to the student's academic, developmental, and functional characteristics simply makes the evaluation more specific. Moreover, the evaluation team still needs to determine the "relative contribution" of "cognitive, behavioral, physical, and developmental factors" to a student's educational needs. Thus, three characteristics, or domains, become the focus of an evaluation under the IEP: academic (consistent with NCLB), developmental, and functional (consistent with the "alternate assessment" provisions of IDEA). The four contributing factors—cognitive (a surrogate for academic), behavioral, physical, and developmental—must be evaluated and taken into account, separately and collectively.

Section 614(d) retains the *appropriate education* principle by setting out the required content of a student's IEP—the theory being that if the content standard is met, the student's education will "benefit" the student and thus meet the *Rowley* definition of "appropriate."

Section 615(f), however, minimizes the "process" component of the *Rowley* definition by providing that a procedural violation constitutes the denial of a free, appropriate public education only if it impedes the student's right to such an education, significantly impedes the parents' opportunity to participate in decision making, or causes a deprivation of educational benefits. This provision seems to codify case law: no significant procedural harm, no substantive foul.

Several sections of the 2004 IDEA restate the *least restrictive environment* principle. Section 612(a)(5) and Sections 614(b)(2)(A) and (c)(1)(B)(iv) continue to ensure that the student may participate and have the opportunity to make progress in the general curriculum. They also retain the requirement that the student's IEP must advance the student's participation in the general curriculum, extracurricular, and other school activities, consistent with the principle of the least restrictive environment.

Likewise, two sections of IDEA (2004) retain the *procedural due process* principle. Section 614 retains the procedural safeguards related to evaluation, program, and placement, and Section 615 retains the procedural due process protections related to grievances, although, as noted earlier, it adds new provisions regarding dispute resolution and mediation and makes it more difficult for a student to resist unilateral placement (see the "unique circumstances" provision) and to prove manifestation of a disability.

Finally, Sections 614 and 615 retain the *parent participation* principle by conferring opportunities on the parents to participate in decisions affecting their child's education.

By retaining its original six principles, IDEA remains a foundation for the 18 core concepts and the related nine overarching principles of disability policy. For example, the zero rejection principle reflects the core concept of *antidiscrimination*. The nondiscriminatory evaluation principle reflects the core concept of *classification*. The appropriate education principle reflects the core concept of *individualized appropriate services*. The least restrictive environment principle reflects the core concept of *integration*. The procedural due process principle reflects the core concept of *accountability*. The parent participation principle reflects the core concept of *empowerment and participatory decision making*.

These core concepts reflect constitutional principles (*life, liberty,* and *equality*) and ethical principles (*dignity, family as foundation,* and *community*). Thus, for example, the NCLB principles of accountability, highly qualified teachers, and scientifically based instruction reflect the core concepts of accountability, professional and system capacity development, and individualized appropriate services, respectively. The principle of local flexibility reflects the core concept of accountability. The principle of safety reflects the core concept of protection from harm. The principle of parental participation and choice reflects the core concept of empowerment and participatory decision making.

The fact that NCLB reflects some of the same core concepts of disability policy as IDEA is significant: It shows how very universalistic and less exceptionalistic IDEA has become. It is "mainstream" disability policy, of course, but it also has become part of the mainstream of education policy.

Two Preludes to IDEA as Accountability Policy

Two reports predicted that the reauthorized IDEA would focus far more on student and parental accountability than it had in the past. The first was *Rethinking Special Education for a New Century.* The second was the report of the President's Commission on Excellence in Special Education (2002). Both reports made similar critiques of special education, and both sought similar improvements to IDEA. Both focused on outcome rather than process, on a model of prevention rather than failure, and on children with disabilities as "general education children first" (President's Commission, 2002). Both reports paid attention to IDEA as an education law but less attention to IDEA as a civil rights law. Most significantly, both reports argued that IDEA leads students with disabilities to have unacceptable outcomes, low expectations, and a diminished sense of personal responsibility.

The point about personal responsibility was made most directly in *Rethinking*, in the chapter by Horn and Tynan, who argued that one of IDEA's "unintended negative consequences" included the "application of an accommodation philosophy to populations better served with prevention or intervention strategies." The "accommodation model," when applied to some "low- and under-achieving students," replaces a goal of "independence" with one of "lifetime dependence on special accommodations, often at tax-payers' expense." The accommodations, and especially the discipline provisions, have been "teaching students in special education that they are entitled to operate under a different set of rules than everyone else." These accommodations constitute "encouragement for special education students to see their disability as rationale for a life-time entitlement to special accommodations." The consequence of these accommodations is that the "end game" of independence has been forgotten: "special education in far too many instances serves to separate, not integrate, through the use of special rules and procedures not available to non-disabled students." Special education "seems focused on encouraging a lifetime entitlement to special accommodations." The "true victims" are the students themselves; they learn that there are "two standards" and they are "encouraged to rely upon special accommodations rather than being challenged to achieve at high levels."

Horn and Tynan's critique has a basic message: IDEA creates dependency. That message is consonant with the messages given by welfare law reform during the last decade, as the following discussion makes clear.

IDEA as Welfare Law

By analyzing the messages that Congress and the Supreme Court have been giving in welfare and disability policy during the past decade, and by bearing in mind Horn and Tynan's critique, it becomes obvious that IDEA extends the basic message of personal responsibility that was the core of welfare reform. This message also relates as much to personal responsibility as it does to social obligations and the social contract.

Congress, the Supreme Court, and the Principle of Personal Responsibility

Congress reformed welfare programs in 1996 by enacting the Personal Responsibility and Work Opportunity Reconciliation Act (PRWORA). This law targeted a subpopulation that allegedly had "learned" to be dependent—namely, families who had been supported by aid-to-dependent-families programs. PRWORA authorized time-limited and conditional cash grants, requiring the head of family to enroll in some educational program or work and entitling the family to receive the grants for only 2 years.

In a nutshell, PRWORA declared an end to learned dependency and imposed responsibilities on heads of families; it taught welfare beneficiaries that they should not continue to expect different treatment from other citizens. It signaled that people should expect less from their government and more from themselves. It proclaimed the renaissance of self-reliance and a work-ethic policy that asserts that everyone has a responsibility to contribute to society.

Similarly, IDEA reflects the theory that special education "teaches" students with disabilities to expect "different" treatment in society. This is a fundamental premise of the Finn et al. report and the Horn and Tynan chapter: The discipline provisions "teach" students with disabilities that they are different, can behave in different (and less acceptable, less conforming) ways and still expect to be treated differently ("no cessation" under Section 612, and special procedural safeguards, including manifestation determinations, under Section 615). The reauthorized IDEA sent a different message, as the many provisions cited earlier demonstrate.

In PRWORA and IDEA, Congress did more than restate the "responsibility" principle. Fundamentally, it restated the quid pro quo of the social contract: Society will do something for you if you cannot do it for yourself, but you first must be responsible for yourself. Self-reliance precedes social support. Personal responsibility precedes social dependency.

The Supreme Court also has advanced the principle of personal responsibility, principally (in its disability-law cases) in *Sutton v. United Air Lines* (1999). In this case, the court held that in determining whether the ADA protects a person, it is permissible to take into account whether the person can or does mitigate his or her disability. If a person's impairment is or can be mitigated, that person does not have a disability. *Sutton's* message and subtext is clear: If you can mitigate your disability, you should, and if you do not, ADA will not cover you.

Following *Sutton,* the Supreme Court made a deliberate effort to reduce the number of people that the ADA covers. The best example is its decision in *Williams v. Toyota.* There, the court declared that the "major life activities" that a person's impairment must significantly limit are performing household chores, bathing, and brushing one's teeth; those activities do not include being able, with accommodations, to perform a particular job. By reducing the number of people who are entitled to accommodations because they have disabilities, the court adopted the premise of *Rethinking* and the President's Commission (2002), namely, that too many people have been included as "disabled" and that it is better social policy to restrict admission to disability entitlements than to allow people to enter the disability category easily. . . .

The Supreme Court's message, then, is congruent with Finn et al., the report of the President's Commission (2002), and the reauthorized IDEA (2004): Disability policy and law should benefit fewer, not more people, and it should teach those who do qualify and those who seek to qualify as having a disability that they have obligations as well as rights and entitlements.

IDEA and the Principle of Personal Responsibility

The reauthorized IDEA (2004) restates the principle of personal responsibility in at least two ways. In this respect, IDEA is consistent with the message that Congress sent in PRWORA and the Supreme Court sent in the ADA employment cases.

First, as noted earlier, IDEA grants a variety of rights to students' parents to participate in decisions about their child's education, but it also imposes duties on them as they do participate. Moreover, IDEA also makes the personal responsibility theme explicit, . . . with respect to the students themselves. Here, Congress declares that students' education can be made more effective when educators have "high expectations" of them and enable them to "meet their developmental goals," to meet the "challenging expectations that have been set for all children," and to "be prepared to lead productive . . . adult lives." . . . Under an analysis of IDEA as welfare law, the provisions about meeting "developmental goals" arguably refer to students' behavior, not just to their academic achievement. Likewise, under the same analysis, the provisions about "lead[ing] productive . . . adult lives" arguably refer to being economically self-sufficient, working and contributing to the nation's economy, or making other socially valued contributions.

Second, as also explained earlier, IDEA allows LEAs to take into account "any unique circumstances on a case-by-case basis" when determining whether to order a change in a student's placement because of conduct that violates school rules. . . . This provision is a Damoclean sword: The "unique circumstances" are a thin hair that can protect the student or, if it is cut, cause the sword of discipline to strike the student. In either event, it permits LEAs to take into account whether the student chose to act responsibly or was incapable of making that choice.

The reauthorized IDEA (2004) also makes it more difficult for students to defend themselves against a disciplinary sanction by alleging "manifestation." As pointed out above, the reauthorized law requires students to prove that their conduct was "caused by" or had a "direct and substantial relationship" to their disability. It also removes the lax standard that the student's services were not delivered "consistent" with the IEP and replaces it with the standard that the LEA must fail to implement the student's IEP and thereby directly cause the student's conduct.

Rights and Responsibilities Within IDEA: Teaching New Lessons

The changes in IDEA's parent participation and student discipline provisions impose a duty of responsibility on parents and students alike. These beneficiaries must either follow new, highly specific procedures and standards or justify why they do not.

The new IDEA, then, teaches parents and students that they have responsibility for their own actions. It intends to shape their behavior by causing them to unlearn their alleged sense of entitlement to act in certain ways. It seeks to reduce their dependency on the schools and to increase their dependency on themselves. It calls on them to be more self-reliant and self-governing. It bears repeating: Section 601(c)(5)(A) proclaims that students' education can be made more "effective" if there are "high expectations" for them (including both behavioral expectations and academic expectations) and ways of "strengthening the role and responsibility of parents." . . .

IDEA, Title I of ESEA, and the New Morbidity

It is not just in its parent and student rights provisions that IDEA reveals that it is a welfare law. There is also a clear line between (a) IDEA and its concern with student outcomes, especially outcomes for ethnically and linguistically diverse students . . . (b) NCLB and the special provisions for Title I schools (i.e., for "poor students" in school); and (c) the "new morbidity." The term *new morbidity* refers to evidence that disability has a positive correlation with poverty and other demographic factors, such as family structure, ethnicity/culture, language, and geography.

IDEA and NCLB focus especially on students whom the new morbidity affects—under IDEA, students from minority populations (Sec. 601(c)(10)–(13)), and under NCLB, the Title I eligible ("poor") students. PRWORA and welfare reform focused on these students' families. Together, IDEA and NCLB continue the PRWORA welfare reform policies passed nearly a decade ago and the *Sutton* line of cases.

Conclusion

It seems unseemly to argue that the reauthorized IDEA is, at its core, part of the reforms that PRWORA and *Sutton* launched more than half a decade before Congress turned its attention to IDEA. Somehow, the notion that students' and parents' rights were sacrosanct had become the conventional wisdom. Yet the transitory nature of "conventional wisdom" is apparent in the very terms that define the concept itself: *Conventional* refers to the conventions, the mores, of a certain time, place, and culture. As our country's history shows, conventions and mores change; the underlying principles (the so-called six principles of IDEA and the so-called core concepts of disability policy) may not have changed, but the ways in which they are expressed in practice and codified in law do.

So it seems to be with the reauthorized IDEA. The conventional notion that rights are paramount now seems to be descendant, not ascendant. At the same time, the notion that rights entail responsibilities is ascendant; this notion does not supersede the importance of rights, but it does assert that, in our society, rights and responsibilities go hand in hand. This is a message of paramount importance to the special education and disability communities. Whether these communities will hear that message—which is sure to be repeated in debates about Social Security, Medicaid, and ADA—and how they will respond to it if they hear it are the stuff of the future.

Tom E. C. Smith

NO

IDEA 2004: Another Round in the Reauthorization Process

The Individuals with Disabilities Education Act (IDEA; 1997) has once again been reauthorized. Although the reauthorization was thought to be on a fast track when it was initially begun in 2001, the law was finally passed in November 2004 and signed by President Bush in December 2004. The Individuals with Disabilities Education Improvement Act (2004), still to be referred to as IDEA, contains some significant changes; however, after careful review, the changes may not be as significant as first thought.

Certainly, the lives of children with disabilities in this country have been forever altered as a result of federal legislation. Beginning with the passage of Public Law 94-142, the Education for All Handicapped Children Act, in 1975, federal policies and federal dollars have been an integral component of special education. Overall, there is no doubt that the lives of children with disabilities have improved significantly. Let us review some of the major changes that have resulted from this law; some of the changes made in previous reauthorizations; and finally, some of the major changes associated with IDEA 2004.

Public Law 94-142

When Public Law 94-142 (the Education for All Handicapped Children Act) was passed in 1975, the state of special education was vastly different from what it is today. Prior to its passage, Congress found that up to 1 million of the estimated 8 million children with disabilities in the United States were excluded from public school services, and another 3 million were being served inappropriately. The original four purposes of P.L. 94-142 included

- to assure that all children with disabilities have available to them . . . a free appropriate public education which emphasizes special education and related services designed to meet their unique needs
- to assure that the rights of children with disabilities and their parents . . . are protected
- to assist States and localities to provide for the education of all children with disabilities
- to assess and assure the effectiveness of efforts to educate all children with disabilities

From *Remedial and Special Education,* vol. 26, no. 6, November/December 2005, pp. 314–319. Copyright © 2005 by Pro-Ed, Inc. Reprinted by permission via Copyright Clearance Center.

Public Law 94-142 resulted in many changes in the way children with disabilities were identified and provided with services. Prior to its passage, special education was a mere footnote in U.S. educational statistics. There were fewer than 3.5 million children with disabilities served in public schools, mostly in isolated, self-contained settings; and teacher preparation for special education was a minor activity. Some of the major requirements of P.L. 94-142 included the following:

- Child Find. Schools were required to locate children with disabilities and initiate the referral process to determine their eligibility for services under this act.
- Individualized Education Program (IEP). Every child served in special education must have an IEP. Although not intending to do so, the IEP requirement resulted in massive amounts of paperwork for special education teachers.
- Least Restrictive Environment (LRE). To the maximum extent appropriate, children with disabilities should be educated with their nondisabled peers. This resulted in "mainstreaming" and the practice of including many students with disabilities in general education settings.
- Nondiscriminatory Assessment. All children must be given a comprehensive assessment prior to determining their eligibility for special education, and this assessment must be administered in such a way as not to discriminate against individuals from different cultural/language groups.
- Related Services. Services that are necessary for a child to benefit from special education, such as physical therapy or transportation, must also be provided.
- Due Process Rights. Children with disabilities, and their parents, must be afforded certain due process rights, including the right of notice and consent prior to actions affecting their child and the right to a due process hearing to resolve complaints and disagreements between parents and the school.
- Funding. Congress said that the federal government would eventually fund up to 40% of the excess costs of educating students with disabilities. Although Congress still has not come close to the 40% level, hundreds of millions of dollars have supported programs under this legislation.
- Free, appropriate public education (FAPE). Schools were required to provide a free, appropriate public education to all students with disabilities. This includes determining the eligibility of children and developing and implementing an IEP for each child. All of the services to children under this act must be provided without cost to the parents.

Although there were many other provisions in the original P.L. 94-142, these were the ones having the greatest impact.

Since P.L. 94-142 was passed, there have been several reauthorizations that have made changes in the law. Although some of these changes have been significant, they have not altered the basic requirements of the

Table 1

Key Components of Reauthorizations of P.L. 94-142/IDEA

Reauthorization	Key components
1983 (P.L. 98-199)	1. Provided incentives for states to serve preschool children with disabilities. 2. Required states to collect information and address issues related to students transitioning from school to post-school.
(P.L. 101-457)	1. Mandated services for children 3-5 lowering all of the requirements of P.L. 94-142 to include 3-5 year old children. 2. Provided for attorney's fees in due process or court cases where parents prevailed.
(P.L. 101-476)	1. Added autism and traumatic brain injury to the list of disabilities covered under IDEA. 2. Changed the name of the act from the Education for All Handicapped Children Act to the Individuals with Disabilities Education Act. 3. Required schools to initiate transition services no later than age 16.
1997 (P.L. 105-17)	1. Required schools to initiate transition planning no later than age 14. 2. Required schools to include behavior intervention plans for students with behavior problems.

original legislation. All children with disabilities must be referred, evaluated, and determined to be eligible or not; all eligible students must have IEPs; and all must be provided with a free, appropriate public education, meaning they must be served in the least restrictive environment. Some of the major changes associated with successive reauthorizations up to 1997 are included in Table 1.

IDEA 2004

The reauthorization of IDEA in 2004 included a name change: The word "improvement" was inserted, making the official title of the legislation the "Individuals with Disabilities Education Improvement Act." However, the law is still referred to as IDEA. Several significant changes were included in the reauthorization. The following section will describe these changes and discuss the actual implications of the changes.

Highly Qualified Teachers

IDEA 2004 includes a requirement that special education teachers meet the "highly qualified" mandate introduced in the No Child Left Behind Act (NCLB; 2001) legislation. This is the first reauthorization of IDEA that includes any specific requirements related to teacher qualifications. Until this act, determining the qualifications of teachers had always been left to the states. IDEA 2004 now requires teachers to be "highly qualified." Highly qualified means that

1. All special education teachers must be highly qualified under the NCLB definition; also, special education teachers must have a state special education certification; not hold an emergency, temporary, or provisional certification; and have at least a bachelor's degree.
2. Special education teachers who teach content courses and are the teachers of record for those courses must meet the NCLB *highly qualified* requirements. This means that they must be licensed in the subjects taught, similar to general classroom teachers under NCLB.

The ramifications of this addition to the legislation are just now being understood. The Council for Exceptional Children (CEC) has referred to this component of the law as "an extraordinary federal intrusion into what has been the domain of States and the profession." CEC has added that these requirements are bureaucratic, impractical, unsound, and intrusive. Many special education teachers have been involved in providing instruction and support to students in subject areas, especially in middle and high schools. Getting these teachers licensed in these content areas will undoubtedly cause many problems. Teachers are allowed to become licensed through state high objective state standard of evaluation (HOUSSE) options, which is a way states can license teachers under NCLB; however, for the immediate future, these requirements will create problems for many teachers, local districts, and states.

Funding

Finally, more than 30 years since the passage of P.L. 94-142, Congress appears to be ready to meet its promise of full funding for IDEA. P.L. 94-142 said that Congress would fund special education programs under the law at a rate up to 40% of excess costs for educating children with disabilities. Congress has never come close to the 40% level. In fact, federal funding for IDEA has never reached the 20% level. IDEA 2004 lays out a path for full funding. The law authorizes Congress to fund IDEA for $12.36 billion for fiscal year 2005 and an additional $2.3 billion each year through 2011, when full funding will be achieved.

Individualized Education Programs

The level of paperwork associated with special education has increased significantly since the passage of P.L. 94-142. In some cases, special education professionals seem to spend as much time on paperwork as on programs for their students. Excessive paperwork has actually been cited by some teachers as their primary reason for leaving the teaching profession. The 2004 reauthorization has made some changes directly targeting a reduction in paperwork. One of the changes incorporated in IDEA 2004 is deleting the requirement that IEPs include short-term objectives, except for students who are assessed using alternative assessment procedures that are aligned with alternate achievement standards. Eliminating short-term objectives hopefully will not have a negative impact on appropriate programming but will result in a reduction of paperwork.

Another change in IEPs relates to transition requirements. Whereas IDEA 1997 required schools to include transition planning in IEPs when the child reached 14 years of age, IDEA 2004 only requires schools to include a statement of transition goals based on age-appropriate transition assessments beginning with the first IEP that will be in effect when the child reaches 16 years of age.

IDEA 2004 also provides some flexibility in attendance at IEP meetings by permitting team members not to attend if their area of expertise is not needed, as agreed by other team members, and not to attend if they provide written information related to the IEP meeting prior to the meeting, again with team approval. IEPs can also be modified during the year without the entire team being present if the school and parents agree to a written amendment after the original IEP is developed. These provisions should help limit the number of times that complete teams have to get together to develop and modify IEPs. It also keeps some school personnel from having to attend meetings when their expertise is really not needed.

Finally, relative to the IEP, IDEA 2004 has established a 15-state pilot program for multiyear IEPs. States can apply for participation in the pilot program. Under the pilot program, states can develop IEPs for up to 3 years on a trial basis. Whereas students' progress toward achieving their 3-year goals would have to be measured annually, IEPs would not have to be rewritten on an annual basis. This pilot program, advocated by many professionals and some professional organizations, will determine if students can receive FAPE using multiyear IEPs, just as they receive FAPE using annual IEPs. If the results of the pilot program are positive, it is likely that all states will be able to move to multiyear IEPs.

Due Process Requirements

The original P.L. 94-142 included specific due process requirements, including the right to notice and consent and the right to a due process hearing. Parents must give consent prior to the initial evaluation and placement of their child in special education, and they must be notified prior to other actions dealing with their child. IDEA 2004 continues to require that schools obtain consent prior to initial evaluation and placement. If parents refuse their consent for initial evaluation, schools may pursue this denial through due process. However, parental refusal of consent to special education placement may not be pursued by the school through due process. In this situation, the child is not considered a child with a disability under IDEA, and the school district is not responsible for ensuring FAPE for the child.

IDEA 2004 also includes some significant changes related to due process hearings. Parents have been able to recoup attorney fees in situations where they prevailed in due process hearings and court cases, but the schools have not been able to recoup attorney fees in situations where they prevailed. IDEA 2004 enables schools to recoup costs in certain situations from the parents and parents' attorneys.

Specifically, IDEA 2004 says that the court may award fees to the prevailing state education agency (SEA) or local education agency (LEA) against parents' attorneys who (a) file a complaint or other cause of action that is frivolous, unreasonable, or without foundation or (b) continue to litigate after litigation clearly has become frivolous, unreasonable, or without foundation. The prevailing SEA or LEA may also be awarded fees by the courts against the parents' attorney or against the parents if the complaint or subsequent cause of action was presented for any improper purpose (e.g., to harass, cause delay, or increase the cost of litigation).

It is hoped that these provisions will reduce the number of complaints, due process hearing requests, and court actions, unless the situation truly merits those actions. Schools have complained in the past that some parents are filing complaints to retaliate against a school or school personnel and that often parents or their attorneys continue the litigation process to enhance the level of attorney fees. The fact that parents and their attorneys can be held accountable for these fees in situations where the courts think their actions are unwarranted may reduce the level of complaints.

Expulsion and Suspension

Disciplinary procedures for students with disabilities have been a highly debated topic for many years. In fact, disagreements on disciplining students with disabilities have been a major stumbling block in successfully reauthorizing IDEA on several previous occasions. Advocates for children with disabilities have resolutely supported students and opposed disciplinary procedures for this group of children that did not take the effect of the child's disability into consideration. This has resulted, correctly, in schools having to consider the impact of the disability on the behavior. If a suspension was for fewer than 10 days, and the student did not already have a series of suspensions that might add up to 10 days, then the school could suspend the student, similar to suspending any other student. However, if the suspension or expulsion added up to more than 10 days, the schools had to conduct a manifestation determination to determine the relationship, if any, between the disability and the inappropriate behavior. If a relationship was found to exist, then the school could not remove the student. If no relationship was found, the child could be removed from the school but the school had to continue to provide FAPE.

IDEA 2004 makes some changes to the disciplinary procedures for children with disabilities. Similar to IDEA 1997, prior to any suspension or expulsion for more than 10 days, a manifestation determination must be made. If no relationship is found, then the school may suspend or expel the student, similar to a student without disabilities. In this case, however, the school must continue to provide FAPE to the student. If there is a relationship between the disability and the behavior, then the school may not expel or suspend the student. A relationship is found if the behavior was caused by or had a *direct and substantial* relationship to the child's disability, or if the school had failed to implement the child's IEP. IDEA 2004 adds the *direct and substantial* language, possibly making it more difficult to determine that the behavior is related to the disability. If the manifestation determination concludes that there is a relationship between the disability and the behavior, then a functional behavior assessment is conducted and a behavior intervention plan is developed. The child is returned to the original placement unless both parties agree to a change of placement. The parents or the school may appeal a decision. In this case, the student will remain in the alternative placement until appeals are exhausted. An expedited hearing process is held.

In certain instances (e.g., the child has a weapon, is using or in possession of drugs, or inflicts serious bodily injury on someone), the child may be removed for up to 45 school days without regard to whether the behavior is a manifestation of the disability. This action can be taken without a hearing officer's involvement. IDEA 1997 said that a child could be removed for 45 days; by changing this to 45 *school* days, IDEA 2004 in effect allows a substantial increase in the period of time the child can be removed. Again, parents may appeal this decision and have an expedited hearing. While under appeal, the student remains in the placement that resulted from the inappropriate behavior, not the student's placement before the behavior occurred.

Eligibility for Students Classified as Having LD

Overidentification of students as having learning disabilities (LD) has been a concern for many years. Indeed, with more than 50% of all students with disabilities in this classification, many professionals have long been concerned about the use of a discrepancy formula to determine eligibility. Some have agreed that the use of this formula, which requires a severe discrepancy between IQ and achievement scores, has led to overidentification. Although IDEA has never required a discrepancy formula, many states and local education agencies have adopted this model of LD.

IDEA 2004 makes a point that a discrepancy between achievement and aptitude is not required to classify a student as having LD. It further states that schools may use a child's response to intervention as part of their eligibility process. Therefore, a school may choose to implement intervention programs, such as reading programs, and, if a child responds positively to the program, determine that a child is not eligible under IDEA. IDEA 2004 gives schools this flexibility. This language was added to IDEA 2004 in an attempt to limit the number of students identified as eligible for special education services who may simply be experiencing difficulties resulting from inappropriate instruction. If interventions are successful, there is no reason to identify the child as having LD and being eligible for special education.

Other Changes

In addition to the aforementioned changes in IDEA 2004, there are many other changes that schools will be implementing. These include:

- changing definitions of *assistive technology device*

- optional establishment of a risk pool with up to 10% of IDEA funds reserved for state-level activities for high-cost activities and supports
- allowing up to 15% of a school's IDEA funds for prereferral interventions
- flexibility in using Part C funds
- including homeless children in child-find activities
- allowing reevaluations of students not more than once each year and not more than every 3 years, unless school and parents agree it is not necessary
- conducting evaluations in the language or form most likely to yield accurate results, not necessarily in the child's native language

Conclusions

IDEA 2004 includes some significant changes to IDEA 1997; however, in many instances, practices will remain relatively similar. The basic requirement of IDEA—to provide a free, appropriate public education to children with disabilities—has not changed. There are numerous changes, but some of the notable ones include (a) adding NCLB language related to highly qualified special education teachers; (b) increasing funding to the authorized 40% level over a period of years through 2011; (c) changing eligibility for classification as having LD; (d) adding flexibility to attendance at IEP meetings; (e) creating a pilot demonstration for multiyear IEPs; (f) deleting the requirement for short-term objectives on the IEP; and (g) modifying suspension and expulsion requirements.

These notable changes may or may not have a significant impact on schools. Obviously, one change that could negatively affect schools is the requirement that special education teachers meet the NCLB *highly qualified* standard. With special education teachers already in short supply, adding this bureaucratic requirement could only exacerbate the situation, without improving educational opportunities for children with disabilities. Only time will determine the impact of this requirement, as school personnel and professional organizations lobby for a change. Increasing funding for special education could have a dramatic impact on services. However, the first budget proposal from the White House after the passage of IDEA 2004 added only $500 million to the IDEA budget, as opposed to the more than $2 billion called for in the legislation. Therefore, although it initially looked like a movement toward full funding would be made, reality has already set in that the likelihood of such an increase is low.

Changes made in the IEP requirements appear to be major. However, it is unlikely that, previously, all individuals participated in IEP development and changes at every meeting. In practice, IEPs were often developed by one individual or a small number of individuals and were likely changed without a formal IEP meeting. The changes in IDEA 2004 only legitimize those actions. Not having to include objectives might reduce some of the paperwork associated with IEPs; however, there still must be ongoing efforts to ensure that adequate progress is being made toward the student's annual goals. Finally, the multiyear IEP seems to be an idea that could significantly reduce paperwork. However, this is only a pilot program for up to 15 states, and even in schools that participate in the program, school personnel must determine if progress is being made toward the multiyear goals on at least an annual basis.

So, finally, IDEA has been reauthorized once again. Although the 3 years of debate focused on many of the same issues that have been dealt with in each reauthorization—discipline, due process rights, attorney fees, overidentification—the result is similar in many ways to the "old" law. As always, the changes do not satisfy everyone and, in fact, may not satisfy anyone. Hopefully, however, with each reauthorization of IDEA, realizing the original intent of P.L. 94-142 becomes more likely: meeting the needs of each child with a disability in the most appropriate way.

POSTSCRIPT

Does IDEA 2004 Contain Substantial Changes?

Contemplate IDEA 2004 in light of the recommendations of *Rethinking Special Education (Rethinking)* and the PCESE. As noted, these pre-reauthorization documents called for substantial changes to increase accountability, reduce paperwork, and reign in what each perceived as rampant litigation.

In today's climate of standards-based assessment, accountability is defined by whether students demonstrate increased academic performance. Writing on IDEA's 25th anniversary, Katsiyannis, Yell, and Bradley (*Remedial and Special Education,* 2001) declared that IDEA had met its initial goal of providing access to education for students with disabilities. They predicted that future reauthorizations needed to secure increased educational quality to improve achievement. Clearly, IDEA 2004 embraces a results-driven philosophy.

Not everyone is happy with this change. Writing earlier, Turnbull and Turnbull (*Education Next,* 2002) comment that special education encompasses more than academics, including efforts to help students succeed in the larger arenas of work, communication, and socialization. They worry that parents might lose confidence in a system that ignores these domains.

Two *Rethinking* papers (Horn and Tynan, 2001; Lanigan, 2001) maintained that confidence and accountability must be reciprocal. Parents desiring supports from IDEA must assume personal responsibility in the educational process. According to Turnbull's selection, IDEA 2004 "makes accountability a bilateral concept." Parents and students (as well as schools) must now be more accountable for their actions.

Reactions to these changes are mixed. Some feel the regulations are overly complicated, asking parents to waive rights that help their children (Cleveland, www.thearc.org, 2005; Sabia, www.ndss.org, 2005). Others, like Peter Wright (http://www.wrightslaw.com/idea/art/goodlaw.optimist.pw.htm, 2005), a high-profile advocate, express no concern about the changes. Wright was actually surprised by his positive response.

Paperwork is the bane of everyone's existence, especially if you would prefer to spend your time teaching. Several contributors to *Rethinking* noted that special education has become consumed with documenting compliance with reams of paper.

IDEA 2004 seems to take paperwork reduction seriously. Meetings are streamlined, short-term objectives have been eliminated for most students, and pilot projects for multi-year IEPs will be funded.

Smith holds out hope that elimination of objectives will stem the paperwork tide. However, he maintains that many other provisions sound more dramatic than they are, and will make little difference in the daily lives of teachers. He is not alone.

Looking at IEP changes, Gartin and Murdick (*Journal of Special Education Leadership,* 2005) feel the elimination of objectives for most students responds to paperwork complaints from both parents and teachers. Simultaneously, they are haunted by the possibility that paperwork may actually increase as teachers document other aspects of IDEA 2004, including agreements for excusing colleagues from team meetings.

Smith's predictions seem fulfilled in other arenas. The heralded multi-year paperwork reduction pilots have hit a snag. Apparently, documenting the efforts of these projects demands a workforce exceeding the capacity of any state (Samuels, *Education Week,* 2006). Furthermore, districts must submit "massive" amounts of data documenting progress on issues such as parent involvement and disproportional representation (Samuels, *Education Week,* 2005). If the paperwork burden is shifted from teachers to administrators, not much will have changed (Weatherly, *In CASE,* 2005) and administrators will have even less time to help teachers meet student needs.

Two final contrasting views complement the main selections: one from parents; the other from teachers. From the standpoint of the Center for Law and Education, IDEA 2004 "undermines" hard-won rights, reduces school accountability, and punishes parents for seeking the best for their child (Boundy, www.cleweb.org, 2006). Reflecting the teacher's perspective, Pardini's interviewees felt the daily practice of teaching is so far removed from the law, they doubt any changes will make a difference (www.rethinkingschools.org, 2002).

Think about the changes in IDEA 2004. Have they, as Turnbull predicts, modified our behavior or, as Smith says, do the alterations "not satisfy everyone and, in fact, may not satisfy anyone?"

ISSUE 3

Is Eliminating Minority Overrepresentation Beyond the Scope of Public Schools?

YES: M. Suzanne Donovan and Christopher T. Cross, from "The Committee on Minority Representation in Special Education," *Minority Students in Special and Gifted Education* (National Academy Press, 2002)

NO: Daniel J. Losen and Gary Orfield, from *Racial Inequity in Special Education* (Harvard Education Press, 2002)

ISSUE SUMMARY

YES: M. Suzanne Donovan and Christopher T. Cross, researchers representing the findings of a National Research Council (NRC) study on minority students in special and gifted education, believe overrepresentation issues are complex and not easily resolvable. While teachers can make a difference, environmental factors and poverty have a large impact and require interventions beyond schools.

NO: Daniel J. Losen and Gary Orfield, both policy experts, present the results of research commissioned by the Civil Rights Project (CRP) of Harvard University. While agreeing with some of the NRC recommendations, these findings suggest that patterns will change with stricter enforcement of federal and state regulations.

As far back as 1968, Dunn (*Exceptional Children*, 1968) examined the developing field of special education and voiced concern that African American children were disproportionately placed in special education, resegregated into substantially separate classes for the mentally retarded.

Accurate analysis is affected by the complexity of both racial designation and disability definitions. Racial designations, reported by individuals, are shaped by the categories provided on official forms. As more people have a multi-racial heritage (think of Tiger Woods), choosing one racial "category" may become irrelevant. Additionally, eligibility qualifications for disabilities differ across states. Some use no discrete categories.

Several procedures are used to calculate special education enrollment statistics. Some compare the percentage of each racial group in the overall school population with their proportion in special education. Others study the racial composition of individual disability categories.

Despite varying reporting options and definitional complications, there is overall agreement that children of color are disproportionately represented in special education. This seems so especially in the socially defined disabilities of mental retardation, emotional disturbance, and learning disabilities. The challenge is deciding why disproportionality exists and what remedies can reduce it.

Two influential reports were issued in 2002. Because of their depth, their continuing relevance, and their contrasting recommendations, these form the readings for this Issue.

M. Suzanne Donovan, a researcher in education and public policy, and Christopher Cross, who has been active in government and local board of education associations, edited a report representing the work of over a dozen scholars who are members of the National Research Council (NRC) Committee on Minority Representation in Special Education. Directed by NRC and Congress to update NRC's 1982 study of this same issue, their work was expanded to consider racial underrepresentation in gifted and talented programs. The committee reviewed existent research studies to determine why disproportionality exists. Their conclusions and recommendations highlight environmental variables, suggesting that there may be reasons for overrepresentation that extend into the classroom.

Daniel Losen and Gary Orfield share a professional commitment to studying the impact of law and public policy on the opportunities available for communities of color. Both have been heavily involved in designing and guiding policy formation, with a particular connection to the Civil Rights Project (CRP) at Harvard University. The impetus for their study was provided by the compelling voices of community leaders concerned about children wrongly placed in special education. To broaden the knowledge base, CRP commissioned leading scholars to analyze conditions and contributing factors and to generate solutions. The collective findings led to recommendations that racial disproportionality should become a top school priority, facilitated (if necessary) through federal and state enforcement of school practices.

Federal regulations endeavor to address disproportionality in special education, considering both overrepresentation and underrepresentation. IDEA 97 mandated that states collect and report special education enrollment information by race and ethnicity. IDEA 2004 requires that states and districts establish policies and procedures to "prevent the inappropriate overidentification or disproportionate representation by race and ethnicity of children as children with disabilities", examine data to determine if disproportionality exists, use federal funds to provide "early intervening services" to reduce overrepresentation, and document their efforts (and results) at reducing disproportionality (*Dialog Guides for IDEA 2004 Regulations*, http://www.ideapartnership.org). Not unexpectedly, states reported confusion when formulating their own definitions of "significant disproportionality" and "inappropriate identification" (Burdette, 2007, http://www.nasdse.org).

As you read these selections, discuss their similarities and differences. How do the findings correspond to your own experiences and observations? Does overrepresentation exist in your district? If so, what steps are in place to reduce it?

YES ↩

**M. Suzanne Donovan and
Christopher T. Cross**

Executive Summary

From the enactment of the 1975 federal law requiring states to provide a free and appropriate education to all students with disabilities, children in some racial/ethnic groups have been identified for services in disproportionately large numbers. Public concern is aroused by the pattern of disproportion. In the low-incidence categories (deaf, blind, orthopedic impairment, etc.) in which the problem is observable outside the school context and is typically diagnosed by medical professionals, no marked disproportion exists. The higher representation of minority students occurs in the high-incidence categories of mild mental retardation (MMR), emotional disturbance (ED), and to a lesser extent learning disabilities (LD), categories in which the problem is often identified first in the school context and the disability diagnosis is typically given without confirmation of an organic cause.

The concern is not new. In 1979 the National Research Council (NRC) was asked to conduct a study to determine the factors accounting for the disproportionate representation of minority students and males in special education programs for students with mental retardation, and to identify placement criteria or practices that do not affect minority students and males disproportionately. Twenty years later, disproportion in special education persists: while about 5 percent of Asian/Pacific Islander students are identified for special education, the rate for Hispanics is 11 percent, for whites 12 percent, for American Indians 13 percent, and for blacks over 14 percent. The NRC, at the request of Congress, has been asked to revisit the issue. In this case, however, the Office for Civil Rights in the U.S. Department of Education extended the committee's charge to include the representation of minority children in gifted and talented programs as well, where racial/ethnic disproportion patterns are, generally speaking, the reverse of those in special education.

Current Context

Since the 1982 NRC report, much has changed in general education as well as in special education. The proportion of minority students in the population of school-age children has risen dramatically—to 35 percent in 2000—increasing the diversity of students and of primary languages spoken in many schools. And state standards have raised the bar for the achievement expected of all students. More than 1 in 10 students is now identified for special education services: in the past decade alone, there has been a 35 percent increase in the number of children served under the Individuals with Disabilities Education Act (IDEA). And many more of these students are receiving special education and related services in general education classrooms.

The distribution of students across special education categories has changed as well. Identification rates for students with mental retardation today are about a quarter lower than in 1979. While the decline has applied across racial/ethnic groups, disproportionate representation of black students in that category has persisted. Just over 1 percent of white students but 2.6 percent of black students fall into that category.

Two decades ago, fewer than 3 percent of students were identified with learning disabilities (LD). That number approaches 6 percent of all students today. Only American Indian students are represented in disproportionately large numbers in that category. But for all racial/ethnic groups, the LD category accounts both for the largest number of special education students and for the largest growth rate in special education placements.

While these demographic and policy changes create a somewhat different-context today from that confronting the earlier NRC committee, the problems are conceptually quite similar. At the outset, both committees confronted a paradox: if IDEA provides extra resources and the right to a more individualized education program, why would one consider disproportionate representation of minority children a problem? The answer, as every parent of a child receiving special education services knows, is that in order to be eligible for the additional resources a child must be labeled as having a disability, a label that signals substandard performance. And while that label is intended to bring additional supports, it may also bring lowered expectations on the part of teachers, other children, and the identified student. When a child cannot learn without the additional supports, and when the supports improve outcomes for the child, that trade-off may well be worth making. But because there is a trade-off, both the need and the benefit should be established before the label and the cost are imposed. This committee, like its predecessor, does not view the desirable end necessarily as one in which no minority group is represented in disproportionate numbers, but rather one in which the children who receive special education or gifted program services are those who truly require them and who benefit from them.

Who requires specialized education? Answering that question has always posed a challenge. The historic notion of a child with an emotional or learning disability or a talent conveys a "fixed-trait" model, in which the observed performance is the consequence of characteristics internal to the child. Assessment processes have been designed as an attempt to isolate those children with internal traits that constitute a "disability" or a "gift." And clearly there can be within-child characteristics that underlie placement in one of the high-incidence categories. Neurobiological investigations, for example, reveal different patterns of brain activity in dyslexic and nondyslexic children while reading.

However, in the past few decades a growing body of research has pointed to the critical role that context can play in achievement and behavior. The same child can perform very differently depending on the level of teacher support, and aggressive behavior can be reversed or exacerbated by effective or ineffective classroom management. In practice, it can be quite difficult to distinguish internal child traits that require the ongoing support of special education from inadequate opportunity or contextual support for learning and behavior.

Committee's Approach

The conceptual framework in which the committee considered the issue of minority disproportion in special education and gifted and talented programs, then, is one in which the achievement or behavior at issue is determined by the interaction of the child, the teacher, and the classroom environment. Internal child characteristics play a clear role: what the child brings to the interaction is a function both of biology and of experience in the family and the community. But the child's achievement and behavior outcomes will also reflect the effectiveness of instruction and the instructional environment.

The committee did not view the problem of disproportionate representation in special education as one of simply eliminating racial/ethnic differences in assignment. If special education services provide genuine individualized instruction and accountability for student learning, we consider it as serious a concern when students who need those supports are passed over (false negatives) as when they are inappropriately identified (false positives). Likewise with respect to gifted and talented programs, we consider it a problem if qualified minority students are overlooked in the identification process, but consider it an undesirable solution if minority students are selected when they are not adequately prepared for the demands of gifted and talented programs. The committee's goal, then, was to understand why disproportion occurs. To address our charge, the committee asked four questions:

> 1. *Is there reason to believe that there is currently a higher incidence of special needs or giftedness among some racial/ethnic groups? Specifically, are there biological and social or contextual contributors to early development that differ by race or ethnicity?*

Our answer to that question is a definitive "yes." We know that minority children are disproportionately poor, and poverty is associated with higher rates of exposure to harmful toxins, including lead, alcohol, and tobacco, in early stages of development. Poor children are also more likely to be born with low birthweight, to have poorer nutrition, and to have home and child care environments that are less supportive of early cognitive and emotional development than their majority counterparts. When poverty is deep and persistent, the number of risk factors rises, seriously jeopardizing development.

Some risk factors have a disproportionate impact on particular groups that goes beyond the poverty effect. In all income groups, black children are more likely to be born with low birthweight and are more likely to be exposed to harmful levels of lead, while American Indian/Alaskan Native children are more likely to be exposed prenatally to high levels of alcohol and tobacco. While the separate effect of each of these factors on school achievement and performance is difficult to determine, substantial differences by race/ethnicity on a variety of dimensions of school preparedness are documented at kindergarten entry.

> 2. *Does schooling independently contribute to the incidence of special needs or giftedness among students in different racial/ethnic groups through the opportunities that it provides?*

Again, our answer is: "yes." Schools with higher concentrations of low income, minority children are less likely to have experienced, well-trained teachers. Per pupil expenditures in those schools are somewhat lower, while the needs of low-income student populations and the difficulty of attracting teachers to inner-city, urban schools suggest that supporting comparable levels of education would require higher levels of per-pupil expenditures. These schools are less likely to offer advanced courses for their students, providing less support for high academic achievement.

When children come to school from disadvantaged backgrounds, as a disproportionate number of minority students do, high-quality instruction that carefully puts the prerequisites for learning in place, combined with effective classroom management that minimizes chaos, can put students on a path to academic success. While some reform efforts suggest that such an outcome is possible, there are currently no assurances that children will be exposed to effective instruction or classroom management before they are placed in special education programs or are screened for gifted programs.

> 3. *Does the current referral and assessment process reliably identify students with special needs and gifts? In particular, is there reason to believe that the current process is biased in terms of race or ethnicity?*

The answer here is not as straightforward. The majority of children in special and gifted education are referred by teachers. If a teacher is biased in evaluating student performance and behavior, current procedures provide ample room for those biases to be reflected in referrals. Some experimental research suggests that teachers do hold such biases. But whether bias is maintained when teachers have direct contact with children in the classroom is not clear. For example, research that has compared groups of students who are referred by teachers find that minority students actually have greater academic and behavior problems than their majority counterparts.

Once students are referred for special education, they must be assessed as eligible or ineligible. Whether the assessment process is biased is as controversial as the referral process. However research shows that context, including familiarity with test taking and the norms and expectations of school, may depress the scores of students whose experiences prepare them less well for the demands of classrooms and standardized tests.

Whether the referral and assessment of students for special and gifted education is racially biased or not, are the right students being identified—students who need and can benefit from those programs? Here the committee's answer is "no." The subjectivity of the referral process allows for students with significant learning problems to be overlooked for referral, and the conceptual and procedural shortcomings of the assessment process for learning disabilities and emotional disturbance give little confidence that student need has been appropriately identified. Importantly, current procedures result in placements later in the educational process than is most effective or efficient.

4. Is placement in special education a benefit or a risk? Does the outcome differ by race or ethnic group?

The data that would allow us to answer these questions adequately do not exist. We do know that some specific special education and gifted and talented interventions have been demonstrated to have positive outcomes for students. But how widely those interventions are employed is not known. Nor do we know whether minority students are less likely to be exposed to those high-quality interventions than majority students. What evidence is available suggests that parent advocacy and teacher quality, both of which would be expected to correlate with higher-quality interventions, are less likely in higher-poverty school districts where minority children are concentrated.

At the core of our study is an observation that unites all four questions: *there is substantial evidence with regard to both behavior and achievement that early identification and intervention is more effective than later identification and intervention.* This is true for children of any race or ethnic group, and children with or without an identifiable "within-child" problem. Yet the current special education identification process relies on a "wait-to-fail" principle that both increases the likelihood that children will fail because they do not receive early supports and decreases the effectiveness of supports once they are received. Similarly, the practice of identifying gifted learners after several years of schooling is based on the "wait 'til they succeed" philosophy rather than a developmental orientation.

While this principle applies to all students, the impact is likely to be greatest on students from disadvantaged backgrounds because (a) their experience outside the school prepares them less well for the demands of schooling, placing them at greater risk for failure, and (b) the resources available to them in general education are more likely to be substandard. Early efforts to identify and intervene with children at risk for later failure will help all children who need additional supports. But we would expect a disproportionately large number of those students to be from disadvantaged backgrounds.

The vision we offer in the report is one in which general and special education services are more tightly integrated; one in which no child is judged by the school to have a learning or emotional disability or to lack exceptional talent until efforts to provide high-quality instructional and behavioral support in the general education context have been tried without success. The "earlier is better" principle applies even before the K-12 years. The more effective we are at curtailing early biological harms and injuries and providing children with the supports for normal cognitive and behavioral development in the earliest years of life, the fewer children will arrive at school at risk for failure.

Conclusions and Recommendations

. . . Here we give the conclusions we consider key, along with the recommendations. They are organized here in the following major categories: referral and eligibility determination in special education (SE) and gifted and talented education (GT); teacher quality (TQ); biological and early childhood risk factors (EC); data collection (DC); and expanding the research and development base (RD).

Special Education Eligibility

From our review of the current knowledge base, several important conclusions have led the committee to rethink the current approach to special education:

5. Among the most frequent reasons for referral to special education are reading difficulties and behavior problems.
6. In recent years, interventions appropriate for the general education classroom to improve reading instruction and classroom management have been demonstrated to reduce the number of children who fail at reading or are later identified with behavior disorders.
7. There are currently no mechanisms in place to guarantee that students will be exposed to state-of-the-art reading instruction or classroom management before they are identified as having a "within-child" problem.
8. Referral "for the high-incidence categories of special education currently requires student failure. However, screening mechanisms exist for early identification of children at risk for later

reading and behavior problems. And the effectiveness of early intervention in both areas has been demonstrated to be considerably
greater than the effectiveness of later, postfailure intervention.

These findings suggest that schools should be doing more and doing it
earlier to ensure that students receive quality general education services to
reduce the number of students with pronounced achievement and behavior
problems. The committee's proposed alternative would require policy and
regulatory changes at both the federal and state levels of government.

Federal-Level Recommendations

*Recommendation SE.1: The committee recommends that federal guidelines
for special education eligibility be changed in order to encourage better integrated general and special education services. We propose that eligibility
ensue when a student exhibits large differences from typical levels of performance in one or more domain(s) and with evidence of insufficient response to
high-quality interventions in the relevant domain(s) of functioning in school
settings. These domains include achievement (e.g., reading, writing, mathematics), social behavior, and emotional regulation. As is currently the case,
eligibility determination would also require a judgment by a multidisciplinary
team, including parents, that special education is needed.*

The proposed approach would not negate the eligibility of any
student who arrives at school with a disability determination, or who has
a severe disability, from being served as they are currently. But for children
with milder high-incidence disabilities, the implications for referral and
assessment are considerable. Assessment for special education eligibility
would be focused on gathering information that documents educationally
relevant differences from typical levels of performance, and that is relevant
to the design, monitoring, and evaluation of treatments.

While eligibility for special education would by law continue to depend
on establishment of a disability, in the committee view, noncategorical conceptions and classification criteria that focus on matching a student's specific
needs to an intervention strategy would obviate the need for the traditional
high-incidence disability labels such as LD and ED. If traditional disability
definitions are used, they would need to be revised to focus on characteristics
directly related to classroom and school learning and behavior (e.g., reading
failure, math failure, persistent inattention and disorganization).

State-Level Recommendations

Regulatory changes would be required in most states for implementation
of a reformed special education program that uses functional assessment
measures to promote positive outcomes for students with disabilities.
Some states have already instituted changes that move in this direction
and can serve as examples. These states' rules require a systematic problem-
solving process that is centered around quality indicators associated with
successful interventions.

Recommendation 5E.2: The committee recommends that states adopt a universal screening and multitiered intervention strategy in general education to enable early identification and intervention with children at risk for reading problems. For students who continue to have difficulty even after intensive intervention, referral to special education and the development of an individualized education program (IEP) would follow. The data regarding student response to intervention would be used for eligibility determination.

Recommendation 5E.3: The committee recommends that states launch large-scale pilot programs in conjunction with universities or research centers to test the plausibility and productivity of universal behavior management interventions, early behavior screening, and techniques to work with children at risk for behavior problems. Research results suggest that these interventions can work. However, a large-scale pilot project would provide a firmer foundation of knowledge regarding scaling up the practices involved.

Federal Support of State Reform Efforts

Recommendation SE.4: While the United States has a strong tradition of state control of education, the committee recommends that the federal government support widespread adoption of early screening and intervention in the states.

Gifted and Talented Eligibility

The research base justifying alternative approaches for the screening, identification, and placement of gifted children is neither as extensive nor as informative as that for special education.

Recommendation GT.l: The committee recommends a research program oriented toward the development of a broader knowledge base on early identification and intervention with children who exhibit advanced performance in the verbal or quantitative realm, or who exhibit other advanced abilities.

This research program should be designed to determine whether there are reliable and valid indicators of current exceptional performance in language, mathematical, or other domains, or indicators of later exceptional performance. Research on classroom practice designed to encourage the early and continued development of gifted behaviors in underrepresented populations should be undertaken so that screening can be followed by effective intervention.

School Context and Student Performance

School resources, class size, and indicators of teacher quality are associated with learning and behavior outcomes. However, their influence is exerted primarily through teacher-student interactions. Moreover, in the prevention and eligibility determination model the committee is recommending, general education assessments and interventions not now in widespread use are proposed as standard practice. Key to our proposals, then, are sustained efforts at capacity building, and sufficient resources, time, and coordination among stakeholders to build that capacity.

State-Level Recommendations

Teacher Quality: General education teachers need improved teacher preparation and professional development to prepare them to address the needs of students with significant underachievement or giftedness.

> *Recommendation TQ.l: State certification or licensure requirements for teachers should systematically require:*

> - *competency in understanding and implementing reasonable norms and expectations for students, and core competencies in instructional delivery of academic content;*
> - *coursework and practicum experience in understanding, creating, and modifying an educational environment to meet children's individual needs;*
> - *competency in behavior management in classroom and noninstructional school settings;*
> - *instruction in functional analysis and routine behavioral assessment of students;*
> - *instruction in effective intervention strategies for students who fail to meet minimal standards for successful educational performance, or who substantially exceed minimal standards;*
> - *coursework and practicum experience to prepare teachers to deliver culturally responsive instruction. More specifically, teachers should be familiar with the beliefs, values, cultural practices, discourse styles, and other features of students' lives that may have an impact on classroom participation and success and be prepared to use this information in designing instruction.*

While a foundational knowledge base can be laid in preservice education, often classroom experience is needed before teachers can make the most of instructional experiences.

> - *States should require rigorous professional development for all practicing teachers, administrators, and educational support personnel to assist them in addressing the varied needs of students who differ substantially from the norm in achievement and/or behavior.*
> - *The professional development of administrators and educational support personnel should include enhanced capabilities in the improvement and evaluation of teacher instruction with respect to meeting student's individual needs.*

> *Recommendation TQ.2: State or professional association approval for educator instructional programs should include requirements for faculty competence in the current literature and research on child and adolescent learning and development, and on successful assessment, instructional, and intervention strategies, particularly for atypical learners and students with gifts and disabilities.*

> *Recommendation TQ.3: A credential as a school psychologist or special education teacher should require instruction in classroom observation/assessment and*

in teacher support to work with a struggling student or with a gifted student. These skills should be considered as critical to their professional role as the administration and interpretation of tests are now considered.

Federal-Level Recommendations

This committee joins many others at the NRC and elsewhere in calling for improved teacher preparation. How to move from widespread agreement that change is needed to system reform is a challenge that will itself require careful study.

Recommendation TQ.4: The committee recommends that a national advisory panel be convened in an institutional environment that is protected from political influence to study the quality and currency of programs that now exist to train teachers for general, special, and gifted education. The panel should address:

- *the mechanisms for keeping instructional programs current and of high quality;*
- *the standards and requirements of those programs;*
- *the applicability of instructional programs to the demands of classroom practice;*
- *the long-term influence of the programs in successfully promoting educational achievement for pre-K, elementary, and secondary students.*

Direct comparison to other professional fields (e.g., medicine, nursing, law, engineering, accounting) may provide insight applicable to education.

Biological and Social Risk Factors in Early Childhood

Existing intervention programs to address early biological harms and injuries have demonstrated the potential to substantially improve developmental outcomes. The committee concludes that the number of children, particularly minority children, who require special education can be reduced if resources are devoted to this end. In particular, the committee calls attention to the recommendation of the President's Task Force on Environmental Health Risks and Safety Risks to Children to eliminate lead from the housing stock by 2010.

Federal-Level Recommendations

The committee also looked at social and environmental influences on development with no clear biological basis that might differ by race or ethnicity. Because there is evidence that early intervention on multiple fronts, if *it is of high quality*, can improve the school prospects for children with multiple risk factors and reduce the likelihood that they will require special education, the committee recommends a substantial expansion and improvement of current early intervention efforts. Our recommendation is addressed to federal and state governments, both of whom currently play a major role in early childhood education.

Recommendation EC.l: The committee recommends that all high-risk children have access to high-quality early childhood interventions.

- *For the children at highest risk, these interventions should include family support, health services, and sustained, high-quality care and cognitive stimulation right from birth.*
- *Preschool children (ages 4 and 5) who are eligible for Head Start should have access to a Head Start or another publicly funded preschool program. These programs should provide exposure to learning opportunities that will prepare them for success in school. Intervention should target services to the level of individual need, including high cognitive challenge for the child who exceeds normative performance.*
- *The proposed expansion should better coordinate existing federal programs, such as Head Start and Early Head Start, and IDEA parts C and B, as well as state-initiated programs that meet equal or higher standards.*

While much is known about the types of experiences young children need for healthy development, improving the quality of early childhood programs will require refinement of the knowledge base in ways that are directly useful to practice, and bridging the chasm between what is known from research and best practice and is done in common practice. This will require a sustained vision and a rigorous research and development effort that transforms knowledge about what works and what does not work into field-tested program content, supporting materials, and professional development.

Recommendation EC.2: The committee recommends that the federal government launch a large-scale, rigorous, sustained research and development program in an institutional environment that has the capacity to bring together excellent professionals in research, program development, professional development, and child care/preschool practice for students from all backgrounds and at all levels of exceptional performance.

Improving Data Collection and Expanding the Research Base

The data documenting disproportionate representation are difficult to interpret in a variety of respects that make them a weak foundation on which to build public policy. Moreover, the data provide little if any insight into factors that contribute to placement or services that students receive.

Federal-Level Recommendations

Recommendation DC.1: The committee recommends that the Department of Education conduct a single, well-designed data collection effort to monitor both the number of children receiving services through the Individuals with Disabilities Education Act or through programs for the gifted and talented, and the characteristics of those children of concern to civil rights enforcement efforts. A unified effort would eliminate the considerable redundancy, and the burden it places on schools, in the current data collection efforts of the Office for Civil Rights and the Office of Special Education Programs.

While a more careful data collection effort of the sort outlined here would improve the understanding of who is being assigned to special education and gifted and talented programs, it would do little to further understanding of the reasons for placement, the appropriateness of placement (or nonplacement), the services provided, or the consequences that ensue.

> *Recommendation DC.2: The committee recommends that a national advisory panel be convened to design the collection of nationally representative longitudinal data that would allow for more informed study of minority disproportion in special education and gifted and talented programs.* The panel should include scholars in special education research as well as researchers experienced in national longitudinal data collection and analysts in a variety of allied fields, including anthropology, psychology, and sociology.

In our study of the issues related to the representation of minority children in special education and gifted and talented programs, the existing knowledge base revealed the potential for substantial progress. We know much about the kinds of experiences that promote children's early health, cognitive, and behavioral development and set them on a more positive trajectory for school success. We know intervention strategies that have demonstrated success with some of the key problems that end in referral to special education. And we know some features of programs that are correlated with successful outcomes for students in special education.

Between the articulation of what we know from research and best practice, and a change in everyday practice, lies a wide chasm. It is the distance between demonstrating that vocabulary development is key to later success in reading, and having every Head Start teacher trained and equipped with materials that will promote vocabulary development among Head Start children. It is the distance between knowing that classroom management affects a child's behavior, and the school psychologist knowing how to help a specific teacher work with a specific child in the classroom context. It is the distance between those who are most knowledgeable and experienced agreeing on what teachers need to know, and every school of education changing its curriculum. Bridging the chasm will require that we become better at accumulating knowledge, extending it in promising areas, incorporating the best of what is known in teacher training efforts and education curricula and materials, and rigorously testing effectiveness. It will require public policies that are aligned with the knowledge base and that provide the support for its widespread application.

> *Recommendation RD.1: We recommend that education research and development, including that related to special and gifted education, be substantially expanded to carry promising findings and validated practices through to classroom applicability. This includes research on scaling up promising practices from research sites to widespread use.*

For medical problems like cancer, federal research programs create a vision, focus research efforts on areas with promise for improving treatments, conduct extensive field tests to determine what works, and facilitate the movement of research findings into practice. If the nation is serious about reducing the number of children who are on a trajectory that leads to school failure and disability identification as well as increasing the number of minority students who are achieving at high levels, we will need to devote the minds and resources to that effort commensurate with the size and the importance of the enterprise.

Daniel J. Losen and
Gary Orfield

→ **NO**

Introduction: Racial Inequity in Special Education

Before Congress passed the Education for All Handicapped Children Act—now known as the Individuals with Disabilities Education Act (IDEA)—nearly half of the nation's approximately four million children with disabilities were not receiving a public education. Of the children who were being educated in public schools, many were relegated to a ghetto-like existence in isolated, often run-down classrooms located in the least desirable places within the school building, or sent to entirely separate facilities. Since its passage in 1975, the IDEA has brought tremendous benefits: today, approximately six million children with disabilities enjoy their right to a free appropriate public education. IDEA's substantive rights and procedural protections have produced significant and measurable outcomes for students with disabilities: their graduation rates have increased dramatically, and the number of these students who go on to college has almost tripled since 1978 (though it is still quite low).

Despite these improvements, the benefits of special education have not been equitably distributed. Minority children with disabilities all too often experience inadequate services, low-quality curriculum and instruction, and unnecessary isolation from their nondisabled peers. Moreover, inappropriate practices in both general and special education classrooms have resulted in overrepresentation, misclassification, and hardship for minority students, particularly black children.

A flood of concerns expressed by community leaders about minority children being misplaced in special education prompted The Civil Rights Project at Harvard University to commission the research for [our] book. Since the early 1970s, national surveys by the Office for Civil Rights (OCR) of the U.S. Department of Education have revealed persistent overrepresentation of minority children in certain disability categories. The most pronounced disparities then were black children who, while only 16 percent of the total school enrollment, represented 38 percent of the students in classes for the educationally mentally retarded. After more than twenty years, black children constitute 17 percent of the total school enrollment and 33 percent of those labeled mentally retarded—only a marginal improvement. During this same period, however, disproportionality in the area of emotional disturbance (ED) and the rate of identification for both ED and specific learning disabilities (SLO) grew significantly for blacks.

To better understand this persistent overrepresentation trend, as well as growing reports of profound inequities in the quality of special education, The Civil Rights Project set out to find the best research available. In the original call for papers we asked leading scholars from around the country to document and clarify the issues for minority students with regard to special education. As researchers pursued this task and analyzed possible contributing factors, our fears about the persistence of these problems, the complexities of the contributing factors, and the lack of proven solutions were confirmed.

Our primary purpose in presenting this information is to identify and solve the problem, not to assign blame. This research is intended to inform the debate on special education and racial justice and to provide educators, researchers, advocates, and policymakers with a deeper understanding of the issues as they renew their efforts to find workable solutions. Using national-, state-, district-, and school-level data, these studies document the current trends for minority students regarding identification and restrictiveness of placement. They explore some of the most likely causes, dispel some myths and oversimplified explanations, and highlight the complex interplay of variables within the control of educators at all levels of government. Recognizing the critical role that advocacy has played in securing the rights of all children to educational opportunity, [our] book also provides analysis of the evolving role of the law in stopping inappropriate practices that harm children of color, and in guaranteeing equitable benefits from special education.

The findings [here] point to areas where much improvement is needed and offer an array of ideas for remedies and suggestions for continued research. It is important to recognize that concerns about special education are nested in concerns about inequities in education generally. Special education overrepresentation often mirrors overrepresentation in many undesirable categories—including dropping out, low-track placements, suspensions, and involvement with juvenile justice—and underrepresentation in desirable categories such as gifted and talented. Because special education inequities are often tied to general education issues, remedies should address shortcomings in both special and general education. The recommendations, which are aimed at improving policy and practice, were developed through extensive analysis of the efforts and experiences of educators, policymakers, attorneys, and civil rights enforcement agents. We hope the recommendations will help prevent harmful misidentification and inappropriate placements of minority students, and encourage effective and equitable leadership, enforcement, and distribution of resources to ensure that all children who need special education support receive appropriate and high-quality services.

Issues Explored and Findings

Much of the empirical research . . . explores patterns of overrepresentation of minority children by disability category and whether, once identified, they experience relatively less access to the general education classroom than similarly situated white children. The evidence suggests that black overrepresentation is substantial in state after state. The studies reveal wide differences in disability identification between blacks and Hispanics and between black boys and black girls that cannot be explained in terms of social background or measured ability.

Both the statistical and qualitative analyses . . . suggest that these racial, ethnic, and gender differences are due to many complex and interacting factors, including unconscious racial bias on the part of school authorities, large resource inequalities that run along lines of race and class, unjustifiable reliance on IQ and other evaluation tools, educators' inappropriate responses to the pressures of high-stakes testing, and power differentials between minority parents and school officials.

[We] . . . examine whether the numerous causes of overrepresentation are likely race linked, which is a distinctly different inquiry from whether intentional racial discrimination is the primary cause. Absent a blatantly discriminatory (i.e., illegal as written) policy or practice, to establish that different treatment is purposeful and racist requires specific proof of intent, which is usually discovered through legal enforcement proceedings. The research [here] is obviously not specific enough to explore questions of intent.

Overidentification

On October 4, 2001, the U.S. House of Representatives Committee on Education and the Workforce convened hearings about the overidentification of minority students in special education. In his testimony, Representative Chaka Fattah concluded with the following story of Billy Hawkins:

> For the first fifteen years of his life Billy Hawkins was labeled by his teachers as "educable mentally retarded." Billy was backup quarterback for his high school football team. One night he was called off the bench and rallied his team from far behind. In doing so, he ran complicated plays and clearly demonstrated a gift for the game. The school principal, who was in the stands, recognized that the "retarded boy" could play, and soon after had Billy enrolled in regular classes and instructed his teachers to give him extra help. Billy Hawkins went on to complete a Ph.D. and is now Associate Dean at Michigan's Ferris State University.

Students like Billy Hawkins seldom get the "call off the bench" and an opportunity to shine in front of their principal. Instead, they are removed from the mainstream and never realize their talent. Unfortunately, some in Congress responded to findings we released in earlier reports and to stories like Dr. Hawkins' by opposing efforts to guarantee and fully fund special education at the level Congress originally intended, claiming a need to "fix" special education before providing more funds. [We address] discrete areas of deep racial inequity within a much larger system of special education. It would be wrong to restrict or withhold promised expenditures for all students with disabilities in every state of the nation based on the issues identified in this research.

Of the inequalities in education experienced by minority school-children, those in special education are better documented than most. In 1998, approximately 1.5 million minority children were identified as having mental retardation, emotional disturbance, or a specific learning disability. More than 876,000 of these were black or Native American, and black students were nearly three times as likely as white students to be labeled mentally retarded. Mental retardation diagnoses are relatively rare for all children, and the last twenty years have witnessed a modest decrease in the percentages of students labeled mentally retarded for nearly all racial groups.

Despite this fact, U.S. Department of Education data from 2000–2001 show that in at least thirteen states more than 2.75 percent of all blacks enrolled were labeled mentally retarded. The prevalence of mental retardation for whites nationally was approximately 0.75 percent in 2001, and in no state did the incidence among whites ever rise above 2.32 percent. Moreover, nearly three-quarters of the states with unusually high incidence rates (2.75–5.41%) for blacks were in the South. This is arguably a continuation of the problem as a southern phenomenon that was first observed in the National Research Council's data from 1979, although both then and now many northern states also exhibit remarkably high rates. One positive sign is that southern states exhibited the largest decreases in sheer percentages since 1979.

The data in these studies are generally analyzed in one of three ways. In one, a given minority group's percentage enrollment in the general population is compared to that group's percentage identification in a given disability category. In the second, the actual risk level for a minority group is calculated by dividing the number of students from a given racial group with a given disability by the total enrollment of that racial group. And in the third way, these risk levels are calculated for each minority group and then compared. These comparisons are described as risk ratios and are usually reported in comparison to white children.

. . . Tom Parrish, a senior research analyst with the American Institutes for Research, calculates risk levels using U.S. Department of Education data based on the number of children eligible for special education reported by each state for children between the ages of six and twenty-one in 1998, and compares that with census estimates of children of the same age for each state for the same year. Parrish then calculates the risk ratios for each minority group by cognitive disability category for every state and for the nation.

He finds that black children are 2.88 times more likely than whites to be labeled mentally retarded and 1.92 times more likely to be labeled emotionally disturbed.

Blacks are the most overrepresented minority group in every category and in nearly every state. The gross racial disparities that exist between many minority groups and whites in terms of mental retardation also exist in other cognitive disability categories, but are less pronounced. Nation-wide, blacks and Native Americans are less often overidentified for specific learning disabilities (i.e., black children are more than twice as likely as white children to be found to have a specific learning disability in only nine states).

Parrish also shows the extent of overidentification of other minorities in the ED and SLD categories. In the SLD category, for example, only in Hawaii are Asian Americans/Pacific Islanders identified at nearly twice the rate of whites. On the other hand, Native American children in six states are identified at more than twice the rate of whites.

Latinos and Asian Americans are generally underidentified compared to whites in most states and in most categories, raising the possibility of inadequate attention to their special needs; however, the state-level data may underreport the problem for some groups. According to a 1982 National Research Council (NRC) report, district-level data on Hispanics from 1979 suggested that a wide variety of both over- and underrepresentation tended to cancel each other out in aggregate state-level data. Neither the 2002 NRC report, "Minority Students in Special and Gifted Education," nor the studies [here] conducted a district-level analysis with national data comparable to that contained in the 1982 study of Hispanic identification rates. However, Alfredo Artiles, Robert Rueda, Jesus Jose Salazar, and Ignacio Higareda, in their analysis of large urban school districts in California, reveal that disproportionate representation in special education is far more likely for (predominantly Latino) English-language learners in secondary school than in elementary school. Thus, the problem may even be hidden when elementary and secondary school data are aggregated at the district level.

Edward Fierros and James Conroy's research . . . , which does examine district-level data from throughout Connecticut and from selected U.S. cities, suggests that the state data may miss disturbing trends for minority overrepresentation in a given category or educational setting. Generally speaking, the most serious racial disparities (both under- and overrepresentation) become apparent when data on minority children are disaggregated by race/ethnicity subgroups, cognitive disability category, gender, and placement—at least down to the district level.

Educational Placement
Readers should not forget that students with disabilities are entitled to receive supports and services in a setting best suited to their individual needs, and not to be automatically assigned to a separate place, subjected to low expectations, or excluded from educational opportunities. While substantially separate educational environments are certainly best for some individuals, it is equally well established in research that students with disabilities benefit most when they are educated with their general education peers to the maximum extent appropriate, and this is reflected in the law.

Fierros and Conroy's work demonstrates that, once identified as eligible for special education services, both Latinos and blacks are far less likely than whites to be educated in a fully inclusive general education classroom and far more likely to be educated in a substantially separate setting. The data Fierros and Conroy explore show a consistent trend toward less inclusion for minority children at the national, state, and district levels. The relationship between race and greater exclusion, also not examined in the NRC's 2002 report, suggests that, among students with disabilities, black and Latino children with disabilities may be consistently receiving less desirable treatment than white children. Fierros and Conroy further disaggregate the racial data by disability type for the state of Connecticut and find a lower level of inclusion for blacks and Hispanics compared to whites among each of the three disability types examined (students with mental retardation, emotional disturbance, and specific learning disabilities).

The concern with the overrepresentation of minorities would be mitigated if the evidence suggested that minority children reaped benefits from more frequent identification and isolation. But as government officials acknowledge and as data demonstrate, this does not appear to be the case.

Low-Quality Evaluations, Supports, and Services

In their chapter, David Osher, Darren Woodruff, and Anthony Sims illustrate how the issue is often not as simple as the false identification of a nondisabled minority child. Many minority children do have disabilities but are at risk of receiving inappropriate and inadequate services and unwarranted isolation. Osher et al. point out that, for some children, receiving inappropriate services may be more harmful than receiving none at all. For others, not receiving help early enough may exacerbate learning and behavior problems. Both problems are reflected in disturbing statistics on outcomes for minority children with disabilities. As Donald Oswald, Martha Coutinho, and Al Best report in the opening lines of the book's first chapter, there are dramatic differences in what happens to minority students with disabilities after high school:

> In the 1998–1999 school year, over 2.2 million children of color in U.S. schools were served by special education (U.S. Department of Education, 2000). Post–high school outcomes for these minority students with disabilities are strikingly inferior. Among high school youth with disabilities, about 75 percent of African American students, as compared to 47 percent of white students, are not employed two years out of school. Slightly more than half (52%) of African Americans, compared to 39 percent of white young adults, are still not employed three to five years out of school. In this same time period, the arrest rate for African Americans with disabilities is 40 percent, as compared to 27 percent for whites (Wagner, D'Amico, Marder, Newman, & Blackorby, 1992).

In addition to these patterns, Osher, Woodruff, and Sims provide new data depicting substantially higher rates of disciplinary action and placement in correctional facilities for minority students with disabilities still in school. Based on their review of the data and other research, they suggest that investments in high-quality special education and early intervention are sorely needed and could reduce the likelihood that minority students with disabilities will develop serious discipline problems or eventually wind up in correctional facilities.

Racial Discrimination and Other Contributing Factors

In a society where race is so strongly related to individual, family, and community conditions, it is extremely difficult to know what part of the inequalities are caused by discrimination within the school. These studies, however, do uncover correlations with race that cannot be explained by factors such as poverty or exposure to environmental hazards alone. While the scope of this research does not attempt to depict a definitive causal link to racial discrimination, the research does suggest that unconscious racial bias, stereotypes, and other race-linked factors have a significant impact on the patterns of identification, placement, and quality of services for minority children, and particularly for African American children.

The researchers recognize that factors such as poverty and environmental influences outside of school contribute to a heightened incidence of disability in significant ways. All analysts who attempt to sort out the causes of inequality in U.S. institutions of course face the dilemma that some of the differences in subtracted control variables are themselves products of other forms of racial discrimination. For example, if a researcher determined that 40 percent of the association between race and shorter life expectancy could be explained by poverty, we have to understand that the poverty in question may be influenced by employment discrimination or be due in part to a second-generational effect of segregated schooling. Therefore, despite the importance of statistical controls, it is well established that many controls will lower the estimates of the effect of race when race is examined as an isolated variable. What happens in school is only a subset of the far more pervasive impact of racial discrimination that affects minority families and their children.

Even when researchers assume that poverty is independent of race and subtract race and other background variables, many of the trends highlighted by this research appear to contradict the theory that poverty is primarily to blame and that race is not a significant factor. Those trends include the following: (a) pronounced and persistent racial disparities in identification between white and black children in the categories of mental retardation and emotional disturbance, compared with far less disparity in the category of specific learning disabilities; (b) a minimal degree of racial disparity in medically diagnosed disabilities as compared with subjective cognitive disabilities; (c) dramatic differences in the incidence of disability from one state to the next; and (d) gross disparities between blacks and Hispanics, and between black boys and girls, in identification rates for the categories of mentally retarded and emotionally disturbed.

The data on disproportionate representation is compatible with the theory that systemic racial discrimination is a contributing factor where disparities are substantial. Moreover, the trends revealed in [our] book are consistent with the theory that different racial groups, facing different kinds of stereotypes and bias, would experience racial disparities differently. States with a history of racial apartheid under de jure segregation, for example, account for five of the seven states with the highest overrepresentation of African Americans labeled mentally retarded—Mississippi, South Carolina, North Carolina, Florida, and Alabama. This trend suggests that the "soft bigotry of low expectations" may have replaced the undeniable intentional racial discrimination in education against blacks that once pervaded the South. In contrast, no southern state was among the top seven states where Hispanic children deemed mentally retarded were most heavily overrepresented.

The effects of poverty cannot satisfactorily explain racial disparities in identification for mental retardation or emotional disturbance. Regression analysis suggests that race, gender, and poverty are all significant factors. Oswald, Coutinho, and Best specifically asked whether, "taking into account the effects of social, demographic, and school-related variables, gender and ethnicity are significantly associated with the risk of being identified for special education." Their examination of each factor at the district level (based on all of the districts surveyed in OCR's database combined with the National Center for Education Statistics, Common Core of Data) finds that, although disability incidence often increases with poverty, when poverty- and wealth-linked factors are controlled for, ethnicity and gender remain significant predictors of cognitive disability identification by schools. Specifically, wealth-linked factors included per pupil expenditure, median housing value, median income for households with children, percentage of children in households below the poverty level, and percentage of adults in the community who have a twelfth-grade education or less and no diploma.

Most disturbing, was that in wealthier districts, contrary to the expected trend, black children, especially males, were *more likely to be labeled* mentally retarded. Moreover, the sharp gender differences in identification within racial groups, also described in the 2002 NRC report, are not explained by the poverty theory.

Large demographic differences among minority groups are also discussed by Parrish and by Fierros and Conroy, and each confirms that the influence of race and ethnicity is significant, and apparently distinct from that of poverty. For example, Parrish reviews the data for each racial group across all fifty states and finds that, in comparison to whites, each minority group is at greater risk of being labeled mentally retarded as their percentage of the total enrolled population increases.

That poverty does account for some of the observed racial disproportions in disability identification comes as no surprise. Certain minority groups are disproportionately poor. Logically, one would expect poverty to cause a higher incidence of "hard" disabilities (e.g., blindness and deafness) among members of low-wealth minority groups, due to the impact of poor nutrition and inadequate prenatal care. But the most recent research shows that blacks in any given state are substantially less likely to be overrepresented in these hard categories.

Finally, the theory that poverty and socioeconomic factors can explain all or most of the observed racial disparities fails to account for the extreme differences between black overrepresentation and Hispanic underrepresentation, differences that are even more significant in many states than disparities between blacks and whites. For example, blacks in Alabama and Arkansas are more than seven to nine times as likely as Hispanics to be labeled mentally retarded. Moreover, nationally and in many other states, the disparity in identification rates for mental retardation and emotional disturbance between blacks and Hispanics is greater than the disparity between blacks and whites. Yet Hispanics, like blacks, are at far greater risk than whites for poverty, exposure to environmental toxins in impoverished neighborhoods, and low-level academic achievement in reading and math. Thus, the high variation in identification rates among minority groups with similar levels of poverty and academic failure casts serious doubt on assertions by some researchers that it is primarily poverty and not bias that creates these deep racial disparities.

Multiple Contributing Factors

Most students with disabilities enter school undiagnosed and are referred by regular classroom teachers for evaluations that may lead to special education identification and placement. Therefore, the cause of the observed racial disparity is rooted not only in the system of special education itself, put also in the system of regular education as it encompasses special education. Most students referred for evaluation for special education are deemed in need of services. If differential referral is a key element, then the perceptions and decisions of classroom teachers, as well as school-level policies and practices that have an impact on students in regular classrooms, are, likewise, key elements.

Based on years of research, Beth Harry, Janette Klingner, Keith Sturges, and Robert Moore conclude in their chapter that "[t]he point at which differences [in measured performance and ability] result in one child being labeled disabled and another not are totally matters of social decisionmaking." Special education evaluations are often presented to parents as a set of discrete decisions based on scientific analysis and assessment, but even test-driven decisions are inescapably subjective in nature. The existence of some bias in test *content* is not the primary concern. Harry et al.'s research, for example, describes how subjective decisions creep into all elements of the evaluation *process*, including whom to test, what test to use, when to use alternative tests, how to interpret student responses, and what weight to give results from specific tests. All of these alter the outcomes. As Harry et al. point out, "a penstroke of the American Association on Mental Retardation (AAMR)" lowered the IQ score cutoff point for mental retardation from 85 to 70, "swiftly curing thousands of previously disabled children."

School politics, power relationships between school authorities and minority parents, the quality of regular education, and the classroom management skills of the referring teacher also introduce important elements of subjectivity that often go unrecognized. Other race-linked forces at work include poorly trained teachers who are disproportionately employed in minority schools (some of whom use special education as a disciplinary tool), other resource inequalities correlated to race, beliefs in African American and Latino inferiority and the low expectations that accompany these beliefs, cultural insensitivity, praise differentials, fear and misunderstanding of black males, and overcrowded schools and classrooms that are disproportionately located in school districts with high percentages of minority students. Add to these forces the general phenomenon of white parents' activism, efficaciousness, and high social capital exercised on behalf of their children compared to the relative lack of parent power among minority parents, and one can understand how the combination of regular education problems and the special education identification process has had a disparate impact on students of different races and ethnicities.

Sweeping reforms may also trigger harmful outcomes. For example, Artiles et al.'s preliminary examination of the "Unz Initiative," which eliminated bilingual education in California, suggests that English-language learners whose access to language supports is limited are more likely to be placed in restrictive special education settings. And as Jay Heubert describes in detail in his chapter, over the last ten years the use of high-stakes testing may have disproportionately punished poor and minority students, students with disabilities, and English-language learners: "There is evidence that states with high minority enrollments in special education are also likely to have high-stakes testing policies." Heubert goes on to cite evidence that "promotion testing is . . . likely to increase, perhaps significantly, the numbers of students with disabilities and minority students who suffer the serious consequences of dropping out." He points out that the National Research Council has described simple retention in grade as "an ineffective intervention." The aspirational benefits of raising standards aside, Heubert concludes that minority students with disabilities are at "great risk . . . especially in states that administer high-stakes promotion and graduation tests. . . ."

The Status of the Law and Enforcement Policy

Beginning with *Brown v. Board of Education*, litigation and enforcement under civil rights law has been essential to improving racial equity in education. Title VI of the Civil Rights Act of 1964 provided an important lever for racial justice in education that was especially effective when the federal government made enforcement a high priority. Critically important was that, under the Title VI regulations, plaintiffs could use statistical evidence to prove that even a policy that was race neutral on its face had an adverse and unjustifiably disparate impact on children of color in violation of the law. As Daniel Losen and Kevin Welner describe in their chapter, the legal landscape shifted dramatically following the U.S. Supreme Court's 2001 ruling in *Alexander v. Sandoval* which declared that there is no implied private right of action to bring legal challenges under "disparate-impact" theory. Therefore, court challenges that would rely on serious statistical disparities to prove allegations of discrimination are nearly extinguished today. Although the government and individuals filing complaints with government agencies may still use the Title VI regulations to redress the racially disparate impact of neutral policies, enforcement of disparate impact regulations is more vulnerable to an administration's enforcement policy preferences than ever before.

Untouched by *Sandoval* is the potential to challenge policies or practices where the racial disparities in special education identification or placement arise in the context of hearings on school desegregation. For example, in Alabama in 2000, a court review of consent decrees in that state resulted in a settlement yielding comprehensive state- and district-level remedies for overidentification of minorities.

Losen and Welner point out that disability law is becoming a relatively stronger basis for leveraging remedies from states and school districts where overidentification, underservicing, or unnecessarily restrictive placements are an issue. They explain further how systemic legal actions are better suited for seeking effective comprehensive remedies that could address contributing factors in both regular and special education. In her chapter, Theresa Glennon closely examines and evaluates the Office for Civil Rights' enforcement efforts where disability law and Tide VI converge. Glennon's recommendations include better coordinated investigations and interagency information sharing, clearer guidance for schools, and more comprehensive compliance reviews by well-trained investigators.

Sharon Soltman and Donald Moore provide an extensive analysis of how to fashion a remedy through litigation in a case known as *Corcy H.* Their thorough chapter combines many years of research on effective practices with models of school improvement. They set forth a roadmap for school district reform to ensure that children with disabilities in Illinois be educated in the least restrictive environment as required by law. The multitiered *Corey H.* remedy entails a ten-year process for change, in one set of schools each year. The plaintiffs also won a large infusion of state funding to make implementing the *Corey H.* requirements a fully funded mandate. Further research on the efficacy of the court-ordered remedy should prove extremely useful to policymakers and others seeking to guarantee that minority children with disabilities have appropriate educational opportunities.

The only study in this volume that explores restricting federal funds as a remedy does so in the context of analyzing the viability of the Department of Education's Office for Special Education Programs' (OSEP) enforcement mechanisms for redressing racial disproportionality. In that study, Thomas Hehir argues forcefully for more frequent exercise of partial withholding by enforcement agents that is narrowly targeted to leverage compliance by specific states or districts in certain areas. As Hehir points out, partial withholding would allow OSEP to ratchet up its enforcement efforts without wholesale withdrawal of federal funds, which would heighten the risk of political backlash and have a negative impact on students in properly run programs. Likewise, federal policymakers should improve IDEA imple-mentation and civil rights enforcement without imposing wholesale limi-tations on federal special education funding, which would have a negative impact on children with disabilities nationwide. Of course, there may be extreme cases in noncompliant districts where the only way to end seri-ous violations is to cut off general funds, which proved very effective in spurring the desegregation of southern schools.

Moreover, Tom Parrish's research suggests that some state funding formulas are contributing to problems of overidentification. Some of these formulas fail to follow the federal model, which relies on U.S. Census data to determine allocations. The most problematic state formulas in-stead channel funds by disability identification and/or program and are suspected of creating incentives for overidentification.

Recommendations

Theses studies and the NRC's 2002 report both suggest that special edu-cation issues faced by minority children often begin with shortcomings in the realm of general education well before teachers or parents seek an evaluation for special education eligibility. Therefore, policy solutions that fail to consider the connection with general education classrooms will un-likely bring about significant change.

A New Federal Initiative With Implications for State Accountability

Our nation's education policy is at a crossroads. Leaders demand an end to the "soft bigotry of low expectations" and our government has promised to improve the achievement of all children in 2002 through the new edu-cation reform act, known as the No Child Left Behind Act. Racial equity is rooted in the commitment to teach all children well, with particular attention to meeting the needs of minority children.

To tackle racial disparities in achievement and graduation rates, the president and Congress embraced three reform approaches: public report-ing, accountability at all levels (school, district, and state), and mandatory enforcement. These three reform approaches could be used to address the gross racial disparities in special education identification, restrictiveness of placement, and quality of services.

For policymakers, there is no need to pinpoint a specific cause or al-lege race discrimination in order to achieve racial equity. Scholars report that many schools today still operate under a deficit model, where school authorities regard students with disabilities as the embodiments of their particular disability and ask only *what the special educators are required to do in order to accommodate the student's problem.* A universal commitment to equity in special education would help erode this deficit model by shifting the focus to *what all public educators should do to improve educational oppor-tunities and outcomes for all children.*

There is bipartisan acknowledgement that special education issues faced by minority children need a federal legislative response. This apparent consensus holds promise for effective federal reform. Reform attempts in the recent past can be improved upon. In 1997 the IDEA was amended to require states to collect and review data on racial disproportionality in both identification and placement and to intervene where disproportionality is significant. Before that, in 1995, the Office for Civil Rights made racial disproportionality in special education a top priority. The persistence of this problem suggests that states' legal obligations under IDEA and our civil rights enforcement priorities have not been met.

OCR was once a major force in the effort to desegregate our nation's schools, suggesting that the agency's efficacy is related to political will as much as it is to resources. It is apparent that there is a glaring need for stepped-up enforcement and oversight by both federal and state agencies. These actions must be geared toward encouraging the active participation of educators at all levels if there is to be any hope of meaningful and lasting improvement. Most important, aggressive efforts to remedy these issues are only the starting point. The efficacy of enforcement interventions and attempted reforms must be evaluated in terms of the outcomes for minority children.

Both general and special education teachers and administrators need better training to deliver effective instruction in the least restrictive, most inclusive environment appropriate. Meeting this need, along with the need for better data collection on racial and ethnic disparities and enhanced civil rights enforcement, would require an infusion of special education funds, which could be expected to result in net gains in education outcomes and savings in juvenile justice expenditures in the long term. By increasing federal oversight and by encouraging states to intervene where appropriate, the federal government could help improve the quality of instruction, supports, and services received by minority students in both regular and special education.

Although OCR still does not collect national data to determine racial disparities in the educational environment, the 1997 IDEA amendments obligate the states to collect sampled data. If the government required every state and school district to collect disaggregated data by race with disability category and educational setting (all three together), research on overrepresentation would benefit tremendously.

Moreover, much general education reform law is predicated on the concept that public pressure at the local level from parents and community stakeholders will stimulate meaningful improvements. To generate local reform pressure, the Bush education program requires public reporting of test achievement by a number of student subgroups, including disability status and major racial and ethnic subgroups. Policymakers could likewise stimulate meaningful improvements in special education by amending the IDEA to require public reporting of racial disparities in special education identification and placement.

IDEA should also require states to intervene under specified circumstances (they now have complete discretion) and to provide technical assistance to effect reforms. Such required intervention and assistance would likely foster greater self-reflection and improvement at the district level. While adopting mandatory interventions would be helpful, given the context of shrinking state education budgets, an emphasis on rewards and continued supports to foster successful efforts must be an integral part of any new enforcement efforts.

Finally, new mechanisms for minority children to exercise their rights under IDEA, including legal services support, would help considerably.

Toward Comprehensive Solutions to Systemic Problems at the District Level

The research and analysis presented in [the] volume are intended to serve educators, advocates, and policymakers alike. In addition to raising awareness of the issues, suggesting changes in legislation, and improving the enforcement of existing requirements, much can be accomplished with greater determination by school leadership.

For communities of color, disproportionate representation in special education is just one facet of the denial of access to educational opportunity. Denial begins in the regular education setting with school segregation, low tracking, test-based diploma denial and retention, overly harsh discipline, less access to programs for the gifted, and resource inequalities that have a distinctly racial dimension. Education leaders who suspect a problem at their school can accomplish a great deal by clearly stating that this problem is one that they and their staff can do something about, and that it has a racial dimension. By squarely shouldering responsibility and resolving to improve outcomes for all children as they tackle the racial disparities, school leaders can also reduce racial tensions among staff and in their school community and recover lives and talents that would otherwise be wasted. Tackling these issues should be a shared responsibility, not the duty of the principal or special education administrator alone. Furthermore, technical assistance can be sought from state and federal agencies, including OCR and OSEP, without triggering legal action. School leaders concerned with the issues raised above can also renew their efforts to involve parents and community in innovative ways. Some suggested methods include entering into partnerships with community organizations in order to boost minority parent involvement, and engaging school-based councils that would share decisionmaking power, working more closely with social service agencies to ensure that at-risk students receive high-quality services and that social workers and teachers are collaborating effectively, and increasing direct outreach to families.

Moreover, teachers need support to change their practice and improve classroom outcomes. In many cases regular classroom teachers have received little or no training in working with students from diverse backgrounds or with special education students, or have had little practicum experience in inclusive classrooms. Similarly, many special education teachers have not had the degree of training in the core curriculum or on how to work in a full-inclusion setting. Without both academic and multicultural training and time for special education and regular education teachers to collaborate, it is unrealistic to expect significant improvement.

Protecting the civil rights of all students benefits society at large. Obviously, it is much better if this problem is solved within the school than through external enforcement. Strong leadership at all levels could make an important difference. There is a great deal of work that can and should be done by schools, by districts, by states, and by federal lawmakers and enforcement agents that would improve educational opportunities for minority children in general, and make tremendous progress in solving the specific problems highlighted [here].

There are no quick fixes. The problems [we explore] have many roots, and creating better outcomes requires difficult changes at many levels. Far more research is needed on the practices that produce inequality and the reforms that can successfully correct them. We need to reach the point at which every child is treated as if he or she were our own child, with the same tirelessly defended and protected life possibilities. In schools where we can predict the racial makeup of a special education class before we open the door, we must have leadership, if possible, and enforcement, if necessary, to ensure that each child receives the quality academic support and special services he or she truly needs without diminishing any of the opportunities that are any child's right in American society. We hope [our] book will contribute to that dream.

POSTSCRIPT

Is Eliminating Minority Overrepresentation Beyond the Scope of Public Schools?

These selections provide only a glimpse into the projects they represent. Reading both reports in their entirety delivers a much more textured appreciation of their extensive treatment of disproportionality.

The studies share common concerns about the issues surrounding overrepresentation. Their opening words, however, signal their differences. Donovan and Cross do not necessarily want to end disproportionate representation, if it delivers a benefit. Losen and Orfield would like schools to end disproportionality, asserting that minority children in special education have not received that hoped-for benefit.

In their literature review, Donovan and Cross find there may be external reasons for overrepresentation. Citing risks inherent in poverty, including environmental hazards, they conclude that children who have encountered these conditions come to school at a greater risk. There are actual differences in school readiness. Schools can address student performance, but environmental issues are matters of "political priority."

Losen and Orfield agree that environmental circumstances affect school readiness and performance, but raise two compelling puzzles. First, if environmental issues are causal, why is there not overrepresentation in every disability category? Second, why do Hispanic children, who generally share economic status with African Americans, experience less overrepresentation?

Racial bias is hard to evaluate, say all the authors. The NRC study notes that the effects of prejudice are often subtle and intangible. Losen and Orfield comment that it is difficult to determine whether disproportionality results from intentional, biased behaviors, but describe what happens in schools as a "subset" of racial impacts in society. Both sets of researchers agree educators must re-examine an evaluation process that can be subjective and influenced by cultural differences.

Manning and Gaudelli (*Teacher Education and Special Education*, 2007) speak passionately about "modern myths of poverty and special education." Asserting that the origins of the achievement gap reside neither in schools nor in students, the authors say that holding schools responsible masks the "history of negligence that has plagued poor children in our society." The current expectation for uniform academic achievement exacerbates the problem. To resolve overrepresentation, the authors urge special education teachers to openly challenge elementary teachers and administrators about their referrals.

Both studies agree that responsive general education programs are critical. To what extent is overrepresentation affected by poor schools with inexperienced teachers and principals?

Although doctors identify the most visible disabilities, approximately 90 percent of referrals to special education are made by general education teachers: 73–90 percent of those referred are found eligible (Harry & Klingner, *Why Are So Many Minority Students in Special Education?*, 2007). Dismayed that special education is often redefined as the appropriate option for any children whom the regular education system finds too difficult to serve, the authors ask if it would not make more sense to simply help struggling learners, rather than seek a disability label.

First-year teachers remarked that they were overwhelmed by the diversity in their new classrooms, even though they gave high marks to their preparation programs (*Lessons Learned*, http://www.publicagenda.org, 2008). Novices had the same reaction to the number of students with special needs. The report notes that these responses might be related to the fact that new teachers are often assigned the "hardest-to-reach" students. Could new teachers be reaching out for any available assistance?

Is disproportionality an issue for schools to solve or a broader societal challenge? If poverty and environmental problems were alleviated, what differences would we see? Will the uniform expectations from NCLB ensure general education attention to the needs of all children or motivate educators to seek assistance through special education? Will stricter governmental oversight relieve disproportionality? These challenging questions must be raised and addressed, for the benefit of all children.

ISSUE 4

Can Whole School Reform Reduce Discipline Problems?

YES: Howard S. Adelman and Linda Taylor, from "Rethinking How Schools Address Student Misbehavior and Disengagement," *Addressing Barriers to Learning* (Spring 2008)

NO: William C. Frick and Susan C. Faircloth, from "Acting in the Collective and Individual 'Best Interest of Students:' When Ethical Imperatives Clash with Administrative Demands, *Journal of Special Education Leadership* (March 2007)

ISSUE SUMMARY

YES: Howard S. Adelman and Linda Taylor, co-directors of the UCLA School Mental Health Project, based in the Center for Mental Health in Schools, believe that many discipline problems could be eliminated by whole school initiatives that create and sustain an environment that addresses positive social and emotional development as well as academics.

NO: William C. Frick and Susan C. Faircloth, assistant professors at the University of Oklahoma and The Pennsylvania State University, respectively, present dilemmas faced by principals torn between balancing the needs of one particular student who exhibits disruptive behavior with those of the rest of the student body, whose learning is affected by the single student's actions.

IDEA ensures a free and appropriate public education for students with disabilities. Students with emotional/behavioral disabilities are among those accorded this right. These students typically experience difficulty complying with general school rules and social conventions. Some may internalize conflict, withdrawing, and perhaps, hurting themselves. Others react aggressively, externalizing their conflict. While both types of behavior must be addressed, externalizing behavior is usually the most visible, and therefore the most problematic for teachers.

Educators encounter a dilemma when students with a disability violate school norms. The behavior (e.g., starting a fight) breaks the rules, but the student starting the fight has a disability that prevents him from restraining his impulses. Repeated suspensions for the same behavior could effectively expel the student, depriving him of his legally protected education and services, constituting a change of placement.

In its early authorizations, IDEA emphasized academic access; there was no mention of "the troublesome topic of discipline" (Osborne & Russo, *ELA Notes,* 2007). IDEA 97 remedied that oversight by stipulating that students should not be removed from school for behavior that was a manifestation of their disability or the result of an inappropriate Individualized Education Program (IEP). Behavior unrelated to the disability could receive the standard consequence. Unfortunately, IDEA 97 contained no precise definition of the term manifestation (Osborne & Russo). Often the appropriateness of the IEP became the primary focus of discussion, removing or delaying disciplinary consequences.

IDEA 2004 tightened legal requirements regarding manifestation determination, making it easier to discipline students with disabilities (Zirkel, *Journal of Special Education Leadership,* 2006). The emphasis has shifted from whether the IEP was appropriate to whether it has been implemented. A tougher standard exists for finding specific behavior directly related to the disability. Schools have broader latitude to send students with disabilities to short-term alternate facilities for longer periods of time. Parents now bear the burden of proof if they disagree with the school's determination regarding manifestation.

Boyd (*Children's Rights,* 2006) voices concern about the impact of these changes, especially on students with mild/moderate disabilities. She notes that some might act out in frustration as they struggle with tasks that are confusing or beyond their current capabilities. Observing that teachers may impose disciplinary consequences without recognizing the impact of a mild/moderate disability, she worries that these students will become "isolated and left with nothing but frustration and an inability to learn."

Howard Adelman and Linda Taylor agree that disciplined students might become disengaged, unmotivated to continue learning. Acknowledging the pressures on teachers, Adelman and Taylor advocate school improvement efforts that seek to identify the reasons for difficult behavior, incorporate positive behavioral supports to minimize the occurrence of undesirable behavior, and re-engage troubling students, whether or not they have a disability.

William Frick and Susan Faircloth analyze the words of high school principals struggling to balance the needs of the whole student body with those of individual students with disabilities. These leaders are comfortable providing instructional accommodations and adaptations to meet student needs, but unsettled by the ethical dilemmas they face when trying to be fair to everyone in disciplinary matters.

As you read these articles, think about how your school approaches behavior and discipline. Are there consistently applied schoolwide standards and expectations? How do educators work to understand the reasons behind inappropriate behavior? How is inappropriate behavior addressed? Are all students treated fairly?

YES ↵

Howard S. Adelman
and Linda Taylor

Rethinking How Schools Address Student Misbehavior and Disengagement

The essence of good classroom teaching is the ability to create an environment that first can mobilize the learner to pursue the curriculum and then can maintain that mobilization, while effectively facilitating learning. The process, of course, is meant not only to teach academics, but to turn out good citizens. While many terms are used, this societal aim requires that a fundamental focus of school improvement be on facilitating positive social and emotional development/learning.

Behavior problems clearly get in the way of all this. Misbehavior disrupts. In some forms, such as bullying and intimidating others, it is hurtful. And, observing such behavior may disinhibit others. Because of this, discipline and classroom management are daily topics at every school.

Concern about responding to behavior problems and promoting social and emotional learning are related and are embedded into the six arenas we frame to encompass the content of student/learning supports. How these concerns are addressed is critical to the type of school and classroom climate that emerges and to student engagement and re-engagement in classroom learning. As such, they need to be fully integrated into school improvement efforts.

Disengaged Students, Misbehavior, and Social Control

After an extensive review of the literature, Fredricks, Blumenfeld, and Paris conclude: *Engagement is associated with positive academic outcomes, including achievement and persistence in school; and it is higher in classrooms with supportive teachers and peers, challenging and authentic tasks, opportunities for choice, and sufficient structure.* Conversely, for many students, disengagement is associated with behavior and learning problems and eventual dropout. The degree of concern about student engagement varies depending on school population.

From *Addressing Barriers to Learning,* vol. 13, no. 2, Spring 2008, pp. 1–2, 4–6. Copyright © 2008 by UCLA Center for Mental Health in Schools. Reprinted by permission. http://smhp.psych.ucla.edu

In general, teachers focus on content to be taught and knowledge and skills to be acquired—with a mild amount of attention given to the process of engaging students. All this works fine in schools where most students come each day ready and able to deal with what the teacher is ready and able to teach. Indeed, teachers are fortunate when they have a classroom where the majority of students show up and are receptive to the planned lessons. In schools that are the greatest focus of public criticism, this certainly is not the case.

What most of us realize, at least at some level, is that teachers in such settings are confronted with an entirely different teaching situation. Among the various supports they absolutely must have are ways to re-engage students who have become disengaged and often resistant to broad-band (non-personalized) teaching approaches. To the dismay of most teachers, however, strategies for re-engaging students in *learning* rarely are a prominent part of pre- or in-service preparation and seldom are the focus of interventions pursued by professionals whose role is to support teachers and students. As a result, they learn more about *socialization* and *social control* as classroom management strategies than about how to engage and re-engage students in classroom learning, which is the key to enhancing and sustaining good behavior.

Reacting to Misbehavior

When a student misbehaves, a natural reaction is to want that youngster to experience and other students to see the consequences of misbehaving. One hope is that public awareness of consequences will deter subsequent problems. As a result, a considerable amount of time at schools is devoted to discipline and classroom management.

An often stated assumption is that stopping a student's misbehavior will make her or him amenable to teaching. In a few cases, this may be so. However, the assumption ignores all the research that has led to understanding *psychological reactance* and the need for individuals to maintain and restore a sense of self-determination. Moreover, it belies two painful realities: the number of students who continue to manifest poor academic achievement and the staggering dropout rate in too many schools.

Unfortunately, in their efforts to deal with deviant and devious behavior and to create safe environments, too many schools overrely on negative consequences and plan only for social control. Such practices model behavior that can foster rather than counter the development of negative values and often produce other forms of undesired behavior. Moreover, the tactics often make schools look and feel more like prisons than community treasures.

In schools, short of suspending a student, punishment essentially takes the form of a decision to do something that the student does not want done. In addition, a demand for future compliance usually is made, along with threats of harsher punishment if compliance is not forthcoming. The discipline may be administered in ways that suggest the student is seen as an undesirable person. As students get older, suspension increasingly comes into play. Indeed, suspension remains one of the most common disciplinary responses for the transgressions of secondary students.

As with many emergency procedures, the benefits of using punishment may be offset by many negative consequences. These include increased negative attitudes toward school and school personnel. These attitudes often lead to more behavior problems, anti-social acts, and various mental health problems. Because disciplinary procedures also are associated with dropping out of school, it is not surprising that some concerned professionals refer to extreme disciplinary practices as "pushout" strategies.

In general, specific discipline practices should be developed with the aim of leaving no child behind. That is, *stopping misbehavior must be accomplished in ways that maximize the likelihood that the teacher can engage/ re-engage the student in instruction and positive learning.*

The growing emphasis on positive approaches to reducing misbehavior and enhancing support for positive behavior in and out-of-the-classroom is a step in the right direction. So is the emphasis in school guidelines stressing that discipline should be reasonable, fair, and non-denigrating (e.g., should be experienced by recipients as legitimate reactions that neither denigrate one's sense of worth nor reduce one's sense of autonomy).

Moreover, in recognizing that the application of consequences is an insufficient step in preventing future misbehavior, there is growing awareness that school improvements that engage and re-engage students reduce behavior (and learning) problems significantly. That is why school improvement efforts need to delineate:

- efforts to prevent and anticipate misbehavior
- actions to be taken during misbehavior that do minimal harm to engagement in classroom learning
- steps to be taken afterwards that include a focus on enhancing engagement. . . .

Focusing on Underlying Motivation to Address Concerns About Engagement

Moving beyond socialization, social control, and behavior modification and with an emphasis on engagement, there is a need to address the roots of misbehavior, especially underlying motivational bases. Consider students who spend most of the day trying to avoid all or part of the instructional program. An *intrinsic* motivational interpretation of the avoidance behavior of many of these youngsters is that it reflects their perception that school is not a place where they experience a sense of competence, autonomy, and or relatedness to others. Over time, these perceptions develop into strong motivational dispositions and related patterns of misbehavior.

Misbehavior Can Reflect Proactive (Approach) or Reactive (Avoidance) Motivation

Noncooperative, disruptive, and aggressive behavior patterns that are *proactive* tend to be rewarding and satisfying to an individual because the behavior itself is exciting or because the behavior leads to desired outcomes (e.g., peer recognition, feelings of competence or autonomy). Intentional negative behavior stemming from such approach motivation can be viewed as pursuit of deviance.

Misbehavior in the classroom may also be *reactive*, stemming from avoidance motivation. This behavior can be viewed as protective reactions. Students with learning problems can be seen as motivated to avoid and to protest against being forced into situations in which they cannot cope effectively. For such students, many teaching situations are perceived in this way. Under such circumstances, individuals can be expected to react by trying to protect themselves from the unpleasant thoughts and feelings that the situations stimulate (e.g., feelings of incompetence, loss of autonomy, negative relationships). In effect, the misbehavior reflects efforts to cope and defend against aversive experiences. The actions may be direct or indirect and include defiance, physical and psychological withdrawal, and diversionary tactics.

Interventions for Reactive and Proactive Behavior Problems Begin with Major Program Changes

From a motivational perspective, the aims are to (a) prevent and overcome negative attitudes toward school and learning, (b) enhance motivational readiness for learning and overcoming problems, (c) maintain intrinsic motivation throughout learning and problem solving, and (d) nurture the type of continuing motivation that results in students engaging in activities away from school that foster maintenance, generalization, and expansion of learning and problem solving. Failure to attend to motivational concerns in a comprehensive, normative way results in approaching passive and often hostile students with practices that instigate and exacerbate problems.

After making broad programmatic changes to the degree feasible, intervention with a misbehaving student involves remedial steps directed at underlying factors. For instance, with intrinsic motivation in mind, the following assessment questions arise:

- Is the misbehavior unintentional or intentional?
- If it is intentional, is it reactive or proactive?
- If the misbehavior is reactive, is it a reaction to threats to self-determination, competence, or relatedness?
- If it is proactive, are there other interests that might successfully compete with satisfaction derived from deviant behavior?

In general, intrinsic motivation theory suggests that corrective interventions for those misbehaving reactively requires steps designed to reduce reactance and enhance positive motivation for participation. For youngsters highly motivated to pursue deviance (e.g., those who proactively engage in criminal acts), even more is needed. Intervention might focus on helping these youngsters identify and follow through on a range of valued, socially appropriate alternatives to deviant activity. Such alternatives must be capable of producing greater feelings of self-determination, competence, and relatedness than usually result from the youngster's deviant actions. To these ends, motivational analyses of the problem can point to corrective steps for implementation by teachers, clinicians, parents, or students themselves.

Promoting Social and Emotional Learning

One facet of addressing misbehavior proactively is the focus on promoting healthy social and emotional development. This emphasis meshes well with a school's goals related to enhancing students' personal and social well being. And, it is essential to creating an atmosphere of "caring," "cooperative learning," and a "sense of community" (including greater home involvement).

In some form or another, every school has goals that emphasize a desire to enhance students' personal and social functioning. Such goals reflect an understanding that social and emotional growth plays an important role in

- enhancing the daily smooth functioning of schools and the emergence of a safe, caring, and supportive school climate
- facilitating students' holistic development
- enabling student motivation and capability for academic learning
- optimizing life beyond schooling.

An agenda for promoting social and emotional learning encourages family-centered orientation. It stresses practices that increase positive engagement in learning at school and that enhance personal responsibility (social and moral), integrity, self-regulation (self-discipline), a work ethic, diverse talents, and positive feelings about self and others.

It should be stressed at this point that, for most individuals, learning social skills and emotional regulation are part of normal development and socialization. Thus, social and emotional learning is not primarily a formal training process. This can be true even for some individuals who are seen as having behavior and emotional problems. (While poor social skills are identified as a symptom and contributing factor in a wide range of educational, psychosocial, and mental health problems, it is important to remember that symptoms are correlates.)

What is Social and Emotional Learning?

As formulated by the Collaborative for Academic, Social, and Emotional Learning (CASEL), social and emotional learning (SEL) "is a process for helping children and even adults develop the fundamental skills for life effectiveness. SEL teaches the skills we all need to handle ourselves, our relationships, and our work, effectively and ethically. These skills include recognizing and managing our emotions, developing caring and concern for others, establishing positive relationships, making responsible decisions, and handling challenging situations constructively and ethically. They are the skills that allow children to calm themselves when angry, make friends, resolve conflicts respectfully, and make ethical and safe choices."

CASEL also views SEL as "providing a framework for school improvement. Teaching SEL skills helps create and maintain safe, caring learning environments. The most beneficial programs provide sequential and developmentally appropriate instruction in SEL skills. They are implemented in a coordinated manner, school-wide, from preschool through high school. Lessons are reinforced in the classroom, during out-of-school activities, and at home. Educators receive ongoing professional development in SEL. And families and schools work together to promote children's social, emotional, and academic success."

Because of the scope of SEL programming, the work is conceived as multi-year. The process stresses adult modeling and coaching and student practice to solidify learning related to social and emotional awareness of self and others, self-management, responsible decision making, and relationship skills.

Natural Opportunities to Promote Social and Emotional Learning

Sometimes the agenda for promoting social and emotional learning takes the form of a special curriculum (e.g., social skills training, character education, assets development) or is incorporated into the regular curricula. However, classroom and school-wide practices can and need to do much more to (a) capitalize on *natural* opportunities at schools to promote social and emotional development and (b) minimize transactions that interfere with positive growth in these areas. Natural opportunities are one of the most authentic examples of "teachable moments."

An appreciation of what needs more attention can be garnered readily by looking at the school day and school year through the lens of goals for personal and social functioning. Is instruction carried out in ways that strengthen or hinder development of interpersonal skills and connections and student understanding of self and others? Is cooperative learning and sharing promoted? Is counterproductive competition minimized? Are interpersonal conflicts mainly suppressed or are they used as learning opportunities? Are roles provided for all students to be positive helpers throughout the school and community?

The Center's website offers specific examples of natural opportunities and how to respond to them in ways that promote personal and social growth . . .

The Promise of Promoting Social and Emotional Learning

Programs to improve social skills and interpersonal problem solving are described as having promise both for prevention and correction. However, reviewers tend to be cautiously optimistic because so many studies have found the range of skills acquired are quite limited and so is the generalizability and maintenance of outcomes. This is the case for training of specific skills (e.g., what to say and do in a specific situation), general strategies (e.g., how to generate a wider range of interpersonal problem-solving options), as well as efforts to develop cognitive-affective orientations, such as empathy training. Reviews of social skills training over several decades conclude that individual studies show effectiveness, but outcome studies often have shown lack of generalizability and social validity. However, the focus has been mainly on social skills training for students with emotional and behavior disorders.

Recent analyses by researchers involved with the Collaborative for Academic, Social, and Emotional Learning (CASEL) suggest that "students who receive SEL programming academically outperform their peers, compared to those who do not receive SEL. Those students also get better grades and graduate at higher rates. Effective SEL programming drives academic learning, and it also drives social outcomes such as positive peer relationships, caring and empathy, and social engagement. Social and emotional instruction also leads to reductions in problem behavior such as drug use, violence, and delinquency."

Promotion of Mental Health

Promotion of mental health encompasses efforts to enhance knowledge, skills, and attitudes in order to foster social and emotional development, a healthy lifestyle, and personal well-being. Promoting healthy development, well-being, and a value-based life are important ends unto themselves and overlap primary, secondary, and tertiary interventions to prevent mental health and psychosocial problems.

Interventions to promote mental health encompass not only strengthening individuals, but also enhancing nurturing and supportive conditions at school, at home, and in the neighborhood. All this includes a particular emphasis on increasing opportunities for personal development and empowerment by promoting conditions that foster and strengthen positive attitudes and behaviors (e.g., enhancing motivation and capability to pursue positive goals, resist negative influences, and overcome barriers). It also includes efforts to maintain and enhance physical health and safety and *inoculate* against problems (e.g., providing positive and negative information, skill instruction, and fostering attitudes that build resistance and resilience).

While schools alone are not responsible for this, they do play a significant role, albeit sometimes not a positive one, in social and emotional development. School improvement plans need to encompass ways the school will (1) *directly facilitate* social and emotional (as well as physical) development and (2) *minimize threats* to positive development (see references at end of this article). In doing so, appreciation of differences in levels of development and developmental demands at different ages is fundamental, and personalized implementation to account for individual differences is essential.

From a mental health perspective, helpful guidelines are found in research clarifying normal trends for school-age youngsters' efforts to feel *competent, self-determining,* and *connected with significant others.* And, measurement of such feelings can provide indicators of the impact of a school on mental health. Positive findings can be expected to correlate with school engagement and academic progress. Negative findings can be expected to correlate with student anxiety, fear, anger, alienation, a sense of losing control, a sense of hopelessness and powerlessness. In turn, these negative thoughts, feelings, and attitudes can lead to externalizing (aggressive, "acting out") or internalizing (withdrawal, self-punishing, delusional) behaviors.

Clearly, promoting mental health has payoffs both academically and for reducing problems at schools. Therefore, it seems evident that an enhanced commitment to mental health promotion must be a key facet of the renewed emphasis on the whole child by education leaders.

Concluding Comments

Responding to behavior problems and promoting social and emotional development and learning can and should be done in the context of a comprehensive system designed to address barriers to learning and (re)engage students in classroom learning. In this respect, the developmental trend in thinking about how to respond to misbehavior must be toward practices that embrace an expanded view of engagement and human motivation and that includes a focus on social and emotional learning.

Relatedly, motivational research and theory are guiding the development of interventions designed to enhance student's motivation and counter disengagement. And, there is growing appreciation of the power of intrinsic motivation.

Now, it is time for school improvement decision makers and planners to fully address these matters.

William C. Frick and
Susan C. Faircloth

 NO

Acting in the Collective and Individual "Best Interest of Students:" When Ethical Imperatives Clash With Administrative Demands

The focus of this investigation was on how secondary principles inter-pret the experience of leadership decision making as a moral activity in relation to a specific ethical lens, the Ethic of the Profession, and its associ-ated Model for Promoting Students' Best Interests. This ethical framework elevates the profession of educational leadership by positing a central moral ideal in the form of an injunction of special duty: "serve the best interests of the student" whereby "promoting the success of all students" by focus-ing on the individual needs of children. The Ethic of the Profession is an eclectic framework incorporating established ethical paradigms of justice, care, critique, and community not as totally distinct, incommensurable moral reasoning, but as complementary—a "tapestry of ethical perspec-tives that encourage . . . rich human response to . . . many uncertain ethi-cal situations." The Ethic of the Profession indicate that a disparity exists between diverse ethical perspectives related to the education of students, professional codes meant to inform decision making and conduct, and the personal moral values of administrators that influence their judgment and behavior. When reflective school leaders attempt to integrate established ethical paradigms and professional and personal codes of ethics, the result is often moral dissonance, or a "clashing of codes." In responding to this inevitable discord, the Ethic of the Profession is grounded in a reasoned consideration of the educational shibboleth "serve the best interests of the students."

The student's best interests are the focal point of the Ethic of the Profession. A model for determining the best interests of the student consists of a robust focus on the essential nature of individual rights, the duty of responsibility to others for a common interest, and respect as mutual acknowl-edgment of others as having worth, value, and dignity unto themselves.

An important consideration for this investigation was the distinc-tion practicing secondary school administrators make between the best

From *Journal of Special Education Leadership*, 20(1), March 2007, pp. 21–22, 23, 24, 25–29 (excerpts). Copyright © 2007 by Council of Administrators of Special Education (CASE). Reprinted by permission.

interests of the student (one) and the best interests of the students (all or most). In reviewing the literature on the best interests of students, Walker indicates that "the interests of children supersede the interests of all other interests." Walker argues, however, that it may be very difficult to know with precision and appositeness what the best interests of students might be. The Ethic of the Profession and its Model for Promoting Students' Best Interests clearly and intentionally refer to the best interests of the student (one) as opposed to the best interests of students (group, many, or all). This ethical frame does not recognize a difference between the two perspectives and purports that

> if the individual student is treated with fairness, justice, and caring, then a strong message is sent to all students that they will be treated with similar justice and caring and that they should treat others similarly. Thus, rights carry with them responsibilities, so much so that the rights of one individual should not bring harm to the group.

The (individual) student's best interests are at the center of the Ethic of the Profession and, according to this decision-making framework, individuals (particularly students) possess inherent worth and dignity unto themselves and they need not strive to maintain their value. With this said, educational leaders must first decide if the individual is acting responsibly in asserting his or her rights. If not, there are opportunities to teach responsibility, which is challenging and requires vigilance, but the potential is great for students to share responsibility for their own development.

Purpose of the Study

. . . [The] primary intent in this study was to pilot the use of this frame in the field of education leadership to test the explanations and definitions of what professional moral practice entails, the defined by the Ethic of the Profession and its Model for Promoting Student's Best Interests, compared to the explanations and definitions practitioners use. The focus was on practicing administrators' understanding of the expression "the best interests of the student" and additional aspects of moral practice and reasoning removed from classroom or seminar settings.

Method

As part of the overall study from which this specific research is derived, verification was sought as to whether or not educational leaders could relate experiences of discord between organizational policies and professional expectations meant to inform judgment, decision making, and conduct and their own personal moral values (whether held privately or expressed publicly). In addition, this research investigation sought to known and understand how the expression "the best interests of the student" was defined and used in decision making. . . .

Participants

. . . A range of people occupying the position of secondary school principal were sought as participants for this research. Secondary principals were selected because of their work in managing the size, scale, and level of problems associated with a complex and often bureaucratic service organization. This range of participants constituted a broad variety of individual and contextual factors and backgrounds. . . . Three female and eight male principals participated in this study. One male and one female were black and the other nine were white. Participants ranged in age from 35 to 55 years old and had worked in their administrative role from 2 to 19 years. The size of student enrollment in participants' respective schools ranged from 80 to 2200, with two principals serving in rural schools, three serving in suburban schools, three serving in suburban/metro schools, and three in urban schools. . . .

Findings

As a result of the focus and stamina required to lead an entire school organization, each participant in this study indicated in some fashion a sharp distinction and clear difference between the best interests of individual students and the best interests of students as a group. The distinction administrators made was markedly different from the conceptual framework guiding this study. They viewed the work of deciding and acting in the best interests of the student body as being qualitatively different from working with individual students. Participants indicated that balancing the two priorities was difficult, but essential, within the confines of a bureaucratic institution.

In their daily work, most principals thought about the best interests of students in general, as a corporate body, and when specific student-related issues came to their attention they would alter their perspective on students' best interests and focus on unique, individual student needs. This pattern of thought was prevalent and consistent across participants in terms of their interpretation of the expression "the best interest of the student." . . .

A young, male high school principal put it this way: "You look at each situation, and I think [about] a decision: How many kids can I impact versus how many may I not impact, across the board?" A similar attitude was expressed by a veteran high school administrator who said:

> I think there are times when you have to do things in the collective best interests. There is no question you have to do things sometimes that a student may have to have an issue sacrificed for the benefit of the entire student body, or for the safety of the student body, or for a variety of reasons. And because we do work within a system, we're not working in a private setting where we can handle each student individually: we're working in a system where we have to handle the entire global group. So yeah, people are sometimes, I hate to say people are

sacrificed, but their issue may be sacrificed for the benefit of all. That's
a bureaucratic issue.

Another principal communicated the view of focusing primarily on
individual student needs and best interests as specified in the Model for
Promoting Students' Best Interests when he explained, "Given certain circumstances, you can send a message to the entire student body based on
what happens to an individual." Although he believed focusing on a case
by case treatment of individual students can have some effect on the best
interests of the entire student body, this level of individual interaction was
not sufficient for ensuring a complete consideration of the best interests of
all students under his supervision.

Although the principals' first order of business was considering,
deciding, and acting in the best interests of students as a group, they were
cognizant of the potential danger of the distinction, especially when,
according to one participant, "you just give people what they need" at an
individual rather than a group level. The perspectives participants held
about balancing what was in the best interests of one student as opposed
to an entire group were diverse. Most believed that public schooling was
becoming increasingly individualized and student centered, with planning and interventions designed to address the needs and talents of every
student, whereas other principals expressed their frustration with public
education and organizational life where "political correctness" and a "one
size fits all approach" dictated how to respond when addressing students'
needs or seeking to serve their best interests.

The majority of the principals focused on special education policy to
illustrate the qualitative difference, in their view, between the best interests of the student (one) and the best interests of the students (all or most).
It was difficult for principals to address the best interests of the student
(one), although they would have liked to, because of policies and protections for groups of students. One aspect (instructional) of the policies and
protections resonated with their moral notions of equity, fairness, and social justice whereas the other aspect (discipline) was morally troubling and
restrictive and did not address the best interest of the individual student.

The two contrasting views, one of student centered discretion and
the other a one size fits all way of doing business, were fueled by the same
source—special education mandates and the provisions of the Individuals
with Disabilities Education Improvement Act (IDEIA) and the No Child
Left Behind Act (NCLB). Most principals fully supported IDEIA and the
current direction of public education. For example, a female high school
principal indicated that "what's best for all is not necessarily what's best
for the individual. Education these days is working toward the needs of
each child, [such as] differentiation of instruction and curriculum in the
classroom. This is a good thing." This view was also held by a young,
male, rural high school principal who imagined that public education will
eventually remake itself into an endeavor centered on serving individual

student needs, promoting each student's success, and attending to "best interests" at an individual/personal level. He said:

> I think we're always going to make [decisions for] the best interests of the whole. That's been the direction of education, but then we are prescribing more of what is in the individual best interests of certain students, and it's likely to continue on that track. I think we're going to be doing more of that now. . . . Every day we think about our services for special education; what we're doing in special education. I think we've got to service kids. I think we're obligated to do that, [but] I think we're overprotective of special education. I think it's a copout when we put the responsibility to work with low achieving or special needs kids on special education teachers. I think it's everybody's responsibility to work with those special needs kids. . . . I think there'll be a point where, I mean people keep laughing about this, and they've been laughing about this 10, 15, 20 years ago when they said, "Every kid is going to have an IEP. I think we're headed that way, I really do. We're headed in a direction where we're really individualizing a lot of decision making and the way things are being done.

Other principals took a completely different perspective on the "direction education was headed." One middle school principal believed that the balance between the individual and the group was skewed more toward the group, particularly in instructional matters. He was deeply disturbed by this type of attitude and indicated that uniform treatment of all students did not achieve the goals and purposes of public education. He said:

> I think we have a philosophy in education today that we believe that one size fits all. . . . There needs to be more recognition of the uniqueness of mankind and individual needs in that one size doesn't fit all—people haven't sensed that uniqueness or that specialness in a sea of numbers. And I think that sometimes we lose messes because that's not occurring.

Expressing this position in a more critical tone, a veteran high school principal did not mince words about his viewpoints when it came to the restrictions placed on him by special education policy when desiring to make decisions in, what he believed to be, the best interests of students. He spoke primarily about student discipline and how the balance between individual and group is skewed because of the standards of uniform treatment he must comply with based on federal, state, and district policy. His frustration was about treating every student in a protected class the same way, or within the parameters of restrictive policy mandates, without being granted the administrative discretion and decision making necessary to respond to students in their best interests. . . . He indicated:

> Public education dictates to you what you can and can't say, or do, or feel, or be; because you are all things to all people—that's the nature of public education. And a result of that, being all things to all people . . . my own personal positions are inconsequential for the most part, unless

it's a major philosophical issue. There are many things that are [a major philosophical issue], but because we live in a politically correct world, we cannot deal with things that are actual . . . and so as a result of that, we cannot act on what we know to be true, we have to act on what the public perceives to be acceptable, so that is a dilemma sometimes.

The same principal illustrated the tension he feels when complying with special class protections and his desire to respond morally, decide and act ethically, and deal with students as individuals. The extended quote that follows illustrates the importance, for this principal, of engaging and responding to students on a personal and individual level rather than being forced to decide and act in the best interests of students as a group. According to this participant, there is a moral danger in dictated and uniform prescriptions for attending to and managing students as a group that essentially ignore or do away with administrative discretion.

I have special education questions every single day. What's best for the child? Well in this building we have 470 special education students. So there's a large group, and I think the moral questions come every day: What's right for those particular students? I think, in weighing that out [it] combines with What's right then for regular education students? You look at them as separate tracks. Clearly the moral dilemma is there: 'How can I treat two people who do the same thing totally differently and still acquire some integrity of fairness?' The answer is you can't. So you do the best you can. Knowing the fact that if I have a special education student sitting here, he has a knife on him; he's OK to have that knife on him because he is a special education student. And I have a regular education student with the same knife on him, and I have to expel him for a year and this [special education] kid doesn't get anything because it's OK—that's a moral dilemma for me. It's a moral dilemma for me when I have a special education student extort money from a student in the hallway, and I have a regular education student extort money in the hallway, and I have to suspend one or expel one and not the other. It's a moral dilemma when . . . I have a special education student punch a teacher in a fight and a regular education student punch a teacher in a fight [and] one's expelled for assaulting staff, the other one gets nothing because the parent won't agree to a suspension. That's a moral dilemma for me—that's a problem for me, because that's wrong. No matter how you cut that up in my mind that's wrong. I know there's somebody . . . somewhere that could cut that up in their own mind and make that right. I can't do that, and I've not been able to do that over 32 years' time. Pretty sure it won't change in the next five or ten.

More than half of the principals in this study focused on special education policy to illustrate the qualitative difference, in their view, between the best interest of the student (one) and the best interests of the students (all or most). Results of this study, specific to handling special education student issues, indicate that it is difficult to address the best interests of the student (one), although the participants would have liked to, because of educational policies and protection for groups of students. Although the instructional aspects of the policies and protections resonated with participants' moral notions of equity, fairness, and social justice, the disciplinary aspects of the same policies and protections were morally troubling and restrictive and did not address the best interest of the individual student.

Discussion

The turbulent intersection of education policy, professional ethics, and personal morality became evident as participants talked about working with students on an individual basis. . . . Serving the best interests of the student meant being fair and acting fairly, and in the eyes of participants who talked about fairness as a principle or virtue, the rule or quality was immensely important. However, fairness required responding with personal investment to each student based on their unique needs, not being inextricably tied to formulaic procedures or regulations that did not allow for reasonable distinctions between equality and equity. As one respondent indicated, "You just give people [students] what they need" at an individual level. It seems that participants would not want to be questioned about why they were not doling out the same treatment or responding and acting in the same, uniform manner toward every student.

. . . The principals in this study described the difficulties they experienced, both externally by way of publicly defending their decisions and actions to others and internally as a moral struggle between their own sense of fairness as equity and the uniform procedures and policies that were to be applied equally to all students.

Principals expressed, in a variety of ways, the importance of treating students equitably. . . . Another principal put the matter this way:

> I think we struggle with what is fair and consistent. We have to treat everybody as an individual, but we have to be consistent with our discipline. I know sometimes we have to weigh it. How is it going to be looked at by the rest of the kids or the faculty if one thing happens to this kid who did the same behavior as another kid? See, they don't get the background information. . . . You definitely have to keep your faculty happy; you have to be supportive and let them know you're backing them up, but they don't know that we can't treat everybody the same sometimes for the same behavior because there's circumstances out there. I wish some people would just understand that and even parents too.

Implications

Implications for Practice

This study raises important questions regarding . . . preparing building-level administrators, to respond to the dilemmas that arise when the best interests of the individual student clash with the best interests of students as a whole. The potential for such dilemma is clearly illustrated by the increasing demand on school leaders to meet the individual needs of children with special educational needs as mandated by the IDEIA and the often competing demands of NCLBA which may be described as being directed toward the more collective interests of students as a group rather than individual students.

Implications for Policy

To assist school leaders in navigating these potential ethical and administrative dilemmas, policy makers must give increased attention to the ways in which the implementation of current and future policies affects school leaders' abilities to respond to individual student needs as well as fosters and sustains inclusive learning environments for all students. An example such action includes recent federal policy discussions pertaining to the use of the Response to Intervention (RTI) model, which may have the potential to assist educators in more effectively addressing student academic and learning needs as well as disciplinary and behavioral issues. Using the RTI model may assist building level principals and their staff in mitigating what principals, such as those in this study, identify and experience as qualitative differences between responding to the best interests of the student (one) and responding to the best interests of the students (all or most). As noted earlier in the findings, in addition to the instructional aspects of special education policies and protections, it may be easier for some school leaders to equate the provision of instructional accommodations and adaptations with the moral notions of equity, fairness, and social justice, whereas the disciplinary aspects may be viewed as morally troubling, restrictive, and at odds with the practice of meeting the best interest of the individual student. Again, this illustrates the potential for both administrative and ethical dilemmas for school leaders. . . .

Conclusion

As discussed, principals in this investigation expressed satisfaction in their press for equitable responses to student learning needs, particularly for those students identified as requiring special instructional services. In contrast, participants reported a significant unsettledness with special class protections that dismiss, and thereby limit, the principal's ability to take fair and just disciplinary actions. These findings suggest that secondary principals, who play a significant role in special education leadership in their respective building assignments, experience a moral tension between serving the best instructional interests of each identified student under their supervision and care and the disciplinary policies and procedural regulations that limit, according to participants' perspectives, moral discretion, ethical judgment, and reasonable retributive justice pertaining to student disciplinary matters. Although special education disciplinary policies and procedural regulations were created and enforced to preserve students' rights to a free and appropriate education as a protected class, some principals ironically view these policies and regulations as morally and ethically inadequate in addressing individual student needs.

Given the complexity of today's educational system, it is imperative that school leaders be skilled in balancing the competing demands that emerge from the challenge to meet the best interests of the students as well as the best interests of all students. According to Donaldson, leadership that builds commitment to mutual moral purposes positions school leaders to respond justly and equitably to "increasingly diverse student needs and increasingly demanding societal needs . . . as agents of a 'free, appropriate education' for every American child" (pp. 49–50). Building such a commitment in the face of "pluralistic pressures" from a wide range of constituencies is one matter (Gardner, 1990), but attending to the best interests of the student in face-to-face encounters must be the first order of the day for school administrators. Before building broad and lasting collective commitment to moral purposes, principals need to find ethical satisfaction in the decisions they make, about individual students.

POSTSCRIPT

Can Whole School Reform Reduce Discipline Problems?

Arter (*Teaching Exceptional Children*, 2007) agrees with Frick and Faircloth's principles: traditionally schools have treated behavioral and academic difficulties differently. However, student misbehavior may be a reaction to academic difficulties; the time students spend out of class for discipline causes them to fall farther behind academically. Unless the cycle is broken, the spiral continues downward. The behavior becomes increasingly unacceptable.

In the full text of their article, Adelman and Taylor present an exhibit on positive behavioral interventions and support (PBIS). Like response to intervention (RTI), PBIS encompasses a range of interventions designed to model and support positive behavior rather than focus on punishing negative behavior. Trussell (*Intervention in Schools and Clinic,* 2008) comments that PBIS schools create environments that support both social and learning outcomes, preventing the emergence of problem behaviors.

Two key resources support educators interested in pursuing a PBIS model. The federally funded technical assistance Web site (www.pbis.org) contains extensive resources and links to state PBIS contacts. Second is a comprehensive guide to mental **health and school improvement, developed by Adelman and Taylor** (http://smhp.psych.ucla.edu/mhbook/mhbookintro.htm, 2008). The authors emphasize the importance of including counselors, psychologists, and school social workers in school reform to create an array of proactive practices that do not depend on a disability label for access. This vision of school reform is rare, but promising.

A driving force for this type of reform might be the reality that some students just do not thrive in traditional schools, exceeding the tolerance level of teachers and administrators (Quinn, Poirier, Fuller, Gable, & Tonelson, *Preventing School Failure,* 2006). These students often flourish in alternative learning environments, which provide a unique blend of structure, support, and flexibility.

Alternative schools have seen a dramatic increase recently, perhaps due to mismatches between today's expectations and student performance. Students with disabilities account for 12–19% of alternative school enrollment (Bullock, *Preventing School Failure,* 2006). There is no one definition of an alternative school, but Tissington (*Preventing School Failure*, 2006) identified three varieties. Type I schools focus on educational specialties, such as magnet schools; Type II schools address disciplinary issues and are sometimes seen as the last chance before expulsion; Type III alternatives are therapeutic, delivering specialized treatment for students with disabilities.

The specialized focus of alternative schools helps students become re-engaged with academics while simultaneously working with their families to improve social and emotional skills (Hughes & Adera, 2006). Although alternatives strike a balance between safe schools and keeping troubling children in school, Van Acker (*Preventing School Failure,* 2007) cautions that grouping children with behavioral issues in one place eliminates role models and could exacerbate negative behavior.

Troubling, aggressive, unacceptable behavior might begin with bullying—playground pushing, shoving, and rude language. This behavior is often overlooked. It is stressful for teachers and more difficult to address than instructional challenges. Unfortunately, without intervention, bullies can become increasingly aggressive and antisocial (Crothers & Kolbert, *Intervention in School and Clinic,* 2008).

Quinn and Poirier (in Rutherford, Quinn, & Mathur, 2004) highlight the cost of not addressing unacceptable behavior. Without intervention, delinquent behavior leads to substance abuse, school failure, and criminal activity. Prisons are expensive. Lost happiness and productivity also come with a substantial cost.

Several options to address troubling behavior exist. Doing nothing is not one of them. What will your school do to develop and support positive behavior? Are alternative schools part of these options?

ISSUE 5

Does School Choice Open Doors for Students with Disabilities?

YES: Marcus A. Winters and Jay P. Greene, from "Vouchers and Special Education; Vouchers for Special-Ed Students: The Politics of Special-Ed Vouchers," *Washington Times* (April 29 and 30, May 1, 2008)

NO: Barbara Miner, from "Vouchers: Special Ed Students Need Not Apply," *Rethinking Schools Online* (vol. 18, no. 2, 2003)

ISSUE SUMMARY

YES: Marcus A. Winters and Jay P. Greene are both senior fellows of the Manhattan Institute; Jay Greene is also a department head at the University of Arkansas. Winters and Greene found that Florida's McKay voucher program for special education students has improved education for those who remain in public schools.

NO: Barbara Miner, a freelance writer and former managing editor of *Rethinking Schools,* shares frustrating experiences with the pioneering Milwaukee voucher system. Her interviewees claim that exclusionary policies and practices limit access for students with disabilities who seek entry into voucher schools.

School choice, a major component of education reform, offers parents alternatives to their neighborhood school. States determine the range of choice available. Intra-district options range from open-enrollment programs to magnet schools focusing on thematic education. Charter schools are funded by direct transfers of funds from public schools; depending on state law, these may be considered part of a school district or a distinct district in themselves. Finally, voucher programs grant families an amount of money that they can use across district lines to enroll in their chosen program, even in a private (sometimes religious) school. Each option endeavors to offer unique programs. Some critics hope that this will, as a by-product, stimulate creativity in public schools.

Charter and private schools are exempt from many of the rules that structure (some say bind) public schools. Freedom from union contracts and many state regulations is balanced by strict accountability for student performance.

Together, these will, ideally, result in more desirable alternatives for all children than those found in bureaucracy-laden neighborhood public schools.

School choice is intended to change public schools. The possibilities offered through charter schools and vouchers are intended to serve as competition, motivating public schools to move beyond their traditions. Some worry that choice options will "skim the cream," enrolling top students and leaving public schools with the most needy students and fewer resources.

Although free from many regulations, privately funded and charter schools must abide by federal laws ensuring equal educational opportunities for students with disabilities. This requirement provides protection from discrimination through the Americans with Disabilities Act, but generally not the more specific protections of IDEA (Samuels, *EducationWeek*, 2007). Lively discussions have emerged about how students with disabilities will fare in the world of school choice.

Marcus Winters and Jay Greene highlight findings from their recent report on Florida's McKay Scholarship Program (Greene & Winters, http://manhattan-institute.org, 2008). The first to focus specifically on students with disabilities, McKay enrollment grew from 970 students in 2000 to over 18,000 in 2006; disgruntled parents have an alternative to fighting public schools for decent services. Winters and Greene found that McKay's existence not only provided new opportunities for students with disabilities who used the vouchers, but also improved the education experienced by students with disabilities who remained in public schools.

The Milwaukee Parental School Choice Program, begun in 1993, is the nation's oldest voucher initiative. The number of voucher schools dramatically increased in response to a 1998 Wisconsin Supreme Court decision that religious schools could be included in this program. Barbara Miner investigated voucher schools in Milwaukee and cites evidence that all is not rosy in the world of school choice—especially for students with disabilities. She talked with parents and researchers who revealed that many voucher schools find reasons not to be available to students with disabilities even those as little as a year below grade level.

As you read the following selections, consider the options open to students with disabilities and their parents. Does school choice offer the promise of better education, regardless of setting? Is innovative programming worth giving up IDEA's legal protections? Will children with disabilities have a fair chance at finding the answer?

YES

Marcus A. Winters
and Jay P. Greene

Vouchers and Special Education; Vouchers for Special-Ed Students: The Politics of Special-Ed Vouchers

Special education has grown dramatically over the last two decades and shows no signs of slowing. To date, about 14 percent of public school students have been diagnosed with a disability and receive special education services. In response to the disappointing educational experiences of these students, five states have now adopted voucher programs specifically tailored to disabled students. In a new study for the Manhattan Institute, we find evidence that Florida's special-education voucher program has improved the education that the public schools provide to the disabled students who remain in the public schools.

The first of its kind, the McKay program has offered vouchers to any disabled student in a Florida public school since 1999. Students can use these scholarships to pay tuition at any public or private school that is willing to admit them. The generous voucher is worth the lesser of the tuition at a private school or the amount that the public school would have spent on the child if he remained in public school. The McKay program has grown rapidly and with 18,273 participants is currently the largest school voucher program in the United States.

Most agree that vouchers probably help those students who use them. In fact, several randomized field trials—the "gold standard" of social science research—have found that voucher students benefit when they use them to attend a private school of their choice. Rather, the debate over school choice for both regular enrollment and disabled students now centers on the impact it has on the public school system. Many people worry that vouchers harm public schools by depriving them of resources. Others contend that vouchers might improve public schools by forcing them to compete for students.

In the first quantitative evaluation of a voucher program for disabled students of which we are aware, we found that those students with relatively mild disabilities—the vast majority of special-education students in the state and across the nation—made larger academic gains when the number of private options nearby increased. Students with more severe disabilities were neither helped nor harmed by the addition of McKay scholarship-receiving private schools near their public school.

Students diagnosed with the mildest form of disability, known as a Specific Learning Disability (SLD), benefited the most from the availability of school choice. About 61 percent of students in special education have been identified as having an SLD, and many of these kids are not much different from non-disabled students. We found that the average student with an SLD who remained in the public school system made an additional 0.05 and 0.07 standard deviation improvement in math and reading, respectively, than he would have made without the McKay program.

We cannot know for sure how exactly McKay improved public schools in Florida. It could be that public schools saw that their disabled students were leaving for private alternatives in search of a better education and responded to the challenge by improving their efforts. On the other hand, if special education students are as much of a financial burden for public schools as some argue, then as students leave public schools may be better able to utilize their resources to help the students who remain. From a policy perspective, the reason for the effect doesn't matter. What we know from our study is that rather than harming public schools, vouchers improve the education that they provide to their disabled students.

Our findings for special education vouchers are consistent with a growing body of research focused on school choice programs for regular education students. Despite conventional wisdom, several previous studies indicate that school choice from voucher programs and charter schools actually improves the performance of public schools. Our new study is consistent with that literature and specifically shows that school choice has a positive effect even for those students who are the most challenging to educate.

Florida's McKay program combines two of the least commonly understood aspects of education policy: vouchers and special education. Although we still have a great deal to learn about these policies, the evidence from Florida suggests that vouchers improve the education that public schools offer to disabled kids. Expanding these programs across the nation could substantially improve the lives of the nation's nearly 7 million disabled students.

⋘◦⋙

The Individuals with Disabilities Education Act (IDEA), the federal law governing special education, requires a school system to enter into a legally binding contract that specifies the services it must provide to each individual disabled student. Parents who believe the school system fails to provide these services can seek remedy of that failure through a legal process. But this right is only as meaningful as one's ability to enforce it. Frustrated parents face the unappealing prospect of engaging in a legal fight with the same people who care for their children each day. Given the psychological and financial difficulty of pursuing the legal path and given how frequently public schools win those disputes, most disgruntled parents come to terms with sub-par services.

But a new way of structuring special education holds the promise of changing this situation. Under special-education voucher programs that now exist in five states, instead of going to court, disabled students can use a voucher to pay for the cost of attending another public school or a private school. Rather than fighting, they can walk out the door and take the money that is spent on them with them.

As we described in this space yesterday, the disabled students who remain in public schools benefit academically from Florida's special-education voucher program, called the McKay Scholarship. In a new study we found that the quality of special education seems to improve when students gain more options to leave their public school. But these expanded options also benefit the students who choose to leave with a voucher, the public schools from which they leave and the taxpayers.

It is true that private schools are not legally required to provide particular services to disabled students in the same way that public schools are under IDEA. But in reality, no one loses any rights when they use a voucher to attend a private school. If their private school does not serve them well, families can always pursue appropriate services from their assigned public school through the legal system. Families simply gain another mechanism to make their right a reality.

Further, private schools appear more willing to provide necessary services than public schools, even though they are not contractually mandated to do so. Parents of disabled students participating in Florida's McKay program report that they are almost three times as likely to receive all promised services from their McKay private school as from their previous public school (86 percent vs. 30 percent).

More than 90 percent of parents participating in the McKay program report that they are satisfied or very satisfied, while only about a third of them were similarly satisfied with their previous public school. What is it that they like about their experience? For starters, disabled students participating in McKay benefit from significantly smaller classes when they take a voucher to a private school. On average, their class size drops from 21.8 students in their previous public school to 12.7 students in the private school they attend with a McKay Scholarship. And the rates at which disabled students are bullied for their disability drop from almost half in the public school to about one in twenty in the private school with a voucher.

Even the public schools that students leave benefit. Schools no more relish legal battles with parents than parents do. By giving dissatisfied parents an exit option other than litigation, special-education vouchers reduce the financial and administrative burden on school districts.

Lastly, taxpayers benefit because McKay Scholarships are capped at the amount that the public schools spend on students or private-school tuition, whichever is less. Since the tuition at many private schools is less than the spending on disabled students at public schools, the financial burden on taxpayers is reduced. The average amount of a McKay voucher in Florida is only $7,206, far below the average per-pupil amount spent on a disabled student in the public schools.

The current special-education system is an arrangement that only lawyers could love. It creates rights that can only be enforced in court—if then. It creates conflict between families and schools. It is all about process and not about results. Adding vouchers to the mix changes all of that by giving families an alternative mechanism for getting what they need, reducing costs and conflict, and ensuring better results for all disabled students.

With some courage, Sen. John McCain has made school choice a pillar of his presidential campaign's education platform. However, to date it is unclear what type of school choice policy he might consider as president. Heated opposition from the teacher unions would almost certainly block or subvert any proposal for a national voucher program of the conventional style. Instead, Mr. McCain should consider embracing a fresh approach to school choice that would allow parents of disabled students to use federal special-education dollars in any public or private school they see fit. Altering the federal special-education law in this way overcomes both vested and principled forms of opposition and would dramatically expand school choice without substantially increasing the federal role in education.

Federal spending for the nation's nearly 7 million disabled students under the Individuals with Disabilities Education Act (IDEA) currently goes to state school systems based on their special-education enrollments. We could instead redirect this more than $11 billion to parents and allow them to use the money to pay tuition at a public or private school of their choice. No additional taxpayer dollars need be raised and few new federal regulations would be required. In fact, since private-school tuition is routinely lower than public-school per-pupil revenues, we could save millions of taxpayer dollars.

In the previous two days, in this space generously provided by The Washington Times, we have argued that school choice can improve the academic achievement of disabled students and help reform the legalistic burdens of the current IDEA system. We have pointed to evidence, including our new study for the Manhattan Institute, finding that Florida's voucher program for special-education students improves the academic gains of those who remain in the public schools. But even we social scientists realize that it is not enough for a policy to be effective; it must be politically viable as well. Reforming IDEA to target its dollars into the hands of parents passes this political test.

Voucher programs for disabled students are more politically popular than are universal programs or those constrained to low-income students. Special-education voucher programs have spread to five states in less than a decade at a time when the growth of traditional voucher programs for regular education students has slowed. Another sign of their political appeal is that while other voucher programs face legal challenges from the unions, and courts have thrown some of them out, special-education vouchers have mostly escaped challenge. Teachers' unions don't relish the image of dragging disabled kids into courts to compel them to return to public schools that were serving them poorly.

Another important political virtue of special-education vouchers is that they benefit the rich and poor, minority and white students, alike. Voucher programs for low-income students have clienteles with little political power. But special education, like Social Security, touches the lives of Americans of all incomes, creating powerful constituencies for support.

In 2003, we surveyed parents participating in Florida's special-education voucher program. The demographic profile of families receiving special-education vouchers was roughly representative of all families in Florida. About a quarter of enrolled parents reported that they had a household income above $60,000 and about a third of them had earned at least a college degree. If presented to them properly, there is a natural support for special-education vouchers among this all-important middle-class demographic, many of whom have struggled with the current system themselves.

Finally, once enacted a federal special-education voucher program would have little to fear from the legal challenges that are the bane of statewide voucher programs. Recent court cases against voucher programs are now most often filed when the state has what is known as a Blaine Amendment; amendments present in many state constitutions, which are the product of anti-Catholic sentiment in the 19th century, explicitly banning taxpayer dollars flowing to religious institutions in any way. But a federal program would be immune to such challenges since the U.S. Constitution does not contain such an amendment and the U.S. Supreme Court has ruled that federal law does not prohibit taxpayer dollars from being spent on religious private school tuitions if that is the uncoerced choice of parents.

The teachers' unions would almost certainly deter any Democratic nominee from campaigning for such a sensible rethinking of policy and reallocation of resources, so the proposal will probably have to come from the Republican nominee. If Mr. McCain is serious about school choice, he would do well to consider targeting IDEA dollars to parents as part of his education policy platform.

Barbara Miner   ➡ **NO**

Vouchers: Special Ed
Students Need Not Apply

Susan Endress is into her second decade of demanding, cajoling, threatening, and doing whatever it takes to ensure that Milwaukee schools honor the rights of special education students.

On a recent afternoon, she shakes her head in weary frustration as she reads a summary of the special ed services provided (or, more likely, not provided) by Milwaukee voucher schools that receive public dollars yet operate as private schools.

"What do they mean, they can't serve children more than a year below grade level?" she says of one school's description. "That's terrible."

"Oh, here's a good one," she says as she continues reading. "'We cannot serve wheelchair-bound students.' And look at this one, it cannot serve 'students who are unable to climb stairs.'" She turns to a young man in a wheelchair working in the office with her at Wisconsin FACETS, a special education advocacy and support group for families. "Make sure you're bound to your wheelchair," she tells him good-naturedly. "And better learn to climb stairs."

Her moment of humor over, Endress turns serious again.

"You have to remember, it's only been a little over 25 years that special needs children have even had the right to attend a public school," she says. "And here we're moving backwards with the voucher schools, not forward. I'm personally scared to death of where this might lead."

Milwaukee's voucher program, the country's oldest, has long been seen as a prototype for what, in essence, is a conservative strategy to privatize education under the guise of "choice." With the U.S. Congress poised to start the first federally funded voucher program . . . in the Washington, D.C., schools, vouchers have once again jumped to the fore of educational debate.

Although Milwaukee's voucher schools receive tax dollars, they operate as private schools and thus can ignore almost all of the requirements and accountability measures that public schools must follow. They do not, for example, have to hire certified teachers, nor administer the same tests as public schools, nor report their students' academic achievement.

Nor do they have to provide the special education services required of public schools. While voucher supporters portray vouchers as a new Civil Rights Movement, disability activists see a different reality.

Jim Ward, president of ADA Watch and the National Coalition for Disability Rights in Washington, D.C., warns that voucher programs threaten the rights of students with special needs. He cites a 1998 survey by the U.S. Department of Education that between 70 and 85 percent of private schools in large inner cities would "definitely or probably" not participate in a voucher program if required to accept "students with special needs such as learning disabilities, limited English proficiency, or low achievement." Among religious schools, the figure was 86 percent.

"The Supreme Court's 1954 *Brown vs. Board of Education* decision struck down 'separate but equal' schools, but voucher programs threaten to usher in a new form of segregation," Ward warns.

Milwaukee's voucher program shows that Ward's fears are well-founded. At a time when the percentage of special education students in the Milwaukee Public Schools (MPS) hovers around 16 percent and is projected to reach 19 percent by 2007, voucher schools are not legally obliged to provide special education services to their students.

The only official data on special ed and Milwaukee voucher schools is from a 2000 report by the Wisconsin Legislative Audit Bureau. It found that only 3 percent of the students in voucher schools in 1998–99 had previously been identified as needing special education services. It also noted that voucher schools likely served children with "lower-cost" needs such as speech, language, and learning disabilities.

Current data is sketchy, at best, because voucher schools do not have to collect or release information. The little information that's available paints a bleak picture.

A voluntary, unaudited survey by the Public Policy Forum in October 2002 found that almost half of the voucher schools provide no special ed services, even for students with mild learning disabilities. A significant number reported programs such as "Title I" or "smaller classes" that are generally not considered special education services. Some note that they work with MPS, which provides the special education services. One school said that special needs students are served through its "Jesus Cares Ministry."

A look at a website hosted by the University of Wisconsin-Milwaukee is even more revealing. The site has information on most Milwaukee schools, private and public, and has a section where schools report on "categories of students which the school cannot serve." Some voucher schools do not report anything. Or, like Marquette University High School, they say the information is "n/a."

Many voucher schools succinctly note that they cannot serve "LD, ED, children with physical disabilities"—referring to learning disabled (LD) and emotionally disabled (ED). Some explanations are more elaborate. Blessed Sacrament, for example, says: "We believe that students who are 2–3 years below grade level cannot be realistically brought up to grade level because we do not have a tutorial/learning center to accommodate their needs. Students who have severe emotional or behavioral problems need specific programs to assist them—we do not have a counselor or social worker."

Some schools send mixed messages. St. Adelbert says: "We do not have specific services for ED students though we do have ED students. We do not have an elevator. However, we do have physically disabled students. We do have sight- and hearing-impaired students. We cannot service severe MR [mental retardation]."

A few voucher schools note they provide some special ed services, in particular for children with mild learning or physical disabilities. St Gregory the Great, for instance, says, "We are able to accommodate most children with learning disabilities."

Services for special education students seem to be particularly limited at voucher high schools. Messmer, which had 398 voucher students last year, specifically notes on the EPIC website that it has "no special [ed] classes." Learning Enterprise, which had 175 voucher students, likewise said it cannot serve special education students. Pius XI, meanwhile, with 199 voucher students last year, is making an effort. While it says it cannot serve ED or EMR [educable mentally retarded] students, it provides services for LD students.

The Milwaukee voucher program is expected to cost about $76 million in taxpayer dollars this year, bringing the total to almost $350 million since its inception in 1990. This year it will serve almost 13,000 students, providing up to $5,882 for each child.

Funding Special Ed

Voucher proponents sometimes argue that voucher schools do not provide special education services because they do not get money to do so. But Endress of Wisconsin FACETS doesn't buy the money argument, whether it comes from public schools, charter schools, or voucher schools.

She understands why all schools may not be equipped to deal with students needing a full-time aide, such as medically fragile students or those with multiple physical, emotional, and medical needs. But such students are the exception, she says. Most special education students can be served without extraordinary accommodations.

"The main thing they have to do is have a teacher on staff that is licensed in special education that is cross categorical," she says. "There is no reason why these voucher schools can't have just one teacher. Think of all the support they could provide not just the students but also other teachers. To me, it just makes good educational sense."

The money argument assumes that public schools receive adequate funding for special education. But they don't. In MPS, for example, special ed spending is about $164 million this year, according to Michelle Nate, director of finance. Since the state and federal governments reimburse only 66 percent of that money, MPS must take $55 million from its overall budget to fund special education.

The Milwaukee Archdiocese, which oversees the largest bloc of voucher schools, does not have figures on special education. Nor does the Archdiocese provide special education teachers for its schools. Dave

Prothero, superintendent for the Milwaukee Archdiocesan schools, says special education issues are dealt with at the school level. "Any parent that calls and says that their child has special needs, the response will be, 'Please come in to the school and talk about the specific needs of your child to see if we can meet those needs.'"

Special education experts, based on anecdotal evidence, say this often means that special ed children are "counseled out" of applying, or encouraged to leave if already enrolled, on the grounds that the school is not a good match.

"I think they are oftentimes discouraged from the very beginning," says Dennis Oulahan, an MPS teacher who provides special education assessments for bilingual children in both private and public schools. "The message might be, 'Don't apply.'"

Voucher schools are legally prohibited from discriminating in admissions against children with special needs and are only required to provide services that require "minor adjustments." Until the definition of "minor adjustments" is tested in the courts, it is doubtful that voucher schools will significantly change their practice.

As Oulahan notes, "Voucher schools don't have to deal with special ed. They are private schools. And as long as they don't have to deal with it, I don't think they are going to volunteer."

POSTSCRIPT

Does School Choice Open Doors for Students with Disabilities?

The authors of these two selections paint startlingly contrasting pictures of the impact of school choice on students with disabilities. Their differences are typical of the current state of discussion.

Greene and Winters note that, to their knowledge, theirs is the first study to examine the impact school choice has on students who remain in public schools. In their full report, the authors note that they decided to focus on this population for a number of reasons, not the least of which was that they could use a reliable data set from the Florida Department of Education that permitted them to study the same students for a number of years. They reasoned that if voucher schools were reticent to enroll students with disabilities, there would be no programmatic competition and student performance in public school experiences would not change over time. Greene and Winters were happy to discover the positive change in public schools, but acknowledge their study was not designed to identify the reasons for the improvement.

Consider next an extensive study of the Milwaukee Parental Choice Program, which examined whether voucher-driven competition improved student achievement in public schools (Carnoy, Adamson, Chudgar, Luschei, & Witte, www.epi.org, 2007). Although performance increases were seen about the time that religious schools entered the voucher pool, the authors could not determine what schools did to effect that change. Over eight years, it was impossible to measure whether voucher students performed better than those who remained in public schools because the state did not provide a mechanism for this comparison. Estimating the effects of competition by comparing student gain scores, Carnoy et. al. found no evidence that competition resulted in better achievement.

Students with disabilities were not mentioned in the Wisconsin study. They were also invisible in a pair of analyses reported in the *Wall Street Journal* (Tomsho, 2006). The Educational Testing Service re-examined data from the 2003 National Assessment of Educational Progress (NAEP), which had previously been studied by the National Center for Educational Statistics. In both reviews, fourth graders in traditional schools outscored charter school peers. These were national data, however, not separated by individual states. Could students with disabilities be doing better than their typical peers?

Students with disabilities were very much present in a study of charter school statutes and special education (Rhim, Ahearn, & Lange, *Journal of*

Special Education, 2007). This descriptive review documented "policy tensions and basic challenges" associated with addressing special education in charter schools. State regulations and funding differ widely. Charter school administrators, accustomed to their relative freedom, had little knowledge of special education laws and their complexity. Clear evaluation of the outcomes for students with disabilities is hindered by their small numbers, often below the minimum subgroup size identified by the state for NCLB purposes.

In contrast, Estes (*Preventing School Failure,* 2006) reported that Texas charter schools were enrolling increasing numbers of students with behavioral/emotional problems, perhaps reflecting state efforts to increase knowledge on the subject. Curiously, she reports finding that charter schools were beginning to use resource room services and other practices "increasingly similar to traditional public schools."

How does school choice really affect students with disabilities? Do they find doors that are open or tightly closed? If their numbers are too small to examine, how will anyone know how they are faring? How will the opinions of America's 44th president change the doorways?

ISSUE 6

Do Funding Systems Create a Perverse Incentive to Place Students in Special Education?

YES: **Jay P. Greene and Greg Forster**, from *Civic Report No. 32: Effects of Funding Incentives on Special Education Enrollment* (Center for Civic Innovation at the Manhattan Institute, December 2002)

NO: **Kanya Mahitivanichcha and Thomas Parrish**, from "Do Non-Census Funding Systems Encourage Special Education Identification? Reconsidering Greene and Forster," *Journal of Special Education Leadership* (April 2005)

ISSUE SUMMARY

YES: Jay P. Greene, senior fellow, and Greg Forster, senior research associate, both with The Manhattan Institute for Policy Research, assert that the number of students identified as disabled is increasing at an excessive rate, especially in states where funding systems provide a "perverse incentive" in favor of placement.

NO: Kanya Mahitivanichcha, research analyst, and Tom Parrish, managing director for the Education and Human Development Program, both at the American Institutes for Research, maintain that funding formulas are only one reason behind increases in special education placement.

T hirty years ago, approximately 8 percent of school children were in special education. Thousands more lived in institutions, spent their days at home, or struggled in school with little, if any, assistance. Today, approximately 13 percent of school-age children are enrolled in special education across the nation.

The percentage of children in special education has risen consistently over time. Curiously, there is enormous variation among states, ranging (in 2000–01) from 9.4 percent in California to 17.8 percent in Rhode Island (Mahitivanichcha and Parrish).

Thirty years ago, legislators knew that establishing and maintaining programs for students with disabilities would cost money. No one knew how much or approached an accurate prediction. Passage of the first special education law came with Congress' promise to pay up to 40 percent of the cost of educating children with disabilities. Annually determined through Capital Hill negotiations, the actual amount appropriated has never come close to this promise. From 1998 to 2003, the federal share rose from 8 percent to 13 percent of the spending.

Once budget wrangling ends, checks are sent to each state. Since FY 2000, this allocation has been determined primarily by the state's school-aged population, with an additional factor reflecting the state's relative poverty. After retaining some funds for the operation of its own special education activities, each state disperses the remaining federal money among school districts.

To qualify for these funds, districts maintain detailed records documenting compliance with special education laws and regulations. Students are counted annually, along with the extent of their time in special education. These figures are reported to the state and then to the U.S. Department of Education.

Two types of funding systems exist. Census-based mechanisms distribute money in accordance with the overall number of children in a district. Another option is a weighted strategy, allotting funds based on the number of children receiving special education services. While states alter their funding mechanisms periodically, most are currently using weighted systems.

Jay Greene and Greg Forster are troubled by the continuing increase in the percentage of children receiving special education services. Rejecting competing explanations, they hold that schools are responding to the "bounty" provided by weighted systems for placing children in special education. Results of their analyses maintain that using census (or lump sum) mechanisms would save $1.5 billion annually.

Kanya Mahitivanichcha and Thomas Parrish share the concern about rising special education numbers, but disagree that census-based funding mechanisms are the clear solution. Their own analyses doubt the magnitude of Greene and Forster's findings and point to more complex interactions.

As you read these articles, note that both studies consider expenditures for children from ages 6 to 21. Many districts serve children as young as age 3; at least one state extends services to the twenty-sixth birthday. Ask yourself whether funding formulas are "culprits," encouraging schools to increase the number of children in special education. How does anyone determine the "right" number of children who deserve these services?

YES ↵

Jay P. Greene and
Greg Forster

Effects of Funding Incentives on Special Education Enrollment

. . . Over the past decade, the U.S. special education enrollment rate has increased from 10.6% of all students to 12.3%. The rate of growth is accelerating and shows no sign of slowing down, and policy makers are anxious to determine why. Critics of the U.S. special education system argue that it creates perverse financial incentives to label children as disabled. School districts have traditionally received state funding based on the size of their special education programs, so in effect they receive a bounty for each child they place in special education. Critics claim that this rewards schools for placing students in special education unnecessarily. Some defenders of the system argue that special education enrollment is growing because the real incidence of disabilities in children is growing, but this explanation does not withstand scrutiny very well. A number of researchers are now pointing towards still another culprit: perverse incentives arising not from funding systems but from high-stakes testing. When schools are held accountable for students' performance on standardized tests, they have an incentive to remove the lowest-scoring students from the testing pool by placing them in special education, where they will be exempt from testing requirements.

Several states, struggling to cope with the ever-accelerating growth of special education, have adopted new funding systems that eliminate the bounty for new special education students. An even larger number of states have adopted high-stakes testing, in the hope that it will improve education outcomes. However, no national statistical studies have attempted to measure what effect these new lump-sum funding and high-stakes testing policies are having on special education enrollment.

This study finds that funding systems have a dramatic effect on special education enrollment, while high-stakes testing has no significant effect. We estimate that in the states that adhere to the traditional bounty system, over the last decade the rate of special education enrollment grew a total of 1.24 percentage points more than it would have if these states had lump-sum funding systems, accounting for a full 62% of these states' total increase in special education enrollment. This represents approximately 390,000 extra students placed in special education because of the bounty system, resulting in additional spending of over $2.3 billion per year. Using another method that is more sensitive to the timing of changes in states' funding systems, we estimate that if all bounty system states had switched to lump-sum systems in the 1994–95 school year, their special education enrollments in the 2000–01 school year would have been lower by an average of 0.82 percentage points. This margin represents a difference of roughly 258,000 students and over $1.5 billion per year in extra spending. In light of these findings, reforms that would remove the perverse incentives of bounty funding systems—such as switching to lump-sum systems or offering private school scholarships to disabled children—are urgently needed.

Previous Research

Enrollment in special education has been growing steadily for decades, and the rate of growth has been accelerating for the past ten years. Already high—over 10% of the student population—at the beginning of the 1990s, special education enrollment is now approaching 13% and shows no sign of slowing down. Since special education students are a significantly greater burden on schools than regular students because of the individual attention and specially trained staff they require, this expansion of the special education population is becoming a more and more urgent concern for U.S. education. Indeed, the percentage of students in special education has been going up at a time when the average cost of special education per student has also been rising, exacerbating the problem further.

Unfortunately, any effort to address this problem must first overcome sharp disagreement over what is causing it in the first place. At least three different culprits have been identified: greater real incidence of disabilities, the advent of high-stakes testing, and the financial incentives created by special education funding.

Defenders of the U.S. special education system argue that the growth of enrollment in special education reflects growth in the real incidence of disabilities in children. According to this explanation, there are simply more disabled students than there used to be, and those students have more costly disabilities. . . . Berman, . . . Davis, . . . Koufman-Frederick, and . . . Urion argue that increases in special education enrollment and spending "have been primarily due to the increased numbers of children with more significant special needs who require more costly services." They attribute this alleged growth in student disabilities to social forces over which schools have no control, pointing to three factors in particular: improvements in medical technology, deinstitutionalization of children with serious difficulties, and increases in childhood poverty.

However, this account is not consistent with the facts. The authors argue that there are now more children with mental retardation because improved medicine saves more low-birth-weight babies. While it is true that the number of such babies expected to exhibit retardation has grown, the actual number of students classified as mentally retarded has dropped remarkably—from about 961,000 in 1976–77 to about 599,000 in 2000–01. Improvements in prevention of mental retardation have more than offset any growth in mental retardation caused by increased numbers of surviving low-birth-weight babies. As a general matter, while medical improvements will certainly cause some number of children to survive with disabilities where in a previous era they would have died, it will also cause other children to avoid developing disabilities where in a previous era they would have become disabled. From improved prenatal medicine to safer child car seats to reductions in exposure to lead paint, medical improvements have saved untold thousands of children from disabilities. Furthermore, the decline in the number of students with mental retardation, as well as those with other severe types of disability, also disproves the argument that deinstitutionalization of students with severe problems is driving increases in special education enrollment. As for childhood poverty, it hasn't actually increased. For children under 6, it was 17.7% in 1976 when federal law first required special services for disabled students, and it was 16.9% in 2000. Even that understates the case, since the standard for what counts as "poverty" goes up over time as society gets richer.

If the real incidence of childhood disabilities isn't going up, then more students are being classified as disabled when there has been no change in the number of students who actually are disabled. Some of this change may be caused by improved diagnosis of existing disabilities. For example, growth in the number of students classified as autistic may be attributable to improved diagnosis. Likewise, growth in the number of students placed in special education under the category of "other health disorders" may be attributable to more widespread recognition and diagnosis of attention-deficit disorder and related disorders—though most students with such disorders are not placed in special education, some students with severe cases are.

But it is extremely unlikely that improved diagnosis is the most important cause of the last decade's overall growth in special education. Autism represents only a tiny fraction of total special education enrollment, and the category of "other health disorders," though larger, is not large enough to even come close to explaining the explosive growth in special education enrollment. As for other categories, we have no reason to believe that between 1990 and 2000 schools dramatically improved their ability to accurately identify students with most types of disabilities.

This leaves us with a less benign explanation—that schools are increasingly diagnosing students as disabled and placing them in special education for reasons unrelated to those students' genuine need for special education services. This would help explain not only the growth of special education enrollment, but also the recent increase in graduation rates for special education students—if more students who aren't truly disabled are being placed in special education, we would expect to see improvements in the academic performance of students in special education.

Why would schools place more students in special education when they didn't truly need it? Some researchers are now identifying high-stakes testing as a possible cause. More and more states have adopted test-based accountability programs in which significant consequences, such as student promotion and graduation or school funding cuts, are attached to performance on a standardized test. The goal of such programs is to provide schools with a firm incentive to improve performance—if students do poorly on the test, schools can be held accountable. But these programs can also create a perverse incentive: an incentive to game the system by getting low-performing students out of the testing pool altogether. By labeling such students as disabled and placing them in special education, schools can exempt them from mandatory testing. In some states, special education students who are considered testable are included in mandatory testing, but schools could still game the system by labeling special education students untestable (that is, too disabled to take the test). When low-performing students are exempt from testing, schools' average test scores go up, which makes the schools look better.

Examining a high-stakes statewide test in Texas, Deere and Strayer found that students who failed the test in one year were more likely to be classified as exempt from the test (either as special education students or limited English proficient students) the next year; that schools were more likely to classify minority students as exempt if this would reduce the number of minority students tested to a low enough level that the school's minority test scores would not be reported; and that when the state started counting the scores of special education students who did take the test towards schools' accountability ratings, the percentage of special education students who were classified as exempt from the test went up, reversing a downward trend. Figlio and Getzler, examining a high-stakes test in Florida, found that special education enrollment went up after the introduction of the test, that students in tested grades were more likely than students in untested grades to be placed in special education, that lower-scoring students were more likely to be placed in special education, and that severe disability categories did not rise after the introduction of the test. Jacob, studying Chicago schools, found that the percentage of students exempted from testing through special education rose faster after the introduction of high-stakes testing, and most quickly among lower-scoring students.

These findings are limited to various extents by research methodology. Most obviously, all these studies are confined to one state or city. None of them attempts to control for the national trend in special education enrollment, or otherwise compare states with high-stakes testing to states without high-stakes testing (although a few of the findings do compare students who are and are not subject to high-stakes testing within the same state). Special education enrollment was increasing nationwide throughout the 1990s, and the nationwide rate of growth increased as the decade progressed. Thus, finding that special education enrollment in a state or city grew faster after it adopted high-stakes testing does not, in itself, prove that high-stakes testing caused faster growth; it only proves that the state or city in question behaved in a manner consistent with the national trend.

Likewise, correlations between low test scores and special education enrollment are of limited value. If low-performing students are more likely to be enrolled in special education programs, it may well be that schools are pushing those students into special education to remove them from the testing pool. But it is also possible that those students' low test scores are indicative of genuine disabilities, for which they were subsequently diagnosed and enrolled in special education. Deere and Strayer try to account for this by comparing more than one set of paired years—that is, they look not only at whether students are more likely to be enrolled in special education one year after performing poorly on the test, but also at whether they are more likely to be enrolled in special education after two or three years of performing poorly. However, this does nothing to overcome the problem; it only proves that when schools put low-performing students into special education, they do not always do so after only one year of low performance. In fact, this is exactly what schools are supposed to do—they are not supposed to put students into special education based solely on a low test score. Deere and Strayer's finding is simply a multi-year correlation between low test scores and special education enrollment, which is still just as easily attributable to real disabilities in low-performing students as it is to schools' desire to remove those students from the testing pool.

Hanushek and Raymond conducted the only prior national study of high-stakes testing and special education enrollment, covering 1995–2000. They looked only at states with high-stakes testing, but they controlled for the national trend in special education enrollment. This control serves to implicitly compare states with high-stakes testing to states without high-stakes testing, a significant advantage over previous research. They found that when the control for the national trend was applied, the significant statistical relationship between high-stakes testing and special education enrollment disappeared entirely.

In explaining surging enrollment in special education, there is another possible culprit besides high-stakes testing. School districts have traditionally received state funding for special education, which makes up the bulk of all special education funding, in such a manner that they receive more money if their special education programs are larger. This provides school districts with a financial reward—a bounty, so to speak—for placing students in special education. Critics of the U.S. special education system have long argued that this creates a perverse financial incentive to put as many students as possible into special education.

Defenders of the system often argue that funding for special education cannot create perverse incentives because placing a student in special education creates costs at least equal to the new funding it generates. This misrepresents what truly is and is not a "cost" of placing a child in special education. A true cost is an expenditure that the school would not have made otherwise. Some services that a school would have provided to a particular child no matter what can be redefined as special education services if the child is placed in special education; these services are not truly special education costs because they would have been provided anyway.

For example, if a school provides extra reading help to students who are falling behind in reading, the school must bear that cost itself. But if the same school redefines those students as learning disabled rather than slow readers, state and federal government will help pick up the tab for those services. This is financially advantageous for the school because it brings in new state and federal funding to cover "costs" that the school would have had to pay for anyway. Furthermore, there are many fixed costs associated with special education that do not increase with every new child. For example, if a school hires a full-time special education reading teacher, it will pay the same cost whether that teacher handles three students a day or ten. However, the school will collect a lot more money for teaching ten special education students than it would for teaching three.

Although there have been no national statistical studies of this question, and in particular no studies directly comparing states with and without bounty system funding, there has been a study of the relationship between financial incentives and special education enrollment. Cullen studied how school districts in Texas responded to changes in financial incentives arising from court-mandated restructuring of the state education financial system. She found that after the court order took effect, in districts where the amount of money provided for placing a student in special education went up, special education enrollment also went up. Specifically, she found that a 10% increase in the bounty for placing a student in special education could be expected to produce a 1.4% increase in a district's special education enrollment rate. The relationship between changes in financial incentives and changes in special education enrollment was strong enough that Cullen found it explained 35% of the growth in special education in Texas from the 1991–92 school year through the 1996–97 school year.

Method

To perform the study, we needed two types of enrollment data for each state: enrollment of students served in special education under . . . [IDEA] and total public school enrollment during the school years from 1991–92 through 2000–01. We obtained special education enrollment data from the Annual Report to Congress on the Implementation of the Individuals with Disabilities Education Act, published each year by the U.S. Department of Education's Office of Special Education Programs. We obtained total enrollment data from the Digest of Education Statistics, published by the U.S. Department of Education's National Center for Education Statistics. All these figures included students between the ages of 6 and 21. For each state in each year, we divided special education enrollment by total enrollment to determine the special education enrollment rate.

To obtain information on special education funding systems, we contacted each state's education department and asked three questions: what kind of funding system was in place, whether the system had been changed since the 1991–92 school year (and if so, when and from what kind of system), and whether there had been any other major changes in special education funding since 1991. For each state, we classified the funding system as a bounty system if it caused state funding to vary significantly by the size of each district's special education program. This included systems that distributed funds according to the number of special education students in each district, the number of special education staff in each district, or the level of special education spending in each district. Systems that did not cause state funding to vary significantly by the size of each district's special education program, which typically distributed funds according to the total student population in each district, were classified as lump-sum systems.

We also collected information on high-stakes testing in each state. A test was considered high-stakes if any of the following depended upon it: student promotion or graduation, accreditation, funding cuts, teacher bonuses, a published school grading or ranking system, or state assumption of at least some school responsibilities. . . .

Our first method of analysis was a linear regression. To provide a measurement of growth in special education enrollment to serve as the dependent variable, we plotted each state's special education enrollment rates for the years included in the study, fitted a line to these data points using the ordinary least squares (OLS) method, and determined the slope of the line. The OLS line represents the closest possible approximation of the state trend in special education enrollment; the slope of the OLS line serves as a measurement of the rate at which special education enrollment grew during the study period. The independent variables in our analysis (that is, factors that might explain growth in special education enrollment rates) were both binary measurements: whether or not the state had a lump-sum system during the study period, and whether or not the state had a high-stakes test.

This regression analysis has the advantage of identifying the difference in the rates of special education growth in states with different funding systems. However, it is not sensitive to when changes in funding systems occurred during the study period. Of the states that had lump-sum systems in the 2000–01 school year, only a few had those systems since the 1991–92 school year; the rest switched from a bounty system to a lump-sum system at some point in between. The regression analysis counts all of these states as lump-sum states; it does not differentiate between states that had lump-sum systems for the whole decade and states that had lump-sum systems for only part of that period.

To capture the difference that changes in state funding systems may have made during the study period, we performed another analysis using a method that keeps track of which states had lump-sum systems in each specific year. First, we determined that the average school year in which states adopted lump-sum systems (counting the four states that had always had such systems during the study period as if they had switched in 1990–91) was 1994–95. In that year, seven states had lump-sum systems, a sufficiently large number for meaningful analysis. For each year from 1994–95 onward, for all states that had lump-sum systems in that year we subtracted that state's special education enrollment rate for the previous year from its special education enrollment rate in that year. For example, for each state that had a lump-sum system in 1994–95 we subtracted that state's special education enrollment rate in 1993–94 from its enrollment rate in 1994–95. This gave us the change in enrollment rate for each state with a lump-sum system in each year. We then calculated the average change in enrollment rate for all lump-sum system states in each year.

Turning to the remaining states—those that had bounty systems for the entire study period—we took each state's special education enrollment rate in 1993–94 and added the average change in enrollment rate for lump-sum states in 1994–95. This gave us projected values for the enrollment rates that those bounty states would have had in 1994–95 if they had switched to lump-sum systems in that year. We then added the average change for lump-sum states in 1995–96 to get a projected value for that year, and so on through 2000–01. This gave us projected values for the enrollment rates that bounty states would have had in 2000–01 if they had switched to lump-sum systems in 1994–95. By subtracting each state's projected 2000–01 rate from its actual 2000–01 rate and taking the average difference for all bounty states, we were able to estimate the average effect it would have had if all bounty states had switched to lump-sum systems in 1994–95.

Results

. . . Four states had lump-sum systems for the entire study period, twelve states began with bounty systems and switched to lump-sum systems during the study period, and 33 states (plus the District of Columbia) had bounty systems for the entire study period. Twenty-nine states (plus the District of Columbia) had high-stakes testing and 21 states did not. By far the most common type of high-stakes testing was a requirement that students pass a certain test to be promoted to the next grade or graduate from high school.

Hawaii and the District of Columbia each have only one school district. Rather than classifying them according to the system by which funds are distributed to school districts, we classified them according to the system by which the school district distributes funds to individual schools. Though the incentives are at a different organizational level, they work the same way.

One state, New Hampshire, did not have any state-level funding of special education until 1999. In that year, to comply with a court order, it created a new state program that funds special education by a bounty system. To prevent distortion of our results by this unusual case in which there was no state funding system of any kind for many years, we excluded New Hampshire from all calculations.

The national special education enrollment rate is shown in Figure 1. It grew from 10.6% of all students in the 1991–92 school year to 12.3% in the 2000–01 school year. The rate of growth has accelerated consistently during the past decade.

Figure 1

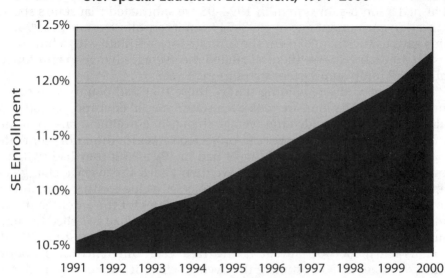

Figure 2 shows the special education enrollment rate over the same period, with figures separated into enrollments under lump-sum systems and bounty systems. Special education enrollment under lump-sum systems grew from 10.5% in the 1991–92 school year to 11.5% in the 2000–01 school year, an increase of one percentage point. Meanwhile, special education enrollment under bounty systems grew from 10.6% to 12.6% in the same period, an increase of two percentage points.

In interpreting Figure 2, we must bear in mind that it represents enrollments under the two types of funding systems rather than enrollments in two fixed sets of states. Enrollment figures in states that changed from bounty to lump-sum systems during the study period were included in the "bounty system" set for years before the state changed, and in the "lump-sum system" set for years after the change. The line for enrollment under lump-sum systems includes four states in 1991–92, but this rises to 16 states by 2000–01. We must also bear in mind that these rates are based on total figures rather than averages, so they are population-weighted. The 1998 funding system change in California will produce a much larger impact on these figures than the 1995 funding system change in Rhode Island. Figure 2 represents national totals for each funding system type.

Figure 3 shows average special education enrollment rates in lump-sum system states and bounty system states. The average special education

Figure 2

Special Education Enrollments under Bounty
and Lump-Sum Systems, 1991–2000

Figure 3

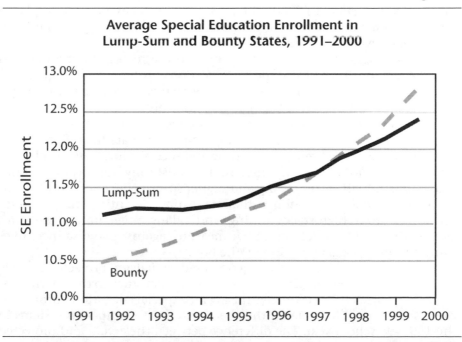

Average Special Education Enrollment in
Lump-Sum and Bounty States, 1991–2000

enrollment rate for states that had lump-sum systems at any time during the study period grew from 11.1% in the 1991–92 school year to 12.4% in the 2000–01 school year, an increase of 1.3 percentage points. In the same period, the average special education enrollment rate for states that maintained bounty systems for the entire study period grew from 10.5% to 12.8%, an increase of 2.3 percentage points.

In Figure 3, state classifications are fixed. The line for enrollment in lump-sum system states always includes the same states: the 16 states that had lump-sum systems in the 2000–01 school year. Also, Figure 3 shows the average special education enrollment rate for the states in each group, rather than the total rate in each group. This means the population of each state has been factored out; all states are equally weighted. Thus, Figure 3 represents a population-controlled comparison of two sets of states, rather than population-weighted national totals for the two system types.

Our regression analysis found a statistically significant relationship between a state's special education enrollment rate and whether or not that state had a lump-sum system during the study period. The regression coefficient for funding systems was 0.124. This means that every year, bounty system states experienced 0.124 more percentage points of growth in special education enrollment than they would have experienced if they had lump-sum systems. Over a ten-year period this adds up to 1.24 percentage points of additional special education enrollment because of the bounty system. The 33 states (plus the District of Columbia) that adhered to the bounty system saw special education enrollment grow by two percentage points over the study period, so a full 62% of that growth can be attributed to the effects of the bounty system. Also, 1.24% of total enrollment in bounty states in 2000–01 represents 390,000 extra students placed in special education because of the bounty system, resulting in additional spending of over $2.3 billion per year.

As for high-stakes testing, not only did the regression analysis find that the relationship between special education enrollment and high-stakes testing was not statistically significant, the regression coefficient for high-stakes testing was negative. That is, states with high-stakes testing actually had lower rather than higher rates of special education enrollment, although not so much so that we can be highly confident that this reflects a real relationship between high-stakes testing and special education enrollment. This study cannot tell us why there isn't a statistically significant relationship between high-stakes testing and higher special education enrollment, but one possible explanation is that states may be anticipating perverse incentives from high-stakes testing and taking preventative measures against them, but not taking similar measures against perverse incentives from funding special education by the bounty system.

. . . [Our] second analysis . . . [compared] actual and projected average special education enrollment rates in the states that stuck to the bounty system. The projected rate estimates the average special education enrollment these states would have had if they had switched to lump-sum systems in the 1994–95 school year. The difference between the actual and projected rates represents the average extra enrollment in these states attributable to the bounty system. In the 2000–01 school year this difference is 0.82 percentage points. In these states, 0.82% of total enrollment in 2000–01 represents roughly 258,000 additional students in special education, which would generate over $1.5 billion per year in extra spending.

Conclusion

State funding systems are having a dramatic effect on special education enrollment rates. In states where schools had a financial incentive to identify more students as disabled and place them in special education, the percentage of all students enrolled in special education grew significantly more rapidly over the past decade. By contrast, high-stakes testing appears to be having no significant effect on special education enrollment. This is contrary to the findings of previous studies that have looked only at individual cities or states and have not controlled for national trends, but agrees with the finding of the only previous national study.

The ever-accelerating growth of special education enrollment is becoming an urgent problem for American education, drawing off more and more billions of dollars that could otherwise be spent on better education for all students. The finding that state funding systems are responsible for the bulk of the past decade's growth in special education enrollment suggests how this problem could be curtailed. The most obvious policy solution would be for bounty system states to adopt lump-sum funding systems, removing the perverse financial incentive to place students in special education. However, state funding reform is not the only way to remove that incentive.

There are several ways in which the federal government could help alleviate the problem of perverse funding incentives. One approach would be to provide private school scholarships to all special education students, on the model of Florida's popular McKay Scholarship Program. This would mitigate perverse incentives from state special education funding, since placing a student in special education would not automatically bring more money into a school district's budget. It would also have the advantage of potentially providing the other benefits of school choice to families with disabled students, such as the ability to choose for themselves which school will provide the best education for their children.

If full-scale private school scholarships are not politically feasible, there are several smaller steps that could be taken in this direction. For example, existing federal IDEA funding could be made portable. Under such a system, families could choose either to continue receiving special education services from their public school, in which case federal money would continue to go to that school, or to take their federal dollars to another service provider of their choice. In cases where only limited special education services are needed, families choosing to seek services elsewhere could even leave their children in public school for regular educational services.

Another way to combat the effects of perverse state funding incentives would be to begin federal auditing of special education placements.

The federal government could identify districts with especially high or especially low rates of special education placement, either generally or for certain groups. Other districts could be chosen for audits at random. Independent experts could then make their own diagnoses of students in special education in those districts, to determine how frequently students have been misdiagnosed. This would serve to expose to the public the true extent to which students without disabilities have been placed in special education; at the very least, such exposure would generate much stronger political pressure for reform of the system.

Finally, Congress could redirect its spending priorities when considering how new IDEA funds should be structured. Giving higher financial priority to types of disability that have more clearly objective diagnostic standards—such as autism, visual impairments, and hearing impairments—would send a clear message to states that the federal government will not provide infinite amounts of money for out-of-control special education programs. It would also have the beneficial effect of directing new federal money towards disability categories that place larger financial burdens on schools.

Kanya Mahitivanichcha
and Thomas Parrish

 NO

Do Non-Census Funding Systems Encourage Special Education Identification? Reconsidering Greene and Forster

Over the past 25 years, special education as a percentage of total enrollment has risen significantly across the nation. In 1975–76, special education made up about 8% of the school-age population. This figure rose to 10.6% in 1991–92, and was 12.2% by 2001–02. Rising enrollments have led to increased spending, with an estimated national expenditure of $50 billion on special education services during the 1999–2000 school year.

These growing numbers have garnered increased public attention and raised questions as to whether the type of special education funding formula used by states may be affecting rising special education identification rates. One perspective is that the same federal provisions govern special education identification throughout the country, and that each identified student undergoes extensive scrutiny by a multidisciplinary team of professionals prior to being deemed eligible for special education. These professionals often have no knowledge of underlying fiscal provisions, so their professional eligibility decisions would not be affected by them.

On the other hand, in 2000–01 the percentage of students identified for special education services in Rhode Island (17.8%) was nearly twice the identification rate for California (9.4%). Why are one state's identification criteria and procedures for students in special education so different from another? As the same federal provisions, the Individuals with Disabilities Education Act (IDEA), pertain, what combination of state policies and circumstances result in such broad variation? What role might the state's type of special education funding formula play, if any?

One analysis that was fairly widely publicized concluded that the nation could save over $1.5 billion per year in special education spending if all states were to adopt funding formulas free of fiscal incentives to identify additional special education students. A savings of this magnitude appears to be counter to the prevailing, but also fairly limited, research previously conducted on this topic. While other studies, some of which are briefly described in this article, have found evidence of the effects of funding

From *Journal of Special Education Leadership,* vol. 18, no. 1, April 2005, pp. 38–45. Copyright © 2005 by Council of Administrators of Special Education (CASE). Reprinted by permission.

incentives on special education practice, most have concluded that fiscal provisions are just one set of a complex array of factors explaining the large range in identification rates across states. No prior report reveals the type of unequivocal relationship that Greene and Forster claim to have found, or suggests the extensive changes in practice and resultant savings that would result from adopting what they refer to as an "incentive-free" approach to special education funding.

Rather than favoring one type of funding formula over another, this article argues that incentive-free approaches to special education funding do not exist, since all formulas place fiscal premiums on some behaviors over others. The real question addressed by this article is the extent to which evidence can be found that special education providers actually alter behavior in response to these fiscal incentives. This article briefly explores existing research about the relationship between alternative types of funding systems and special education identification rates, re-examines the analysis and findings of Greene and Forster, and provides some independent analyses related to the possible impact of special education fiscal incentives.

To the degree that fiscal incentives impact policy and practice, the questions addressed in this article are important. According to a survey on state special education funding systems conducted by the Center for Special Education Finance (CSEF) in 1999–2000, more than half of the responding states (28 of 46) said they had altered the way they fund special education since 1994–95. Additionally, almost half of the responding states said they were considering further changes. These findings point to the dynamic nature of the mechanisms through which states allocate special education funds and the ongoing opportunity to inform policy. If $1.5 billion can be saved per year, as claimed by Greene and Forster, all states should adopt the type of funding system they advocate.

Fiscal Incentives in the Context of Special Education Funding

Greene and Forster argue that all states should adopt the special education funding systems that are based on the total number of children living in a state or the total number of students enrolled in a district. These formulas are not directly related to special education enrollments or the types or levels of service provision. However, they may be adjusted to reflect variations in measures of student need that cannot be directly affected by district practice, such as student poverty (as found in the federal special education formula), or an external estimate of student severity (as used in California). These formulas are sometimes referred to as "census-based" or "population-based." Such formulas are used by the federal government in allocating a growing portion of IDEA funds, as well as by states such as Pennsylvania, Massachusetts, and California.

A second category of formulas, which is more predominant across the states, is based on some measure of special education provision. Examples include formulas in which the amount of state aid is based on varying funding "weights" (or amounts) associated with each special education student, formulas where districts are reimbursed for a certain percentage of their special education expenditures, or formulas in which funding is based on the allocation of specific special education resources such as classroom units or teachers.

The major distinction between these two categories of formulas is that under non-census systems, the amount of funds allocated is based on some measure of the degree of special education services provided, while under census systems they are not. Greene and Forster posit that the non-census systems create incentives to identify more students for special education than the census-based approaches. They further claim that their analyses strongly confirm the hypothesis that higher special education identification rates occur under non-census types of formulas.

Review of the Prior Literature

Although there has been much speculation regarding fiscal incentives in special education, relatively few studies have directly examined the association between fiscal incentives and special education identification rates. Among the most recent is the work of Cullen, in which the author utilized data from Texas from the early- to the mid-1990s to quantify the relationship between changes in fiscal incentives and student disability rates. According to these findings, fiscal incentives explained about 40% of the increase in disability rates among school districts in Texas during the study's period.

In a study by Kane and Johnson, the authors evaluated the first three years of implementation of Act 230 in Vermont. Under Act 230, the special education funding system was changed so that the block grant portion was based on total student membership rather than special education enrollment. Act 230 also included other changes in the funding system that increased flexibility and decreased incentives to identify children as disabled. The authors found that special education enrollment in Vermont over the first three years of implementation of Act 230 decreased by over 17%.

Thus, these two studies did find a relationship between fiscal incentives and special education identification patterns in Texas and Vermont. In Pennsylvania, Hartman also initially found evidence that the shift to a census funding formula appeared to slow special education identification across the state. In contrast with nationwide trends throughout the 1990s, Pennsylvania actually experienced initial decreases in special education as a percentage of total public school enrollment. However, this series of decreases in Pennsylvania was followed by increases in the mid- to late-1990s. By the 2000–01 school year, Pennsylvania's special education percentage was once again slightly above the national average.

Other studies, however, have pointed to the complexity of these relationships and the need to also consider the influence of such factors as the organizational structure, program constraints and regulations, characteristics

of advocacy groups, commitment and leadership of staff, legal requirements, and variation in funding from other sources that are available to
states and school districts. Such factors may interact with fiscal incentives
created by funding formulas, resulting in behaviors and responses that are
much less predictable.

Magnetti found relationships between governing agencies, such as
the collaboration between special education programs and welfare services,
affect special education identification. Weikart found that variables such
as the organization of the state department of education, priorities of state
leadership, and the relative effectiveness of federal monitoring influence
the placement patterns of students in special education.

In his paper examining issues of reliability, validity, and usefulness of
disability assessments on special education identification and classification,
Reschly pointed out that disability classification is not uniform across states.
Assessing disabilities is a complex task, and professional judgment may vary
across districts and states. Identical characteristics may be interpreted and
classified differently depending on the state in which the student resides.

In summary, although research evidence can be found that funding
formulas may create fiscal incentives that sometimes influence the provision of special education services, the literature also suggests that these incentives need to be understood in conjunction with other factors such as
the historical context, impact of advocacy groups, organizational structure,
professional judgment, program constraints, and government regulations.

Reconsidering Greene and Forster

In examining the association between fiscal incentives in funding mechanisms and special education enrollment, Greene and Forster classified state
funding systems into the census and non-census categories previously
described. Figure 1 replicates their analysis showing enrollment figures
under the two funding systems over ten years. It is important to note that
each point on the chart represents a weighted average of the percentage
of students in special education across all the states having one type of
funding system as opposed to another in a given year. This type of weighted
approach results in very large states having a vastly larger impact than very
small ones. The resulting averages are, therefore, much more susceptible to
what happens in a few large states as opposed to reflecting a true average
of 50 varying state experiments regarding the relationship between funding
policies and special education enrollments. It is also important to note
that the states included in each category of funding differ across the years
as they change from one type of funding system to another.

For example, California had a non-census system up until 1998, and
therefore is included in the non-census averages shown in Figure 1 from
1991–97. After changing its funding policy in 1998, California is reflected
in the figures representing the census system. Given this change and the
fact that the weight generated by a single state with a very large student
enrollment has the capacity to substantially alter aggregate trends, it is

Figure 1

Replication of Greene and Forster's Population-Weighted Analysis

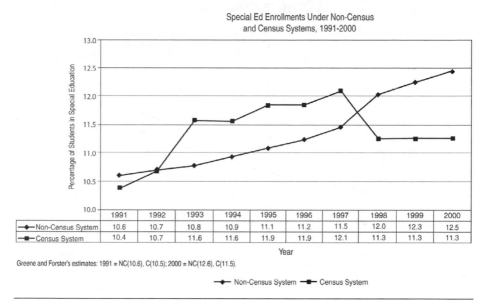

Special Ed Enrollments Under Non-Census
and Census Systems, 1991-2000

	1991	1992	1993	1994	1995	1996	1997	1998	1999	2000
Non-Census System	10.6	10.7	10.8	10.9	11.1	11.2	11.5	12.0	12.3	12.5
Census System	10.4	10.7	11.6	11.6	11.9	11.9	12.1	11.3	11.3	11.3

Year

Greene and Forster's estimates: 1991 = NC(10.6), C(10.5); 2000 = NC(12.6), C(11.5).

Non-Census System   Census System

important to question whether the sudden drop shown for 1998 in Figure 1 is simply a result of California's shift from a non-census to a census system during that year. As California's represents one-eighth of the nation, this state alone may have driven the observed aggregate trend, which Greene and Forster cite as evidence that census funding systems result in lower special education identification rates.

Figure 2 . . . is a replication of the same chart with California removed from the analysis. As can be seen, without California the trends in total special education enrollment rate representing each funding system look quite different. Greene and Forster concluded from Figure 1 that the states with a non-census system exhibit an increase in special education enrollment rate of about 1.9 percentage points over the ten-year period, while the census system saw an increase of about 0.9 percentage points. With the removal of California, Figure 2 . . . tells a different story: The non-census states now show an increase of about 1.6 percentage points over the ten-year period, while the census states saw an increase of 2.3 percentage points over the the ten-year period. Hence, the trends reverse when removing the "California effect."

A further argument against the Greene and Forster approach shown in Figure 1 is that the trends associated with the two funding systems are more appropriately examined through the calculation of unweighted averages, treating each state as an independent experiment regarding the relationship between state funding policies and special education identification

Figure 2

Modification of Greene and Forster's Population-Weighted Analysis Without California

Special Ed Enrollments Under Non-Census and Census Systems Without California, 1991-2000

	1991	1992	1993	1994	1995	1996	1997	1998	1999	2000
Non-Census System	10.9	11.0	11.1	11.2	11.4	11.6	11.8	12.0	12.3	12.5
Census System	10.4	10.7	11.6	11.6	11.9	11.9	12.1	12.4	12.5	12.7

Year

Greene and Forster's estimates: 1991 = NC(10.6), C(10.5); 2000 = NC(12.6), C(11.5).

Non-Census System   Census System

rates. The results of such analyses are shown in Figure 3. . . . With each state weighed equally, the non-census states saw an increase of 1.9 percentage points over the ten-year period, while those designated as using a census system saw an increase of 2.3 percentage points. On the other hand, the non-census states showed slightly higher identification rates over the past few years. Overall, however, the relationship observed from tracking the two lines in Figure 3 is far from stable, and does not appear to warrant any clear conclusions about the impact of one type of funding system over another on special education enrollments.

Regression Analysis

Greene and Forster also used Ordinary Least Squares (OLS) analyses to test their basic premise regarding the impact of alternative funding systems. They used special education growth from 1991–92 to 2000–01 as the dependent variable. From these analyses, they reported a statistically significant, positive correlation between non-census funding and growth in special education enrollment. According to the authors, these systems were associated with an additional increase of 1.24 percentage points in special education enrollment over this ten-year span. They also concluded from these findings that disability rates would be lower by an average of

Figure 3

Unweighted Analysis of States in Non-Census and Census Systems

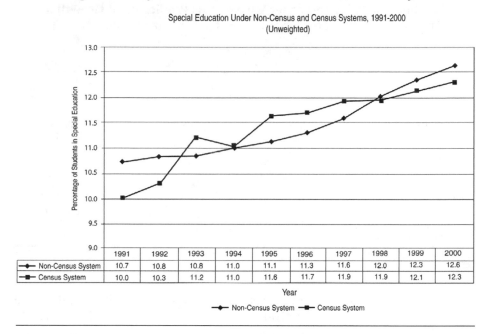

Special Education Under Non-Census and Census Systems, 1991-2000
(Unweighted)

Year	1991	1992	1993	1994	1995	1996	1997	1998	1999	2000
◆ Non-Census System	10.7	10.8	10.8	11.0	11.1	11.3	11.6	12.0	12.3	12.6
■ Census System	10.0	10.3	11.2	11.0	11.6	11.7	11.9	11.9	12.1	12.3

◆ Non-Census System ■ Census System

0.82 percentage points if states with non-census systems were to switch to census formulas.

To test these results, using the same data as Greene and Forster we first ran similar analyses, only modifying the independent (predictor/explanatory) variables somewhat. We retained the variable indicating whether the state had a census system at any point in time during the study period. However, we replaced their independent variable indicating whether the state had a "high stakes" testing system with the poverty rate among children in each state Greene and Forster's rationale for including the "high stakes" testing variable was that special education identification rates might be affected by the existence of "high stakes" testing (i.e., there may be an incentive for placing low-performing students in special education to avoid exposure to the tests that may pull down average district or state test scores). However, their analyses showed this variable to be statistically insignificant in explaining growth in special education enrollment. Hence, we replaced this variable with a poverty measure to reflect the established relationship between poverty and the need for special education services. Indeed, we found poverty to be a significant predictor of special education identification rate.

Table 1 compares regression results from Greene and Forster with two alternative model specifications. Model 1 shows that after controlling for poverty, the differential effect on identification rates associated with the two

Table 1

Replication and Modification of Greene and Forster's OLS Regression: Funding Formulas and other Variables as Predictors of Growth in Special Education Enrollment over the Ten-Year Period (N = 51)

	Replication of Greene & Forster	Model 1	Model 2
Census	−0.122*[a] (0.040)	−0.090* (0.039)	–
Five-Year Census	–	–	−0.080 (0.044)
High Stakes	−0.066 (0.038)	–	–
Poverty	–	0.006* (0.003)	0.007* (0.003)
Adjusted R-sq.	0.146	0.177	0.145

*p < 0.05, standard errors in parentheses.
[a]Greene and Forster's estimate = −0.124*

types of funding formulas becomes less pronounced, with the estimated effects on special education enrollment growth associated with census systems dropping from 1.24 to 0.9 percentage points (p < 0.05). However, the difference between our estimate in Model 1 and that of Greene and Forster is not statistically significant.

Model 2, as shown in Table 1, includes a different definition for determining whether a state is classified as census or non-census in the analysis. In this case, states were only classified as census if they had such a system in place for at least five years during the study period. This contrasts with Greene and Forster's approach, which designated states as census if they had a census formula in place in any single year over this ten-year span. This modification was based on the assumption that if a state had nine years of non-census funding and one year of census funding, it made little sense to include them in the census grouping. Assuming that some period of implementation would be needed before any program effect would occur, a state was labeled as census or non-census, based on the prevailing system through the ten-year period.

Using this revised definition of census states and poverty as predictors (see Model 2 in Table 1), the census variable shows up as statistically insignificant. In other words, the analysis suggests that there are no statistically reliable correlations between states' special education growth rates and states' having census systems for at least five years. Estimates on the poverty variable, however, showed up as statistically significant in both Models 1 and 2.

In deciding how to classify states in our regression models, we also used a model in which states were classified as having a census system if they had a census system in place for three years or more. The resulting estimates were identical to those reported by Greene and Forster, because all states with a census system in place at any point in time had had it for at least three years. In an attempt to further test the resiliency of the relationship between the funding system and identification rates, we applied the five-year definition, whereby only states that have had the census system for at least five years were categorized as having a prevailing census system. The rationale is that if an influence is seen under the census system, the longer it is in place the more pronounced the effect should be. However, as shown in Model 2, we found that the relationship seemed to disappear when we applied the five-year test. This suggests that with the small sample size (limited by the number of states), the results are more a reflection of how states are classified, than a measure of any relationship between the census funding systems and special education identification rates.

An Alternative Regression Analysis

In addition to re-examining Greene and Forster's methodology, an alternative regression approach for considering the relationship between funding systems and special education identification was applied. Specifically, a repeated measures regression analysis was conducted, using special education enrollment rates for each of the ten years across 50 states and the District of Columbia, resulting in 510 cases (see Table 2).

Repeated measures analysis takes into consideration that the observations across years for each state may be correlated with one another and account for such intrastate dependence. The predictor variables in this analysis include a poverty measure; a continuous year variable (to reflect special education enrollment growth over the ten-year period); a binary variable classifying whether the state has a census system for each respective year; and an interaction term, "census × year." This interaction term captures average growth (per year) in special education enrollment over the ten-year period associated with the census system relative to the non-census system.

Applying this repeated measures regression model, the estimate on the census variable shows up as statistically insignificant. This suggests that states with census systems do not have significantly lower special education enrollment rates relative to states with non-census systems, after filtering out the effects of poverty. However, the interaction term shows up as significant ($p < 0.01$). That is, the average growth (per year over the ten-year period) in special education enrollment rate in a census system is 0.06% lower than in a non-census system. This finding is consistent with, but considerably less pronounced, than that of Greene and Forster.

Implications for Policymakers

What are the policy implications of these varying results? As mentioned earlier, a number of states, as well as the federal government, have altered the basis on which special education funds have been allocated over the past ten years. In addition, the Center for Special Education Finance reports

Table 2

Repeated Measures Analysis: Funding Formulas and Poverty as Predictors of Special Education Enrollment over the Ten-Year Period (N = 51)

Variables	Estimated Coefficients on Special Education Enrollment Rate
Census	−0.00082 (0.002699)
Year	0.00223** (0.000081)
Census × Year	−0.00059* (0.000201)
Poverty	0.000018 (0.000459)

$*p < 0.05$.
$**p < 0.01$, standard errors in parentheses.

continuing evidence that future changes are likely. States report that one factor driving change is concern about rising special education enrollments and costs. As states continue to actively consider future funding provisions, it is important for policymakers to understand the possible program implications of alternative funding policies.

All of the formula options from which policymakers may choose contain fiscal incentives in relation to one another. Census formulas, which do not base funding received on any measure of special education provision, contain a fiscal incentive to identify fewer students for special education and to provide lower levels of service as compared to non-census formulas in which the allocation of funds is clearly based on these factors.

Some states may adopt census-based systems specifically in an attempt to dampen growing special education enrollments. There are also many other reasons why a state may wish to choose one type of formula over another. Thus, in considering the relative merits of alternative formulas, perhaps the operative question is not whether varying fiscal incentives for special education identification are contained in them, but whether these incentives have any effect on practice. Greene and Forster seemed to extend a clear call to action by arguing that the nation could save over $1.5 billion per year in special education spending if all states were to adopt census-based funding formulas.

After a review of prior research in this area, a re-examination of Greene and Forster's methods and results, and an attempt at a more rigorous empirical examination of this question, there appears to be mild evidence that the choice of a census-based funding system alone may have a slight affect on future special education enrollments. However, little evidence is found that this relationship is as clear or close to the magnitude claimed by Greene and Forster. Rather, the findings in this paper seem to substantiate evidence from the prior literature that fiscal provisions are among many factors that appear to affect varying patterns of special education enrollment.

POSTSCRIPT

Do Funding Systems Create a Perverse Incentive to Place Students in Special Education?

Special education costs stimulate many heated arguments. Everyone agrees it would be better not to have such high expenses.

Many parents struggle to have their children qualify for special education, convinced that intensive academic attention is essential for their success. Many say their struggle is due to districts' reluctance to spend money on services. Everyone agrees it would be better if their children learned effortlessly and did not require supports.

All four authors agree that special education numbers are rising. They all use complex statistical analyses to discover the "culprit." They disagree about what fuels the growth.

Greene and Forster staunchly believe that funding systems are to blame. Maintaining that even 10% of children in special education is too many, they provide powerful illustrations of how state expenses have changed. Their models suggest that impressive savings could be easily realized by implementing systems that do not tempt districts.

Mahitivanichcha and Parrish analyze the data differently and reach other conclusions. Removing "California effect" of size, they found smaller discrepancies between the funding systems. Additionally, although agreeing that special education numbers in census-based states are slightly lower, they present evidence that poverty is a compelling element affecting these enrollments.

Competing demands for funds always cause financial tension between general and special education. The *Journal of Special Education Leadership (JSEL)* focused its entire April 2005 issue on this topic. The centerpiece was the recently released Special Education Expenditure Project (SEEP). Mandated by IDEA 97, SEEP was conducted by the American Institutes for Research (http://csef.air.org), with which Mahitivanichcha and Parrish are affiliated.

Initial SEEP analyses made an unexpected discovery (Chambers, Perez, Harr, and Shkolnik, *JSEL*, 2005). While expenditures varied widely, the last comprehensive study, conducted in 1985–86, calculated the annual expense of educating a child in special education to be 2.28 times that of educating a typical child. SEEP, using data from the 1999–2000 school year, found that ratio had fallen to 1.90:1. This amount is lower than the 1.92:1 figures gathered in 1968–69.

Special education costs have increased (108 percent). General education costs have risen even more (110 percent). Agreeing with all of this issue's authors, SEEP finds that larger expenditures are due to added numbers of students with mild needs.

Harr and Parrish (*JSEL*, 2005) echo Parrish's statement—every funding system contains incentives. Census-based systems reward districts for identifying fewer students. Weight-based systems reward identification. Which preference will result in better outcomes for all our students?

In the same issue, Brian Benzel, superintendent of the Spokane (WA) public schools, notes that his district has rising special education numbers despite a funding ceiling. Although proud of his district's attention to students, he worries about how to afford services. One of his suggestions is a funding system based on a defined set of services that could be standardized across the country. This, and fulfillment of the federal funding promise, would help Spokane.

Are there ways to determine a standard level of services in special education? What about general education? Is it possible that increased numbers in special education are driven by fewer services available to all children?

There is agreement that special education numbers are rising and that services to these children are costly. Is this controversy about the number of children in special education, the cost to educate these children, or the limited resources for all of education?

Internet References . . .

No Child Left Behind

Use this U.S. Department of Education Web site to learn everything you want to know about No Child Left Behind. Information encompasses the following: text of the statute, updates on hearings, notices of changes in the regulations, and resources for teachers. A newsletter is also available to deliver information as soon as it becomes available.

http://www.ed.gov/nclb/landing.jhtml

What Works Clearinghouse

The What Works Clearinghouse was established in 2002 by the U.S. Department of Education's Institute of Education Sciences to provide educators, policymakers, researchers, and the public with a central and trusted source of scientific evidence of what works in education.

http://www.whatworks.ed.gov/

National Center on Educational Outcomes

The National Center on Educational Outcomes (NCEO), based at the University of Minnesota, is a primary research site for the participation of students with disabilities in large-scale testing. This Web site contains current resources on the status of testing in all statutes as well as information on the ways in which students with disabilities participate. Links include numerous printable NCEO publications.

http://education.umn.edu/nceo/

National Dissemination Center for Children with Disabilities (NICHCY) Research Center for Children with Disabilities

A new resource for educators and parents of students with disabilities, this site provides comprehensive information on the research process. One element, The NICHCY Research-to-Practice Database, enables readers to access research about techniques and practices that might be useful in their work with children with disabilities. An update feature announces added topics or updated pages

http://nichcy.org/

Circle of Inclusion

This Web site, funded by the U.S. Office of Special Education Programs, is targeted at providing information and resources about the effective practices of inclusive educational programs for children from birth through age eight. Links to additional resources and videoclips can be found on the home page.

http://www.circleofinclusion.org/

Intervention Central

Designed and maintained by a New York school psychologist and school administrator, this site contains strategies, publications, and tools to assist in classroom intervention and assessment. A free online newsletter updates readers about additions to the site.

http://www.interventioncentral.org

Access and Accountability

*T*hirty *years ago, special education was concerned with getting students with disabilities into schools. Next, the conversation turned to opening classroom doors, so students with disabilities had access to typical peers and were included in school experiences. Current deliberations revolve around access to the general curriculum—the real work of schools. With access has come accountability. Now that the doors are open, we all must be accountable for the learning that goes on inside. As this new step in inclusionary practice takes shape, we must retain the careful attention to individuals that is the hallmark of special education.*

- Is Response to Intervention (RTI) Ready for Implementation?

- Does NCLB Leave Some Students Behind?

- Will NCLB Requirements Produce Highly Qualified Special Education Teachers?

- Can Scientifically Based Research Guide Instructional Practice?

- Should Students with Cognitive Disabilities Be Expected to Demonstrate Academic Proficiency?

- Have Schools Gone Too Far in Using Accommodations?

- Can One Model of Special Education Serve All Students?

- Is Full Inclusion the Least Restrictive Environment?

ISSUE 7

Is Response to Intervention (RTI) Ready for Implementation?

YES: Rachel Brown-Chidsey and Mark W. Steege, from *Response to Intervention: Principles and Strategies for Effective Practice* (The Guilford Press, 2005)

NO: Douglas Fuchs and Donald D. Deshler, from "What We Need to Know About Responsiveness to Intervention (and Shouldn't Be Afraid to Ask)," *Learning Disabilities Research & Practice* (May 2007)

ISSUE SUMMARY

YES: Rachel Brown-Chidsey and Mark W. Steege, faculty members at the University of Southern Maine, who have conducted extensive research in the area of student assessment, describe Response to Intervention (RTI) as a systematic way for educators to help all children experience appropriate educational practices.

NO: Douglas Fuchs and Donald D. Deshler, professors at Vanderbilt University and the University of Kansas, respectively, prolific scholars, and co-directors of the National Research Center on Learning Disabilities, urge educators to identify and explore unresolved aspects of RTI before wholesale implementation.

Struggling learners waiting to fail so they could receive special education, rising numbers of children identified as learning disabled, and overrepresentation of minorities in special education—these were among the problems legislators wanted to address when reauthorizing IDEA.

RTI was identified as a remedy that would help more children learn effectively in the general education classroom. Key elements of RTI include the following: an integrated system that uses performance data to drive high-quality instruction, a problem-solving approach to student learning, and a progressive, multi-tiered system of interventions.

Echoing NCLB, RTI emphasizes a connection between scientifically based instructional practices and continuously monitored student progress. Every student's progress is to be systematically and regularly measured. Careful attention to each child's rate of learning alerts educators to developing difficulties. If a student does not progress, then instruction must change.

Slow progress is viewed as a problem to be addressed by a team of educators, who pool their expertise to identify interventions that will help the student's learning improve. Although this sounds like the traditional pre-referral process, there is a key difference. Instead of signaling the prelude to special education referral and services, RTI focuses on documenting a student's responses to significant interventions within general education.

Intervention tiers correspond to instruction and assessment that are increasingly individualized. For the purposes of illustration, three levels are described here; no specific design is specified by IDEA. In Tier 1, children experience effective classroom instruction. All students are screened regularly; teachers are appropriately prepared to use scientifically based teaching methods; educators scrutinize assessment data to identify students who are not progressing adequately. In Tier 2, groups of students showing some difficulty are given additional focused, short-term instruction and assessments. Tier 3 is reserved for individual students who do not respond to Tier 2 and require longer, and more intense, instruction. The tiers are expected to be fluid. As students respond to intervention, they return to a less intense tier.

While there is agreement that instruction in Tiers 1 and 2 is delivered by general education teachers, more variation exists about Tier 3 implementation. Some see Tier 3 as a further level of intensity within general education; others envision it delivered by special education faculty; still others view Tier 3 as the opportunity to evaluate whether a student has a disability (NASDSE, 2006).

Brown-Chidsey and Steege view RTI as a responsive approach to children and a way to ensure that schools deliver the kinds of services that students need. Emphasizing the strength of the problem-solving model, they cite evidence from states that found a reduction in special education numbers after implementing RTI procedures. Even though it is a new solution, Brown Chidsey and Steege encourage educators to adopt RTI and, in the rest of their book, provide guidance on how to do so.

Fuchs and Deshler are concerned that educators will be pressured to adopt RTI before critical questions are answered. They compare interpretations of many elements, including the problem-solving model, the essentials of appropriate Tier 1 instruction, and the nature of non-responders. Fuchs and Deshler advise educators to thoroughly explore these issues before formulating their own response to this intervention strategy.

As you read these articles, consider your own level of knowledge about RTI. How is RTI being implemented in your neighborhood school? Have educators resolved the questions raised in these selections?

YES ↵

Rachel Brown-Chidsey
and Mark W. Steege

What Is Response to Intervention (RTI)?

Consider the case of Sean. Sean is a first grader who has not yet developed important prereading skills that he will need if he wants to succeed in school, graduate, go to college, or get a well-paying job in the future. His parents, his teacher, his principal, and the superintendent of his school district want him to learn how to read. So Sean keeps plugging away in school, sitting attentively when his teacher reads to the class, pointing to pictures in books when his parents read to him at home, and "borrowing" answers from other student's worksheets when completing class assignments. At the end of Sean's first-grade year he takes a test to show what he has learned during the year. The test shows that he knows his colors and shapes, but he still cannot read.

Sean's teacher makes a note about his reading problems in his file before it is sent on to the second-grade teacher. When Sean starts the second grade his teacher is already concerned about his reading difficulties, and she works with him closely for several weeks. At the end of October, his teacher has concluded that Sean must have a learning disability, so she refers him for evaluation. In early January an individualized education plan (IEP) meeting about Sean is held. At the meeting, results from the evaluation are reported. These results show that Sean scored in the low end of the average range on both academic achievement and cognitive (IQ) testing. As a result of these highly consistent scores, Sean's parents are told that their son does not have a learning disability. The parents are relieved to hear that, but then ask, "Who will help our son learn to read?" The assistant principal who is chairing the meeting regretfully tells Sean's parents that, because his school does not have Title I funding and Sean did not qualify for special education, he will have to keep "trying" to learn to read in his current class. Sean's mom starts to cry and his dad stands up and states angrily, "This is crazy! Our son cannot read, but you won't do anything to help him! We're leaving and I'm calling the superintendent."

The foregoing scenario is neither uncommon nor unlikely. In our experience as educators and psychologists we have evaluated and met with the parents of many students who had clear and specific learning needs but could not obtain additional school assistance to meet those needs. The described example is sometimes known as a "waiting-to-fail" model, because Sean may eventually qualify for special education if he continues to lag behind in reading and cannot engage with or participate in reading-based classroom activities. The tragedy of this model is that by the time Sean meets the criteria for special education eligibility, the best years for teaching him to read will have passed.

The good news for students like Sean is that the instructional methods and educational policies needed to get him the reading (or math, or writing) instruction that he needs are available. The instructional methods and assessment procedures most likely to benefit students like Sean are known as *response to intervention* (RTI). RTI is an assessment–intervention model that allows schools to deliver sound instructional methods to students like Sean who otherwise might fall through the cracks. This book is designed to provide knowledge, skills, and resources for using RTI methods in schools. RTI is a relatively new term for an approach to understanding and addressing students' school difficulties. For the purpose of clarity . . . we developed the following definition. First, let's define the important words in the term:

Response: 1. The act of responding
                  2. An answer or reply
Intervention: 1. The act of intervening; interposition
                  2. Any interference that may affect the interests of others, especially of one or more states with the affairs of another; mediation

Essentially, RTI is an objective examination of the cause–effect relationship(s) between academic or behavioral *intervention* and the student's *response* to the intervention. For example, a student's *response* to a specific reading instruction *intervention* can be measured using oral reading fluency indicators. When the core terms *response* and *intervention* are put together, a more general set of educational practices and procedures can be defined. Such practices include providing a specific *intervention* (an interference that affects others) for one or more students and measuring the student(s)' *response* (answer or reply) to the intervention. Put more succinctly, RTI is a systematic and data-based method for identifying, defining, and resolving students' academic and/or behavior difficulties. This definition has certain inherent limitations. For example, it includes only academic and behavior problems. We chose to include only academic interventions because this is an important and emerging application of RTI procedures. Specifically, the most recent version of the Individuals with Disabilities Education Improvement Act included RTI references related to identification of learning disabilities. This use of RTI has widespread implications for many aspects of education . . . Importantly, RTI is designed to take the guesswork out of the assessment and intervention process as it is implemented first in general education, and then, for a small number of students, in special education.

History

The components that make up RTI methods have been used in schools for many years but have not been understood as part of the larger system now known as RTI. For example, teachers have routinely used targeted methods of instruction to help individual students develop certain skills. Likewise, as standard practices, schools have reported on student progress at regular intervals. What makes RTI different from these prior means of helping students is that the assessment and instruction practices are integrated into an objective data-based system with built-in decision stages. This is in contrast to past models of student assessment in which students were assumed to be doing OK unless identified otherwise. In RTI, all students are screened and monitored for specific educational outcomes, and those needing additional assistance are given targeted intervention that is monitored systematically using scientifically based data recording procedures. In essence, RTI integrates high-quality teaching and assessment methods in a systematic way so that students who are not successful when presented with one set of instructional methods can be given the chance to succeed with the use of other practices.

Key Features of RTI

As described in the RTI definition above, there are two main components that distinguish RTI from other teaching and assessment practices. These essential components are *systematic* and *data-based* activities. A conceptual framework of our RTI model . . . reflects three tiers of intervention in RTI. Tier 1 . . . reflects the general education curriculum. This tier is designed for and provided to all students in each grade level. Tier 1 is comprehensive and universal. . . . Tier 1 activities are selected on the basis of effectiveness. Still, not all students will respond to Tier 1 instruction with success. Tier 2 . . . represents those students who need more intensive and specific instruction in order to be successful in school. Importantly, . . . data are the only connecting point, or pathway, between each tier. A student can cross between tiers only when data indicate that it needs to happen. A third tier . . . represents a small subset of students who do not respond to the interventions provided in Tiers 1 and 2. Tier 3 activities include comprehensive assessment to identify whether a student has a specific disability and meets the criteria for special education. Notably, Tier 3 does not include special education services; rather, it is a transition point for those students who have not yet found success in school.

Our model of RTI is built upon previous work related to school assessment and instruction. An early precursor to RTI methods is Deno's "cascade" model of special education service delivery. In this model Deno conceptualized students' educational progress as "developmental capital" that could yield dividends in response to appropriate instruction in the least restrictive environment. Deno's "cascade" features increasingly small instructional groupings matched to the individual student's specific needs. Deno's model was used as a core framework for the implementation of special education regulations during the 1970s and 1980s. While this model helped to make special education a reality for many students, one of the problems seen in special education, starting in the 1980s, was the rapid increase in students identified as having learning disabilities.

In part to address the rapid increase in special education placements, several programs and initiatives have been implemented to address the needs of students before they are given special education services. The first of these attempts was known as the regular education initiative, or REI. This federal policy focused on having as many students as possible remain in "regular" education. Drawing from Deno's cascade model, the idea was to focus on determination of what constituted the least restrictive environment for students with disabilities. Instead of assuming that all students with disabilities would need separate specialized teaching, the REI effort pushed teachers and administrators to keep as many children in their original classrooms as possible.

The REI was criticized from its first days, with concerns ranging from lack of teacher training to violation of student rights. . . . Analysis showed that the REI was not very effective in reducing the number of students receiving special education services. Soon after REI measures were put into place, a second major push to reform special education was begun. Known as "inclusive education," this movement had longer-lasting effects than REI. This effort to change special education policies and practices was focused more on establishing the rights and needs of students with disabilities than reducing the overall number of students receiving special education services. The inclusion movement led to examinations of how special education services were being provided. As with RTI, many researchers suggested that additional training was needed by general education classroom teachers. Most notably, educators were reported to be philosophically supportive of special education but not adequately trained to meet the needs of students with disabilities in inclusive classrooms.

Although the inclusion movement has not totally disappeared, recent efforts to address the large number of students in special education have shifted to using RTI methods as the primary mechanism. Additionally, the reduction efforts are now squarely focused on reducing the number of students identified with learning disabilities rather than reducing special education enrollments overall. Kavale and Forness have suggested that the reason why both REI and inclusion failed to bring about the desired changes in general and special education is that they failed to utilize empirical evidence of effective practices and instead focused on philosophical issues about the moral imperative to educate all children. Of note, Kavale expressed opposition to adoption of RTI policies at the federal level until more evidence was produced that such practices systematically result in desired outcomes. Kavale's criticism of current RTI methods appears to be an extension of the arguments made against REI and inclusion. Kavale and others have argued that until there is clear and substantial evidence that RTI methods produce large-scale improvements in educational outcomes, RTI should not be used at the state or national level.

The problem with waiting to implement RTI on a large scale is that the only way to determine whether it will achieve its promise is to implement it at the state or national level. Such implementation needs to be done with the rights and needs of students uppermost in mind. Importantly, RTI methods include certain "safety net" features that can prevent negative consequences. For example, unlike REI and inclusion, RTI is by definition data-driven, so no decisions are made without evidence to support them. Most importantly, RTI is not simply one intervention or method. It is a set of scientifically based procedures that can be used to make decisions about educational programs. In light of the history of efforts to improve educational outcomes for all students, it is important that current and future such initiatives not get bogged down in rhetoric. . . . [Early] intervention has a huge effect on long-term outcomes. . . .

RTI and Problem Solving

By their nature, RTI methods are problem-solving activities. Although many students and teachers in schools may not perceive their daily experiences as "problems," they do engage in ongoing assessment and reflection. In the course of daily events, teachers (and students) are generally pleased when teaching and learning activities go as expected. Under such circumstances, no major "problems" are evident. When a teacher notices that a student's work is not what was expected, a different reaction is likely to occur. If the teacher find the student's work to be exemplary, he or she may offer additional praise. If the teacher finds the work to be below expectations, he or she may believe that a learning problem is present. Such a problem could include academic skills such as reading, writing, or math, or it could relate to behavioral expectations such as whether the student is able to stay seated, stand in line, or play with others at recess. Regardless of the event, teachers and students tend not to notice school problems until they occur, and then they are very apparent. As a result of efforts to help all students be successful in school, researchers have developed specific problem-solving methods designed to assist teachers and specialists when school difficulties arise.

RTI methods are closely linked with problem-solving models for school difficulties. . . . Deno's five-part data-based problem-solving model will be used as part of the RTI stages and activities. . . . This model includes (1) problem identification, (2) problem definition, (3) designing intervention plans, (4) implementing the intervention, and (5) problem solution. . . . [Each] of these steps is aligned with specific assessment and instructional activities designed to reduce or eliminate a student's school difficulties. This model is designed to be used continuously and interactively. As one step ends, the next begins. In some cases, not all steps will be implemented. In other cases, each step will be utilized multiple times to help identify the best way to help a student be successful in school. An important feature of this problem-solving model is that it recognizes that schools cannot be problem-free. Instead, it offers a way of dealing with problems when they happen so that the long-term negative impact is minimized.

Problem Identification

The first step begins with problem identification activities. Such activities include any and all moments when a student's school difficulties are initially identified. To help explain this step and the other steps of the model, the metaphor of radar will be used. Problem identification may be likened to the moment when something is first detected on a radar screen. Those monitoring the screen do not know what's causing the "blip" on the screen, but they know it needs to be addressed. A number of different people may participate in problem identification activities. Teachers, parents, students, administrators, bus drivers, and/or cafeteria staff members may help to bring problems to greater attention and put them on the "radar screen." Problem identification is not an end unto itself. Instead, this first step activates a process by which more data about a student's school difficulties can be collected.

Problem Definition

The second step of the problem-solving model is problem definition. This step includes evaluating the nature and magnitude of the problem and determining whether the problem requires an intervention or might resolve itself on its own. This is similar to what sea-farers and aviators must do in order to determine whether the radar signal is from a large attack ship or a small unarmed private vessel. How the pilot responds will be based on the nature of the object identified by the radar. In the same way, educators can help students by defining the nature of the student's problem. Problem definition activities include evaluating the student's skills in certain areas and comparing them to what is expected. Such definitions include measurements such as reading fluency, frequency of on-task behaviors, and rate of homework completion. Only once a student's current behaviors have been identified is it possible to know the magnitude and importance of the problem identified in Step 1. Some problems may be very small and likely to resolve on their own over time. Alternatively, other problems may be of immediate concern. If the difference between a student's current performance and what is expected is large, that student is likely to have a serious school problem that needs to be resolved.

Designing Intervention Plans

The third step of the problem-solving model includes putting in place specific activities and procedures designed to reduce significantly the difference between what a student can currently do and what he or she is expected to do. The development of such intervention plans is similar to how a pilot of a boat or plane might respond to information concerning the source of a radar signal. If the captain of a small sailboat is charting a course and finds that he or she is steering toward a much larger vessel, changing course is the prudent thing to do, especially if the larger ship is an aircraft carrier or oil tanker. Educators can help students to chart a new course by designing ways to improve their skills so that they can be successful in school. . . . [All] interventions need to be empirically validated with evidence of effectiveness in school settings. Effective interventions include methods such as direct instruction of specific skills, positive behavior support plans, and peer-assisted learning strategies. . . . A specific time frame and plan for implementing the intervention, what personnel will be involved, and how data will be collected provide crucial links to the next steps of the problem-solving process.

Implementing the Intervention

This step of the model has two major components: implementation and progress monitoring. The intervention should be implemented as planned and intended. If a well-designed intervention is put into action incorrectly, it may be impossible to know whether it could have worked. For this reason, the intervention plan should include some form of treatment integrity check to document whether the plan was implemented as intended. If an intervention is implemented as planned but does not work, it can be changed, but information about initial ineffectiveness is needed in order to design effective alternatives. If some portions of the intervention did work, these might be retained and used with additional new components. The only way to know if an intervention works is to collect data. This is the critical second component of problem-solving step 4. From the very first moment that an intervention is put into place, data concerning the outcomes must be collected. This is no different from a pilot who would monitor the radar screen as well as other sources of information to verify that the threat posed by a larger vessel is reduced as a result of someone changing course. Data collection methods can include recording the frequency, rate, accuracy, duration, and intensity of a behavior or skill. (Determination of what type of data recording procedure to use is based on the specific nature of the problem. Students who are often off-task can be monitored according to the frequency of on-task behaviors. Students with reading difficulties can be monitored by checking and recording oral or silent reading fluency). Progress monitoring also involves ongoing data analysis. Single-case experimental designs are typically used in the analysis of data.

Problem Solution

As mentioned earlier the problem-solving model is organized in such a way that it can be used to solve a wide range of school problems. It is set up to account for the reality that there will always be problems in schools. Thankfully, many school problems are solvable, and this model has an identifiable end step that documents when a problem is resolved. The specific way that each school problem will be solved will always differ according to the strengths and needs of each child. The important aspect of the fifth, and final, step of the model is that it allows for recognition of school success by noting when certain preset criteria for success are met. Just as the captain of a boat lets out a sign of relief when a new course results in being out of harm's way, students and their support teams can determine a performance level that will mark problem solution and celebrate when it is met. As noted above, the problem-solving model is set up to be used continuously, as needed. For some students, one intervention may be all it takes to achieve problem solution. For others, the problems may be greater in size and number, and multiple problem solution parties will be shared on the pathway to greater success. Importantly, problem solution provides all members of the school team with the chance to identify what has been successful and develop new goals and plans.

RTI and Special Education

As described [earlier], RTI methods share a legacy with prior efforts to improve special education programs. It is impossible to separate RTI completely from special education because RTI activities occur in a sequence along a continuum. When empirically validated interventions are used, it is expected that most students school progress will be appropriate. Still, RTI methods include steps to be taken for students who continue to struggle in school despite attempted interventions. For some students, RTI activities will result in evaluation and eligibility for special education services. Indeed, . . . RTI methods have been included in the most recent reauthorization of the Individuals with Disabilities Education Act. Such methods also fit with other recent education policies such as the No Child Left Behind Act and related state programs. Importantly, RTI methods were developed with the goal of spreading a wide net for identification of students having difficulty in school. This net is designed initially to identify a larger number of students who need help than will end up in special education. The goal is to provide student at risk or already experiencing school difficulties with interventions that prevent additional problems.

An example of the wide-net approach included in RTI is the Texas Primary Reading Instrument (TPRI). This instrument is part of a statewide effort to identify and define the needs of students at risk of reading problems. It is organized such that scores on the TPRI will yield a list of students who may have reading problems. This list is used to design and implement reading interventions that will be monitored over time. It is expected that most students will show reading improvement as a result of the intervention. Those students who do not show improvement are provided with additional intervention that is developed in response to the data collected during the earlier program. Students who consistently struggle to learn to read despite multiple empirically based reading interventions are evaluated to determine whether they are eligible for special education services. Similar programs also have been used in Iowa and Massachusetts. Data from early reading RTI programs in Iowa showed that fewer students were ultimately placed in special education programs after RTI methods were used than before.

RTI and General Education

The success of RTI as a means of reducing the number of students who receive special education services is important for those concerned about too many students being identified as disabled. The more important aspect of RTI data thus far is how many students have found greater school success as a result of data-based educational programming. Yes, fewer students have been labeled as disabled; however, these same students have developed critical basic skills that increase the likelihood they will be successful in school and life. For this reason, RTI is really a general education initiative. RTI activities begin and end in general education. They may serve as a pathway for "child find" activities for some students, but they provide systematic, data-based decision making for far more general education students. Some researchers have noted that general educators are not prepared for the demands that are implicit in RTI methods. Nonetheless, there is emerging evidence that RTI methods are very effective as part of general education, and the U.S. Department of Education's *Reading First* grant program is organized according to several RTI principles.

In order for RTI to become a routine part of general education, teachers, administrators, and specialists will need to learn how to implement and interpret RTI methods and data. Some teachers may not have received much, if any, training in data analysis. Others may worry that RTI is another "add-on" to what they are already doing and fear that there are not enough hours in the school day to incorporate RTI practices. Importantly, RTI does not require "adding on" to what is already being done in the classroom. Instead, it involves reviewing current classroom practices to identify those that yield evidence of effective instruction as well as those that do not. RTI methods call for teachers to *replace* those practices that do not yield student improvement with those that do. When using RTI, general education teachers will remain the most important part of students' school success.

RTI and Public Policy

RTI has already become part of several educational policies and is likely to be incorporated into future programs as well. The rationale for having RTI as a central focus of public education policy is that it is a population-based system for determining which students need more assistance. Population-based decision making comes from the field of public health. Examples of population-based policies already widely in place include mandatory immunization of all school children, review and recall of beef, pork, and poultry by the Department of Agriculture, and warnings about alcohol use on beer, wine, and liquor labels. All of these policies are designed to protect the public health and welfare through systematic procedures, recalls, and warnings. Although population-based decision making has been widely used in health, food, and safety policies for many years, it has been less utilized in school settings. RTI represents a major application of population-based policy in education because it calls for screening of the entire school population for identification of possible school difficulties.

Just as there are many public welfare benefits from immunizations, meat recalls, and alcohols labels, RTI applications in schools are likely to yield important gains for all students. The universal nature of RTI methods mean that all students are reviewed regularly to determine if school problems are present. This prevents students from "slipping through the cracks." Those students who need additional assistance are provided with interventions previously shown to be effective, just as physicians use treatments validated in research studies. The data-driven nature of RTI means that decisions about school practices are derived from students' actual performance in class. New interventions are provided only as needed when data show that existing practices are not working. In the end, RTI is designed to enhance all students' educational outcomes by providing continuous progress monitoring of all students and specialized assistance to those who need it.

Big Ideas About RTI

There are three main components to RTI, high-quality instruction, frequent assessment, and data-based decision making. Each of these components connects to a "big idea" about educational policy. High-quality instruction is based on the idea that all children deserve effective instruction that leads to achieving functional skills. Frequent assessment is based on the idea that continuous assessment leads to skill improvement. Instructional decision making relates to the idea that adjustments to instruction must be based on data. When the three components of RTI are put together with the problem-solving assessment model, decisions about a student's progress toward education goals are much easier to make. . . .

Douglas Fuchs and
Donald D. Deshler

 NO

What We Need to Know About Responsiveness to Intervention (and Shouldn't Be Afraid to Ask)

In May 2006, David Tilly and seven of his colleagues sent a letter to the Office of Special Education and Rehabilitation Services (OSERS), which was subsequently given to us by one of the authors. The letter writers chided OSERS on several counts, including that, in their view, the agency wrongly promotes a notion that researchers and practitioners need to understand more about responsiveness to intervention (RTI) to ensure its successful implementation. Tilly and associates expressed an opposite belief, claiming that practitioners have all necessary and sufficient information to conduct RTI competently. They wrote, "University- and field-based research strongly supports the use of Problem-Solving/RTI as the service delivery model that results in the most equitable outcomes for the diverse learners in the United States today. . . . RTI implementations have improved outcomes in all students and [have] shown reductions in referrals for special education. . . . The [only remaining] problem is one of scaling, which is a different research question than . . . whether practices like RTI are effective or implementable" [sic].

This "we-know-all-we-need-to-know" message about RTI implementation has also been delivered at conferences and in-service programs across the nation. The obvious intent of the message is to instill confidence among teachers and administrators about RTI implementation and to encourage them to get on with the difficult work of reforming service delivery. A less obvious intent seems to be to characterize those raising questions about RTI as uninformed or (worse) temporizing or (much worse) attempting to obstruct wider use of RTI through passive–aggressive intellectualizing.

We join Tilly and company—and virtually everyone else—in wishing to see stronger and earlier intervening practices in general education. We support a multitiered approach to provide increasingly intensive help to our most academically vulnerable children. We also believe practitioners and researchers know a good deal about how to conduct RTI. Nevertheless, the "we-know-it-all" message strikes us as an exaggeration and counterproductive. It is an exaggeration because the message is factually incorrect.

From *Learning Disabilities Research & Practice*, 22(2), May 2007, pp. 129–135 (refs. omitted). Copyright © 2007 by Council for Exceptional Children. Reprinted by permission of Wiley-Blackwell Publishing.

We do not have all necessary technical information to ensure that RTI, to quote Tilly and colleagues, improves outcomes "in all students"—a fact of which at least some teachers, administrators, and researchers are well aware. The message is counter-productive because practitioners must understand what we collectively *do not* know so they can avoid costly mistakes. Moreover, by recognizing what we do not know, practitioners and researchers can work diligently to find solutions, thereby strengthening our shared capacity to implement RTI successfully on a wide scale.

A case in point is work at the National Research Center on Learning Disabilities (hereafter "LD Center"), which, for the past 5 years, has focused in part on how best to identify nonresponders to Tier 1 instruction who are in need of more intensive and costly instruction at Tier 2. Many advocates of RTI propose use of a one-time universal screen to identify these children. In such an approach, all children in a given school are assessed on a brief measure at the beginning of the school year. Those scoring below a norm-referenced cut point (e.g., 25th percentile on the Woodcock Reading Mastery Tests—Word Identification) or below a performance benchmark associated with poor long-term outcome (e.g., 15 on curriculum-based measurement word identification fluency at the beginning of first grade) enter Tier 2 intervention. The assumption is that low performance relative to the normative cut point or the performance benchmark at the start of the school year constitutes necessary and sufficient evidence that the child has failed to respond to Tier 1 instruction in the previous year and requires more intensive help.

However, in our research at the LD Center, 50 percent of first-grade students identified as nonresponsive to Tier 1 instruction by a one-time universal screen given in early fall "recovered" spontaneously. That is, they made unanticipated satisfactory progress in reading throughout their first-grade year without Tier 2 instruction. The number of these "false positives" (i.e., children who appear at risk but are not) was reduced considerably when, as part of our research, we used data from five weeks of weekly progress monitoring following the universal screen to further specify the nonresponders. On the basis of this research finding, we have been encouraging practitioners to combine the use of a one-time universal screen (to identify at-risk children) with short-term progress monitoring (to identify nonresponders for Tier 2 instruction). We predict that this two-step procedure will save school districts many thousands of dollars by helping them provide Tier 2 instruction to only those students who truly need it. This LD Center research, we believe, illustrates how asking and exploring technical questions can increase our knowledge about RTI implementation and provide practitioners with practical payoffs.

The importance of asking questions—of knowing what we don't know—about RTI implementation is underscored by recently released federal regulations that are bereft of procedural detail. Practitioners across the nation are looking for guidance, and the best they will get will help clarify for them what is known and unknown. It is in this spirit that we wrote this article. Our intent is not to disparage RTI or diminish its value by identifying questions that need answers. Nor is our intent to discourage its implementation. Rather, we wish to say to practitioners, "When implementing RTI, bring as much good knowledge to bear as you can, including the recognition that we don't know everything important about it." Following are a handful of important questions that still need answers. We begin at a general level and move to the more specific.

What's the Purpose of RTI?

Practitioners need to agree on the purpose of RTI—at least practitioners in the same school district or state need to agree. Some who have written about RTI say it should be only about early intervention, while others say "disability identification." Still others say, "both." Those believing RTI should be synonymous with early intervention argue for three or more instructional tiers exclusive of special education.

Implicit in this belief about RTI is a view of education reform that reminds us of the Regular Education Initiative, which emerged in the mid-to-late 1980s. Its leaders had three goals. The first was to merge special and general education into one inclusive system. The second goal was to dramatically increase the number of children with disabilities in mainstream classrooms by use of large-scale, full-time mainstreaming. The third goal, implicit in the first two, was to strengthen the academic achievement of students with high-incidence disabilities, as well as of low-achievers without disabilities. To wit: "Local schools should be encouraged to experiment and evaluate the effectiveness of a variety of educational approaches in solving the widespread persistent problem of how to achieve more productive learning for all students". In short, as general education became better resourced, it would become more resourceful; as it became more "expandable," special education would become more "expendable."

Indeed, this Regular-Education-Initiative-like assumption drives the part of the most recent IDEA reauthorization that gives general education 15 percent of special education monies. The special education law seems to say to practitioners and other stakeholders: "Front load special education dollars into general education to strengthen prevention efforts, and fewer children will require special education on the back end." Notwithstanding the logic and confidence reflected in this message, it is unclear just how preventive and expandable general education can become. Which brings us to the work of Mary Wagner and her colleagues.

Wagner and her associates compared nationally representative high-school students with LD from the mid 1980s to same-age students with LD in 2001–2002. Thus, students in the earlier of the two national studies participated in pre-Regular-Education-Initiative schools; those in the later investigation were more likely to have participated in more inclusive schools. Consonant with our assumption, Wagner, Newman, and Cameto found a greater percentage of the nationally representative 2001–2002 cohort taking more challenging academic courses—courses more frequently conducted in general education settings. Further, whereas only 2 percent of the high schoolers in the mid 1980s earned "mostly As" and only 56 percent graduated, 19 percent in 2001–2002 had "mostly As" and 74 percent graduated.

However, according to Wagner, Newman, Cameto, Levine, and Marder in 2001–2002, class participation of students with LD was much lower than that of their non-disabled peers, and they earned average standard scores of only 86 (20th percentile) and 88 (28th percentile) on the passage comprehension and math calculation subtests, respectively, of the Woodcock–Johnson III Research edition. For passage comprehension, 74 percent of the nationally representative high-school students with LD performed in the bottom quartile; for math calculations, 53 percent were in the bottom quartile. Thus, despite the more inclusive classroom practices apparently engendered by the Regular Education Initiative, the reading and math performance of many high-school students with LD in the 2001–2002 cohort was still poor, raising questions about general education's capacity to accommodate these students' special learning needs.

Wagner and associates' findings are not necessarily cause for pessimism or skepticism about RTI because there are important differences in principle between RTI and the Regular Education Initiative. Rather, results from Wagner and associates' national, longitudinal studies suggest the magnitude of the challenge involved in attempting to make K-12 classrooms substantially more accommodating of greater academic diversity.

Returning to the start of this section, we see RTI as potentially providing both strong early intervention and more valid means of disability identification—not just one or the other. We encourage practitioners and researchers to recognize that assessment and identification are (or should be) inextricably connected to early intervention; to a school district's or school building's capacity to provide more intensive and costly help to its most vulnerable, academically unresponsive children. An assessment and identification process with strong predictive validity is likely to enhance the effectiveness and efficiency of early intervention, as well as strengthen the public's support of it.

What Conditions Support RTI's Successful Implementation?

When practitioners read about effective RTI models in the literature or hear about their successful implementation at professional conferences, they need to understand the conditions, or contextual factors, in the school or district in which RTI was successfully implemented. In other words, educational innovations like RTI gain most traction in settings that provide the necessary conditions to support their use. Less successful implementations elsewhere may be caused by an absence of supporting conditions, rather than because of the particular RTI procedures, per se.

Because RTI consists of numerous components (e.g., multiple instructional tiers, progress monitoring), it must function as a well-orchestrated system to be effective. Effective implementation is dependent upon:

1. Significant and sustained investments in professional development programs to provide teachers with the array of skills required to effectively implement RTI as well as to deal with ongoing staff turnover.
2. Engaged administrators who set expectations for adoption and implementation of RTI, provide the necessary resources, and support the use of procedures that ensure fidelity of implementation.
3. District level support to hire teachers who embrace RTI principles and possess the pre-requisite skills to implement it effectively in their classes.
4. A willingness of teaching and ancillary staff (e.g., school psychologists) to have their roles redefined in ways to support effective implementation.
5. The degree to which staff is given sufficient time to "make sense of" and accommodate RTI into their instructional framework, and have their questions and concerns addressed.
6. Whether decisions regarding the adoption of RTI have been influenced by the thoughts and beliefs of practitioners at the grassroots level versus decisions made exclusively by those on high.

In short, failure to ask questions about the factors that surround and support RTI implementation may prevent practitioners from understanding the complete picture. This may lead to adoption of another site's RTI model based on the incorrect assumption that the success of the other site's model (as reported in the literature) is due to what happens in the classroom during the RTI implementation process. In reality, there are many situational factors—inside and outside the classroom—that support and account for its successful implementation. These factors are as important to identify and understand as are the components of the RTI model itself.

What Is the Nature of Tier 1 Instruction?

Practitioners and researchers almost always refer to classroom instruction as Tier 1. Many also describe the importance of classroom teachers using "scientifically validated" instruction. Yet there is widespread uncertainty about what this means. "Scientifically validated" refers to a process of experimentation by which the importance of an instructional procedure or curriculum has been tested. Most rigorous testing involves the use of randomized control trials, whereby students or classrooms, typically, are assigned at random to two or more study groups, including a no-treatment control group or comparison group. Randomized assignment is meant to help prevent or reduce the likelihood of non-treatment forces from influencing findings and complicating their interpretation. Use of randomized control trials, in short, is critically important to program or curriculum development and evaluation.

Randomized control trials or not, there is no instructional program or curriculum that has been validated for use with all children. Hence, when we say that an instructional approach or curriculum is "scientifically validated," we mean it's a "good bet" for many children. It should be considered seriously by practitioners for adoption, but it comes with no guarantees. No instructional program or curriculum is valid for all students or for all time. They must be implemented and evaluated by local practitioners.

The good news here is that there is a large handful of instructional procedures and curricula that have been rigorously tested and that should be considered "good bets" by practitioners for use in Tier 1 settings. Many other instructional procedures and curricula available to practitioners have not been tested rigorously. This doesn't mean that they will be ineffective if used. Rather, there is no scientific basis to know whether they will fail or succeed. They are *not* good bets. All districts or states should establish a vetting process to help teachers and administrators distinguish good bets from bad ones. As we write, few have thought seriously about how to establish such a vetting process.

What Is "Problem Solving" and Does It Promote Academic Achievement Among Children with Severe Learning Problems?

An example of the importance and complexity of understanding the term "scientifically validated" involves "problem solving." Problem solving is an oft-used and sometimes confusing term in the context of RTI. By our count, it is currently used in three ways: first, to describe a process by which differentiated instruction is developed, child-by-child, at Tiers 1 and 2 in general education; second, to signify the data-based, recursive, individualized instruction that special educators should be using with their schools' most difficult-to-teach students; third, to refer to how building-based teams operate to provide support to general educators with academically at-risk students.

Problem solving as a process to develop, implement, and evaluate interventions in general education was conceptualized and first researched by John Bergan and colleagues more than 30 years ago. It is a behavioral approach to school consultation. Its most frequently studied application has been to help teachers of students with conduct problems, such as talking or moving about the classroom without permission, or with "work productivity" problems, including inattentive or undermotivated behavior. Research indicates problem solving can be effective when applied to such student behaviors. Currently, however, some RTI proponents are advancing problem solving as a means of helping classroom teachers deal with students with severe learning problems that go beyond inattention and low motivation despite that it has not been scientifically validated for this purpose.

We need to know whether problem solving in general education identifies or leads to the development of instruction that accelerates the learning of children with severe learning problems not caused by poor attention and motivation. This will require researchers who recognize a need for documenting fidelity of treatment implementation, which will be more challenging than usual because the treatments in a problem-solving process are constructed on a case-by-case basis and often involve the use of combined interventions that have never been tested scientifically. Appropriate measures of fidelity-of-treatment-implementation must be constructed as part of the research process.

Who Are Responders and Nonresponders?

Research on instruction at Tiers 1 and 2 has documented these facts: (a) many students benefit from this instruction, especially when standard treatment protocols (i.e., explicitly scripted activities) drive the activity; (b) there are nonresponders—or students who do not respond to scientifically valid instruction, even when its intensity comes close to that of instruction in a good special education program and is implemented with strong fidelity. Estimates of nonresponders at Tier 2, when the instruction is conducted by researchers, range from 2 to 6 percent of the general school population.

RTI Methods of Identification

Once Tier 2 instruction is delivered, practitioners evaluate student responsiveness. More specifically, performance must be categorized as responsive or nonresponsive. The research literature suggests at least five RTI methods of defining these terms. The first method, which we term "median split," was introduced by Vellutino et al. They measured students on the Woodcock Reading Mastery Tests several times during a multiyear tutoring program and used hierarchical linear modeling to obtain slope of improvement for each child. To derive a cut point for designating responsiveness, the slopes were rank ordered, and the median was determined. Any student whose slope was at or above this median was designated responsive to the tutoring; those whose slopes were below the median were labeled nonresponsive.

Torgesen et al. used an alternative, "normalization" method. He and his colleagues tested students on the Woodcock Reading Mastery Tests at the end of their tutoring intervention and computed standard scores. Those scoring at or above a standard score of 90—the 25th percentile—were designated responsive; those below the 25th percentile, nonresponsive. A third method is also based on performance at the end of tutoring but it employs a criterion-referenced benchmark associated with appropriate future performance. We refer to this as the "final benchmark" method. Good, Simmons, and Kaméenui (2001) followed this approach when they measured students at the end of first-grade intervention with the Dynamic Indicators of Basic Early Literacy Skills (DIBELS) oral reading fluency measure. To define responsiveness, they compared raw scores on this measure against a criterion-referenced benchmark associated with future success on the Oregon highstakes third-grade assessment. First-grade students with final

DIBELS scores exceeding 39 were designated responsive. Those with scores below 40 were recognized as unresponsive.

Fuchs and Fuchs developed a fourth method, "dual discrepancy." It is illustrated in the research of Speece and Case, who used curriculum-based measurement passage reading fluency to test students weekly and at treatment's end. "Treatment" was defined as the core reading program in the general classroom. Speece and Case summarized student response in two ways: slope of improvement during treatment and performance level at the end of treatment. Nonresponders were required to demonstrate both slope and performance levels at the end of treatment more than 1 standard deviation (*SD*) below that of classroom peers.

A fifth method of operationalizing responsiveness and nonresponsiveness is based entirely on students' slope, and we refer to it as the "slope discrepancy" method. Students are measured periodically; a slope of academic improvement is computed; students above a normative cut point, referenced to the classroom, school, district, or nation, are deemed responsive, and others are designated nonresponsive. This approach is illustrated in the work of Fuchs, Fuchs, and Compton.

Before proceeding, we wish to point out that alternative RTI methods, measures, testing frequencies, and cut points may be applied in various combinations. For example, recall that Speece and Case used a dual discrepancy method with passage reading fluency determined weekly and at the end of treatment. Their cut point required nonresponders to score 1 *SD* or more below classroom peers on both slope and final level of performance. Alternatively, a school might collect curriculum-based measurement word identification fluency (rather than passage reading fluency) data on a monthly (not weekly) basis, with same-grade school (not classroom) peers providing the normative framework and with a cut point of 0.75 *SD* (rather than 1 *SD*) on slope and final level of performance. The very important question here is, Do different RTI identification methods . . . with alternative measures and testing frequencies, yield the same or different subgroups of responsive and nonresponsive children with similar or dissimilar profiles of disability?

LD Center Research

As part of our LD Center research, we designed a prospective, longitudinal study for which we recruited 42 first-grade teachers who were using the same core reading program. Based on September performance on Woodcock Reading Mastery Tests—Word Identification, Rapid Letter Naming, and teacher judgment, we identified the six lowest-performing first-grade children per class as potentially at-risk for learning disabilities. These 252 children were assigned randomly, within class, to receive tutoring or not. We delivered tutoring in small groups, three times per week for 10 weeks, while monitoring weekly progress on curriculum-based measurement word identification fluency. The children were post-tested at the end of tutoring, at the end of first grade, and at the end of second grade. In first grade, we applied seven traditional and RTI methods for designating reading disabilities: "initial" (beginning of first grade) low achievement, "final" (end of first grade) IQ-achievement discrepancy, median split, final normalization, final benchmark, slope discrepancy, and dual discrepancy. For each of these methods of identification, we considered the impact of using alternate measures.

Our findings indicated that, for our traditional *non-RTI methods*, an initial low achievement definition of reading disabilities, especially in conjunction with the Woodcock Reading Mastery Tests—Word Identification, provided reasonable prevalence estimates, acceptable "specificity" (the degree to which a measure identifies children at low risk for disability status), and good "hit rates" (the proportion of children correctly identified as at risk). But it also produced poor "sensitivity" (how well a measure correctly identifies children at risk for disability status), suggesting that many children appearing at risk but who are not would receive unnecessary first-grade tutoring. By contrast, IQ-achievement discrepancy at the end of first grade, a "traditional" approach to LD identification, provided unrealistically low prevalence estimates and poor sensitivity. It did, however, produce good hit rates and strong specificity. But too many children were not identified at end of first grade although they showed a need for reading intervention, as revealed by their end-of-second-grade reading disabilities status.

In terms of *RTI methods*, final normalization resulted in an acceptable reading disabilities prevalence rate but produced mixed hit rates, mixed sensitivity, and mixed specificity. Benchmark and median split methods overidentified reading disabilities. Curriculum-based measurement word identification fluency slope and dual discrepancy over-identified reading disabilities but resulted in acceptable hit rates, sensitivity, and specificity.

An important conclusion from our LD Center study was that both traditional methods and RTI methods for defining and distinguishing responsiveness and nonresponsiveness result in different groups of children designated "reading disabled," with each method resulting in varying prevalence rates, severity, and stability. All of this suggests an urgent need for a data-based consensus about what RTI methods of disability identification (in combination with which measures, testing frequencies, and cutpoints) will be most useful. With such consensus, greater consistency in "reading disability" and "learning disability" designations across schools, districts, and states might be achieved.

Is There Need of Formal Testing by Multidisciplinary Teams?

This question creates two camps. The group that answers "no" makes at least two important points. First, it says that a multi-tiered instructional process will generate all information necessary to understand the learner and her academic needs. Second, the formal testing of working memory, receptive language, processing speed, and the like, will not yield information with strong instructional relevance. Hence it asks why should we measure such cognitive processes? This second point resonates; the first point less so because it reflects a failure to recognize that students chronically unresponsive to multiple tiers of increasingly intensive instruction need something different. That is, implementing "x" instruction or "y" curriculum with greater fidelity, or in groups of three and not five, or providing a token economy instead of verbal praise, is not likely to make learners from chronically nonresponsive students. There is strong need for instructional research that explores whether and how knowing more about cognitive processing leads to more effective teaching and learning.

More of What We Need to Know

1. How relevant is RTI to middle and high schools? If we define RTI's purpose in part as delivering early intervention, then how should we think about RTI for a 10th-grade student reading at a 2nd-grade level? Do we perhaps need a very different model for at-risk students in middle school and high school?
2. Most RTI intervention research has involved early reading. What do we know about effective multi-tiered instruction that addresses reading comprehension? Writing? Social studies? Science?
3. If classroom teachers implement scientifically validated instruction at Tier 1, who will conduct Tier 2 instruction? If school psychologists, then who will conduct formal evaluations and re-evaluations? If special education teachers, who will work most intensively with chronically nonresponsive children? If para-professionals, who will prepare them?
4. What criteria should practitioners use in school buildings and districts to evaluate the success of their RTI implementation? Student achievement on high-stakes tests? Progress monitoring data? Information on the fidelity with which interventions are implemented? Special education enrollments and costs? In a related way, who should aggregate a school building's data or school district's data, and how should this be accomplished, so practitioners can effectively and responsibly answer the question, "is RTI working?"
5. Where in the RTI process does due process occur?

Conclusion

Like Ed Kaméenui . . . we believe it is constructive and important to think hard about what we know and don't know about RTI, and it is in this spirit that we've written this article. We are not suggesting that there is a paucity of knowledge because, in fact, researchers and practitioners collectively know a good deal about aspects of RTI, like how to monitor student progress accurately and meaningfully. But it is untrue and misleading to claim that we currently have a necessary and sufficient knowledge base to guide the implementation of RTI as a process of early intervention and disability identification across all grades, for all academic skills, in all content areas, and for all children and youth. It behooves teachers, administrators, and researchers to understand what we don't know.

If we were to prioritize areas in which more knowledge is needed, our priorities would be these: First, practitioners need scientifically-validated instructional protocols that are likely to accelerate student progress in pivotal skills aside from early reading (e.g., math and writing) and in content areas (e.g., social studies and science). Generally effective instructional protocols are critical because in an RTI framework instruction is the "test" against which student response is measured. Without validated instruction (implemented with fidelity by practitioners), RTI cannot be a valid method of disability identification or early intervention. Second, practitioners require a validated means of determining "responsiveness" and "nonresponsiveness." As indicated, there is a handful of possibilities but no consensus about which are preferable. If practitioners across the nation choose different RTI methods of identification, there may be as much or greater variation in number and type of children identified as having LD than the variation produced by use of IQ-achievement discrepancy.

In part because of the under-specification of the most recent federal regulations on RTI, and an absence of necessary and sufficient technical information, we're in a kind of *de facto* de-regulated environment when it comes to RTI. This can mean greater flexibility and discretionary decision making; more room for innovation. At the same time, it contributes to confusion and uncertainty. It also provides opportunity to those who would use this situation for their own purposes. In such circumstances, especially, practitioners must educate themselves by asking tough questions— of themselves and others—as they organize to deliver stronger prevention services and more valid methods of disability identification through RTI implementation.

POSTSCRIPT

Is Response to Intervention (RTI) Ready for Implementation?

Decrying the large numbers of students in special education, one assistant secretary for the Office of Special Education and Rehabilitative Services identified three flaws in the educational system: many children cannot receive needed help because they do not meet eligibility guidelines, poor school performance is often equated with a disability, and early intervention services are unavailable (Will, *Exceptional Children*, 1986).

Yes, you read the date correctly. 1986. The speaker was Madeline Will, who recommended a partnership between general education and special education to build "a more powerful, more responsive educational system" (Will, 1986). RTI is today's remedy for very similar problems.

It is difficult to find someone completely opposed to RTI (Wright, Dude Publishing, 2007). How can any educator object to using information to make decisions about student learning?

Both selections describe RTI as a significant change in general education. Brown-Chidsey and Steege reassure classroom teachers that RTI will not mean adding extra tasks, just using available information more effectively. Examining student work carefully helps teachers intervene early, rather than waiting until a student fails. Fuchs and Deshler wonder how much prevention can be delivered by a general education teacher, who must balance many compelling priorities.

The scarcity of RTI-related research is frequently mentioned. Most studies have focused on the acquisition of decoding skills in elementary-level children (Gersten & Dimino, *New Directions in Research,* 2006). There is little evidence about the best interventions or the optimal duration of each. Nevertheless, since there is consensus on RTI's basic elements, some see this as part of the process of development rather than a "fatal flaw" (Wright, 2007).

Since RTI is part of existing law, perhaps the question is not whether educators should implement RTI, but how to do so. Although some fret because the U.S. federal government does not specify one model, this gives educators the latitude—and the responsibility—to design RTI programs that respond to their particular community of students (Kame'enui, *Teaching Exceptional Children,* 2007).

One goal of RTI is to reduce the overrepresentation of minorities in special education. Educators must use existing flexibility to consider what RTI means for culturally diverse students, English language learners, and those who live in poverty (NCCREST, 2005). One essential resource is the

National Center for Culturally Responsive Educational Systems (NCCRESt, http://www.nccrest.org), sponsored by the U.S. Department of Education. NCCRESt is dedicated to exploring and disseminating information that helps educators identify and implement "effective literacy and behavioral interventions for students who are culturally and linguistically diverse." The newsletter and Web site are rich sources of technical assistance and professional development. The NCCRESt position statement on RTI cautions that an intervention system that does not consider the complexity of today's students risks being no more than "old wine in a new bottle." Very little will have changed, except the label.

RTI has the potential to be a new way of examining student learning. The outcome could be a comprehensive array of school supports other than special education (Adelman & Taylor, *Addressing Barriers to Learning,* 2006). One thing is certain, the questions about RTI are likely to lead to an array of designs and, perhaps, to the kind of solution Madeline Will envisioned 30 years ago.

As you weigh these perspectives, consider other questions. Does RTI reform special education, or is special education being used as a tool to reform general education practices? If RTI is based in the general education classroom, why isn't it part of NCLB? If RTI does not achieve its goals because of implementation challenges, will special education be held accountable? And, most importantly, what does all this mean for children who struggle?

ISSUE 8

Does NCLB Leave Some Students Behind?

YES: Jennifer Booher-Jennings, from "Rationing Education in an Era of Accountability," *Phi Delta Kappan* (June 2006)

NO: U.S. Department of Education, from "Working Together for Students with Disabilities: Individuals with Disabilities Education Act (IDEA) and No Child Left Behind Act (NCLB)," http://www.ed.gov/admins/lead/speced/toolkit/index.html (December 2005)

ISSUE SUMMARY

YES: Jennifer Booher-Jennings, a doctoral candidate at Columbia University, finds the accountability pressures of No Child Left Behind (NCLB) are leading some administrators to advise teachers to focus only on those children who will improve their school's scores; other students don't count much.

NO: The U.S. Department of Education FAQ Sheet on IDEA and NCLB advises readers that the link between these two statutes is sound, emphasizing how they work together to ensure that every student's performance and needs receive appropriate attention.

The No Child Left Behind Act of 2001 (NCLB), a reauthorization of the Elementary and Secondary Education Act (ESEA), has changed the vocabulary and practice of educators in every publicly funded school in America.

More familiarly known as Title I, ESEA has long provided funds to districts to improve the educational performance of children from low-income families. In the reauthorization now known as NCLB, the U.S. federal government demands a return on its investment.

Four key principles form the foundation of NCLB.

- Schools must be accountable for student performance and teacher qualifications.
- States and districts must set growth targets and have the latitude to achieve them.

- Parents must have more information about their schools and broader educational options if their schools do not reach growth targets.
- Schools must use research-based instructional strategies.

The principle most on the minds of educators is accountability. States may set their own educational standards, but all students must be proficient in math and reading/language arts by 2013–2014. Some states designed high-level academic programs to meet world class standards. Others preferred literacy standards, measuring the basic skills students will need to be successful in the world of work. Some have formulated separate sets of standards for students with severe disabilities.

States determine specific benchmark goals, staged to reach proficiency. Regular testing determines if a school is making Adequate Yearly Progress (AYP) toward the target: students must be assessed in reading/language arts and math annually in grades 3–8, and at least once in grades 9–10. Beginning in 2007–08, students must be assessed in science at least once in grades 3–5, 6–9, and 10–12.

Some schools appear to be successful, but small groups within their walls do markedly less well than others. To hold schools accountable for the achievements of all students, NCLB identifies particular subgroups including: students from low-income families; students from major racial and ethnic groups; those with limited English proficiency; and those with disabilities. Unless each subgroup makes AYP, a school is deemed not making total AYP.

Schools that do not make AYP are subject to an array of interventions. Their leadership must take actions to improve. Parents must be notified of the status and have the option of transferring to higher-performing schools. Supplemental educational services must be available. In the extreme, schools are subject to "corrective actions" under the guidance/supervision of external experts.

These expectations and consequences are taken seriously by all educators. While striving to meet goals, some wonder if all students will be part of the race or if some, especially students with disabilities, will be left behind.

Jennifer Booher-Jennings, after studying NCLB implementation in one Texas school, found teachers were encouraged to focus their attention on "the kids who count" because their improvement could increase school scores. Since students with disabilities didn't "count", or because they were "hopelessly" unlikely to do well, they were not deemed worthy of teachers' energy.

The U.S. Department of Education, in responses to frequently asked questions, maintains that NCLB and IDEA work in concert to ensure that every child with a disability reaches high standards. The FAQ notes that most children with disabilities are in general education placements. The information gleaned from frequent assessments should "shine a light on student needs and draw attention to how schools can better serve (them)."

As you read these articles, ask yourself how the schools in your neighborhood are implementing NCLB. Are all subgroups participating meaningfully or are some more important than others?

YES

Jennifer Booher-Jennings

Rationing Education in an Era of Accountability

Meet Mrs. Dewey, 46 years old and a veteran fourth-grade teacher at Marshall Elementary School. Mrs. Dewey entered the teaching profession in the wake of *A Nation at Risk* and has weathered the storm ever since. For the last 20 years, she has survived the continuous succession of faddish programs that has characterized American education reform. Year after year, administrators have asked Marshall teachers to alter their practice to conform to the latest theory. Mrs. Dewey's colleagues, frustrated by the implementation of such silver-bullet approaches, have often flouted the administrative directives and chosen instead to serve as the sole arbiters of their classroom practice.

But it is the newest of the new solutions that worries Mrs. Dewey most. The language of accountability is swift and uncompromising: hold educators responsible for results. Identify those teachers who, as President Bush says, "won't teach." Fair enough, Mrs. Dewey thinks. The consummate professional, Mrs. Dewey always looks for the silver lining.

Like other reforms, accountability requires teachers to embrace a new strategy. Data-driven decision making, a consultant told the faculty at a professional development session, is the philosophy Marshall teachers must adopt. The theory is simple. Give students regular benchmark assessments; use the data to identify individual students' weaknesses; provide targeted instruction and support that addresses those areas. Mrs. Dewey remembers nodding approvingly. After all, this approach—gathering textured information on each student to guide instructional activities—was one she had been using for 22 years.

The consultant moved on. "Using the data, you can identify and focus on the kids who are close to passing. The bubble kids. And focus on the kids that count—the ones that show up at Marshall after October won't count toward the school's test scores this year. Because you don't have enough special education students to disaggregate scores for that group, don't worry about them either." To make this concept tangible for teachers, the consultant passed out markers in three colors: green, yellow, and red. Mrs. Dewey heard someone mutter, "What is this? The traffic light theory of education?"

From *Phi Delta Kappan*, June 2006, pp. 756–761. Copyright © 2006 by Phi Delta Kappan. Reprinted by permission of Phi Delta Kappan and Jennifer Booher-Jennings.

"Take out your classes' latest benchmark scores," the consultant told them, "and divide your students into three groups. Color the 'safe cases,' or kids who will definitely pass, green. Now, here's the most important part: identify the kids who are 'suitable cases for treatment.' Those are the ones who can pass with a little extra help. Color them yellow. Then, color the kids who have no chance of passing this year and the kids that don't count—the 'hopeless cases'—red. You should focus your attention on the yellow kids, the bubble kids. They'll give you the biggest return on your investment."

As the bell tolls a final warning to the boisterous 9-year-olds bringing up the rear of her class line, Mrs. Dewey stares blankly into the hallway. Never did she believe that the advice offered by that consultant would become Marshall's educational mantra. Focus on the bubble kids. Tutor only these students. Pay more attention to them in class. Why? It's data-driven. Yet this is what her colleagues have been doing, and Marshall's scores are up. The community is proud, and the principal has been anointed one of the most promising educational leaders in the state. At every faculty meeting, the principal presents a "league table," ranking teachers by the percentage of their students passing the latest benchmark test. And the teachers talk, as they always do. The table makes perfect fodder for faculty room gossip: "Did you see who was at the bottom of the table this month?"

Mrs. Dewey has made compromises, both large and small, throughout her career. Every educator who's in it for the long haul must. But this institutionalized policy of educational triage weighs heavily and hurts more. Should she focus only on Brittney, Julian, Shennell, Tiffany, George, and Marlena—the so-called bubble kids—to the exclusion of the other 17 students in her class? Should Mrs. Dewey refuse to tutor Anthony, a persistent and eager little boy with no chance of passing the state test this year, so that she can spend time with students who have a better shot at passing? What should she tell Celine, a precocious student, whose mother wants Mrs. Dewey to review her entry for an essay contest? Celine will certainly pass the state test, so can Mrs. Dewey afford the time? What about the five students who moved into the school in the middle of the year? Since they don't count toward Marshall's scores, should Mrs. Dewey worry about their performance at all?

In her angrier moments, Mrs. Dewey pledges to ignore Marshall's approach and to teach as she always has, the best way she knows how. Yet, if she does, Mrs. Dewey risks being denounced as a traitor to the school's effort to increase scores—in short, a bad teacher. Given 22 years of sacrifices for her profession, it is this reality that stings the most.

Mulling over her choices, Mrs. Dewey shuts her classroom door and begins her class.

Unintended Consequences of Accountability Systems: Educational Triage

Test-based accountability systems aim to direct the behavior of educators toward the improvement of student achievement. The No Child Left

Behind (NCLB) Act codified accountability as our national educational blueprint, requiring schools to increase test scores incrementally so that all students are proficient in reading and math by 2014. Yet, despite the stated intent of NCLB to improve outcomes for all students, particularly those who have been historically neglected, educators and others may adopt a series of "gaming" practices in order to artificially inflate schools' passing rates. Such practices include giving students a special education classification to exclude them from high-stakes tests, retaining students in grade to delay test-taking, diverting attention away from subjects not evaluated on high-stakes tests, teaching to the test, and cheating.

In what follows, I discuss two of the dilemmas presented by a less well-known gaming practice: educational triage. The insights offered here derive from an ethnographic study of an urban elementary school in Texas, to which I have assigned the pseudonym "Beck Elementary." Educational triage has become an increasingly widespread response to accountability systems and has been documented in Texas, California, Chicago, Philadelphia, New York, and even England. By educational triage, I mean the process through which teachers divide students into safe cases, cases suitable for treatment, and hopeless cases and ration resources to focus on those students most likely to improve a school's test scores. The idea of triage, a practice usually restricted to the direst of circumstances, like the battlefield or the emergency room, poignantly captures the dynamics of many schools' responses to NCLB. In the name of improving schools' scores, some students must inevitably be sacrificed. And the stakes are high—for schools, which face serious sanctions for failing to meet adequate yearly progress targets; for students, who increasingly face retention if they do not pass state tests; and for teachers, who are judged by the number of students they "save."

Dilemma 1. *Data can be used to improve student achievement, but they can also be used to target some students at the expense of others.* Data-driven decision making has become something of a sacrosanct term in education policy circles. Who could be against it? The public face of data-driven decision making—identifying the needs of each individual child and introducing interventions to remediate any learning difficulties—is sensible and beyond question.

But the Achilles' heel of education policy has always been implementation. When I listened closely to the conversations that educators at Beck Elementary School had about "being data-driven," the slippage between evaluating the individual needs of every student and deciding which students to target to maximize school performance quickly became evident. As I moved closer and closer to the classroom, the administrators' ideal version dissipated and gave way to a triage-based understanding of data-driven decision making. Teachers were most attuned to the chasm between administrators' theoretical proclamations and how the same administrators expected them to operate: teachers understood that the bottom line in this numbers game was the percentage of students who passed. Because of the unrelenting pressure to increase test scores, one mode of using data became dominant at Beck: the diversion of resources (e.g., additional time in class; enrichment sessions with the literacy teacher; and after-school, Saturday, and summer tutoring) to students on the threshold of passing the test, the "bubble kids."

All my questions about which students received extra help were met with the deferent maxim, "It's data-driven." When I asked one teacher how the school allocated additional services to students—for example, the reading specialist or after-school and Saturday tutoring—she provided the following response:

> It's all data-driven. . . . We do projections—how many of them do you think will pass, how many of them do you think will need more instruction, how many teachers do we have to work with, what time limit do we have? Based on that, who are we going to work with? It comes down to that. . . . We really worked with the bubble kids . . . that's the most realistic and time-efficient thing we can think of.

In this conception of data-driven practice, the choice to privilege one group of students over another is viewed as neutral and objective. The decision to distribute resources to those most advantageous to the school's pass rates is not understood as a moral or ethical decision. Instead, it is seen as a sterile management imperative. Protected by its scientific underpinnings, the data-driven focus on the bubble kids is difficult for teachers to attack. In sum, at Beck Elementary, the invocation of the phrase "data-driven" obscures, neutralizes, and legitimates a system of resource distribution that is designed to increase passing rates rather than to meet the needs of individual students.

The blunt vocabulary of triage infiltrated every corner of Beck. The tenor of the phrases used to describe students—"the ones who could make it" and "hopeless cases"—speaks not only to the perceived urgency to improve test scores but also to the destructive labeling of those children who find themselves below the bubble. Driven by the pressure to increase the passing rate, teachers turned their attention away from these students. As one teacher related in an interview:

> I guess there's supposed to be remediation for anything below 55%, but you have to figure out who to focus on in class, and I definitely focus more attention on the bubble kids. If you look at her score [pointing to a student's score on her class test-score summary sheet], she's got a 25%. What's the point in trying to get her to grade level? It would take two years to get her to pass the test, so there's really no hope for her. . . . I feel like we might as well focus on the ones that there's hope for.

To say that hope is absent for a 10-year-old child is a particularly telling comment on how dramatically the accountability system has altered the realm of imagined possibility in the classroom. Now, with an unforgiving bottom line for which to strive, teachers can retain hope only for those perceived as potential passers. To assert that students below the bubble are just too low-performing to help establishes that the only worthwhile improvement in this brave new world is one that converts a nonpasser to a passer.

The problem is that those students who arrive at school as the most disadvantaged are often the lowest scoring. And since the focus on the bubble kids at Beck Elementary begins not in the third grade—the first year that students take state tests—but the moment students enter kindergarten, they are branded as "hopeless cases" from the very first days of their schooling.

An important shift occurs in a system focused on the percentage of students above a particular threshold. When a low-performing student enters a teacher's classroom, he or she is seen as a liability rather than as an opportunity to promote individual student growth. As Michael Apple trenchantly wrote, the emphasis changes "from student needs to student performance, and from what the school does for the student to what the student does for the school."

Certainly one can imagine uses of data that could turn attention to the individual needs of each and every student. However, the current monolithic discourse on data-driven decision making begs for a discussion of unintended consequences. Data can be used to target some students at the expense of others, and it is happening today.

When we blindly defer to "the data," we abdicate responsibility for tough decisions, all the while claiming neutrality. But data are not actors and cannot do anything by themselves. Data do not make decisions; people make decisions that can be informed by data. Decisions about resource allocation are ethical decisions with which educators and communities must grapple and for which they must ultimately take responsibility.

What we need above all is a sustained discussion among educators and the broader polity about the very real tradeoffs involved in schools' responses to accountability systems. If schools adopt the practices of educational triage in response to NCLB, the consequence may be suboptimal outcomes for students "below the bubble," as well as for their peers who are mid-level and high-achieving students. And all of these unintended consequences can happen while official pass rates increase.

Dilemma 2. *It is unfair to hold schools accountable for new students or for subgroups that are too small to yield statistically reliable estimates of a school's effectiveness; however, the consequence of excluding some students may be to deny them access to scarce educational resources.* Educational triage does not end with the diversion of resources to the "bubble kids." Because of the fine print in NCLB, all students are not equally valuable to a school's test scores. Subgroups are not disaggregated if the number of test-takers does not meet a minimum size requirement, and students are not counted at all in a school's scores if they are not enrolled in a school for a full academic year. For example, in Texas, the scores of students who arrive at the school after the end of October do not count toward schools' scores. Such a definition is logical, for it attempts to isolate the impact of schools on students. Including students who have not attended the school for a reasonable period of time might bias estimates of the school's quality and unfairly penalize schools serving more mobile students.

However, if resources flow only toward those students who affect a school's outcomes, students who do not "count" may be denied access to scarce educational resources. I found that another pithy term, "the accountables"—those students who count toward a school's scores—was incorporated into the lexicon of Beck educators. Teachers engaged in a second kind of educational triage by focusing resources on the "accountables," to the virtual exclusion of students who "did not count." In accountability's ultimate contradiction, the protean word "accountable" retained only a semblance of its intended meaning—taking responsibility for each and every student.

How many students are affected by the mobility provisions of NCLB? Take the Houston Independent School District as an illustrative example. Serving 211,157 students, this district is the largest in Texas and the seventh largest in the nation. The average Houston school excludes 8% of its students from its "accountables." Almost one-third of Houston schools (31%) exclude more than 10% of their students from scores used for accountability. By any measure, this is not an insignificant number of students. Moreover, because mobility is not uniformly distributed across the population, some demographic groups have much higher numbers of mobile—and thus unaccountable—students. In Houston, an average of 16% of special education students and 11% of African American students are not counted in schools' scores because they have not been enrolled in a school for a full academic year. Ironically, the very students NCLB was designed to target are often those least likely to be counted.

A second way that students may "not count" stems from states' definitions of the subgroup size required for disaggregation. If states define subgroup size expediently, the scores of various subgroups will continue to be buried in schoolwide averages. Again, Texas is a good example of artful definition of subgroup size. Under the Texas state accountability system, subgroups must include at least 30 students and account for at least 10% of all students—or include 50 or more students—to be evaluated. Under Texas' NCLB implementation plan, subgroups must include at least 50 students and make up at least 10% of all students—or include 200 or more students—to be evaluated. Under the state system, 82% of Houston schools with African American test-takers disaggregate scores for African American students, while for the purposes of NCLB, only 66% do.

Though Texas does not include a special education subgroup in its state system, the impact of using the 50 and 10% or greater than 200 definition rather than the lower threshold is significant. Shifting the definition upward reduces the percentage of Houston schools that disaggregate scores for special education from 55% to 24%. Other states have similarly gamed the subgroup-size provision of the law. In 2005, the U.S Department of Education allowed Florida to change its minimum subgroup size to 30 students who also make up 15% of test-takers. Because special education students rarely account for more than 15% of a school's population, very few schools in Florida will be required to disaggregate scores for these students.

There is an irreconcilable tension between accurately measuring school effects and forestalling the potential negative consequences of excluding some students from accountability calculations. If accuracy of measurement is privileged, some students will necessarily be excluded from accountability calculations. In order to best estimate school effects, a school should not be responsible for students who attend it for a short period of time. Similarly, small subgroups may yield statistically unreliable estimates of the school's efficacy with a particular group of students. Moreover, mainstream state tests may be inappropriate measures for some English-language learners or special education students. In other words, there are valid reasons, from a measurement perspective, for excluding students from schools' scores. On the other hand, the consequence of excluding these students may be to deny them access to scarce educational resources.

Better Choices?

So Mrs. Dewey can choose to teach all of her students, regardless of their potential contribution to her school's bottom line, or she can participate in educational triage. If she refuses to focus her time and attention on those students most likely to raise the school's scores, she risks not only the school's survival but her professional reputation as a good teacher and, potentially, her job.

Mrs. Dewey should not be asked to make such choices, and it is unconscionable to question her ethics when she does what she has little choice but to do. Systems of public policy cannot be designed solely for those with the moral certitude to qualify them for sainthood.

Educators will respond to systemic incentives, and NCLB's current incentives structurally induce behaviors that are inimical to broader notions of equity and fairness. In many cases, these perverse incentives turn educators' attention away from NCLB's intended beneficiaries. Until these issues are addressed, we can expect to see educational triage practices flourish across the country.

Working Together for Students with Disabilities: Individuals with Disabilities Education Act (IDEA) and No Child Left Behind Act (NCLB)

1. Are *NCLB* and *IDEA* in conflict with each other?

No. Both laws have the same goal of improving academic achievement through high expectations and high-quality education programs. *NCLB* works to achieve that goal by focusing on school accountability, teacher quality, parental involvement through access to information and choices about their children's education, and the use of evidence-based instruction. *IDEA* complements those efforts by focusing specifically on how best to help students with disabilities meet academic goals.

NCLB aims to improve the achievement of all students and recognizes that schools must ensure that all groups receive the support they need to achieve to high standards. That is why *NCLB* requires that schools look at the performance of specific subgroups of students, including students with disabilities, and holds schools accountable for their achievement. By including students with disabilities in the overall accountability system, the law makes their achievement everybody's business, not just the business of special education teachers. Shining the light on the needs of students with disabilities draws attention to the responsibility of states, districts, and schools to target resources to improve the achievement of students with disabilities and to monitor closely the quality of services provided under *IDEA*.

2. If *NCLB* focuses on school performance while *IDEA* focuses on individual students, how can a student's individual rights not be compromised under *NCLB*?

The requirements of *NCLB* do not infringe on the rights of students with disabilities under *IDEA*.

IDEA requires that schools provide special education and related services to meet the individual needs of each student with a disability. To provide these services, a team of educators and parents develop a plan

From http://www.ed.gov/admins/lead/speced/toolkit/index.html, December 2005. Published by the U.S. Department of Education.

(referred to as an "Individualized Education Program," or IEP) for each student with a disability that maps out what achievement is expected and what services are needed to help the student meet these expectations. With the appropriate supports and services, students with disabilities can and should be held to high standards.

NCLB is designed to ensure that schools are held accountable for educational results so that each and every student can achieve to high standards. Setting the bar high helps all students, including students with disabilities, reach those standards. The expectation of *NCLB* is that students with disabilities can achieve to high standards as other students, given the appropriate supports and services.

3. Was *NCLB* the first federal law to require states to include students with disabilities in the state's assessment system?

NCLB is the first law to hold schools accountable for ensuring that all students participate in the state assessment system, but it is built on earlier law. The 1997 amendments to the *IDEA* required that students with disabilities participate in state and district assessments and that their results be reported publicly in the same way and with the same frequency as those of other students. The federal law that preceded *NCLB*, the *Improving America's Schools Act of 1994*, required schools to include the assessment results of students with disabilities in accountability decisions for Title I schools. *NCLB* and the 2004 *IDEA* amendments strengthened a commitment to this requirement, and now all states are paying attention to testing students with disabilities and are using those results to hold schools accountable for the performance of these students.

Data indicate that participation and achievement levels are rising each year. Data from the National Council on Educational Outcomes (NCEO) show that in 2003, most states had 95 percent to 100 percent participation in state math and reading assessments by students with disabilities in elementary school, middle school, and high school. By including students with disabilities in the assessment and accountability systems, we raise our expectations for them while giving schools the data they need to help all of their students to be successful. *NCLB* is helping special education programs and each child's IEP team know what academic goals children need to achieve so that they are given the appropriate supports and services. *NCLB* tells us what we're working towards, while *IDEA* brings to bear multiple resources and services to help students attain the learning standards.

4. My school did not make Adequate Yearly Progress (AYP) because students with disabilities did not score well on the state test. Is that fair?

Only by holding schools accountable for *all* students will the spotlight of attention and necessary resources be directed to those children most in need of assistance and most often left behind academically.

Schools need to be accountable for all students. To achieve that goal, AYP is intentionally designed to identify those areas where schools need to improve the achievement of their students. What we are learning is that some schools perform well on average, but they may miss their AYP goals as a result of the student achievement of one or a few groups of students. The requirement for states, districts, and schools to disaggregate their data (i.e., separate their assessment data by the results of the different subgroups of students) is one of the fundamental principles of *NCLB*. This ensures that all schools and districts are held accountable for the performance of subgroups of students, not just the school as a whole.

The Department recognizes the challenges educators face in helping all children achieve to high standards. But allowing overall school performance to mask the lower performance of particular groups of students who need additional academic assistance would be *unfair* to those struggling groups of students.

5. Why should students with disabilities be tested and included in accountability systems?

Students with disabilities deserve the same high-quality education as their peers. Ever since Congress enacted the 1997 amendments to the *IDEA*, the nation has been working to improve the participation of students with disabilities in state assessments and provide students with disabilities with access to the general education curriculum. Many states have been committed to this goal for an even longer period of time. The purpose of requiring participation in assessments is to improve achievement for students with disabilities. As Secretary Spellings has said on more than one occasion, "What gets measured gets done." Too often in the past, students with disabilities were excluded from assessments and accountability systems, and the consequence was that they did not receive the academic attention and resources they deserved.

Students with disabilities, including those with the most significant cognitive disabilities, benefit instructionally from such participation. One state explains the instructional benefits of including students with the most significant cognitive disabilities in its assessment system in the following way: "Some students with disabilities have never been taught academic skills and concepts, for example, reading, mathematics, science, and social studies, even at very basic levels. Yet all students are capable of learning at a level that engages and challenges them. Teachers who have incorporated learning standards into their instruction cite unanticipated gains in students' performance and understanding. Furthermore, some individualized social, communication, motor, and self-help skills can be practiced during activities based on the learning standards."

To ensure that adequate resources are dedicated to helping these students succeed, appropriate measurement of their achievement needs to be part of school and district accountability systems. Furthermore, when students with disabilities are part of the accountability system, educators' expectations for these students are more likely to increase. In such a system, educators realize that students with disabilities count and that they can learn to high standards, just like students without disabilities.

6. Is it fair to make students with disabilities take a test that they cannot pass?

For too long in this country, students with disabilities have been held to lower standards than their peers and unjustly routed through school systems that expected less of them than of other students. Several states have found that once students with disabilities are included in the assessment system and expected to achieve like other students, performance improves. In 2005, for example, 60 percent of fourth-graders with disabilities in Kansas were proficient in reading. This represented an increase over 2003, when 51 percent of students with disabilities were proficient.

Students with disabilities can achieve at high levels. That is why *NCLB* requires states and school districts to hold all students to the same challenging academic standards and have all students participate in annual state assessments. We test students to see what they are learning, identify academic needs, and address those needs. The purpose is not to frustrate children. Rather, it is to shine a light on student needs and draw attention to how schools can better serve their students.

If students are excluded from assessments, they are excluded from school improvement plans based on those assessment results. If all students are to benefit from education reforms, all students must be included. Only by measuring how well the system is doing will we clearly identify and then fill the gaps in instructional opportunities that leave some students behind.

We do, however, need to improve tests for students with disabilities. We need tests that measure what students know and can do without the interference of their disability. The Department is currently looking at ways to make tests more accessible and valid for a wider range of students so that all students can participate and receive meaningful scores. For more information about this work, please refer to item 13 of this document and to the proposed regulation that was released in December 2005. . . .

7. Why can't a student's Individualized Education Program (IEP), instead of the state assessment, be used to measure progress?

There are several reasons why IEPs are not appropriate for school accountability purposes. In general, IEP goals are individualized for each student and may cover a range of needs beyond reading/language arts and mathematics, such as behavior and social skills. They are not necessarily aligned with state standards, and they are not designed to ensure consistent judgments about schools—a fundamental requirement for AYP determinations. The IEP is used to provide parents with information about a student's progress and for making individualized decisions about the special education and related services a student needs to succeed. Assessments used for school accountability purposes must be aligned to state standards and have related achievement standards.

8. **Students in special education get extra privileges in taking the state tests. Some of them get more time and get tested by themselves or in small groups. Isn't this unfair?**

These "privileges" are called "accommodations." Accommodations are changes in testing materials or procedures, such as repeating directions or allowing extended time, that, by design, do not invalidate the student's test score. In other words, accommodations help students access the material but do not give students with disabilities an unfair advantage. These accommodations instead help level the playing field so that a test measures what the student knows and can do and not the effect of the child's disability. It is not unfair to allow valid accommodations during a test because these accommodations allow a test to measure the student's knowledge and skills rather than the student's disability.

The state is responsible for analyzing accommodations to determine which are acceptable on the basis of the test design. It is important for the state to make sure that students use only those accommodations that result in a valid score. For example, if the assessment is supposed to measure how well a student decodes text, reading the test aloud to the student would result in an invalid score.

9. **Isn't it unrealistic to expect *all* students with disabilities to meet grade-level standards? Students are in special education for a reason.**

Students receive special education services for a reason. They are in special education because a team of professionals has evaluated the child using a variety of assessment tools and strategies to gather relevant functional, developmental, and academic information about the child, including information provided by the parent, and determined that the child has a disability and needs special education services. Their achievement on grade-level standards is only part of the picture. It does not determine whether or not they need services. Assessments and other evaluation materials include those tailored to assess specific areas of education need. The child must be assessed in all areas related to the suspected disability including, if appropriate, health, vision, hearing, social and emotional status, general intelligence, academic performance, communicative status, and motor abilities. The impression that students are receiving special education services because they cannot pass a state test is a misunderstanding of what it means to be eligible for *IDEA* services.

Being in special education does not mean that a student cannot learn and reach grade-level standards. In fact, the majority of students with disabilities should be able to meet those standards. Special education provides the additional help and support that these students need to learn.

This means designing instruction to meet their specific needs and providing supports, such as physical therapy, counseling services, or interpreting services, to help students learn alongside their peers and reach the same high standards as all other students.

10. What about students with significant cognitive disabilities? Is it realistic to expect them to meet the same level of achievement as all other students?

The expectation of *NCLB* is that the majority of students with disabilities can and should participate in and achieve proficiency on state assessments. We understand, however, that there is a small percentage of students with disabilities who may not reach grade-level standards, even with the best instruction. These are students with the most significant cognitive disabilities (about 10 percent of all special education students). The Title I regulations allow these students to take an alternate assessment based on alternate achievement standards that is less difficult and more tailored to their needs. Their proficient scores can be counted in the same way as any other student's proficient score on a state assessment. The Department has developed certain safeguards around this policy to help prevent students from being placed in an assessment and curricula that are inappropriately restricted in scope, thus limiting their educational opportunities (see item 11).

11. It seems like the Department has said the following: "Only 1 percent of students with disabilities can take an alternate assessment based on alternate achievement standards." Is this true?

The Department has not made such a statement. In fact, it reflects several common misunderstandings about federal education policy. Current Title I regulations permit a student's proficient score on assessments based on alternate achievement standards to count the same as any other student's proficient score on a state assessment, subject to a 1.0 percent cap at the district and state levels. If more than 1.0 percent of proficient scores come from such assessments, then the state must establish procedures to count those scores as non-proficient for the purposes of school accountability.

MYTH.   The Department expects that only 1 percent of students with disabilities should take a test based on alternate achievement standards (1 percent cap).

FACT.   The 1.0 percent cap reflects the following: 1 percent of *all* students represents about 10 percent of students with disabilities. While all children can learn challenging content, evaluating that learning through the use of alternate achievement standards is appropriate only for a small, limited percentage of students who are within one or more of the existing disability categories under the *IDEA* (e.g., autism, multiple disabilities, traumatic brain injury), and whose cognitive disability prevents them from attaining grade-level achievement standards, even with the very best instruction. The 1 percent cap (or approximately 10 percent of students with disabilities) is based on current incidence rates of students with the most significant cognitive disabilities, allowing for reasonable local variation in prevalence.

MYTH.   IEP teams are limited in the number of students with disabilities that they may determine need an alternate assessment based on alternate achievement standards.

FACT.   The cap is a limit on the number of proficient scores that may be included in AYP decisions at the district and state levels. The cap is not a limit on the number of students who may take such an alternate assessment based on alternate achievement standards.

FACT.   IEP teams must make informed and appropriate decisions for each individual student, based on each student's unique needs. If more than 1 percent of all students in a district need to take an assessment based on alternate achievement standards, then all such students may take them. To protect students from inappropriate, low standards, however, districts and states are limited in the use of proficient scores based on alternate achievement standards in making AYP decisions.

FACT.   Alternate assessments based on alternate achievement standards must only be given to students with the most significant cognitive disabilities. States must develop guidelines to help IEP teams determine which assessment is most appropriate for a student with a disability to take. If those guidelines are appropriately developed and implemented, IEP teams should be making the right decisions for their students.

12. Don't such "caps" interfere with IEP decisions?

No. The policies on including students with disabilities in assessment and accountability systems do not affect the IEP team's role in making specific individual decisions about how to best address the needs of children with disabilities. The policies do not restrict the number of students who can participate in an alternate assessment. Instead, the policy restricts, solely for purposes of calculating AYP for school accountability, the number of scores that can be counted as proficient or advanced based on alternate achievement standards on alternate assessments.

13. How will the Department's recent proposed regulations change the policy on assessing and including students with disabilities in school accountability?

Since the regulation permitting a state to develop alternate achievement standards for students with the most significant cognitive disabilities was issued, information and experience in states, as well as important recent research, indicate that there may be an additional number of students who, because of their disability, have significant difficulty achieving grade-level proficiency, even with the best instruction, within the same time frame as other students.

The best available research and data indicate that this group of students comprises about 2 percent of the school-age population (or approximately 20 percent of students with disabilities). The progress of these students with disabilities in response to high-quality instruction, including special education and related services designed to address the students' individual needs, is such that the students are not likely to achieve grade-level proficiency within the school year covered by the students' IEPs.

The Department is publishing proposed regulations to address how these students may be included in a state's assessment and accountability systems. The proposed regulations would permit a state to (1) develop modified achievement standards, that is, standards that are aligned with the state's academic content standards for the grade in which a student is enrolled, but may reflect reduced breadth or depth of grade-level content; (2) develop assessments to measure the achievement of students based on such modified achievement standards; and (3) include the proficient and advanced scores based on modified achievement standards in determining AYP for school accountability purposes only, subject to a cap of 2.0 percent at the district and state levels.

The goal of the proposed regulations is to recognize, based on research, the specific needs of an additional group of students with disabilities while ensuring that states continue to hold schools accountable for helping these students with disabilities meet challenging standards that enable the students to approach, and even meet, grade-level standards. The proposed regulations would require certain safeguards, such as requiring that modified achievement standards provide access for students with disabilities to grade-level curricula and do not preclude a student from earning a regular high school diploma. They would also require a state to develop clear and appropriate guidelines for IEP teams to apply in determining which students should be assessed based on modified achievement standards and to ensure that parents are informed that their child's achievement will be measured on those standards. The proposed regulations would also permit a state, in determining AYP for the students with disabilities subgroup, to include, for a period of up to two years, the scores of students who were previously identified as having a disability but who are no longer receiving special education services.

The proposed regulation affects both *IDEA* and *NCLB* by ensuring that the requirements for participation in state assessment systems are the same. With this proposed change, students with disabilities must participate in an assessment that results in a valid score.

14. How will *IDEA* and *NCLB* work together for students with disabilities in the future?

IDEA and *NCLB* reinforce and strengthen the goal of accountability for all children. Both laws require states to include students with disabilities in state assessments and to report publicly the achievement of students with disabilities. In addition, state performance goals under the *IDEA* must be aligned with the state's definition of AYP. Such consistency across these two laws will facilitate greater collaboration between special education and general education teachers and realize the goal of considering children with disabilities as general education students first. One of the ways that *IDEA* supports this effort is through new provisions added by the 2004 reauthorization of the *IDEA* that allow local education agencies (LEAs) to use federal special education funds to provide early intervention services for students who are at risk of later identification and placement in special education. (There is nothing precluding state funds from also being used for this purpose.) This provides an opportunity for educators to work together to implement scientifically based instructional practices like curriculum-based measurement to identify and address academic problems early.

POSTSCRIPT

Does NCLB Leave Some Students Behind?

"Mrs. Dewey" dislikes being told to focus on students whose performance will lead to higher scores; this contradicts her professional ethics. Yet, she worries that teaching every child brands her as not contributing to the school's targets.

Secretary Spellings' words would puzzle "Mrs. Dewey":

> "Special education is no longer a peripheral issue. IDEA and NCLB have put the needs of students with disabilities front and center. We've torn down the final barrier between special and general education. And now everyone in the system has a stake in ensuring students with disabilities achieve high standards." (Spellings, 2005)

If so, "Mrs. Dewey" might ask, "Why is my group of students with disabilities too small to matter?"

Subgroups and their sizes engender much discussion. Scores from a very small number of students may not be statistically valid or reliable. Additionally, with small subgroups, privacy can be compromised when scores become public. These issues are particularly relevant in small and/or rural schools (McLaughlin, Embler, Hernandez, & Caron, *Rural Special Education Quarterly*, 2005).

Under NCLB, states set their own minimum subgroup size. If a subgroup falls below the minimum size, it is considered as having met AYP, regardless of student scores.

An extensive study on subgroup size and confidence intervals (another statistical tool for evaluating scores) found minimum subgroup sizes vary widely nationwide, from 10 to at least 80 (Simpson, Gong & Marion, http://www.nciea.org, 2005). Sometimes different subgroups had different minimum sizes. The authors noted that larger minimum subgroup sizes mask the performance of students with disabilities. Schools meet their targets without being accountable for these students.

Diverse groups have signified strong opposition to this practice (*Joint Organizational Statement on NCLB,* www.fairtest.org, 2004; National Conference of State Legislatures, 2005; Commission on No Child Left Behind, 2006). It continues. Does it lead to statistically accurate results or deny access to some students?

Authors of the Department of Education FAQ sheet might say schools who manipulate subgroup sizes violate the spirit of NCLB. The FAQ Sheet would advise "Mrs. Dewey's" administrators to believe their students with disabilities can meet high expectations and to use assessment results and services to pursue that target. In support, the Commission on No Child Left Behind (2006) found that disability subgroup scores were "very often not the sole reason a school is identified as not making AYP."

Yell, Katsiyannis and Shiner (*TEACHING Exceptional Children*, 2006) express confidence that NCLB provides tools and guidance to meet its ambitious challenge. Inspired by its belief in students and educators, Faust (*In CASE*, 2006) finds "kernels of gold" in NCLB: opportunities for systemic change and growth.

Most people agree that students with disabilities should be included in education reform. Few would like to see these students relegated to shabby classrooms with outdated books. One quote strikes a jarring note:

> "Nobody thinks kids with significant cognitive disabilities should be expected to reach the same standards as everyone else; it's hard if not impossible to find anyone in the Administration or on Capitol Hill who claims credit for the idea of including special education students as an NCLB subgroup in the first place. Once it was embedded in the law, however, special ed advocates seized on its potential, making it impossible to move. Spellings – and Secretary Paige before her – have been carefully walking federal policy back from this brink since the Act's ink was dry. (Petrilli, *The Education Gadfly, 2005*).

Is it possible that NCLB targets were painted with little thought of students with disabilities?

Is NCLB a leap forward; holding schools accountable for the performance of all students? Or does NCLB represent a step backward; creating loopholes (varying subgroup sizes, alternate and modified standards, alternate assessments, safe harbor provisions) that exclude students whose parents and teachers trusted the promise that no child would be left behind?

ISSUE 9

Will NCLB Requirements Produce Highly Qualified Special Education Teachers?

YES: Rod Paige, from "Remarks at the Education Department's First Annual Teacher Quality Evaluation Conference" (June 11, 2002)

NO: James McLeskey and Dorene D. Ross, from "The Politics of Teacher Education in the New Millennium: Implications for Special Education Teacher Educators," *Teacher Education and Special Education* (Fall 2004)

ISSUE SUMMARY

YES: Rod Paige, then-Secretary of the U.S. Department of Education, and former Houston, Texas superintendent, believes the promise of No Child Left Behind can be realized by mandating that every teacher be highly qualified, by increasing their focus in the content areas they teach and decreasing time spent on pedagogical skills.

NO: James McLeskey and Dorene D. Ross, teacher education faculty at the University of Florida, present competing views of what constitutes "highly qualified" special education teachers, one based on deregulation and one based on professionalization; they encourage ongoing consideration to determine the value and impact of each.

T he No Child Left Behind Act of 2001 (NCLB) holds high expectations for student achievement. Every child must be proficient in reading and math by 2014. To help each student reach that goal, NCLB also sets high expectations for teachers.

The first selection is the speech, made by then-Secretary of the U.S. Department of Education Rod Paige, that accompanied the release of his first Secretary's Annual Report on Teacher Quality (www.title2.org, 2002). With affection and passion, Paige acknowledges the critical role teachers play in the lives of their students. With equal intensity, Paige laments the current quality of teachers and teacher-education programs. His vision of a highly qualified teacher has spent many educational hours studying fields of concentration (what to teach) and very little time on theory and pedagogy (how to teach).

NCLB requires that all teachers must be highly qualified. To be considered as such, teachers must have a bachelor's degree, hold full state certification or licensure, and demonstrate competence in each subject they teach. The latter can be done by either a graduate degree or a "rigorous" test. Elementary teachers can demonstrate content competence through a "rigorous" test. Both new and veteran teachers must be highly qualified.

These requirements were relatively easy to understand as they applied to secondary teachers assigned to a specific subject-area. Less clear was how special education teachers would be deemed highly qualified, especially those responsible for teaching an array of subjects to groups of middle/secondary students with significant disabilities.

Striving for consistency with NCLB, IDEA 2004 requires that the highly qualified special education teacher providing consultative services or support services possess at least a bachelor's degree and hold full state certification in special education. However, a special education teacher responsible for primary instruction in any core academic subject (English, reading or language arts, math, science, foreign languages, civics and government, economics, arts, history, and geography) must also demonstrate competence in each subject-area taught. Competence could be established through any of the methods available to general education teachers. This requirement extends to special education teachers in substantially separate settings for students with complex disabilities.

In this Issue's second selection, James McLeskey and Dorene D. Ross, who study programs of teacher preparation, as well as teach in them, discuss two competing perspectives about the kind of training that leads to a well-qualified special education teacher. Those favoring deregulation, including NCLB proponents, have little use for traditional courses of study that highlight adaptations and/or strategies addressing student behavior and learning patterns. In contrast, numerous professional associations call for rigorous standards that include content, but also stress the critical importance of demonstrated teaching practices which respond to the unique needs of students with disabilities. While McLeskey and Ross favor the professionalization argument, they maintain there are insufficient research findings to enable us to embrace either one of these perspectives to the exclusion of the other.

As you read these articles, consider whether you think the increased emphasis on subject-area content is a wise direction for special education teachers. Should time developing teaching skill be replaced by courses in content areas to enhance access to the general curriculum? Can this expand options for students? Will a highly qualified special education teacher be highly competent to address the learning and behavior needs of students for whom learning poses significant challenges?

YES ↙

Rod Paige

Education Secretary Paige Addresses First Annual Teacher Quality Evaluation Conference

I want to thank all of you for coming and for being a part of this, the first annual Teacher Quality Evaluation Conference.

For those who have come from out of town, I hope you get a chance to visit some of our national treasures and see for yourself what an incredibly beautiful and vibrant place our nation's capital is.

More than a year later, I am still in awe seeing Lincoln and Jefferson in the early morning light—or Lady Freedom standing sentry on the Capitol dome. There is a special feeling when you pass the White House and see families peering through the fence, hoping for a glance of their president or first lady or first dogs.

Every day I'm reminded what an honor it is to live here and to serve as U.S. Secretary of Education.

One of the things you learn right off the bat is that children are going to write and ask for favors. Three of the most popular requests are: shorter school days, less homework and better cafeteria food.

Some write to ask me to come visit their schools and *to please bring the president with me!*

But most of their letters include well-thought out questions—like the one from a New Jersey eighth grader named Brianna who wrote to ask: "What do you believe are the most important issues facing elementary or high school education in the United States today?"

That's a great question—in fact, it goes to the very heart of our new education reforms signed into law by President Bush on January 8.

I believe the *No Child Left Behind* Act of 2001 will go down in history as the key piece of public policy that finally slammed close the achievement gap between those who have and those who don't—between those who are hopeful and those who are hopeless.

Our nation has been called to commit itself to a bold goal—the goal of creating an education system that insists on accountability, results, teacher quality and reading programs that work so all children in our public schools get the excellent education their parents sent them there for.

From speech at Department of Education's First Annual Teacher Quality Evaluation Conference, June 11, 2002.

And it all started because we have a president who believes that the most sacred duty of government is to educate its children. They are our future.

Yet national report cards in recent years show we are destroying that future—one child at a time.

- Two out of three fourth-graders can't read proficiently
- Seven out of 10 inner-city and rural fourth graders can't read at the most basic level
- Nearly a third of college freshmen need remedial classes before they can handle entry level courses
- America's twelfth graders rank among the lowest in math and science achievement among their counterparts in other industrialized nations

These are more than just statistics. They are a grim picture of the human toll of an education system that is failing too many African-American, Hispanic and low-income children in our nation's classrooms.

Soon after President Bush took office, he called on Congress to fundamentally change the structure of education—and enact the most sweeping change in education in 35 years.

Never before have we as a nation made the commitment to all children in our public schools that every one of them can and will learn. *Every single child*. Regardless of race, income or zip code.

The *No Child Left Behind* law also recognizes that just throwing money at a problem won't make it go away. Over the last half-century local, state and federal taxpayers have spent more than $10 trillion on our public schools. $10 trillion.

And what have we got to show for it?

Every year we did the same thing: spent more money. And every year we got the same result: mediocre student performance—or worse.

It was Albert Einstein who said insanity is "the belief that one can get different results by doing the same thing."

It doesn't take an Einstein to see the truth is that all the money in the world won't fix our schools if your *only* plan is to throw more money at the problem.

To solve the problem, you must first create a framework for change.

And our new education reforms provide that framework by insisting on accountability and results; by providing local control and flexibility; by empowering parents to take a lead in their children's education; and by insisting on teaching methods that work.

The basics work. Research-based reading programs work. Testing works.

Defenders of the status quo hate the idea of testing. But parents don't. Recent polls show the American people standing shoulder to shoulder with the president on annual testing. Moms and dads want the best for their children. They understand that the only way to know if teachers are teaching and their children are learning is to measure for results—and to hold schools accountable.

Their own children agree. A Public Agenda poll shows 95 percent of students are not obsessing over the idea of tests.

No Child Left Behind provided the framework for change. And it provided historic levels of funding to get the job done—including the largest education budget for disadvantaged children in U.S. history.

The big difference now is that taxpayers know what they're getting for their money. And parents know if their children are learning.

And if a school is failing its mission, moms and dads no longer have to helplessly stand by and watch every last spark of curiosity die in their children's eyes.

Thanks to *No Child Left Behind* they can choose one-on-one tutoring, or after-school help or enroll their children in a better public school.

Our new education reforms depend on high standards and accountability—and teaching every child to read. Most of all, our new education reforms depend on who's standing at the front of the classroom teaching.

Most of us can remember a favorite teacher. President Bush loved teachers so much he married one.

I had two favorite teachers: my parents. By day, they taught other children in Monticello, Mississippi. But on nights and weekends, they taught me and my sisters and brothers.

Books filled our house, and so did love—for learning, for our faith, for our country and for each other. Their example inspired me to become a teacher as well.

And it was while working in the classroom that I discovered the truth in the words of World War II General Omar Bradley when he said: "The teacher is the real soldier of democracy. Others can defend it, but only he can make it work."

Very few people have the influence over our lives that teachers do. And that is why the president, the Congress and I are determined to meet the goal of a quality teacher in every classroom by 2006.

Today, I am sending Congress a report on the state of teacher quality in America that spells out the challenges states face in achieving this goal. And we have a few:

- Too many teachers are not qualified in the subject they're teaching
- Too many states do not test to make sure teachers know what they're teaching
- Too many states that do test set the bar for passing way too low
- Too many education programs require too much focus on theory and pedagogy, and too little focus on fields of concentration—like math, history or science.
- Too many barriers are built into the system that keep talented people out of the classroom and force districts to fill vacancies with teachers on waivers

Clearly, there is much work to do.

Fortunately, we have a growing body of scientific research that tells us what it takes to be an effective teacher, and we must listen.

And we must do several things:

First, we must strengthen academic standards for teachers.

Research confirms that the most effective teachers are those who are smart and who know the subject they're teaching—inside and out. How much teachers know determines how well students learn.

Yet academic standards for teachers are low. Not all states test potential teachers on content knowledge. And many states that do test use tests that are not rigorous enough.

California, for example, requires teachers to take the California Basic Educational Skills Test that is set at roughly the 10th grade level.

Other states set the bar so low that even teachers who scored in only the 20th percentile passed certification.

Sadly, it's the children who need help most—those in inner-city and rural schools—who are *least* likely to have well-prepared teachers.

- 43 percent of math teachers in high poverty schools have neither majored nor minored in math-related fields, compared to 27 percent of middle class schools
- 25 percent of disadvantaged children are taught English by teachers who don't have a degree in English, compared to only 11 percent of middle class children.

Not only is this troubling to me. It's troubling to teachers.

Some months back, Mrs. Bush held a White House conference on teacher preparation. At that conference, Sandra Feldman, the president of the American Federation of Teachers, said: "Good teachers need to be really well educated . . . They need to know—deeply—the subject they teach. Prospective teachers should complete an academic major and have a solid foundation in the liberal arts. You can't teach what you don't know well."

Some states have embraced meaningful standards—I think of Pennsylvania and Virginia.

But *all states* need to take a hard look at how they decide who's qualified to teach and who's not.

Which brings me to my second point: we must tear down barriers preventing talented men and women from entering the teaching profession.

At a time when we desperately need strong teachers in our classrooms, we should be doing all we can to attract and keep the best and the brightest candidates. A good place to start is by drawing from nontraditional sources.

For example, Teach For America is a program that recruits gifted and talented students from our nation's college campuses to teach in inner-city schools.

Transition to Teaching matches talented mid-career professionals with schools with the greatest need.

And Troops to Teachers is a program that taps retired service men and women for the classroom—people like Army Sgt. Art Moore.

Sgt. Moore served our country for 21 years. When he retired, he wanted to keep serving. So he contacted Troops to Teachers about alternative certification. And for the past seven years, Sgt. Moore has been a special education teacher in Baltimore.

Another teacher who took a different route to the chalkboard is Col. Chauncey Veatch.

After 25 years serving our country, Col. Veatch left the Army to teach children of migrant workers in California.

In April, President Bush and I had the honor of joining Chauncey in the Rose Garden as he was named the 2002 National Teacher of the Year.

We must streamline the process to encourage more people like Art and Chauncy to help fill the need in our nation's classrooms.

Finally, states must improve the quality of teacher education programs to ensure that new teachers are prepared to be effective in the classroom.

I've been a dean of a school of education. And I know the special problems these schools face and the responsibilities they bear.

But I am also mindful of what Diane Ravitch of New York University said during the White House conference on teachers. She said the original idea behind colleges of education was to create rigorous professional training for teachers—just like doctors and lawyers.

Yet here we are—a century later—with research showing many teachers fresh out of college lack what they need to meet the challenges of the classroom. More than one in five will give up and leave the profession within their first three years.

In one study, less than 36 percent surveyed said they felt "very well prepared" to teach and help their students meet performance standards. Less than 20 percent said they felt prepared to meet the needs of diverse students or those with limited English proficiency.

Despite this, many schools of education have continued, business-as-usual—focusing heavily on pedagogy—how to be a teacher—when the evidence cries out that what future teachers need most is a deeper understanding of the subject they'll be teaching—of how to monitor student progress and of how to help students who are falling behind.

It got so bad in the Elk Grove school district in California, that its Superintendent—David Gordon—took the matter into his own hands. David is with us today. Where are you David?

Working with a local university that was willing to "think outside the box," David started a fast-track teacher credential program called the Teacher Education Institute. They set high standards for prospective teachers and then provided intensive training to meet those high standards.

You know what happened? Even though he raised the bar for achievement for both students and teachers—and even though a teacher shortage loomed Elk Grove schools began filling its classrooms with top-quality and well-trained people who were up to the challenge of the rigorous curriculum.

Student achievement soared. And the number of college-bound students has more than doubled.

Future teachers certainly need to learn the basics of teaching and managing a classroom, but that should not be the main focus of teacher preparation.

We must be open to innovative approaches and rethink traditional methods that may not work anymore.

There is no doubt that we ask a lot of our teachers—and we owe them something in return. We owe them our respect for the professionals they are. We owe them our support. And we owe them the training and tools to succeed.

The *No Child Left Behind* Act gives schools greater flexibility to use federal funds where the local need is greatest: to recruit new teachers, to improve teacher training, or to increase teacher pay in critical need areas.

President Bush's 2003 budget calls on Congress to:

- Increase funding for teacher development to help teachers succeed
- Increase funding to train and recruit teachers in math and science
- Provide tax relief to help teachers defray expenses
- Expand loan forgiveness for those who teach in high need schools

President Bush's $2.85 billion Teacher Quality Initiative represents the largest and most comprehensive federal investment in preparation, training and recruiting teachers and principals.

These resources—and the ideas I've laid out—will help states as they work to ensure a highly qualified teacher in every classroom, and to implement our new education reforms.

Some defenders of the status quo are resisting our new education reforms. And, frankly, I don't understand that.

How can they possibly argue with a plan that says we want to provide more resources and better instruction for disadvantaged children?

Maybe the critics are like those people Sam Rayburn used to talk about when he said, "Any jackass can kick over a barn. It takes a carpenter to build one."

We're talking about helping children so far down on the achievement scale they're not even a blip on the radar.

We're talking about helping children who show up in national report cards that say 40 percent of white fourth graders can read while only 12 percent of black fourth graders can read.

In the 19 years since *A Nation at Risk* set off a wave of well-intentioned school reform efforts, we still have too many children—mostly urban and mostly African American—falling through the cracks.

The reforms of *No Child Left Behind*, when implemented, will provide a safety net to catch these children and get them back on track academically.

To be sure, there are pockets of excellence all around our country. As I travel our country I see many inspiring examples of schools and teachers and students rising to the challenges, of moms and dads getting involved in their children's schools.

No Child Left Behind is not just a law, it's a revolution. A profound moment of change. And all of us—as educators, policymakers, community leaders and those of us in public life—have a role to play.

Years from now, people will look back and say: That's when they raised the bar and student achievement began to soar. That's when leadership triumphed over politics and no child was left behind. That's when the American people realized they could create great schools worthy of a great nation.

God bless you all. And God bless America.

James McLeskey
and Dorene D. Ross

NO

The Politics of Teacher Education in the New Millennium: Implications for Special Education Teacher Educators

Over the last several years, teacher education has become a 'front burner' political issue in Washington, DC and in most statehouses. This new found status has resulted largely from the widespread agreement that highly qualified teachers make a significant difference in the academic achievement of students. The National Commission on Teaching and America's Future has argued that what teachers know and do makes a difference in their impact on students and student learning. Research by Sanders and Horn provides robust evidence to support this claim. Specifically, Sanders and Horn found that over a period of years, the quality of the teacher contributes more to student achievement than any other factor, including class size, class composition, or student background. This research, coupled with calls at the federal level and in most states for 'tougher academic standards', led to the inclusion of the mandate in the recently passed No Child Left Behind (NCLB) Act that all content area teachers in Title I schools be "highly qualified" by 2005–06. . . . [A] similar mandate will be included in the next reauthorization of the Individuals with Disabilities Education Act (IDEA), requiring that all special education teachers be highly qualified.

The current highly politicized context for teaching and teacher education creates both challenges and opportunities for teacher educators. Two questions emerge as central in this debate: (1) What is the definition of "highly qualified" teacher? (2) What are the characteristics of high quality teacher education which produce highly qualified teachers? Although educational researchers have frequently engaged these questions, the distinction in today's context is that each issue is being debated and defined within a highly charged political context. Acknowledging and understanding the implications of the way these issues are being defined and the potential solutions that are being proposed is critical to the work of teacher educators over the next decade. . . .

From *Teacher Education and Special Education,* vol. 27, no. 4, 2004, pp. 342–349 (excerpts). Copyright © 2004 by the Teacher Education Division of the Council for Exceptional Children. Reprinted by permission.

What Is the Definition of "Highly Qualified Teacher"?

While all agree on the need for highly qualified teachers, there is disagreement about what 'highly qualified' entails. Two camps control the discussion regarding this issue. One group is calling for the deregulation of teacher education, while a second group argues for the professionalization of teaching. Both of these positions exert considerable pressure on state departments of education and teacher education programs and have a significant influence on who enters the classroom as a beginning teacher. . . .

The leading advocate to deregulate teacher education has been Rod Paige, former Superintendent of the Houston (TX) Independent School District, and current Secretary of the U.S. Department of Education. In a paper addressing the need for highly qualified teachers, the Secretary made his position clear by stating that "rigorous research indicates that verbal ability and content knowledge are the most important attributes of highly qualified teachers. In addition, there is little evidence that education school course work leads to improved student achievement." This perspective on teacher quality is reflected in [NCLB], which provides alternate definitions for "highly qualified teachers", including an option to fully certify as "highly qualified" those who (a) complete a bachelor's degree and pass a test of subject knowledge (for middle and secondary level teachers) or (b) complete a bachelor's degree and pass a test or tests of subject knowledge and teaching skills (elementary teachers). In this way NCLB gives the force of law to alternative certification routes currently in place in many states which do nor hold participants to the same high standards as other state approved teacher education programs . . . that are typically based in Institutions of Higher Education. . . .

Much of the support for the 'deregulation' position has come from the work of private foundations. . . . In a position paper that provided the basis for the Secretary's position, the Abell Foundation contended that there is no research to support the perspective that teacher certification leads to improved student outcomes. Furthermore, in this report Walsh contended that teacher certification requirements are unnecessary regulatory hurdles that prevent many potentially well-qualified individuals from becoming teachers. Similar to NCLB, the Abell Foundation recommended that "the only fixed requirement (for teacher certification) should be a bachelor's degree and a passing score on an appropriate teacher's exam." Chester Finn and colleagues from the Heritage and Fordham Foundations took similar positions, and also called for a dramatic increase in alternate routes to certification, which circumvent the regulatory hurdles that exist for traditional preparation programs.

The positions taken by Secretary Paige and others cited above lead to the conclusion that the image they have of a 'highly qualified' teacher is "a technician who faithfully implements the highly sequenced instructional techniques stipulated in government-approved texts and materials, which are based on the results of 'scientific research'." This contrasts sharply to the perspective taken by those who support the professionalization of teaching and a broadened and more complex definition of "highly qualified teacher."

Professional education groups, including the National Council for the Accreditation of Teacher Education (NCATE), the National Board for Professional Teaching Standards (NBPTS), the American Association of Colleges for Teacher Education (AACTE), the Interstate New Teacher Assessment and Support Consortium (INTASC), and the Council for Exceptional Children (CEC), among many others, are major representatives of those who seek to professionalize teaching. The most influential of these groups has been the National Commission on Teaching and America's Future (NCTAF). . . . This group has called for more rigorous standards for teachers. These standards have been produced by the NBPTS and INTASC, and incorporated into teacher education program approval by NCATE and CEC. While these standards include and emphasize knowledge of subject matter, as the deregulationists recommend, they also include knowledge of teaching and demonstration of this knowledge through teacher performance in the classroom. These groups advocate the use of high, national standards for the preparation and certification of teachers, as well as uniform assessments to ensure that teachers can demonstrate mastery of these standards through classroom performance.

Research to support the professionalization agenda has primarily been reviewed by Darling-Hammond and Wilson. These investigators . . . concluded that pedagogical preparation enhances teacher quality and results in increased student achievement. These investigators also reported a significant relationship between teacher certification and student achievement. Finally, while these investigators conclude that research supports the importance of subject matter preparation for teachers, they did not find that subject matter preparation was more important than knowledge of how to teach as a factor influencing student achievement.

The image of a teacher that emerges from the perspectives taken by those who seek to professionalize teaching contrasts sharply with those who seek to deregulate teaching. This image reflects the perspective that the teacher "knows subject matter (what to teach) and pedagogy (how to teach) but also knows how to learn and how to make decisions informed by theory and research from many bodies of knowledge and also is informed by feedback from school and classroom evidence in particular contexts."

What Are the Characteristics of High Quality Teacher Education Which Produces Highly Qualified Teachers?

For teacher educators, among others, it follows logically that the quality of a beginning teacher is influenced by her or his teacher education program. However, this has not been the conclusion reached by all, as the contrasting definitions of "highly qualified" teacher reveal. Indeed, the simultaneous calls for deregulation and increased professionalization in teaching and teacher education have played out in state departments of education across the U.S. in two distinctive ways. First, the deregulation movement has resulted in a range of alternative teacher preparation programs in every state. In some instances these alternative certification programs are held to the same standards as . . . teacher education programs . . . based in Institutions of Higher Education . . . , while in others they are not held to these same high standards. The most extreme example of lowering standards has been the option of becoming certified through receipt of a bachelor's degree with any major, and subsequently passing a test of content and/or instructional knowledge, as proposed in NCLB. . . . At least one state currently has a test-based alternative to traditional certification (Florida), and a national test is being developed for this purpose by the American Board for Certification of Teaching Excellence.

In many of the same states that have lowered standards through alternative paths to teacher certification, departments of education have responded to the professionalization of teaching agenda by changing and often raising standards for traditional, Institution of Higher Education . . . based teacher preparation programs. For example, in Florida, more specific requirements for general education course work have been added to teacher education requirements, along with specific course requirements in classroom management, assessment, reading, and ESOL. In addition, rigorous outcomes measures, which must be demonstrated through course work and in field experiences, have been added. . . .

The major weakness in the arguments made by advocates for both sides of this debate is the lack of definitive research evidence to guide decision making about how best to prepare and credential teachers. Rice noted that the current debate is largely ideological, because there is so little robust research to guide policy decisions. It is important to acknowledge that teacher education is still a relatively new research field, and therefore it is hardly surprising that we lack definitive answers to the many important questions that would allow an informed response to the professionalism/deregulation debate.

As is characteristic of many emerging fields, the very nature of our research questions has progressed over time as we have gained knowledge about teaching and teachers. Cochran-Smith provides a brief review of the history of teacher education research, noting that we have moved from research on the attributes of good teachers (1950s and 1960s), to research about the kinds of instructional strategies used by good teachers (1960s to mid-1980s), to syntheses that focused on the domains of knowledge essential for good teaching (1980s to 1990s), to research about the outcomes of teacher education and the links to student learning (1990s to today). While one might wonder why we have not yet developed strong linkages between teacher education and student outcomes, it is important to remember that such studies require longitudinal cross-institutional research and access to student achievement data bases in ways that link achievement data to specific teachers. Unfortunately, until recently there has been little funding for this kind of evaluative research, nor has there been the availability of and access to databases needed to conduct such studies.

At present, teacher education researchers are working to distill from available, peer-reviewed research clear conclusions about the impact of the full range of teacher preparation programs or paths and, more specifically, the impact of components of teacher education programs on teacher quality and student outcomes. . . . (Researchers are working to determine what we KNOW about the practices most likely to prepare high quality teachers.)

While Rice finds sufficient research to conclude that "there is no merit in large-scale elimination of all credential requirements," Shulman has pointed out that neither teacher education nor certification can be considered a variable, because both are ill-defined and vary from setting to setting. Instead, he argues that teacher education researchers need to document the impact of various components of teacher education on both teacher and student learning. Thus, the most important question for teacher education researchers is, "What components of teacher education programs (whether traditional or alternative) are critical to produce highly qualified teachers?"

Recent reviews of available research in both general and special education teacher education suggest that currently available research provides more questions than answers. At this point, the available research evidence suggests:

- Content knowledge is important for teachers, particularly those in secondary education. However, developing subject matter knowledge is more complex than completing a major in one's discipline or taking some specified number of courses. Research does not tell us how much content preparation is sufficient or whether certain courses provide better preparation than others. Additionally, most content related studies have been done in the areas of math and science, and provide little guidance related to teachers in other content areas, or in elementary or special education.
- Pedagogical preparation strengthens the skills of teachers. In fact, Goldhaber and Brewer found that pedagogical preparation of teachers had a larger impact on student achievement in math and science than content preparation. Similarly, Rice concludes that "it appears that having subject matter expertise is necessary but not sufficient. A number of Studies . . . suggest that teachers must learn and practice how to apply that knowledge in classroom settings, implying an important role for pedagogical training." However, studies of this issue do not tell us how much or what kinds of pedagogical preparation teachers need, nor do they tell us whether pedagogical knowledge is better developed in a general course (e.g. an instructional strategies course), or as part of content specific courses. Available research suggests that subject specific preparation is of critical importance for high school mathematics teachers, but the impact of subject specific pedagogical preparation for other content areas, elementary education, or special education is less apparent, and in some cases even negative.

- Preservice teachers learn more from focused, well-structured clinical experience than from other kinds of field experiences. . . . While available research provides evidence that field experience provides opportunity to "learn the profession" and reduces the anxiety of beginning teachers we know little about the impact of different forms of clinical experience on the practice of novice teachers and the learning of their students. In addition, we know little about the contribution of fieldwork versus the contribution of course work on the development of knowledge and skills in novice teachers.

Clearly, our knowledge about the components of effective teacher education is still emerging. One of the challenges to further developing this area of research is that there are few cross-institutional studies available and that the studies that do exist seldom link findings to future classroom practice or to subsequent student outcomes. . . .

What Are the Implications of the Current Political Climate for Teacher Education and Special Education?

The national discussions regarding the definition of a "highly qualified" teacher and what constitutes high quality teacher preparation have significant implications for special education. Recent research indicates that the shortage of fully certified teachers in special education is greater than in any other area, including mathematics, science, and foreign language. Currently, 47,532 or 11.4% of all special education teachers in the U.S. lack full certification for their current teaching assignment. These teachers provide instruction for 800,000 students with disabilities. Thus, the greatest shortage of 'highly qualified' teachers is in the area where students have the greatest need for teachers with the most expertise, special education.

To address this severe shortage of special education teachers, some states have lowered standards for obtaining certification in keeping with NCLB, to allow anyone who has a bachelor's degree and can pass a test to be certified. Moreover, many states have approved quick, alternative paths to certification via routes that do not meet the standards of traditional teacher education programs or the characteristics of intensive, high quality alternative routes to licensure. These actions will result in the placement of many teachers into special education classrooms who are called "highly qualified", yet in many instances lack the most basic preparation for successfully teaming students with disabilities. Furthermore, these actions may well exacerbate shortages in special education, as the attrition rates for graduates of short-cut routes to certification are significantly higher (up to three times greater) than those of graduates from traditional teacher education programs.

At the same time that states have lowered requirements for certification via some routes, the movement toward demanding increasingly higher standards for all students, coupled with the professionalization movement in teacher education has resulted in increasing requirements for traditional . . . program approval in these same and many other states. These higher requirements will likely result in *fewer* prospective teachers in traditional teacher education programs, as these candidates seek out alternative paths to certification that are less time-consuming and less demanding.

With these ideas in mind, it seems highly likely that the reform agendas that are currently playing out in Washington and in statehouses across the U.S. will result in *fewer* special education teachers who have the qualifications to successfully teach students with disabilities, rather than more 'highly qualified' teachers. . . .

While teaching and teacher education have always been influenced by national policy and legislation, many educators currently contend that the controls set by policymakers are both more intrusive and more troubling than has ever been the case. Special educators do not have a long history of research in teacher education. In fact most research in special education has focused on the nature and impact of specific interventions on the learning or behavior of children. Clearly, this research has been and continues to be highly important. However, if we are to have an impact on policy related to teacher education, which is setting (and will continue to set for the foreseeable future) policy that will shape the nature and training of teachers in special education classrooms, it is time for more special educators to study the education of our teachers, so that we will have research based evidence to influence these policy decisions.

POSTSCRIPT

Will NCLB Requirements Produce Highly Qualified Special Education Teachers?

The call for highly qualified special education teachers comes during a critical teacher shortage. A comprehensive study revealed that a nation-wide scarcity of special education teachers has existed for 15 years and is greater than shortages in mathematics and science (McLeskey, Tyler, and Flippin, *The Journal of Special Education,* 2004).

Unease about this predicament comes from several fronts. Margaret Spellings, Paige's successor, noted that staffing problems in self-contained special education classes remain among the most persistent (*Key Policy Letter,* October, 2005). Her concern is echoed by administrators in both rural (Hardman, Rosenburg, and Sindelar, *Rural Special Education Quarterly,* 2005) and urban (Nagle and Crawford, *Journal of Special Education Leadership,* 2005) settings. In its fourth report studying NCLB implementation, the Center on Education Policy (www.cep-dc.org, 2006) found states cite locating highly qualified special education teachers as their biggest challenge.

In his *Second Annual Report on Teacher Quality,* Paige (2003) advocated a "high standards, low barriers" approach to improving teacher quality. Acknowledging particular staffing stresses in urban and rural areas, Paige encouraged alternative preparation programs to offer streamlined paths to the classroom. These would attract nontraditional candidates who bring content expertise with them.

McLeskey and Ross emphasize that alternative routes often are held to looser standards than are traditional programs. They are concerned that a bachelor's degree and a passing test score will not guarantee someone capable of successfully teaching students with disabilities. Similar concerns are expressed by other researchers (Gelman, Pullen, & Kauffman, *Exceptionality,* 2004; Torff, *Phi Delta Kappan,* 2005).

Others are troubled about the "highly qualified" expectations, themselves. Describing the regulations as nothing more than pretense, Rebell and Hunter (*Phi Delta Kappan,* 2004) find NCLB's intentions weakened because state licensing standards differ widely. They observe that NCLB does not require anyone to demonstrate that they can "translate their academic knowledge into effective instruction for even the easiest-to-educate students." And yet, they note that the groups most targeted by NCLB—including students with disabilities—demand the most skillful instruction.

McCormick (*TEACHING Exceptional Children,* 2005) concedes that experienced chemists might transfer their knowledge to advanced high school students. However, he objects strenuously to reducing elements of strong traditional programs: training to assess students with disabilities, modify learning environments, adapt curricula, and select and implement appropriate behavioral supports. He is concerned that a shift in emphasis sacrifices the essence of special education, leading to distrust and litigation.

Viewing highly qualified teacher requirements from their legal perspective, Jameson and Huefner (*Journal of Law and Education*, 2006) hypothesize that current tensions between teacher quality, student achievement, and educational placement might ultimately be resolved through litigation. Several court cases have supported education in the least-restrictive environment. Will parents prefer supported inclusive environments or those with the most content-trained teachers? If parents pursue a combination of opportunities, will a new model of inclusion be ordered—successfully blending the content expertise of a general education teacher with the instructional expertise of a special educator?

Perhaps general education teachers will need more competence in special education knowledge and strategies. A noted scholar of special education teacher attrition and retention, Billingsley (*Journal of Special Education Leadership*, 2005) observes that principals must actively support meaningful, effective collaboration between general education and special education teachers through consistent planning time and mentoring.

Can co-teaching teams blend the talents of two highly qualified teachers to create ideal programs? Will NCLB's content emphasis create special education teachers unable to deliver the specially designed instruction that is the hallmark of IDEA?

ISSUE 10

Can Scientifically Based Research Guide Instructional Practice?

YES: Samuel L. Odom, Ellen Brantlinger, Russell Gersten, Robert H. Horner, Bruce Thompson, and Karen R. Harris, from "Research in Special Education: Scientific Methods and Evidence-Based Practices," *Exceptional Children* (Winter 2005)

NO: Frederick J. Brigham, William E. Gustashaw III, Andrew L. Wiley, and Michele St. Peter Brigham, from "Research in the Wake of the No Child Left Behind Act: Why the Controversies Will Continue and Some Suggestions for Controversial Research," *Behavioral Disorders* (May 2004)

ISSUE SUMMARY

YES: Samuel L. Odom, Ellen Brantlinger, Russell Gersten, Robert H. Horner, Bruce Thompson, and Karen R. Harris, all college faculty members and educational researchers, begin their article with definitive support for research-based methodology. They herald proposals for quality indicators, to establish rigor in an array of research methods that can identify effective educational practices.

NO: Frederick J. Brigham, associate professor at the University of Virginia, Charlottesville; William E. Gustashaw III and Andrew L. Wiley, both doctoral candidates at the University of Virginia, Charlottesville; and Michele St. Peter Brigham, a special education practitioner, believe that disagreement, mistrust, and the shifting general education environment preclude the usefulness of scientifically based research to guide daily instruction.

Dismayed by decades of flat results on the National Assessment of Educational Progress, the framers of No Child Left Behind (NCLB) emphatically state that educators must use interventions based on scientifically based research "that involves the application of rigorous, systematic, and objective procedures to obtain reliable and valid knowledge" (NCLB, 2001). Interventions encompass educational practices, strategies, curriculum, and programs.

A profusion of educational materials now claim to be scientifically based. Close comparison with NCLB requirements may reveal that, although some may rely on the research done by others, they do not measure up to NCLB standards. This issue explores the controversy swirling around the application of these standards.

Two resources are available to assist educators in understanding the meaning and application of scientifically based research: *Identifying and Implementing Educational Practices Supported by Rigorous Evidence: A User Friendly Guide* (Institute of Educational Sciences, 2003) and the What Works Clearinghouse (http://www.whatworks.ed.gov). A third resource, the NICHCY's Research Center (http://research.nichcy.org) debuted in February 2006, focusing solely on special education.

Noting that many educational practices have been supported by "poorly-designed studies and/or advocacy-driven studies" (p. iii), the authors of *Identifying and Implementing* "seek(s) to provide educational practitioners with user-friendly tools to distinguish practices supported by rigorous evidence from those that are not" (p. iii).

This useful guide begins by defining NCLB's "gold standard" of evidence: randomized controlled trials (RCT), which are "studies that randomly assign individuals to an intervention group or to a control group, in order to measure the effects of the intervention" (p. 1). Briefly, students, similar on critical variables, are randomly assigned into two groups. One receives the intervention; the other does not. If the first group significantly outperforms the second, the intervention can be said to be effective. Similar students ensure that no other factors could account for the results. Random assignment of these students ensures that no bias differentiated the groups.

The What Works Clearinghouse (WWC), an online resource, "collects, screens, and identifies studies" on topic areas such as middle school mathematics, and reports "on the strengths and weaknesses of those studies against the WWC Evidence Standards so that you know what the best scientific evidence has to say." In addition to using RCT, the strongest evidence comes from studies that have lasted at least a semester, have outcome measures, and have been published in peer-reviewed journals.

Educational researchers have risen to this challenge. A number of prominent research-based journals have published thematic issues on the topic of scientifically based methodologies.

Our first selection is the lead article in one of these thematic issues. Odom, Brantlinger, Gersten, Horner, Thompson, and Harris review the considerable history of special education research. Embracing the use of scientific data to guide practice, Odom et al. discuss research stages, each of which requires specific methods to identify scientifically supported interventions.

In the second selection, Brigham, Gustashaw, Wiley, and Brigham argue that even gold-standard evidence will not resolve the controversies surrounding practices in special education. They believe competing motives, perspectives, and goals will not be eliminated by evidence. They also wonder if today's research findings will be relevant in the rapidly changing schools of tomorrow.

As you read these articles, ask yourself if the methods used in your school could stand up to gold-standard scrutiny. Can the assistance of *The User Friendly Guide* and WWC help you make better choices? Will parents, teachers, and administrators agree on the choices? What happens if they disagree?

YES ↵ Samuel L. Odom et al.

Research in Special Education: Scientific Methods and Evidence-Based Practices

Should science guide practice in special education? Most individuals would say "Yes." However, the "devil is in the details." Major initiatives in other disciplines such as medicine, the allied health professions, and psychology are attempting to identify and disseminate practices that have scientific evidence of effectiveness. In education, national policies such as the No Child Left Behind Act (NCLB) require that teachers use scientifically proven practices in their classrooms. Yet, there is concern about the quality of scientific research in the field of education and disagreement about the type of scientific information that is acceptable as evidence. An oft-cited report from the National Research Council (NRC) states that science in education consists of different types of questions and that different methodologies are needed to address these questions. In contrast, other agencies and research synthesis organizations (e.g., the What Works Clearinghouse [WWC]) have focused primarily on the question of whether a practice is effective and proposed that the "gold standard" for addressing this question is a single type of research methodology—randomized experimental group designs (also called randomized clinical trials or RCTs).

In January 2003, the Council for Exceptional Children's (CEC) Division for Research established a task force to address these devilish details as they apply to special education. The operating assumptions of this task force were that different types of research questions are important for building and documenting the effectiveness of practices, and that different types of methodologies are essential in order to address these questions. The task force identified four types of research methodologies in special education: (a) experimental group, (b) correlational, (c) single subject, and (d) qualitative designs. The task force was to establish quality indicators for each methodology and to propose how evidence from each methodology could be used to identify and understand effective practices in special education. . . .

This article provides a context and rationale for this endeavor. We begin with a discussion of the importance of multiple scientific methodologies in special education research. Next, we examine efforts to identify

From *Exceptional Children*, vol. 71, no. 2, Winter 2005, pp. 137–148. Copyright © 2005 by Council for Exceptional Children. Reprinted by permission. www.cec.spend.org

high-quality research methodology and then examine initiatives in the fields of medicine and education to identify evidence-based practice. In conclusion, we propose that research and development on effective practices in special education exists on a continuum, with each methodology matched to questions arising from different points of the continuum. Also, it is important to acknowledge that although basic research serves as the foundation for the development of effective practices and is critically important for our work in special education, the issues addressed in this article will be most relevant for applied research.

Rationale for Multiple Scientific Research Methodologies in Special Education

The rationale for having different research methodologies in special education is based on the current conceptualization of research in education and the complexity of special education as a field. The history and tradition of special education research, when employing multiple methodologies, has resulted in the identification of effective practices.

Current Conceptualization of Research in Education

A primary emphasis in education policy today is to improve the quality of education for all of America's children. This policy, exemplified by NCLB, compels educators to use "teaching practices that have been proven to work." However, a general concern has been voiced about the quality of research in education. To address this concern, the National Academy of Sciences (NAS) created a committee to examine the status of scientific research in education. An operating assumption of this committee was that research questions must guide researchers' selections of scientific methods. The NAS committee proposed that most research questions in education could be grouped into three types: (a) description (what is happening?); (b) cause (is there a systematic effect?); and (c) process or mechanism (why or how is it happening?). The committee conveyed two important points about these types of research and their associated questions. First, each type of question is scientific. Second, the different types of questions require different types of methodologies. It follows that each type of methodology that empirically, rigorously, and appropriately addresses these questions is also legitimately scientific. Scientists and social philosophers as diverse as B. F. Skinner, John Dewey, and J. Habermas have emphasized that the appropriate match between question and methodology is an essential feature of scientific research.

Complexity of Special Education as a Field

In his commentary on the NAS report on scientific research in education and the policy emphasizing use of RCTs implied by NCLB, Berliner noted that such a conceptualization of science is based on hard sciences, such as physics, chemistry, and biology. He proposed that science in education is not a hard science but it is the "hardest-to-do science." Berliner stated,

> We [educational researchers] do our science under conditions that physical scientists find intolerable. We face particular problems and must deal with local conditions that limit generalizations and theory building—problems that are different from those faced by the easier-to-do sciences [chemistry, biology, medicine].

Special education research, because of its complexity, may be the hardest of the hardest-to-do science. One feature of special education research that makes it more complex is the variability of the participants. The Individuals with Disabilities Education Act (IDEA) identifies 12 eligibility (or disability) categories in special education (Office of Special Education and Rehabilitation Services [OSERS]), and within these categories are several different identifiable conditions. For example, in addition to "typical" learning disabilities, attention deficit/hyperactive disorder is often subsumed under the Specific Learning Disabilities category. Autism is now widely conceptualized as a spectrum consisting of four disorders. Mental retardation varies on the range of severity. Emotional and behavioral disorders consist of externalizing and internalizing disorders. Visual and hearing impairments range in severity from mildly impaired to totally blind or profoundly deaf. Physical impairment can be exhibited as hypotonia or hypertonia. Other health impaired may incorporate health conditions as distinct and diverse as asthma, epilepsy, and diabetes. Adding to this variability is the greater ethnic and linguistic diversity that, unfortunately, occurs in special education because of overrepresentation of some minority groups.

A second dimension of complexity is the educational context. Special education extends beyond the traditional conceptualization of "schooling" for typical students. Certainly many students with disabilities attend general education classes. However, the continuum of special education contexts is broader than general education. At one end of the chronological continuum, infants, toddlers, and many preschoolers receive services in their home or in an inclusive child care setting outside of the public school settings (e.g., Head Start Centers). For school-age students with disabilities, placement sometimes occurs in special education classes or a combination of special education and general education classes. For adolescents and young adults with disabilities, special education may take place in community living or vocational settings in preparation for the transition out of high school and into the workplace.

Complexity in special education has several implications for research. Researchers cannot just address a simple question about whether a practice in special education is effective; they must specify clearly for whom the practice is effective and in what context. The heterogeneity of participant characteristics poses a significant challenge to research designs based on establishing equivalent groups, even when randomization and stratification is possible. Certain disabilities have a low prevalence, so methodologies that require a relatively large number of participants to build the power of the analysis may be very difficult or not feasible. In addition, because IDEA ensures the right to a free appropriate public education, some research and policy questions (e.g., Are IEPs effective in promoting student progress?) may not be addressable through research methodologies that require random assignment to a "nontreatment" group or condition. Last, in special education, students with disabilities are often "clustered" in classrooms, and in experimental group design, the classroom rather than the student becomes the unit on which researchers base random assignment, data analysis, and power estimates.

History of Special Education Research

Special education research has a long history in which different methodologies have been employed. In the early 19th century beginning with Itard's foundational work, *The Wild Boy of Aveyron,* there was a tradition of discovery, development, experimentation, and verification. Initially, the research methods employed in the field that was to become special education research were derived from medicine. Many of the early pioneers in services for individuals with disabilities (Itard, Seguin, Montessori, Fernald, Goldstein) were physicians. Similarly, early services for individuals with disabilities occurred in residential facilities and training schools, which were based on the medical tradition of care.

As psychology, sociology, and anthropology became academic disciplines, they provided methodological tools for research in special education. For example, Skeels's and Kirk's works, respectively, on early experiences and preschool education for infants and young children with mental retardation employed experimental and quasi-experimental group designs prominent in psychology. Edgerton's research on individuals with mental retardation who left institutions and moved to the community, drew from methods in sociology and anthropology. In academic instructional studies, Lovitt and Haring based their methodology on the then newly created single-subject design methodology of the time. Farber's important early work on families of children with disabilities and continuing through work by Blacher and Dunst had its roots in family sociology. Many of the current special education research tools now frequently employed, such as sophisticated multivariate designs, qualitative research designs, and program evaluation designs, have their roots in general education and educational psychology. Today a range of methodological approaches are available to researchers in special education as a result of this rich history.

More than One Research Methodology
Is Important in Special Education Research

A current initiative of the U.S. Department of Education is to improve the quality of research in the field of education, with the rationale that improved research will lead to improved practice. A major effort to improve quality has come through the establishment in 2003 of the

Institute of Education Sciences (IES), whose mission is to expand fundamental knowledge about education. A central theme advocated by IES is to focus research on the questions of effectiveness and to employ high-quality research methods to address these questions. The gold standard for research methodology that addresses these issues is the use of RCT methodology. The IES acknowledges that different methodologies are important for addressing different questions.

The increased use of RCT methodology, when conducted well, will undoubtedly enhance the quality of research in education and special education. Rigorously conducted RCT studies have greater capacity to control for threats to internal validity than do quasi-experimental designs that are often used in special education. Because of this greater experimental control, Gersten et al. propose that random assignment to experimental groups is one indicator of high-quality group design research. The IES and Department of Education policy of encouraging RCT studies may well move the field closer to the goal of identifying evidence-based special education practices. But again, there are devilish details that challenge the near exclusive use of this methodology for investigating effective practices in special education.

In special education, other methodologies, such as single-subject designs, are experimental and may be a better fit for some research contexts and participant characteristics. Powerful correlational methodologies may suggest causal relationships by statistically controlling for competing hypotheses and may be essential for addressing causal-like questions when researchers are not able to conduct experimental group or single-subject design studies. The discovery and development of new effective practices may require researchers to work in naturalistic contexts where they may not be able to exert experimental control and/or in design experiments, or where they have the flexibility of changing certain elements of an intervention based on students' responses. Such descriptive and process-oriented research may require the use of qualitative methods. Educational researchers have acknowledged the value of mixing methodologies to provide a complementary set of information that would more effectively (than a single method) inform practice.

Quality Indicators of Research Methodology

Quality indicators are the feature of research that represents rigorous application of methodology to questions of interest. They may serve as guidelines for (a) researchers who design and conduct research, (b) reviewers who evaluate the "believability" of research findings, and (c) consumers who need to determine the "usability" of research findings. High-quality research is designed to rule out alternative explanations for both the results of the study and the conclusions that researchers draw. The higher the quality of research methodology, the more confidence the researcher and readers will have in the findings of the study.

Textbooks on educational research describe the methodology that investigators should follow, but they usually do not provide a succinct or understandable set of indicators that are useful for individuals who lack graduate training on research methodology. Several professional organizations have developed standards for describing and, in some cases, evaluating research. Division 16 of the American Psychological Association (APA) and the Society for the Study of School Psychology have established criteria for evaluating group design, single-subject design, and qualitative methodology used in research on practices in school psychology. Similarly, APA Division 12 Task Force on Psychological Interventions has established criteria primarily for experimental group designs studies used to provide support for therapies in clinical psychology and clinical child psychology. The CEC Division for Early Childhood (DEC) created procedures for describing research methodology for studies using group, single-subject, and qualitative research methodology, which they used to determine recommended practices for early intervention/early childhood special education. These standards have been used to determine the quality of research methods employed; however, they have not been published as quality indicators that other researchers could use.

In their work on summarizing evidence for effective practices, which will be described in the next section, some research synthesis organizations have established evaluation criteria and methods for determining the quality of research. For example, the WWC created an evaluation instrument, called the Design and Implementation Assessment Device (DIAD), with which a rater could conduct an extremely detailed evaluation of a research article. At this writing, a DIAD has only been created for experimental and quasi-experimental group design, but the WWC reports that DIADs are also being constructed for single-subject and qualitative group designs. Other research synthesis organizations, such as the Campbell Collaboration and the Evidence for Policy and Practice Information Centre (EPPIC), have somewhat similar research evaluation procedures.

Efforts described here illustrate the progress that professional and governmental organizations have made toward establishing standards for quality in research. To date, however, such quality indicators have not been identified specifically for research in special education. As noted, the purpose of the work conducted by this task force was to establish a set of quality indicators that were clearly stated, understandable, and readily available for use as guides for identifying high-quality research in special education. These quality indicators are presented in the articles appearing in this special issue.

Evidence-Based Practice

The type and magnitude of evidence needed to verify a practice as evidence-based is a prominent issue in the discussion of scientific research and effective educational practices. These devilish details are critical for policymakers, practitioners, educational researchers, and consumers. Current endeavors to establish standards for evidence-based practice as well as to identify the evidence-based-practices themselves, are occurring through two different, but related, initiatives. In this section, we describe briefly the history of identifying effective practices first in medicine and then other social science fields, efforts by professional organizations to identify effective practices, and similar efforts being conducted by research synthesis organizations.

Identifying Evidence-Based Practice

Like the evolution of special education research methods noted previously, the search for evidence-based practice originated in the field of medicine. Although the practice of evidence-based medicine extends back to the mid 19th century, the modern era of evidence-based practice emerged in the early 1970s and 1980s and came into fruition in Great Britain in the early 1990s. Cutspec tracked the evolution of evidence-based medicine from a movement that began with the intent to address the gap between research and practitioners' provision of medical care, moved to the use of the literature to inform practice decisions, and then became an approach to practicing medicine. Evidence-based practice is now a central part of medical education, education in allied health professions such as nursing, and counselor education.

General and special education have followed suit in adopting scientific evidence as the appropriate basis for selecting teaching practices. The impetus for the current evidence-based movement in education is similar to that in medicine: A concern that effective educational practices, as proven by research, are not being used in schools. This current concern reflects a long-standing discussion in the field of special education regarding the distance between research and practice. In response, a large number of initiatives have been established to identify practices that will generate positive outcomes for children. Two types of groups are sponsoring these initiatives: research synthesis organizations and professional associations that propose standards for practice.

Research Synthesis Organizations.   Research synthesis organizations systematically evaluate and aggregate findings from the research literature in order to inform practitioners. Perhaps the largest and longest standing synthesis organization is the Cochrane Collaboration . . . , located in Great Britain and founded in 1963. This organization, which focuses on medical and health research, consists of over 50 collaborative review groups and has completed over 1,300 reviews. Following this model, the Campbell Collaboration . . . was established in the United States in 1999 to assist individuals in education and the social sciences to make informed decisions about what works based on high-quality research and reviews. In Great Britain, EPPIC at the University of London Institute of Education . . . was created in 1993 to conduct systematic reviews of research on social interventions. This organization was recently funded to conduct reviews specifically on educational practices, which it plans to make available through their Research Evidence in Education Library. . . .

In the United States, the IES has established the WWC . . . , which is jointly managed by the Campbell Collaboration and the American Institutes for Research. WWC conducts reviews of educational practices supported by high-quality research and makes this information available to practitioners through Web-based databases. The U.S. Department of Education funds the Research and Training Center on Early Childhood Development (CED) . . . , which is conducting a set of practice-sensitive research syntheses on the effectiveness (and ineffectiveness) of practices for infants and young children with disabilities and their families. Whereas other organizational efforts primarily provide evidence that a practice is effective, the CED has created a more functional operational definition by stating that evidence-based practices are informed by research, in which the characteristics and consequences of environmental variables are empirically established and the relationship directly informs what a practitioner can do to produce the desired outcome.

To examine the effectiveness of programs for children with autism, a committee formed by NAS established guidelines for the strength of evidence provided by individual studies. The dimensions of the studies evaluated were internal validity, external validity, and generalization, with strength of evidence (i.e., from I to IV) evaluated for each.

A key feature in these research synthesis initiatives is the methodological criteria established to select or exclude research studies for the synthesis. Most organizations confined evidence of effectiveness to research studies that have employed RCT methodology or rigorously constructed quasi-experimental designs. The CED researchers took a broader view of the empirical linkage between a practice and an outcome and looked for descriptions of the process of the intervention practices that led to the outcome. The leadership of the WWC has noted that qualitative research may provide information about the ways in which interventions work and can be used to substantiate "promising practices" in education, although they proposed that clearly efficacious practices would require verification through RCTs. For the EPPIC, Oakley reported that they incorporated qualitative research in their reviews, but they had encountered multiple problems in their evaluation of qualitative studies.

Professional Associations.   Professional associations and groups have also examined the literature to determine effective practices. These groups have often established the level of evidence needed to identify a practice as effective. For example, the Child-Clinical Section of Division 12 of the APA established the Task Force on Empirically Supported Psychosocial Interventions for Children. They proposed the types and amount of evidence needed to identify a practice as (a) well-established (i.e., two well-conducted group design studies by different researchers or nine well-conducted single-subject designs); or (b) "probably efficacious" (i.e., two group design studies by same investigator or at least three single-subject design studies).

The Division for Early Childhood of CEC established a process for identifying recommended practices that incorporated evidence from the research literature. Mentioned previously, DEC conducted an extensive literature review to identify support for recommended practices and also to incorporate information from focus groups of experts, practitioners, and family members in the final identification of practices. The level or type of evidence needed to support a recommended practice was not identified.

The American Speech-Language-Hearing Association (ASHA) proposed that different types of evidence may be important for different clinical activities. For questions of treatment efficacy, they propose that different frameworks are available for evaluating the level of evidence that documents efficacy. They provide as an example one such framework developed by the Oxford Centre for Evidence-based Medicine. This system could be used to classify practices according to four levels of evidence:

- Level I evidence derives from meta-analyses including at least one randomized experimental design or well-designed randomized control studies.
- Level II evidence includes controlled studies without randomization and quasi-experimental designs.
- Level III consists of well-designed nonexperimental studies (i.e., correlational and case studies).
- Level IV includes expert committee report, consensus conference, and clinical experience of respected authorities.

The ASHA policy emphasizes that other frameworks are currently available or evolving and could be useful for specific questions related to treatment efficacy.

To date, the special education community has yet to develop systematic guidelines for specifying the types and levels of evidence needed to identify a practice as evidence-based and effective. The Division for Learning Disabilities (DLD) and the Division for Research (DR) jointly published a document entitled *Alerts,* in which an expert from the field reviews the literature relevant to a specific practice and describes the evidence or lack of evidence that underlies the practice. These alerts, however, have been based on individual authors' reviews of the literature and, although quite useful, different authors may well be using different criteria for the evidence they include. The second goal of the current DR Task Force, therefore, was to describe the types of results generated by each research methodology and to recommend guidelines for using the results as evidence of effectiveness, or lack of effectiveness, of practices in special education.

Where Do We Go from Here?

The Department of Education is under pressure to prove to Congress that there are educational practices that have evidence of effectiveness and that supporting educational research is a good investment of public funds. In specifying RCT methodology as the gold standard for research, the Department of Education is investing the bulk of research funding in addressing the question of effectiveness, which is clearly important. However, Berliner urges us to avoid confusing science with a specific method or technique. It is more important to look at the broader goal of using science to improve education for all children.

To accomplish such a goal, educational science might be more appropriately seen as a continuum rather than a fixed point. Levin, O'Donnell, and Kratochwill suggest that a program of educational research might be thought of as occurring in four stages. The first stage would involve observational, focused exploration and flexible methodology, which qualitative and correlational methods allow. Stage 2 would involve controlled laboratory or classroom experiments, observational studies of classrooms, and teacher-researcher collaborative experiments. Design experimentation involving qualitative methodology, single-subject designs, quasi-experimental and/or RCT design could be useful at that stage. Stages to design well-documented interventions and "prove" their effectiveness through well-controlled RCT studies implemented in classroom or naturalistic settings by the natural participants (e.g., teachers) in the settings. We propose that single-subject design studies could also accomplish this purpose.

If research ended here, however, the movement of effective, evidence-based research into practices that teachers use on Monday morning would likely fail. A further step in the development process (Stage 4) would be to determine the factors that lead to adoption of effective practices in typical school systems under naturally existing conditions. That last step would require research into organizational factors that facilitate or impede adoption of innovation in local contexts. The research methodologies that would generate this information are more likely qualitative, correlational, and mixed methods, as well as RCT and large-scale, single-case designs. Researchers may well draw from such disciplines as sociology, political science, economics, as well as education, in this research. Research at this stage may best occur though a partnership among researchers from education, researchers from other disciplines, local education agencies, and teachers. Indeed, an initiative is emerging from another panel convened by the NRC, which is proposing a broad federal initiative that would create just such a partnership.

Conclusion

If different methodologies are appropriate for addressing important questions in special education, then we, as a field, need to be clear about (a) the match between research questions and methodology, (b), the features of each methodology that represent high quality, (c) and the use of research findings for each methodology as scientific evidence for effective practices in special education. To date, we have numerous texts and papers that describe each methodology, but they are not a coordinated, clear index of how each contributes to the present research-to-practice challenge. . . .

Frederick J. Brigham et al. **NO**

Research in the Wake of the No Child Left Behind Act: Why the Controversies Will Continue and Some Suggestions for Controversial Research

The unique and sometimes competing interests of key stakeholders, which often drive the development of educational policy, may lead to misunderstanding and confusion. For example, policies espoused by educational advocates and the pragmatic management procedures of educational administrators are sometimes difficult to understand for educators who advocate the adoption of scientific practices. This is because science and advocacy have different traditions and purposes. Scientists begin from a position of doubt and collect evidence, whereas advocates are more likely to begin from a position of certainty. A different point of view yet is held by administrators and policymakers, who must work within the political system and deal with the realities of compromise and communication that affect policy development.

Given the differing perspectives and traditions of the stakeholders in educational reform, it is unlikely that any major educational policy will be without controversy. However, if a coherent educational policy is to be developed, controversial issues must be decided according to some framework. Failure to adopt a coherent position is likely to lead to a hodge-podge of competing initiatives rather than a broadened range of educational opportunities.

In 2001, the interests of various stakeholders were brought together in the passage of the No Child Left Behind (NCLB) Act. A crucial component of NCLB was the requirement that educators use practices that are validated through scientific research. This presents a useful opportunity for individuals concerned with the education of children with emotional or behavioral disorders (E/BD) to introduce scientifically validated practices into the classroom and collect data related to a number of important questions—mainly questions regarding better ways of providing instruction in academic skills. However, the history of educational practice suggests that consensus will be elusive at best, even with the soundest of

From *Behavioral Disorders*, 29(3) May 2004, pp. 300–310. Copyright © 2004 by CCBD Publications. Reprinted by permission.

scientific evidence. With this in mind, in this article we (a) describe reasons why educational practices will remain controversial even with the call for scientifically validated procedures and (b) suggest areas of research opportunities that NCLB may provide.

Policies, Science, Uncertainty, and Justification

To withstand debate, policies must often be crafted in such a way that people with different perceptions and purposes can recognize their interests in them. One way of creating such policies is to make the wording vague and, therefore, its meaning elusive. As a result, a variety of interpretations and actions are likely to follow from policy statements crafted into law. No Child Left Behind is no exception. For example, according to the U.S. Department of Education, "Under *No Child Left Behind,* states and school districts have unprecedented flexibility in how they use federal education funds, in exchange for greater accountability for results." Whether the flexibility provided by NCLB is real or illusory is debatable. It is clear, however, that this law, like most other policies, is open to a number of conflicting interpretations except for the bottom line—academic accountability.

One way of dealing with the uncertainty that accompanies large-scale policies is to analyze them with respect to a particular philosophical orientation. For example, the impetus for initiatives such as inclusion or whole language can be viewed as primarily philosophical rather than scientific because they are based not on data but on a sense of what should be. From this perspective, actions in violation of a philosophical orientation are irresponsible. Regrettably, acting according to philosophical principles has led to some unfortunate and ludicrous behaviors. For example, consider the behaviors exhibited by virtually any cult. The philosophic stances proclaimed by some cult leaders have led to mass suicides, killings, or other atrocities, often in the name of justice. In education, the whole language movement is probably the best known of the failed philosophies. However, movements such as facilitated communication and full inclusion are better seen as philosophical rather than scientific and empirical in their orientation. Although the evidence in support of these activities is lacking, proponents claim that they are worth implementing because they are consistent with their beliefs. However, in a zero-sum environment such as education, funds devoted to one thing are necessarily diverted from other options. Spending money on disproven programs such as facilitated communication is simply folly. A philosophical orientation, while important, is insufficient to protect the field from folly.

Scientists are more likely to endorse the position that it is foolish to act in a manner that fails to conform to the available data. This position is far from invulnerable to failure and unfortunate outcomes. Fortunately, science possesses a self-correcting mechanism that, over time, eliminates wishful thinking, self-serving bias, and erroneous beliefs from the body of accepted scientific belief. Although it has become fashionable in some circles to decry science as merely a sociopolitical activity, such a position drastically underestimates the power of science to serve society and, just as dramatically, overestimates the alternative approaches to guide decisionmaking.

The social aspects of scientific inquiry are actually a major part of science's self-correcting mechanism. The self-correcting mechanism is the major component that unifies all forms of scientific inquiry. This self-correcting mechanism limits the amount of effort expended on ideas that are unlikely to be productive and also limits the lifespan of ideas that do not produce consistent results. For example, through the self-correcting mechanism of science, strong genetic and environmental positions with regard to human behavior have given way to a more balanced interactionist perspective that accommodates both positions. In academic instruction, the idea that children would improve their spelling by drawing boxes around words and examining their shape has virtually disappeared from serious educational literature because the evidence failed to support it.

As Shermer put it:

> Science is a social process, where one is trained in a certain paradigm and works with others in the field. A community of scientists reads the same journals, goes to the same conferences, reviews one another's papers and books, and generally exchanges ideas about the facts, hypotheses, and theories in that field. Through vast experience they know, fairly quickly, which new ideas have a chance of succeeding and which are obviously wrong. Newcomers from other fields, who typically dive in with both feet without the requisite training and experience, proceed to generate new ideas that they think—because of their success in their own field—will be revolutionary. Instead, they are usually greeted with disdain (or more typically, ignored) by the professionals in the field. This is not because (as they usually think is the reason) insiders don't like outsiders (or that all great revolutionaries are persecuted or ignored), but because in most cases those ideas were considered years or decades before and rejected for perfectly good reasons.

Although the data are not always conclusive and the implications of data in social science are not always readily apparent, the absence of scientifically collected data fails to absolve policymakers and administrators from the need to act. In the absence of scientific advice, however, policymakers, administrators, practitioners, and other concerned parties often turn to influences such as tradition, currently popular ideas, ideas that are expedient at the moment, and various philosophical positions that they may hold. Sometimes the actions taken are counterproductive and actually undermine the responsible and ethical intentions of the policymakers.

If it were easy to undo these counterproductive actions and change course, we could chalk it up to learning through experience. When such policies are in place, however, they are very difficult to change even if they turn out to be unworkable. There are several reasons for this, including the following two: First, certain stakeholders have vested interests in keeping the policies intact. Second, people tend to develop justifications for their actions. Reasoning that has the appearance of rational scientific discourse is often used toward that end. In other words, it is common to find irrational actions supported by seemingly rational justifications. Thus, individuals are unlikely to engage in behavior that works contrary to their own interests (e.g., support a teacher licensing bill that would eliminate their jobs), and they are quite likely to develop elaborate ideational schemes to justify self-interested action as actually pursuant to larger and more noble motives.

Shermer provided an analysis of the ways in which people justify beliefs in "weird things." He defined weird things as:

(1) a claim unaccepted by most people in that field of study,
(2) a claim that is either logically impossible or highly unlikely, and/or
(3) a claim for which the evidence is largely anecdotal and uncorroborated

It is clear that people who are superstitious, foolish, or desperate are especially vulnerable to beliefs that fit these criteria. However, they are not the only people who fall victim to such beliefs. Smart people can also hold irrational beliefs and behave in a stupid manner. Shermer suggested that "smart people believe weird things because they are skilled at defending beliefs they arrived at for non-smart reasons." He proposed two forms of biased thinking—attribution bias and confirmation bias—that are primarily responsible for the maintenance of irrational beliefs by ostensibly rational individuals.

Attribution Bias

Attribution bias occurs when a behavior exhibited by both oneself and another person, even though identical, is suggested to have occurred for different reasons. Most often attribution bias is self-serving. That is, individuals perceive their own actions to have been for good and just reasons, whereas the same actions taken by others are dismissed as unjust and unjustifiable. Areas in which attribution bias have been noted include religious beliefs, vigilante behavior, interpersonal aggression, aggressive acts between nations, and even interpersonal relations among scientists. Ironically, even though science is described as having a major social component, Kramer found that scientists ascribed trustworthy and collegial intent to their own efforts to share resources, data, and the like with others but often believed that attempts to obtain resources, data, and the like by others were the result of untrustworthy and sinister motives.

Attribution bias in relation to NCLB is likely to result in proponents of any action being viewed with suspicion, even by others who support similar ideas. For example, suggestions that students should be excused from the state-wide and district-wide assessment requirements of both NCLB and the 1997 reauthorization of the Individuals with Disabilities Education Act (IDEA) may be viewed as serving the interests of a child by one group and as an attempt to inflate a school's test scores by another. Whereas the extreme positions are easily identified, the likelihood is that the truth lies somewhere between these polar opposite.

We suggest that the production of scientific data is the best way to identify the most probable location of the truth between the self-serving poles of any debate. It must be noted, however, that scientific data can be determined as good or useful only in relation to a specific purpose or set of purposes. Therefore, the initial task facing producers of scientific research is to decide which goal or set of goals is most important to pursue. This is a difficult task that is far from being accomplished in education.

The implication of attribution bias is that, as individuals, we tend to attribute to ourselves greater nobility in purpose than we do our fellow citizens, and, as a nation, we are less than clear and unified about our educational goals. Thus, the call for scientifically based practices in education will probably do little to lessen the conflict surrounding any instructional method or decision.

Confirmation Bias

Confirmation bias, as it is commonly used in psychological literature, refers to the seeking or interpreting of evidence in ways that conform to existing beliefs, expectations, or a hypothesis in hand. According to Shermer, people often believe weird things because they have a "tendency to seek or interpret evidence favorable to already existing beliefs, and to ignore or reinterpret evidence unfavorable to already existing beliefs." As a result, people tend to find what they are looking for even if it is not there.

Confirmation bias is often the result of determining the truth by checking only positive and not negative instances. Although it is certainly more pleasant to examine the reasons for our successes, a full understanding can be reached only if we consider the reasons for our failures as well. Many of the controversial treatments for disabilities appear to be supported by confirmation bias. Rather than providing clear data obtained under replicable conditions, proponents of less-accepted treatments (and some popular but refuted treatments, e.g., modality-based instruction) use anecdotal evidence about how the treatment worked for them or a given child to assure decisionmakers that it will, therefore, work for others as well.

The evidence regarding the practice of coteaching appears to be one such product of confirmation bias. Weiss and Brigham pointed out that the studies that purportedly support coteaching were highly flawed in that they often failed to define coteaching, employed only teachers who were satisfied with their instructional arrangements, employed such vague outcome indicators as "improved" or "more accepted," and failed to describe what the teachers involved in coteaching did. Weiss concluded that coteaching was often used to meet the needs of students with disabilities despite the absence of supportive evidence. In addition, she pointed out that many examples of coteaching were actually outside of the recommendations found in the literature. Nevertheless, when we discuss this evidence with teachers and parents of students with disabilities, we are often informed that the evidence may say one thing but their experience or the experience of their friends is different.

One unfortunate outcome of confirmation bias is that by focusing on information that supports a given belief, an individual's views are rarely challenged. For example, the World Wide Web, although holding the potential to open unlimited stores of information to vast numbers of people, can also have the opposite effect. Rather than focusing on a variety of viewpoints, some users simply look for statements in agreement with a given predisposition and, through repetition, reinforce the predisposition. Still another form of confirmation bias results when individuals amass large stores of information that are unified around a given proposition. Such individuals can become so entrenched in a point of view or a way of doing things that it becomes hard to see things differently.

The Impact of Attribution Bias and Confirmation Bias on Educational Research

No Child Left Behind's step in the direction of clarifying educational goals by forcing attention on academic outcomes focuses on only one of the possible goals of a school—academic achievement. Whether or not the strength of the current emphasis on academics is desirable can only be answered by science with the response "It depends." It depends on the balance that is held between academics and other ostensible goals for any given community, school, or student. The exact nature of this balance is probably better analyzed politically or economically than scientifically. Once the goals are established, science can provide substantial assistance in reaching them. However, even if a unified set of goals could be established for all children in all U.S. schools, controversies would continue to erupt.

We have described two forms of bias, attribution bias and confirmation bias, that affect individual judgment regarding any source of data. Knowing that these forms of bias (and there are more that we have not discussed here) exist can help individuals guard against them. However, knowledge of the threat alone is a necessary but insufficient cure to the problems arising from bias. The self-correcting methods of scientific inquiry can, over time, mediate these forms of bias if decisionmakers and their constituents will trust data collected with due rigor and appropriate methods and expose their own beliefs to doubt and questioning. However, "issues of belief and doubt get into some very partisan ruts." Thus, NCLB may ask more of educational leaders, educators, and parents than it does of schoolchildren.

Suggestions for Research in the Wake of No Child Left Behind

Special education practice is highly dependent on the conditions present in general education. Moreover, influences such as statewide testing and budget constraints that affect general education personnel and program managers also affect special educators. Students with mild disabilities are most often called to the attention of school officials because they have been unsuccessful in meeting the demands of general education in some way. Many of the current special education regulations and initiatives have their roots in the past 3 or 4 decades in which general education programs were expanding the number of options available to students in U.S. schools. No Child Left Behind focuses attention squarely on academic achievement as the measure of educational accountability. It is a bottom-line, outcome-driven approach to educational decisionmaking. As such, it differs in many ways from earlier approaches to educational accountability. Furthermore, the unit of analysis applied by NCLB is actually the school and its disaggregated populations, rather than the individual, as was the case historically in special education.

The trend toward academic monitoring has already affected special education programs for many students. For example, educational programs for students with severe disabilities have moved from a developmental model to a functional model and subsequently to a model that attempts to link instructional activities to academic skills taught in the general education curriculum. Although such a trend can be viewed as opening up academic avenues that previously were closed to many students, it also closes off the opportunities for developmental and functional curricula by reallocating resources and attention to other issues. Whether or not this proves to be a positive step remains to be seen. However, the focus on academic outcomes is clearly related to enabling children to fit in to the general education environment in a more satisfactory manner. Similar trends can be seen relative to the educational programs of students with E/BD. With the emphasis on general education goals, it is difficult to imagine that programs (or remediation and community-based or vocational education will receive the support necessary to serve the populations for which they were created. Rather than isolated developments in the special education community, such trends are better understood as responses to changes in the general education program.

The NCLB focus of accountability on the academic achievement of groups of students within schools will, in our opinion, call into question earlier research findings and policy decisions made relative to IDEA. This is because the nature and focus of the general education program under NCLB is different from the nature and focus under IDEA. How these differences will manifest themselves has yet to be settled. Nevertheless, changes in the general education program will, of necessity, prompt special educators to reevaluate the findings and recommendations made earlier if they wish their research findings to remain consistent with improving student performance relative to the general education curriculum. In the following sections, we suggest some specific areas of educational research that will benefit from additional scrutiny given the requirements of NCLB.

Planning and Service Delivery

Impact of Students with Disabilities on General Education

Inclusion of students with disabilities developed in an era of mostly expanding curriculum offerings and emphasis on tolerance of individual differences. The pressures to align resources with curricular areas that are measured in state- and district-wide tests appear to be narrowing the curriculum offerings of many schools in the United States. This reduction in the number of classes, coupled with the IDEA requirement of access to the general education curriculum and pressures for inclusion, suggest that more students with disabilities will be present in classes in which teachers are already experiencing increased pressure to raise their students' achievement. Students with E/BD will likely be seen as adding unnecessary impediments to the education of other students in the general education classroom. Rather than speaking of a special education student's right to receive an individualized program of special education and related services, researchers and advocates need to be able to respond with data examining the performance of students with E/BD in classes under these new pressures and curricular demands and to provide clear evidence that the education programs of other students are unaffected. Some evidence of this currently exists; however, the extent to which the conditions under which this evidence was collected reflect conditions in schools facing the bottom-line academic accountability of NCLB is unclear.

Individualized Education Programs

The backbone of a student's special education program is the individualized education program (IEP). In an era in which developmental and functional approaches prevailed, it made a great deal of sense to single out things that a given student would be learning that were different from the curriculum presented to most students. The result of the coupling of NCLB with IDEA's access to the general education curriculum clause appears to be that more students with disabilities are taking core academic classes and are to be measured by the same standards and at the same frequency as are students who have no disabilities. Under such conditions, the traditional IEP, with its detailed mapping of goals and objectives that form the curriculum for a particular student, seems redundant because the academic program delivered for students in a given classroom or course of study is dictated by the state curriculum standards. However, there may be specific benefits to this redundancy that would be better defended through data than through insistence that IEPs are clearly needed and beneficial. For example, rather than focusing on *what* a student with E/BD will do in a particular class, the IEP may still serve a useful function in describing *how* (e.g., the conditions and timelines) a student will fulfill the requirements. While it is certainly possible to craft an IEP focusing on such aspects of a student's educational program, there is little empirical evidence that educators currently know how to do so.

Another research issue related to IEPs is the extent to which they are actually individualized. Research conducted in the past several years has not been particularly supportive of the extent to which IEPs actually reflect students' educational needs or vary according to their characteristics. Indeed, our own experience with several school districts that pride themselves on the quality of their IEPs suggests that the "I" in IEP could more accurately stand for "interchangeable." Perhaps the interchangeability of IEPs is a necessary reflection of the movement to include students in the general education curriculum; perhaps it is the result of limited time, imagination, or training. Under the NCLB opportunities, it seems prudent to examine the functionality and uniqueness of the benefits of these documents relative to their costs.

Intervention

Appropriateness of a Standard Intervention Protocol for Students with Emotional or Behavioral Disorders

By *standard intervention protocol,* we mean a set of clearly defined and well-documented treatments that should be employed as a matter of course for students with behavior problems as well as for students whose problems are serious enough to warrant identifying them as having E/BD. Multiple gating procedures in E/BD, as well as "failure to respond to treatment" models for students with learning disabilities, are predicated on the proposition that children who fail to respond to interventions that would support most students are the students who are most likely in need of special education services. In that regard, it seems imperative to have a clear idea of what the word *treatment* means.

In regard to behavioral issues, treatment could mean anything from poorly executed and inconsistent reprimands to well-designed reinforcement or cognitive behavior management programs. For newly identified students, the efforts to manage problematic student behaviors are recorded in documents such as prereferral intervention plans, reports from teacher assistance teams, and other, similar reports. With proper assistance and support, teachers have been able to create useful and effective interventions for some students who otherwise would have been referred needlessly for special education evaluation. Most classroom teachers, however, are on their own in developing and maintaining behavior management programs for their classes and treatments for individual students. It is not at all clear that most school-based practitioners possess the expertise or the time and support to develop and implement unique behavior intervention programs for individual students. Furthermore, given the relatively consistent advice about general behavior management techniques provided by different tests in the field, it is not clear that unique treatments need to be developed as a first or even second step in dealing with problematic behavior.

Efforts at creating school-wide discipline programs have established baseline conditions that could be considered essential before individual treatments are implemented. Research data could be used to establish a "what to do next" category of treatment that would be recommended for students once general school-wide and class-wide efforts had failed. Such practices are commonly found in medical treatment models but have not yet taken hold in educational settings. The enormous advantage of such a system is that students would receive effective treatments more quickly and teachers would have additional guidance and assurance that they were, indeed, providing appropriate educational services to their students.

Preferred Target Domains

The obvious focus of intervention for students with E/BD is their behavior. However, behavior can serve a variety of functions, and the relationship of behavior to academic instruction is often underplayed in discussions of students with E/BD. One of the major functions of unacceptable behavior in classrooms is escape. We know that well-designed instruction is a mediator of students' behavior, yet we see little attention paid to the academic structure of the classrooms in which the misbehavior occurs.

Research on academic instruction as an antecedent is available to scholars and policy-makers. It is clear that providing students with well-designed instruction that is within their ability to master reduces the incidence of behavior problems in the classroom. However, after NCLB's changes in academic emphasis, the extent to which teachers are able or believe that they are able to deviate substantially from state curriculum guides and time-lines related to covering material before a certain test date is unknown. It is possible that little has changed since NCLB. It is also possible that the current emphasis on performance relative to test-linked standards makes general education teachers unwilling to make substantial curriculum adaptations.

The current popularity of coteaching as a service delivery model may also mediate the ability of special education teachers to provide instruction that is supportive of students with E/BD. Through coteaching arrangements, students with E/BD are considered to have their special education programs delivered to them in the general education classroom. However, as previously discussed, the model of coteaching is poorly supported for students with special education needs. In addition, the general education classroom may be a less hospitable place to deliver special education services after NCLB than it was prior to this legislation. One reason for this is the pressure exerted on teachers to cover specific content objectives regardless of student readiness or mastery of the material covered. Many special education teachers that we work with report that they and their general education colleagues experience great pressure from their district administrators to cover the content regardless of student mastery. While it is unlikely that many students will demonstrate mastery of content that has not been taught, content-coverage approaches are likely to result in incomplete teaching and partial mastery of material, particularly for nonperforming or disengaged students. As such, the NCLB standards may actually increase rather than decrease the range of achievement outcomes for students in diverse classrooms. We suggest that it is better to find out than to wonder whether this is the case.

Possible Research Outcomes

We have suggested that a number of the traditional elements of special education programming for students with E/BD should be reexamined in light of the requirements of NCLB and the changes in general education programs that are likely to evolve from implementation of that legislation. With regard to the relationship of general and special education, it is possible that the NCLB requirements place pressures on teachers that make the general education environment a less welcoming place than it was previously. It is also likely that such changes will make the general education environment a less desirable goal for students with E/BD. Another possible outcome is that NCLB actually will result in no detectable change in general education classrooms that will be relevant to the education of students with E/BD.

We also suggest that IEPs should be reexamined to determine their necessity, function, and actual ability to promote individualized treatment for students with E/BD. Related to this question, it is possible that researchers will document the necessity of the IEP for ensuring educational treatments for students with E/BD. Conversely, it is possible, given the pressure toward a standards-based curriculum and the previous evidence that IEPs are rarely *individualized*—that they no longer serve their intended function. Another possible outcome might be documentation that the important functions of IEPs could be served by a much shorter document than is typically found in the folders of students with E/BD. If that were the case, researchers could turn their attention to the essential elements of IEPs that need to be maintained or new elements that need to be created, as well as those that are superfluous to effective intervention for students with E/BD.

Finally, we suggest that the traditional target domains of E/BD intervention may be affected by NCLB-prompted changes in the general education classroom. The flexibility of general education teachers or special education teachers working in inclusive settings or under coteaching models may be far more limited in NCLB-compliant classrooms than it was previously. It may be that teachers perceive their flexibility to be curtailed but that they would be able to offer flexible instruction with appropriate guidance. Researchers could provide a great service to the field by documenting what supports are most helpful to teachers under the pressures of test-linked standards.

We suggest that NCLB has the potential to make substantial changes in the educational landscape. The direct changes are clearly established in the legislation. Other changes may emerge as indirect effects of the legislation and will benefit from the attention of educational researchers to identify and describe them as well as to validate effective methods for dealing with these changes on behalf of students with E/BD.

Conclusion

No Child Left Behind offers a number of opportunities to the educational profession in return for a strong focus on academic accountability. One of the more commonly celebrated themes of NCLB is the call for educators to use practices that have been scientifically validated by research in their efforts to serve students with disabilities.

Although the call to use scientifically validated practices appears straightforward and within our grasp given the extant body of research, several factors suggest that it will be a more difficult and demanding task than many educators and policymakers believe. One of the difficulties affecting this enterprise is the impact of attribution and confirmation biases on the judgment of decisionmakers. Such biases work to maintain the status quo by allowing individuals to believe that their motives are somehow different from and more noble than the motives of those who disagree with them and by insulating them from evidence that contradicts or undermines personal beliefs. Furthermore, scientifically validated practices for students with disabilities are effective or ineffective in inclusive schools only relative to their interaction with the programs and expectations present in the general education curriculum. By altering the emphasis of educational programs to a predominant emphasis on performance on test-linked standards, NCLB will probably result in substantial changes in the actions, climate, and expectations of general education classrooms. How these changes will affect the service delivery, instructional, and behavioral options recommended for special education teachers has yet to be seen.

Whereas many of the findings of educational research may hold true after NCLB, others may not, and the way that they are used in the classroom may need adjustment. Components of effective special education practice interact with general education programs in much the same way that notes and scales interact with key changes in musical performance. When the rest of the orchestra changes key, it is in best interests of all the players to change at the same time. Those who do not wish to do so are better advised to be soloists or to write their own music. Special educators must respond to the key changes in general education. Transposing from one key to another can take a line of music from the comfortable range of an instrument or singing voice to a range that is impossible for the performer or vice versa. If the data suggest that the NCLB changes make general education a more productive and supportive place for students with E/BD, special educators should certainly play in the orchestra. If not, it may be time to reconsider "solo projects" and resurrect the dedicated service delivery models that have faded in recent years. In either case, we should let the data, rather than our biases, guide our actions.

POSTSCRIPT

Can Scientifically Based Research Guide Instructional Practice?

Odom and his colleagues identify "devilish details" complicating research efforts in special education: the heterogeneity of disability (consider the range within the autism spectrum alone) and the complexity of the contexts of special education (preschool to young adult; home, school, and work). To conquer these challenges, and continue the necessary pursuit of scientifically gathered data, they introduce articles that present quality indicators to establish rigor within a variety of research methods.

This range of acceptable methodology is actually encouraged by the Institute for Education Sciences, which agrees that "research designs and methods (must be) appropriate to the research question posed" (WWC, *What Is Scientifically Based Research?*). Still, to fully satisfy the gold standard, findings from other methodologies must be verified through RCT.

Originally skeptical about RCT, Forness (*Behavioral Disorders,* 2005) was convinced by its successful application in mental health. Agreeing with WWC standards, Forness believes that, despite their challenges, RCT studies are the only way to control variables and discover whether an intervention makes a critical difference.

Brigham and his co-authors maintain that controversies over instruction cannot be guided by scientific research until stakeholders agree on the purpose of education. Today's policymakers see academic achievement as the goal; special educators seek improved functioning and participation in society.

Consider inclusion, an educational practice supported by IDEA and a focus of many school interventions. Under NCLB, the efficacy of inclusion must be established through RCT studies. Could control groups be identified?

Every good study must begin with an agreement of the target phenomenon. A modest survey of preservice and practicing teachers revealed no universally agreed upon definition or model of inclusion (Snyder, Garriott, and Aylor, *Teacher Education and Special Education,* 2001). Variable definitions make conducting and analyzing research challenging indeed (Simpson, *Behavioral Disorders*, 2004).

In two districts involved in a project to increase inclusionary practices, models changed as teams developed and responded to student experience (Burstein, Sears, Wilcoxen, Cabello, and Spagna, *Remedial and Special Education,* 2004). Perhaps this change itself should be studied.

In *Improving Outcomes for Students with Disabilities* (National Council on Disability, 2004), a researcher asks, "Which is more valid, the work of an evidence-based research center or the experiences of families of children with disabilities? What is the basis for the criteria? Someone's [research] numbers or someone's real life experience?" (p. 4). For advocates, inclusion is a belief system, not a program or a research-based strategy (Villa and Thousand, 2005).

And yet, at least one researcher has devised a study of inclusionary practices within an RCT model. Russell Gersten (*Learning Disabilities Theory & Practice,* 2005), takes readers "behind the scenes," describing the complex, but rewarding, process of developing and conducting a gold-standard research project on inclusion. Other articles in this issue extend the discussion of this collaboration.

Intense partnerships with funded researchers are unavailable to most teachers. Networking through professional organizations, and the journals they publish, enables educators to become informed consumers in this evidence-driven era (Simpson, LaCava, and Graner, *Intervention in School and Clinic,* 2004). What is a teacher to do, though, when a resource such as WWC has not studied any special education methodologies?

Scientists seek evidence. Parents seek change and growth. Teachers want to use the best possible techniques to help students learn. Sometimes parents may want the school team to implement a promising treatment. Is the school compelled to reject the request if it has not been validated against a control group? Or might the successes of one child stimulate a line of research inquiry that could identify a method that would help many?

If medicine and mental health use RCT, can education become more credible by doing the same? In this high-stakes time, can we afford not to do so? Can special education research be conducted in shifting school environments and be published fast enough to help teachers?

ISSUE 11

Should Students with Cognitive Disabilities Be Expected to Demonstrate Academic Proficiency?

YES: Kevin S. McGrew and Jeffrey Evans, from *Expectations for Students with Cognitive Disabilities: Is the Cup Half Empty or Half Full? Can the Cup Flow Over?* (National Center on Educational Outcomes, December 2004)

NO: James M. Kauffman, from *Education Deform: Bright People Sometimes Say Stupid Things About Education* (The Scarecrow Press, 2002)

ISSUE SUMMARY

YES: Kevin S. McGrew, educational researcher and director of the Institute for Applied Psychometrics (IAP), and Jeffrey Evans, consultant and educational researcher for IAP, are wary that stereotypes of individuals with cognitive disabilities are used to form limited (and limiting) expectations and self-fulfilling prophecies.

NO: James M. Kauffman, professor emeritus of education at the University of Virginia, Charlottesville, and special education philosopher-researcher, believes that educators and parents must acknowledge that some students with cognitive disabilities cannot reach high academic standards and are best served by programs that develop other skills.

Beginning with IDEA 97, districts were required to include students with disabilities in all large-scale testing programs. NCLB increased the stakes. Districts must report, and be held accountable for, the academic performance of students with disabilities.

Previously, the very fact that a student had a disability often meant they—and their performance—were excluded from testing programs. This was the case whether the student had a mild learning disability, moderate mental retardation, or a complex combination of sensory, physical, and cognitive issues. The existence of the disability was sufficient to preclude participation. Some thought this was the right thing to do; it spared students the frustration of testing on the general curriculum, which everyone knew they could not master.

To comply with IDEA and NCLB, IEP teams now decide not whether a student with a disability participates in district testing, but the way in which they can best demonstrate what they know and can do. Although parents may contest the manner of testing, they cannot ask for students to be exempt from the process. The following participation options are open:

- Regular assessment (that is administered to all students in that grade)
- Regular assessment with accommodations
- Alternate assessment based on grade-level achievement standards
- Alternate assessment based on alternate achievement standards
- Assessment based on modified achievement standards

States determine academic standards and assessment programs as well as their own method of alternate testing. In contrast to the familiar multiple choice test, some use portfolios; others select out-of-level testing, a method in which a test from a lower grade is used. All alternate assessments must be based on state academic standards.

Every school is held accountable for the adequate yearly progress of all students toward the goal of proficiency by 2013–2014. All children are expected to reach that target. States are permitted to count as "proficient" a limited number of students who take an alternate assessment based on modified or alternate achievement standards.

Should demanding standards really apply to all students? Educators generally agree that blanket exclusion of all students with disabilities was not wise and did not provide an accurate view of the accomplishments of all students. Now, some ask whether it is wise to expect all students to reach the same targets. Should students with cognitive or complex disabilities (e.g., mental retardation, traumatic brain injury, deaf-blindness) even participate if they are not expected to achieve these goals?

This issue's selections are somewhat longer than is typical for *Taking Sides*. Their length reflects the complexity of this critical controversy.

Kevin McGrew and Jeffrey Evans caution there are dangers in relying on disability labels or IQ scores to anticipate what a student might achieve. They discuss the powerful impact expectations can have on accomplishments and worry that stereotypes will limit possibilities for students with cognitive disabilities.

James Kauffman maintains that some students, particularly those with cognitive disabilities, simply will not be able to reach high academic standards. He sees this as a reality that should be accepted and urges people to focus on what these individuals can do, offering programs to develop their strengths.

As you read these articles, ask yourself if you believe all students can reach academic proficiency. Will students with cognitive disabilities surprise us all if only we raise our expectations? Or should we focus on functional, work-related areas for these students? Are lower academic expectations ever reasonable? Who decides?

YES

Kevin S. McGrew and
Jeffrey Evans

Expectations for Students with Cognitive Disabilities: Is the Cup Half Empty or Half Full? Can the Cup Flow Over?

Introduction

Over the past 30 years the United States has slowly and steadily clarified the meaning of access to a free and appropriate public education for students with disabilities. . . . Unfortunately, there is still limited consensus among educators regarding appropriate achievement expectations for students with disabilities, particularly those with cognitive disabilities.

A concern about low expectations and the need for high expectations was reflected in the IDEA's 1977 Preamble: "Over 20 years of research has demonstrated that the education of children with disabilities can be made more effective by . . . having high expectations for such children and ensuring their access to the general education curriculum to the maximum extent possible. . . ." IDEA 1997 clarified that all students with disabilities are to have access to instruction focused on the same skills and knowledge as all other students, and that their achievement is to be measured with the same district and statewide assessment programs as used for all students (and, adding an alternate assessment for those students unable to participate in the general assessment).

The *No Child Left Behind (NCLB) Act of 2001* further clarified that schools are to be held accountable for the adequate yearly progress (AYP) of all groups of students. NCLB specifically requires the disaggregation of assessment data for specified subgroups, including students with disabilities. The intended purpose of NCLB is "to ensure that all children have a fair, equal, and significant opportunity to obtain a high quality education and reach, at a minimum, proficiency on challenging State academic achievement standards and state academic assessments." In other words, the expected educational outcomes for students with disabilities . . . are the same high expectations held for all students.

McGrew, K.S., Evans, J. (2004). *Expectations for Students with cognitive disabilities: Is the cup half empty or half full? Can the cup flow over?* (Synthesis Report 55). Published by University of Minnesota, National Center for Educational Outcomes. http://education.umn.edu/NCEO/OnlinePubs/Synthesis55.html

Although data show that some students with disabilities are reaching the state-determined level of proficiency, many students with disabilities are still far from performing at this level. . . .

Many educators have grown increasingly concerned about the performance of students with cognitive disabilities who are appropriately working toward grade-level achievement standards, but whose current performance is far from a proficient level on grade-level achievement standards as measured by current statewide assessments. Considerable controversy surrounds the issue of what can and should be expected for these students. Some people argue that the vast majority of students with disabilities, when given appropriate access to high quality curriculum and instruction, can meet or exceed the levels of proficiency currently specified. Many special education advocates believe that subscribing to the same high expectations and accountability for student progress will ultimately lead to improved instruction and learning for all students. Others argue that a student's disability will ultimately prevent the student from attaining gradelevel achievement standards, even when provided appropriate instruction and accommodations. This latter group believes that it is unjust to punish schools when these students fail to perform at the proficient level.

The discrepant "expectations" arguments reflect very different perspectives regarding the nature of cognitive disabilities. These two perspectives have existed for many years. To make informed decisions about the best instruction and assessments for students with cognitive disabilities, several questions need to be answered. For instance, how many students with cognitive disabilities can be expected to achieve the same level of proficiency as other students? To what extent can we predict who these students are? Can we discern whether a student's failure to meet proficiency is due to the student's disabling condition or lack of appropriate instruction? Finally, what effects do teacher expectations have on student achievement?

This report was prepared to begin to address these issues. It includes an analysis of nationally representative cognitive and achievement data to illustrate the dangers in making blanket assumptions about appropriate achievement expectations for individuals based on their cognitive ability or diagnostic label. . . .

Overview

Few would argue that the concept of intelligence (IQ), and tests that measure the construct, have played a long and significant role in education, and special education in particular. The use of practical IQ tests is typically traced to the beginning of the century when Alfred Binet developed a battery of tasks to help identify children with learning difficulties. Binet's goal was to develop a means by which to identify struggling students who would then receive remediation via "mental orthopedics." Clearly, Binet did not believe that his measure of intelligence quantified an innate or "fixed" ability. Binet was an optimist who believed that the ability "glasses" of children with lower ability were half full, and that their vessels could be filled further.

In stark contrast to Binet's optimistic position was that of English psychologist Sir Cyril Burt, [whose] . . . work was based on the then popular view that intelligence was a genetically based fixed entity. Burt's ideas influenced the design of educational systems that segregated children in different educational tracks based on ability. According to Burt, "capacity must obviously limit content. It is impossible for a pint jug to hold more than a pint of milk; and it is equally impossible for a child's educational attainments to rise higher than his educable capacity permits." Clearly Binet and Burt viewed the proverbial half-filled glass differently.

A final view, based on the 1994 feel-good movie *Forrest Gump*, can be considered the "cup overflowing" perspective. Briefly, this movie portrayed the fictitious life history of Forrest Gump, an individual who was classified in the mental retardation range early in school. The exchange between the school principal and Forrest's mother clearly illustrated an educational approach grounded in the Burt philosophy:

School principal: "Your boy's . . . different, Miz Gump. His IQ's 75."

Ms. Gump: "Well, we're all different, Mr. Hancock. He might be a bit on the slow side. He's not going to a special school to retread tires!"

Ms. Gump's response, and the subsequent string of life achievements of her son Forrest (e.g., star football player in college, world class ping pong player, Vietnam war hero, CEO of successful shrimp company) reflects the "cup flowing over" perspective on IQ test scores. That is, Forrest's achievements were beyond his measured IQ (which was below the average sized "jug" according to Burt).

When faced with students whose classroom performances or achievement test scores surpass their measured . . . IQ scores by significant amounts, laypersons and professionals (e.g., educators and psychologists) frequently demonstrate an implicit subscription to a Burt philosophy that a person can achieve only up to his or her level of intelligence when they characterize Gump-like students as "overachievers." Ms. Gump's implicit intelligence conception, which was subsequently manifested in Forrest's accomplishments, would suggest that there is more to school learning than the size of a child's "IQ cup or jug"—other variables contribute to achievement.

Half-full or half-empty? Filled to-the-brim or the cup flowing over? Which intelligence-learning metaphor is correct? Burt versus Binet/Gump? Who should be believed during the current standards-driven educational reform fueled by the mantra that "no child shall be left behind" (NCLB), and that all children should reach grade level standards. More importantly, which philosophy should guide educational expectations for students whose primary special education classification is tied closely to IQ scores below the normal range (i.e., students with mental retardation or cognitive disabilities)? Should educational expectations for students with cognitive disabilities be grounded in a Burt philosophy (i.e., expect academic performance and achievement no higher than the student's estimated cognitive ability), or should expectations be based on the more optimistic Gump philosophy (i.e., it is possible for students with cognitive disabilities to achieve higher than their IQ test score and at grade level)? . . .

Diversity within Disability Distributions

Probably no environment elicits individual differences sooner in life than formal education. In classrooms teachers strive to arrange conditions to elicit optimal performance among a diverse class of unique learners. However, due to the only true "law" in psychology (the law of individual differences), optimal learning conditions and techniques are not universal across learners.

This holds true for all learners—those with and without disabilities. It is important that students with disabilities not be saddled with group-based stereotyped low academic expectations. Just as the diversity of learning rates for students without disabilities is acknowledged, so it should be for students with disabilities. . . .

The federally funded *Special Education Elementary Longitudinal* (SEELS) study, the first ever nationally representative longitudinal investigation of elementary students with disabilities (ages 6 to 12), recently provided empirical support for the diversity of achievement levels of students with disabilities. According to the SEELS project director . . . the data indicate that "you can find kids with disabilities who are scoring right near the top—above the 80th percentile—and you'll find some in the middle . . . and then a lot more kids in the lowest quartile. So it's heavily weighted toward the low end but there's quite a bit of diversity." Although students with disabilities, as a group, tend to achieve in the lower half of the distribution of achievement, "individuals with disabilities can be found across the full range of academic performance." . . .

IQ and Disability: The Misunderstood Common Denominator

Despite their diversity of characteristics, the majority (58%) of students receiving special education services under IDEA share a common experience—most have been classified as having a learning disability or cognitive impairment (mental retardation) with the aid of an intelligence test. Despite many disputes over competing theoretical conceptualizations of intelligence and the utility of intelligence test scores, even the most ardent critics recognize that IQ tests "predict certain forms of achievement—especially school achievement—rather effectively."

Despite a defensible rationale for their early development and continued deployment in the schools, many people have developed . . . the inaccurate belief, often reinforced by court decisions, that measured intelligence is a genetically determined, largely fixed, global, and enduring trait that explains most of a student's success (or failure) in school learning. Such a Sir Cyril Burt conceptualization of intelligence can doom a student to low expectations if his or her IQ score is significantly below the norm. This fixed entity view of intelligence, summarized in the belief in the predictive power of the single global IQ score, represents the mental jug or cup being "half-empty" or "filled to the brim" philosophy. According to this view, to expect more academic achievement than a person's estimated or measured IQ score is simply not possible.

A recent *Education Week* (2004) national survey (*Count me in: Special Education in an Era of Standards*) of 800 special and general education teachers suggests that most educators implicitly subscribe to the Burt IQ-potential philosophy. Eighty-four percent of surveyed teachers did not believe that students in special education should be expected to meet the same set of academic standards as students without disabilities. In addition, approximately 80% of the teachers felt that students with disabilities should not be included in the same state tests as students in general education, especially if the results are used for accountability purposes.

The surprising extent to which educators appear to hold alternative (and typically lower) standards and expectations for students with disabilities, although appropriate for many of these students, is troubling given the empirical reality of the predictive power of IQ test scores—scores that are often at the root of lowered expectations. Sir Cyril Burt's IQ-fixed potential legacy appears to be alive and well in America's schools (albeit not typically adopted maliciously or explicitly articulated).

Fortunately, decades of research on intelligence tests have repeatedly converged on a near unanimous consensus on the predictive accuracy of IQ test scores[;] it is time to "leave the Burt IQ-potential philosophy behind."

Reality of the IQ-Achievement Relationship: Statistics Made Simple

In an era of standards-driven educational reform, educators and policy-makers must recognize the truth about IQ test scores and the resulting disability categories that are based on a continuum of IQ test scores. . . . The reality is simple. Given the best available theoretically and psycho-metrically sound, nationally standardized, individually administered intelligence test batteries, three statements hold true. Each of these can be explained in depth. . . . For greater conciseness here, the statements that hold true are:

- IQ test scores, under optimal test conditions, account for 40% to 50% of current expected achievement.
- Thus, 50% to 60% of student achievement is related to variables "beyond intelligence."
- For any given IQ test score, half of the students will obtain achievement scores at or below their IQ score. Conversely, and frequently not recognized, is that for any given IQ test score, half of the students will obtain achievement scores at or *above* their IQ score.

. . . Using the general IQ and Total Achievement (average across reading, math, and written language) scores for "real" norm subjects from the standardization of the *Woodcock-Johnson Battery Third Edition* (WJ III, . . . there is a strong linear relation between IQ and achievement, as evidenced by a strong correlation of .75. . . .

[However,] . . . even IQ tests that demonstrate some of the strongest correlations with achievement . . . cannot be used to provide perfect estimates of predicted achievement for *individual* students. . . . [For] subjects with IQs from 70–80, expected achievement scores range from a low of approximately 40 to a high of approximately 110. . . . [Half] of the individuals with IQs between 70–80 achieve at or below IQ-predicted achievement, and the other half . . . score at or *above* IQ-predicted achievement.

[These] data . . . suggest that the proper metaphor for the IQ-achievement prediction relationship is that the "cup can flow over." The carte blanch assumption that all students with disabilities should have an alternative set of educational standards and an assessment system is inconsistent with empirical data. . . .

The current reality is that despite being one of the flagship developments in all of psychology, intelligence tests are fallible predictors of academic achievement. IQ test scores (and associated IQ-based disability category labels) are adequate, but not nearly sufficient metrics, by which to make reasonably precise predictions about any particular *individual* student's future expected achievement progress. It simply cannot be done beyond a reasonable doubt.

The fallibility of IQ tests, coupled with the enduring presence of the ghost of Sir Cyril Burt's deterministic IQ-achievement educational philosophy, in the context of today's high-stakes educational accountability environment, raises the specter of many children with disabilities being denied the right to appropriate and demanding expectations. Stereotyping students with disabilities (often on the basis of disability label or test scores) as a group that should be excluded from general education standards and assessments is not supported by the best evidence from current science in the field of psychological and educational measurement. The potential soft bigotry of setting a priori IQ or disability label-based low academic expectations (for students with disabilities) needs to be recognized, understood, and minimized, if all children are not to be left behind.

Expectancy Effects: A Brief History and Literature Review

Since the 1970s, the notions of the "self-fulfilling prophecy" (SFP), the "Pygmalion Effect," . . . and more recently, "expectancy effects" (EE), have become commonplace in the educational psychology literature. In general, these terms refer to similar phenomena. . . .

Merton is recognized as the first to coin the term "self-fulfilling prophecy" which has now evolved into the more general phenomena of "expectancy effects." According to Merton, SFP occurs when an inaccurate definition of a situation elicits new behaviors which, in turn, make the originally inaccurate conception a reality. SFP is a compelling theory, largely because of its potential implications and elegant simplicity.

> The concept is simple enough: If we prophesy (expect) that something will happen, we behave (usually unconsciously) in a manner that will make it happen. We will, in other words, do what we can to realize our prophecy.

In most EE research, it is usually a person in a position of authority (e.g., an employer, medical professional, parent, teacher, . . .) who holds expectations about an individual (or group) under their supervision. According to the EE research, expectations expressed by an authority figure via verbal and nonverbal communication often influence the self-image and the behavior of the supervised person in such a way that the expectations held come to pass.

Origins of Expectancy Effects

. . . SFP is also often referred to as the "Pygmalion Effect" which was drawn from the title of the original book (Rosenthal & Jacobson, *Pygmalion in the Classroom*) that reported the phenomenon. SFP first appeared in early psychological research studies where it was demonstrated that experimenters could unwittingly influence the behavior of animal and human subjects during an experiment. In 1968, Rosenthal and Jacobson substituted teachers for experimenters in order to investigate the effects of teachers' expectancies on the intelligence test scores of their pupils. The Rosenthal and Jacobson study was designed to measure "whether those children for whom the teachers held especially favorable expectations would show greater intellectual growth than the remaining or control-group children" when evaluated . . . months later. Cotton provided a succinct summary of the original Pygmalion study:

> The Rosenthal/Jacobson study concluded that students' intellectual development is largely a response to what teachers expect and how those expectations are communicated. The original Pygmalion study involved giving teachers false information about the learning potential of certain students in grades one through six in a San Francisco elementary school. Teachers were told that these students had been tested and found to be on the brink of a period of rapid intellectual growth; in reality, the students had been selected at random. At the end of the experimental period, some of the targeted students—and particularly those in grades one and two—exhibited performance on IQ tests which was superior to the scores of other students of similar ability and superior to what would have been expected of the target students with no intervention.

The Rosenthal and Jacobson report suggested that teacher expectations could increase or decrease . . . IQ . . . test scores. Understandably, this report created a media sensation. The possibility that teachers could effect change (either positive or negative) in a student's IQ scores held considerable popular interest and appeal. . . .

Expectancy Effects and Intelligence

It would be an understatement to describe the EE research focused on the relations between teacher's expectations and intelligence as contentious. Post hoc re-analysis of the . . . Rosenthal and Jacobson investigation raised many questions about the study's methodology. Numerous attempts to replicate the Pygmalion effect . . . have proven unsuccessful. . . . In many of the subsequent follow-up studies the control groups often gained more IQ points than the experimental groups. . . .

Many . . . researchers have continued to examine the teacher-student expectancy effect. A clear connection between [EE] and IQ has not been established. However; *expectancy effects and academic achievement do appear to correlate positively.*

Expectancy Effects: How Large?

A frequently quoted estimate of the magnitude of Expectancy Effects (EE) in education is that 5% to 10% of student achievement performance might be ascribed to the influence of differential teacher expectations. More recently, average expectancy effect sizes from 0.1 to 0.3 have been reported. On first inspection, effect sizes of 0.1 to 0.3 appear to be of little practical import. This is wrong. According to Jussim et al., when discussing students who are the "targets" of EE, "a naturally occurring effect of 'only' .2 means, that on average, of all targets of high expectations, 10% show substantial improvement; and of all targets of low expectations, 10% show substantial decreases in performance." . . .

To reassure the reader of the importance of what appear to be significant, yet small correlations or effect sizes, one only needs to be reminded that many significant public and social policy decisions have been made on the strength of relations between variables that are of the same magnitude or lower than those reported for EE. . . . [A] special American Psychological Association . . . *Psychological Assessment Work Group* . . . provided the following examples:

- The reduction of the risk of dying from a heart attack by taking aspirin is based on $r = 0.02$
- The impact of chemotherapy on breast cancer survival; $r = .03$
- The value of antihistamines for reducing sneezes and a runny nose; $r = .11$
- The impact of Viagra on improved sexual functioning; $r = .38$

Furthermore, much like the long-term insidious effect of long-term exposure to subclinical levels of lead, asbestos, second-hand smoke, and other toxins, some research studies have suggested that even small EE can result in larger cumulative effects over time. Small EE could exert a substantial influence on student achievement, particularly for more vulnerable and "at risk" students.

Expectancy Effects and Student Characteristics

In the field of special education, EE was first investigated . . . with regard to the potential negative consequences of being labeled "mentally retarded." In general, this "stigma" research suggested that being labeled mentally retarded often led to changes in the behavior of adults who encouraged "learned helplessness." These studies reported that the attribution for success or failure for a mentally retarded person was more frequently assigned to the person's inherent low ability, while failure attribution for others was more frequently assigned to the person's effort.

Researchers have found that, in general, EE in classrooms are often related to a number of different student characteristics. "Teachers overestimate the achievement of high achievers, underestimate that of low achievers, and predict least accurately the responses of low achievers." Although low-achieving students have been found to receive more learning support, they also are communicated lower expectations via less pressure to achieve than high achieving students. Additional student characteristics associated with teacher expectations include race, ethnicity, SES, physical appearance or attractiveness, . . . use of standard English . . . , prior negative comments or evaluations about a student by other teachers, readiness/maturity, and grouping/tracking effects. Similar to the early MR-stigma research, some teachers have been found to associate success to inherent ability in the case of high achieving students and luck or chance for perceived low achievers. . . .

Expectancy Effects: Educator Behaviors

Although the claim that teacher expectancies can raise student intelligence has been effectively rebuked, most . . . critics have expressed the belief, supported by research, that expectancy effects do influence teacher-to-student performance and behavior. . . .

Expectancies can be expressed both verbally and non-verbally. Although most teachers report that they can fully control their behavioral affect and deceive students whenever necessary, at times the two primary modes of communication can send mixed signals. . . .

Even brief exposure to a teacher's face or body movements (e.g., differences in voice inflection) can provide a student with enough information to communicate expectancies. Teacher behaviors associated with the communication of low achievement expectancies to low achievement students have included:

- The provision of fewer opportunities to learn new material.
- Less "wait" time provided to answer questions.
- Providing answers or calling on someone else.
- Inappropriate feedback (more frequent and severe criticism for failure; insincere praise), limited reinforcement (e.g., giving reinforcement that is not contingent on performance), or rewarding more incorrect answers or inappropriate behavior.

- Providing less attention and more interaction in private settings.
- Providing differential treatment in grading (less frequently giving "the benefit of the doubt") and personal interactions (e.g., teachers less friendly or responsive; making less eye contact; giving fewer smiles).
- Providing briefer and less informative feedback.
- Providing less stimulating, and lower-level cognitive questions.
- Providing less effective (but time consuming) instructional methods.

Expectancy Effects: Why Do They Occur?

Although the original research on [EE] was based primarily on studies where educators were provided false information regarding student potential, "most researchers have concluded that teacher expectations are not generally formed on the basis of 'false conceptions.'" Rather, they are based on the best information available about the students. Furthermore, even if the initial expectations a teacher forms for a student are realistic and appropriate, student learning and self-concept development can be limited as a result of *sustained expectation effects*. The adverse impact of sustained expectations can occur when teachers continue to engage in behaviors that result in the maintenance of previously formed low expectations (e.g., by giving low-expectation students only drill work). . . .

Attribution Theory

Certain beliefs about intelligence and learning may lead to lowered expectations for low achieving students and students with cognitive disabilities . . . [Contemporary] social cognitive psychology research has suggested that *attribution theory* is a "useful framework for exploring teachers' response to children's academic outcomes, such as success or failure, in the general education classroom."

Briefly, attribution theory research has demonstrated that individuals (e.g., teachers) tend to attribute success or failure for an individual (e.g., students) to one of two different human characteristics—*ability* or *effort*. Graham and Weiner's studies found that the initial response of many classroom teachers to a negative student outcome is either anger or pity. Furthermore, the elicitation of anger or pity was differentially linked to the degree to which teachers perceived the student as responsible for his or her failure. Typically, when faced with student failure, a teacher pity response was elicited for students of low abilities while anger was the more frequent response to high ability students (due to a perceived lack of effort or motivation). Furthermore, these researchers found that the anticipation of future failure for students was directly related to the perceived stability of the cause of the student failure. "Failure due to causes that are viewed as stable, such as low ability, will result in a high expectation that failure will recur, whereas failure due to unstable causes, such as effort or task difficulty, will result in a lower expectation of repeated failure. . . ."

Clark found . . . [that when] students use attribution information to make inferences about their own ability and effort, these inferences are manifest in the students' self-esteem, expectations for their own future successes and failures, and their classroom performance." . . .

Group Stereotyping

Expectancy effects may also reflect the differential treatment of an individual based on group membership stereotypes. Group-based self-fulfilling prophecies differ from individual-based self-fulfilling prophecies and are relevant to the educational practices of grouping, tracking, and institutionalized segregated instruction (e.g., separate special education classrooms). . . .

Researchers have reported the communication of differential expectations as a function of placement in different ability or tracked groups in classrooms. According to Cotton's research synthesis, "students in low groups and tracks have been found to get less exciting instruction, less emphasis upon meaning and conceptualization, and more rote drill and practice activities than those in high reading groups and tracks." . . . In general, . . . tracking or ability grouping "may lead to the type of rigid teacher expectations that are most likely to evoke self-fulfilling prophecies and perceptual biases. Teachers often prepare more for and are more supportive toward students in high ability groups."

Stereotype-based low expectations for "different" students . . . can beset anyone who belongs to a group with a specific reputation. When the stereotype or reputation is pejorative, . . . the effects can be significantly disruptive to individual development. Stereotypes have two salient characteristics: (1) they polarize perceptions and sharpen differences, and (2) they are rigidly held, readily fixated and resistant to change. Thus, the development of stereotypically-based differential student academic expectations (based on group membership or label) can serve to fixate and exaggerate existing differences. . . .

Probably one of the more potentially insidious forms of stereotype-based expectation formation is that which results from the attachment of diagnostic labels (e.g., learning disabled, mentally retarded, emotionally disturbed, . . .) to students. Although all forms of social stereotypes (e.g., gender, social class, race, ethnicity, . . .) can produce harmful effects, diagnostic educational or medical disability labels almost always have the authoritative stamp of approval by a credible expert (e.g., psychologist, doctor). This major source of lowered teacher expectations has been repeatedly demonstrated in the special education research literature. Based on the previously summarized *Education Week* national survey of teachers, lowered expectations for all students with disabilities continues to be a latent force in many of America's classrooms, and may be exacerbated by the current wave of high stakes educational accountability.

Beware of Silent, Shifting Standards

Research during the past decade has revealed that group-based stereotypes can be conceptualized as functioning as "standards against which individual members of stereotype groups are judged." Briefly, *stereotyping effects* occur when individual group members are evaluated in a direction consistent with group-based expectations or stereotypes. "For example, a man is judged a better leader than a woman; a physician is judged more intelligent than a hairdresser . . . these types of effects certainly indicate that stereotypes have been used to judge individuals and that the outcome is *assimilation*." The self-fulfilling prophesies previously described are examples of the commonly recognized assimilative stereotype effect.

Research on the "shifting standards model" suggests that assimilative effects alone fail to capture the complexity and extent to which stereotyped-based expectations operate in group settings: "Less well recognized is the fact that stereotyping can also be manifested in other ways, most notably in counter-stereotypical or contrast effects."

Within-category standards are typically used when a person evaluates or judges an individual . . . of a stereotyped group . . . on stereotyped dimensions. For example, given the stereotype that students with mental retardation are "slower learners" than students of normal intelligence, one is likely to judge the learning capability of a particular student with mental retardation relative to (lower) standards for students with mental retardation and, the learning ability of a particular non-retarded student relative to (higher) standards of competence for non-retarded students. . . . "Good" does not mean the same thing for the student with mental retardation and the student of normal intelligence. . . .

Probably the most pernicious masked effect of the shifting standards model is that "evidentiary standards are lower for members of the group stereotyped as deficient on an attribute." When an individual . . . is a member of a group that is stereotyped as deficient on a trait or attribute (i.e., intelligence), evidentiary standards or expectations are often shifted in the direction of leniency, less challenge, and minimal competencies. [This] shift, . . . in turn, often produces behavior in the evaluator in the opposite direction of the stereotype. This shifting of standards "activates low (patronizing) minimizing standards that are more readily surpassed, producing a subjective sense of positivity—a 'wow' effect. That this positivity is not borne out in outcomes that matter for the target (getting a job or the key fielding position) suggests that the favorable treatment is more apparent and ephemeral than real." The essence of this phenomena is captured in the words of Alexa Pochowski, the assistant commissioner for learning services in the Kansas education department, . . . quoted in *Education Week* as saying:

> For too long, we held these students to lower standards . . . I hate to say it: I think we almost felt sorry for them."

. . . In summary, for students with cognitive disabilities, expectancy effects can be viewed as a form of **standards-based stereotyping**. This

stereotyping can either produce direct . . . or indirect "hidden" stereotyping effects, both of which can exert negative influences on academic
performance. The silent, subjective shifting (towards lower) evidentiary
academic standards (for students with disabilities) represents a subtle, yet
potentially potent force operating against the goal of "leaving no child
behind."

Education Expectations: Caveats and Concerns

Teachers, like all humans, develop personal beliefs, opinions, and stereotypes. During most teacher preparation programs, educators are taught to
become aware of potential expectancy effects and how to control their
overt day-to-day teaching behavior to be more equitable, and to refrain
from dispensing differential praise and criticism.

Given the popularity of the expectancy effects and self-fulfilling prophesies in the educational and psychological research and popular press, one
could be led to believe that these negative influences are pandemic in school
classrooms. This is not the case. Although some researchers have concluded
that differential treatment of students is widespread, most researchers have
concluded that the majority of educators (particularly experienced teachers
and teachers who are very familiar with their students) form expectations
based on the initial available information and "tweak" or adjust their expectations and instruction based on changes in student performance.

It is inappropriate to infer that the majority of educators are biased
simply because they may hold differential expectations for some students.
Often, differential treatment of students represents the appropriate implementation of individualized adaptive instruction responsive to the individual differences in a classroom. . . .

It is important to note that educators who may hold inappropriately
low expectations for some students "are rarely acting out of malice; indeed,
they are often not even aware that their low expectations have developed
based on specious reasoning."

Nevertheless, the literature raises numerous issues that are directly relevant to today's educational context for students with disabilities in which
both IDEA and NCLB are requiring improved performance. Particularly for
those students with cognitive disabilities, the information on expectancy
effects should cause us much concern. Is it possible that expectancy effects
have been holding students back in the past? Are we under the influence
of silently shifting standards—especially for students with cognitive disabilities? These and other questions are ones that states, districts, schools,
administrators, and teachers need to ask themselves and others—as our
nation strives to improve the performance of all of its students, including . . .
those with cognitive disabilities.

James M. Kauffman **NO**

Education Deform: Bright People Sometimes Say Stupid Things about Education

Test Bashing Is Part of the "Progressive" Rhetoric that Thwarts Progress

Standardized testing has become the Great Satan of education in the minds of some, a "monster" that must be put out of schools. For example, Alfie Kohn condemns standardized testing—not just certain tests or the misuse of tests, but standardized tests as tools. . . . His suggestions for fighting standardized tests include not only civil disobedience by educators but printing bumper stickers with slogans such as "Standardized Testing Is Dumbing Down Our Schools." Like most slogans in education, this one, too, in my opinion, is vapid. Standardized testing can, indeed, be stupid or be used stupidly, but I doubt very seriously that it is the ogre responsible for dumbing down our schools. And rejecting standardized tests can only deprive parents, teachers, school officials, and governing bodies of an important tool in monitoring students' performance. . . .

Now it is undoubtedly true that some standardized tests are poorly made or misused, as are many teacher-made tests and other forms of "alternative assessment" such as portfolios. In fact, *any* form of assessment of which I'm aware can be (and has been) crudely made and badly used. So, why the seething hostility toward "standardized" testing? The answer is not simple, but I think much of the outrage over standardized tests is prompted by fears of comparisons of various individuals and groups who take the tests. Furthermore, educational theory has become, to some, a matter of religious conviction in which evidence doesn't matter. Too many educators—and, as well, too many people who are not educators—embrace "progressive" theory that relies on pet phrases and terminology for its defense of educational "quality" that tests are said not to be able to measure. These "reformers," who actually hold educational theories originated nearly a century ago, call for "real learning" that standardized tests are assumed not to be able to assess. . . .

Kohn and others who take a position against standardized tests also often raise the specter of uniformity across schools and states, which they see as being overly rigid. Even such politically conservative opinion writers as George F. Will suggest that America probably should not have a standard examination for high school graduation or a national curriculum. Perhaps it is inevitable that people of nearly all political persuasions will figure out some day that math and reading and much of what we need to know about science and geography and the United States government is not really different in different places. People might figure out that uniformity of expectations and curricula and testing might actually be beneficial in a society in which children move often to different localities or states. But it may take decades for people to arrive at these conclusions.

All the more reason, in my opinion, that standardized testing has a valuable role to play in measuring students' progress. . . . [One] argument against standardized testing is that comparisons of schools and states—perhaps of individuals as well—are insidious. No one is to be "left behind." . . . [Any] measure of progress—but most obviously a standardized measure—produces a distribution that by nature finds some to have performed better than others; for any measure that is not simply "yes/no" or "pass/fail" or in some other way a truncated range, there is a bottom fourth (first quartile) as well as a top fourth (or any other percentage of the sample one wishes to examine). So alternative assessment procedures that obscure if not obviate comparisons seem, to some, a godsend. Such alternative measures can help maintain the fiction that all students are excellent or give the misimpression that nobody is actually behind. The "progressive" idea seems to be that an "authentic" assessment will show that everyone and everything is cool—nobody can fail.

For some purposes there is no good substitute for the test that is standardized and can be failed—normed on a large sample of test takers by which we want to judge the achievement of individuals and groups. It is easier to shoot the messenger that brings unwelcome tidings than to confront the differences among individuals and groups that tests may reveal. . . . And it is easy to overlook the advantages of standardized tests while describing the tests themselves as monsters to be driven from our schools.

Some scholars have pointed out that the current popularity of standardized testing is really based on public concern about standards or accountability. The standards of performance that a state or school adopts are nearly always linked to a standardized test, and for this reason some writers refer to "test-linked standards." We do, I think, want to know how a student's performance compares to others' and to be able to compare average student performances across schools and states. It is only through such comparisons that we can address some problems, including the problem of how well we're doing and the problem of equity. Nevertheless, some people seem to be in favor of accountability—but without knowing how students are doing on any standardized test. To them, standardized tests seem to be a way of holding people responsible for teaching a standard curriculum, which they find anathema.

Mary Anne Raywid has voiced a familiar complaint: "One problem with the vast majority of tests, of course, is that they are curriculum-based." Well, it seems to me that we do want curriculum and testing to be aligned. That is, we want to teach what students are going to be tested on and to test what we teach. In fact, curriculum-based assessment is what some of us are after. It makes no sense to test students on things they haven't been taught, and it makes good sense to base assessment on the curriculum. The curriculum could determine what is tested; the tests could determine what is taught. But, either way, it only makes sense for the two to be in sync. In fact, one is not likely to be developed without the other: Testing and curriculum *should* influence each other. To me, it makes little difference which comes first, as long as what is taught is really important stuff for students to learn. I suppose the question actually becomes what we think is important for students to know. Another way of putting it is to ask whether we think there is a common core of knowledge that most students should learn. I think there is this common content that most students should be expected to master, and I see no reason not to check up on how well we're doing it—to test it with a standardized instrument.

Others, particularly E. D. Hirsch, Jr., have described eloquently how having a core body of knowledge or core curriculum increases equity among groups of students differing in ethnicity or social privilege—or, at least, opportunities for achieving such equity. Standardized tests were invented, at least in part, to be fairer to students without social privileges—to focus on a student's performance rather than his or her genetic or social heritage that brought privilege in spite of what a student could do. Standardized tests *can* be used to increase equity if they measure important knowledge and if all schools and individuals are provided the resources needed to allow them to attain a reasonable standard. Standardized tests *can* be used to improve the clarity of schools' objectives and focus on instruction. Standardized tests *can* be used to allocate resources more efficiently, and they *can* be used as a common metric—a common, readily understood language of measurement—for communicating educational outcomes.

Please notice that I have *not* suggested that *all* students should learn exactly the same thing or be taught exactly the same way. I suggested that *most* students would benefit from a standard, core curriculum. . . . Some students are not going to be successful in the regular, general curriculum that may be right for the majority of students. I think it's essential that we provide alternatives for those students who cannot reasonably be expected to learn the core curriculum and be tested on it. . . . But, of course, here's the problem: Who should decide, and on what basis, that an alternative to the core curriculum is a better choice for a given student? Here are some givens, in my opinion: First, the decision should not be based on the student's ethnicity, gender, or social privilege. Second, the decision should be based on the student's estimated ability to learn the core curriculum. Third, there are no perfect decision makers. Any decision making scheme we can devise will produce some false positives (students thought to be able to learn the core curriculum but who cannot) and false negatives (students who are thought to be unable to learn the core curriculum but who can). The goals should be to make as few errors of judgment as possible in either direction and to correct errors as soon as they can be detected by changing the student's curriculum. But don't miss this given: Assuming that any core curriculum should be studied and mastered by *all* students simply guarantees a very large number of false positives. For a substantial number of kids and a significant percentage of the student population, it's not in the cards. The majority of the students I'm referring to have disabilities of one kind or another, although some of those with disabilities can and should learn the standard—general, core—curriculum.

Standardized tests, like every other human invention and some natural phenomena, will be abused. That is a given. We are well advised to recognize abuses without proscribing the use of the instruments that are abused, to use instruments responsibly. Obscuring or hiding differences on good standardized measures merely locks in place the social inequities that anti-testing forces say they oppose. We cannot address inequities that we will not admit are real and important. . . . [I] think we have yet to invent a better or more reliable way than standardized testing of finding out fairly what someone knows. The fact that some test questions are bad and that some people use scores unwisely should not be used as an excuse for bashing the very notion of standardized testing.

Every educational policy has a downside as far as I know, standardized testing and test-linked standards included. It is possible to narrow a curriculum unreasonably in efforts to prepare students for tests, and this is true for standardized tests or any other kind of assessment. It is possible to define good teaching simply as that which maximizes test performance—standardized tests or any other type of assessment. It is possible to use standardized test performance to devalue those who do not score well on them, but the same is true for any type of assessment—kids can be devalued because their performance is judged to be inferior, not up to expectations, not acceptable. And standardized tests or any other type of assessment can preclude certain opportunities for students who fail to meet expectations. Any kind of assessment of performance—standardized test or any alternative—can create anxiety in the person being assessed. Alternatives to standardized tests, such as "portfolio assessment" in which a student's work is judged in some way, have their downsides, too. They are cumbersome, extremely time-consuming, and present problems of reliability, validity, and comparisons across individuals and groups.

If our schools are being "dumbed down," I doubt that it's because of standardized tests. Much more likely, I think, is that the dumbing down is a result of fumbled thinking about issues in education, including mindless rhetoric that misleads people's thinking about the tools we use to assess educational progress. And make no mistake about this, either: *Standardized testing cannot take the place of the type of frequent teacher monitoring or assessment that is an essential part of good teaching.* Imagining that standardized testing provides sufficient early warning for failing students is similar to imagining that reporting tornado damage provides sufficient early warning of severe weather. Standardized tests can assess instructional success or failure long after the fact, and for that they're important, but they can't be relied upon to guide the instruction of individuals. . . .

Some who write about education policy see the advantages of good standardized testing but suggest "criterion-referenced" tests that set "benchmarks" of performance. Sometimes, these individuals even suggest that an advantage of such criterion-referencing is that the test does not rely on norms, that students' performance is simply compared to the criterion, not to other students' performance. This is quite a misleading interpretation of "criterion" or "benchmark." A reasonable person would, I think, have to ask something like this: How'd we come up with this criterion or benchmark?

A criterion or benchmark can be pulled out of the air or be based simply on someone's opinion of what a student should know at a particular age. But "pull-them-out-of-the-air" criteria are ultimately seen as arrogant and unworkable. Eventually, people come to their senses and inquire about what most students know at a given age. The criterion is then set based on a comparison to what most students can do. Otherwise, it is unreasonably high or unreasonably low.

People I think should know better than to refer to criterion-referenced tests as not comparative or non-normative. They're right in only a very restricted way—a student is judged to perform acceptably or not based only on comparison to the criterion or benchmark of performance. However, a reasonable person has to ask where the criterion comes from, and this inevitably takes us back to a normative sample or normative comparison. Witness the difficulties various states or school districts have in deciding on a "cut point" or benchmark on a standards of learning test. If the criterion is something that too few students can reach, then it's abandoned as unreasonable (and for good reason). If the criterion is something just about every student reaches without difficulty, then it's abandoned as too low (and with good reason). A criterion-referenced test does force the issue of manufacturing failure (just how much is enough, desirable, or too much?). But here's something I think you can go to the bank on: If a criterion is set that results in what is deemed a reasonable rate of failure and a few years down the road we find that nearly every child is passing it, we will see efforts to raise the bar because the benchmark is now judged too low.

Criterion-referencing might be a good idea. That is, it might be a good idea to set a standard that we think merits promotion to the next grade or graduation or the need for remediation. But nobody should be fooled into thinking that the criterion isn't based on some comparison to a normative group. And nobody should be fooled into thinking that every last student will reach whatever criterion is set. Some students will fail to reach the benchmark unless it is set at zero, and some will find reaching the benchmark ridiculously easy. That's one of the reasons we need special education. . . .

Failure of Some Students with Disabilities to Reach a Standard Is Predictable

Why is the failure of some exceptional students to profit from standard educational programs utterly predictable? The answer seems obvious to me. It is because they differ significantly from the modal or typical student in instructionally relevant ways. Standard programs are designed for modal (most frequently occurring) students, not those at the extremes of a distribution. These standard educational programs simply cannot, and can't be expected to, accommodate extreme differences in instructionally relevant characteristics, like abilities to read, perceive, organize, store, retrieve, and apply information to the solution of particular problems. Some students with disabilities are going to fail to meet standard educational goals regardless of the instructional strategies a teacher uses.

Some students with disabilities can meet state testing standards, but not with the standard instructional program or in the standard amount of time or by the typical chronological age. And some students who are gifted will be bored out of their minds by having to repeat and by being expected to *appear* to learn things they learned long ago.

Pixie Holbrook described the futility and cruelty of requiring all students with disabilities to take state-mandated examinations that are appropriate for the majority of students. She describes the agony for herself and one of her pupils, Sarah, a fourth-grader with a learning disability. Sarah is a good and diligent student, but because of her learning disability she hasn't the skills required for the test.

> She knows she doesn't know. And she knows that I know she doesn't know. This is so very humiliating.
>
> Her eyes are wet now, but she's silent and stoic. I check in, and she re-assures me she's fine. She appears to be on the verge of weeping, but she will not be deterred. I cannot help her in any way; I can only sit nearby and return a false smile. I can offer a break, nothing more. Later, I calculated the reading level of this selection. Sarah reads like a second-grader, and the poem is at the high end of the fifth-grade scale. Her eyes are not just scanning the paragraphs. I know she has stopped reading and is just glancing and gazing. It's meaningless, and it hurts. Yet she attempts to answer every question.
>
> It is now 2 ½ hours, and my anger is growing. This is immoral and has become intolerable. And it's only the first day.

. . . Teachers and school administrators have, it seems to me, a moral obligation to recognize the fact that many special education students should not be required to take state competency exams.

Moreover, teachers have to be allowed, even encouraged, to recognize the limits of their instructional competence. Teachers should decline to teach students for whom their training is inadequate and decline to teach a curriculum that isn't right for their students. . . .

. . . [For] the life of me I can't figure out how someone . . . can . . . argue that teachers in elementary and secondary schools should just try to teach all students, regardless of students' characteristics. And, so some argue, if a teacher has a student that he or she can't seem to teach and manage or one who seriously interferes with teaching the rest of the class, then that teacher should just suck it up and learn to deal with it, never work to get the student taught in a special class or school. Maybe that teacher could ask for help, so the full-inclusion or merge-general-and-special-education argument goes, but not give up responsibility for the student and turn education of that student over to someone else.

I try to make this add up with any other profession's attitudes toward its clients, and I can't. What would we think of a dentist who said, "Well, no, I don't know what to do here, but I'm not going to refer you to someone else, because I am responsible for treating *all* of my patients? So I'll ask another dentist what to do and then do my best to follow the advice I get." Would we not want to wring the neck, if not sue, a mechanic or plumber or builder or lawyer who was in over his or her head—didn't have the skills demanded of the case and knew it—yet wouldn't give the job over to someone with the necessary skills?

Knowing the limits of one's knowledge and skill and being given the responsibility for refusing clients whose problems don't match one's training and skills are rather basic professional and moral responsibilities, it seems to me. Those who do not want teachers to decline to teach a child for whom they are not prepared believe one of two erroneous things, I think: (a) teachers shouldn't be professionals in any true sense or (b) students don't actually differ much in what's required to teach them. Teaching is teaching, they seem to believe, and if you can teach one student you can teach any student. I find that kind of denial maddening.

Students Who Fail at Certain Things Aren't Total Failures

Some people fail at few things, others at many. We have a tendency to write people off as failures if they fail at anything we think is important, regardless of the values or abilities of the person whose performance we judge to be failing. Much as we are too quick to judge someone who makes a vapid statement a stupid person, we overgeneralize. Surely, there are people whom failure seems to dog, and I believe there are people who could be described as *being* failures or as having failed generally at life. But those cases are, I think, rare. And, although some people may act like test scores are everything, we know that they're not—and we need to act like they're not.

Some people fail at something because of a disability, and their disability is then used against them in an unfair manner. True, we can't eliminate failure, and we can't and shouldn't "protect" people from confronting their own and other people's failures. But keeping failure at a particular thing or things in perspective is also important. Dan Hallahan and I, as well as many of our colleagues in special education, have noted that although people with disabilities can't do certain things (and, thus, could be said to fail in some respect) it is essential that we focus on what they *can* do, which for most people with disabilities is most of the things we consider normal or expected.

Failure at something doesn't make a person bad, nor does success make them a good person. Sometimes I think people misunderstand this and suppose that those who are gifted are better people and those who are disabled are not as good as others. Achievement or success at something doesn't make someone a better person, but it does enhance a person's opportunities. The more you know and are able to do, the more opportunities you have to learn and succeed. We do want to give students the greatest opportunity we can, and that means teaching them things that will open up new opportunities. I tried to make this clear in a previously published essay.

> Clearly, we do not want a human's worth to be measured simply by what he or she can do. That criterion would, for example, result in very little worth being attached to infants and young children. Yet, what someone can do is not a trivial matter. A just and humane society does not value people *for* what they can do, but it does unequivocally value peoples' ability to do certain things. If we do not value what people can do, then we have no reason to teach anyone anything. We value what people can do because of what accomplishment does for them, the additional opportunities it brings them—not because it makes them better people but because it makes them people who are better off.

Certainly, assuming that the test score is all that matters is perverse. It's the kind of perversion and stupidity we would be much better off without. We want kids to be happy and go to school excited about learning. Those objectives aren't incompatible with test scores unless we act as if, and teach kids that, test scores are all that matter. Still, avoiding test scores is just a way of evading reality.

One more thing here: It's important to note that failure once doesn't mean failure always. Most people can and do learn lots of things. Sometimes they have to try again, sometimes many times, before they learn a particular thing. Sometimes things just start to "click," and away they go. Sometimes people just seem to hit a "wall" and don't progress beyond it. Anyone who's practiced a musical instrument or sport knows the phenomenon most people call a learning "plateau," a point at which progress seems to stop. But persistence usually pays off, in that progress resumes with repeated practice—sometimes people experience a "breakthrough" in their progress, but not unless they're persistent. Yes, people differ in aptitudes for particular things and in skill in picking them up, but we have to be really careful not to assume that because a person is progressing only slowly (or rapidly) they'll always continue at that rate. . . .

Exceptional Students Need Options for Curriculum, Instruction, and Placement

Because public education must serve all children's educational needs, the largest part of general education must be designed for the modal (most frequently occurring) characteristics of students and teachers. Public education is by definition a service designed for the masses. Any product or service intended for the public at large has to be designed around the typical characteristics of consumers. Economies of scale alone require this. The size, shape, and abilities of the typical citizen fall within a fairly narrow band of variability around the mean, and simple economics demand that things be designed with this in mind.

Surely, what some call "universal design" is important, and good design will accommodate a large range of individual characteristics. But, like "all," "universal" has its limits, often unspoken, sometimes not even recognized. If "universal" design can accommodate a larger segment of the population, that is all well and good. But remember that it is neither economically feasible nor necessary to eliminate all stair steps because some people can't use them or to design and equip every car so that a person with quadriplegia can drive it. Neither is it feasible or desirable to design a reading program for most children that will be appropriate for students with severe mental retardation.

Education has to be designed for what the average teacher and the average student can be expected to do, not what the exceptionally able or those with disabilities can accomplish. I'm not suggesting that the performance of the average teacher or student can't be improved, simply that expectations in the general education program can't outstrip what the average teacher can do with appropriate training or what the typical student can do with good instruction.

Because public education must address all children's educational needs, it must include explicit structures ensuring the accommodation of exceptional students. By definition, exceptional students require an extraordinary response from educators—something different from the ordinary, even if the ordinary is good. The standard educational program can serve most students very well, but it can't serve exceptional students without additional, explicit components—special structures that go beyond the normal or routine in such matters as goals, lines of authority, roles and responsibilities of personnel, budgets and purchases, allocation of time and space, modification of curriculum, evaluation of performance, and assignment of students to classes. Failure to create these explicit structures to accommodate students at the extremes of the performance distribution inevitably results in their neglect. They are forgotten. They don't just fail a little. They fail a lot, and their noses are rubbed in their failures.

The requirement of alternative educational goals and programs must be explicit for exceptional students. It's as simple as this, I think: When the interests of students with disabilities or those who are gifted are not explicitly mandated, they get lost in the shuffle. The implicit or explicit assumption that standard educational goals and programs will accommodate the needs of exceptional students is not just logically untenable. It also places the onus of proof that the program is inappropriate wholly on the student when questions arise about his or her performance. However, if there is an explicit requirement of alternative goals and programs for exceptional students, then the burden of proof is at least partly on the school to show that those alternatives are available to students for whom the typical program is unsatisfactory and in which an exceptional student cannot be expected to make satisfactory progress.

Alternative goals and programs must be expressed as alternative curricula and educational methods for exceptional students. It is not enough to have a separate place—a special class or school. Some exceptional learners need to learn something other than the standard curriculum, not just learn the standard curriculum in a different way or in a different place. And they may need instructional or behavior management procedures that are not needed by most students.

People not familiar with instruction may miss the distinctions of method that are important for exceptional students. For example, students with disabilities may require more trials, more examples, a different pace, smaller steps in a sequence, more reinforcement (praise, encouragement, or other rewarding consequences, more careful monitoring, more structure (e.g., higher predictability, more explicit instructions, more immediate consequences) than is desirable for typical students. There may be other distinctions that I have not listed here, but at least all of these are involved in more precise teaching. In short, the instruction of students with disabilities may need to be considerably more precise than the instruction that produces good results for typical students.

In many types of performance, it is the precision with which something is done that makes the difference, not the basic operation. This is true in driving, flying, playing music, shooting guns, and so on. Just consider the differences in level of performance of the same basic operations in the following comparisons: the typical drive to work versus driving in a high-speed race; flying from city A to city B versus flying with a stunt team; playing in a municipal band versus playing in one of the world's virtuoso combos; shooting targets in the backyard versus sharp-shooting for a SWAT team. Highly expert, precision performance requires extensive training. You don't give all soldiers the competence of the Special Forces by giving them a beret. You don't make every teacher a special educator by telling them good teaching of exceptional children is just good teaching because, after all, kids are more alike than they are different and good teachers use the same basic operations regardless who their students are.

POSTSCRIPT

Should Students with Cognitive Disabilities Be Expected to Demonstrate Academic Proficiency?

People sometimes live up to our expectations for them—or down to those same expectations. The power of positive thinking motivates many to unimagined levels of success. McGrew and Evans remind us not to let IQ scores limit the opportunities offered to children with cognitive disabilities.

Testifying at an NCLB hearing, Martha Thurlow (2004), a noted scholar of including students in large-scale testing, emphasized that the existence of a disability should not automatically mean students cannot reach high standards. Expectations must be raised.

Listen to the voices of teachers who have used alternate assessments to engage their students in academic standards. "My attitude [about her abilities] was denying her the opportunity to succeed." "Now I look at the possibilities instead of the limitations." "He is doing things I didn't realize he could do." These optimistic comments represent the findings of Moore-Lamminen and Olsen (Alliance for Systems Change, n.d.), who documented the positive experiences of teachers who have stretched their students to excel.

James Kauffman would likely be pleased that these teachers and their students had found success. Simultaneously, he would doubt that this increased academic focus will bring all students to proficiency.

A New Jersey high school teacher (Karp, *Rethinking Schools Online*, 2004) bemoans the fact that the proficiency hurdle masks significant student change. "On a test . . . where a passing score is 200, helping a bilingual, special education student from a low income household raise his/her test score from, say, a 50 to 199 counts for nothing. . . . Moving a student from 199 to 200 is success."

U.S. Secretary of Education Margaret Spellings appears to have acknowledged that holding all students to one standard may not be the best way to reflect a school's progress. Holding firm to the "bright-line principles" that all students must participate and reach proficiency targets, she has announced pilots for growth models of accountability.

These pilots, approved through a peer-reviewed process, will track the achievement of individual children from year to year. Schools receive credit for the progress of each child, instead of the number of students who reach targets. Such a model, first approved in Tennessee and North Carolina, would address Karp's concerns and also document the incremental growth of students with disabilities.

Growth models are receiving initial approval. Some are pleased that schools will be held accountable for steady progress of each student (Hershberg, *Phi Delta Kappan,* 2005). The Council for Exceptional Children (CEC) (http://www.cec.sped.org), an international professional association, has long advocated a longitudinal growth model to document and validate the progress of students who may not reach grade-level standards.

Even with growth models, can all students reach proficiency? The *Education Week* study (Olson, 2004), cited by McGrew and Evans, noted discrepant opinions among the participating teachers. The majority of special education teachers surveyed were more optimistic about their students' content progress than were general education teachers. In addition, the special education teachers felt more prepared to tackle the content challenge than the general education teachers felt about teaching students with disabilities. Which group is optimistic? Which is realistic? How will these different opinions affect student performance?

Do expectations hold students back, or do they set reasonable, reachable targets that make a productive adulthood more likely? Can higher academic standards for schools raise our expectations for students with cognitive disabilities? Will growth models accurately reflect individual performance or reinforce lower expectations?

Have Schools Gone Too Far in Using Accommodations?

YES: James M. Kauffman, Kathleen McGee, and Michele Brigham, from "Enabling or Disabling? Observations on Changes in Special Education," *Phi Delta Kappan* (April 2004)

NO: MaryAnn Byrnes, from "Accommodations for Students with Disabilities: Removing Barriers to Learning," *National Association of Secondary School Principals Bulletin* (February 2000)

ISSUE SUMMARY

YES: James M. Kauffman, a faculty member at the University of Virginia, along with Kathleen McGee and Michele Brigham, both special education teachers, maintain that special education has pursued its goal of normalization to an extreme. The emphasis has shifted from increasing competence to perpetuating disabilities through the unwise use of accommodations.

NO: MaryAnn Byrnes, a University of Massachusetts–Boston faculty member, former special education administrator, and editor of this *Taking Sides*, argues that relevant accommodations are necessary to ensure that people with disabilities have a fair chance to demonstrate what they know and can do.

Have you ever used a curb-cut to ease the passage of your bike or a stroller? Have you pushed the automatic door opener button when your arms were full? Did you know that the now-ubiquitous food processor was designed to meet the cooking needs of a one-handed cook?

All of the above are accommodations. Originally designed to make the world more accessible for people with disabilities, they often make life easier for the rest of society. Federal laws require that reasonable accommodations like these be provided so that people with disabilities have fair and equal access to normal life activities.

Think about Braille texts and ramps in school. Amplification systems that expand the range of hearing aides in classrooms. Are they reasonable and acceptable accommodations to make school more accessible for children who have sensory or motoric disabilities? Most people would say they are.

Now think about scribes to transfer the words of a student into print. Or extended time for assignments and exams. Or permitting some students to submit a video or taped project instead of a written report. These are accommodations as well—for people who have difficulty writing or processing material quickly or sustaining attention. Do you accept them as easily? Many people pause here, wondering if these cross the line into making school a little too easy. Are these unreasonable accommodations?

Accommodations in school are adjustments to setting, timing, presentation mode, and/or response mode that allow students with disabilities to demonstrate what they know and can do. Their purpose is to make the task accessible. They are not intended to change the nature of a task, make it easier, or ensure that a student passes.

The issue of accommodations achieved controversial status with the advent of high-stakes testing and school accountability that includes students with disabilities. Federal laws require that schools provide appropriate accommodations to students with disabilities so they can participate fully in educational and assessment activities.

The argument is whether these accommodations are fair, just, and reasonable, or whether they go beyond leveling the playing field to create a whole new game that is just not fair to everyone else, including the students with disabilities.

Kauffman, McGee, and Brigham feel that accommodations have gone too far. Citing a number of powerful examples, they make the case that accommodations are being used indiscriminately. Bowing to threats from parents and their lawyers, educators extend accommodations that attempt to disguise a disability. In doing so, they abandon the commitment to hold students to high standards and responsibility.

Byrnes asks educators and parents to be thoughtful about the use of accommodations, choosing them to remove a barrier to learning. In her view, accommodations are to be selected carefully and matched with learning challenges so that students' disabilities don't stand in the way of acquiring, and demonstrating, knowledge and competence.

As you read these articles, ask yourself what you have seen, read, or heard about accommodations in schools. Do you think they help or hinder? Do educators and parents want to create opportunities or give excuses? In this era of high stakes, are people tempted to give the benefit of the doubt, extending accommodations in hopes of raising scores and granting diplomas? If so, does this create a climate of learned helplessness? Will students feel entitled rather than responsible?

YES ↵

James M. Kauffman, Kathleen McGee, and Michele Brigham

Enabling or Disabling? Observations on Changes in Special Education

Schools need demanding and distinctive special education that is clearly focused on instruction and habilitation. Abandoning such a conception of special education is a prescription for disaster. But special education has increasingly been losing its way in the single-minded pursuit of full inclusion.

Once, special education's purpose was to bring the performance of students with disabilities closer to that of their nondisabled peers in regular classrooms, to move as many students as possible into the mainstream with appropriate support. For students not in regular education, the goal was to move them toward a more typical setting in a cascade of placement options. But as any good thing can be overdone and ruined by the pursuit of extremes, we see special education suffering from the extremes of inclusion and accommodation.

Aiming for as much normalization as possible gave special education a clear purpose. Some disabilities were seen as easier to remediate than others. Most speech and language disorders, for example, were considered eminently remediable. Other disabilities, such as mental retardation and many physical disabilities, were assumed to be permanent or long-term and so less remediable, but movement *toward* the mainstream and increasing independence from special educators were clear goals.

The emphasis in special education has shifted away from normalization, independence, and competence. The result has been students' dependence on whatever special programs, modifications, and accommodations are possible, particularly in general education settings. The goal seems to have become the *appearance* of normalization without the *expectation* of competence.

Many parents and students seem to want more services as they learn what is available. Some have lost sight of the goal of limiting accommodations in order to challenge students to achieve more independence. At the same time, many special education advocates want all services to be available in mainstream settings, with little or no acknowledgment that the services are atypical. Although teachers, administrators, and guidance counselors are often willing and able to make accommodations, doing so is not always in students' best long-term interests. It gives students with disabilities what anthropologist Robert Edgerton called a cloak—a pretense, a cover, which actually fools no one—rather than actual competence.

In this article, we discuss how changes in attitudes toward disability and special education, placement, and accommodations can perpetuate disability. We also explore the problems of ignoring or perpetuating disability rather than helping students lead fuller, more independent lives. Two examples illustrate how we believe good intentions can go awry— how attempts to accommodate students with disabilities can undermine achievement.

"But he needs resource. . . ." Thomas, a high school sophomore identified as emotionally disturbed, was assigned to a resource class created to help students who had problems with organization or needed extra help with academic skills. One of the requirements in the class was for students to keep a daily planner in which they entered all assignments; they shared their planner with the resource teacher at the beginning of class and discussed what academic subjects would be worked on during that period.

Thomas consistently refused to keep a planner or do any work in resource (he slept instead). So a meeting was set up with the assistant principal, the guidance counselor, Thomas, and the resource teacher. As the meeting was about to begin, the principal announced that he would not stay because Thomas felt intimidated by so many adults. After listening to Thomas' complaints, the guidance counselor decided that Thomas would not have to keep a planner or show it to the resource teacher and that the resource teacher should not talk to him unless Thomas addressed her first. In short, Thomas would not be required to do any work in the class! When the resource teacher suggested that, under those circumstances, Thomas should perhaps be placed in a study hall, because telling the parents that he was in a resource class would be a misrepresentation, the counselor replied, "But he *needs* the resource class."

"He's too bright. . . ." Bob, a high school freshman with Asperger's Syndrome, was scheduled for three honors classes and two Advanced Placement classes. Bob's IEP included a two-page list of accommodations. In spite of his having achieved A's and B's, with just a single C in math, his mother did not feel that his teachers were accommodating him appropriately. Almost every evening, she emailed his teachers and his case manager to request more information or more help for Bob, and she angrily phoned his guidance counselor if she didn't receive a reply by the end of the first hour of the next school day.

A meeting was scheduled with the IEP team. When the accommodations were reviewed, Bob's mother agreed that all of them were being made. However, she explained that Bob had been removed from all outside social activities because he spent all night, every night, working on homework. The accommodation she demanded was that Bob have *no* homework assignments. The autism specialist agreed that this was a reasonable accommodation for a child with Asperger's Syndrome.

The teachers of the honors classes explained that the homework in their classes, which involved elaboration and extension of concepts, was even more essential than the homework assigned in AP classes. In AP classes, by contrast, homework consisted primarily of practice of concepts learned in class. The honors teachers explained that they had carefully broken their long assignments into segments, each having a separate due date before the final project, and they gave illustrations of their expectations. The director of special education explained the legal definition of accommodations (the mother said she'd never before heard that accommodations could not change the nature of the curriculum). The director also suggested that, instead of Bob's sacrificing his social life, perhaps it would be more appropriate for him to take standard classes. What Bob's mother was asking, he concluded, was not legal. She grew angry, but she did agree to give the team a "little more time" to serve Bob appropriately. She said she would "be back with her claws and broomstick" if anyone ever suggested that he be moved from honors classes without being given the no homework accommodation. "He's too bright to take anything less than honors classes, and if you people would provide this simple accommodation, he would do just fine," she argued. In the end, she got her way.

Attitudes Toward Disability and Special Education

Not that many decades ago, a disability was considered a misfortune—not something to be ashamed of but a generally undesirable, unwelcome condition to be overcome to the greatest extent possible. Ability was considered more desirable than disability, and anything—whether a device or a service— that helped people with disabilities to do what those without disabilities could do was considered generally valuable, desirable, and worth the effort, cost, and possible stigma associated with using it.

The disability rights movement arose in response to the widespread negative attitudes toward disabilities, and it had a number of desirable outcomes. It helped overcome some of the discrimination against people with disabilities. And overcoming such bias and unfairness in everyday life is a great accomplishment. But the movement has also had some unintended negative consequences. One of these is the outright denial of disability in some cases, illustrated by the contention that disability exists only in attitudes or as a function of the social power to coerce.

The argument that disability is merely a "social construction" is particularly vicious in its effects on social justice. Even if we assume that disabilities are socially constructed, what should that mean? Should we assume that socially constructed phenomena are not "real," are not important, or should be discredited? If so, then consider that dignity, civil rights, childhood, social justice, and nearly every other phenomenon that we hold dear are social constructions. Many social constructions are not merely near and dear to us, they are real and useful in benevolent societies. The important question is whether the idea of disability is useful in helping people attain dignity or whether it is more useful to assume that disabilities are not real (i.e., that, like social justice, civil rights, and other social constructions, they are fabrications that can be ignored when convenient). The denial of disability is sometimes expressed as an aversion to labels, so that we are cautioned not to communicate openly and clearly about disabilities but to rely on euphemisms. But this approach is counterproductive. When we are able only to whisper or mime the undesirable difference called disability, then we inadvertently increase its stigma and thwart prevention efforts.

The specious argument that "normal" does not exist—because abilities of every kind are varied and because the point at which normal becomes abnormal is arbitrary—leads to the conclusion that no one actually has a disability or, alternatively, that everyone has a disability. Then, some argue, either no one or everyone is due an accommodation so that no one or everyone is identified as disabled. This unwillingness to draw a line defining something (such as disability, poverty, or childhood) is based either on ignorance regarding the nature of continuous distributions or on a rejection of the unavoidably arbitrary decisions necessary to provide special services to those who need them and, in so doing, to foster social justice.

Another unintended negative consequence of the disability rights movement is that, for some people, disability has become either something that does not matter or something to love, to take pride in, to flaunt, to adopt as a positive aspect of one's identity, or to cherish as something desirable or as a badge of honor. When disability makes no difference to us one way or the other, then we are not going to work to attenuate it, much less prevent it. At best, we will try to accommodate it. When we view disability as a desirable difference, then we are very likely to try to make it more pronounced, not to ameliorate it.

Several decades ago, special education was seen as a good thing—a helpful way of responding to disability, not something everyone needed or should have, but a useful and necessary response to the atypical needs of students with disabilities. This is why the Education for All Handicapped Children Act (now the Individuals with Disabilities Education Act) was written. But in the minds of many people, special education has been transformed from something helpful to something awful.

The full-inclusion movement did have some desirable outcomes. It helped overcome some of the unnecessary removal of students with disabilities from general education. However, the movement also has had some unintended negative consequences. One of these is that special education has come to be viewed in very negative terms, to be seen as a second-class and discriminatory system that does more harm than good. Rather than being seen as helpful, as a way of creating opportunity, special education is often portrayed as a means of shunting students into dead-end programs and killing opportunity.

Another unintended negative consequence of full inclusion is that general education is now seen by many as the *only* place where fair and equitable treatment is possible and where the opportunity to learn is extended to all equally. The argument has become that special education is good only as long as it is invisible (or nearly so), an indistinguishable part of a general education system that accommodates all students, regardless of their abilities or disabilities. Usually, this is described as a "unified" (as opposed to "separate") system of education. Special education is thus something to be avoided altogether or attenuated to the greatest extent possible, regardless of a student's inability to perform in a general setting. When special education is seen as discriminatory, unfair, an opportunity-killing system, or, as one writer put it, "the gold-plated garbage can of American schooling," then it is understandable that people will loathe it. But this way of looking at special education is like seeing the recognition and treatment of cancer as the cause of the problem.

The reversal in attitudes toward disability and special education—disability from undesirable to inconsequential, special education from desirable to awful—has clouded the picture of what special education is and what it should do for students with disabilities. Little wonder that special education stands accused of failure, that calls for its demise have become vociferous, and that contemporary practices are often more disabling than enabling. An unfortunate outcome of the changing attitudes toward disability and special education is that the benefit of special education is now sometimes seen as freedom from expectations of performance. It is as if we believed that, if a student has to endure the stigma of special education, then the compensation should include an exemption from work.

Placement Issues

Placing all students, regardless of their abilities, in regular classes has exacerbated the tendency to see disability as something existing only in people's minds. It fosters the impression that students are fitting in when they are not able to perform at anywhere near the normal level. It perpetuates disabilities; it does not compensate for them.

Administrators and guidance counselors sometimes place students in programs for which they do not qualify, even as graduation requirements are increasing and tests are mandated. Often, these students' *testing* is modified although their *curriculum* is not. The students may then feel that they have beaten the system. They are taught that the system is unfair and that the only way to win is by gaming it. Hard work and individual responsibility for one's education are often overlooked—or at least undervalued.

Students who consistently fail in a particular curriculum must be given the opportunity to deal with the natural consequences of that fact as a means of learning individual responsibility. For example, social promotion in elementary and middle school teaches students that they really don't have to be able to do the work to pass. Students who have been conditioned to rely on social promotion do not believe that the cycle will end until it does so—usually very abruptly in high school. Suddenly, no one passes them on, and no one gives them undeserved credit. Many of these students do not graduate in four years. Some never recover, while others find themselves forced to deal with a very distasteful situation.

No one wants to see a student fail, but to alter any standard without good reason is to set that same student up for failure later in life. Passing along a student with disabilities in regular classes, pretending that he or she is performing at the same level as most of the class or that it doesn't really matter (arguing that the student has a legal "right" to be in the class) is another prescription for disappointment and failure in later life. Indeed, this failure often comes in college or on the job.

Some people with disabilities do need assistance. Others do not. Consider Deborah Groeber, who struggled through degenerative deafness and blindness. The Office of Affirmative Action at the University of Pennsylvania offered to intercede at the Wharton School, but Groeber knew that she had more influence if she spoke for herself. Today, she is a lawyer with three Ivy League degrees. But not every student with disabilities can do or should be expected to do what Groeber did. Our concern is that too many students with disabilities are given encouragement based on pretense when they could do much more with appropriate special education.

Types of Accommodations

Two popular modifications in IEPs are allowing for the use of calculators and granting extended time on tests and assignments. Calculators can be a great asset, but they should be used when calculating complex problems or when doing word problems. Indiscriminate use of a calculator renders many math tests invalid, as they become a contest to see if buttons can be pushed successfully and in the correct order, rather than an evaluation of ability to do arithmetic or use mathematical knowledge.

Extended time on assignments and tests can also be a useful modification, but it can easily be misused or abused. Extended time on tests should mean *continuous* time so that a test is not studied for first and taken later. Sometimes a test must be broken into smaller segments that can be completed independently. However, this could put students with disabilities at a disadvantage, as one part of a test might help with remembering another part. Extensions on assignments need to be evaluated each time they are given, not simply handed out automatically because they are written into an IEP. If a student is clearly working hard, then extensions may be appropriate. If a student has not even been attempting assignments, then more time might be an avoidance tactic. Sometimes extended time means that assignments pile up and the student gets further and further behind. The result can then be overwhelming stress and the inability to comprehend discussions because many concepts must be acquired in sequence (e.g., in math, science, history, and foreign languages).

Reading tests and quizzes aloud to students can be beneficial for many, but great caution is required. Some students and teachers want to do more than simply read a test. Reading a test aloud means simply reading the printed words on the page *without* inflections that can reveal correct answers and without explaining vocabulary. Changing a test to open-notes or open-book, without the knowledge and consent of the classroom teacher, breaches good-faith test proctoring. It also teaches students dependence rather than independence and accomplishment. Similarly, scribing for a student can be beneficial for those who truly need it, but the teacher must be careful not to add details and to write only what the student dictates, including any run-on sentences or fragments. After scribing, if the assignment is not a test, the teacher should edit and correct the paper with the student, as she might do with any written work. But this must take place *after* the scribing.

How Misguided Accommodations Can Be Disabling

"Saving" a child from his or her own negative behavior reinforces that behavior and makes it a self-fulfilling prophecy. Well-intentioned guidance counselors often feel more responsibility for their students' success or failure than the students themselves feel. Sometimes students are not held accountable for their effort or work. They seem not to understand that true independence comes from *what* you know, not *whom* you know. Students who are consistently enabled and not challenged are never given the opportunity to become independent. Ann Bancroft, the polar explorer and dyslexic, claims that, although school was a torment, it was disability that forged her iron will. Stephen Cannell's fear for other dyslexics is that they will quit trying rather than struggle and learn to compensate for their disability.

Most parents want to help their children. However, some parents confuse making life *easier* with making life *better* for their children. Too often, parents feel that protecting their child from the rigors of academic demands is in his or her best interest. They may protect their child by insisting on curricular modifications and accommodations in assignments, time, and testing. But children learn by doing, and not allowing them to do something because they might fail is denying them the opportunity to succeed. These students eventually believe that they are not capable of doing what typical students can do, even if they are. Sometimes it is difficult for teachers to discern what a student actually can do and what a parent has done until an in-class assignment is given or a test is taken. At that point, it is often too late for the teacher to do much remediation. The teacher may erroneously conclude that the student is simply a poor test-taker.

In reality, the student may have been "protected" from learning, which will eventually catch up with him or her. Unfortunately, students may not face reality until they take a college entrance exam, go away to college, or apply for a job. Students who "get through" high school in programs of this type often go on to flunk out of college. Unfortunately, the parents of these students frequently blame the college for the student's failure, criticizing the postsecondary institution for not doing enough to help. Instead, they should be upset both with the secondary institution for not preparing the child adequately for the tasks to come and with themselves for their own overprotection.

The Benefits of Demands

Many successful adults with disabilities sound common themes when asked about their ability to succeed in the face of a disability. Tom Gray, a Rhodes Scholar who has a severe learning disability, claims that having to deal with the hardest experiences gave him the greatest strength. Stephen Cannell believes that, if he had known there was a reason beyond his control to explain his low achievement, he might not have worked as hard as he did. Today, he knows he has a learning disability, but he is also an Emmy Award-winning television writer and producer. Paul Orlalea, the dyslexic founder of Kinko's, believes God gave him an advantage in the challenge presented by his disability and that others should work with their strengths. Charles Schwab, the learning-disabled founder of Charles Schwab, Inc., cites his ability to think differently and to make creative leaps that more sequential thinkers don't make as chief reasons for his success. Fannie Flagg, the learning-disabled author, concurs and insists that learning disabilities become a blessing *only if you can overcome them*. Not every student with a disability can be a star performer, of course, but all should be expected to achieve all that they can.

Two decades ago, special educators thought it was their job to assess a student's achievement, to understand what the student wanted to do and what an average peer could do, and then to develop plans to bridge the gap, if possible. Most special educators wanted to see that each student had the tools and knowledge to succeed as independently as possible. Helping students enter the typical world was the mark of success for special educators.

The full-inclusion movement now insists that *every* student will benefit from placement in the mainstream. However, some of the modifications and accommodations now being demanded are so radical that we are doing an injustice to the entire education system. Special education must not be associated in any way with "dumbing down" the curriculum for students presumed to be at a given grade level, whether disabled or not.

Counselors and administrators who want to enable students must focus the discussion on realistic goals and plans for each student. An objective, in-depth discussion and evaluation must take place to determine how far along the continuum of successfully completing these goals the student has moved. If the student is making adequate progress independently, or with minimal help, special education services might not be necessary. If assistance is required to make adequate progress on realistic goals, then special education may be needed. Every modification and every accommodation should be held to the same standard: whether it will help the student attain these goals—*not* whether it will make life easier for the student. Knowing where a student is aiming can help a team guide that student toward success.

And the student must be part of this planning. A student who claims to want to be a brain surgeon but refuses to take science courses needs a reality check. If a student is unwilling to attempt to reach intermediate goals or does not succeed in meeting them, then special education cannot "save" that student. At that point, the team must help the student revisit his or her goals. Goals should be explained in terms of the amount of work required to complete them, not whether or not the teacher or parent feels they are attainable. When goals are presented in this way, students can often make informed decisions regarding their attainability and desirability. Troy Brown, a university dean and politician who has both a doctorate and a learning disability, studied at home with his mother. He estimates that it took him more than twice as long as the average person to complete assignments. Every night, he would go to bed with stacks of books and read until he fell asleep, because he had a dream of attending college.

General educators and special educators need to encourage all students to be responsible and independent and to set realistic expectations for themselves. Then teachers must help students to meet these expectations in a more and more independent manner. Special educators do not serve students well when they enable students with disabilities to become increasingly dependent on their parents, counselors, administrators, or teachers—or even when they fail to increase students' independence and competence.

Where We Stand

We want to make it clear that we think disabilities are real and that they make doing certain things either impossible or very difficult for the people who have them. We cannot expect people with disabilities to be "just like everyone else" in what they can do. . . .

In our view, students with disabilities *do* have specific shortcomings and *do* need the services of specially trained professionals to achieve their potential. They *do* sometimes need altered curricula or adaptations to make their learning possible. If students with disabilities were just like "regular" students, then there would be no need whatever for special education. But the school experiences of students with disabilities obviously will not be—*cannot* be—just like those of students without disabilities. We sell students with disabilities short when we pretend that they are no different from typical students. We make the same error when we pretend that they must *not* be expected to put forth extra effort if they are to learn to do some things—or learn to do something in a different way. We sell them short when we pretend that they have competencies that they do not have or pretend that the competencies we expect of most students are not important for them.

Like general education, special education must push students to become all they can be. Special education must countenance neither the pretense of learning nor the avoidance of reasonable demands.

MaryAnn Byrnes

 NO

Accommodations for Students with Disabilities: Removing Barriers to Learning

Think about taking a driver's test without wearing glasses (if you do, that is). Not fair, you say; you need the glasses to see. You have just identified an accommodation that you need. Wearing glasses does not make a bad driver better or make driving easier; rather, wearing glasses makes driving possible. Glasses are so much a part of our lives that we do not even consider that they remove a barrier caused by a disability.

Secondary school teachers encounter students every day on an Individualized Education Plan (IEP) or 504 Plan, both of which address programs for students with disabilities. Most likely, the person charged with monitoring this plan has indicated that particular students need changes in teaching style, assignments, or testing strategies.

It is usually easy to understand the need for glasses or wheelchairs or hearing aids. These sound like changes the student must make. Other adjustments, modifications, or accommodations on these plans, such as extended time, may not be as clear.

What Is an Accommodation?

An accommodation is an adjustment, to an activity or setting, that removes a barrier presented by a disability so a person can have access equal to that of a person without a disability. An accommodation does not guarantee success or a specific level of performance. It should, however, provide the opportunity for a person with a disability to participate in a situation or activity.

Think of that pair of glasses, or the time you broke your leg and could not drive. Think of how your life was affected by these conditions. Your competence did not change. Your ability to think and work did not change. Your ability to interact with (have access to) the reading material may be very limited without your glasses. Your ability to get to (have access to) work or the grocery store may be very limited without someone to transport you. The support provided by the glasses—or the driver—made it

From *NASSP Bulletin*, 84(613), February 2000, pp. 21–27. Copyright © 2000 by National Association of Secondary School Principals. www.principals.org. Reprinted by permission via Rightslink.

possible for you to use your abilities without the barrier presented by less than perfect vision or limited mobility.

The accommodations in IEPs or 504 Plans serve the same purpose. They identify ways to remove the barrier presented by a person's disability.

Why Do We Need to Provide Accommodations?

Accommodations are required under Section 504 of the Federal Rehabilitation Act of 1974 as well as the Americans with Disabilities Act. Both these federal laws prohibit discrimination against individuals who have a disability. Situations that limit access have been determined to be discriminatory.

Accommodations must be provided not just by teachers to students, but by employees for workers and governments for citizens. Curbs have been cut to provide access. Doors have been widened and door handles altered to provide access to people for whom the old designs posed a barrier. Employers provide computer adaptations or other adjustments in work schedules and circumstances.

For employers and schools, individuals with disabilities may have a document called a 504 Plan, which details the types of accommodations that are required. Students who have a 504 Plan will not require special education services, just changes to the environment or instructional situation.

Students who have a disability and require special education services in addition to accommodations will have this information contained in an IEP, which also details the types of direct services that need to be provided and the goals of these services. Accommodations will be listed within this IEP.

With the recent changes in IDEA '97, the federal law governing special education, you will be addressing accommodations that must be made so a student with a disability can participate in large-scale districtwide or statewide assessment systems as well as classwork and school life.

Who Needs Accommodations?

According to Section 504, an individual with a disability is any person who has "a physical or mental impairment that limits one or more major life activities." IDEA '97, the federal special education law, lists the following disabilities: autism, deaf-blindness, deafness, hearing impairment, mental retardation, multiple disabilities, orthopedic impairment, other health impairment, serious emotional disturbance, specific learning disability, speech or language impairment, traumatic brain injury, and visual impairment.

Some conditions are covered by Section 504, but not special education. These can include attention deficit disorder—ADD, (also attention deficit hyperactivity disorder—ADHD); chronic medical conditions (such as cancer, Tourette Syndrome, asthma, or epilepsy); communicable diseases; some temporary medical conditions; physical impairments; and disorders of emotion or behavior. To qualify, there must be a demonstrated and substantial limitation of a major life activity.

Students (or adults) who have disabilities may require accommodations to have equal access to education. Not every student with a disability will require accommodations, and not every student with a disability requires the same accommodation all the time.

Think of Jim, a student who has limited mobility in his hands, affecting his ability to write. This disability will present a barrier in a class that requires the student to take notes quickly or write long essays in class. In a class that does not require either of these activities, no barrier may be present. Equal access is possible without accommodation. The student can learn and demonstrate what he knows and can do unaffected by his disability.

What Kind of Accommodations Are There?

Just as there is no limit to the range of disabilities, there is no limit to the range of accommodations. The point is to understand disability and determine if it presents a barrier to equal access. If so, decide whether an accommodation can be identified to remove the barrier—and make sure the accommodation is implemented.

Think of the student described above. The limited mobility in Jim's hands presents a barrier in a class that requires rapid note taking or the writing of long essays in class. There are several accommodations that can result in equal access. Jim might tape the lesson and take notes later. These notes could be written or dictated into a computer. Essays could be composed verbally at a computer workstation or dictated into a tape recorder or to a scribe. A computer might be adapted so typing becomes an effective way to record information on paper. In yet another type of accommodation, essays could be replaced by oral reports.

Are There Some Accommodations That Should Not Be Used?

Like many difficult questions, the answer depends on the context. An accommodation should not alter the essential purpose of the assignment. If the skill you want to measure is the ability to make multiple rapid hand movements, then there is probably no accommodation that is appropriate. Jim will not do well because of his disability. Alternately, if the purpose of a task is to see if someone has perfect vision without glasses, using those glasses is not an appropriate accommodation. If the purpose is to see if you can read, the glasses become a reasonable accommodation.

Who Decides about Accommodations?

The team that writes IEPs and 504 Plans reviews the disability and determines what accommodations, if any, are necessary. These are then written into the IEP or 504 Plan.

Once more, return to Jim. As you consider the requirements of your class, think of the most appropriate way to remove the barrier that is presented by the limited mobility Jim has in his hands.

If We Use Accommodations, How Will the Student Ever Be Prepared for Independent Life in College or the World of Work?

Some people are concerned that the supports provided in school will result in the student being unable to work productively when he or she leaves school. As a matter of fact, Section 504 applies to colleges and employers as well. Colleges offer support centers and provide accommodations upon documentation that a disability exists. Employers are required to provide reasonable accommodations to any person who is otherwise qualified to fulfill the elements of the job.

If companies remove barriers at the workplace, educators should be willing and able to take barriers out of the school activities that prepare a student for the workplace. Teachers can help a student identify the type of accommodation that will be the least cumbersome for everyone, and those that will permit the student to be most independent.

Don't Accommodations Just Make School Easier?

That depends on how you view the world. Does wearing glasses make driving easier? Not really—for a person with limited vision, wearing glasses makes driving *possible*. With or without glasses, you need to be able to drive to pass the test. The same is true of an academic accommodation; whether or not the accommodation is provided, the students still must demonstrate that they know required material.

Think about the important elements of your class: Is it more important that Jim take notes in class or understand the material? Is it more important that Jim demonstrate good handwriting or the ability to communicate thoughts in print? Often, when you identify the main purpose of your assignments and consider the skills and abilities of a student, you will see that an accommodation lets you determine more clearly what a student knows, understands, and can do.

Does a Student Need to Follow the IEP Accommodations in All Classes?

The IEP or 504 Plan needs to address any area in which the student's disability affects life in school. Sometimes this means in all classes, but not always. For example, a student who was blind would need to use Braille in all classes dealing with written material. Jim, our student with limited mobility in his hands, might not require accommodations in world languages or physical education.

Can We Make Accommodations without Having Students on an IEP?

Many accommodations are just different ways of teaching or testing. You should be able to have this freedom in your classes. In some cases, the way in which a class is taught makes accommodations unnecessary. Accommodations change the situation, not the content of the instruction. However, accommodations on standardized tests must be connected to IEP's or 504 Plans.

May Teachers Give Different Assignments on the Same Content as a Way to Meet the Needs of Different Learning Styles without Lowering Standards?

Absolutely. The point is to remove the barrier of the disability; this is one way to accomplish that. Some teachers find they tap student knowledge best in active projects; others find that written work is best. Many secondary schools are using portfolios or performance activities to document student learning.

These assessment activities can be very compelling and they do tap different methods of expression. A student like Jim, for example, might communicate depth of understanding and analysis to a social studies debate that might be difficult to capture in an on-demand written test. A student with a disability in the area of speech or language might find barriers in the performance activities that do not exist on a paper-and-pencil task.

What If Accommodations Are Not Implemented?

Since accommodations allow equal access, refusing to provide them can be viewed as discrimination. Individuals who knowingly refuse to implement accommodations make themselves personally liable for legal suit.

This sounds serious, and it is serious. Once the accommodations are found to be necessary, everyone must implement them in situations where the student's disability poses a barrier that prevents equal access.

If no barrier exists in your class, the accommodation is not necessary. No one has the option, however, of deciding not to implement a necessary accommodation. Telling students they could not wear glasses or use a hearing aid is unthinkable. Just as inappropriate is a decision not to allow Jim to use accommodations to remove the barrier posed by his disability, even though it means making some changes to your own work.

Questions About Specific Accommodations

Now that the issues underlying accommodations have been addressed, it is time to talk about frequently-encountered accommodations that raise questions and concern. All these questions have come from secondary school faculty members in a variety of school systems.

Why Is It Fair to Read Material Aloud to Some Students?

Some students have a learning disability that makes it difficult for them to decode print. They can understand the concepts; they can comprehend the material when they hear it; they can reason through the material. They just can't turn print into meaning. If the task is to determine if the student can read, you already know they will have difficulty. If the task is to determine if the student has content knowledge, reading material aloud removes the barrier of the learning disability. Reading material aloud to a student who does not understand the material will not result in a higher grade.

Why Is It Fair to Give Some Students Extra Time on Tests?

Some students have motor difficulties that make writing an enormous challenge. They may not be able to form the letters correctly. They may not be able to monitor their thoughts while they work on the physical act of writing. They understand the material, and they know what they want to respond; it just takes longer to write the answer. If the task is to determine how quickly the student can respond, you already know they will have difficulty. If the task is to determine if the student has the knowledge, providing extra time removes the barrier of the motor disability. Providing extra time to a student who does not understand the material will not result in a higher grade.

Why Is It Fair to Permit Some Students to Respond Orally to Tests?

Think about the example above. For some students, responding orally would be a comparable accommodation. In this case, allowing an oral response will not result in a higher grade if the student does not know the material.

The Bottom Line

It all comes down to deciding what is important. Think about your assignment and expectations. Think about the disability. If the disability provides a barrier, the accommodation removes it. The accommodation does not release a student from participating or demonstrating knowledge—it allows the student to be able to participate and demonstrate knowledge. And isn't that what school is all about?

POSTSCRIPT

Have Schools Gone Too Far in Using Accommodations?

The authors agree that accommodations are necessary and can be an important educational tool. Kauffman and colleagues feel special education randomly tosses about accommodations to make life "easy" for students and, thereby, limiting opportunities to learn and excel. Byrnes says that wisely chosen accommodations provide the opportunity for students to demonstrate their capacity to achieve high standards.

Two questions are at the heart of the debate. When should accommodations be provided? Which accommodations should be provided?

Horn and Tynan (Fordham Foundation, 2001) agree with Kauffman and colleagues that accommodations are used too widely. They believe accommodations made sense early on when the intention was to ensure that students with significant sensory or motor disabilities had access to a free and appropriate public education. Now, they say, their use has been broadened to create a "lifetime of dependence," often at taxpayers' expense.

Writing in *Education Week's* 2004 Quality Counts edition focusing on the state of special education in a standards-based environment, Olson observes that states differ widely in their definition of acceptable accommodations. She references the continuing challenge of deciding whether a particular accommodation helps or gives an unfair advantage. The difficulty of selecting appropriate accommodations makes it easy to identify too many, too few, or incorrect options.

Extending the significant work of the National Center on Educational Outcomes, Bolt and Thurlow (*Remedial & Special Education*, 2004), emphasize the need to provide appropriate accommodations to ensure students with disabilities are included in the curriculum and assessment changes of education reform. Educators must determine which accommodations enhance access without changing demands.

Some say that anyone would do better if they had more time, a reader, or a computer. The evidence seems to say that is not so. To be appropriate, an accommodation must confer a "differential boost." It must result in a gain for students with disabilities, without enhancing the scores of typical learners. This would show that students could demonstrate knowledge, once the impact of a disability was removed. Reviewing research on the differential impact of the most commonly allowed accommodations, including extended time, Bolt and Thurlow (2004) uncovered mixed results. Some had very little impact. Elliott and Marquart (*Exceptional Children*, 2004) found that extended time on math tests did not provide an advantage to students with disabilities. It did, however, help everyone feel more relaxed and provided them more time to check the accuracy of their responses.

The point, say Fuchs and Fuchs (*The School Administrator,* 1999), is to choose accommodations that result in valid, rather than optimal, performance. It is not always easy to make this determination. Students and disabilities are different. Task demands differ. The Fuchs have developed the Dynamic Assessment of Testing Accommodations (DATA) to help educators determine which accommodations are most appropriate to choose. While this evidence-based method holds much promise, it requires a substantial investment of time.

Because this field is so new, research evidence is not comprehensive. Because students differ dramatically, research is difficult to conduct. Would you want your child in the control group? Because stakes can be so high for students and schools, correct decisions are critical. How can we all be sure we make the right choices as we continue to provide meaningful education? And can we ensure that we provide appropriate accommodations when they are needed; teach required skills; and remove the accommodations when the student no longer needs them?

ISSUE 13

Can One Model of Special Education Serve All Students?

YES: Wayne Sailor and Blair Roger, from "Rethinking Inclusion: Schoolwide Applications," *Phi Delta Kappan* (March 2005)

NO: Naomi Zigmond, from "Where Should Students with Disabilities Receive Special Education Services? Is One Place Better Than Another?" *The Journal of Special Education* (vol. 37, no. 3, 2003)

ISSUE SUMMARY

YES: Wayne Sailor, professor of education and associate director of the Beach Center on Disability at the University of Kansas–Lawrence, and Blair Roger, an educational consultant based in Oakland, California, believe that a school-based model of support services for all students would successfully increase inclusionary practices.

NO: Naomi Zigmond, professor of education at the University of Pittsburgh, maintains that promoting one model of services over another is the wrong approach and advocates that educators and researchers need to focus attention on individual students.

When special education laws began, people focused on getting students with disabilities into school. Initially, many children with mild disabilities received their specially designed instruction in small self-contained rooms, with little connection to their age mates. Over time, some children were enrolled in typical classes, but "pulled out" to receive help from a specialist. School focused on intensive instruction and remediation. The goal was to help students conquer the basic skills so they could return to their "regular" classes. When this remediation occurred, students often missed the curriculum and activities of the general classroom. Two separate educational systems existed. Many thought the standards and expectations of small classes were far too low.

In 1986, Madeline Will, then-Assistant Secretary of Education, launched the Regular Education Initiative (*Exceptional Children*, 1986). Acknowledging that the first 10 years of mandated special education had provided opportunities for many children, she decried the separate nature of special education. She challenged general education administrators to take responsibility for the education of students with mild to moderate disabilities and accept "the general applicability of special education techniques beyond the confines of the special education class." In words that could have been spoken yesterday, Secretary Will predicted that less segregated programming would "prepare *all* children to identify, analyze and resolve problems as they arise; to increase their ability to cope in a flexible manner with change . . . and to enter the community as informed and educated citizens who are capable of living and working as independent and productive adults."

Note that Secretary Will's emphasis was on students with mild to moderate disabilities. The *Annual Reports to Congress* indicate that the percentage of children with disabilities increased consistently from 1988 to 2000, especially students identified as having learning disabilities. In general, these students are considered to have mild disabilities. The services and supports they need are not viewed as intense. These children were the focus of Secretary Will's words.

The impact of a learning disability is deceptive. Although children might look, think, and behave much like their typical peers, they encounter significant challenges mastering the basic building blocks of reading, writing, and/or math. Educators and researchers labor mightily to identify specialized teaching methods that overcome the hurdles posed by nimble minds stymied by tasks others master so easily. Teachers identify these children as needing special education because they have not responded to traditional classroom methods.

Echoing Will's words, Wayne Sailor and Blair Roger criticize the separation that still exists. They claim that special education continues to be disengaged from general education—too focused on individuals. Sailor and Roger present a whole-school support model, in which previously specialized services improve the learning of all students.

Naomi Zigmond notes that inclusion conversations, which once focused on access to peers, now emphasize access to the general curriculum. She has discovered no compelling reason to focus on *where* education takes place. Instead, she urges that we strive to do what is best for individual learners— and that may take place in specialized educational settings.

Sailor and Roger think special educators focus on the trees and miss the forest of the whole school. Zigmond thinks we need to focus on the trees to ensure they grow strong. As you read these articles, ask yourself which approach will provide the best education for students with disabilities.

YES

Wayne Sailor and
Blair Roger

Rethinking Inclusion: Schoolwide Applications

As a field, special education presents an excellent case study of the paradox of differentiation and integration, wherein we seek solutions through increased specialization but, in so doing, we redefine a problem in terms of discrete parts at the expense of the whole. As Thomas Skrtic pointed out more than a decade ago, a large and ever-widening gap exists between the purpose of special education—to provide needed supports, services, adaptations, and accommodations to students with disabilities in order to preserve and enhance their educational participation in the least restrictive environment—and its practice. And that practice has evolved over three decades into a parallel and highly differentiated educational structure, often with only loosely organized connections to the general education system.

Having disengaged from general education early on, special education began to undergo a process that, at times, has seemed to mimic cell division. At one point in its ontogeny, the field could list some 30 distinct eligibility categories for special education services (e.g., learning disabilities, behavioral disorders, severe disabilities, autism, and so on). Many of these early categories further subdivided, with autism, for example, splitting into a host of subcategories lumped under "autism spectrum disorders."

How has all of this come about? The paradox of differentiation and integration—with its tensions in practice and contradictions in policy—offers a reasonable hypothesis. In our efforts to better meet the educational needs of specific identifiable groups, we have promoted differentiation at the expense of integration. If such a policy produced exemplary outcomes, the only remaining questions would concern how to direct scarce resources to meet the needs of a few individuals, and the values underlying special education would no doubt resolve the tension in favor of customization and differentiation. But the positive outcomes don't seem to be there.

In its early days, special education embraced the diagnostic/prescriptive model characteristic of modern medicine, and disability was viewed as pathology. Psychology, with its partner the test industry, became the "gatekeeper" for special education. Students referred by teachers and parents were diagnosed in one of the categories of disability and tagged for separate (highly differentiated) treatment. Indeed, special education policy handbooks at the

From *Phi Delta Kappan*, March 2005, pp. 503–509. Copyright © 2005 by Phi Delta Kappan. Reprinted by permission of Phi Delta Kappan and Wayne Sailor and Blair Roger.

district level came to resemble the *Diagnostic and Statistical Manual* of the American Psychiatric Association.

Then in the 1980s, the U.S. Department of Education began to advance policy reforms designed to slow the growth in the number of special education categorical placements and practices. These initiatives occurred against a backdrop of publications citing positive outcomes from integrated practices and a corresponding barrage of studies associating separate classrooms and pullout practices with negative outcomes.

The first of these reforms was called the Regular Education Initiative and was designed to stimulate the provision of special education supports and services in general education classrooms. It generated enormous controversy within special education. Indeed, a special issue of the *Journal of Learning Disabilities* was devoted entirely to an attempt to refute the research underlying the policy. Framing the reform of special education policy as general education policy ("regular" education initiative) failed completely within the community of special education.

More recently, federal policy has advanced "inclusion" as recommended practice and has expended significant funds for training, research, and demonstration purposes. This initiative, too, has failed to significantly change special education placement and service configurations, over about a 15-year period. Again, the policy has drawn fire from within special education and has failed to attract interest and enthusiasm from general education.

The No Child Left Behind (NCLB) legislation, for all its problems, does offer special education an opportunity to pursue once again the pathway to integration. First, NCLB makes clear that *all children* in public education are general education students. Second, the law is firmly anchored in accountability, even going so far as to define "evidence" and to restrict scientific inquiry to approved methodologies. If students identified for special education are placed in general education settings and provided with specialized services and supports, and if evidence for academic and social outcomes is to be evaluated according to approved methodologies, then there is an opportunity to achieve a measure of integrated education policy. And the sum of available evidence overwhelmingly supports integrated instructional approaches over those that are categorically segregated, regardless of the categorical label or severity of the disability.

A Schoolwide Approach

That inclusion policy has failed to garner much support from general education can be partially attributed to the way "inclusion" has been defined. Virtually all definitions begin with a general education classroom as the unit of interest and analysis for the provision of supports and services. The problem with a general-classroom-based model is that it doesn't seem credible to the general education teacher, whose job is usually seen as moving students as uniformly as possible through the curriculum. Students whose disabilities impede them from progressing at the expected rate and who, as a result, fall whole grade levels behind their classmates on various components of the curriculum seem to belong elsewhere. Special education has usually been there to oblige with separate categorical placements, particularly when "inclusion" has been tried and has "failed."

Alternatively, when inclusion is a core value of the school program, students with IEPs (individualized education programs) who cannot function in various components of the classroom curriculum often find themselves at tables, usually in the back of the classroom, with paraprofessionals who, in a one-on-one approach, work with them on "something else." This practice not only segregates special education students within the general education classroom but also creates a distraction that has a detrimental effect on general and special education students alike.

But does inclusion need to be tied to a classroom-based model? If the objective is to avoid separate, categorical placements as the chief alternative to general education placements, then can we shift the unit of analysis from the classroom to the school? So if Joey is a student who, because of his disabilities, cannot progress at grade level in the third grade, then we can ask, For those portions of the third-grade curriculum that Joey cannot successfully engage, even with support, where should he be? With whom? And doing what? The problem then becomes one of scheduling, personnel deployment, and the use of space, not one of alternative placement.

A schoolwide approach is not a variation on the older "pull-out" model. Under emerging schoolwide models, students with IEPs are not removed from general education classrooms to receive one-on-one therapies and tutorials or to go to "resource rooms." Following the logic of integration, all services and supports are provided in such a way as to benefit the maximum number of students, including those not identified for special education. Indeed, in recent years, special education has developed evidence-based practices that have been shown to work for general education students as well. Learning strategies, positive behavior support, and transition planning are three excellent examples. Here's a good summary of this new kind of thinking:

> In a transformed urban school, then, learning and other educational supports are organized to meet the needs of all students rather than historical conventions or the way the rooms are arranged in the building. Creative reallocation of even limited resources and innovative reorganization of teachers into partnerships and teams offer ways to break old molds and create the flexibilities needed to focus on student learning and achievement. Previously separate "programs," like special education, Title I, or bilingual education, come together to form a new educational system that delivers necessary additional supports and instruction in the same spaces to diverse groups of students. The new system anchors both organizational and professional effort in student content, performance, and skill standards that are owned by local communities and families while informed by national and state standards, curriculum frameworks, and effective assessment strategies.

The Individuals with Disabilities Education Act (IDEA) contains language in its "incidental benefits" section that encourages applications of special education that hold promise for general education students. This approach enables special educators to support students with special needs by means of integrated arrangements.

Three decades of comprehensive special education have produced an extraordinary wealth of pedagogical adaptations and strategies to enhance learning. This unique set of conditions came about through the provision of set-aside funds for research under IDEA, and much of that research has focused on problem-solving strategies that can benefit any hard-to-teach students. Today, NCLB exhorts us to teach all students to the highest attainable standards. Special education has designed instructional enhancements that can facilitate this outcome, but for these research-based enhancements to benefit all students, special education needs to be integrated with general education. Emerging schoolwide approaches and the call for a "universal design for learning" represent early efforts in this direction.

When a schoolwide approach is applied to "lowperforming" schools, such as those sometimes found in isolated rural settings or in inner-city areas affected by conditions of extreme poverty, mounting evidence suggests that integrated applications of special education practices can yield positive outcomes for all students. For example, when fully integrated applications of learning strategies designed originally for students with specific learning disabilities have been implemented, scores on NCLB-sanctioned accountability measures for all students have increased. Where social development is at issue, the use of schoolwide positive behavior support has led to higher standardized test scores for general education students in low-performing schools.

SAM

To illustrate how an integrated model works in practice, we describe below our own version of such an approach, called SAM for Schoolwide Applications Model, which is being implemented and evaluated in eight California elementary and middle schools and in one elementary school in Kansas City, Kansas. We describe this model in terms of six "guiding principles," which can be broken down into 15 "critical features." Each feature can be evaluated over time using SAMAN (Schoolwide Applications Model Analysis System), an assessment instrument designed to enable schools themselves to link specific interventions to academic and social outcomes for all students. While this approach can appear to mimic comprehensive school reform in some ways, it is specifically designed to be integrated into the existing values and culture of each individual school. In other words, under SAM, a school that wishes to unify its programs and resources is presented with the 15 critical features and instructed to use team processes to implement them according to its own culture and time lines. Across our nine research sites, we are seeing great diversity and creativity on the part of school teams.

Guiding Principles and Critical Features

Guiding Principle 1.   General education guides all student learning. As a fully integrated and unified model, SAM proceeds on the key assumption that all student learning is guided by a district's framework for curriculum, instruction, and assessment and is thus aligned with state standards. Four critical features support this principle: 1) all students attend their regularly assigned school; 2) all students are considered general education students; 3) general education teachers are responsible for all students; and 4) all students are instructed in accordance with the general education curriculum.

Most teacher training programs today continue to encourage general education teachers to expect special education teachers to assume primary responsibility for students with IEPs. Special education departments at colleges and universities reinforce this notion by training special education teachers in self-contained classrooms and by having little overlap with general education departments, such as departments of curriculum and instruction. An integrated schoolwide model, on the other hand, essentially requires teachers to see their role differently. At SAM schools, the general education teacher is the chief agent of each child's educational program, with support from a variety of others. Using SAM, general education teachers have primary responsibility for all students, consider themselves responsible for implementing IEPs, and collaborate with special education professionals to educate students with disabilities.

Furthermore, this guiding principle encourages schools to avoid such alternative placements as special schools for students who need extensive services and supports. Through SAM, schools welcome these students and configure any funding that comes with them to benefit a variety of students through integrated applications.

At our research sites, it is school policy to encourage parent participation and involvement, and parents are given extensive information about the schoolwide model. In those rare cases when parents feel strongly that their child requires a separate, self-contained placement—and the district concurs—the student may be referred to a comparable non-SAM school that offers self-contained classes for students with disabilities.

SAM does not allow for separate classes for students with disabilities at the school site, so the challenge is to focus on how such students can be supported in the general education classroom, how they can be supported in other environments, and how specialized therapies and services can be provided. The use of space, the deployment of support personnel, and scheduling issues become significant. At SAM schools, very little attention is focused on the existence of disabilities among some students. Every effort is made to foster friendships and positive relationships among students with and without disabilities.

SAM differs from traditional inclusion models by ensuring that students with IEPs are pursuing goals and objectives matched to and integrated with the curriculum being implemented in the general education classroom. Under SAM, no student with disabilities would be found at the rear of a classroom, engaged with a paraprofessional on some task that is unrelated to what the rest of the class is doing. If the class is engaged in a higher-level curricular activity, say, algebra, and a student with disabilities cannot engage that material with measurable benefit, then that student might be assigned to an integrated grouping outside of the classroom for that period. In that case, instruction in remedial math would take place with general education students who are also operating at the same curricular level.

There are times, of course, when one-on-one instruction is appropriate in the general education classroom, but this option would be available to any student who could benefit rather than restricted solely to students identified for special education. For example, any child who needs intensive instruction in reading might receive a 30-minute tutorial session in the school's learning center while the rest of the class is engaged in a reading exercise.

Guiding Principle 2.   All school resources are configured to benefit all students. Three critical features support this principle: 1) all students are included in all activities; 2) all resources benefit all students; and 3) the school effectively incorporates general education students in the instructional process.

In traditional schools, students in special education often do not accompany general education students on field trips; attend sporting events, assemblies, performances, and after-school programs; or take part in specialized reading, math, and science programs or enrichment programs in the arts. SAM schools seek to overcome such barriers to inclusion in all regular school events. All students with IEPs are members of age-appropriate, grade-level classrooms, and they attend all non-classroom functions with their classmates.

Large SAM schools, particularly secondary schools, also make use of small-group arrangements at the classroom level and small learning communities at the school level. Cooperative learning groups, student-directed learning, peer tutorials, peer-mediated instructional arrangements, and so on can greatly enhance outcomes for all students in integrated instructional settings. In addition, particularly in large middle schools and high schools, teams of general and support teachers skilled in math or literacy can use learning centers to support any student's needs. The learning center becomes flexible space for tutorial services offered by teachers or volunteer members of the National Honor Society, as well as a place to make up tests, complete homework with assistance, see a missed film, find resources for a paper or project, and so forth.

Guiding Principle 3.   Schools address social development and citizenship forthrightly. A single critical feature undergirds this principle: the school incorporates positive behavior support (PBS) at the individual, group, and schoolwide levels. PBS was originally developed as specialized instruction in social development for students with behavioral disabilities. But it has demonstrated its efficacy for all students, particularly those in schools challenged by urban blight and poverty. SAM schools incorporate schoolwide PBS as a comprehensive intervention package to help meet the social development needs of all students.

Guiding Principle 4.   Schools are democratically organized, data-driven, problem-solving systems. Four critical features support this principle: 1) the school is data-driven and uses team processes; 2) all personnel take part in the teaching/learning process; 3) the school employs a noncategorical lexicon; and 4) the school is governed by a site leadership team.

SAM schools are encouraged to upgrade district software to enable the leadership team to make use of all available databases that affect the social and academic performance of students. Through a process called school-centered planning, SAM schools use a variety of performance data fields, disaggregated at the district level, to make decisions regarding priorities related to school improvement.

SAM schools recognize that all salaried personnel at a school can contribute to the teaching/learning process. A custodian may have hidden talents for vocational training, or a speech therapist may be skilled in musical composition. The trick is to enable all school personnel to contribute to the primary mission of the school and not to be completely constrained by bureaucratic specifications of roles. SAM schools also seek to move away from such categorical descriptors as "learning disabilities," "inclusion," "specials," and so on. There are just two kinds of teachers in a SAM school: classroom teachers and support teachers.

A site leadership team is established at each SAM school. It represents all school personnel and may include parents and members of the local community. This team undertakes the process of school-centered planning to evaluate data related to student academic and social performance, to prioritize specific interventions to improve outcomes, and to advance the mission of the school through full implementation of SAM.

Guiding Principle 5.   Schools have open boundaries in relation to their families and communities. Two critical features support this guiding principle: 1) schools have working partnerships with their students' families; and 2) schools have working partnerships with local businesses and service providers.

SAM schools go beyond the traditional structure of parent/teacher organizations and solicit the active participation of family members in the teaching/learning process. Some SAM sites have made the establishment of a family resource center at the school a top priority. Some have even created a "parent liaison" position.

SAM schools also reach beyond the "business partnership" relationship that has characterized some school reform efforts. Schools undertake a "community mapping" process to understand their respective communities. Under many circumstances, the school community may not be geographically defined. But the point is to engage the school's constituents in the life of the school.

Furthermore, effective community partnerships set the stage for meaningful service-learning opportunities and open up possibilities for community-based instruction for any student. Students with IEPs, for example, who cannot engage a secondary-level, classroom-based math curriculum, might take part in "community math" in real-life applied settings such as banks and stores. Other students who are chronically unmotivated by school may reconnect with the learning process through community-based learning opportunities.

Guiding Principle 6. Schools enjoy district support for undertaking an extensive systems-change effort. Just one critical feature is necessary here: schoolwide models such as SAM that offer a significant departure from traditional bureaucratic management and communication processes must have district support. One way to garner such support is to set up pilot projects with the understanding that expansion to additional sites is contingent on documented gains in measured student academic and social outcomes. District-level support may be expected to increase following successful demonstrations and sharing results across schools over time.

Measurement Strategies

Each SAM school employs a package of psychometrically established instruments with which to assess progress related to the priorities that were established through the school-centered planning process. These instruments include a schoolwide evaluation tool to assess support for positive behavior, SAMAN to assess the 15 critical features of SAM, and EVOLVE to assess the training of paraprofessionals and the ways they are deployed.

Districts are encouraged to use the COMPASS Data Analyzer as an adjunct to the districtwide data system to enable each SAM school to receive feedback about its own priorities and specific data of interest. The program also facilitates reporting to the other teams and committees at the school.

Structural Elements of SAM

SAM is a fully integrated and unified approach to the education of all students. As a process, it is intended to enable schools to engage in collaborative, team-driven decision making that is focused on interventions designed to enhance academic and social outcomes for students. The process of educating all students together presents both challenges and opportunities. The SAM approach requires certain structural elements to be in place. As touched upon earlier, two elements, a site leadership team and school-centered planning, must be present at the school level. And two more elements, a district leadership team and a district resource team, must be present at the district level.

Site leadership team. The SLT, usually with between eight and 12 members, evaluates schoolwide data on student progress; sets priorities, goals, and objectives for each school term; and networks with and reports to the other teams and committees that function at the school. The principal is usually a member of the SLT but does not need to be its chair. Membership on SLTs is usually determined by a combination of internal teacher nominations, with elections for one-year renewable terms; principal appointments; and invitations to specific parents and community members. Expenses incurred by parent and community participants, the cost of substitutes for participating teachers who attend out-of-class meetings, the cost of supplies, and so on, can become budget items for SLTs. SLTs follow strict team procedures with regard to agenda, floor time, minutes, and so on, so that precious time is not wasted. SLTs meet at least biweekly and undergo full-day "retreats" at least twice a year, prior to the beginning of each new term. The school-centered-planning process takes place during these retreats.

School-centered planning. The SCP process is patterned after empowerment evaluation. Using this process, a facilitator, supplied by the district or arranged through a university partnership, assists the SLT to begin with a vision for why the school decided to become a SAM school. A set of goals is derived to make the vision real, and a set of specific objectives for the coming term is spelled out for the various school/community personnel. Measurement strategies are identified for each objective so that subsequent planning and objective setting can take account of data on pupil performance that are linked to specific measurable processes. The SLT holds interim meetings to review progress in the implementation of each SCP action plan for the term.

District leadership team. The DLT consists of district personnel with an interest in implementing SAM. The superintendent may well be a member but usually will not be the chair. DLTs are frequently chaired by the head of curriculum and instruction, since SAM processes are driven primarily by general education. Other members of the DLT typically include the head of pupil support services, the special education director, the Title I director, and the director of programs for second-language learners. The superintendent may appoint other members as needed. The DLT usually meets three or four times a year to review SAM school-site plans and to consider requests for approval of policy and budget items arising from these plans.

District resource team. The final structural component is the DRT. This team is usually made up of district-level staff members who work closely with the schools, such as regional special education personnel, grade-level specialists, the parent support coordinator, and transportation officials. The function of the DRT is to help the DLT consider requests for resources from each school site for the coming term. If, for example, a SAM site requests two additional paraprofessionals to implement one or more objectives on its plan for the coming term, the DRT will consider the request, balance the needs of that site against the collective needs of all district schools, and make recommendations to the DLT. Typically, DRTs with several SAM sites in the district will meet on a fairly frequent basis to help the district stay ahead of the curve of systems change.

The Schoolwide Applications Model is a work in progress. It represents an effort to integrate all aspects of comprehensive school reform with a new and innovative approach to the delivery of special education supports and services. Research must continue if we are to determine whether the premise of SAM holds: namely, that de-differentiated educational practices can support personalized learning—in and outside of classrooms—while creating a sense of unity and a culture of belonging in the school.

Naomi Zigmond

NO

Where Should Students with Disabilities Receive Special Education Services? Is One Place Better than Another?

The question of where special education students should be educated is not new. Lloyd Dunn raised the question in 1968, and response to his article spurred the adoption of resource room services in place of special day classes in the 1970s. The question was raised again in 1975 with the passage of the Education for All Handicapped Children Act, later known as the Individuals with Disabilities Education Act (IDEA), and its balanced support for both a continuum of services and placement in the least restrictive environment. The Act required that procedures be established

> to assure that, to the maximum extent appropriate, handicapped children . . . are educated with children who are not handicapped and that . . . removal of handicapped children from the regular educational environment occurs only when the nature or severity of that handicap is such that education in regular classes with the use of supplemental aids and services cannot be achieved satisfactorily.

The very first annual report to Congress by the U.S. Department of Health, Education and Welfare provided a succinct summary of this balanced position. The argument went as follows. In 1819, in *McColloch v. Maryland,* the courts maintained that the government's purpose should be served with as little imposition on the individual as possible—if less dramatic means for achieving the same basic purpose could be found, they should be taken. Years later, this court decision was interpreted to mean that children with disabilities should be educated in as mainstream a setting as possible. That interpretation was supported by the wave of civil rights litigation in the late 1960s and early 1970s, most notably *Brown v. Board of Education* (1954) and *Pennsylvania Association for Retarded Children (PARC) v. Commonwealth of Pennsylvania* (1972). *PARC*, and the subsequent *Mills v. Board of Education of the District of Columbia* (1972) case, established the proposition that children with disabilities should be placed in the least

From *Journal of Special Education,* vol. 37, no. 3, October 2003, pp. 193–199. Copyright © 2003 by Pro-Ed, Inc. Reprinted by permission via Copyright Clearance Center.

drastic, or most normal, setting appropriate, with as little interference and as normal an educational process as possible.

Court cases established the principle of least restrictiveness, but they were only part of the story. State and federal legislation reiterated the principle. Well before the federal legislation became effective, the principle of least restrictiveness embodied in the *PARC* agreement was clearly established in the laws, statutes, or regulations of at least 20 states. In fact, in its first annual report to Congress, the U.S. Department of Health, Education and Welfare proudly proclaimed that even in 1976–1977, the school year preceding full implementation of the new federal law, "many handicapped children are already receiving their education in a regular classroom setting and appropriate alternative placements are in most cases available to accommodate children with special needs." During the following decades, efforts would be made to move services for students with disabilities out of separate schools and into regular schools, with these students being integrated (mainstreamed) into general education classes for part of the school day and provided with pull-out itinerant, resource, or part-time special education services for the rest of the day.

The question of where students with disabilities should be educated was hotly debated again in the mid-1980s, as essays on the failure of pull-out special education began to proliferate. The theme was consistent: Fundamental changes in the delivery model for special education were needed to increase the accomplishments of students with disabilities. Even Madeline Will, then Assistant Secretary of Education and head of the Office of Special Education Programs, joined the fray: "Although well intentioned, the so-called 'pull out' approach to the educational difficulties of students with learning problems has failed in many instances to meet the educational needs of these students." Will and other advocates of the regular education initiative called for children with learning problems to have completely integrated educational experiences in order to achieve improved educational outcomes.

The 1997 IDEA amendments raised the question of where students with disabilities should be educated with a new urgency. Whereas earlier definitions of *restrictiveness* had focused on access of students with disabilities to nondisabled peers, the new focus defined this in terms of their access to the general education curriculum. With the additional requirement that students with disabilities participate in (and perform respectably on) statewide assessments and accountability procedures, pressures to favor one kind of placement (e.g., inclusion in the general education classroom) over any other (e.g., providing pull-out services in some other place) mounted.

A decade earlier, McKinney and Hocott had explained that "part of the rationale for totally integrated [as compared to pull-out] programs for mildly handicapped students is based on research that questions the efficacy of special education." How solid is the research evidence indicating that any one particular place, or service-delivery model, can achieve better outcomes for students with disabilities, though? In this article I review research studies and research reviews that address the question of place. I argue, as many others have before me, that research evidence on the relative efficacy of one special education service delivery model over another is scarce, methodologically flawed, and inconclusive. But I will also argue that, in practical terms, the question of where students with disabilities should be educated is misguided. That question is antithetical to the kind of individualized planning that is the hallmark of special education for students with disabilities. I will argue for new ways of thinking about the issue of place and the conduit of research on special education placements before progress can be made on improving results for students with disabilities.

Although I limit myself to the research literature in which students with mild and moderate disabilities are studied, I strongly believe that the arguments I make have merit across the entire range of students with disabilities promoted and protected by IDEA and that these arguments have important implications for the rhetoric of the next IDEA reauthorization.

Efficacy Studies on Place

For more than 3 decades, special education researchers and scholars have conducted research, and synthesized research, on the relative usefulness of one place or another for serving students with disabilities. Dunn concluded, on the basis of several studies conducted in the 1960s and a review of research published by Kirk, that there was no empirical support for educating students with high-incidence disabilities in special classes: "Retarded pupils make as much or more progress in the regular grades as they do in special education [and] efficacy studies on special day classes for other mildly handicapped children, including the emotionally handicapped, reveal the same results." Although Dunn called for the abandonment of special day classes for students with high-incidence disabilities, he also argued persuasively for part-time pull-out special education services to meet their special educational needs.

Ten years later, in a narrative review of 17 studies, Sindelar and Deno concluded that resource rooms were more effective than general education classrooms in improving academic achievement of students with learning disabilities (LD). At about the same time, a meta-analysis of efficacy studies completed by Carlberg and Kavale reported more complex results. Carlberg and Kavale's calculations of effect sizes showed that students with mental retardation in special class placements performed academically as well as those placed in general education classrooms. However, they also concluded that students with learning or behavior disorders in special classes (both self-contained and resource programs) had a modest academic advantage over those remaining in the general education classrooms. Leinhardt and Pallay also concluded from their research review that resource rooms were better than general education classrooms for students with LD. In addition, 1 year later, Madden and Slavin reviewed seven studies on the efficacy of part-time resource placements compared to full-time special education classes and full-time placement in the mainstream and concluded that if increased academic achievement is the desired outcome, "the research favors placement in regular classes . . . *supplemented by well designed resource programs*" (p. 530, italics added).

Research support for supplemental resource room services was, however, overlooked in the national frenzy to reshape special education that swept the country in the mid-1980s. With the introduction of newer, more inclusive service-delivery models, the early research comparing special pull-out placements with general education placements seemed dated and irrelevant. In those earlier studies, it was easy to draw stark contrasts between general education placements, in which no special services were available to students with disabilities, and pull-out services staffed by trained teachers who provided special instruction. In the newer service-delivery models, particularly the full inclusion models for students with mild/moderate disabilities that employed special education teachers in consulting or co-teaching roles, students with disabilities were supposed to be receiving specially designed instruction or supplemental aids and services right in the general education classroom. Research documenting student progress in these new inclusive settings was needed, and it proliferated.

Some studies showed positive trends when students were integrated into general education classrooms, including that full-time placement in a general education classroom resulted in student academic progress that was just as good as that achieved by students in separate settings in elementary schools. Others, however, reported disappointing or unsatisfactory academic and social achievement results from inclusion models. It should come as no surprise, then, that in a review of research on these newer special education service-delivery models, Hocutt reported equivocal findings. She concluded that "various program models, implemented in both general and special education, can have moderately positive academic and social impacts for student with disabilities." However, no intervention in the research literature eliminated the impact of having a disability. That is, regardless of the place of the intervention, students with disabilities did not achieve even at the level of low-achieving nondisabled peers, and no model was effective for *all* students with disabilities.

Manset and Semmel compared eight inclusion models for elementary students with high-incidence disabilities, primarily LD, reported in the research literature between 1984 and 1994. They reiterated Hocutt's conclusions: Inclusive programs can be effective for some, although not all, students with high-incidence disabilities. Waldron and McLeskey agreed with this conclusion. In their research, students with severe LD made comparable progress in reading and math in pull-out and inclusion settings, although students with mild LD were more likely to make gains commensurate with nondisabled peers when educated in inclusive environments than when receiving special education services in a resource room.

Holloway reviewed five studies conducted between 1986 and 1996 that compared traditional pull-out services to fully inclusive service-delivery models and models that combined in-class services with pull-out instruction. His conclusions did not offer strong support for the practice of full inclusion. Reading progress in the combined model was significantly better than in either the inclusion-only model or the resource room-only model.

In very recent research, Rea, McLaughlin, and Walther-Thomas used qualitative and quantitative methods to describe two schools and their special education models, one fully inclusive and one with more traditional supplemental pull-out services. Results showed that compared to students in the more traditional schools with pull-out programs, students served in inclusive schools earned higher grades, achieved higher or comparable scores on standardized tests, committed no more behavioral infractions, and attended more school days.

In a specific review of co-teaching as the inclusive service-delivery model, Zigmond and Magiera found only four studies that focused on academic achievement gains. In the three elementary studies, co-teaching was just as effective in producing academic gains as was resource room instruction or consultation with the general education teacher; in the high school study, students' quiz and exam grades actually worsened following the co-teaching experiment. Murawski and Swanson, in their meta-analysis of the co-teaching research literature, found six studies from which effect sizes could be calculated; dependent measures were grades, achievement scores, and social and attitudinal outcomes. Murawski and Swanson reported effect sizes for individual studies ranging from low to high, with an average total effect size in the moderate range. Both literature reviews on co-teaching concluded that despite the current and growing popularity of co-teaching as a service-delivery model, further research is needed to determine whether it is an effective service-delivery option for students with disabilities, let alone a preferred one.

Conclusions Derived From the Empirical Research Base

There is no simple and straightforward answer to the question of where students with disabilities should receive their special education instruction. The efficacy research reviewed here, which spans more than 3 decades, provides no compelling research evidence that place is the critical factor in the academic or social progress of students with mild/moderate disabilities. There are probably many reasons for reaching this conclusion, but I suggest only two. The first has to do with the body of research evidence itself. The second has to do with the appropriateness of the question.

Explanation 1: Research Base Is Insufficient

Despite the fact that the efficacy research literature on the places where special education services are provided spans more than 3 decades and that dozens of studies have been reported in refereed special education journals, Murawski and Swanson are right to ask where the data are. Studies worthy of consideration in a meta-analysis or narrative literature review, with appropriate controls and appropriate dependent measures, are few and far between.

Of course, research on the efficacy of special education placements is very hard to conduct at all, let alone to conduct well. For example, definitions of service-delivery models or settings vary from researcher to researcher, and descriptions of the treatments being implemented in those models or settings are woefully inadequate. Random assignment of students to treatments is seldom an option, and appropriately matched (sufficiently alike) samples of experimental and control students and teachers are rare. As a result, *where* special education occurs is not a phenomenon that lends itself to precise investigation, and funding for research studies and publication of results in refereed journals are difficult to achieve.

Methodologically Flawed Research.   Research designs used to explore the effectiveness of different service-delivery models often employ pre-post treatment group designs. The limitations of these research designs for studying the efficacy of special education have been reported in numerous previous research reviews, most notably in Kirk and Semmel, Gottlieb, and Robinson. Some studies use control groups, often samples of students experiencing "traditional" programs (sometimes referred to as "business as usual" programs) in nonexperimental schools. In some studies, the researchers manage to achieve random assignment of students to treatments, but most use intact groups of students assigned to the teacher or the school building who volunteered to participate in the experimental treatment program. Often the experimental treatment is well described, although degree of implementation is not. Descriptions of the control treatment and its degree of implementation (if indeed a control group is used) are rarely provided. Most often, replication is hindered by inadequate descriptions of the treatments and insufficient monitoring of treatment implementation. Thus, even if reliable achievement changes are demonstrated in one research study, difficulty in identifying critical treatment variables makes replicability impossible in virtually all cases. Achievement gains, or lack thereof, cannot be related to replicable interventions, and the fundamental question of whether Place A is better than Place B cannot actually be answered.

Inconclusive Research.   The accumulated evidence to date has produced only one unequivocal finding: Languishing in a general education class where nothing changes and no one pays you any attention is not as useful to students with mild/moderate learning and behavior disorders as is getting some help, although it does not seem to matter for students with mild mental retardation. All other evidence on whether students with disabilities learn more, academically or socially, and are happier in one school setting or another is at best inconclusive. Resource programs are more effective for some students with disabilities than are self-contained special education classes or self-contained general education classes, but they are less effective for other students with similar disabilities. Fully inclusive programs are superior for some students with disabilities on some measures of academic or social skills development and inferior for other students or on other measures. The empirical research not only does not identify one best place but also often finds equivalent progress being made by students with disabilities across settings; that is, the research reports nonsignificant differences in outcomes. Interpreting nonsignificant findings can be tricky. Do we conclude that the proverbial cup is half full or half empty? Do we acknowledge that it does not matter where students receive their special education services and allow parents or school personnel wide berth in making choices? Or do we proclaim that one setting is preferred over another for philosophical or moral reasons with empirical evidence that it "doesn't hurt"?

Explanation 2: Efficacy Studies Have Been Asking the Wrong Question

Failure to Specify "Best for Whom?" Special education has evolved as a means of providing specialized interventions to students with disabilities based on individual student progress on individualized objectives. The bedrock of special education is instruction focused on *individual* needs. The very concept of "one best place" contradicts this commitment to individualization. Furthermore, results of research on how groups of students respond to treatment settings does not help the researcher or practitioner make an individualized decision for an individual student's plan. A better question to ask, if we dare, is "best for whom?" or best for which individual students with which individual profiles of characteristics and needs? Answering this question requires that we abandon the rhetoric in which we call for *all* students to do this, or *all* students to learn that, or *all* students be educated in a certain place.

Special educators understand about individual differences. Special educators understand that no matter how hard they try or how well they are taught, there are some students who will never be able to learn on the same schedule as most others, who will take so long to learn some things that they will have to forego learning other things, or who will need to be taught curricular content that is not ordinarily taught. Special educators understood this when they fought hard for the legal requirement of the Individualized Educational Program for children with disabilities, to permit formulation of unique programs of instruction to meet unique individual needs. By continuing to ask, "What is the best place?" we are ignoring what we know.

Restating the question as "best for whom?" would also require new research designs and data analysis. A first step in that direction might be to reanalyze group design data at the individual student level. For example, Zigmond et al. collected achievement test data for 145 students with LD in three full inclusion programs and for many of these students' nondisabled classmates. Rather than reporting average growth of the students with LD, the researchers reported the number and percentage of students with LD who made reliably significant gains (i.e., gains exceeded the standard error of measurement of the reading test) during the experimental year. They also reported on the number and percentage of students with LD whose reading gains matched or exceeded the average gain of their grade-level peers. Finally, they reported on the number and percentage of students with LD whose achievement status (i.e., their relative standing in the grade-level peer group) had improved during the school year. These analytic techniques allowed for exploration of setting effects at an individual level. Waldron and McLeskey followed this same tactic. Unfortunately, neither group of researchers took the final step of describing individual participants in enough detail to permit generalization of the findings or extrapolation of the findings to the individual case. Nevertheless, this approach seems more promising than the traditional approaches that have been used to date in terms of answering the question "best for whom?"

Failure to Specify "Best for What?" Different settings offer different opportunities for teaching and learning. The general education classroom provides students with disabilities with access to students who do not have disabilities; access to the curricula and textbooks to which most other students are exposed; access to instruction from a general education teacher whose training and expertise are quite different from those of a special education teacher; access to subject matter content taught by a subject matter specialist; and access to all of the stresses and strains associated with the preparation for, taking of, and passing or tailing of the statewide assessments. If the goal is to have students learn content subject information or how to interact with nondisabled peers, the general education setting is the best place.

Pull-out settings allow for smaller teacher–student ratios and flexibility in the selection of texts, choice of curricular objectives, pacing of instruction, scheduling of examinations, and assignment of grades. Special education pull-out settings allow students to learn different content in different ways and on a different schedule. A pull-out special education setting may be most appropriate if students need (a) intensive instruction in basic academic skills well beyond the grade level at which nondisabled peers are learning how to read or do basic mathematics, (b) explicit instruction in controlling behavior or interacting with peers and adults, or (c) to learn anything that is not customarily taught to everyone else.

If educators value education that is different and special and want to preserve that feature of special education, it is legitimate to ask whether the general education classroom can be transformed to support this desire. Or, as Fuchs and Fuchs asked, "Can general education become special education?" Their experience (and mine) strongly suggests that the answer to this question is "no." Attempts to transport teaching methods that were developed and validated in special education to general education settings have not been successful. Instructional practices that focus on individual decision making for individual students and improve outcomes of students with severe learning problems are not easily transposed into practices that can survive in a general education classroom. General educators will make instructional adaptations in response to students' persistent failure to learn, but the accommodations are typically oriented to the group, not to the individual, and are relatively minor in substance, with little chance for helping students with chronically poor learning histories.

Over and over again, researchers and staff development personnel have come to recognize that general education teachers have a different set of assumptions about the form and function of education than do special educators. General educators cannot imagine focusing intensively on individual students to the extent that different instructional activities for different students are being implemented at the same time. This is simply impractical in a classroom of 25 to 35 students. Moreover, special education's most basic article of faith, that instruction must be individualized to be truly effective, is rarely contemplated, let alone observed, in most general education classrooms. Mainstream teachers must consider the good of the group and the extent to which the learning activities they present maintain classroom flow, orderliness, and cooperation. In addition, they generally formulate teaching plans that result in a productive learning environment for 90% or more of their students. General education settings are best for learning what most students need to learn.

For many of the remaining 10% of students, however, a different orientation will probably be needed. These students need to learn something different because they are clearly not learning what everyone else is learning. Interventions that might be effective for this group of students require a considerable investment of time and effort, as well as extensive support. Special education in a pull-out setting, with its emphasis on empirically validated practices and its use of data-based decision making to tailor instruction to the individual students' needs, might be better for teaching these students.

Conclusion

As early as 1979, federal monitoring of state programs was put into place to guard against not only too much segregation of students with disabilities but also "inappropriate mainstreaming." Although most would agree that students with mild and moderate disabilities should spend a large proportion of the school day with peers without disabilities, research does not support the superiority of any one service-delivery model over another. Furthermore, effectiveness depends not only on the characteristics and needs of a particular student but also on the quality of the program's implementation. A poorly run model with limited resources will seldom be superior to a model in which there is a heavy investment of time, energy, and money. Good programs can be developed in any setting, as can bad ones. The setting itself is less important than what is going on in the setting.

Reflecting on the 35 years of efficacy research on the settings in which special education is delivered that I have reviewed in this article, what do we know? We know that what goes on in a place, not the location itself, is what makes a difference. We know that you learn what you spend time on and that most students with disabilities will not learn to read or to write or to calculate if they are not explicitly taught these skills. We know that some instructional practices are easier to implement and more likely to occur in some settings than in others. We know that we need more research that asks better and more focused questions about who learns what best where. In addition, we know that we need to explore new research designs and new data analysis techniques that will help us bridge the gap between efficacy findings and decision making on placements for individual students.

In response to the query of what is special about special education, I can say with some certainty that place is not what makes special education "special" or effective. Effective teaching strategies and an individualized approach are the more critical ingredients in special education, and neither of these is associated solely with one particular environment. Educators must also remember that research has shown that typical general education environments are not supportive places in which to implement what we know to be effective teaching strategies for students with disabilities. Considering the research evidence to date, it is clear that placement decisions must continue to be made by determining whether a particular placement option will support the effective instructional practices that are required for a particular child to achieve his or her individual objectives and goals.

The search for the best place in which to receive special education services has tended to be fueled by passion and principle, rather than by reason and rationality. Until educators are ready to say that receiving special education services in a particular setting is good for some students with disabilities but not for others, that different educational environments are more conducive to different forms of teaching and learning, that different students need to learn different things in different ways, and that traditional group research designs may not capture these individual differences in useful ways, we may never get beyond the equivocal findings reported here. We may even fail to realize that, in terms of the best place to receive special education and related services, we have probably been asking the wrong questions.

POSTSCRIPT

Can One Model of Special Education Serve All Students?

Research findings supply grist for this controversy. According to Wehmeyer, Lattin, Lapp-Rincker, and Agran (*Remedial and Special Education*, 2003), inclusive settings provided students with mental retardation greater access to the general curriculum. However, the authors question whether access translates into greater progress, wondering whether the curriculum itself presents insurmountable barriers. Like Sailor and Roger, they advocate using universal design to increase meaningful learning.

Comparing two schools in the same district, outcomes for students with learning disabilities were significantly more favorable in an inclusive setting (Rea, Laughlin, and Walther-Thomas, *Exceptional Children*, 2002). Could the disability make a difference?

Sailor and Roger feel strongly that initiatives to increase inclusive programming have not garnered support from either special education or general education professionals. Using NCLB as a lever, their schoolwide service model extends special education supports to reach all children, instead of concentrating on a few in separate environments.

Supporting Sailor and Roger, and contrary to popular opinion, McLeskey, Hoppy, Williamson, and Rentz (*Learning Disabilities Research & Practice*, 2004) found that the drive toward inclusion is an illusion, virtually nonexistent for students with learning disabilities. Increases were slight and attributable to a few states. The most successful ventures accompanied long-term school change.

Zigmond would have educators concentrate on learners and outcomes rather than schools. Finding no one model effective for all students, and "no compelling research evidence" that *place* is the critical variable, she doubts that general education classrooms can be sufficiently restructured to make a difference. She urges educators to ask what works best for each learner. And each learner's goals.

Placement debates often occur in hearing rooms, with schools and parents supporting their preferred program. The direction of preference is unpredictable. Schools frequently advocate for services delivered in the general education environment. At other times, the same school favors a more restrictive, separate program. Some parents feel the "regular" classroom is key to learning and growth. Others believe a separate, intensive program will ensure success for their child.

Curtis (2005) was surprised by the anger of parents seeking assistance through a special education law clinic. Usually, the issue at stake was the delivery of effective services. He found general education teachers "effectively rebelling" against inclusion. Feeling they lacked the knowledge, skills, or time to take on inclusion responsibilities, some teachers did not always implement IEPs as written. Would a whole-school approach eliminate this problem? Or would it dilute specialized services for the most needy learners?

IDEA never mentions *inclusion*, although it clearly prefers the most typical setting. Yell and Katsiyannis review legal requirements for placement decisions (*Preventing School Failure*, 2004). Supporting Zigmond's recommendations, they note that IDEA requires IEP teams to consider each learner's needs first; next, appropriate goals. Only then should the team determine the appropriate setting. Decisions based on disability category, service availability, or administrative preference are not permissible.

Inclusion is an imposing endeavor. Done well, it requires hard work. Despite some opinions, it does not save money or reduce staff. Does it increase educational access or limit opportunities for targeted instruction?

Could initiatives like SAM (Schoolwide Application Model) make a difference? Would whole-school options create the best climate for all students: a well-staffed, coordinated, child-centered school? With more attention to all students, perhaps fewer needs would develop. But what about those students who need more? SAM does not "allow" separate classes in its schools.

How do the schools you know address inclusion? What is considered when making placement decisions? How are inclusion efforts supported? Have opinions and practices changed with the advent of high-stakes testing?

ISSUE 14

Is Full Inclusion the Least Restrictive Environment?

YES: Rosalind Vargo and Joe Vargo, from "Voice of Inclusion: From My Friend Ro Vargo," in Richard A. Villa and Jacqueline S. Thousand, eds., *Creating an Inclusive School*, 2nd ed. (Association for Supervision and Curriculum Development, 2005)

NO: Amy Dockser Marcus, from "Eli's Choice," *The Wall Street Journal* (December 31, 2005)

ISSUE SUMMARY

YES: Rosalind and Joe Vargo, parents of Ro, use their voices to tell a powerful story of their daughter's success in fully inclusive educational programs, from kindergarten through college.

NO: Amy Dockser Marcus, staff reporter at *The Wall Street Journal*, records the voices of Eli's parents and teachers as they react to his message to leave a fully inclusive program in favor of a separate special education class.

Ask a group of people about the definition of "inclusion," and they will usually come up with a statement like, "all children being educated in the same school." Ask again, "Do you mean *all* children?" The reply is likely to be a bit less certain, "Well, maybe not *all*." Probe a bit further and someone is likely to admit (with a bit of trepidation) that inclusion should mean all students except. . . . The words that follow might vary, but usually there are exceptions for students with severe cognitive challenges—those who have mental retardation or those who have disabilities in multiple areas and require complex and broad levels of support in order to communicate, move, and learn. So inclusion, for many people, really does not include *all* children.

Proponents of full inclusion have a very different answer. They say—and mean—*all* children being educated in the same school. Full inclusion advocates proclaim that all children, regardless of level of need, have a moral and legal right to attend their home school, be enrolled in general education classes, and receive all necessary supports within those classes. In a full inclusion environment, students don't need to fit into the school; the school needs to adapt to all students. Services are brought to the child; children are not sent out (or away) because what they need is not available or difficult to deliver.

Those who oppose full inclusion cite the difficulties of adapting instruction, meeting student needs, and acquiring material, training, and professional supports. Accustomed to traditional academic curriculum for some students and vocational, life-skills–based curriculum for others, they ask how the demands of both can be met.

The challenge of full inclusion is perhaps greatest at high schools, with their focus on distinct academic disciplines and college hopes. Communication between teachers is complicated by the increased number of people who interact with each student and the large numbers of students taught by each educator. The conversation has become even more intense with the advent of high-stakes testing, causing some to wonder if the needs of every child can be met within a typical classroom.

This issue presents the compelling voices and experiences of two sets of parents who have had much in common. They each had a child—now grown—with a significant disability. Both chose fully inclusive educational programs for their children. By their accounts, both children flourished. Then their experiences diverge.

Rosalind and Joe Vargo, parents of a young woman who communicates through sign language and uses a wheelchair, describe Ro's inclusive schooling experiences, from kindergarten through university. They share vivid illustrations of how Ro was recognized for her capabilities rather than judged by her appearance.

Amy Dockser Marcus communicates the reactions of Eli's parents, who were also strongly committed to inclusion. The selection relates their surprise when their son, who has Down syndrome, reaches high school and actively rejects inclusion to be with his friends with disabilities. Although Eli's parents abide by his choice, they have different questions about the outcome of the decision.

As you read these articles, consider the experiences of both these families. What successes and challenges did they experience? Why did their paths diverge? What would you think if you were in their shoes?

YES

**Rosalind Vargo and
Joe Vargo**

Voice of Inclusion: From My Friend, Ro Vargo

It was Tuesday, a beautiful autumn morning at Syracuse University. Ro had just finished her class "Topics in American Music—20th Century" in Bowne Hall and was walking back to the car (with my assistance) to go home. Joe, Ro's dad, was waiting in the car. He and I looked at each other and at Ro and wondered how we had gotten here. After all, it seemed like only yesterday. . . .

Kindergarten

Among our vivid memories is kindergarten and Ro's first invitation to a birthday party. Kristen's mother phoned to ask if she should make any special arrangements for Ro to attend. Fighting back tears, we responded, "No, but thanks for asking." Kristen's mom said her daughter was so looking forward to Ro coming. Then we said it: "We love Ro because she's our daughter. But do you know why other kids like her?"

The mom replied, "Well, I can speak only for my daughter, Kristen. She says she likes Ro's smile and that Ro is someone you can really talk to . . . and that she wears really neat clothes." Kristen's mom continued, "I think kids like Ro because she isn't a threat to them; they can just be themselves around her."

2nd Grade

In 2nd grade, we invited several kids to Ro's birthday party. Because we would be picking them up at school, we needed to know who would be coming. The night before the party, we called Eric's mom and politely asked, "Is Eric coming to Ro's party tomorrow?"

She said, "I'm sorry I didn't call you, but Eric said he just told Ro in school yesterday that he was coming. Was that all right?" It was more than all right! To Eric, the fact that Ro couldn't talk didn't mean that she couldn't understand him. . . .

4th Grade

In 4th grade, a time when pressure to have the "right" clothes and hairstyles had already begun, Ro was voted "Best Friend" by her 25 "typical"

4th-grade classmates. Somehow, Ro's inclusion in the school life was making a tremendous difference in many kids as well. Her "giftedness" was recognized and celebrated.

We recall another night when a puzzling phone call came for Ro. Sharing the same nickname as my daughter, I thought the call was for me and I replied, "Speaking."

The young girl at the other end of the line clarified, "No, I'd like the Ro who goes to Ed Smith School."

I said, "Hold on," and exclaimed to Joe, "Someone wants to talk with Ro on the phone!" We got Ro from the dinner table and put the phone to her ear. Immediately recognizing the voice of her friend Ghadeer, Ro started laughing. She then nodded her head to indicate "yes" and followed with a head shake indicating "no." Curiosity got the best of me and I took the phone, reporting to Ghadeer, "Ro's listening and nodding her head."

Ghadeer said, "Great, I'm asking her advice about a birthday present for a friend. Now, did she nod 'yes' for the jewelry or 'yes' for the board game?"

Ro's 11th Birthday

We remember with pleasure Ro's 11th birthday party. Before the party, the mother of one of Ro's friends called to ask if the present she had picked out for Ro was OK. Apparently, her daughter hadn't been with her when she went shopping. She had just wrapped it and given it to her daughter to take to school that morning. She wasn't sure if the gift was the "in" thing and feared that her daughter would die of embarrassment if it weren't.

She had bought a jump rope for Ro—a deluxe model. Without hesitation, I said that it was a wonderful idea and a gift that Ro would love using with her sisters.

With a sigh of relief, the mom responded, "Well, I am glad. I was hoping that Ro was not handicapped or anything. Is she?"

For the life of me, I wanted to say "No" and save this mom obvious embarrassment. So I said, "Well, a little bit." After many of her apologies and my reassurances, we got off the phone as friends. She had made my day, my week, my life! The thought that an 11-year-old girl had received a birthday party invitation, wanted to go, and asked her mom to buy a present, *never thinking it important to mention that her friend had a disability*, still makes me cry with wonder and happiness. . . .

When Ro unwrapped the jump rope, all the girls were elated, shrieking, "I hope I get one of those for my birthday," and "Oh, cool." The girls immediately dragged Ro down the stairs and outside to the driveway, where they tied one end of the jump rope to her wrist. With the strength of her twirling partner, Ro was able to rotate the rope for her friends. It was Ro's best adaptive occupational therapy activity in months.

A Gift for Ghadeer

Probably the most profound testimony to inclusive education occurred in January 1993. Ghadeer, Ro's friend who had called to ask for advice on gift selection, suffered a cerebral hemorrhage, or severe stroke. At the age of 12, she was comatose for almost four weeks. . . . [After] weeks of having family, teachers, and friends read at her bedside, Ghadeer miraculously, although not completely, recovered. Her voice and articulation were so severely impaired that she could not communicate orally. To the amazement of the child's doctors and nurses, her disability did not stop her from communicating; she began to use sign language. An interpreter was quickly found who asked Ghadeer, "Where did you learn sign language?"

Ghadeer replied in sign, "From my friend, Ro Vargo!"

After four months of intensive rehabilitative therapy, Ghadeer returned to school, but now as a "special education" student requiring speech and language services plus physical and occupational therapy. Her family proudly reports that Ghadeer turned away the "special" bus and rode the regular school bus on her first day back to school. Furthermore, she advocated for herself to get a laptop computer to assist her with her schoolwork. Inclusive education enabled Ghadeer to get to know someone like Ro and to learn about augmentative communication systems and her rights, particularly her right to be part of her school, class, and friendship circle. She had learned that a person can still belong even if something unexpected—like a disability—happens.

What's Hard About Being Ro's Friend?

Ghadeer was one of many of Ro's friends who became quite capable of articulating for themselves what Ro meant to them and the kinds of things that they learned at school with her. That relationship became clear when Ro and a group of her friends responded to questions from parents and teachers in a session titled "Building Friendships in an Inclusive Classroom" at a national education conference that they attended.

Tiffany said, "I think Ro should be in class with all of us because how else is Ro going to learn the really important stuff? Besides, we can learn a lot from her."

Teachers asked Ro's friends some unusual questions, such as, "'Have you ever discussed her disability with her?'"

Stacey replied, "No, I know she is different, but I never thought it important to ask. Like, for instance, I never thought to go up to a black kid in my class and say, 'You're black. How come you're different?'"

A "popular" question among teachers and parents—judging by their nods—was "What is the hardest thing about being Ro's friend?" As Ro's parents, we held our breath, waiting for responses such as "She drools," "She walks funny," or "She's a messy eater."

But again Stacey spoke up, saying, "The hardest thing about being Ro's friend is that she always has a parent or an adult with her." Ouch! That hurt. But Stacey's observation taught us, Ro's parents, an important lesson that will surely have a positive effect on our daughter's future.

Transition to Middle School

The transition from elementary to middle school was tough socially for Ro, as it can be for any adolescent. For Ro, the first months were spent in isolation, but her isolation was not one of physical proximity. Ro attended a regular 6th grade program and had to gain acceptance from her new middle school peers. Initially, she was ignored or stared at; a few classmates even teased her. When Ro was assigned to a work group, no group members complained out loud, but Ro noticed non-verbal signs of rejection. In those first months, we began to doubt our decision to include Ro in middle school. We recalled the comment a teacher from the previous year had made: "Middle school kids don't like themselves. How can you expect them to like your kid?"

Mauricha, a classmate, became Ro's closest new friend. It was Mauricha who broke the social barrier. Asked how the two became friends, Mauricha said, "I saw her. She saw me. We've just been friends ever since." One night when I was taking Mauricha home, she looked at me and touched my arm. "You know, Mrs. Vargo," Mauricha said, "lots of teachers think I'm friends with Ro cuz it gets me more attention. That isn't true. The truth is, I need her more than she needs me."

Ro's father and I would have to summarize Ro's middle school experience as fairly typical. When reflecting on our other daughters' experiences in middle school, we realized that there were many of the same issues: isolation at times, hot and cold friendships, recognition of and a growing interest in boys, physical changes, teasing, challenging class work, and parents who didn't know anything! Oh, yes. Ro went to her first dance and danced with Jermaine. . . .

Arrival at High School

. . . Ro and six other students with disabilities entered Henninger High School. Early on, Ro communicated, "I like . . . zoology . . ., and the kids and I have learned a lot. I have had some classes I didn't like. It is hard for me when classes have no small groups and no homework for me. Sometimes there is too much information. The worst is when neither the kids nor the teachers talk to me." . . .

Inclusive education in high school was offering Ro a whole new world of opportunities and choices. She joined the Key Club. . . . She accrued service hours through her volunteer job at a . . . fully inclusive day care. Ro was acting as a role model for many young students with disabilities, as well as for the whole class and her fellow workers.

During her early high school years, Ro communicated many things to us in various ways. . . . Her "voice" gave us a clearer vision of where and what Ro wanted to do with her life. . . .

On the afternoon of her first volunteer job, Ro had to fill out an application. Her teaching assistant completed it with Ro's input. However, 10 minutes later, Ro totally dissolved into a full-blown temper tantrum.

The panicked teaching assistant questioned Ro, "Does it have anything to do with the application?"

Ro nodded, "Yes."

"Was it #1, #2, #3 . . . ." until the question, "What has been your biggest challenge?"

Without consulting Ro, the teaching assistant had written "Rett syndrome." That was the one! Ro wanted it removed. Yes, the line about Rett syndrome.

Another time that Ro clearly expressed her thoughts was when she was nominated by her teachers for Student of the Month. She had to complete an information sheet for the committee who would select the winner. After much deliberation, Ro opted not to include any of her work with local university students and their numerous papers on her life experiences or any of her work with other girls with Rett syndrome. Basically, her nomination went in with just her name, age, and favorite teacher. Ro was making it clear that she didn't think that Rett syndrome was something important to share about herself. It wasn't really who she was, or what she did, or even what she wanted to have. . . .

The voice of Ro's peers was also becoming clearer and louder. While on the zoology trip to New York City, Ro and her dad struggled for three days to keep up with the fast pace of a very busy itinerary. Ro's classmates seemed oblivious to her tiring easily and to the locomotion problems that caused her to lag behind. It appeared that they hardly noticed her at all that weekend—at least that was Joe's observation. Ro still enjoyed the trip, and it was a wonderful bonding experience for her and dad.

Months later, we came to understand the ramifications and the benefits of Ro's participation in that trip. Students in the class began to vocalize, without our knowledge, concerns about Ro's support person in school. They complained to their teacher at first about how they thought the teaching assistant was disrespectful to Ro. When the teacher heard their complaints, she notified the principal. When there was no action, kids went to their parents and parents came to us. When the school administration failed to act, Ro's peers did!

The vision for inclusive education was a reality. We had hoped that the kids who sat in class with Ro would not seek to harm her now or in the days to come. We had hoped that they would protect her and take care of her, seek the social and legislative reforms to support the inclusive lifestyle that she had grown accustomed to, and gladly be her neighbors and her friends because they had shared the same space, the same hopes, and the same dreams. Ro and her peers in an inclusive high school setting were already living out the dream, and there was no going back for any of us.

After Ro's third year in high school, . . . Ro was clearly envious of the planning and choices that her sister Josie was engaging in. College visits, college applications, and senior pictures were taking place. We were unclear about what Ro's choices could be, and she communicated that the situation was not fair.

One night I read about an inclusive college setting in Kentucky. The ONCAMPUS program had been initiated as a collaborative effort between the Inclusive Elementary and Special Education Program of Syracuse University (SU) and the Syracuse City School District. . . . ONCAMPUS brought six high school students . . . with moderate to severe disabilities to the SU campus where they would participate with other SU students in . . . learning experiences.

Ro. . . . actively communicated her absolute delight with her peers that she was going to attend SU next year. She decided which courses to take, what clubs to belong to, and where she would eat lunch.

However, getting a handicapped parking permit proved to be no easy task. After much discussion and hassle, Ro was secured her permit. When I picked it up, the receptionist asked, "Oh, is this for Ro Vargo who went to Henninger High School?"

"Yes," I replied.

"Tell her I said 'Hi.'"

"You know Ro?" I asked.

"Yeah, I graduated with her from Henninger last year."

Inclusive education . . . another voice heard and in all the right places . . . another confirmation.

Syracuse University Students

Jacqueline [,] . . . a sophomore at SU in the School of Social Work. She began to spend time with Ro on campus through her job as a residential habilitation counselor. She shared with Ro the names of all the good professors and the courses she should pass up! . . . Jackie was a member of SU's jazz and pep band, as well as the dance band. She would clue Ro in on any musical performances on campus. . . .

Justine had seen Ro on campus. . . . She was a senior in the Maxwell School of Communication at the time. As part of her final grade, Justine had to produce a short documentary. She approached Ro and asked if she would be willing to be part of a presentation highlighting the ONCAMPUS program. Ro agreed. A relationship developed that spanned a whole year. Justine introduced Ro to Gregg, another senior, who would be the codirector. They met frequently to talk and shoot videotape.

The final project culminated in a video titled *Ro*. Justine and Gregg's perspective was clearly evident in their work. It was respectful, serious, and funny, and Ro's hopes and dreams of being on a university campus were unfolded in the video. The images were searing and thought-provoking as Ro traversed the campus. Justine and Gregg's voice on this tape will last forever, and so will Ro's voice.

Ro's inclusion in high school and college settings has certainly caused my daughter some pain as she acknowledged her limitations and struggled to belong. Yet inclusion also prompted Ro's self-actualization, self-determination, and self-acceptance and her growing belief that there is nothing that she cannot do. Placing herself in a "regular" environment was a risk that Ro was willing to take.

Inclusive education has always been an emotional and physical risk for all of us, especially Ro. But it has clearly been worth it! . . . Today, Ro uses adult services, and we're starting all over again: justifying, rationalizing, sharing vision, relaying data and information.

When parents of children with disabilities become lonely and fatigued, their voices can become silent. There are limited routes of appeal and no federal mandates to support Ro's inclusive lifestyle. Frankly, we are exhausted and frustrated. Nothing prepared us for this new fight to belong in a community outside of school. This adult, segregated mentality has taken its toll. We have been diligent advocates, articulate spokespersons. We've awakened—not only in Ro but also in many other students—the idea that inclusive education can mean college.

The impact of Ro's inclusive education is made clear by the relationships she forged along the way. Ghadeer called Ro to attend Ghadeer's high school graduation party. . . . Ro received a Christmas card from Mauricha, the middle school friend who broke the social barrier for Ro. The note began, "Hi, Ro. I know you probably don't remember me, but I have never forgotten you." Mauricha explained that she was working as a home health aide and taking a sign language course at night.

Kristen, Ro's teaching assistant, married Gavin. Ro was invited to the wedding, and she reminisced with the bridal party about the last time that they had all been in a limo together! . . . In a newspaper article highlighting the . . . high school graduations in the area, Kristen told a reporter that . . . "Ro was the sister I never had."

The Future?

Our "severely impaired" child has already accomplished more than we had ever thought possible, and she continues to grow. . . . We believe in those young adults who sat in class with Ro. They will not seek to harm her but will be her community—the ones who will protect and care for her. They will advocate social and legislative reform to support the inclusive lifestyle to which Ro and they have grown accustomed. They will gladly be her neighbors, caretakers, job coaches, and friends because they shared the same classes, space, hopes, and dreams.

Eli's Choice

For years, Eli Lewis was the only student in his class with Down syndrome.

The genetic condition, which causes a range of cognitive and physical impairments, made it harder for him to do his school work. But his parents felt strongly that he could succeed. They hired a reading tutor. An aide worked with his teachers to modify tests and lessons so that he could be in the same classroom as everyone else. He participated in his middle school's award-winning chorus and was treated as a valued member.

But when all the other kids in his class were making plans to go to the local high school this fall, Eli, 14 years old, said he didn't want to go. He wanted to be in a small class with other students like him. "I don't want to get lost in a big crowd," Eli says.

Eli's declaration surprised his parents. Then his mother recalled the many times she stopped by the school to check on her son, only to find him eating by himself. Once, when she came to pick him up from a dinner that chorus members attended, she says she found Eli sitting with his aide, while the other students sat at a different table.

"The kids liked him, they knew him, they spoke to him," says his mother, Mary Ann Dawedeit. "They just didn't think of him as a peer." Eli, she says, was tired of "being the only kid who was different."

Federal law mandated in the 1970s that children with disabilities be offered a "free and appropriate public education" in the "least restrictive environment," rather than being separated only in special schools or institutions. Over the years, advocacy and additional laws resulted in efforts to get children with disabilities placed in regular classrooms, with proper support, whenever possible. The process, called "inclusion" or "mainstreaming," has largely been an academic success.

Studies have shown benefits for all children, not only those with disabilities, who study together. Many researchers argue this is one reason why people with Down syndrome have made such remarkable progress in recent decades. People with Down syndrome who learn in regular classrooms do much better academically, research has found. They also have significantly higher rates of employment after they graduate and earn more money than peers who studied mainly in self-contained classes.

And yet, Eli Lewis's experience poses a difficult dilemma, one that is only now starting to be recognized and addressed. With help, he had succeeded academically in a regular classroom. But he felt isolated. In a book to be published next year, researchers at the Center for Social Development and Education at the University of Massachusetts in Boston say that although people with intellectual disabilities made enormous gains academically due to inclusion, their social integration at school "remains stagnant."

In a survey of 5,600 seventh- and eighth-grade students from 70 schools across the country, more than half of the youths said they were willing to interact with students with intellectual disabilities at school. But only one-third said they would be willing to invite such students to their house or go to the movies with them, according to the survey done by the University of Massachusetts center and the Washington-based opinion firm, ORC Macro. "Student attitudes continue to remain the most formidable barrier to inclusion," the researchers concluded.

At first, Ms. Dawedeit and her husband, Howard Lewis, thought Eli might change his mind. The couple—who have two other sons who don't have Down syndrome—felt there were many advantages to Eli staying in a regular classroom, including greater independence and more interaction with the general student body. But eventually, Mr. Lewis says he began to recognize that having Eli in a regular classroom might not be "as important to Eli as it is to me."

Ms. Dawedeit remained reluctant. She talked with a friend who had a son with Down syndrome, who was also learning in a regular classroom. "I felt like I had let her down," Ms. Dawedeit says. "I had preached a mantra for so long to so many."

In May, at the science exposition at Eli's middle school, her feelings changed. The eighth-graders took over the school hallway and parents were invited to visit. Some students demonstrated elaborate experiments they had been working on. Eli worked with his aide to do research online about the chemical properties of silver. He learned where to find it on the periodic table. For the exposition, he printed out some of the documents he had found.

When his mother came to see his project, Eli again raised the subject of where he was going to high school. For Ms. Dawedeit, the contrast was sharp. Here was Eli, successfully participating in a science exposition with peers who didn't have disabilities—but still talking about wanting to be with other people with Down syndrome.

She says she realized she needed to try to accommodate her son's desire for a social group. "I really had to step back from my personal beliefs," she says.

In the fall, Eli enrolled in the ninth grade at Bethesda's Walter Johnson High School, a sprawling building of over 2,000 students. He is in a special program with 20 other students who have disabilities, including one who gets around in a wheelchair and has difficulty talking. Six of the students in the class have Down syndrome. Eli already knew some of the kids from various extracurricular activities, such as drama class and Special Olympics, where he participated in soccer, basketball, swimming and bowling.

Getting out of the mainstream has meant trade-offs. His school is about 10 miles from Eli's house, farther than the local high school that his older brother attends. (The local high school doesn't have a separate special-education program.) A special-education bus now comes each day to pick up Eli, along with other students with disabilities.

"This was one of our big compromises," says his mother. In middle school, Eli walked to a bus stop and rode a regular school bus. "Other kids knew him," says Ms. Dawedeit. "Now he's a special-ed kid on a bus."

One evening in November, after a dinner of chicken burritos and salad, Eli helped his brothers, ages 12 and 17, clear the dishes. Then his parents watched him, as he started making his way through his homework—a worksheet to practice using nouns and verbs. Since Eli was born, they had fought to have him included in regular classrooms. Now it sometimes felt as if Eli might end up outside the world they had tried so hard to keep him in.

All along, they shared a similar goal: for their son to be able to live independently. But Mr. Lewis, a lawyer, began to worry that the academic gap between Eli and other classmates was getting wider in the regular classroom as he grew older, and might be too difficult to bridge in high school. "I'm not married to inclusion at the expense of Eli's getting the skills he needs," he says.

Ms. Dawedeit, a manager at a retail store, was less certain. She knew how much Eli, like all kids his age, wanted to belong. But without spending significant amounts of time in regular classrooms, how would he ever learn the skills he needed to reach the goal of living on his own? "The truth is he has to go out and get a job," she says. "If he's educated with his regular peers, then maybe a regular peer will hire him."

Eli finished his English worksheet, and got up to take a break. He came over and gave his father a hug. "Are you meeting any new kids at school, Eli?" his dad asked. "Not just yet, Dad," Eli answered. "Why are you hanging out only with the kids in your class?" his father queried. "Because I know them," Eli answered, and went into the kitchen to get some cookies.

At his new school, the Parent Teacher Student Association has put the issue of how to promote the inclusion of students with disabilities in extra-curricular activities on the agenda for its January meeting. A student group that pairs students with disabilities with a buddy without disabilities has already scheduled several activities for the coming months, including ice skating and bowling.

Still, for most of his school day, Eli is now in a separate classroom from the general school population. Last month, ninth-graders in the general-education classes were reading the novel, "To Kill a Mockingbird." In the special-education classroom, the teacher was going over worksheets that had been adapted from the book, with some related questions.

Eli was signed up for a regular physical-education class, but asked his parents if he could switch to one with only special-education students. His mother was reluctant to change, because it was one of his only chances to meet kids in the general-student population. She offered a compromise: He could switch to the special-education gym class with his friends, if next semester he took weight-training as part of the regular class. Eli agreed.

Janan Slough, the assistant principal who oversees the special-education department at Eli's school, says the school has difficulty finding certified special-education teachers because of a national shortage.

The school tries to foster as many opportunities as possible for those with disabilities to be in general classrooms, she says. Still, she adds, "I feel caught" between juggling the need for socializing with the need to teach basic, crucial tasks, such as handling money. On one field trip, the special-education kids went to a grocery store; they were supposed to buy something their family might use at home, pay for it, and make sure they got correct change.

Most of the kids with disabilities need to focus on independent-living and job skills, rather than college preparation. "I'm charged with thinking about where they are going to be at 21," she says. "I don't want parents to come back and say, 'It's nice they were socially included and had parallel instruction, but you didn't prepare them for the world of work.'"

For now, Eli has only one class—ceramics—that he attends with the general school population. On a recent morning, Eli sat next to a boy assigned to help him. The students were designing tiles, and from time to time his peer assistant would look at what he was doing, or go with him to get more clay. For much of the class, the boy bantered with one of his friends, who had pulled up a chair next to him and was regaling him with a story. From time to time, Eli made a joke and the boys all laughed together.

But when they walked Eli back to the special-education classroom, there was no suggestion that they meet up again that day. When Eli was asked if he enjoyed spending time with his assigned partner, he shrugged and said, "It's OK."

Eli has a lot of ideas about what he wants to do after high school. In middle school, he took a media class and worked in the school's TV studio. Along with the other kids in the class, he was given a homework assignment to make a public-service announcement. Eli made one about the Special Olympics. "I want to be a director," he said, when asked about his plans after high school.

"Eli has serious career aspirations for himself that may not have anything to do with what the rest of the world sees for him after high school," said his mother, one afternoon last month, while waiting for him at a drama class he takes outside of school. The class, made up of students with and without disabilities, was planning a variety show, and Eli was excited about performing. Every night, he went to his room to work on a dance routine he had created to accompany a song from the soundtrack of the movie, "Holes."

His girlfriend, whom he met in elementary school and also has Down syndrome, had invited him to be her date to the upcoming Winter Ball at her private school. Next month, Eli will turn 15 and is planning a big party. The only kids he plans to invite also have disabilities, his mother says.

While she's glad he has found a social circle, she still wonders about what he's missing by going to special-education classes instead of staying in regular classes. "I go back and forth on it all the time," she says. For instance, his school has a state-of-the-art TV studio with editing facilities and a control room, where a class is given. Eli's parents wanted him to be in that class, but it's not possible right now, because he needs to attend the special-education math class, which is held during the same period.

On a recent morning at school, Eli weaved around the teenagers lining the hallway. Some sprawled on the floor, catching up on homework. Others joked with each other by their lockers, or rushed to get to their next class. Eli didn't talk to any of the students. He walked with purpose, heading to the special-education room.

When he got there, his face brightened when he saw one of his friends. "This is my best friend," he said, throwing his arm around the other boy, who also has Down syndrome. He pressed his face close to his friend's until their cheeks almost touched. Eli smiled. "What table are you sitting at lunch today?" he said as they walked together down the hall. "Come on, make sure you sit with me."

POSTSCRIPT

Is Full Inclusion the Least Restrictive Environment?

How can we not respond to the compelling narratives of these parents? Eli and Ro come alive in their words. The road was not always easy and branches into two different paths.

The inclusion literature abounds with stories that melt hearts and open eyes. Horowitz and Klein (*Educational Leadership*, 2003) describe their efforts to include a child with Down syndrome into their religious school kindergarten. They discovered that, through working to include Michael, they learned to see the potential in every child and the interconnectedness of us all.

Proponents of the wisdom of full inclusion, Villa and Thousand (2005) maintain that inclusionary programs acknowledge the right of each of us to belong. No one should have to "fit in" or prove their worthiness to be part of everyday life experiences.

Taking one step further, Sapon-Shevin (*Educational Leadership*, 2003) portrays inclusion as an opportunity to teach social justice. In her eyes, building successful inclusive schools challenges people to actively create the inclusive, democratic society we envision for our children.

Most writers acknowledge that successful full inclusion is far from easy to achieve. In two instructive articles, Villa and Thousand (*Educational Leadership*, 2003) and McLeskey and Waldron (*Phi Delta Kappan*, 2002), provide numerous examples of lessons learned through schools' efforts to become inclusive. Their practical suggestions emphasize that successful inclusive programs require collaborative, sustained partnerships between administrators, teachers, and parents.

Drawing on student voices, Chadsey and Han (*TEACHING Exceptional Children*, 2005) address the peer connections essential to successful inclusion. The students think "segregation is unfair" and urge educators to provide opportunities where friendships can flourish naturally, as they would between any students.

Another group of students (Moore and Keefe, *Issues in Teacher Education*, 2004) found friendships—and inclusion—less important than their educational environment. These high school students, asked about their educational experiences, favored separate programs. Although disliking the accompanying stigma, they felt special education classes offered a more responsive environment that attended to their learning requirements.

Teachers, too, are concerned about the full inclusion learning environment. Kavale and Mostert (*Exceptionality*, 2003) reviewed several studies that explored the "empirical evidence" of full inclusion. Teachers embraced the democratic, just goals of full inclusion, but were concerned about its responsibilities. Their enthusiasm often moderated as they struggled to meet daily challenges.

How are such divergent experiences possible? Zigmond (*The Journal of Special Education*, 2003) suggests the answer may lie in our questions. Instead of asking whether full inclusion is desirable for all, perhaps we should return to the individual focus that has been the hallmark of special education to ask: For whom is full inclusion the best course? What instructional goals are best served by full inclusion?

Ro's and Eli's parents regain common ground when they speak of the future. The Vargos believe Ro's typical peers "will be her community—the ones who will protect and care for her. They will advocate social and legislative reform to support the inclusive lifestyle." Eli's mother hopes "The truth is he has to go out and get a job. If he's educated with his regular peers, then maybe a regular peer will hire him."

All teachers seek to prepare students to be successful adults. In partnership with parents, we endeavor to support and guide the young people we share along this journey. Is there one road to this ultimate destination? If not, how can any of us know which is the path best taken?

Internet References . . .

Council for Exceptional Children

The Council for Exceptional Children (CEC) is the largest international professional organization addressing issues surrounding education of students with disabilities, as well as those who are gifted and talented. CEC's site introduces you to current events in the field, recent legislative developments, and an array of specialized divisions focused on particular aspects of special education.

http://www.cec.sped.org

National Research Center on Learning Disabilities

This joint project of researchers at Vanderbilt University and the University of Kansas is funded by the U.S. Department of Education, Office of Special Education Programs. Activities include the development, study, and dissemination of best practices associated with RTI, including SLD determination.

http://www.ncrld.org

Children and Adults with Attention-Deficit/Hyperactivity Disorder

Children and Adults with Attention-Deficit/Hyperactivity Disorder (CHADD), founded in 1987 by families seeking information about this disorder, is now a national organization linked to a variety of activities. The CHADD Web site contains extensive information on ADHD and ADD and is helpful to anyone who wants to learn more about these conditions.

http://www.chadd.org

Autism Society of America

The mission of the Autism Society of America is to promote lifelong access and opportunity for all individuals within the autism spectrum, and their families, to be fully participating, included members of their community. Education, advocacy at state and federal levels, active public awareness, and the promotion of research form the cornerstones of ASA's efforts. This Web site contains a wide range of information regarding autism, treatments and supports for families.

http://www.autism-society.org

National Institute of Mental Health

A branch of the National Institutes of Health, the National Institute of Mental Health (NIMH) is focused on generating and disseminating information regarding mental health conditions. This site contains information regarding the full range of behavioral disorders and conditions as well as up-to-date research information related to their existence, causes, and treatment.

http://www.nimh.nih.gov

National Association for Gifted Children

The National Association for Gifted Children is a professional association dedicated to increasing public awareness about gifted learners, their needs and appropriate services. This Web site contains extensive information about gifted services in each state as well as resources for parents, teachers, and administrators.

http://www.nagc.org

Exceptionalities

*E*arlier sections of this book focused on global issues regarding the education of children who learn differently than their peers. In addition to the arenas of law, policy, and practice, exist controversies about the reality of particular exceptionalities and the efficacy of unique methodologies. The fervent desire of parents and educators to help children nurtures the development of approaches that promise success. The challenge of evaluating new ways of thinking will be with us as long as there are children who need extra support to realize their potential.

- Can Brain Scans Unravel the Mystery of Learning Disabilities?

- Can RTI Reduce the Numbers of Children Identified with Specific Learning Disabilities (SLD)?

- Is Attention Deficit (Hyperactivity) Disorder Overdiagnosed?

- Are There Scientifically Effective Treatments for Autism?

- Is Mental Health Screening an Unwarranted Intrusion?

- Do Gifted and Talented Students Need Special Schools?

ISSUE 15

Can Brain Scans Unravel the Mystery of Learning Disabilities?

YES: Sally E. Shaywitz and Bennett A. Shaywitz, from "Reading Disability and the Brain," *Educational Leadership* (March 2004)

NO: Gerald Coles, from "Danger in the Classroom: 'Brain Glitch' Research and Learning to Read," *Phi Delta Kappan* (January 2004)

ISSUE SUMMARY

YES: Sally E. and Bennett A. Shaywitz, codirectors of the National Institute of Child Health and Human Development—Yale Center for the Study of Learning and Attention, and Yale University professors, summarize their recent research findings suggesting that advances in medicine, together with reading research, can virtually eliminate reading disabilities.

NO: Gerald Coles, an educational psychologist and former member of the Robert Wood Johnson Medical School, University of Medicine and Dentistry of New Jersey, contests the claim that neurological procedures can identify reading disabilities and identify the methods to help children read.

Specific learning disability:

> A disorder in one or more of the basic psychological processes involved in understanding or in using language, spoken or written, that may manifest itself in an imperfect ability to listen, think, speak, read, write, spell, or to do mathematical calculations, including conditions such as perceptual disabilities, brain injury, minimal brain dysfunction, dyslexia, and developmental aphasia. This does not include learning problems that are primarily the result of visual, hearing or motor disabilities, of mental retardation, of emotional disturbance, or of environmental, cultural, or economic disadvantage. (IDEA 2004)

Have you ever met a student who seems to be very capable in many ways—can communicate, compute, and reason well—but who struggles to read? Or who is proficient in all academic areas except for the ability to compose a coherent narrative? The puzzle is that the student seems so competent—except in one specific area. Motivation, family support, and good teaching have all been present, but performance in this one area persistently lags behind success in others.

Curiosity and frustration about this student have been the source of discussion for the last century. In 1963, Samuel Kirk formalized thinking into a condition he termed "learning disabilities." Education has never been the same since.

Since the advent of special education law, educators, parents, and attorneys have argued over the shape and meaning of specific learning disabilities, a set of conditions that seem to be defined mostly by what they are not. The federal definition cited above describes a disability that is most apparent while learning academic subjects and occurs in a child who appears to have the background and capability to learn easily. For much of the twentieth century, researchers sought to identify specific neurological differences hypothesized to be the basis for learning disabilities.

More than half the children receiving special education services have been identified as having a specific learning disability. Most frequently, reading is identified as the primary area of difficulty.

No Child Left Behind (NCLB) sets a goal of having all children learn to read by the end of third grade, emphasizing the use of "effective, research-based reading programs." How do children with learning disabilities fit into this goal?

Sally E. Shaywitz and Bennett A. Shaywitz are prolific researchers in the area of learning. They, along with Reid Lyon, have been instrumental in shaping the reading foundation of NCLB. Shaywitz and Shaywitz believe that learning disabilities exist. In their research, results of functional magnetic resonance imaging (fMRI) identified "glitches" in the brains of struggling readers. They cite evidence that the right type of instruction can eliminate these glitches.

Gerald Coles, a pioneer researcher in the area of learning disabilities, feels that fMRI data do not provide a clear link between brain functioning and reading. He is concerned that the scientific glitz of new technology leads people to think that a glitch exists. By focusing only on brain activity, he fears that critical information about how and why children struggle to learn may be overlooked.

As you read the articles, decide whether or not you think that advances in medical technology have found the long-sought-for neurological cause of learning disabilities.

YES ⤹

Sally E. Shaywitz and
Bennett A. Shaywitz

Reading Disability and the Brain

The past decade has witnessed extraordinary progress in our understanding of the nature of reading and reading difficulties. Never before have rigorous science (including neuroscience) and classroom instruction in reading been so closely linked. For the first time, educators can turn to well-designed, scientific studies to determine the most effective ways to teach reading to beginning readers, including those with reading disability (National Reading Panel, 2000).

What does the evidence tell us? Several lines of investigation have found that reading originates in and relies on the brain systems used for spoken language. In addition, accumulating evidence sheds light on the nature of reading disability, including its definition, prevalence, longitudinal course, and probable causes. Although the work is relatively new, we have already made great progress in identifying the neural systems used for reading, identifying a disruption in these systems in struggling readers, and understanding the neural mechanisms associated with the development of fluent reading.

Reading and Spoken Language

Spoken language is instinctive—built into our genes and hardwired in our brains. Learning to read requires us to take advantage of what nature has provided: a biological module for language.

For the object of the reader's attention (print) to gain entry into the language module, a truly extraordinary transformation must occur. The reader must convert the print on the page into a linguistic code: the phonetic code, the only code recognized and accepted by the language system. Unless the reader-to-be can convert the printed characters on the page into the phonetic code, these letters remain just a bunch of lines and circles, totally devoid of meaning. The written symbols have no inherent meaning of their own but stand, rather, as surrogates for the sounds of speech.

To break the code, the first step beginning readers must take involves spoken language. Readers must develop *phonemic awareness*. They must discover that the words they hear come apart into smaller pieces of sound.

As seen in *Educational Leadership*, March 2004, based on the book *Overcoming Dyslexia* by Sally E. Shaywitz (Knopf, 2003). Grateful acknowledgement is made to Sally Shaywitz, c/o Writers' Representatives LLC (to whom all inquiries should be directed for permission to reprint).

On the basis of highly reliable scientific evidence, investigators in the field have now reached a strong consensus: Reading reflects language, and reading disability reflects a deficit within the language system. Results from large and well-studied populations with reading disability confirm that in young school-age children and in adolescents, a weakness in accessing the sounds of spoken language represents the most robust and specific correlate of reading disability. Such findings form the foundation for the most successful, evidence-based interventions designed to improve reading (National Reading Panel, 2000).

Understanding Reading Disability

Reading disability, or *developmental dyslexia*, is characterized by an unexpected difficulty in reading in children and adults who otherwise possess the intelligence, motivation, and education necessary for developing accurate and fluent reading. Dyslexia is the most common and most carefully studied of the learning disabilities, affecting 80 percent of all individuals identified as learning disabled and an estimated 5–17 percent of all children and adults in the United States.

Incidence and Distribution of Dyslexia

Recent epidemiological data indicate that like hypertension and obesity, reading ability occurs along a continuum. Reading disability falls on the left side of the bell-shaped curve representing the normal distribution of reading ability.

Dyslexia runs in families: One-fourth to one-half of all children who have a parent with dyslexia also have the disorder, and if dyslexia affects one child in the family, it is likely to affect half of his or her siblings. Recent studies have identified a number of genes involved in dyslexia.

Good evidence, based on surveys of randomly selected populations of children, now indicates that dyslexia affects boys and girls equally. Apparently, the long-held belief that only boys suffer from dyslexia reflected bias in school-identified samples: The more disruptive behavior of boys results in their being referred for evaluation more often, whereas girls who struggle to read are more likely to sit quietly in their seats and thus be overlooked.

Longitudinal studies indicate that dyslexia is a persistent, chronic condition rather than a transient "developmental lag." Children do not outgrow reading difficulties. The evidence-based interventions now available, however, can result in improved reading in virtually all children.

Neurobiological Origins of Dyslexia

For more than a century, physicians and scientists have suspected that dyslexia has neurobiological origins. Until recently, however, they had no way to examine the brain systems that we use while reading. Within the last decade, the dream of scientists, educators, and struggling readers has come true: New advances in technology enable us to view the working brain as it attempts to read.

Perhaps the most convincing evidence for a neurobiological basis of dyslexia comes from the rapidly accumulating and converging data from functional brain imaging investigations. The process of functional brain imaging is quite simple. When we ask an individual to perform a discrete cognitive task, that task places processing demands on specific neural systems in the brain. Through such techniques as functional magnetic resonance imaging (fMRI), we can measure the changes that take place in neural activity in particular brain regions as the brain meets those demands. Because fMRI uses no ionizing radiation and requires no injections, it is noninvasive and safe. We can use it to examine children or adults on multiple occasions.

Using functional brain imaging, scientists around the world have discovered not only the brain basis of reading but also a glitch in the neural circuitry for reading in children and adults who struggle to read. Our studies and those of other investigators have identified three regions involved in reading, all located on the left side of the brain. In the front of the brain, Broca's area (technically the inferior frontal gyrus) is involved in articulation and word analysis. Two areas located in the back of the brain are involved in word analysis (the parieto-temporal region) and in fluent reading (the occipito-temporal region, also referred to as the word form area).

Studies of dyslexic readers document an underactivation of the two systems in the back of the brain together with an overactivation of Broca's area in the front of the brain. The struggling readers appear to be turning to the frontal region, which is responsible for articulating spoken words, to compensate for the fault in the systems in the back of the brain.

Researchers have observed this neurobiological signature of dyslexic readers across cultures and across different languages. The observation of this same pattern in both children and adults supports the view that reading difficulties, including the neural disruption, do not go away with maturity. To prevent failure for students with reading disability, we must identify the disability early and provide effective reading programs to address the students' needs.

The Importance of Fluency

In addition to identifying the neural systems used for reading, research has now revealed which systems the brain uses in two important phases in the acquisition of literacy.

Beginning reading—breaking the code by slowly, analytically sounding out words—calls on areas in the front of the brain (Broca's area) and in the back of the brain (the parieto-temporal region).

But an equally important phase in reading is fluency—rapid, automatic reading that does not require attention or effort. A fluent reader looks at a printed word and instantly knows all the important information about that word. Fluent reading develops as the reader builds brain connections that eventually represent an exact replica of the word—a replica that has integrated the word's pronunciation, spelling, and meaning.

Fluency occurs step-by-step. After systematically learning letters and their sounds, children go on to apply this knowledge to sound out words slowly and analytically. For example, for the word "back," a child may initially represent the word by its initial and final consonants: "b—k." As the child progresses, he begins to fill in the interior vowels, first making some errors—reading "back" as "bock" or "beak," for example—and eventually sounding out the word correctly. Part of the process of becoming a skilled reader is forming successively more detailed and complete representations of familiar words.

After the child has read the word "back" correctly over and over again, his brain has built and reinforced an exact model of the word. He now reads that word fluently—accurately, rapidly, and effortlessly. Fluency pulls us into reading. A student who reads fluently reads for pleasure and for information; a student who is not fluent will probably avoid reading.

In a study involving 144 children, we identified the brain region that makes it possible for skilled readers to read automatically. We found that the more proficiently a child reads, the more he or she activated the occipito-temporal region (or word form area) in the back of the brain. Other investigators have observed that this brain region responds to words that are presented rapidly. Once a word is represented in the word form area, the reader recognizes that word instantly and effortlessly. This word form system appears to predominate when a reader has become fluent. As a result of this finding, we now know that development of the word form area in the left side of the brain is a key component in becoming a skilled, fluent reader.

Helping Struggling Readers Become More Fluent

Our study of 144 children also revealed that struggling readers compensate as they get older, developing alternate reading systems in the front of the brain and in the *right* side of the brain—a functioning system, but, alas, not an automatic one. These readers do not develop the critical left-side word form region necessary for rapid, automatic reading. Instead, they call on the alternate secondary pathways. This strategy enables them to read, but much more slowly and with greater effort than their classmates.

This research evidence of a disruption in the normal reading pathways provides a neurobiological target for reading interventions. In a new study, we hypothesized that an evidence-based, phonologically mediated reading intervention would help dyslexic readers develop the fast-paced word form systems serving skilled reading, thus improving their reading accuracy and fluency. Under the supervision of Syracuse University professor Benita Blachman, we provided 2nd and 3rd grade struggling readers daily with 50 minutes of individual tutoring that was systematic and explicit, focusing on helping the students understand the *alphabetic principle*, or how letters and combinations of letters represent the sounds of speech.

Students received eight months (105 hours) of intervention during the school year in addition to their regular classroom reading instruction. The experimental intervention replaced any additional reading help that the students might have received in school. Certified teachers who had taken part in an intensive training program provided the tutoring.

Immediately after the yearlong intervention, students in the experiment made significant gains in reading fluency and demonstrated increased activation in left hemisphere regions, including the inferior frontal gyrus and the parieto-temporal region. One year after the experimental intervention ended, these students were reading accurately and fluently and were activating all three left-side brain regions used by good readers. A control group of struggling readers receiving school-based, primarily nonphonological reading instruction had not activated these reading systems.

These data demonstrate that an intensive, evidence-based reading intervention brings about significant and durable changes in brain organization so that struggling readers' brain activation patterns come to resemble those of typical readers. If we provide intervention at an early age, then we can improve reading fluency and facilitate the development of the neural systems that underlie skilled reading.

Evidence-Based Effective Reading Instruction

In addition to new neurological research on the nature of reading, educators can draw on a body of rigorous, well-designed, scientific studies to guide reading instruction. In 1998, the U.S. Congress mandated the National Reading Panel to develop rigorous scientific criteria for evaluating reading research, apply these criteria to existing reading research, identify the most effective teaching methods, and then make findings accessible for parents and teachers. As a member of the Panel, I can attest to its diligence. After two years of work, the Panel issued its report (2000).

The major findings of the report indicate that in order to read, all children must be taught alphabetics, comprising phonemic awareness and phonics; reading fluency; vocabulary; and strategies for reading comprehension. These elements must be taught systematically, comprehensively, and explicitly; it is inadequate to present the foundational skills of phonemic awareness and phonics incidentally, casually, or fragmentally. Children do not learn how letters represent sounds by osmosis; we must teach them this skill explicitly. Once a child has mastered these foundational skills, he or she must be taught how to read words fluently.

Good evidence now indicates that we can teach reading fluency by means of repeated oral reading with feedback and guidance. Using these methods, we can teach almost every child to read. It is crucial to align all components of a program with one another—for example, to provide so-called decodable booklets that give the student practice in the specific letter-sound linkages we are teaching. The use of decodable booklets enables the repeated practice necessary to build the automatic systems in the word form region that lead to fluent reading.

Neuroscience and Reading Research Agree

We are now in an era of evidence-based education. Objective scientific evidence—provided by brain imaging studies and by the National Reading Panel's rigorous scientific review of the literature—has replaced reliance on philosophy or opinion.

In considering a reading program, educators should ask several key questions:

- Is there scientific evidence that the program is effective?
- Was the program or its methodology reviewed by the National Reading Panel?
- In reading instruction, are phonemic awareness and phonics taught systematically and explicitly?
- How are students taught to approach an unfamiliar word? Do they feel empowered to try to analyze and sound out an unknown word first rather than guess the word from the pictures or context?
- Does the program also include plenty of opportunities for students to practice reading, develop fluency, build vocabulary, develop reading comprehension strategies, write, and listen to and discuss stories?

Children are only 7 or 8 years old once in their lifetime. We cannot risk teaching students with unproven programs. We now have the scientific knowledge to ensure that almost every child can become a successful reader. Awareness of the new scientific knowledge about reading should encourage educators to insist that reading programs used in their schools reflect what we know about the science of reading and about effective reading instruction.

Gerald Coles

NO

Danger in the Classroom: 'Brain Glitch' Research and Learning to Read

Did you know that recent studies of the brain and reading support the reading instruction mandated in George W. Bush's No Child Left Behind (NCLB) legislation? And did you know that this research also supports the legislation he has proposed to dismantle Head Start's comprehensive approach to preschool education? And were you aware that, thanks to this brain research, we now know how children learn to read and which areas of the brain must first be stocked to promote skilled reading? Did you realize that we now have strong brain-based evidence that the best reading instruction is heavily prescriptive, skills-emphasis, building-blocks teaching that starts with small pieces of written language and proceeds to larger ones—and teachers are fortunate because these features are contained in reading programs like Open Court?

You didn't know all that? Good, because none of it is true, although you would never know that if you just listened to the President, the educators and assorted researchers who support his educational agenda, and the media who repeat their assertions.

Over 25 years ago, when I began appraising theories about faulty brain wiring in beginning readers, my criticism of the research then being conducted was limited to ersatz explanations of so-called brain dysfunctions in children called "learning disabled," "reading disabled," or "dyslexic." Contrary to the assertions made then, the research had never shown that the overwhelming number of these children did not have normal brains. Certainly a portion of poor readers had problems that were the result of exposure to such toxins as lead and cadmium, to food additives, and to other environmental influences. But, I argued, there was no evidence that they accounted for more than a small portion of the large numbers of children given these labels and shunted into special education programs.

At some point, thanks to increased, widespread criticism of these "brain-based" explanations, I had thought a change had started toward more informed, measured interpretations. However, my naive thinking has long been gone. Not only are explanations about "brain glitches," to use the term employed by reading researcher Sally Shaywitz, now being applied more forcefully to "dyslexics," but they have also been reworked to explain how all children learn to read, what single method of instruction must be used to teach them, and why the single method mandated in Bush's Reading First, part of the NCLB legislation, is a wise, scientifically based choice. Thus never have these "brain glitch" explanations been more pervasively intrusive for all beginning readers and their teachers in classrooms across the nation. . . .

A new best seller, *Overcoming Dyslexia*, by Sally Shaywitz, who has received considerable NICHD [National Institutes of Child Health and Human Development] funding for her research, claims to present "the advances in brain science" that inform what "at last we know," which are "the specific steps a child or adult must take to build and then reinforce the neural pathways deep within the brain for skilled reading." Shaywitz served on the panel whose findings, she proudly explains to readers, "are now part of the groundbreaking No Child Left Behind Legislation,". . .

In this article I will argue that, despite all the unbridled assertions about the wonder of it all, this new "brain glitch" research is theoretically, empirically, and conceptually deficient, as was the deficit-driven work that preceded it by decades. . . . More than ever, claims about the research constitute an ideological barrier to a sounder understanding of the connections between brain activity and learning to read. More than ever, this work is a danger in the classroom both because it applies unproven labels to an ever-larger number of children and because it promotes a single kind of instruction that, based on the actual empirical evidence mustered for it, contains no promise for leaving no beginning reader behind. To all of this, add the false and cruel expectations that these claims generate in parents.

To help illustrate my critique, I will use as an example a recent, highly publicized study on reading and brain activity whose co-authors include Reid Lyon, Sally Shaywitz, and several other researchers whose work argues for building-blocks teaching and has been used as evidence for Reading First instruction. (For convenience I call it the Shaywitz/Lyon study).

Is the Brain "Reading"?

Functional magnetic resonance imagery (fMRI) is a valuable diagnostic and investigative technology that can measure blood flow in the brain and thereby provide information about certain kinds of brain activity when someone is performing a task. However, like every technology used in research, its value and the information it produces are never better than the initial theory and concepts that steer its application. Perhaps the biggest misrepresentation in the "brain glitch" research is that the color scans produced by fMRI provide information about "reading." In fact, they provide no such thing, because the "reading" tasks under study are largely a person's performance on simple sound and sound/symbol (phonics) tasks with words and parts of words, rather than performance in reading as conventionally defined, that is, reading and comprehending sentences and paragraphs. (The same misrepresentation appears in claims about "reading" contained in the report of the National Reading Panel, the chief research document cited in the Reading First legislation.)

The puny definition of reading used in this research appears not to concern the investigators, though, because they design their studies on the assumption that these simple tasks involving words and parts of words embrace the core requirements for beginning readers: that is, mastery of phonological awareness (distinguishing and manipulating sounds in words) and sound/symbol relationships. As the Shaywitz/Lyon study explains, there is now "a strong consensus" (that is, a broad unanimity of professional opinion) that phonological awareness is the first building block within the sequence and that reading disability reflects a deficit in this "lower level component" of "the language system." Only after mastering this component can beginning readers effectively continue to master other reading skills.

That's the claim. The reality is that the so-called strong consensus does not exist. I and others have published thorough research reviews that critique—and dismiss—the "lower level component" model and the supposed empirical evidence showing the superior effect of early, direct, and intensive instruction in word sounds on later reading. As I have also argued, this narrow, do-as-you're-told instruction not only pushes aside numerous issues that bear on beginning literacy—such as children's backgrounds, interests, problem-solving approaches, and definitions of "reading" —it also masquerades as a bootstrap policy solution for poor children that takes off the table all other policies required to address the many needs that influence learning success or failure. However, for the advocates of this "strong consensus," especially those linked to the political power pushing these claims, conflicting views are never allowed to ruffle their harmony.

Hence, an experiment, such as those reported in the Shaywitz/Lyon study, can be designed in which subjects do "lower level component" tasks, such as deciding if nonwords rhyme ("Do leat and bete rhyme?") or making judgments requiring both phonological and semantic knowledge ("Are corn and rice in the same category?"), and the researchers can claim that the data generated tell us a great deal about "reading," the reading process, and the best kinds of instruction. The conclusions in this work display no awareness of the self-fulfilling prophecy at play when the research focuses solely on "lower level components" decontextualized from a full appraisal of reading, uses no other model of reading and instruction, and then concludes that these components are the initial and key ones in learning to read.

A Real "Brain Glitch"?

Looking more deeply into the research design of the "brain glitch" studies, we find a problem that dyslexia researchers have long encountered but not overcome when organizing an experiment so that data on brain activity can be meaningfully interpreted: the experiment must start by grouping dyslexics separately from other kinds of poor readers. This distinction is required because even in studies using the fMRI, the data are about brain activity associated with the word-level tasks, not about micro brain damage. Therefore, fMRI differences in brain activity among a group of unsorted poor readers would not provide information about the cause and meaning of the various differences in activity.

To solve the problem, these studies and previous ones employing simpler technologies try first to separate from a group of poor readers those whose problems are assumed to have non-neurological causes, such as emotional, familial, social class, and similar "exclusionary" influences, as they have been called. If these poor readers are excluded, researchers have reasoned, the probability is high that the reading problems of those who remain are caused by a "brain glitch." While this might make sense in theory, in practice it has not worked, because researchers have not created evaluation methods and criteria for separating the two groups of poor readers.

Even worse, for decades, researchers have frequently stated that they have used a thorough process of distinguishing between the two groups, but the assertion has rarely been accompanied by evidence. In the Shaywitz/Lyon study, for example, dyslexics were supposedly identified after the researchers had determined that the subjects' reading problems were not caused by emotional problems or "social, cultural, or economic disadvantage." Yet the researchers, so dedicated to obtaining and reporting a surfeit of brain data, offered not a whit of information on this process of elimination. Presumably, readers of the published study were expected to accept without question the assertion that genuine dyslexics had been identified and that these children could then be compared to "nonimpaired" readers (an odd term, since it refers to normal or average readers but is used in the study to underline a priori the assumption that the dyslexics' brains were impaired).

The need to provide evidence of thorough appraisals of the roots of subjects' reading problems is usually obvious to anyone who has actually taught poor readers and, therefore, knows that there can be numerous contextual causes of poor reading in middle-class children that will not be readily apparent. In my extensive work with children, young adults, and adults with severe reading problems, I have found that causes can be uncovered only after spending considerable time *both* evaluating and teaching a student, with the latter especially necessary. Poor teaching—such as using a one-size-fits-all reading program, insufficient individualized instruction, too much phonics, too little phonics—is just one of the many influences that can produce reading problems in a variety of ways, but those problems will not be apparent without thorough analysis of a person's instructional history and current active reading.

Many unusual family circumstances and stresses can impair a child's early reading progress. A parent losing a job, a family moving to another city in the middle of the first grade, overworked parents, grandparents dying around the time a child began school are all examples of problems I have identified. These experiences hinder reading development by distracting and stressing a child, but they are not overt "emotional" problems. Even when a poor reader comes from a family that appears "normal," only an extensive exploration of the family dynamics can determine whether this appearance might cloak problems that have affected a child's beginning reading.

By not providing criteria and evidence that the "dyslexics" are different from other poor readers, the brain research studies use another self-serving, self-fulfilling prophecy: because the fMRI shows differences in brain activity between "dyslexic" and "nonimpaired" readers, the differences in brain activity must be visual demonstrations of impairment and nonimpairment. How do we know the fMRI data reveal impairment? Because one of the groups was initially identified as impaired. How do we know the group was impaired? Because the group was first identified as impaired and the fMRI data corroborated the impairment. No other explanations can explain the dyslexics' different brain activity. Impaired, for sure! No question about it. . . .

Fixing the "Brain Glitch"

Beyond finding "brain glitches," researchers have reported other good news: building-block skills instruction can remedy the glitch. "An effective reading program" can produce "brain repair," Shaywitz reports. "The brain can be rewired.". . .

Nearly 20 years ago, Leonide Goldstein and I published a study on differences in brain hemisphere activation in adult beginning readers as they were learning to read. We found that these adults, when they were poor readers or nonreaders, did, indeed, demonstrate brain activation that was different from that found among good readers. However, as their reading improved, through the use of a holistic, comprehensive teaching approach over many months, their brain activation changed toward that commonly found in good readers. We interpreted these data as evidence that new knowledge and competencies were linked to concomitant changes in brain structure and functioning, as one would expect for *all kinds of learning*. There was nothing in the data to suggest that these beginning readers started learning to read with anything other than normal brains that were configured as they were at the beginning of the study because the students had not learned to read; no data suggested that the educational intervention we provided somehow repaired or circumvented dysfunctional brain areas.

To restate a central point for appraising these glitch-fixing interventions: although researchers insist that the training programs they use repair or ameliorate brain hardware or glitches, there is no evidence in any of their studies that this rewiring was different from that which is concomitant with the learning that continues throughout our learning lives. Nor does this so-called repair demonstrate that phonological processing is the *initial* key component in learning to read. The subjects apparently lacked this ability and then learned this ability, and their brain processing changed accordingly. Using modern technology to identify and track brain changes related to changes in reading ability is an extraordinary achievement. Using the achievement for ideological ends is not.

Emotionless "Cognition"

Like the assumed "consensus" on building-blocks instruction, "brain glitch" research assumes that cognition—that is, the process that creates images, concepts, and mental operations—is not a construct but an independent reality that actually describes the brain processes associated with reading. Ignored in this assumption is the ever-growing evidence suggesting that thinking is an inseparable interaction of both cognition and emotion (feelings, desires, enthusiasms, antipathies, etc.) . . .

Unfortunately, none of this new perspective on the "continuous and interwoven cognitive-emotional fugue," . . . has entered the "brain glitch" research. As a result, the question of whether diminished activity in a portion of the brain of someone doing a reading task might be a consequence of an emotional response, in that emotional memories can exert a powerful influence on "thought processes," remains unaddressed. By purging emotions and focusing only on cognition, the "brain glitch" research also purges the alternative: a holistic instructional approach based on the assumption that classrooms are filled with whole children for whom learning is always grounded in the fugue of cognition and affect.

How the Brain Works: Modules?

The interrelationships and interactions missing from the narrow cognitive model of "brain glitch" research lead us to a final concern. A chief premise of this research holds that the brain has specific modules for specialized operations that work in sequence with other modules in learning written language and that foremost of these is at least one module that can process basic sound and sound/symbol skills. This kind of modular model has a certain palpable, visual appeal (not unlike "building-blocks instruction"), but the actual existence of such modules is a theory, not a fact, that has increasingly been questioned. Most likely, the modular model is not one that explains how the brain actually works.

For instance, Merlin Donald, a psychologist who has written extensively on human consciousness, rejects the explanation that modules perform "specialized operations," such as deciphering portions of language. While language areas of the brain, such as those related to aspects of reading, are important in processing particular functions, all are intertwined in extensive networks (a polyphony) of brain areas that are simultaneously and interactively communicating and constructing and reconstructing particular areas within the whole. Yes, the brain has fundamental mechanisms for beginning to learn written language, but it does not begin with a "fixed pattern of connectivity." Instead, the "connectivity pattern is set by experience" with "countless interconnection points, or synapses, which connect neurons to one another in various patterns." In other words, learning and experience create and shape the brain's circuits and how they are used in learning to read; the circuits are not predetermined.

Linguist Philip Lieberman has also criticized modular explanations, calling them "neophrenological theories," that is, theories that "map complex behaviors to localized regions of the brain, on the assumption that a particular part of the brain regulates an aspect of behavior." In these theories, he remarks, the functional organization of the brain is run by "a set of petty bureaucrats each of which controls a behavior." Like Donald, Lieberman proposes that converging behavioral and neurobiological data indicate that human language is composed not of a hierarchical system but of neural networks, including the traditional cortical "language" areas (Broca's and Wernicke's areas), formed through circuits that link populations of neurons in neuroanatomical structures that are distributed throughout the brain. Lieberman stresses, "Although specific operations may be performed in particular parts of the brain, these operations must be integrated into a *network* that regulates an observable aspect of behavior. And so, a particular aspect of behavior usually involves activity in neuroanatomical structures distributed throughout the brain" (emphasis in original). . . .

The view of a "connectivity pattern" that emerges and is activated as children learn to read contrasts with the model of step-by-step progression from module to module. If the former is an accurate model of brain organization and functioning, it suggests that the connectivity pattern should be the focus of research because only by looking at the overall pattern can researchers begin to determine the functioning and interrelationships of any part and the causal, consequential, or interactive function of that part within the entire pattern.

From the perspective of a connectivity pattern model, not only do the brain areas involved in grasping the sound/symbol correspondence *not* have to be primed first before other areas of the pattern can become effectively operable, the creation and functioning of these areas depends on connections within the entire pattern. And because the pattern is not innately fixed, if instruction were to stimulate certain areas more than others, a particular connectivity pattern would emerge. That specific pattern, however, might not necessarily be the sole one required for reading success and might not be superior to other connectivity patterns. Moreover, a more complex connectivity pattern could be created through richer written language learning. None of this is addressed in the "brain glitch" research.

Conclusion

Philip Lieberman offers a caveat worth emphasizing when appraising "brain glitch" research, learning to read, and the Bush agenda for education: "We must remember that we stand on the threshold of an understanding of how brains really work. The greatest danger perhaps rests in making claims that are not supported by data." Unfortunately, not only have "brain glitch" researchers seldom been guided by such a caveat, they have tended to misconstrue the data and have drawn conclusions that serve to justify unwarranted beliefs, instructional policy, and the politics that have driven the research in the first place. . . .

For research on the brain and reading to become productive, what is needed most is the discarding of fundamental assumptions that have not been validated. Building-blocks instruction has not been proved to be the best way to teach reading. Phonological awareness has not been proved to be the initial, essential component that determines reading success. Thinking does not involve "cognition" alone. The modular organization of the brain is, at best, a disputed theory. Brain activation differences do not necessarily reflect "brain glitches." Dyslexia remains no more a proven malady among a substantial percentage of beginning readers than when Glasgow ophthalmologist James Hinshelwood first discussed it as "congenital word-blindness" at the end of the 19th century.

To make research on the brain and reading work, it must be informed by the complexity of reading acquisition, and it must begin to address such questions as: Will alternative teaching approaches configure brain activity in alternative ways? Will children's differing assumptions about what it means to "read" correspond to differing brain activity and organization? How do different aspects of reading, such as comprehension, syntax, and word analysis, interact in certain reading tasks and what kinds of brain activity do the interactions produce? How does the knowledge children bring to literacy learning affect brain activity?

These and similar questions can begin to contribute to a better understanding of the relationship between brain function and reading acquisition, which in turn can help promote ecological approaches that are grounded in an understanding of the unified interrelationships of brain, active child, and learning environment. They can also begin to help identify genuine brain-related reading impairments. Developing this kind of understanding of integrated interrelationships will require that we eschew views that are either "brain based" or conceive of the brain as an extraneous "black box."

By adding to the current pretensions about the superiority of one brand of "scientifically based" reading instruction, "brain glitch" research remains a danger in the classroom. Unfortunately, because of the political power connected to this sham science and brainless instruction, a mighty effort is required to end that danger.

POSTSCRIPT

Can Brain Scans Unravel the Mystery of Learning Disabilities?

By Christmas of the first-grade year, parents and teachers alike begin to worry about children who don't seem to be catching on to the magic of reading—understanding the connection between the sounds we make and their written symbols. Heated disputes about the best way to help struggling readers have existed for hundreds of years.

The latest round of this debate was sounded with the release of the National Reading Panel Report (2000). Using a tool called meta-analysis, the National Reading Panel (NRP) reviewed a number of research studies. Based on this analysis, the NRP concluded that most children would learn to read with systematic and intensive instruction, emphasizing phonemics and phonics.

The NRP report generated much controversy, especially from theorists who believe in a more holistic, literature-based method of reading instruction. Researchers argued (and continue to argue) about the studies selected and the studies eliminated from consideration. They argued about types of students included in the studies and criticized the fact that many of the studies did not seem to include struggling readers. They argued about the definition of reading—is it decoding individual words or gaining meaning from the print? The fervor increased when NCLB authors used the NRP's findings to set expectations for the type of research-based instruction schools should be using.

The drive to help all children learn to read easily has generated so much disagreement that it has often been termed "The Reading Wars." A promising method is identified, only to be dashed in a few years in a headline proclaiming reading researchers failed, yet again, to solve the reading crisis. In an attempt to define common ground, Rona Flippo (2004, 1999, 1998) surveyed "The Experts." Working for over 10 years, she learned that 11 prominent researchers with varying philosophies agreed on a number of points. One was that there is no "one best method" of teaching reading. The experts agreed that it was critical for teachers to match instructional methods to individual children, in response to their specific needs, interests, and learning styles.

Shaywitz and Shaywitz use fMRI results to provide evidence that brain "glitches" exist and can be corrected with the right kind of reading instruction. They strongly believe that the type of reading instruction advocated by NCLB can help "virtually" all students learn to read, even those with disabilities. Shaywitz and Shaywitz have great confidence that "teaching matters and good teaching can change the brain."

Coles cautions that demonstrating differences in brain activity is not enough—brains change as they learn. Some students have difficulty reading, he notes, because they have not had sufficient language support or because they might be preoccupied with troubled lives. According to Coles, the reasons for reading problems are not always simple—neither are the solutions. He is wary that the results of a few studies have been used to further a political agenda that dictates specific reading methodologies for use by all schools.

In the next 10 years, what will we discover about reading and the brain? Will fMRI (or its successor) unlock the mysteries of thinking and learning? Will in-school testing be replaced by visits to the neurologist? Will research identify teaching techniques to match with brain scan patterns? Or will the next set of studies find that the puzzle of reading disability has multiple explanations and solutions?

ISSUE 16

Can RTI Reduce the Numbers of Children Identified with Specific Learning Disability (SLD)?

YES: Lynn S. Fuchs, from *NRCLD Update on Responsiveness to Intervention: Research to Practice* (National Research Center on Learning Disabilities, 2007)

NO: Cathy G. Litty and J. Amos Hatch, from "Hurry Up and Wait: Rethinking Special Education Identification in Kindergarten," *Early Childhood Education Journal* (February 2006)

ISSUE SUMMARY

YES: Lynn S. Fuchs, a prolific scholar in the area of learning disabilities, and one of the several researchers in the National Research Center for Learning Disabilities, explains how Research to Intervention (RTI) strategies can separate a struggling learner from one with specific learning disability (SLD).

NO: Cathy G. Litty (Western Carolina University) and J. Amos Hatch (University of Tennessee) discuss the increasing academic pressures for kindergarten children; they believe special education services should be provided as soon as possible to students who will eventually be found eligible.

Specific learning disabilities (SLD), defined elsewhere in this book, is the disability designation for the majority of students covered by IDEA. It is the only disability specifically defined in IDEA, and the only one for which assessment methodology is addressed.

Students with SLD encounter substantial learning difficulties not attributable to other disabilities, such as mental retardation or a sensory impairment. They have not experienced environmental, cultural, or economic disadvantage. They have received quality instruction. In other words, all the conditions for learning are present, but learning is not occurring at a developmentally typical rate.

Assessment to determine SLD has traditionally focused on the concept of severe discrepancy. Educators and psychologists looked for a significant difference between the student's ability (usually measured by an IQ test) and academic achievement. Many complain that this process requires students to "wait to fail," since the discrepancy often does not become significant during the earliest years of school.

Prevalence rates for SLD vary from under 3% of all students in Georgia to 7% in Rhode Island (LD Summit Consensus, 2001). This variation likely reflects inconsistent approaches to identification, using SLD as "the sociological sponge that wipes up the spills of general education" (Gresham, LD Summit, 2001).

Courts have found a lack of evidence in favor of the discrepancy model as well as documented standardized test bias against minority children and English language learners (Zirkel, *CEC*, 2006). These challenges, along with concern for the sheer numbers of students in this category, led Congress to address SLD identification directly.

IDEA 2004 signaled a dramatic shift in the way schools could identify students as having SLD. Districts are now directed not to require that teams rely solely on finding an ability/achievement gap. Instead, teams "may use a process which determines if a student responds to scientific, research-based intervention." Schools can use the approaches in combination.

Briefly, assessment through RTI involves gathering student progress information on a consistent basis, beginning with universal screening. All students are to experience research-based classroom instruction (Tier 1). Students whose regular in-class assessments show an unsatisfactory rate of growth would receive more intense general education services and progress-monitoring (Tier 2). Those who do not respond to this level of assistance move on to Tier 3 or higher. If formal evaluation rules out the exclusionary factors listed above, the student could be identified with SLD and be considered for special education.

Diagnosis through RTI accomplishes two ends. RTI acts as a prevention tool, focusing teacher attention on students who are progressing slowly. Interventions address difficulties before they become large enough to warrant disability status. Students and teachers no longer need wait for the discrepancy to reach significance.

Lynn Fuchs, whose research identifies both benefits and risks in using RTI, believes the number of students found to have SLD will be reduced by effective general education intervention. Checking student progress on a regular basis, and providing data-based help as soon as it seems needed, will help many children learn successfully without resorting to special education.

In the second selection, Cathy Litty and J. Amos Hatch, university faculty members, describe the hurried academic pace of today's kindergartens. Even though teachers can monitor student progress, and adjust teaching strategies, Litty and Hatch fear this just delays necessary special education services for students who need them.

As you read these articles, consider the viewpoints they present. Will RTI be the key to reducing SLD numbers? Or will it merely postpone the inevitable?

YES ⤶

Lynn S. Fuchs

NRCLD Update on Responsiveness to Intervention: Research to Practice

What RTI Is

Students with SLD make up the majority of school-age individuals with disabilities. The number of students with SLD has increased (from 1.2 million in 1979–1980 to 2.9 million in 2003–2004). Many policymakers and school administrators are concerned about the increasing numbers of students with SLD. The concern is that some of these students may be capable of learning without special education if they are provided effective general education.

The usual method for identifying SLD relies on the difference between IQ and achievement. Research now shows that this method has many problems. For example, children who read poorly have similar characteristics, regardless of whether they have a discrepancy between IQ and achievement. Also, the size of discrepancy does not indicate the severity of the SLD. Moreover, data obtained through an assessment of the IQ-achievement discrepancy do not inform instruction in important ways.

RTI is a promising model for a new way to identify SLD as a student's failure to respond to teaching methods that research has shown to work well for most students.

Here is one example of an RTI process.

STEP 1: All students in a school are given short tests. The aim is to identify those students whose scores are low and so seem to be at risk of developing a learning disability.

STEP 2: The progress of these at-risk students is checked for five to eight weeks. A short test is given each week. Students whose progress is low in response to *general education instruction (Tier 1)* are identified.

STEP 3: These students receive *small-group instruction (Tier 2 and Beyond intervention)* for nine to 20 weeks. This instruction usually consists of three to four sessions per week. Each instructional session lasts 30 to 40 minutes. Each week, a short test measures the student's progress. They also are tested at the end of instruction. *Students who*

From *National Resource Center on Learning Disabilities,* Winter 2007. Published in 2007 by U.S. Office of Special Education Programs/Department of Education. www.nrcld.org

respond well to the intervention return to Tier 1 (general education) instruction. Responding well means the student has improved each week during instruction and has a satisfactory achievement score at the end of the intervention. Student progress continues to be checked to catch any student who is not able to keep up a good rate of learning while back in general instruction.

STEP 4: *Students whose response to small-group instruction is poor are given a comprehensive evaluation.* A poor response is a low rate of improvement each week and a low achievement score at the end of the intervention.

STEP 5: To answer questions that arose during Tier 2 and Beyond, a *comprehensive evaluation* is conducted using valid and reliable data collection measures that are targeted specifically to student needs. The aim is to determine whether it is correct to identify the student as having a learning disability. A student may be identified as having some other disability—for example, mental retardation, speech/language delay, or emotional or behavioral disorder.

STEP 6: *Special education is delivered with a more intensive instructional program.* Progress continues to be checked each week. If at any time data indicate that the student is not progressing adequately with the instructional program, the special educator changes the program. *Once a student has a strong rate of learning and reaches a satisfactory performance level, the student exits special education and returns to Tier 1 general education instruction.* The student's progress in Tier 1 instruction continues to be checked so that corrective action may be taken as needed.

The reasoning behind this RTI method of identifying learning disabilities is this: When a student does not respond to generally effective interventions both at Tier 1 and at Tier 2 and Beyond, the quality of instruction is not a likely reason for poor academic progress and, instead, may provide evidence of a disability.

Benefits

An RTI model may offer several benefits. First, an RTI model for identifying students with SLD has the benefit of *early identification and intervention.* Students at risk for SLD can be screened as early as January of kindergarten or September of first grade. This decreases the likelihood that students will slip through the system without detection of their learning problems.

A second potential benefit of an RTI model of SLD identification is *systematic screening, which reduces screening bias.* Systematic screening, which involves testing all students, decreases reliance on teacher-based referral. This reduces possible teacher bias and reduces the variability in SLD identification practices. Referral and identification for SLD vary in part because teachers differ in their views about how students perform and why they may be learning poorly. This variability in teachers' views and attributes results in missed opportunities to serve students with SLD.

A final potential benefit of RTI is *linking identification assessment with instructional planning.* Presently, the assessment process for documenting a discrepancy between IQ and achievement takes a lot of resources. At the same time, the resulting test scores have little connection with planning effective instruction. Many special and general education teachers find results from traditional tests are not much help in designing instruction. Using RTI to identify students as having SLD keeps the assessment focus on the student's learning. The RTI model switches the emphasis from assessment for identification to instructionally relevant assessment. It involves monitoring student progress and systematic testing of changes in instruction.

Risks

Despite the promise of an RTI model for identifying learning disabilities, key conceptual issues need to be sharpened. RTI methods need to be further specified and studied.

One potential pitfall of RTI is *whether strong intervention models and measures are available to produce strong learning outcomes.* For schools and teachers to be able to use RTI, instructional procedures that are shown to be effective across teachers and schools must be available. In addition, measures are required to follow learning over time. These tools are available for some, but not all, academic areas. They are better developed at some grade levels. For example, a fair amount of work has been accomplished in beginning reading to provide the groundwork for both RTI intervention and measurement procedures. By contrast, in math, spelling, and writing, measurement procedures for tracking growth are well established, but more research is needed on validated intervention methods for testing responsiveness to instruction. More information is available at the early grades than for older students.

A second potential pitfall concerns *having enough trained professionals available.* To use an RTI model in the thousands of school districts in this country, large numbers of trained professionals are required. They will need the knowledge and skills to put in place defined tutoring methods or to solve problems through research. They also will need the knowledge and skills to monitor student learning, to interpret the assessment results, and to make decisions about eligibility. Moreover, using RTI requires a new way of thinking about assessment and instruction for many professionals, including school psychologists, special and general educators, and principals. To date, RTI models have been implemented only on a small scale by highly trained personnel in research settings. Using RTI on a large scale, in many school systems and many states, has not yet been tested. It will require developing and carrying out an ambitious training agenda for school professionals.

Finally, *RTI practitioners will need to determine when to begin due process and parental involvement.* Does due process begin with problem-solving adaptations to general education or with the intensive short-term preventive instruction? Is it delayed until the student is found to be unresponsive to instruction and a special education classification is imminent? On the one hand, due process early in the identification process may be essential to protect against students getting caught in a cycle in which they linger between general education and some layer of services short of special education, without parents being aware or having input. On the other hand, initiating due process early in identification will be costly and will add considerable time and personnel requirements to identification. Clearly, discussions are needed about due process in such a changed identification system.

How NRCLD's Research Is Helping Schools Implement RTI

Two large studies have been conducted, one in *reading* and the other in *math*, in which students were followed over time.

Reading

NRCLD worked in 42 classrooms across 10 schools. Some schools had large numbers of high-poverty families, and other schools had large numbers of middle-class families. Students from these classrooms were selected for taking part based on low scores on brief reading measures given at the beginning of first grade. These 252 students were randomly assigned to receive the instruction or not at the beginning of January, depending on how they actually improved during the fall.

Instruction Group
Students who had been randomly assigned to receive small-group instruction (and who did not improve much in reading during the fall) continued to receive reading instruction in the general education classroom. They also took part in Tier 2 small-group instruction for nine weeks. Small-group instruction consisted of three, 45-minute sessions per week.

Control Group
By contrast, students who had been randomly assigned to the control group (and who did not improve much in reading during the fall) continued to receive all of their reading instruction in the general education classroom. They did not receive small-group instruction.

Findings
At the end of first grade, students who had received small-group instruction read substantially better than students who did not receive small-group instruction. Many fewer students qualified as SLD given the various methods we used to define SLD. The alternative ways of defining SLD at the end of first grade, some based on traditional methods of discrepancy

between IQ and achievement and others based on RTI approaches, designated different students as having a learning disability.

Math

We conducted a study similar to the reading study but not identical. We worked in 41 classrooms across 10 schools. Some schools had large numbers of high-poverty families, and other schools had large numbers of middle-class families. Based on their math scores near the beginning of first grade, students from these classrooms were designated as not at risk for SLD in math (127 children) or as at risk for SLD in math (569 children). The at-risk children were randomly assigned to receive small-group instruction or not beginning in November.

Instruction Group
Students who had been randomly assigned to receive small-group instruction continued to receive math instruction in the general education classroom. They also took part in Tier 2 small-group instruction for 20 weeks. This instruction consisted of three, 30-minute sessions per week.

Control Group
By contrast, students who had been randomly assigned to the control group continued to receive all of their math instruction in the general education classroom. They did not receive small-group instruction.

Findings
At the end of first grade, students who had received small-group instruction computed and understood math concepts substantially better than students who did not receive small-group instruction. Many fewer students qualified as SLD given the various methods we used to define SLD. The alternative ways of defining SLD at the end of first grade, some based on traditional methods of discrepancy between IQ and achievement and others based on RTI approaches, designated different students as having a learning disorder.

Conclusions

From these studies, we draw several conclusions that should influence how schools conduct RTI.

> 1. One-time testing at the beginning of the year does not provide an adequate basis for identifying children who need Tier 2 and Beyond small-group instruction intervention. Instead, one-time testing can be used to identify a pool of students whose progress then needs to be monitored, using brief weekly tests, for five to eight weeks. Then, a slope of improvement (that is weekly rate of gain) can be calculated to determine which children have progressed nicely in response to the Tier 1 general education program and which children require Tier 2 and Beyond intervention.

2. Tier 2 and Beyond small-group instruction can be effective in promoting better achievement. It also can be effective for sorting out children who will learn well with well-designed instruction versus children who require more intensive special education. With Tier 2 and Beyond small-group instruction, fewer children finish first grade with the kinds of academic deficits that make them appropriate for disability certification.
3. This RTI process can provide a sound basis for identifying students to receive a comprehensive special education evaluation.
4. Tier 2 and Beyond instructors need to be well trained and supervised for Tier 2 and Beyond benefits to accrue. With training and supervision, formal teaching certification is not necessary. Continuing problem solving to address the learning needs and behavioral challenges of individual students needs to be provided by a licensed teacher who has a strong teaching background.
5. Different methods for quantifying "fíresponsefl" to Tier 2 and Beyond small-group instruction will result in different numbers of students being identified for comprehensive special education evaluation. Some methods work better than others at identifying students with severe academic deficits. One method that appears to work well is to define adequate response as students demonstrating (a) a strong rate of improvement during small-group instruction as well as (b) adequate final performance at the end of small-group instruction.
6. Some students who demonstrate adequate response to small-group instruction will fall behind again when they return to Tier 1 general education without the continuing support of small-group instruction. For this reason, it is important that schools continue to monitor the progress of these students with brief weekly assessments so that corrective actions may be taken when needed, including returning to Tier 2 and Beyond small-group instruction.

Frequently Asked Questions about RTI

Will this process delay identification? The RTI process takes longer than a traditional one-step comprehensive evaluation. However, beginning at Tier 2, students are receiving services designed to remediate their learning problems—a prevention strategy. The aim is that the prevention built into RTI will reduce the number of students incorrectly identified as having a disability because they have not received strong instruction. It may help many students get on an upward track toward successful academic outcomes. Also, RTI facilitates prevention and identification early in the primary grades. In contrast, the traditional method of identifying a discrepancy between IQ and achievement often occurs later in schooling, since it may be many grades before a sizeable discrepancy accrues.

Does each child have to go through RTI or can a child have a traditional assessment?   Schools honor parent requests for a traditional one-step comprehensive evaluation, in lieu of the RTI process. Legislation suggests that the evaluation of a child suspected of having a disability must include a variety of assessment tools and must not rely on any single measure.

What does "research-based intervention" mean?   A research-based intervention constitutes a set of practices. Each of those practices is tested and evaluated in controlled studies. Each practice must be shown to be effective. In a controlled study, students are matched (found to be similar) according to the criteria important to the study. Students are randomly assigned to a treatment or no treatment group. The outcomes for students in both groups are compared.

Who initiates an RTI process?   Typically, children are identified to take part in Tier 2 and Beyond interventions based on their universal screening scores, when students are tested once, at the beginning of the school year. Many times, such universal screening is supplemented with short-term progress monitoring (for example, over five weeks) to determine the student's response to general education.

What will be required for professional development?   An RTI process of SLD identification will require professional development to prepare school staffs to do the following activities:

- Collect and interpret screening scores using existing data or individually administered brief assessments on all students
- Ensure the quality of general education by selecting strong curricula and by conducting observations to document that those strong curricula have been used well. This requires examining class-wide patterns of response to determine when teachers require assistance to improve the quality of their instructional programs and then providing that assistance
- Collect continuing progress-monitoring data and interpret the data
- Design Tier 2 and Beyond programs that incorporate validated intervention protocols
- Implement those Tier 2 and Beyond programs with fidelity.

Who is responsible for the various activities required to implement RTI as a method of SLD identification?   Faculty in a school building must work collaboratively to implement RTI as a method of SLD identification. In some schools, the work is distributed as shown in the table on the next page.

How long will the comprehensive evaluation be and what professional is likely to give the Step 4 assessment?   The comprehensive evaluation should be specifically targeted to answer questions that arise during Tier 2 and Beyond instruction. It should be done in collaboration with the perspective

Task	Responsibility
Collecting screening data using existing data or individually administered brief assessments on all students	Teachers & trained aides
Interpreting screening data	Special educators & school psychologists
Ensuring the quality of general education	Curriculum specialists at the school or district level, school psychologists, teachers, & parents
Collecting continuing progress-monitoring data	Teachers & trained aides
Interpreting progress-monitoring data	Special educators & school psychologists
Designing Tier 2 and Beyond programs that incorporate validated intervention protocols	Special educators & school psychologists
Implementing Tier 2 and Beyond programs with fidelity	Trained aides under the supervision of special educators & school psychologists
Conducting the Step 4 evaluation	Special educators & school psychologists

of the student's general education teacher. Typically, answering these relevant questions involves only a small number of relatively brief tests. For example, if mental retardation is suspected as the disability category, school psychologists might administer the Vineland Adaptive Behavior Scale along with a two-subtest Wechsler Abbreviated Scale of Intelligence instead of giving a full-blown intelligence test to rule out mental retardation.

What proportion of students is likely to be identified as at risk (for Tier 1 monitoring) and for the Tier 2 and Beyond diagnostic trial? The proportion of students identified for different steps in the RTI process depends largely on the quality of general education. When general education instruction is of questionable quality, research suggests that 20 percent to 25 percent of a school population is likely to be identified as at risk and demonstrate unresponsiveness to Tier 1. Of course, providing the Tier 2 and Beyond diagnostic instructional trial to 25 percent of a school population challenges a school's resources. In contrast, research also suggests that with high-quality general education, only 9 percent to 10 percent of students will be identified as at risk and respond inadequately to Tier 1, with approximately half those students responding to high-quality Tier 2 and Beyond instruction. Clearly, a need exists to ensure high-quality general education. In a similar way, integrity of the RTI process requires a strong Tier 2 and Beyond diagnostic instructional trial.

Are there schools currently carrying out RTI as a method of SLD identification and, if so, how can I learn more about their methods? Yes, some schools are implementing RTI as a method of SLD identification. . . .

Hurry Up and Wait: Rethinking Special Education Identification in Kindergarten

Introduction

The nature of kindergarten is changing, and the needs of young children with disabilities are often being ignored as these changes take place. Kindergarten teachers are being asked to implement standards-based curricula that many believe "hurry"' the academic development of even the most able children. The tradition of most school systems and the policy of some is to delay doing evaluations for special education identification until after the kindergarten year. This traps children who will eventually qualify for special education services into waiting at least an extra year before their special learning needs will be addressed. It also places kindergarten teachers in a difficult position. They face all the complexity associated with teaching children with disabilities, but get none of the support. Although some teachers have the experience, expertise, and confidence to accommodate the needs of children with special learning needs, the system is set up to create a difficult year for many kindergartners and their teachers. In effect, the system is saying to young children with disabilities that are as yet unidentified: *Hurry up* and fit into an academically driven school setting *and wait* a year for the services you need to be successful. To kindergarten teachers, the message is: *You are on your own.*

Today's Kindergarten

The nature and purposes of kindergarten have changed over the past decade. Factors that have in.uenced these changes include: (a) the experience of being a child is vastly different than it was just a generation ago, (b) advances in knowledge about what young children are capable of learning have challenged traditional perspectives on appropriate practice in kindergarten classrooms, and (c) the standards-based accountability movement has worked its way down into early childhood classrooms. Although many teachers and

From *Early Childhood Education Journal*, 33(4), February 2006, pp. 203–208. Copyright © 2006 by Springer Science and Business Media. Reprinted by permission via Rightslink.

others interested in early childhood would like to preserve kindergarten's traditional role of providing a buffer to help smooth young children's transition from home to school, it is a fact of life that kindergartens are becoming more like the first and second grades of the recent past.

Children entering contemporary kindergartens are assumed to bring with them academic knowledge and skills that not long ago were considered appropriate instructional objectives for first grade. Five-year-olds are now assumed to have already acquired social understandings and capacities that used to comprise a central place in the kindergarten curriculum. Kindergartners are now routinely tested and evaluated on the mastery of academic standards that were previously thought to be beyond their developmental understanding. So, what teachers and students spend their time doing in the new kindergarten looks quite different than what they did a few years ago. The curriculum is more rigorous, teaching methods are more direct, and expectations for academic achievement are much higher. While these changes have implications for all children, we are particularly interested in what they mean for young children who may be at risk, especially the thousands of young children with undiagnosed disabilities who enter kindergarten each year.

Special Education Identification

Federal law dictates that teachers refer children about whom they have concerns for special education evaluation, but they must intervene in some way with modified strategies before this can occur. We know that great variability exists across schools and systems regarding how interventions and referrals are carried out, but we believe that current policy and practice concerning the identification of young children for special education services continues to be dominated by the assumption that it is better to wait until first grade than to start the special education identification processes in kindergarten. The basic logic has been that because the administration of standardized instruments is central to the identification process and young children are not developmentally ready for standardized testing experiences, then kindergartners should not be placed in special education programs based on unreliable psychometric data. Further, because kindergarten-aged children are maturing so rapidly, it is hard to make distinctions between normal delays in development and the presence of certain long-term disabilities. Even further, since kindergarten has traditionally been a place where children were gently socialized into the world of school, not much was lost by allowing children who may eventually qualify for special education services to play out the kindergarten year receiving the same program as their age-mates.

In cases where developmental delays are dramatic or behavior in the classroom is uncontrollable, the "wait till next year" rule is sometimes waived. But, these cases are rare. The mode is much more likely to be that teachers who have concerns about their kindergartners' capacities to be successful because of disabilities are put on hold and told to see if they "grow out of it" or "learn how to act in school."

The United States Department of Education (2003) reports that over 13% of children between the ages of three and 21 qualify for special education services. While we recognize that some disabilities may be difficult to identify in early childhood, it is reasonable to assume that a similar percentage of kindergartners qualify for services. We know that thousands of children in kindergartens across the United States will eventually be assessed and receive special services for an identified disability, so the question becomes: *Why wait?*

Why Wait?

The point we are trying to make is simple on its face. If 5- and 6-year-old children are ready for the academic emphasis that defines current kindergarten practice, then they are also ready for the special education identification system. You can't have it both ways. Either young children are cognitively and emotionally mature enough for both, or neither. The same arguments that have been used for years to make the case for developmental as opposed to academic approaches in kindergarten form the basis for arguing against assessing children for special education placement during kindergarten. Those arguments have failed to convince policy makers of the efficacy of developmental approaches. As a result, kindergarten curricula and teaching methods are decidedly academic in nature. Given the state of contemporary kindergarten programs, it no longer makes good sense to argue that kindergartners are not developmentally ready for special education assessment.

Kindergartners and their teachers are part of the accountability system that drives almost everything that happens in contemporary education settings, including preschool and kindergarten classrooms. National, state, and local accountability initiatives mandate standards-based curricula, prescribed instructional approaches, and standardized testing for younger and younger children. Schools and teachers have no choice but to reconstitute kindergarten curricular, instructional, and assessment practices in an effort to meet increasing accountability requirements. Kindergarten children at all ability and maturity levels face the challenges of meeting the expectations of "accountability shove-down" (Hatch, 2002). Since these expectations do not go away because a child may experience difficulties that significantly reduce his or her chances for school success, we believe waiting an extra year for the special education system to begin providing support is no longer justified.

Inadequate Choices

How should teachers and schools deal with the difficulties of working within a system that expects academic performance of all children while delaying extra support for those who will have the most difficulty meeting expectations? We see inadequate options and better options for dealing with the difficulties inherent in the current situation. Among the inadequate choices are: ignoring, delaying, retaining, and redshirting.

It is always a bad choice to act like nothing is wrong when children in our care are put at risk. Pretending that the current climate in early childhood education is a temporary anomaly and that traditional kinder-garten programs will reemerge as standard practice is wishful thinking at best. Hoping that the needs of kindergarten children with disabilities will be met in programs with no provision of special education services also ignores reality. This issue is real for children, teachers, and families. Imag-ining that it will go away only increases the risk for all involved.

Delaying has been institutionalized by the system. However, teachers, schools, and parents make a bad choice when disabilities are suspected and action is delayed. It is understandable that teachers faced with all the com-plexity of teaching in contemporary kindergarten classrooms rely on the prevailing ethos of waiting until next year when considering options for ad-dressing the needs of their students who struggle most. Many are concerned that some young children might be labeled prematurely by the system sim-ply because their rate of development differs from their peers. We share this concern but believe that teachers and other educators responsible for special education referral and evaluation processes can be equipped to make sound judgments based on solid information gathered from a variety of sources (see discussion of monitoring below). Great care should be taken when making decisions about special education referral, but, waiting to act on behalf of children for whom special education services are designed denies those children of help that will have more effect the sooner it is provided.

Another inadequate choice for dealing with this situation is retain-ing children in kindergarten. Unfortunately, this is the unspoken policy of many schools and school systems. Kindergartners who demonstrate clear delays in their academic progress, in effect, "fail" kindergarten and are retained. This approach may have its roots in nativist early childhood perspectives that assume that maturation is the primary determinant of children's readiness for school, but the literature on the effects of retention (and this includes placement in so-called developmental kindergartens or transition classes) consistently shows that it is a bad idea. What retention means for kindergartners with undiagnosed disabilities is that they are set up to receive a "double dose of the same medicine," when what they actually need is special education intervention.

Retention happens after an unsuccessful kindergarten year, red-shirting happens in anticipation of a difficult year. Neither is a good choice for the children we are talking about here. Redshirting is a term used to describe the practice of waiting for an extra year before starting a child in kindergarten. Many parents and some teachers have come to believe that giving children an extra year (to grow, learn, mature) helps children who might otherwise struggle. Just as athletes are held out of the action during their redshirt season, age-eligible kindergartners wait on the sidelines, then start formal schooling one year older than their peers. Like retention, redshirting has failed to demonstrate signifi-cant benefits for children. For children with disabilities that are as yet unidentified, redshirting may provide an escape from inadequate choices discussed earlier. But, if the better choices to follow were implemented, holding a child out of kindergarten for a year would be a bad option.

Better Choices

We have discussed what schools, teachers, and parents should not do, but what should they do in response to a situation in which 5- and 6-year-old children with potential disabilities are denied access to special education services during their kindergarten year? It seems to us that the best choice is to stop delaying the process of identifying eligible children for special services. Where it is formal policy to not assess kindergartners for possible disabilities, a reexamination of that policy is needed. Where informal practices are in place that severely limit special education assessments during kindergarten, honest and open deliberations about the effects of those practices on the life chances of young children with disabilities are essential. Kindergarten has changed, and expectations for kindergartners have escalated. Placing young children with unidentified disabilities in contemporary kindergartens while denying them access to services for which they will become eligible 1 year later seems indefensible. The span of "lost" time when services could be provided is significant in the life of a young child. Parents, educators, and advocates for young children should do everything they can to change policies and practices that perpetuate this flawed approach.

Beyond trying to change the system, what should teachers and schools be doing now? Three better choices are: balancing, monitoring, and adjusting. The balancing we are talking about is good practice in any early childhood classroom. It goes beyond providing equal parts of teacher-directed lessons and child-centered activities. It is more than covering the state-mandated skills in a developmentally appropriate way. The balancing we advocate is about teachers having a strong grasp of the curricular expectations where they work, an in-depth knowledge of the children in their classrooms, and a broad repertoire of teaching strategies for helping kindergartners be successful. Contemporary kindergarten teaching is complex, and teachers make countless decisions that demand special knowledge of curriculum, children, and teaching.

Balancing means making decisions about what will be taught, to whom, and how. In virtually any public school kindergarten, the "what to teach" part will be strongly influenced by district, state, and national curriculum guidelines. Most teachers will have more autonomy in deciding who will work on what parts of the curriculum at a given time. And, most teachers retain some control over the selection of teaching strategies through which children learn the content. Effective kindergarten teachers deal with this array of factors by applying a model of decision making that involves them in drawing on instructional strategies from direct to incidental teaching, and everything in between. Some strategies will work for the whole group, and some will have to be tailored for individuals or small groups. Children who are struggling in kindergarten should be learning every day, just like their peers. Those likely to be identified for special education services in first or second grade may require more creativity and support; but the model is the same. Kindergarten teachers are responsible for balancing curriculum expectations, individual differences among children, and teaching strategies for all their students. Leaving children with potential disabilities out of the balance is wrong and unnecessary.

By monitoring, we mean gathering and using information that helps teachers keep an appropriate balance for every child, including those who are struggling in kindergarten. We include elements of evaluation and assessment in the monitoring construct, but the principal aim is for teachers to collect information that will allow them to better address the needs of all their children. Monitoring begins as soon as information is available. Most systems now administer screening instruments before or soon after kindergarten entry. The information generated by these standardized screening tools can be a valuable source of information for kindergarten teachers as they set up classrooms and make curricular and instructional plans. But early monitoring should include the collection of data that go beyond the screening results. Gathering insights from parents, pre-school teachers, and caregivers is another important avenue for finding out what children are like, what they need to be successful, and what dimensions of their development may need a closer look. These insights can be gathered using information checklists, questionnaires, and direct contact with those who know the children best. Having this information right away will help kindergarten teachers adjust the experiences they provide for children from the beginning of the year, rather than waiting to see what problems arise for which children.

Teachers should continue to monitor throughout the school year. Systematic observation and documentation of the children's behavior within the classroom environment is the best way to keep track of what's going on, what works, and what needs to be changed. Data in the form of anecdotal records, checklists, or rating scales that rfelect children's performance on daily classroom tasks are essential elements of monitoring. Young children should be assessed with tasks that are functional and meaningful, and examples of work that the child has completed are excellent sources of information. Work samples and portfolios can be useful tools to aid the teacher in monitoring a child's skill level and conceptual development. As systematic monitoring processes unfold, careful records should be maintained because these will provide the best evidence available for making sound decisions about referring kindergartners for special education evaluation. This type of assessment can help early childhood professionals to verify the severity of difficulties a child may be having or rule out other possible explanations for performance that is below that of the other children in the class.

Direct evidence of children's activity in the classroom is among the best information for making adjustments to meet the needs of kindergartners, especially those who are struggling. Adjusting means adapting curriculum and modifying instruction so that every child is learning in kindergarten. Based on the understandings gained through the monitoring processes described above, adjusting should be a natural consequence of seeing what children can do and what they need more help to accomplish. Adapting the curriculum may mean changing the pace for some children, starting them at a place farther down on the curriculum skills' hierarchy than where most kindergartners are operating, then moving them forward at a pace that accommodates their capacities.

Modifying instruction is about calling on a wide repertoire of teaching strategies that improve children's chances of being successful. It means putting aside beliefs that a single approach to delivering instruction is best in any and all situations. Modifying instruction includes being strategic and tactical about how to teach particular content to particular children. For example, Hatch (2005) describes teaching strategies that include incidental teaching, thematic teaching, and direct teaching, along with instructional tactics such as grouping, modeling, demonstrating, coaching, tutoring, discussing, practicing, and individualizing. Adjusting curriculum and teaching to address children's strengths and needs is a vehicle for meeting the expectation that teachers will intervene with modifications before referring children for special education evaluation. More importantly, it would go a long way toward insuring that children who will eventually be identified for special education services learn all they can in kindergarten. It is certainly a better choice than allowing them to languish for a year waiting for the special education system to kick in.

Summary

We believe the complex version of a balanced approach described above is good practice in any kindergarten. By providing children who will eventually be identified for special services with a balanced program based on careful monitoring and adjusting, schools can do a lot to change the status quo. This approach is much preferred over the ignoring, delaying, retaining, and redshirting that dominate current practice for (not) dealing with the issue of what to do with children with disabilities that are not identified in kindergarten.

Yes, balancing, monitoring, and adjusting are necessary in kindergarten classrooms that include children with special needs, identified or not. But, no, they are not sufficient for addressing the needs of children with disabilities during their kindergarten year. In response to the changing nature of early experiences, our expanded knowledge base about how children learn and develop, and especially the impact of the accountability movement, kindergartens have changed. Curricula have expanded, expectations for performance have escalated, and definitions of appropriate teaching approaches have broadened. In the face of these changes, all kindergarten children are being forced to "hurry." But, some of these kindergartners (an average of two or three in each class of 20) are at a distinct disadvantage. These children are currently being asked to "wait" for services for which they will qualify once they enter the special education system. It is time to rethink special education identification in kindergarten. It's not fair to the children, their families, or their teachers to continue policies and practices that force young children with disabilities to hurry up and face the consequences of operating in a newly defined kindergarten, but wait at least a year for the support they need to be successful.

POSTSCRIPT

Can RTI Reduce the Numbers of Children Identified with Specific Learning Disability (SLD)?

Compton ("How Should 'Unresponsiveness' to Secondary Intervention Be Operationalized? It's All About the Nudge," *Journal of Learning Disabilities*, vol. 39, pp. 170–173, 2006), talks about "the nudges" necessary to help children learn. Everyoneneeds little nudges from time to time. A need for stronger and longer nudges might signify a disability. RTI is designed as a system of progressively more intense nudges, within the general education environment, enabling students to receive supplementary instruction without a disability label, which some find stigmatizing (Brown-Chidsey, "No More 'Waiting to Fail:' How Response to Intervention Works and Why it Is Needed," *Educational Leadership*, vol. 65, no. 2, pp. 40–46, 2007).

The SLD definition stipulates that the child must have had the opportunity to learn through solid teaching strategies. Lynn Fuchs notes that the strong instruction mandated by RTI might reduce the numbers of students who are inappropriately placed in special education, usually with an SLD diagnosis.

Emerging proficiency in English can contribute to low standardized test scores, which might be misinterpreted as a disability (Klingner, Artiles, & Barletta, "English Language Learners Who Struggle with Reading: Language Acquisition or LD?," *Journal of Learning Disabilities*, vol. 39, no. 2, pp. 108–128, 2006). Careful attention to student progress might also reduce inappropriate SLD determinations in English language learners.

Several supports exist to help educators track student growth over time. The National Center on Student Progress Monitoring (http://www.studentprogress.org) provides an abundance of resources on using Curriculum Based Measurement (CBM) to project student progress. The Research Institute on Progress Monitoring (RIPM) at the University of Minnesota focuses on developing seamless and flexible assessment-tracking strategies. A themed issue of *The Journal of Special Education* (vol. 41, no. 1, 2007), presented RIPM analyses of the CBM research base.

Litty and Amos approve of interventions and monitoring, but are concerned about how long interventions take. Children with disabilities need the big nudge of special education, not delaying tactics that waste valuable time. Chandler (*Washington Post,* December 31, 2007) predicts a backlash from parents who see RTI as a strategy to contain special education costs at the expense of providing needed services to their children.

Late in 2007, several federal agencies jointly hosted an invitational RTI Summit for over 700 stakeholder representatives. Teams of key state educators and parents learned about RTI models and began to develop implementation plans, accessing available federal and state resources.

Written proceedings for the RTI Summit are available at the website for the new National Center on Response to Intervention (http://www.rti4success.org). The Council for Exceptional Children (2008) related highlights of the lively breakout session on using RTI to identify learning disabilities. Nonresponsiveness may occur for many reasons, one of which might be the quality of the intervention (D. Mellard). RTI data are important, but only as one part of a comprehensive evaluation, which requires multiple measurements and a team decision (D. Deshler). Both speakers, Mellard and Deshler, are noted researchers in the SLD field. CEC also reported concerns about the validity of RTI procedures, which have been focused primarily on younger grades and on literacy.

RTI procedures are written into IDEA, yet the majority of RTI teaching and data collection are the responsibilities of general education teachers, delivering a mixed message to educators and to parents. The success of this initiative may rest heavily in the arena of general education (Baskette, Ulmer, & Bender, "The Emperor Has No Clothes! Unanswered Questions and Concerns on the Response to Intervention Procedure," *Journal of the American Academy of Special Education Professionals,* 2006; Bradley, Danielson, & Doolittle, "Response to Intervention," *Journal of Learning Disabilities,* vol. 38, no. 6, 2005).

Will RTI procedures supplant traditional testing to determine SLD? Will the numbers of students identified with SLD diminish as general education options develop? Or will parents decide to by pass RTI intervention periods in favor of special education evaluations, hoping for even more intense services?

ISSUE 17

Is Attention Deficit (Hyperactivity) Disorder Overdiagnosed?

YES: Arthur Allen, from "The Trouble with ADHD," *The Washington Post* (March 18, 2001)

NO: Russell A. Barkley, from *Taking Charge of ADHD: The Complete, Authoritative Guide for Parents*, 2nd ed. (The Guilford Press, 2000)

ISSUE SUMMARY

YES: Arthur Allen, reporter for *The Washington Post*, believes that ADHD exists, but thinks too many children are given this diagnosis, masking other conditions (or simply normal behavior), and resulting in the prescribing of drugs that do more harm than good.

NO: Russell A. Barkley, director of psychology and a professor at the University of Massachusetts Medical Center, addresses several current beliefs about ADHD and maintains that ADHD is under-diagnosed and undertreated in today's children.

ADHD. Four letters that just about everyone knows. They describe a person who moves incessantly, has difficulty concentrating, and is distracted by what happens around him or her. Three types of ADHD are identified: Predominantly Inattentive, Predominantly Hyperactive-Impulsive, and Combined. Here are the official diagnostic criteria for ADHD:

A. Either (1) or (2):
   (1) Six (or more) of the following symptoms of inattention have persisted for at least six months to a degree that is maladaptive and inconsistent with developmental level:
   - often fails to give close attention to details or makes careless mistakes
   - often has difficulty sustaining attention in tasks or play
   - often does not seem to listen when spoken to directly
   - often does not follow through on instructions and fails to finish chores or duties (not due to oppositional behavior or failure to understand)
   - often has difficulty organizing tasks and activities

- often avoids, dislikes, or is reluctant to engage in tasks that require sustained mental effort
- often loses things necessary for tasks or activities
- often forgetful

(2) Six (or more) of the following symptoms of hyperactivity-impulsivity have persisted for at least six months to a degree that is maladaptive and inconsistent with developmental level:
  - often fidgets with hands or feet or squirms in seat
  - often leaves seat unacceptably
  - often runs about or climbs excessively when inappropriate (in adolescents or adults, may feel restless)
  - often has difficulty playing quietly
  - often talks excessively
  - often blurts out answers before questions completed
  - often has difficulty awaiting turn
  - often interrupts or intrudes on others

B. Some symptoms present before age seven
C. Present in two or more settings
D. Clear evidence of clinically significant impairment
E. Symptoms are not due to another disorder

(Adapted from DSM-IV-TR, 2000)

ADHD is one of the most frequently mentioned medical-behavioral disorders. Likely, it is the topic of at least one article in at least one of the magazines in your pediatrician's office. A medical condition, ADHD is often considered by parents and teachers when a child seems to have difficulty in school. Mention of ADHD is frequently accompanied by the name of a frequently used prescriptive medication.

According to the National Institutes of Mental Health (NIMH), between 3 percent and 5 percent of children (www.nimh.nih.gov) have ADHD. The Centers for Disease Control noted that in 2003, 7 to 8 percent of school-aged children were reported to have an ADHD diagnosis (www.cec.gov). Depending on which statistic is used, this translates into one to two children in every classroom. Why does it seem there are so many more?

The authors of both articles in this section believe that ADHD exists. They hold very different opinions about whether the diagnosis is being used appropriately.

Arthur Allen examines the life stories of a number of children, cast in the light of educators, psychologists, and researchers, to identify how easy it is to apply the ADHD label, and prescribe medication to address the "symptoms."

Russell Barkley, in the first chapter of an extensive book, also considers the experiences of children and families. He believes educators and parents are only just beginning to recognize and appropriately treat the challenging problems of the disorder known as ADHD.

As you read these selections, ask yourself how often you have wondered if you or someone you know has ADHD. Is it possible for us to concentrate fully all the time or is there a real, neurological disorder that deserves our attention?

YES ↵

The Trouble with ADHD

It's a struggle for Andrew Fraser just to be here.

He is sitting politely in the dining room of a Silver Spring church, where each Thursday morning all 36 students at the tiny Quaker middle school Andrew attends gather for silent meeting. The season is midwinter and the group, described by the school's headmaster as mostly "bright underachievers," is midway between childhood and teenagerdom. . . . In the opening moments of worship, the room is remarkably quiet.

The silence is finally broken by a teacher who mentions that in this season of short days, ancient cultures treasured light, which explains why winter celebrations center on lavish displays of it. In the Quaker tradition, you pray for someone by "holding him in the light," and the teacher suggests that the students of Thornton Friends Middle School might do that now.

A boy raises his voice to hold his mother and little sister in the light. His father, he says, is leaving the family—"he says he hates me." Soon others chime in, sharing worries about sick grandparents and aggrieved friends. . . . Andrew, a rail-thin eighth-grader, . . . announces he is holding in the light a gym teacher who twisted his knee. . . .

Andrew has been struggling to get into the light his whole life. At 6 months he fell off the growth curve; in his toddler years, rough textures and loud sounds vexed him. When he was in second grade, a psychiatrist declared Andrew to have the worst case of "attention deficit disorder" he'd seen in 27 years. Andrew ricocheted and fidgeted through grade school, unable to tolerate more than a few minutes in class. He couldn't bear to write. He left his seat constantly. He got into scuffles all the time.

Home life wasn't much better. The Fraser home, a Rockville rambler with a sunken den, frequently shook with Andrew's tantrums. One morning, when Andrew was in fourth grade, he went after his older sister with a knife. Another, he was so enraged at life that he ripped the folding doors off his closet and threw them into the back yard, where he stomped them into slivers. Most mornings Andrew was a reptile coiled in his room, so unready to face the cruel exposures of the school day that his father had to dress him.

Yet Andrew could be a nice kid—open, friendly, communicative. For that grace his teachers and therapists never entirely gave up on him. "Through it all, Andrew was liked," says his mother, Wendy.

From *The Washington Post*, March 18, 2001. Copyright © 2001 by The Washington Post Writers Group. Reprinted by permission via PARS International.

His parents took him to a psychiatrist who diagnosed attention deficit hyperactivity disorder (ADHD) with "co-morbidities"—depression and possible conduct disorder. There were drugs to treat each malady.

. . . [W]hen he was all of 11 years old, Andrew was on an enormous dose—70 milligrams—of Ritalin for his ADHD, plus two antidepressants, Prozac and Pamelar, and the anti-hypertensive Clonidine, to counter the side effects of Ritalin. To make sure his heart could stand the stimulation of so much Ritalin, Andrew had his blood pressure checked weekly. Yet he seemed as distracted, irritable and unhappy as ever. Sometimes the drugs seemed to be making things worse. His father, Bruce, . . . and Wendy . . . were at wit's end.

"He'd cry. He'd threaten to jump out of the car. It was hard to see how he'd make it in middle school," Wendy recalls.

That summer, she got a call from counselors at a day camp that Andrew was attending. Her son had threatened to run into the street, they said, and was marauding around the place with a branch, intimidating counselors and other kids. Come get him. So they did. But this time, when they took Andrew to his psychiatrist, it was clear they had arrived at a threshold. The psychiatrist suggested putting him on a fifth drug, the antipsychotic Risperdal, whose side effects, the doctor explained, included tics, tremors and the risk of permanent brain damage.

Andrew's parents were floored. "He didn't try to hard-sell us," Bruce recalls, but it dawned on them that ever-stronger behavioral drugs were all the psychiatrist had to offer. And Risperdal was "the last club in his bag."

Children who are hyperactive and distracted, who can't focus on what's in front of them or control their behavior, have always been with us. They entered the medical lexicon in 1902, when a British physician, George Frederic Still, described a group of children with "morbid defects of moral control." Still thought he could detect a child's moral propensities by taking measurements of his skull. Since then, the medical definition of this disorder has certainly undergone many revisions. But in some ways it has come full circle.

. . . In 1972, Virginia Douglas, a Canadian researcher, characterized it as attention deficit disorder, and her terminology became the accepted way of referring to children like Andrew Fraser. It was part of a turning point in child psychiatry toward defining mental illnesses more on the basis of observable behaviors and less on a patient's life history. This approach located the problem in the child's brain—separated it, in a way, from the child's character. That opened the way for large-scale use of medication to change the behaviors. . . .

The scientists who study ADHD believe these children are predisposed to it by particular patterns of brain chemistry, with most cases having some sort of genetic basis, others possibly the result of environmental factors during pregnancy or after birth.

Because there are no blood-borne proteins that define when a kid has ADHD, no lumps on the head or in it, no physical marks of any kind that clearly distinguish a child with ADHD from anyone else, the diagnosis remains controversial in society at large, even as the number of children—and, increasingly, very young children—who are treated for it is skyrocketing. . . .

Today an estimated 3 million children in this country have been diagnosed with ADHD—including perhaps 200,000 between age 2 and 4. With numbers like these it is not surprising that the diagnosis is controversial or that it has become enmeshed in many of the cultural battles of the past two decades, America's fretful internal argument over the proper way to parent and educate the young.

While scientists struggle to provide a unifying theory of what's different about the brains of children with ADHD, critics charge that it's wrong to view these kids' behavior as pathological in the first place; the fault lies with overcrowded schools, stressed-out parents with little time for the children and a society that wants to dull its rough edges and is intolerant of anything but success. Other, less radical critics of the system still believe that ADHD is severely overdiagnosed in America.

At the heart of the controversy over hyperactive disorder is that most children diagnosed with it get the same treatment: a stimulant. . . .

It wasn't until the 1960s that doctors began regularly treating hyperactive children with methylphenidate—trade name Ritalin. Researchers had long reported that Ritalin at low doses had a paradoxical effect—it was "speed" that slowed children down. Eventually it was recognized that stimulants had the same effect on almost everyone: They improved short-term concentration. It was just that people with ADHD needed more help focusing than the rest of us.

There was a brief backlash against Ritalin in the 1970s, when some studies suggested it might stunt a child's growth, but later research indicated those worries were overblown, and by the early 1990s, when society had generally embraced the idea that many problems could—and should—be dealt with by a pill, Ritalin had taken off again.

Even the biggest proponents of drug therapy agree that drugs work best in combination with behavioral modification and talk therapy. But talk is not cheap in the era of managed health care. And the thing about Ritalin and other stimulants is, they get results. Study after study has shown that low-dose stimulants will improve short-term concentration and reduce impulsivity and fidgetiness in about three-quarters of the kids who get them, as long as they're on them. These kids will often do better in school. They won't anger and alienate friends and teachers as much. That makes their parents saner. As a result of these things, the children often feel better about themselves.

How does Ritalin work? As with much about ADHD, no one is exactly sure, but it is evident that Ritalin increases the availability of dopamine, a chemical that's key to movement and attention and other nervous functions, to certain cells in the brain. By adding to the dopamine pool, the drug seems to speed the flow of impulses through the circuits that help people control the instinct to respond to each and every stimulus. In a way, you could say that Ritalin strengthens willpower.

Or, as Ellen Kingsley, the mother of a 13-year-old who has been on ADHD drugs since age 5, puts it: "It enables him to do the things he wants and needs to do and would not be able to do." Kingsley, . . . who . . . puts out a magazine about ADD, says her son T.K. would never have made it through school without drug therapy. Like many parents of children with ADHD, Kingsley is impatient with people who don't recognize that kids like hers are deeply impaired and need help. "I could give him all the therapy in the world, but it won't sink in without medication because he can't attend to the task," Kingsley says.

Parents with a morbidly hyperactive or inattentive child, most specialists agree, should be no more reluctant to try Ritalin than to give eyeglasses to a nearsighted child, if Ritalin will calm their child and improve his or her life. But among the millions of parents who have put their children on a permanent ration of behavior-modification drugs, many have undoubtedly had to overcome an initial queasiness and feeling of guilt. Laura and Barney Gault certainly did last fall, when a pediatrician suggested that their son, Sam, might need to be medicated.

"My first thought was denial," recalls Barney, Sam's father. "He's a kid—you aren't going to do this to my son. And then I was a little sad. I was thinking, 'Are we going to alter his personality?'"

It is a dreary winter evening in the [school] cafeteria . . . , and Sam's den leader, Jeff Bush, is attempting to get Sam and eight other rambunctious 9-and-10-year-old Webelos to drill for their civics merit badge. The den leader's presentation isn't really pulling in the audience. The boys, a few in their blue uniforms with yellow kerchiefs, most in ordinary kid clothes, are popping up and down in their seats like ducks in a shooting gallery. They all seem to be talking at the same time, except for the kids who are falling off their chairs. . . .

At the far end of the table, quietly fabricating spitballs and loading them into a straw, sits Sam Gault. You wouldn't necessarily know that he's the one with ADHD. He doesn't seem hyper. And he's very focused—not on Jeff Bush, unfortunately, but he's very focused on his spitballs. He fires across the room at his mother, Laura, and narrowly misses.

Laura . . . is keeping a close eye on her son. . . . On the previous Saturday, the den took a field trip to a firehouse. During the tour Sam got bored and started making silly remarks: "Is this an atomic bomb?" he asked about a high-pressure hose. "Is this a nuclear weapon?" Finally the fire chief turned and scolded him. Laura finds such incidents painful and hopes that, eventually, Sam will be embarrassed, too, and change his behavior. "When kids are continually singled out, it just whittles away at their self-esteem," she says.

It was partly concern about self-esteem that led the Gaults to take Sam in for a psychiatric evaluation more than a year ago, when he was 8 and in third grade. Sam was bright and thoughtful and didn't do poorly in school, but he couldn't sit still. Time and again, his second-grade teacher reported that Sam had trouble following through with her instructions. He raised a ruckus in the halls and played the class clown. He literally climbed the walls at times. Sam was an inquisitive, detail-oriented child, but his mind had a way of meandering from the critical to the banal. You could hear it in his speech as he drifted from one topic to the next—teachers, Game Boys, his ADHD—without clearly completing his thoughts on any of them.

Laura Gault had had forebodings before Sam was diagnosed with ADHD. She felt that Sam's ADHD might have had a hereditary connection—Sam's paternal grandfather . . . probably had ADHD, though in his era, of course, such a thing was not recognized. Even as an adult, he was impatient and impulsive like Sam, and sometimes he blurted out off-color remarks in mixed company.

And that's partly what bothered Laura about her son—the social improprieties. "I noticed that the other kids would be acting out, but they could stop when an adult said stop," she says. "Sam really couldn't stop. He'd just continue to wiggle."

Kids who wiggle too much stand out in a big classroom, where sheer management is a real challenge. Sam's class had 28 other children.

After Sam was diagnosed with moderate ADHD, the Gaults were urged by their pediatrician to start out with a behavioral modification routine. They got his teacher to provide daily reports on Sam, and rewarded good behavior with trinkets: a sleepover for being especially on-task. But within a couple months it was clear this regimen was not enough to motivate Sam. That's when the Gaults turned to Adderall, . . .

"He didn't have the maturity or ability to control his behavior on his own," says Laura. So Sam began taking the drug . . . , and his parents waited to see how it would affect him. Tonight, as his den leader winds up the civics session and the games begin, the effects of Adderall have long since worn off, and Sam is lost in his own world. The boys . . . divide into teams for sock ball, which is dodge ball using balled-up socks. Everyone runs around, yelling and throwing sock bombs at the kids on the opposing team. Sam wads up a pair of socks to make what he calls a "megabomb."

"Throw it, Sam!" shout two of his friends.

Sam does not respond. He is carefully folding the edges of the sock to make a rounder, more compact megabomb. One quality of Sam's mental architecture, it's plain to see, is a certain perfectionism. For better or worse, Adderall hasn't done anything to change that.

"Come on, throw it, Sam!"

Finally he throws and—whack!—the sock bomb smacks a boy named Chris as he attempts to flee.

Teammates cheer. Sam betrays no emotion but lets out a belch of conquest. "He's very proud of that," Laura says, rolling her eyes.

Notwithstanding that ADHD can be a serious disease, the diagnosis of ADHD in America is an inexact science shaped in large part by the socioeconomic milieu of the kid in the middle of it. All it takes is a look at the diagnostic guide to see that.

The guide divides ADHD into three types: inattentive, hyperactive/impulsive or combined. A hyperactive diagnosis requires that the child exhibit six symptoms from a list that includes fidgeting, frequently leaving classroom seat, interrupting often, excessive climbing and running about, excessive talking, inability to quietly engage in leisure activity, acting "as though driven by a motor." An inattentive diagnosis is for children with symptoms that include failure to listen, failure to follow through, tendency to lose things, etc. It's clear that subjective judgment enters into any diagnosis—almost anyone with a child could imagine him or her meeting the diagnostic criteria, on a bad day at least.

To be sure, the diagnostic guide also requires that to be ADHD, the symptoms must exert a significant impact on the child's life at home and school. But "significant impact" requires a context and that's where the controversy about ADHD begins.

Every November, just after parent-teacher conference days in many schools, Barbara Ingersoll, a leading ADHD diagnostician, . . . begins to get calls from parents. Ingersoll, a psychologist, performs assessments of children that parents can use to procure medications, therapy or classroom accommodations—all tools employed to get ADHD children through school with a modicum of success.

"After the parent-teacher conferences, when the honeymoon's over," the parents start seeking assessments, she says. "Wouldn't it be great if we had schools that let them be themselves?" she asks a bit facetiously. "But it ain't going to happen. You can't let them run amok."

Often, it's not the parents but the schools that drive the diagnosis. The principal of an elite . . . private school several years ago gave the parents of a 5-year-old kindergartner a gentle bit of advice that was almost an ultimatum. The child, who had a photographic memory of almost anything ever read to him and who could spend hours working on art and science projects, was unable to sit still in the classroom. The school referred him to another D.C. psychologist—not Ingersoll—for an assessment that lasted three hours, cost about $2,500 and resulted in what the parents viewed as a preordained conclusion: Their son had ADHD. "He may need to be on Ritalin," the principal said, "to stay in the school."

The family decided to get a second opinion. A child psychiatrist at Washington's Children's National Medical Center rolled his eyes when he heard about the diagnosis. ADHD was a "garbage can label," he told them, the diagnosis for any kid who was out of the box. Their boy was too young to be diagnosed definitively, he said, and the diagnosis wasn't a trivial matter.

Ritalin could mask an underlying condition, or it could cause serious side effects. The kindergartner had tics, and children with tics sometimes developed full-blown Tourette's syndrome after going on Ritalin.

Deep in their guts it felt wrong to the parents and they worried it would stifle their son's nascent creativity. When he was reassessed at a clinic two years later, the ADHD label turned out to be wrong. The boy was dyslexic. He wouldn't sit still in school, it turned out, because he couldn't make sense of the words put in front of him. In the meantime, the family had switched their child to a public school. . . .

What almost happened to this family captures society's fear of Ritalin, that the drug is being used to convert spirited children into docile sheep.

But for most children on medication, the real problem isn't that the "meds" turn them into robots; it's that they rarely work as one would hope. At least half of the children diagnosed with ADHD also suffer from complex mixtures of other problems—learning disabilities, anxiety, depression—that can mandate a complex mixture of other drugs.

Theoretically, you can find a drug to treat each symptom. But the relationship between a behavior and the underlying biological facts isn't cut and dried, particularly in children.

Sometimes, Ingersoll acknowledges, she sees children with mood disorders who've been misdiagnosed as ADHD and put on high doses of stimulant that leave them subdued and distant. "You get better behavior, but it's using medicine as a chemical straitjacket," she says. "You get zombies."

Others wonder if some of the "co-morbidities" described by the psychiatrists are caused by the medicines themselves. "Here's the conundrum—I put you on stimulants because you're running around the classroom too much and you're too impulsive and in people's faces," says Julie Magno Zito, a professor at the University of Maryland School of Pharmacy who tracks the growing tendency to prescribe mind drugs for preschoolers. "About three months later, it looks like the treatment works, and then you go home at night and need medication to go to sleep. Enter Clonidine to help you sleep. Now we've gone from one drug to two. I have to worry about interactions, a wider spectrum of side effects. Then after a couple months it becomes apparent that you cry more easily, you're more sensitive. Now somebody says, 'He needs an antidepressant.' Now you're on three drugs. We could call it co-morbid depression. But to me it's equally possible that it's behavioral medicine toxicity. You probably wouldn't have the insomnia and crying if the other drugs were not on board. You can't just keep treating symptom by symptom."

. . . Zito and a colleague, Daniel Safer, a child psychiatrist at Johns Hopkins University, made headlines when they published an article in the *Journal of the American Medical Association* that tracked a threefold increase in the use of stimulants, antidepressants and other psychotropic drugs among 2- to 4-year-old Medicaid patients. . . . The article set off a new round of critical news stories about overuse of psychotropic drugs. And like previous Ritalin scares, the uproar put many physicians and parents who believe the drug can save lives on the defensive.

"When you ask me why I put a child on four drugs, I say look at asthmatics," says Larry Silver, a former NIH [National Institutes of Health] official who now has a large child psychiatry practice in Rockville. "With asthma you have multiple maintenance and emergency drugs, and there's a reason for each of the psychotropic medicines, too."

"The people who tend to criticize the use of these medications," he adds, "are usually in the media, or people who've never had to live with or treat the patients."

For a long time, Andrew Fraser and his parents hewed to this logic and followed the pharmaceutical trail wherever their psychiatrist advised them it led. They spent thousands of dollars and hundreds of hours in therapy and classes and doctor's appointments for Andrew. But when the psychiatrist suggested Risperdal, with its terrible potential side effects, it was a step too far.

"We've got to try something else," Bruce Fraser told his wife.

And so they stepped out of the mainstream and into the . . . office of Peter Breggin, who provided an unexpected answer to the problem of their son.

"Andrew," Breggin said, looking at the thin, . . . boy . . . sitting in front of him, "they say you're mentally ill, my friend. But actually you're a brat."

Peter Breggin, whose office is within mortar distance of the National Institute of Mental Health, is the bete noire of psychiatrists. He has written several books attacking the misdiagnosing and overmedicating of America's children. Some view him as his profession's prickly conscience, but his point of view, that there is no such thing as ADHD, is a fringe one among psychiatrists. Many of them believe that his crusading ways have done more harm than good by driving parents away from treatments that could help sick kids. Yet at least a few parents with difficult children view him as a savior who gives voice to their doubts and worries.

Breggin . . . believes that ADHD is essentially a "bunch of behaviors that make it difficult to teach kids in a big classroom. That's all it is! You wouldn't have a parent coming in and saying, 'Joey squirms in his seat.' What parent would claim that was an illness? It's the teacher saying, 'You're out of control, take some Ritalin.'"

Most of the worst symptoms of ADHD, he believes, are caused by the drugs that are used to treat it. "Once psychiatry went in the direction of drugs, it basically lost its knowledge and skills," he says. "If you look at the leading psychiatric journals today, there's nothing about family therapy, child development, how to handle an out-of-control kid. It's all about drugs. They act as if children don't need parents, they need drugs! Quite literally! We've abandoned our kids."

Breggin is the medical consultant in . . . class action lawsuits . . . on behalf of children medicated with Ritalin. The lawsuits, filed . . . by some of the same lawyers involved in anti-tobacco litigation, accuse[d] Novartis Pharmaceutical Corp., the maker of Ritalin, the American Psychiatric Association, and CHADD [Children and Adults with Attention-Deficit/Hyperactivity Disorder], an advocacy group for people with ADHD, of conspiring to poison America's children. . . .

"Breggin's effect has been to make families wary of medical treatment," says Laurence Greenhill, a Columbia University child psychiatrist who is leading a clinical trial of Ritalin for preschoolers, which he hopes will provide a means of testing Breggin's theory that Ritalin itself causes brain changes that scientists attribute to ADHD. "He feels that the kids don't get enough tender loving care, they aren't hugged enough. But he doesn't believe in evidence-based medicine and that's the standard now."

The Frasers had had enough of evidence-based medicine when they first stepped into Breggin's office . . . , and they instantly took to him and his message. Breggin told them that "in the overload of daily issues we'd failed to pay attention to teaching basic human dignity," Bruce recalls. "Breggin saw a lack of attention had been paid to the basic nurturing of a child. I didn't take umbrage. It sounded reasonable."

. . . Breggin took Andrew off the medications, one by one. In family and individual therapy, . . . he told the Frasers that Andrew had to learn to act civilized. He could learn to check his impulses, to pay attention, to show respect. Willpower was his to grasp. Wendy and Bruce had to love him tough and tender. The Frasers were happy to toss out the biological psychiatry, with its talk of titration and syndromes and EEG patterns. Ceremoniously, in the presence of his parents, Andrew flushed the leftover pills down the toilet: Out with impersonal chemicals! Human beings rule!

But Andrew did not immediately improve. He struggled through a year at a public middle school . . . then a year in a . . . special ed program. Finally, this fall, Andrew began something new—Thornton Friends. The small Quaker school . . . was created expressly for kids with promise who had trouble sitting still or paying attention, kids who got teased or harassed in traditional schools, kids who were a little different—but reachable. Thornton Friends stressed individual growth and community feeling. "We want to help people understand themselves and find a style that works for them," says the headmaster, Michael DeHart.

Roughly one-third of the kids in Thornton's middle school are on psychotropic medications of some kind, DeHart says. He agrees with Breggin, who has written positively about Thornton, that the surge in prescription drug use in children reflects our society's anxiety to produce kids who fit expectations, and its inability to create schools that handle their needs. But he also believes—unlike Breggin—that drugs sometimes are necessary. "It's clear to us that some kids, in order to make it work here, need to be on medication. That's where we kind of part ways with Peter."

When Andrew arrived at Thornton, the administrators were up to the challenge of educating a drug-free Andrew. But it wasn't a lovefest. In his first three months Andrew showed little patience and a lot of anger. In the middle of English once, he'd gotten up and yelled that he hated poetry.

"I'm not going to say Andrew needs to be medicated, and I'm not going to say he doesn't," says Jonathan Meisel, the principal of the middle school. "There have been times when it's been very difficult for him. He's very easily distracted. Does that mean it's not worth continuing to try being off them? I'm not sure. Ultimately, is this the right place for him to be as a student, medication aside? We don't know."

Sitting on the couch in Meisel's office, . . . Andrew says he is embarrassed to tell old friends he goes to this school. "I hate it here," he says matter-of-factly. "A lot of kids here have a lot of problems. They feel like they don't fit in. They are like really big dorks."

At the same time, Andrew, now 13, knows he never wants to take medication again. He hated himself on drugs: "Nothing seemed fun; everything seemed boring." His goal is to get back to public school, which he knows will be impossible unless he shapes up. "I don't want to, but I think I'll end up here," he says. "I'm going to try to make do with what I've got."

Do Andrew and Sam do what they do because of flaws in the wiring of brain circuits that inhibit inappropriate action, or is the apparent difference in their brains more in the nature of an evolutionary mismatch with modern life, an alternate state of readiness that represents a holdover from prehistoric times when extremely alert, impulsive people presumably had advantages in the struggle to survive? These are two of the untestable hypotheses of pop psychology concerning ADHD.

This much is clear: Our brains evolved with a great deal of variation. If children's height was as variable as the size of their brains, some would be giants stooping to get in the classroom door each morning while others would barely be tall enough to reach their computer keyboards.

That fact poses one of the formidable challenges for researchers such as Xavier Castellanos, a doctor who has been studying ADHD for a decade in the child psychiatry branch of the National Institute of Mental Health. . . . "Some kids' brains are twice the volume of those of other kids, with both completely normal and healthy," he says. "There's a wide range in brain volume that we don't understand."

For the past several years, Castellanos has been studying the brains of ADHD children as they appear in magnetic resonance imagery (MRI). He's doing the measurements to see if size can tell us something about the seat of abnormality. The current theory is that ADHD may derive from abnormal neural circuits linking the frontal lobes, the deep brain structures called the basal ganglia, and the cerebellum.

But Castellanos . . . , is the first to admit how few facts have been established. "The problem with neuroscience at this point is that everything in the brain seems to be related to everything else," he says. "It's like you're attempting to make out which notes of a symphony come from the different instruments, but you are listening from the hall through the wall with a stethoscope."

Castellanos and others have found that the brains of children with carefully diagnosed ADHD are approximately 4 percent smaller, on average, than those of healthy children. Some parts of the brains of ADHD children can be particularly small—the posterior-inferior vermis, a tiny segment of the cerebellum, for instance, is 10 to 15 percent smaller, on average. Castellanos doesn't want to make too much of that—or too little. For the record, he doesn't know what that teaspoon-size region of the brain does.

But he was extremely excited when a study . . . found that in macaque monkeys the posterior-inferior vermis was packed with dopamine receptors. That's interesting to Castellanos because an inadequate supply of dopamine is believed to hamper attention and self-control. So the smallness of the posterior-inferior vermis in ADHD kids might mean a shortage of the right neural circuitry.

The smaller the brain size in these children, the worse the ADHD symptoms tend to be. But there's an awful lot of variation, Castellanos says. Two-thirds of the brains of ADHD children are indistinguishable, in size, from those of healthy kids. If you're a skeptic, you say size has nothing to do with it.

Similar caveats cover the genetic work on ADHD so far. "My favorite nightmare is there are going to turn out to be 300 or 500 genes, each of which contributes a couple percent of risk here and there," Castellanos says. The leading candidate gene for ADHD is a variant of the gene known as DRD4. This variant apparently causes a receptor on certain brain cells to have trouble sucking dopamine out of brain synapses. That presumably slows the feedback messages in the brain that inhibit impulses. But you can't call it a defective gene because it turns out fully 30 percent of the U.S. population has it, and not all of those people have been diagnosed with ADHD. And not everyone with ADHD has that particular DRD4 gene variant. . . .

At least two drug companies are said to be working on DRD4-related drugs that could be used to improve the brain circuitry of ADHD patients. But Jim Swanson, one of the UC-Irvine professors involved with the study, has an intriguing hypothesis that the ADHD patients with the suspect DRD4 variant might be the subgroup that benefits most from behavioral modification strategies—rather than medication.

Because it was treatment, rather than diagnosis, that was the most contentious element of the ADHD debate, the National Institute of Mental Health set out to settle the issue of how best to treat ADHD by funding a six-site, 14 month study comparing Ritalin with behavioral modification and combined therapy. The researchers who designed the study included Ritalin advocates . . . and behavioral modification proponents. . . .

. . . The study found that, overall, combined therapy worked best, but drugs alone were significantly more effective than behavioral modification therapy alone.

Swanson was surprised. "We thought intensive behavior modification would meet or beat the medication effects, and it didn't," he says. "We have to face the facts."

But there was another way of looking at the study. More than one-third of the . . . kids in the study who were treated with behavioral techniques alone improved their ADHD symptoms. Which means, in Swanson's words, "If there are 3 million kids medicated in the United States, maybe 1 million of them could have a good response to non-drug therapy."

And that would be a good thing. Because the drugs have side effects, and they don't work perfectly, and there will always be parents who, for a variety of reasons, refuse to give their kids mind-altering chemicals.

Before she started him out on Adderall . . . , Laura Gault wrote a letter to Sam that explained his disorder and compared the drug to the glasses a nearsighted kid would have to wear. She wanted him to have something to look at in case he started to worry about being called ADHD.

Sam tried to avoid telling friends at school that he had the condition; one reason his parents chose to give him Adderall was that it was long-acting. A single dose, it was hoped, would get him through the entire school day. Kids on Ritalin, which the body metabolizes faster, often have to see the school nurse at lunchtime to get a booster dose—and Sam felt that would be embarrassing.

In the first month on the drug, Sam lost four pounds, and he was a skinny boy to begin with. "I was very concerned about that," Laura recalls. "You can tell a child to eat, but you can't make them eat."

"But," she says with a shrug, "it did help with his behavior." Sam no longer seemed compelled to pester his neighbors in class. He could walk from room to room without climbing the walls or rattling a pen along the lockers.

But the tiny blue . . . pill he takes at breakfast wears off by 2 p.m., and from that point Sam's teachers and parents use their wits and wisdom to keep Sam on track. One evening a week, Sam attends a group therapy session with other children with ADHD who need help learning how to act appropriately in social settings. He says he doesn't like it, but he clearly tunes in—you can tell by his recall of some details.

"If you see two people having a conversation there are six things you do," he recites. "First, you stand near them. Then you move closer, and smile. Then you see if they smile back. If they do, then you smile again. Then if you know something about what they're talking about, you join in the conversation, but maybe just a small comment at first."

Laura doesn't give Sam the medication on weekends or evenings, mainly because she worries about his weight. Too, she doesn't want him to be on medication forever. "Our goal is eventually to get him off," she says. "From what I've read, a lot of boys, once they go through puberty can . . . not outgrow it exactly, but the hyperactivity can be less.

"In the meantime I want him to learn how to cope."

For now coping begins with the pills, which clearly have an effect. Sam forgot to take his medication the first day back at school after winter break this year—and the teacher noticed right away. He couldn't sit still and his attention wandered. Which got Laura thinking again about the dosage. "I've been kind of waiting to see if there's a need to increase it," she says.

Before Thornton Friends' two-week winter break, Jonathan Meisel had written up a contract for Andrew. It was a one-page list of do's and don'ts, and it essentially stipulated that if Andrew's behavior didn't improve, he was out of the school.

One thing the contract required was more frequent therapy, and so Andrew began seeing Breggin weekly, instead of every few months. But the new system also made a concession: Instead of writing by hand, which was torture for Andrew as it is for many ADHD kids, he was allowed to bring a laptop to school so he could type his notes.

All in all, it was a challenge.

The family drove to South Carolina to visit Bruce's parents for part of the school vacation. The trip went smoothly. One evening, back in town but before he returned to school, Andrew joined his father and a family friend in a sort of woodshed behind the friend's house. While the adults drank cognac and smoked cigars, they talked with Andrew about his future. "You could just tell how excited he was to be treated as an adult," Bruce says, "and at the end my friend said, 'This is a good kid. He doesn't need to be in special education.'"

Recently, Andrew has begun to feel he has a goal in life. He downloads music from the Internet and burns CDs for his friends, earning a little money that way. He's been thinking he'd like to take a mail-order computer course. "That's what I'd like to do when I'm older," he says, "become a computer programmer."

In written evaluations submitted at the end of the third week of the new trimester, all of Andrew's teachers had noted a remarkable turnaround. "Andrew has developed some qualities in the science classroom since holiday break that I have not usually seen," one teacher wrote, "—improved attentiveness to discussion and explanation, more thoughtful questioning and answering, and decreased distractions with other students. . . ."

His parents are keeping their fingers crossed.

"It took a lot of people—his teachers and friends and therapists and family and him—to get this far," Wendy says. "We feel like he's turned a corner."

Russell A. Barkley **NO**

What Is Attention-Deficit/ Hyperactivity Disorder?

Attention-deficit/hyperactivity disorder, or ADHD, is a developmental disorder of self-control. It consists of problems with attention span, impulse control, and activity level. But, as you will discover here, it is much more. These problems are reflected in impairment in a child's will or capacity to control her own behavior relative to the passage of time—to keep future goals and consequences in mind. It is not, as other books will tell you, just a matter of being inattentive and overactive. It is not just a temporary state that will be outgrown, a trying but normal phase of childhood. It is not caused by parental failure to discipline or control the child, and it is not a sign of some sort of inherent "badness" in the child.

ADHD is real—a real disorder, a real problem, and often a real obstacle. It can be heartbreaking and nerve-wracking.

"Why Don't They Do Something About That Kid?"

It's easy to see why many people find it hard to view ADHD as a disability like blindness, deafness, cerebral palsy, or other physical disabilities. Children with ADHD look normal. There is no outward sign that something is physically wrong within their central nervous system or brain. Yet I believe it is an imperfection in the brain that causes the constant motion and other behavior that people find so intolerable in a child who has ADHD.

By now you may be familiar with the way others react to ADHD behavior: At first many adults attempt to overlook the child's interruptions, blurted remarks, and violation of rules. With repeated encounters, however, they try to exert more control over the child. When the child still fails to respond, the vast majority decide that the child is willfully and intentionally disruptive. Ultimately most will come to one conclusion, albeit a false one: The child's problems result from how the child is being raised. The child needs more discipline, more structure, more limit setting. The parents are ignorant, careless, permissive, amoral, antisocial, unloving, or, in contemporary parlance, "dysfunctional."

"So, Why Don't They Do Something About That Kid?"

Of course the parents often are doing something. But when they explain that the child has been diagnosed as having ADHD, judgmental outsiders typically react with skepticism. They see the label as simply an excuse by the parents to avoid the responsibility of child rearing and an attempt to make the child yet another type of helpless victim unaccountable for his actions. This hypocritical response—viewing the child's behavior so negatively, while at the same time labeling the child as "just normal"—leaves outsiders free to continue blaming the parents.

Even the less censorious reaction of considering ADHD behavior as a stage to be outgrown is not so benign in the long run. Many adults, including professionals, counsel the parents not to worry. "Just hang in there," they advise, "and by adolescence the child will have outgrown it." This is certainly true in some milder forms of ADHD: In perhaps half or more of these very mild cases, the behaviors are likely to be within the normal range by adulthood. If your preschool child has more serious problems with ADHD symptoms, however, such advice is small comfort. Being advised to "hang in there" for 7 to 10 years is hardly consoling. Worse, it is often grossly mistaken, harmful advice. The life of a child whose ADHD is left unrecognized and untreated is likely to be filled with failure and underachievement. Up to 30–50% of these children may be retained in a grade at least once. As many as 35% may fail to complete high school altogether. For half of such children, social relationships are seriously impaired, and for more than 60%, seriously defiant behavior leads to misunderstanding and resentment by siblings, frequent scolding and punishment, and a greater potential for delinquency and substance abuse later on. Failure by the adults in a child's life to recognize and treat ADHD can leave that child with an unremitting sense of failure in all arenas of life.

"Isn't ADHD Overdiagnosed? Aren't Most Children Inattentive, Active, and Impulsive?"

Imagine the toll on society when, conservatively estimated, 3–7%, or more than 2 million school-age children, have ADHD. This means that at least one or even two children with ADHD are in every classroom throughout the United States. It also means that ADHD is one of the most common childhood disorders of which professionals are aware. Finally, it means that all of us know someone with the disorder, whether we can identify it by name or not.

The costs of ADHD to society are staggering, not only in lost productivity and underemployment but also in reeducation. And what of the costs to society in antisocial behavior, crime, and substance abuse? More than 20% of children with ADHD have set serious fires in their communities, more than 30% have engaged in theft, more than 40% drift into early tobacco and alcohol use, and more than 25% are expelled from high school because of serious misconduct. Recently the effects of ADHD on driving have also been studied. Within their first two years of independent driving, adolescents with a diagnosis of ADHD have nearly four times as many auto accidents, are more likely to cause bodily injury in such accidents, and have three times as many citations for speeding as young drivers without ADHD.

Recognition of these consequences has spawned a huge effort to understand ADHD. Besides . . . thousands of scientific papers . . . , more than 50 textbooks have been devoted to the subject, with again as many books written for parents and teachers. Countless newspaper stories have addressed ADHD over the course of the 100 years that clinical science has recognized the disorder as a serious problem. Many local parents' support associations have sprung up, most notably Children and Adults with Attention Deficit Disorder (CHADD), which has grown into a national organization of more than 50,000 members. At least five professional organizations include a number of scientific presentations on the subject in their convention programs each year. . . . All this is hardly what you would expect if the disorder were not "real," as some critics have claimed.

Fact Versus Fiction

. . . [V]arious unsubstantiated claims about the legitimacy of the disorder we call ADHD have been making the media rounds [recently]. Trying to sort through these, in addition to facing the skepticism of friends, family, and teachers, can make it difficult for parents to accept a diagnosis of ADHD and move forward into productive treatment of their child. Here is what we know to date:

Fiction: ADHD is not real, because there is no evidence that it is associated with or is the result of a clear-cut disease or brain damage.

Fact: Many legitimate disorders exist without any evident underlying disease or pathology. ADHD is among them.

Disorders for which there is no evidence of brain damage or disease include the vast majority of cases of mental retardation (various brain-scanning methods reveal no obvious disease or damage in children with Down's syndrome, for example), childhood autism, reading disabilities, language disorders, bipolar disorders, major depression, and psychosis, as well as medical disorders involving early-stage Alzheimer's disease, the initial onset of multiple sclerosis, and many of the epilepsies. Many disorders arise due to problems in the way the brain has developed or the way it is functioning at the level of nerve cells. Some of these are genetic disorders, in which the condition arises from an error in development rather than from a destructive process or an invading organism. The fact that we do not yet know the precise causes of many of these disorders at the level of the molecules in the brain does not mean they are not legitimate. A disorder . . . is defined as a "harmful dysfunction," not by the existence of pathological causes.

As for ADHD, the evidence is quickly mounting that we are dealing in most cases with a disorder in brain development or brain functioning that originates in genetics. Although most cases of ADHD appear to arise from . . . genetic effects and difficulties with brain development and functioning, ADHD can certainly arise from direct damage to or diseases of the brain as well. Fetal alcohol syndrome is known to create a high risk for ADHD in children with that syndrome, and so is prematurity of birth in which small brain hemorrhages may have occurred during delivery. And it is well known that children suffering significant trauma to the frontal part of the brain are likely to develop symptoms of ADHD as a consequence. All of this indicates to scientists that any process that disrupts the normal development or functioning of the frontal part of the brain and its connections to the striatum is likely to result in ADHD. It just so happens that most cases are not due to such damage, but seem to arise from problems in the development of critical brain regions or in their normal functioning. Someday soon we will understand the nature of those problems with greater precision. But for now, the lack of such a precise understanding does not mean that the disorder is not valid or real. If the demonstration of damage or disease were the critical test for diagnosis, then the vast majority of mental disorders, nearly all developmental disabilities, and many medical conditions would have to be considered invalid. Countless people suffering from very real problems would go untreated, and their problems would be unexplored.

Fiction: If ADHD were real, there would be a lab test to detect it.

Fact: There is no medical test for any currently known "real" mental disorder.

Just as we cannot identify any disease or brain damage for ADHD, we cannot give children a test to detect it. Neither is there a test for schizophrenia, alcoholism, Tourette's syndrome, anxiety disorders, or any of the other well-established mental disorders, or for many widespread medical disorders such as arthritis. Yet they are all very real in being harmful dysfunctions.

Fiction: ADHD must be an American fabrication, since it is diagnosed only in the United States.

Fact: Recent studies conducted in numerous foreign countries show that all cultures and ethnic groups have children with ADHD.

Japan has identified up to 7% of children as having the disorder, China up to 6–8%, and New Zealand up to 7%. Other countries may not refer to ADHD by this term, they may not know as much about its causes or treatment, and (depending on the countries' level of development) they may not even recognize it yet as a legitimate disorder. But there is no question that ADHD is a legitimate disorder and is found worldwide.

Remember, the United States is among the few leaders, if not the leader, in the amount of scientific research conducted on childhood mental disorders. It is therefore highly likely that the United States at times comes to recognize disorders and develop treatments for them long before other countries do.

Fiction: Because the rate of diagnosis of ADHD and the prescription of stimulants to treat it have risen markedly in the last decade or two, ADHD is now widely overdiagnosed.

Fact: As the National Institute of Mental Health (NIMH) Consensus Conference on ADHD concluded in late 1998, underdiagnosis and undertreatment of ADHD remain big problems in the United States today.

Several studies indicate that fewer than half of all children who have ADHD are diagnosed or properly treated for the disorder, and that only one-half of these are treated with medication. The greatest problems for our children continue to be that a large percentage of those with legitimate disorders in need of treatment are not being referred, diagnosed, or properly treated, and that services across the United States for children with ADHD are inconsistent, erratic, and often well below what is considered the standard of care for the disorder. So evidence for proclamations that we are overdiagnosing ADHD in the United States and overusing stimulants for its management lack credible scientific evidence.

One possible reason for the rise in diagnosis and stimulant treatment of ADHD is that the prevalence of the disorder has actually increased. However, we do not have a lot of research that has measured the rates of children's mental disorders across multiple generations. The little research we do have indicates that ADHD has not been on the rise over the last two generations of children, but that a few other disorders may be, such as oppositional defiant disorder . . . Mainly what I think we have been witnessing is an increase in the recognition of the disorder by the general population, and therefore an increase in the number of children being referred and diagnosed with the disorder. Tremendous strides have been made to educate the American public about ADHD in the last 20 years. Thanks to a substantial upsurge in research on the disorder, to the various parent advocacy groups raising the level of public and political awareness about ADHD (such as CHADD and ADDA [Attention Deficit Disorder Association] . . . , to increased professional education on the disorder, and to the recognition of ADHD as a legitimate disability in the Individuals with Disabilities in Education Act and the Americans with Disabilities Act, more children with this disorder are getting proper diagnosis and management. But again, we still have a long way to go. A recent study by Dr. Peter Jensen and colleagues at the NIMH found that as many as half or more of children with the disorder in five major regions of the United States that were studied had not been diagnosed or were not receiving appropriate treatment.

The same scenario seems to have been occurring more recently in other countries, such as Australia, Great Britain, and the Scandinavian countries, where greater efforts are under way to educate the public and professional communities about the disorder. The result has been a marked increase in the number of children being referred for professional help, properly diagnosed, and possibly being treated with stimulant medications, among other treatments. So I have to think that most of the increase in diagnosis in the United States is due to greater awareness about the disorder.

In conclusion, a number of facts suggest that we do not have widespread overdiagnosis or overmedication with stimulants, despite the marked rise in both in the United States over the last 10 to 20 years. That is not to say that there may not be some locales within the United States where more children than expected are being diagnosed or where more medication than would be prudent is being prescribed. But these appear to be very local problems and do not indicate a national scandal.

A Question of Perspective

Intense interest in demystifying ADHD has instigated voluminous research. . . . [The] research done by the time [my] book was first published in 1995 led me to a new view of ADHD—a view that has been reinforced by studies undertaken in the last five years. I see ADHD as a developmental disorder of the ability to regulate behavior with an eye toward the future. I believe the disorder stems from underactivity in an area of the brain that, as it matures, provides ever-greater means of behavioral inhibition, self-organization, self-regulation, and foresight. Relatively hidden from view in a child's moment-to-moment behavior, the behavioral deformity this underactivity causes is pernicious, insidious, and disastrous in its impact on a person's ability to manage the critical day-to-day affairs through which human beings prepare for the future, both near and far.

The fact that its daily impact is subtle but its consequences for the child's adaptive functioning are severe has led to many changes in the labels and concepts applied to the disorder over the last century. It explains why clinical science, in its attempts to pin down the nature of the problem, has moved from vague, unfocused notions of defective moral control 100 years ago to sharper, more specific concepts of hyperactivity, inattention, and impulsivity in recent decades. This evolution of our knowledge from the very general to the very specific has taken us leaps forward in understanding the abnormalities of children with ADHD, but it has caused us to lose our perspective on how those behaviors affect the social adaptation of these children over long periods of time.

Now, however, clinical science is stepping back from its microscope on the social moments of children with ADHD and once again peering through its telescope at longer-term social development. We are beginning to understand how these "atoms" of momentary ADHD behavior come to form "molecules" of daily life, how these daily "molecules" form the larger "compounds" of weekly and monthly social existence, and how these social "compounds" form the larger stages or structures of a life played out over many years. As a result, we see that ADHD is not just the hyperactivity or distractibility of the moment or the inability to get the day's work done, but a relative impairment in how behavior is organized and directed toward the tomorrows of life.

This larger, longer view of ADHD clarifies why those with the disorder struggle in their adaptation to the demands of social life and so often fail to reach the goals and futures that they have tried to set for themselves or that others demand of them. If we remember that the behavior of those with ADHD is focused on the moment, we won't judge their actions so harshly. No one would understand half of what we "normal" adults do if these actions were judged solely by their immediate consequences. Many of the actions we take have been planned with the future in mind. Likewise, we don't understand—and are quick to criticize—the behavior of those with ADHD because we are expecting them to act with foresight when they have always focused instead on the moment. We find it difficult to tolerate the way those with ADHD behave, the decisions they make, and their complaining about the negative consequences that befall them because we, who do not have the disorder, can see where it is all leading and use that vision to determine our current behavior while they cannot. Only now is clinical science coming to understand this very important feature of ADHD.

POSTSCRIPT

Is Attention Deficit (Hyperactivity) Disorder Overdiagnosed?

ADHD is firmly established in our society. Information about the disorder and its treatments is readily available. NIMH offers the online booklet *Attention Deficit Hyperactivity Disorder* (www.nimn.nih, 2006), accompanied by extensive references. NIMH describes ADHD as a neurobiological condition with genetic linkages. Environmental toxins can also be contributors.

Allen asks whether ADHD reflects an "inexact science" affected by a busy and demanding society that has little tolerance for individual variation. Allen is dismayed by growing intolerance for childhood exuberance. His view is shared by Olfman (*No Child Left Different*, Greenwood Publishing Group, Westport, CT, 2006), who fears that adults no longer accept what used to be normal childhood immaturity. Both authors deplore the tendency to choose a pill that will ensure compliance instead of teaching children how to behave. They fear that the pharmaceutical industry, in conjunction with managed care pressures, lures adults into thinking the prescription pad holds the solution.

In an easy-to-read book, Bernstein (*10 days to a less distracted child*, Avalon Publishing Group, New York, NY, 2007), offers a "breakthrough program that gets your kids to listen, learn, focus, and behave." A task for "Day One" is to realize that distracting/distractible behaviors are not always the result of ADHD. Bernstein urges adults to look more deeply to determine whether distractibility has a different origin, such as: anxiety/stress over a life event, learning problems, or even media.

Careful evaluation of ADHD-like behavior is urged by Smith, Barkley, and Shapiro (*Assessment of Childhood Disorders*, The Guilford Press, New York, NY, 2007), who describe three levels of assessment. Checklists and brief interviews are minimally sufficient. An extensive "ADHD Checkup" combines assessment (including consideration of the effects of motivation, time of day, and fatigue) and some intervention. The third, and best, type combines the checkup with assessing how the child responds to a series of interventions. Barkley feels medication can be helpful, but can sometimes reduce the motivation to try more complex approaches.

The scientific community has not identified a specific cause or universally effective interventions; few believe ADHD can be cured. Standard treatments include medication, behavioral supports and counseling. A combination of these is usually found to achieve the most significant and long-lasting change.

Anonymous classwide strategies, such as positive behavioral supports and organizational structure, can help the entire class, not just the child with ADHD (Harlacher, Roberts, & Merrill, "Classwide Interventions for Students with ADHD: A Summary of Teacher Options Beneficial for the Whole Class," *Teaching Exceptional Children,* vol. 39, no. 2, 2006). However, formal evaluation of nonmedical interventions is characterized as a "hodgepodge" of studies that do not lend themselves to firm conclusions about effectiveness (Trout, Lienemann, Reid, & Epstein, "A Review of Non-Medication Interventions to Improve the Academic Performance of Children and Youth with ADHD," *Remedial and Special Education,* vol. 28, pp. 207–226, 2007).

Writing in the *Wall Street Journal* (2008, April 17), Shellenberger explores "the silver lining" of ADHD. Interviewing the founders of Jet Blue and Kinko's, she sees signs that their ADHD masked remarkable creativity and ingenuity. Although the negative messages from school could be overwhelming, the outcome was much different because supportive parents reinforced what their child did right.

Deciding whether a problem exists—and what to do about it—is the challenge for all of us. Have we lost our ability tolerate anything other than total compliance and predictability—especially from little boys? Or are we becoming increasingly aware of powerful biomedical conditions which affect our ability to attend, learn and work? Are we running to ADHD (and medication) to make life easier or just beginning to understand its ß and implications?

ISSUE 18

Are There Scientifically Effective Treatments for Autism?

YES: James B. Adams, Stephen M. Edelson, Temple Grandin, and Bernard Rimland, from "Advice for Parents of Young Autistic Children," Autism Research Institute, http://www.autism.org (Spring 2004)

NO: Committee on Educational Interventions for Children with Autism, Division of Behavioral and Social Sciences and Education, National Research Council, from *Educating Children with Autism* (National Academy Press, 2001)

ISSUE SUMMARY

YES: James B. Adams (Arizona State University), Stephen Edelson (Center for the Study of Autism), Temple Grandin (Colorado State University) and Bernard Rimland (Director of the Autism Research Institute) recommend to parents of young children with autism an array of effective treatment options, many of them biomedical based.

NO: The Committee on Educational Interventions, chaired by Catherine Lord, director of the University of Michigan's Autism and Communication Disorders Center, summarizing their examination of research studies of educational treatments for children with autism, found little consistent evidence to support the efficacy claims made by their proponents.

$\mathbf{I}$n 1943, Leo Kanner described a puzzling type of young child who preferred "aloneness" to the company of others. These children did not respond readily to the smiles and speech of adults. They did not react with anticipation when a caretaker reached out to pick them up. They seemed uninterested in people. Kanner identified a combination of social isolation, significant delays in language development, and a tendency to engage in repetitive behavior and resist change; and named this group of behaviors infantile autism.

Early in the recognition of autism, Bruno Bettleheim and other psychoanalytically oriented psychologists posited that the condition stemmed from cold, unloving "refrigerator mothers" who failed to provide warm and responsive parenting. His theory was disproven by other researchers who found no difference between parents of children with autism and those with typical children. In fact, parents of children with autism often had other children who developed with no difficulty.

Autism is referred to as a spectrum disorder, spanning a range of severity. Among the subtypes identified are pervasive developmental disorder (not otherwise specified), childhood disintegrative disorder, and Rett's Syndrome. Individuals exhibiting the characteristics to a lesser degree are identified as having Asperger's Syndrome, sometimes called high-functioning autism.

For the first 30 years, autism occurred two to five times per 10,000 births. Then something changed. Since the mid 1980s', prevalence figures have sky-rocketed. Experts now say autism is identified in 1 of every 150 children. In response to powerful lobbying, IDEA 97 identified autism as a distinct disability category, separate from emotional disturbance.

Some say the exploding numbers are due to more refined diagnostic knowledge and observation (Grinker, *Unstrange Minds*, Basic Books, Philadelphia, PA, 2007). Others assert that something environmental must be behind these increases. Strong educational programming is essential for these children to achieve a productive life.

Reaching agreement on what constitutes good educational programming is another matter entirely. An abundance of Web sites address autism and its causes and therapies. Testimonial books speak powerfully about children who have been "cured" of autism by a specific method, medical treatment, or diet. Some programs cost up to $100,000 per year per child.

The high cost of therapy is compelling enough to stimulate legislative action. As many as 13 states have laws requiring private health insurers to cover autism-related services; another 12 were considering such action as of spring, 2008 (Vocks, www.Stateline.org, 2008). But what treatment should insurance cover?

Bernard Rimland, a pioneering researcher in the field of autism, and his colleagues, all have personal and professional connections with this field. A number of the co-authors are parents of children with autism. Temple Grandin is an adult diagnosed with autism. All have contributed significantly to advancing knowledge and understanding in the field. Offering advice to parents of young children with autism, the authors review a number of methodologies they believe are helpful and supported by research.

At the request of the federal Office of Special Education Programs, the Committee on Educational Interventions for Children with Autism was charged with integrating information from existing research, theory, and policy. This group of skilled researchers concludes that no one method has been substantiated as irrefutably effective for children with autism.

As you read these articles consider that almost everyone speaks to the urgency of beginning services early, sometimes before two years of age. Parents, reeling from the diagnosis of their child, feel compelled to make a rapid choice rather than lose crucial learning time. Educators want to respond to parents, but also to use research-based methods. How can each group make informed decisions? What happens when they disagree?

YES ↵

James B. Adams, Stephen M. Edelson, Temple Grandin, and Bernard Rimland

Advice for Parents of Young Autistic Children

Introduction

This paper is geared toward parents of newly diagnosed autistic children and parents of young autistic children who are not acquainted with many of the basic issues of autism. Our discussion is based on a large body of scientific research. Because of limited time and space, detailed explanations and references are not included.

Receiving a diagnosis of autism can be devastating to some parents, but for others it can be a relief to have a label for their child's symptoms. Many parents can be overwhelmed by fear and grief for the loss of the future they had hoped for their child. No one expects to have a child with a developmental disability. A diagnosis of autism can be very upsetting. Joining parent support groups may help. However, these strong emotions also motivate parents to find effective help for their children. The diagnosis is important because it can open the doors to many services, and help parents learn about treatments that have benefited similar children.

The most important point we want to make is that autistic individuals have the potential to grow and improve. Contrary to what you may hear from outmoded professionals or read in outmoded books, *autism is treatable*. It is important to find effective services, treatments and education for autistic children as soon as possible. The earlier these children receive appropriate treatment, the better their prognosis. Their progress through life will likely be slower than others, but they can still live happy and productive lives.

What Is Autism?

Autism is a developmental disability that typically involves delays and impairment in social skills, language, and behavior. Autism is a spectrum disorder, meaning that it affects people differently. Some children may have speech, whereas others may have little or no speech. Less severe cases may be diagnosed with Pervasive Developmental Disorder (PDD) or with Asperger's Syndrome (these children typically have normal speech, but they have many "autistic" social and behavioral problems).

Left untreated, many autistic children will not develop effective social skills and may not learn to talk or behave appropriately. Very few individuals recover completely from autism without any intervention. *The good news is that there are a wide variety of treatment options which can be very helpful.* Some treatments may lead to great improvement, whereas other treatments may have little or no effect. No treatment helps everyone. A variety of effective treatment options will be discussed below.

Onset of Autism: Early Onset vs. Regression

Autism develops sometime during pregnancy and the first three years of life. Some parents report that their child seemed different at birth. These children are referred to as early-onset autism. Other parents report that their child seemed to develop normally and then had a major regression resulting in autism, usually around 12–24 months. These children are referred as late-onset or regressive autism. Some researchers argue that the regression is not real or the autism was simply unnoticed by the child's parents. However, many parents report that their children were completely normal (e.g., speech, behavior, social) until sometime between 1 and 2 years of age. The possible causative role of vaccinations, many of which were added to the vaccination schedule in the 1980's, is a matter of considerable controversy at present . . .

Prior to 1990, approximately two-thirds of autistic children were autistic from birth and one-third regressed sometime after age one year. Starting in the 1980's, the trend has reversed—fewer than one-third are now autistic from birth and two-thirds become autistic in their second year. The following results are based on the responses to ARI's [Autism Research Institute's] E-2 checklist, which has been completed by thousands of autism families. These results suggest that something happened, such as increased exposure to an environmental insult, possibly vaccine damage, between ages 1 and 2 years.

Several brain autopsy studies have indicated that brain damage occurred sometime during the first trimester of pregnancy, but many of these studies involved individuals who were born prior to 1990. Thus, these findings may not apply to what appears to be the new population of regressive autism.

Speech Development

One of the most common questions parents ask is: Will my child develop speech?

An analysis of ARI's data involving 30,145 cases indicated that 9% never develop speech. Of those who develop speech, 43% begin to talk by the end of their first year, 35% begin to talk sometime between their first and second year, and 22% begin to talk in their third year and after. A smaller, more recent survey conducted by the first author found that only 12% were totally non-verbal by age 5. So, with appropriate interventions, there is reason to hope that children with autism can learn to talk, at least to some extent.

There are several ways to help autistic children learn to talk, including:

- Teaching speech with sign language; it is easy for parents to learn a few simple signs and use them when talking to their child. This is referred to as 'simultaneous communication' or 'signed speech.' Research suggests that the use of sign language increases the chance of children learning spoken language.
- Teaching with the Picture Exchange Communication System (PECS), which involves pointing to a set of pictures or symbols on a board. As with sign language, it can also be effective in teaching speech.
- Applied Behavior Analysis: described in more detail later
- Encouraging child to sing with a videotape or audiotape
- Vestibular stimulation, such as swinging on a swing, while teaching speech
- Several nutritional/biomedical approaches have been associated with dramatic improvements in speech production including dimethyiglycine (DMG), vitamin B6 with magnesium, and the gluten-/casein-free diet. (To be discussed further below.)

Genetics of Autism

Genetics appear to play an important role in causing some cases of autism. Several studies have shown that when one identical twin has autism, the other co-twin often has autism. In contrast, when one fraternal twin has autism, the co-twin is rarely autistic. Studies trying to identify specific genes associated with autism have been inconclusive. Currently, it appears that 20 or more genes may be associated with autism. This is in contrast to other disorders, such as Fragile X or Rett's syndrome, in which single genes have been identified.

A large number of studies have found that autistic individuals often have compromised immune systems. In fact, autism is sometimes described as an autoimmune system disorder. One working hypothesis of autism is that the child's immune system is compromised genetically and/or environmentally (e.g., exposure to chemicals). This may predispose the child to autism. Then, exposure to an (additional) environmental insult may lead to autism (e.g., the MMR vaccine) or mercury-containing vaccine preservatives (i.e., thimerosal).

If parents have a child with autism, there is an increased likelihood, estimated at 5% to 8%, that their future children will also develop autism. Many studies have identified cognitive disabilities, which sometimes go undetected, in siblings of autistic children. Siblings should be evaluated for possible developmental delays and learning disabilities, such as dyslexia.

Possible Environmental Causes of Autism

Although genetics play an important role in autism, environmental factors are also involved. There is no general consensus on what those environmental factors are at this point in time. Since the word "autism" is only a label for people who have a certain set of symptoms, there are likely to be a number of factors that could cause those symptoms. Some of the suspected environmental causes for which there is some scientific evidence include:

- Childhood vaccinations: The increasing number of vaccines given to young children might compromise their immune system. Many parents report their child was normal until vaccinations.
- MMR Vaccine: Evidence of measles virus have been detected in the gut, spinal fluid and blood. Also, the incidence of autism began rising significantly when the MMR was introduced in the US (1978) and in the United Kingdom (1988).
- Thimerosal (a mercury-based preservative) in childhood vaccines. The number of vaccines given to children has risen over the last two decades, and most of those vaccines contained thimerosal, which is 50% mercury. The symptoms of mercury poisoning in children are very similar to the symptoms of autism.
- Excessive use of oral antibiotics: can cause gut problems, such as yeast/bacterial overgrowth, and prevents mercury excretion
- Maternal exposure to mercury (e.g., consumption of seafood high in mercury, mercury dental fillings, thimerosal in RhoGam shots)
- Lack of essential minerals: zinc, magnesium, iodine, lithium, and potassium may be especially important
- Pesticides and other environmental toxins
- Other unknown environmental factors

Prevalence of Autism

There has been a rapid increase in the number of children diagnosed with autism. The most accurate statistics on the prevalence of autism come from California, which has an accurate and systematic centralized reporting system of all diagnoses of autism. The California data show that autism is rising rapidly, from 1 per 2,500 in 1970 to 1 per 285 in 1999. Similar results have been reported for other states by the US Department of Education. Whereas autism once accounted for 3% of all developmental disabilities, in California it now accounts for 45% of all new developmental disabilities. Other countries report similar increases.

We do not know why there has been a dramatic increase in autism over the past 15 years, but there are several reasonable hypotheses. Since there is more than one cause of autism, there may be more than one reason for the increase. A small portion of the increase of autism where speech is delayed may be due to improved diagnosis and awareness, but the report from California reveals that this only explains a minute part of the increase. However, the increase in the milder variant called Asperger's Syndrome may be due to increased diagnosis. In Asperger's Syndrome, there is no significant speech delay and early childhood behavior is much more normal. The major reason for the increase is certainly due to environmental factors, not genetics, since there is no such thing as a 'genetic epidemic.' Some *possible* environmental factors were discussed in the previous section, and an increased occurrence of one or several of those factors probably accounts for the rapid increase in autism. . . .

What is the Difference Between Asperger's Syndrome and Autism?

Asperger syndrome is usually considered a subtype of high-functioning autism. Most of the individuals with Asperger syndrome are described as "social but awkward." That is, they want to have friends, but they do not have the social skills to begin and/or maintain a friendship. While high-functioning autistic individuals may also be "social but awkward," they are typically less interested in having friends. In addition, high-functioning autistic individuals are often delayed in developing speech/language. Those with Asperger syndrome tend not to have speech/language delays, but their speech is usually described as peculiar, such as being stilted and perseverating on unusual topics.

Medical Testing and Treatments

A small but growing number of physicians (many of whom are themselves parents of autistic children) are involved in trying safe and innovative methods for treating the underlying biomedical basis of autism—the Defeat Autism Now! (DAN!) program. . . .

Routine medical tests are usually performed by traditional pediatricians, but they rarely reveal problems in autism that can be treated. Genetic testing for Fragile X syndrome can help identify one possible cause, and this testing is typically recommended when there is mental retardation in the family history. Many physicians do not conduct extensive medical testing for autism, because they believe, incorrectly, that the only useful medical treatments are psychiatric medications to reduce seizures and behavioral problems.

Some of the major interventions suggested by DAN! practitioners include:

- Nutritional supplements, including certain vitamins, minerals, amino acids, and essential fatty acids
- Special diets totally free of gluten (from wheat, barley, rye, and possibly oats) and free of dairy (milk, ice-cream, yogurt, etc.)
- Testing for hidden food allergies, and avoidance of allergenic foods
- Treatment of intestinal bacterial/yeast overgrowth
- Detoxification of heavy metals

Psychiatric Medications

The various topics covered in this overview paper for parents of young autistic children represent, for the most part, a consensus of the views, based on research and personal experience, of all four authors. However, the authors differ in their opinions on the role of psychoactive drugs should play. . . .

Grandin has a relatively accepting position on the use of psychiatric medications in older autistic children and adults. She feels that it is worthwhile to consider drugs as a viable and useful treatment. Rimland and Edelson, on the other hand, are strongly opposed to the use of drugs except as a possible last resort, . . .— [t]hey feel the risks are great and consistently outweigh the benefits. Adams has an intermediate view. . . .

Educational/Behavioral Approaches

Educational/behavioral therapies are often effective in children with autism, with Applied Behavioral Analysis (ABA) usually being the most effective. These methods can and should be used together with biomedical interventions, as together they offer the best chance for improvement.

Parents, siblings, and friends may play an important role in assisting the development of children with autism. Typical pre-school children learn primarily by play, and the importance of play in teaching language and social skills cannot be overemphasized. Ideally, many of the techniques used in ABA, sensory integration, and other therapies can be extended throughout the day by family and friends.

Applied Behavior Analysis Many different behavioral interventions have been developed for children with autism, and they mostly fall under the category of Applied Behavioral Analysis (ABA). This approach generally involves therapists who work intensely, one-on-one with a child for 20 to 40 hours/week. Children are taught skills in a simple step-by-step manner, such as teaching colors one at a time. The sessions usually begin with formal, structured drills, such as learning to point to a color when its name is given; and then, after some time, there is a shift towards generalizing skills to other situations and environments.

A study published by Dr. Ivar Lovaas at UCLA in 1987 involved two years of intensive, 40-hour/week behavioral intervention by trained graduate students working with 19 young autistic children ranging from 35 to 41 months of age. Almost half of the children improved so much that they were indistinguishable from typical children, and these children went on to lead fairly normal lives. Of the other half, most had significant improvements, but a few did not improve much.

ABA programs are most effective when started early, (before age 5 years), but they can also be helpful to older children. They are especially effective in teaching non-verbal children how to talk.

There is general agreement that:

- behavioral interventions involving one-on-one interactions are usually beneficial, sometimes with very positive results
- the interventions are most beneficial with the youngest children, but older children can benefit
- the interventions should involve a substantial amount of time each

week, between 20–40 hours depending on whether the child is in school
- prompting as much as necessary to achieve a high level of success, with a gradual fading of prompts
- proper training of therapists and ongoing supervision
- regular team meetings to maintain consistency between therapists and check for problems
- most importantly, keeping the sessions fun for the children is necessary to maintain their interest and motivation

Parents are encouraged to obtain training in ABA, so that they provide it themselves and possibly hire other people to assist. Qualified behavior consultants are often available, and there are often workshops on how to provide ABA therapy.

Sensory Integration   Many autistic individuals have sensory problems, which can range from mild to severe. These problems involve either hypersensitivity or hyposensitivity to stimulation. Sensory integration focuses primarily on three senses—vestibular (i.e., motion, balance), tactile (i.e., touch), and proprioception (e.g., joints, ligaments). Many techniques are used to stimulate these senses in order to normalize them.

Speech Therapy   This may be beneficial to many autistic children, but often only 1–2 hours/week is available, so it probably has only modest benefit unless integrated with other home and school programs. As mentioned earlier, sign language and PECS may also be very helpful in developing speech. Speech therapists should work on helping the child to hear hard consonant sounds such as the "c" in cup. It is often helpful if the therapist stretches out and enunciates the consonant sounds.

Occupational Therapy   Can be beneficial for the sensory needs of these children, who often have hypo- and/or hyper-sensitivities to sound, sight, smell, touch, and taste. May include sensory integration (above).

Physical Therapy   Often children with autism have limited gross and fine motor skills, so physical therapy can be helpful. May also include sensory integration (above).

Auditory Interventions   There are several types of auditory interventions. The only one with significant scientific backing is Berard Auditory Integration Training (called Berard AIT or AIT) which involves listening to processed music for a total of 10 hours (two half-hour sessions per day, over a period of 10 to 12 days). There are many studies supporting its effectiveness. Research has shown that AIT improves auditory processing, decreases or eliminates sound sensitivity, and reduces behavioral problems in some autistic children.

Other auditory interventions include the Tomatis approach, the Listening Program, and the SAMONAS method. There is limited amount of empirical evidence to support their efficacy. . . .

Computer-based auditory interventions have also received some empirical support. They include Earobics . . . and Fast ForWord. . . . These programs have been shown to help children who have delays in language and have difficulty discriminating speech sounds. Earobics is less much expensive (less than $100) but appears to be less powerful than the Fast ForWord program (usually over $1,000). Some families use the Earobics program first and then later use Fast ForWord.

Computer Software   There are many educational programs available for typical children, and some of those may be of benefit for autistic children. There is also some computer software designed specifically for children with developmental disabilities. One major provider is Laureate. . . .

Vision Training and Irlen Lenses   Many autistic individuals have difficulty attending to their visual environment and/or perceiving themselves in relation to their surroundings. These problems have been associated with a short attention span, being easily distracted, excessive eye movements, difficulty scanning or tracking movements, inability to catch a ball, being cautious when walking up or down stairs, bumping into furniture, and even toe walking. A one- to two-year vision training program involving ambient prism lenses and performing visual-motor exercises can reduce or eliminate many of these problems. . . . More information on vision training can be found on internet Web site of the College of Optometrists in Vision Development. . . .

Another visual/perceptual program involves wearing Irlen lenses. Irlen lenses are colored (tinted) lenses. Individuals who benefit from these lenses are often hypersensitive to certain types of lighting, such as fluorescent lights and bright sunlight; hypersensitive to certain colors or color contrasts; and/or have difficulty reading printed text. Irlen lenses can reduce one's sensitivity to these lighting and color problems as well as improve reading skills and increase attention span. . . .

Relationship Development Intervention (RDI)   This is a new method for teaching children how to develop relationships, first with their parents and later with their peers. It directly addresses a core issue in autism, namely the development of social skills and friendships. . . .

Preparing for the Future

Temple Grandin: "As a person with autism I want to emphasize the importance of developing the child's talents. Skills are often uneven in autism, and a child may be good at one thing and poor at another. I had talents in drawing, and these talents later developed into a career in designing cattle handling systems for major beef companies. Too often there is too much emphasis on the deficits and not enough emphasis on the talents. Abilities in children with autism will vary greatly, and many individuals will function at a lower level than me. However, developing talents and improving skills will benefit all. If a child becomes fixated on trains, then use the great motivation of that fleach reading, use calculating the speed of a train to teach math, and encourage an interest in history by studying the history of the railroads."

Developing Friendships

Although young children with autism may seem to prefer to be by themselves, one of the most important issues for older children and adults is the development of friendships with peers. It can take a great deal of time and effort for them to develop the social skills needed to be able to interact successfully with other children, but it is important to start early. In addition, bullying in middle and high school can be a major problem for students with autism, and the development of friendships is one of the best ways to prevent this problem.

Friendships can be encouraged informally by inviting other children to the home to play. In school, recess can be a valuable time for teachers to encourage play with other children. Furthermore, time can be set aside in school for formal "play time" between children with autism and volunteer peers—typical children usually think that play time is much more fun than regular school, and it can help develop lasting friendships. This is probably one of the most important issues to include in a student's Individualized Education Program (IEP, or education plan for the child). Children with autism often develop friendships through shared interests, such as computers, school clubs, model airplanes, etc. Encourage activities that the autistic individual can share with others.

School Programs

For children younger than 3 years old, there are early intervention programs. For children over 3 years of age, there are pre-school and school programs available. Parents should contact their local school district for information on their local programs. In some cases a separate program for special-needs children may be best, but for higher-functioning children integration into a regular school setting may be more appropriate, provided that there is enough support (a part- or full-time aide, or other accommodations as needed). It is important that parents work with their child's teacher on an Individual Education Plan (IEP), which outlines in great detail the child's educational program. Additionally, meeting with the child's classmates and/or their parents can be helpful in encouraging other students to interact positively with the autistic child.

In some states, home therapy programs (such as ABA and speech therapy) may be funded by the school district, rather than through the state. However, it may take considerable effort to convince the school district to provide those services. Check with your local ASA chapter and other parents about how services are usually provided in your state. . . .

Long-Term Prognosis

Today, most adults with autism are either living at home with their parents or living in a group home. Some higher-functioning people live in a supported-living situation, with modest assistance, and a very few are able to live independently. Some are able to work, either in volunteer work, sheltered workshops, or private employment, but many do not. Adults with PDD/NOS (not otherwise specified) and Asperger's generally are more likely to live independently, and they are more likely to work. Unfortunately, they often have difficulty finding and then maintaining a job. The major reason for chronic unemployment is not a lack of job skills, but rather due to their limited social skills. Thus, it is important to encourage appropriate social skills early on, so they are able to live and work independently as much as possible.

Some of the most successful people on the autism spectrum who have good jobs have developed expertise in a specialized skill that often people value. If a person makes him-/herself very good at something, this can help make up for some difficulties with social skills. Good fields for higher functioning people on the spectrum are architectural drafting, computer programming, language translator, special educator, librarian and scientist. It is likely that some brilliant scientists and musicians have a mild form of Asperger's Syndrome (Ledgin, 2002). The individuals who are most successful often have mentor teachers either in high school, college or at a place of employment. Mentors can help channel interests into careers. Untreated sensory oversensitivity can severely limit a person's ability to tolerate a workplace environment. Eliminating fluorescent lights will often help, but untreated sound sensitivity has caused some individuals on the spectrum to quit good jobs because ringing telephones hurt their ears. Sensory sensitivities can be reduced by auditory integration training, diets, Irlen lenses, conventional psychiatric medications and vitamin supplementation. Magnesium often helps hypersensitive hearing.

It should also be pointed out that the educational, therapy, and biomedical options available today are much better than in past decades, and they should be much better in the future. However, it is often up to parents to find those services, determine which are the most appropriate for their child, and ensure that they are properly implemented. *Parents are a child's most powerful advocates and teachers*. With the right mix of interventions, most children with autism will be able to improve. As we learn more, children with autism will have a better chance to lead happy and fulfilling lives.

Educating Children with Autism

Conclusions and Recommendations

This [selection] summarizes the committee's conclusions about the state of the science in early intervention for children with autistic spectrum disorders and its recommendations for future intervention strategies, programs, policy, and research. The [selection] is organized around seven key areas pertaining to educational interventions for young children with autistic spectrum disorders: how the disorders are diagnosed and assessed and how prevalent they are; the effect on and role of families; appropriate goals for educational services; characteristics of effective interventions and educational programs; public policy approaches to ensuring access to appropriate education; the preparation of educational personnel; and needs for future research.

Diagnosis, Assessment, and Prevalence

Conclusions

Autism is a developmental disorder of neurobiologic origin that is defined on the basis of behavioral and developmental features. Autism is best characterized as a spectrum of disorders that vary in severity of symptoms, age of onset, and association with other disorders (e.g., mental retardation, specific language delay, epilepsy). The manifestations of autism vary considerably across children and within an individual child over time. There is no single behavior that is always typical of autism and no behavior that would automatically exclude an individual child from a diagnosis of autism, even though there are strong and consistent commonalities, especially relative to social deficits.

The large constellation of behaviors that define autistic spectrum disorders—generally representing deficits in social interaction, verbal and nonverbal communication, and restricted patterns of interest or behaviors— are clearly and reliably identifiable in very young children to experienced clinicians and educators. However, distinctions among classical autism and atypical autism, pervasive developmental disorder—not otherwise specified

(PDD-NOS), and Asperger's disorder can be arbitrary and are often associated with the presence or severity of handicaps, such as mental retardation and severe language impairment.

Identifying narrow categories within autism is necessary for some research purposes; however, the clinical or educational benefit to subclassifying autistic spectrum disorders purely by diagnosis is debated. In contrast, individual differences in language development, verbal and nonverbal communication, sensory or motor skills, adaptive behavior, and cognitive abilities have significant effects on behavioral presentation and outcome, and, consequently, have specific implications for educational goals and strategies. Thus, the most important considerations in programming have to do with the strengths and weaknesses of the individual child, the age at diagnosis, and early intervention.

With adequate time and training, the diagnosis of autistic spectrum disorders can be made reliably in 2-year-olds by professionals experienced in the diagnostic assessment of young children with autistic spectrum disorders. Many families report becoming concerned about their children's behavior and expressing this concern, usually to health professionals, even before this time. Research is under way to develop reliable methods of identification for even younger ages. Children with autistic spectrum disorders, like children with vision or hearing problems, require early identification and diagnosis to equip them with the skills (e.g., imitation, communication) to benefit from educational services, with some evidence that earlier initiation of specific services for autistic spectrum disorders is associated with greater response to treatment. Thus, well meaning attempts not to label children with formal diagnoses can deprive children of specialized services. There are clear reasons for early identification of children, even as young as two years of age, within the autism spectrum.

Epidemiological studies and service-based reports indicate that the prevalence of autistic spectrum disorders has increased in the last 10 years, in part due to better identification and broader categorization by educators, physicians, and other professionals. There is little doubt that more children are being identified as requiring specific educational interventions for autistic spectrum disorders. This has implications for the provision of services at many levels. Analysis of data from the Office of Special Education Programs, gathered for school-age children since the autism category was recognized in 1991, would support investigation of whether the dramatic increases in the numbers of children served with autistic spectrum disorders are offset by commensurate decreases in other categories in which children with autistic spectrum disorders might have previously been misclassified or whether these dramatic increases have come about for other reasons.

Although children with autistic spectrum disorders share some characteristics with children who have other developmental disorders and may benefit from many of the same educational techniques, they offer unique challenges to families, teachers, and others who work with them. Their deficits in nonverbal and verbal communication require intense effort and skill even in the teaching of basic information. The unique difficulties in social interaction (e.g., in joint attention) may require more individual guidance than for other children in order to attract and sustain their children's attention. Moreover, ordinary social exchanges between peers do not usually occur without deliberate planning and ongoing structuring by the adults in the child's environment. The absence of typical friendships and peer relationships affects children's motivation systems and the meaning of experiences. Appropriate social interactions may be some of the most difficult and important lessons a child with autistic spectrum disorders will learn.

In addition, the frequency of behavior problems, such as tantrums and self-stimulatory and aggressive behavior, is high. The need for systematic selection of rewards for many children with autistic spectrum disorders, whose motivation or interests can be limited, requires creativity and continued effort from teachers and parents to maximize the child's potential. Although general principles of learning and behavior analysis apply to autistic spectrum disorders, familiarity with the specific nature of the disorder should contribute to analysis of the contexts (e.g., communicative and social) of behaviors for individual children and result in more effective programming. For example, conducting a functional assessment that considers contexts, and then replacing problem behaviors with more appropriate ways to communicate can be an effective method for reducing problem behaviors. . . .

Role of Families

Conclusions
Having a child with an autistic spectrum disorder is a challenge for any family. Involvement of families in the education of young children with autistic spectrum disorders can occur at multiple levels, including advocacy, parents as participating partners in and agents of education or behavior change, and family-centered consideration of the needs and strengths of the family as a unit. Nearly all empirically supported treatments reviewed by the committee included a parent component, and most research programs used a parent-training approach. More information is needed about the benefits of a family-centered orientation or combined family-centered and formalized parent training in helping parents.

It is well established that parents can learn and successfully apply skills to changing the behavior of their children with autistic spectrum disorders, though little is known about the effects of cultural differences, such as race, ethnicity, and social class, nor about the interactions among family factors, child characteristics, and features of educational intervention. For most families, having a child with an autistic spectrum disorder creates added stress. Parents' use of effective teaching methods can have a significant effect on that stress, as can support from within the family and the community. Parents need access to balanced information about autistic spectrum disorders and the range of appropriate services and technologies in order to carry out their responsibilities. They also need timely information about assessments, educational plans, and the available resources for their children. This information needs to be conveyed to them in a meaningful way that gives them time to prepare to fulfill their roles and responsibilities.

In the last ten years the widespread availability of the Internet and media attention to autistic spectrum disorders have increased parents' knowledge but often conveyed perspectives that were not balanced nor well-supported scientifically. Of crucial importance is the question of how to make information available to parents and to ensure their active role in advocacy for their children's education. . . .

Goals for Educational Services

Conclusions

At the root of questions about the most appropriate educational interventions lie differences in assumptions about what is possible and what is important to give students with autistic spectrum disorders through education. The appropriate goals for educational services are the same as those for other children: personal independence and social responsibility. These goals imply continuous progress in social and cognitive abilities, verbal and nonverbal communication skills, adaptive skills, amelioration or behavioral difficulties, and generalization of abilities across multiple environments. In some cases, reports have suggested that particular treatments can foster permanent "recovery." However, as with other developmental disabilities, the core deficits of autistic spectrum disorders have generally been found to persist, to some degree, in most individuals.

Research concerning outcomes can be characterized by whether the goal of intervention is broadly defined (e.g., "recovery" or "best outcome") or more specifically defined (e.g., increasing vocabulary or peer-directed social behavior); whether the design involves reporting results in terms of group or individual changes; and whether the goals are short term (i.e., to be achieved in a few weeks or months) or longer term (i.e., over years). A large body of single-subject research has demonstrated substantial progress in individual responses to specific intervention techniques in relatively short periods of times (e.g., several months) in many specific areas, including gains in social skills, language acquisition, nonverbal communication, and reductions in challenging behaviors. Studies over longer periods of time have documented joint attention, symbolic play, early language skills, and imitation as core deficits and hallmarks of the disorder that are predictive of longer term outcome in the domains of language, adaptive behaviors, and academic skills.

Many treatment studies report postintervention placement as an outcome measure. While successful participation in regular classrooms is an important goal for some children with autistic spectrum disorders, the usefulness of placement in regular education classes as an outcome measure is limited, because placement may be related to many variables other than the characteristics of the child (e.g., prevailing trends in inclusion, availability of other services). The most commonly reported outcome measure in group treatment studies of children with autistic spectrum disorders has been changes in IQ scores, which also have many limitations.

Studies have reported substantial changes in large numbers of children in intervention studies and longitudinal studies in which children received a variety of interventions. Even in the treatment studies that have shown the strongest gains, children's outcomes are variable, with some children making substantial progress and others showing very slow gains. The needs and strengths of young children with autistic spectrum disorders are very heterogeneous. Although there is evidence that many interventions lead to improvements and that some children shift in specific diagnosis along the autism spectrum during the preschool years, there does not appear to be a simple relationship between any particular intervention and "recovery" from autistic spectrum disorders. Thus, while substantial evidence exists that treatments can reach short-term specific goals in many areas, gaps remain in addressing larger questions of the relationships between particular techniques, child characteristics, and outcomes. . .

Characteristics of Effective Interventions

Conclusions
In general, there is consistent agreement across comprehensive intervention programs about a number of features, though practical and, sometimes, ethical considerations have made well-controlled studies with random assignment very difficult to conduct without direct evaluation. Characteristics of the most appropriate intervention for a given child must be tied to that child's and family's needs. However, without direct evaluation, it is difficult to know which features are of greatest importance in a program. Across primarily preschool programs, there is a very strong consensus that the following features are critical:

- Entry into intervention programs as soon as an autism spectrum diagnosis is seriously considered;
- Active engagement in intensive instructional programming for a minimum of the equivalent of a full school day, 5 days (at least 25 hours) a week, with full year programming varied according to the child's choronological age and developmental level;
- Repeated, planned teaching opportunities generally organized around relatively brief periods of time for the youngest children (e.g., 15–20 minute intervals), including sufficient amounts of adult attention in one-to-one and very small group instruction to meet individualized goals;
- Inclusion of a family component, including parent training;

- Low student/teacher ratios (no more than two young children with autistic spectrum disorders per adult in the classroom); and
- Mechanisms for ongoing program evaluation and assessments of individual children's progress, with results translated into adjustments in programming.

Curricula across different programs differ in a number of ways. They include the ways in which goals are prioritized, affecting the relative time spent on verbal and nonverbal communication, social activities, behavioral, academic, motor, and other domains. Strategies from various programs represent a range of techniques, including discrete trials, incidental teaching, structured teaching, "floor time," and individualized modifications of the environment, including schedules. Some programs adopt a unilateral use of one set of procedures, and others use a combination of approaches. Programs also differ in the relative amount of time spent in homes, centers, or schools, when children are considered ready for inclusion into regular classrooms, how the role of peers as intervention agents is supported, and in the use of distraction-free or natural environments. Programs also differ in the credentials that are required of direct support and supervisory staff and the formal and informal roles of collateral staff, such as speech language pathologists and occupational therapists.

Overall, many of the programs are more similar than different in terms of levels of organization, staffing, ongoing monitoring, and the use of certain techniques, such as discrete trials, incidental learning, and structured teaching. However, there are real differences in philosophy and practice that provide a range of alternatives for parents and school systems considering various approaches. The key to any child's educational program lies in the objectives specified in the IEP and the ways they are addressed. Much more important than the name of the program attended is how the environment and educational strategies allow implementation of the goals for a child and family. Thus, effective services will and should vary considerably across individual children, depending on a child's age, cognitive and language levels, behavioral needs, and family priorities. . . .

Public Policies

Conclusions

The Individuals with Disabilities Education Act (IDEA) contains the necessary provisions for ensuring rights to appropriate education for children with autistic spectrum disorders. However, the implementation and specification of these services are variable. Early intervention for young children with autistic spectrum disorders is expensive, and most local schools need financial help from the state and federal programs to provide appropriate services.

The large number of court cases is a symptom of the tension between families and school systems. Case law has yielded an inconsistent pattern of findings that vary according to the characteristics of the individual cases.

The number of challenges to decision-making for programming within school systems reflects parents' concerns about the adequacy of knowledge and the expertise of school systems in determining their children's education and implementing appropriate techniques.

The treatment of autistic spectrum disorders often involves many disciplines and agencies. This confuses lines of financial and intellectual responsibility and complicates assessment and educational planning. When communication between families and school systems goes awry, it can directly affect children's programming and the energy and financial resources that are put into education rather than litigation. Support systems are not generally adequate in undergirding local service delivery programs and maximizing the usefulness of different disciplines and agencies, and transitions between service delivery agencies are often problematic.

A number of states have successful models for providing services to children with autism, and mechanisms are becoming increasingly efficient and flexible in some states. In most cases, existing agencies at state and federal levels can develop appropriate programs without restructuring—with the possible addition of special task forces or committees designed to deal with issues particular to children with autistic spectrum disorders. . . .

Personnel Preparation

Conclusions
The nature of autistic spectrum disorders and other disabilities that frequently accompany them has significant implications for approaches to education and intervention at school, in the home, and in the community. Approaches that emphasize the use of specific "packages" of materials and methods associated with comprehensive intervention programs may understate the multiple immediate and long-term needs of children for behavior support and for instruction across areas.

Teachers are faced with a huge task. They must be familiar with theory and research concerning best practices for children with autistic spectrum disorders, including methods of applied behavior analysis, naturalistic learning, assistive technology, socialization, communication, inclusion, adaptation of the environment, language interventions, assessment, and the effective use of data collection systems. Specific problems in generalization and maintenance of behaviors also affect the need for training in methods of teaching children with autistic spectrum disorders. The wide range of IQ scores and verbal skills associated with autistic spectrum disorders, from profound mental retardation and severe language impairments to superior intelligence, intensify the need for personnel training. To enable teachers to adequately work with parents and with other professionals to set appropriate goals, teachers need familiarity with the course of autistic spectrum disorders and the range of possible outcomes.

Teachers learn according to the same principles as their students. Multiple exposures, opportunities to practice, and active involvement in learning are all important aspects of learning for teachers, as well as students. Many states and community organizations have invested substantial funds in teacher preparation through workshops and large-audience lectures by well-known speakers. While such presentations can stimulate enthusiasm, they do not substitute for ongoing consultation and hands-on opportunities to observe and practice skills working with children with autistic spectrum disorders.

Personnel preparation remains one of the weakest elements of effective programming for children with autistic spectrum disorders and their families. Ways of building on the knowledge of teachers as they acquire experience with children with autistic spectrum disorders, and ways of keeping skilled personnel within the field, are critical. This is particularly true given recent trends for dependence on relatively inexperienced assistants for in-home programs. Providing knowledge about autistic spectrum disorders to special education and regular education administrators, as well as to specialized providers with major roles in early intervention (e.g., speech language pathologists) will be critical in effecting change that is proactive. Findings concerning change in educational and other opportunities suggest that administrative attitudes and support are critical in improving schools. . . .

Needed Research

Conclusions
There are several distinct and substantial bodies of research relevant to young children with autistic spectrum disorders. One body identifies neurological, behavioral, and developmental characteristics. Another body of research addresses diagnostic practices and related issues of prevalence. Another has examined the effects of comprehensive early treatment programs on the immediate and long-term outcomes of children and their families. These treatment studies tended to use some form of group experimental design. An additional body of research has addressed individual instructional or intervention approaches, with many studies in this literature using single-subject experimental methodology. Altogether, a large research base exists, but with relatively little integration across bodies of literature. Highly knowledgeable researchers in one area of autistic spectrum disorders may have minimal information from other perspectives, even about studies with direct bearing on their findings.

Most researchers have not used randomized group comparison designs because of the practical and ethical difficulties in randomly assigning children and families to treatment groups. In addition, there have been significant controversies over the type of control or contrast group to use and the conditions necessary for demonstrating effectiveness. Although a number of comprehensive programs have provided data on their effectiveness, and, in some cases, claims have been made that certain treatments are superior to others, there have been virtually no comparisons of different comprehensive interventions of equal intensity.

Across several of the bodies of literature, the children and families who have participated in studies are often inadequately described. Standardized diagnoses, descriptions of ethnicity, the social class, and associated features of the children (such as mental retardation and language level) are often not specified. Fidelity of treatment implementation has not been consistently assessed. Generalization, particularly across settings, and maintenance of treatment effects are not always measured. Though there is little evidence concerning the effectiveness of discipline-specific therapies, there is substantial research supporting the effectiveness of many specific therapeutic techniques.

POSTSCRIPT

Are There Scientifically Effective Treatments for Autism?

The two sides agree on some points. Autism is a serious disability which can have disastrous consequences. Intensive, early intervention is critical. There are many methods from which to choose. Here is where agreement lessens.

Adams and his colleagues believe strongly in a biomedical cause for autism. Our environment is hurting children. Although educational interventions are important, they advocate medical treatment as well.

The Committee on Interventions holds that the increased numbers are due to changes in diagnostic practices. As the field learns about autism, more children are given this diagnosis instead of another, such as mental retardation or language/communication disability. Noting the wide range of characteristics in this group, the committee says much more systematic research is needed to find the best educational interventions.

Weighing both points of view about increasing numbers, Goode (*New York Times*, February 24, 2004) observes that if the increase is due to environmental problems, numbers are likely to continue to rise unless something changes. If diagnostic knowledge is behind the increase, she posits that "rates should level off as the number of previously overlooked children diminishes."

In the meantime, teachers and parents need to decide what education is best. Unfortunately, attorneys may play the largest role in resolving disagreements through administrative hearings (Drasgow, Yell & Robinson, "Developing Legally Correct and Educationally Appropriate IEPs," *Remedial and Special Education*, vol. 22, pp. 359–373, 2001).

One of the most hotly debated treatments is Applied Behavioral Analysis (ABA). An intensive therapy based on the work of Lovaas and colleagues, ABA methods require many daily hours of 1:1 work, reinforcing children for increasingly complex behaviors. This approach begins with an emphasis on eye contact and basic attention and moves on to academic and social interactions. Supporters proclaim ABA has "cured" their child. Detractors maintain that existing research studies are flawed and that learned behavior does not generalize to new settings.

Equally heated is the debate about whether autism stems from mercury preservatives in vaccines. Some parents report dramatic behavior changes following a routine inoculation. The eighth report of the Immunization Safety Review Committee ("Immunization Safety Review: Vaccines and Autism," National Academy of Sciences, May 17, 2004) "rejected the causal relationship between MMR vaccine and autism." And yet, in 2008, the U.S.

federal government conceded a case, which alleged a vaccine-autism link for a specific child. Some 4000 vaccine-related autism cases are currently pending in federal court.

The conflict between the passionate parental search for a real "cure" and the need for scientific support is poignantly described in "A Father's Fight" (Bernstein, *Health*, 2004). The M.I.N.D. Institute is one of the largest research and treatment centers devoted to autism. This is a unique collaboration: funded by a group of fathers who want their children cured of autism and staffed by researchers committed to the scientific method. Dedicated to the same goal, but driven by different forces, the article describes the institute as a place nurtured by "creative tension." Will this unique collaboration result in solid answers? Will they come soon enough for the children?

How do schools select effective programs? How do parents decide if their school's proposed program is effective? The evidence is clear, but often contradictory. If each child is unique, can research prove the worth of any method? How would you decide for a student? Would you decide differently about your own child?

ISSUE 19

Is Mental Health Screening an Unwarranted Intrusion?

YES: Nathaniel S. Lehrman, from "The Dangers of Mental Health Screening," *Journal of American Physicians and Surgeons* (Fall 2006)

NO: Mark D. Weist, Marcia Rubin, Elizabeth Moore, Steven Adelsheim, and Gordon Wrobel, from "Mental Health Screening in Schools," *Journal of School Health* (February 2007)

ISSUE SUMMARY

YES: Nathaniel S. Lehrman, clinical director (retired) of the Kingsboro (NY) Psychiatric Center warns that new mental health screening requirements, heralded as a way to increase the health of the nation, will intrude on basic freedoms, lead to inappropriate labels, and increase revenue for pharmaceutical companies.

NO: Mark D. Weist, Marcia Rubin, Elizabeth Moore, Steven Adelshiem, and Gordon Wrobel, consultants and researchers in mental health, see this screening as a way to identify those who need early intervention in order to prevent the development of debilitating mental illnesses.

Virginia Tech, Northern Illinois, Columbine: These three schools and countless now-silent adolescents, remind us how fragile our existence can be. Three schools that make us wonder about the students we teach. How many friends, teachers, and parents have worried whether they missed a clue that could have saved a life?

Researchers at the National Institute of Mental Health (*NASET News Alert*, www.naset.org) announced the ability to predict the future development of psychosis by assessing an individual's risk factors. Intervention during a *critical window* could prevent the development of serious mental illness. Who would not want to intervene?

Noting that between 5 percent and 7 percent of all adults and children have a serious mental illness, the President's New Freedom Commission on Mental Health (NFC) observed "(m)ental health ranks first among illnesses that cause disability in the United States, Canada, and Western Europe. This serious public health challenge is underrecognized as a public health burden. In addition, one of the most distressing and preventable consequences of undiagnosed, untreated, or undertreated mental illnesses is suicide" (www.mentalhealthcommission.gov 2003).

The NFC final report lists six goals for an improved quality of mental health in the United States. Goal 4: Early Mental Health Screening, Assessment, and Referral to Services Are Common Practice, includes a recommendation to screen for mental health disorders. This goal would be achieved through regular screenings of children and youth. The intent is to identify those in need and deliver intervention to prevent the development of a mental illness. Seemingly benign, this call for regular screening has engendered much controversy.

In the first selection, psychiatrist Nathaniel Lehrman describes mental health screening as an unwarranted intrusion into individual and family privacy. Acknowledging the good intentions of the NFC, Lehrman is concerned that inadequate screening tools will stigmatize people with unfounded diagnoses. Only the pharmaceutical companies will benefit.

In the second selection, Mark Wiest and colleagues, who practice and conduct research in psychiatry, support systematic mental health screening. They emphasize the effectiveness of early intervention, especially through school mental health services. Wiest and colleagues maintain that, delivered in a timely fashion, mental health interventions can reduce the stigma of mental illness.

Representative Ron Paul (TX), a contender for the Republican presidential nomination, is one of several legislators who introduced a bill (H.R. 2387) prohibiting the use of federal funds for any universal mental health screening. As support for this measure to limit government intrusion into private lives, the authors cite efforts to formalize a diagnosis of "extreme intolerance" as well as the suggestion of one federally funded program that children who share their parents' traditional values may instigate school violence. Like Lehrman, these legislators see such claims as leading to stigmatizing labels which, result in pressure for pharmaceutical treatment.

Responding to an earlier version of H.R. 2387, and in support of screening, the National Alliance on Mental Illness (NAMI) (www.nami.org) appealed to Congress to reject the misinformation provided by antiscreening advocates. To NAMI, the tone of proposed legislation engenders fear, enhances stigma, and keeps people away from needed help. Screening merely identifies those who need more intensive evaluation. This, and any medical treatment, can only happen with full parental involvement and consent.

As you read these articles, consider the powerful issues they raise. What is the best way to balance cherished individual rights and freedoms with the desire to avert a tragedy? Who decides where the line should be drawn?

YES

Nathaniel S. Lehrman

The Dangers of Mental Health Screening

The New Freedom Commission on Mental Health

According to the President's New Freedom Commission on Mental Health (NFC), all American parents will receive notice from their youngsters' schools of the new screening program during the 2005–2006 school year. It will test for mental illness in the 52 million students and 6 million adults working in schools, and expects to find at least 6 million in need of treatment. The force of government will then urge or compel them to receive that treatment.

But children aren't the only targets. The commission's final report looks forward to having both children and adults screened for mental illnesses during their routine physical examinations.

The sale of psychiatric medications—antipsychotics and antidepressants—rose from $500 million to $20 billion between 1987 and 2004, a 40-fold increase. A pharmaceutical stock analyst recently predicted that continuing to widen our definitions of illness will result in increased sales of medications. This amounts to corporate-sponsored creation of illness, to enhance revenue. With the new screening program, the government-sponsored "discovery" of illness will augment the already existing corporate "promotion of undiscovered illness"—which means even more medication sales. And by allowing experts to define peaceful, law-abiding citizens as ill and in need of treatment (which increasingly is becoming involuntary) the program comes to resemble the witchhunts of 16th-century Europe.

Screening and Its Victims

This is how the program works. In December, 2004, as part of the TeenScreen program created to implement the NFC blueprint, Chelsea Rhoades and her Indiana public high school classmates were given a 10-minute, yes-or-no

From *Journal of American Physicians and Surgeons*, 11(3) Fall 2006, pp. 80–82 (refs. omitted). Copyright © 2006 by Association of American Physicians and Surgeons. Reprinted by permission. http://www.jpands.org/

computer test, which had no room for alternate answers or explanations. A few students were not given the test because their parents had opted them out, an option the Rhoades family had not known about in advance.

Shortly after Chelsea took the test, a local mental health center employee told her that she was suffering from obsessive-compulsive disorder because she liked to help clean the house, and from social anxiety disorder because she didn't party much. The worker then suggested that if her condition worsened, her mother should bring her to the center for treatment. Chelsea says all her friends were also told they had something mentally wrong with them. The only youngsters not supposed to be suffering from some mental disorder were those with opt-out slips.

Furious at this intrusion into their privacy and parental rights, the Rhoadeses sounded the alarm. With the help of the Rutherford Institute, they have filed a lawsuit against the school district for failing to inform them about the test or to obtain permission for Chelsea to take it.

Even more frightening was the experience of 13-year-old, black Aliah Gleason, an average, but rather obstreperous seventh-grade student in an Austin, Texas, suburb. After her class was screened for mental illness, her parents were told that she needed further evaluation because she scored high on a suicide rating. She was referred to a university consulting psychiatrist, and thence to an emergency clinic. Six weeks later, a child protection worker appeared at her school, interviewed her, summoned her father to the school, and ordered him to take the girl at once to Austin State (psychiatric) Hospital. When he refused, she took Aliah into emergency custody and had a police officer drive her to the hospital.

During Aliah's five terrible months in the hospital, her parents were forbidden to see or speak to her. While there, she was placed in restraints more than 26 times and given at least 12 different psychiatric medications, many of them simultaneously. After that, she spent four more months in a residential facility, where she received even more psychotropic medications.

Despite her caretakers' uncertainty about her clinical diagnosis (and whether she even had a psychiatric illness), her parents had to go to court to have her released. The professionals they chose for her then tapered her off all medication and successfully addressed problems—both hers and the family's. She is now doing well in school, participating in extracurricular activities, and, according to her psychologist, Dr. John Breeding of Austin, recovering her high spirits.

At a Colorado homeless shelter, 50 percent of the 350 young people given the TeenScreen were found to be suicidal risks, and 71 percent screened positive for psychiatric disorders. Although such youngsters are certainly suffering from residential and social instability, and probably from not eating or sleeping properly, the TeenScreen diagnoses lead to medications instead of appropriate interventions.

The particular purpose of children's mental health screening is supposedly to prevent suicide. But the Columbia University TeenScreen program acknowledged that 84 percent of the teens who tested positive were found to be not really at risk. And, as Sharav points out, an evaluation by the authoritative U.S. Preventive Services Task Force (USPSTF) concluded that screening for suicide failed to demonstrate any benefit at reducing suicide. The report noted that the screening instruments have not been validated. Moreover, there is insufficient evidence that treatment of those identified as high risk reduces either suicide attempts or mortality.

What Is Mental Illness?

What is the mental illness for which we are now screening? Years ago, the term "mental illness" referred only to the insane: people with bizarre ideas who were unable to function socially. Such disabled individuals were social annoyances who might also be dangerous to themselves, others, or both. Other maladaptive psychological patterns such as nervousness or sadness have also been called mental illness, but these produce distress rather than disability. Over the past several decades, however, the term has been expanded to include increasingly more of the thousand natural ills to which the flesh is heir. A recent report from Harvard and the National Institute of Mental Health, for example, says that 46 percent of Americans will at some point in their lives develop a mental disorder.

Many of those thousand natural ills are included among the 400-odd disorders listed in the latest edition of the American Psychiatric Association's (APA) *Diagnostic and Statistical Manual of Mental Disorders,* the DSM. Calling it the psychiatric bible, Herb Kutchins, professor of social welfare at California State University, Sacramento, and Stuart A. Kirk, professor of social welfare at the University of California at Los Angeles (UCLA), point out that since there are no biological tests, markers, or known causes for most mental illnesses, psychiatric diagnosis is based almost entirely on symptomatology—depression, anxiety, disorganization, obsessive thinking, compulsive behavior, and other subjective symptoms.

Depression, for example, has as many causes as there are people suffering from it: job difficulties, failure to attain expectations, and problems in relationships are but a few. Basing psychiatric diagnosis entirely on symptoms can be compared to making fever a definitive diagnosis; symptoms are not disorders in themselves, but products of other psychological and/or physiological phenomena. The cure of depression—a term rarely used today although a common occurrence yesterday—requires that an individual's particular problems be addressed. Psychiatry's dependence on symptom-based diagnostics is a major reason for the specialty's mounting pessimism.

One reason for higher estimates of the prevalence of mental disorders is that the APA keeps adding new disorders and more behaviors to the manual, as Kutchins and Kirk point out. The increase in the number of these disorders, along with the greatly increased use of new medications to treat them, parallels the increase in individuals disabled by these disorders. Rates for psychiatric disability in America have risen from 3.38 per thousand in 1954; to 13.75 in 1987, when the atypical anti-psychotics and SSRI anti-depressants were introduced; to 19.69 in 2003. The number of patient care episodes—the amount of care given, as measured by the number of people treated each year for mental illness at psychiatric hospitals, residential facilities for the mentally ill, and ambulatory care facilities—rose similarly: from 1,028 per 100,000 population in 1955; to 3,295 in 1987; and to 3,806 in 2000. Since the start of the "medication era," the number of mentally disabled people has risen nearly six-fold.

How the History of ADHD Predicts the Effects of Screening

Kutchins and Kirk point out that children are considered to exhibit signs of attention deficit hyperactivity disorder (ADHD) when they are deceitful, break rules, can't sit still or wait in lines, have trouble with math, don't pay attention to details, don't listen, don't like to do homework, lose their school assignments or pencils, or speak out of turn. This common childhood behavior is defined as a disorder by the psychiatry department of the New York University (NYU) School of Medicine. ADHD is now diagnosed in 6 to 9 percent of school-age children and 4 percent of adults. Its "symptoms"—acting impulsively; easy distractibility; interrupting others; constant fidgeting or moving; and difficulty in paying attention, waiting one's turn, planning ahead, following instructions, or meeting deadlines—can be found in any of us. With diagnosis and treatment, the department contends, ADHD symptoms can be substantially decreased.

The process through which ADHD became accepted is important, but little recognized. In 1980, the list of symptoms then called ADD (attention deficit disorder) was first accepted into the DSM. Seven years later, hyperactivity was added, thus making ADHD. Within a year, 500,000 youngsters were assigned this diagnosis.

A few years later, ADHD was classified as a disability, and a cash incentive program was initiated for low-income families with children diagnosed with ADHD. A family could get $450 a month for each child so labeled, and the cost of treatment and medication for low-income children would be covered by Medicaid. Then in 1991, schools began receiving educational grants of $400 annually for each ADHD child. The same year, the U.S. Department of Education classified the disorder as a handicap, which required special services to be provided to each disabled child.

By 1996, close to $15 billion was spent annually on the diagnosis, treatment, and study of this supposed neuropsychiatric disorder. Recently, public health officials in the United States, Canada, and the United Kingdom have issued warnings about previously known but undisclosed risks associated with the stimulant medications used to treat ADHD.

What has happened with ADHD presages what can be expected from government-sponsored mental health screening. One example is the case of the first-grade son of Patricia Weathers. After a school psychologist diagnosed the "disorder," she was pressured into medicating him.

"The medication eventually made him psychotic," she said. But when she stopped giving it to him, the school reported her to state child protection officials for "child abuse." Weathers cofounded AbleChild . . . and filed a lawsuit against school officials.

"We have 1,000 stories like this," she states. Meanwhile, her son is now 15 and "doing fine."

Rep. Ron Paul, M.D., (R-TX) a congressman who has been a physician for more than 30 years, has criticized government agencies for charging parents with child abuse if they refuse to drug their children. Some parents have even had their children taken from them for refusing to give them medications.

Mrs. Weathers's experience is far from unique. According to Dr. Andrew Mosholder of the FDA's Office of Drug Safety, about 2.5 million children in this country between ages 4 and 17 currently take ADHD drugs, 9.3 percent of 12-year-old boys, and 3.7 percent of 11-year-old girls. And although these medications have been used for years, the harm they can cause to the heart and circulatory system, and the psychiatric difficulties they can produce, are only now being publicly discussed.

No matter how we define mental illness in children or adults, it cannot be diagnosed by simple screening. Nobody can, by merely looking at someone else, or even on the basis of a questionnaire, differentiate the transient emotional disturbances we all have from those that last longer.

The ephemeral nature of suicidal ideation and depressive feelings among teens is specifically mentioned by the Columbia TeenScreen report. Screenings won't prevent suicide because those who are contemplating it usually won't tell. Indeed, the screening process itself can produce significant anxiety among those in whom mental illness is being "diagnosed." Such efforts to find their troubles by frightening people, and thus aggravating those troubles, are misdirected. Only when gross insanity exists can mental illness be recognized on inspection, and then we need neither experts nor screening.

Troubled people can indeed benefit from good mental health care. But good treatment requires that a physician actually examine a patient and address that individual's unique problems, with the patient's knowledge and consent. This requires time, and busy practitioners are often under severe time constraints. Thus they are pressured to quickly prescribe medications to relieve symptoms that are often transient even if untreated.

In my opinion, relying on medication as the definitive treatment of psychiatric complaints, rather than addressing their real causes in patients' lives, is responsible for the gross overuse of psychiatric medications, especially among children, but also among seniors:

- Twenty-nine million prescriptions were written last year in the United States for Ritalin and similar medications to treat ADHD, 23 million of them for children.
- From 60 to 70 percent of children in foster care in Massachusetts are now being given psychiatric medications.
- About 40 to 50 percent of students arrive at some colleges with psychiatric prescriptions.

- Approximately 41 percent of prescriptions for one group of 765,000 people over 65 were for psychotropics.
- As many as 75 percent of elderly, long-term-care nursing home residents in another study were being given psychotropics.

The screening program will aggravate this already unfortunate situation.

Conclusions

Good intentions notwithstanding, the mental health screening program created by the president's NFC probably will harm thousands of Americans by giving them stigmatizing diagnoses that can follow them for the rest of their lives. The program's government-sponsored promotion of long-term medications will compound the harm, as the experience with ADHD has shown.

As Sharav points out, screening for mental illness serves no medical or societal purpose. Screening will, however, do much to increase the benefits to the drug manufacturers and to the mental health provider industry. Good psychiatric care is voluntary, and based on trust between patient and physician. The involuntary government-sponsored mental health screening program, as demonstrated by the cases of Aliah Gleason and Chelsea Rhoades, represents psychiatric malpractice.

Their cases also demonstrate how the program undermines basic American freedoms, as parents are coerced to medicate their children, sometimes with severe adverse effects.

We need to start to undo psychiatry's 50 years of overdependence on psychopharmacology, rather than expanding it through mental health screening.

Mark D. Weist, Marcia Rubin, Elizabeth Moore,
Steven Adelsheim, and Gordon Wrobel

 NO

Mental Health Screening in Schools

Background

A significant gap between the mental health needs of children and adolescents and the available services has been well documented. For example, between 12% and 27% of youth might have acting-out behavioral problems, depression, and anxiety; yet, as few as one sixth to one third of these youth receive any mental health treatment. In this context, school mental health (SMH) programs have grown progressively. This growth reflects increasing recognition of the need to address the mental health needs of children and youth and the many advantages of SMH programs. These include reducing barriers to student learning, unmatched access to youth, and ability to engage youth in an array of strategies that can simultaneously address their educational, emotional, behavioral, and developmental needs. In fact, for youth who do receive mental health services, most receive them in schools. In addition, SMH programs can reduce stigma, enhance the generalization and maintenance of interventions, increase opportunities for preventive services, and promote efficiency and productivity of staff and programs. Program evaluation data and early research suggest that *when done well*, SMH services are associated with satisfaction by a number of different stakeholder groups including students and contribute to achieving outcomes valued by families and schools.

Strong federal support for SMH programs and services is found in the US Surgeon General's reports on mental health and child and adolescent mental health; large federal initiatives such as the Safe Schools/Healthy Students Program and the Child and Adolescent Service System Program. *Achieving the Promise: Transforming Mental Health Care in America*, the report issued by the President's New Freedom Commission on Mental Health in 2003, emphasized the large gap between needs and effective services and the lack of a national priority on child and adolescent mental health. The 6 goals and 19 recommendations of the report strongly support SMH,

From *Journal of School Health*, 77(2) February 2007, pp. 53–57 (refs. omitted). Copyright © 2007 by American School Health Association. Reprinted by permission of Wiley-Blackwell Publishing.

including recommendation 4.2 to "improve and expand school mental health programs" and a related recommendation 4.3 to "screen for co-occurring mental and substance use disorders and link with integrated treatment strategies".

Achieving the Promise calls for an approach that connects policy, training, practice, and research on mental health services and that improves behavioral, emotional, and academic functioning of youth. This approach is reflected in a pyramid of programs and services. The foundation aims to improve school environments and broadly promotes health as well as academic success. The second tier encompasses targeted prevention programs and early identification practices that help recognize and refer students with unmet mental health needs. Providing access to effective treatment services for serious and/or chronic disorders occupies the top of the pyramid. This model is congruent with a public health approach to disease prevention and detection. It incorporates a continuum of educational messages that promote health and prevention and incorporates early identification practices that ensure cost-effective treatment for disabling health conditions. This pyramid model for health and mental health promotion has been embraced by the World Health Organization and other groups but unfortunately does not reflect the way programs and services are delivered to children and youth in the United States.

Although historically, school-based mental health services were provided primarily to students qualified for special education services, more recently, schools have expanded mental health and social services for all students as part of their coordinated school health program. Today, there are a number of different models for offering these services in schools, with an array of service components ranging from alcohol and other drug use treatment, case management, individual and group counseling, and referrals to community mental health systems and providers. Despite this, there remain numerous barriers including:

- insufficient funding
- inadequate training and supervision of staff
- difficulty coordinating a full continuum of prevention and intervention services
- maintenance of quality and empirical support of services
- limited evaluation of outcomes of services to improve programs and contribute to policy improvement.

Providing treatment services within school buildings is often challenging for additional reasons, including:

- environmental characteristics (poor office spaces, crowded classrooms)
- frequent changes in personnel (high teacher and administrator turnover)
- distinctive knowledge bases and cultures (education and mental health)

- difficulties in fully engaging families
- academic demands stemming from the No Child Left Behind educational reforms.

These issues are increasingly documented in the published literature, especially in relation to research-based interventions.

Mental Health Screening in Schools

Youth with internalizing disorders such as depression, anxiety, or suicide ideation are not as easily identified as those with acting-out or externalizing disorders. Individuals with internalizing conditions comprise a significant population; the 2003 Youth Risk Behavior Survey, a nationally representative sample of more than 15,000 high school students throughout the United States, found that in the 12-month period preceding the survey, 16.9% had seriously considered attempting suicide, 16.5% had made a plan for attempting suicide, 8.5% had attempted suicide 1 or more times, and 2.9% had made an attempt requiring medical attention. In addition, studies have shown that students contemplating suicide or even those who had previous attempts were not known or detected by school personnel. Furthermore, 90% of teens who commit suicide have a mental health issue at the time of their death but are usually not receiving treatment.

For these reasons, formal screening programs that detect depression and suicide ideation are recommended. The New Freedom Commission on Mental Health recommended screening in multiple settings as a critical component of a public health approach to prevention and early intervention for mental health issues in youth. The Commission went so far as to name the Columbia University TeenScreen program as a model program for identifying at-risk youth and linking them to critical intervention services. TeenScreen is currently implemented in 460 sites in 42 states and involves systematic and supported assessment of youth mental health needs in schools along with technical assistance and guidance on addressing identified needs. Other effective programs such as Dominic and the Signs of Suicide program are also widely available. These recommendations have led to increasing discussion among mental health providers of the need to advance mental health screening in schools. A few states, such as Ohio, Illinois, and New Mexico, have moved to expand screening in multiple settings as part of their efforts to transform their child's mental health system.

However, screening in schools is not without controversy. Some perceive screening as government intrusion, and others describe it as a violation of the family's right to privacy. These concerns appear to be based on the erroneous belief that screening programs in schools require all students to be screened against their wishes or against those of the parents. In fact, "mandatory universal screening" for behavioral health issues does not exist anywhere and has never been recommended by any federal agency or community screening program. All existing mental health screening programs are voluntary and require active informed consent of the family and the assent of the student. It is likely that another factor contributing to the misunderstanding surrounding screening is stigma. The President's Commission acknowledged the pervasive nature of stigma and the need to actively address it.

While there are no currently agreed-upon national standards for mental health screening in schools, a number of federal agencies, professional organizations, and advocacy groups have issued helpful resources. Both the Substance Abuse and Mental Health Services Administration and the National Alliance for the Mentally Ill recently released documents confirming the importance of screening as part of a public health approach to early identification and intervention for behavioral health problems and offering guidelines for the appropriate use of screening. Well-established screening programs such as TeenScreen generally have experientially based recommendations for implementation and strongly recommend active parental consent for any screening in schools. Another helpful resource on screening and assessing mental health and substance use disorders was issued by the Office of Juvenile Justice and Delinquency Prevention of the US Department of Justice, which includes a set of criteria for selecting screening methods. The American Medical Association's Guidelines for Adolescent Preventive Services includes recommendations for screening behavioral and emotional conditions, such as substance abuse, eating disorders, depression, suicide risk, and school or learning problems. All these guidelines and criteria for mental health screening can provide a foundation for developing standards for the school setting.

Other Issues

In trying to decide whether to implement a screening program, there are other factors that districts will need to consider. For example, strategic planning should attempt to gauge the needs of individual schools in relation to the school/community's abilities to respond to those needs. This will require a self-assessment process. In addition, prior to advancing the agenda related to mental health screening in schools, the community should consider:

1. Availability of trained staff and other resources to conduct screening.
2. Availability of mental health providers with training in evaluating and treating those children and youth identified by screening.
3. Need for technical assistance in system development for ensuring parental consent and student assent for participation in screening.
4. Selection of age-appropriate screening measures.
5. Logistics including when to do the screening, finding the right confidential space for screening, and provision of alternative activities for youth who do not have parental permission for screening.
6. Resolution of liability concerns.

First Steps

Once a district has addressed the issues outlined above and decided to move toward implementing a formal screening program, five additional elements will need to be considered: inclusive planning, collaborative relationships, logistics, training and supervision, and integration.

Inclusive Planning

Planning should involve all significant stakeholders including families, education professionals, primary care providers, mental health professionals, and other representatives from the community. Once configured, the planning body might begin with a policy review to ensure that sufficient safeguards are in place to protect privacy and confidentiality. Districts can also benefit from ongoing technical expertise from community agencies that respond to related mental health issues such as substance abuse, child welfare, law enforcement, or other specialty systems.

Collaborative Relationships

To promote collaboration, the sharing of resources, and to address liability concerns, memoranda of agreement should be established between schools and collaborating community agencies to ensure adequate clarification of responsibility. Ideally, local initiatives and agreements between child serving systems should be approved of and supported by state systems, such as state departments of education, mental health, juvenile justice, and child welfare.

Logistics

The time to conduct screening must be determined. Some have recommended transitional years such as sixth and seventh and ninth and 10th grades as critical times when clinical symptoms often linked to increased suicide risk sometimes develop. However, screening efforts at these ages should ideally be part of broader efforts within communities to promote wellness, mental health, and learning success for youth from preschool through young adulthood. Locally collected data such as emergency room data can assist in identifying age groups at particular risk. In the absence of locally available data, state and national data such as the Youth Risk Behavior Survey . . . can be helpful. However, if the planning group determines that there are inadequate resources to provide adequate follow up to the screen, the screening process should be delayed until adequate resources are marshaled and confidence of adequate follow up is increased.

Training, Supervision, and Support

Staff that participate in screening will require adequate training and supervision. Personnel will be needed who can coordinate the work; select age-appropriate and culturally sensitive measurement tools; manage associated technology for administering, scoring, and interpreting the data; and establish and sustain relationships with school and community providers.

Regardless of whether a school implements a systematic screening program, all schools should enhance their capacity to identify youth who present signs of emotional/behavioral disturbance. These disturbances represent barriers to learning and are indicative of the development of serious mental health concerns. Schools should connect these youth to appropriate resources and services. Professional development will be required to raise awareness and increase knowledge of child and adolescent mental health needs, the factors that promote healthy youth development and those that contribute to mental health problems, specific signs of distress, and strategies to assist distressed youth in obtaining help. All staff should have a clear understanding of referral procedures and know how to determine when a youth is in crisis and needs an immediate intervention.

Integration

Mental health screening should be one aspect of a full continuum of effective mental health programs and services in schools. Such programs can only exist when there is a full partnership between families, schools, and child serving systems, particularly the mental health system. There must be strong emphases on quality assessment and improvement, empirically supported practice, and evaluating outcomes of services. Findings from outcome evaluations should be used to continuously improve services and should connect to advocacy and policy agendas.

Conclusion

The President's New Freedom Commission on Mental Health provides specific recommendations to improve and expand school mental health programs and to screen for co-occurring mental and substance use disorders and link with integrated treatment strategies. The New Freedom Initiative and its 19 specific recommendations represent a call to action for communities and states to move beyond fragmented and ineffective approaches to illness care for a small percentage of those in need toward a true public mental health promotion system that ensures quality and effectiveness along a full continuum of services. Consideration of the issues outlined in this article should help schools and communities determine whether they are ready to include screening in schools as part of their SMH program.

When implemented with appropriate family, school, and community involvement, mental health screening in schools has the potential to be a cornerstone of a transformed mental health system that identifies youth in need, links them to effective services, and contributes to positive health and educational outcomes valued by families, schools, and communities.

POSTSCRIPT

Is Mental Health Screening an Unwarranted Intrusion?

The Executive Summary of the NFC's final report, *Achieving the Promise*, begins with this statement: "We envision a future when everyone with a mental illness will recover, a future when mental illnesses can be prevented or cured, a future when mental illnesses are detected early, and a future when everyone with a mental illness at any state of life has access to effective treatment and supports—essentials for living, working, learning, and participating fully in the community." As the outcome of its work, the NFC anticipates transforming the current complex fragmented system of mental health into a more integrated system of care for all.

Four compelling stories illustrate this controversy: Aliah, Rosie, Chelsea, and Courtney. Lehrman sees Aliah's and Chelsea's experiences as examples of the intrusive consequences of screening; Weist et al. would cite Rosie and Courtney as solid reasons to screen.

Lehrman tells Aliah's story: on the basis of an in-school screening and against the wishes of her parents, Aliah was hospitalized, isolated from her parents, and subjected to heavy medication. Compare Aliah to Rosie, the lead named plaintiff in a class action suit against the State of Massachusetts. The suit charged that nine children were hospitalized, or at risk for hospitalization, because Massachusetts did not provide Medicaid-mandated screenings, and necessary home-based mental health services. The court ruled in Rosie's favor, reinforcing the need for these services in hopes that no other children would get "lost in the system" (Kenny, 2007, http://www.massmedicaid.org/briefs_16.html).

Lehrman also shares the experiences of Chelsea Rhoades, said to have mental health problems as a result of a brief in-school screening. Angered that they had not been notified of this intrusion into their lives, Chelsea's parents filed a lawsuit against her school (www.rutherford.org). Contrast this to Courtney, whose experience with in-school screening, and resultant mental health services, led her to say, "I'm not sure where I would be today if I didn't get screened. I'm not even sure I would be here at all" (Friedman, *The New England Journal of Medicine*, 2006).

One key element of this debate focuses on the type of parental permission requested. Methods of participation in any activity can be mandatory or voluntary; granting permission can be either active or passive. A mandatory activity is just that; everyone must participate. Statewide assessment systems are mandatory activities. Active voluntary permission requires a parent/guardian to sign a paper supporting their child's participation. Because permission slips can get lost—in transmission or on the kitchen table—passive/opt-out permission is sometimes employed. In this method an informational permission note indicates that the student will participate in the stated activity unless the parent/guardian sends an objection to the school. *Achieving the Promise* is clear that screening is to be voluntary and that "parents should be included in the process of making choices and decisions for minor children" (Executive Summary). Some suggest a more active permission process would result in fewer children being screened (Effrem, http://www.edaction.org/2005/021405.htm).

Few would deny the benefits of providing help to those in need, especially to avoid a tragic event. It is harder to find agreement on how to identify those in need of services. Does mental health screening pry into personal thoughts and make value judgments about family choices or is it a valuable opportunity to deliver services that can make a life difference?

ISSUE 20

Do Gifted and Talented Students Need Special Schools?

YES: John Cloud, from "Failing Our Geniuses," *Time Magazine* (August 27, 2007)

NO: Susan Winebrenner and Dina Brulles, from *The Cluster Grouping Handbook* (Free Spirit Publishing, 2008)

ISSUE SUMMARY

YES: John Cloud, a staff writer for *Time Magazine* since 1997, profiles a number of extraordinarily gifted young people challenged for the first time in a specialized school that pushes them to reach their potential in a way that public schools could not.

NO: Susan Winebrenner and Dina Brulles work with educators to design and deliver cluster-based programs that address the needs of the gifted within their neighborhood school and provide options for a range of students to reach their potential.

T his *Taking Sides* focuses on individuals who have disabilities and require 504 Plans or special education services. These students struggle the most with learning, requiring supplemental supports and services to make the progress that comes easily to others.

Another group of exceptional learners also require specialized programming and services. These students are at the other end of the bell curve—gifted and/or talented far beyond most of their age-mates.

No Child Left Behind (NCLB) defines the gifted and talented as: "students, children, or youth who give evidence of high achievement capability in areas such as intellectual, creative, artistic, or leadership capacity, or in specific academic fields, and who need services and activities not ordinarily provided by the school in order to fully develop those capabilities." *(Title IX, Part A, Section 9101(22), p. 544.)*

The unique educational needs of gifted/talented students are not addressed by any federal mandates. Despite their need for programming "not ordinarily provided by the school," they are not covered by special education law because they do not have disabilities. There is no federal requirement to identify, or develop programs for, students who have unique gifts and/or talents.

The National Association for the Gifted (NAGC) monitors the status of gifted/talented education. Programs are completely dependent on individual state policies and funding. "(In 2006–07), although 27 states mandate the identification of gifted students and 24 states mandate services, only five states provide funds to all districts by mandate; 10 by discretionary funding based on applications" (http://www.nagc.org). The sole source of federal funding is a grant competition funded by the Jacob K. Javits Gifted and Talented Student Education Program.

Extraordinarily gifted/talented minds have long fascinated psychologists, teachers, and parents. We each know our own children are brilliant, but who exactly is gifted? NAGC publishes a comprehensive reference evaluating existing research and indicating pressing needs in a range of topics, from policy to identification to instructional strategies (Plucker & Callahan, *Critical Issues and Practices in Gifted Education* [P&K], 2008).

One key chapter (Miller, P&K, 2008) reviews several ways giftedness is conceptualized. There is no universal definition. Proponents of Terman looks for an IQ score more than two standard deviations above average. Gardner finds giftedness in one or more of eight independent multiple intelligences, ranging from linguistic to musical to intrapersonal. Renzulli differentiates between the schoolhouse-gifted and those who create/produce original products that impact society.

Educational options vary with the conceptualization of giftedness. A sampling includes: early school admission; curriculum acceleration in small classes; acceleration through grade skipping; enrichment activities based on the standard curriculum; home schooling; mentoring (by professionals or older students); correspondence courses; summer institutes; and advanced coursework.

John Cloud believes the United States is failing our geniuses; stifling them in a bureaucratic system that lacks the knowledge or creativity to support challenging programs. Cloud presents compelling profiles of young learners who have outgrown their neighborhood schools and will wither and fade unless their talents are nurtured and guided. Cloud's students find room to grow at a unique private school.

Susan Winebrenner and Dina Brulles present the Schoolwide Cluster Grouping Model (SCGM): "an inclusion model in which students with exceptional learning needs are integrated into mixed-ability classrooms and teachers are expected to provide appropriate differentiation opportunities for any students who need them." By careful clustering, and attention to teacher professional development, SCGM stimulates the full range of students to flourish without having to leave home.

As you read these selections, ask yourself whether your state acknowledges the needs of gifted students. How does your district conceptualize giftedness? What model do you think works best?

YES ↵

John Cloud

Failing Our Geniuses

In U.S. Schools, the Highest Achievers Are Too Often Challenged the Least. Why That's Hurting America—and How to Fix It

Any sensible culture would know what to do with Annalisee Brasil. The 14-year-old not only has the looks of a South American model but is also one of the brightest kids of her generation. When Annalisee was 3, her mother Angi Brasil noticed that she was stringing together word cards composed not simply into short phrases but into complete, grammatically correct sentences. After the girl turned 6, her mother took her for an IQ test. Annalisee found the exercises so easy that she played jokes on the testers—in one case she not only put blocks in the correct order but did it backward too. Angi doesn't want her daughter's IQ published, but it is comfortably above 145, placing the girl in the top 0.1% of the population. Annalisee is also a gifted singer: last year, although just 13, she won a regional high school competition conducted by the National Association of Teachers of Singing.

Annalisee should be the star pupil at a school in her hometown of Longview, Texas. While it would be too much to ask for a smart kid to be popular too, Annalisee is witty and pretty, and it's easy to imagine she would get along well at school. But until last year, Annalisee's parents—Angi, a 53-year-old university assistant, and Marcelo, 63, who recently retired from his job at a Caterpillar dealership—couldn't find a school willing to take their daughter unless she enrolled with her age-mates. None of the schools in Longview—and even as far away as the Dallas area—were willing to let Annalisee skip more than two grades. She needed to skip at least three—she was doing sixth-grade work at age 7. Many school systems are wary of grade skipping even though research shows that it usually works well both academically and socially for gifted students—and that holding them back can lead to isolation and underachievement. So Angi home schooled Annalisee.

But Angi felt something was missing in her daughter's life. Annalisee, whose three siblings are grown, didn't have a rich social network of other kids. By 13, she had moved beyond her mother's ability to meaningfully teach her. The family talked about sending her to college, but everyone was hesitant. Annalisee needed to mature socially. By the time I met her in February, she had been having trouble getting along with others. "People are, I must admit it, a lot of times intimidated by me," she told me; modesty isn't among her many talents. She described herself as "perfectionistic" and said other students sometimes had "jealousy issues" regarding her.

The system failed Annalisee, but could any system be designed to accommodate her rare gifts? Actually, it would have been fairly simple (and virtually cost-free) to let her skip grades, but the lack of awareness about the benefits of grade skipping is emblematic of a larger problem: our education system has little idea how to cultivate its most promising students. Since well before the Bush Administration began using the impossibly sunny term "no child left behind," those who write education policy in the U.S. have worried most about kids at the bottom, stragglers of impoverished means or IQs. But surprisingly, gifted students drop out at the same rates as nongifted kids—about 5% of both populations leave school early. Later in life, according to the scholarly Handbook of Gifted Education, up to one-fifth of dropouts test in the gifted range. Earlier this year, Patrick Gonzales of the U.S. Department of Education presented a paper showing that the highest-achieving students in six other countries, including Japan, Hungary and Singapore, scored significantly higher in math than their bright U.S. counterparts, who scored about the same as the Estonians. Which all suggests we may be squandering a national resource: our best young minds.

In 2004–05, the most recent academic year for which the National Opinion Research Center (NORC) has data, U.S. universities awarded 43,354 doctorates—more than ever during the 50 years NORC has gathered the data. But the rate of increase in the number of U.S. doctorates has fallen dramatically since 1970, when it hit nearly 15% for the year; for more than a decade, the number of doctorates has grown less than 3.5% a year. The staggering late-1960s growth in Ph.D.s followed a period of increased attention on gifted kids after Sputnik. Now we're coasting.

To some extent, complacency is built into the system. American schools spend more than $8 billion a year educating the mentally retarded. Spending on the gifted isn't even tabulated in some states, but by the most generous calculation, we spend no more than $800 million on gifted programs. But it can't make sense to spend 10 times as much to try to bring low-achieving students to mere proficiency as we do to nurture those with the greatest potential.

We take for granted that those with IQs at least three standard deviations below the mean (those who score 55 or lower on IQ tests) require "special" education. But students with IQs that are at least three standard deviations above the mean (145 or higher) often have just as much trouble interacting with average kids and learning at an average pace. Shouldn't we do something special for them as well? True, these are IQs at the extremes. Of the 62 million school-age kids in the U.S., only about 62,000 have IQs above 145. (A similar number have IQs below 55.) That's a small number, but they appear in every demographic, in every community. What to do with them? Squandered potential is always unfortunate, but presumably it is these powerful young minds that, if nourished, could one day cure leukemia or stop global warming or become the next James Joyce—or at least J.K. Rowling.

In a no-child-left-behind conception of public education, lifting everyone up to a minimum level is more important than allowing students to excel to their limit. It has become more important for schools to identify deficiencies than to cultivate gifts. Odd though it seems for a law written and enacted during a Republican Administration, the social impulse behind No Child Left Behind is radically egalitarian. It has forced schools to deeply subsidize the education of the least gifted, and gifted programs have suffered. The year after the President signed the law in 2002, Illinois cut $16 million from gifted education; Michigan cut funding from $5 million to $500,000. Federal spending declined from $11.3 million in 2002 to $7.6 million this year.

What's needed is a new model for gifted education, an urgent sense that prodigious intellectual talents are a threatened resource. That's the idea behind the Davidson Academy of Nevada, in Reno, which was founded by a wealthy couple, Janice and Robert Davidson, but chartered by the state legislature as a public, tuition-free school. The academy will begin its second year Aug. 27, and while it will have just 45 students, they are 45 of the nation's smartest children. They are kids from age 11 to 16 who are taking classes at least three years beyond their grade level (and in some cases much more; two of the school's prodigies have virtually exhausted the undergraduate math curriculum at the University of Nevada, Reno, whose campus hosts the academy). Among Davidson's students are a former state chess champion, a girl who was a semifinalist in the Discovery Channel Young Scientist Challenge at age 11 (the competition is open to kids as old as 14) and a boy who placed fourth in both the Nevada spelling and geography bees even though he was a 12-year-old competing against kids as old as 15. And last year the school enrolled another talented kid from a town 1,700 miles (some 2,700 km) away: Annalisee Brasil, whose mother moved with her to Reno so Annalisee could attend the school (her father was working in Longview at the time).

The academy is being watched closely in education circles. The Davidsons are well-connected philanthropists who made their fortune in the education-software business—Jan and a friend conceived the hit Math Blaster program in the early 1980s. She and her husband sold Davidson & Associates for roughly $1.1 billion in 1996. They have given millions of dollars to universities and tens of thousands to Republican politicians like George W. Bush and Senator John Ensign of Nevada. Gifted kids often draw only flickering interest from government officials, but Secretary of Education Margaret Spellings attended the Davidson Academy's opening.

At the academy, the battered concept of IQ—complicated in recent years by the idea of multiple intelligences, including artistic and emotional acuity—is accepted there without the encumbrances of politics. The school is a rejection of the thoroughly American notion that if most just try hard enough, we could all be talented. Many school administrators oppose ability grouping on the theory that it can perpetuate social inequalities, but at the

Davidson Academy, even the 45 élite students are grouped by ability into easier and harder English, math and science classes. The school poses blunt questions about American education: Has the drive to ensure equity over excellence gone too far? If so, is the answer to segregate the brightest kids?

How We See Them

As a culture, we feel deeply ambiguous about genius. We venerate Einstein, but there is no more detested creature than the know-it-all. In one 1996 study from Gifted Education Press Quarterly, 3,514 high school students were asked whether they would rather be the best-looking, smartest or most athletic kids. A solid 54% wanted to be smartest (37% wanted to be most athletic, and 9% wanted to be best looking). But only 0.3% said the reason to be smartest was to gain popularity. We like athletic prodigies like Tiger Woods or young Academy Award winners like Anna Paquin. But the mercurial, aloof, annoying nerd has been a trope of our culture, from Bartleby the Scrivener to the dorky PC guy in the Apple ads. Intellectual precocity fascinates but repels.

Educators have long debated what to do with highly gifted children. As early as 1926, Columbia education professor Leta Hollingworth noted that kids who score between 125 and 155 on IQ tests have the "socially optimal" level of intelligence; those with IQs over 160 are often socially isolated because they are so different from peers—more mini-adults than kids. Reading Hollingworth, I was reminded of Annalisee, who at 13 spoke in clear, well-modulated paragraphs, as though she were a TV commentator or college professor. For an adult, the effect is quite pleasant, but I imagine other kids find Annalisee's precision a bit strange.

In Hollingworth's day, when we were a little less sensitive to snobbery, it wasn't as difficult for high-ability kids to skip grades. But since at least the mid-1980s, schools have often forced gifted students to stay in age-assigned grades—even though a 160-IQ kid trying to learn at the pace of average, 100-IQ kids is akin to an average girl trying to learn at the pace of a retarded girl with an IQ of 40. Advocates for gifted kids consider one of the most pernicious results to be "cooperative learning" arrangements in which high-ability students are paired with struggling kids on projects. Education professor Miraca Gross of the University of New South Wales in Sydney has called the current system a "lockstep curriculum . . . in what is euphemistically termed the 'inclusion' classroom." The gifted students, she notes, don't feel included.

We tend to assume that the highly gifted will eventually find their way—they're smart, right? The misapprehension that genius simply emerges unbidden is related to our mixed feelings about intelligence: we know Alex Rodriguez had to practice to become a great baseball player, and we don't think of special schools for gymnasts or tennis prodigies as élitist—a charge already leveled against the Davidson Academy. But giftedness on the playing field and giftedness in, say, a lab aren't so different. As Columbia education professor Abraham Tannenbaum has written, "Giftedness requires social context that enables it." Like a muscle, raw intelligence can't build if it's not exercised.

People often wonder how to tell if their child is gifted. Truly gifted kids are almost always autodidacts. Take Max Oswald-Selis. He moved to Reno from Sydney with his mother Gael Oswald so that he could attend Davidson. Max is 12. The first time I saw him at the academy, he was reading an article about the Supreme Court. He likes to fence. He loves Latin because "it's a very regimented language . . . There's probably at least 28 different endings for any given verb, because there's first-, second- and third-person singular and plural for each tense . . ." He went on like this for some time. Max didn't get along especially well with classmates in Sydney and later Kent, England, where his mother first moved him in search of an appropriate school—and where she says he was beaten on the playground.

Max is Gael's only child, so when he taught himself to read at 3—she says she hadn't even taught him the alphabet—she wasn't sure it was so unusual. Then around age 4, he read aloud from a medical book in the doctor's office, and the doctor recommended intelligence testing. At 4, Max had the verbal skills of a 13-year-old. He skipped kindergarten, but he was still bored, and his mother despaired. No system is going to be able to keep up, she thought.

Gael, a math teacher, began to research giftedness and found that high-IQ kids can become isolated adults. "They end up often as depressed adults . . . who don't have friends or who find it difficult to function," she says. Actually, research shows that gifted kids given appropriately challenging environments—even when that means being placed in classes of much older students—usually turn out fine. At the University of New South Wales, Gross conducted a longitudinal study of 60 Australians who scored at least 160 on IQ tests beginning in the late '80s. Today most of the 33 students who were not allowed to skip grades have jaded views of education, and at least three are dropouts. "These young people find it very difficult to sustain friendships because, having been to a large extent socially isolated at school, they have had much less practice . . . in developing and maintaining social relationships," Gross has written. "A number have had counseling. Two have been treated for severe depression." By contrast, the 17 kids who were able to skip at least three grades have mostly received Ph.D.s, and all have good friends.

At the Davidson Academy, all the kids are skipping ahead quickly—in some cases they completed more than two years of material last year. There's no sixth grade or ninth grade or any grade at the academy, just three tracks ("core," "college prep" and "college prep with research"). The curriculums are individualized and fluid—some students take college-prep English but core-level math. I sat in on the Algebra II class one day, but it wasn't so much a traditional class as a study session guided by the teacher, Darren Ripley. Kids worked from different parts of the textbook. (One 11-year-old was already halfway through; most Americans who take Algebra II do so at 15 or 16.) Occasionally Ripley would show a small group how to solve a problem on the whiteboard, but there was no lecture.

The Founders

Ultimately the academy's most important gift to its students is social, not academic. One of the main reasons Jan and Bob Davidson founded the school was to provide a nurturing social setting for the highly gifted. Through another project of theirs, the Davidson Institute for Talent Development, each year the Davidsons assist 1,200 highly gifted students around the U.S. who need help persuading their schools to let them skip a grade or who want to meet other kids like them. Often the kids are wasting away in average classes, something that drives Bob Davidson crazy: "I mean, that's criminal to send a kid [who already reads well] to kindergarten . . . Somebody should go to jail for that! That is emotional torture!"

Davidson, 64, carries an air of peremptory self-assurance. He unself-consciously enjoys his place in the plutocracy. During a tour of the Lake Tahoe manse he and Jan, 63, call Glen Eagle, he showed me his red Ferrari, his private theater and the two 32-ft. totem poles just inside the entry. They are made from cedar at least 750 years old and feature carvings of the Davidsons and their three kids, who are now grown. Bob sees his work for the gifted as akin to the patronage that sustained the artists and inventors of the Renaissance. His view of giftedness is expressed through simple analogies: Educators often "want people to have equal results. But that's not likely in our world. You know, I would love to be equal to Michael Jordan in my basketball talents, but somehow I never will be."

But such an uncomplicated view of intelligence—one that esteems IQ scores and raw mental power—has had at least one awkward consequence for the Davidson Academy: it doesn't mirror America. Twenty-six of the 45 students are boys; only two are black. (A total of 16 are minorities.) The school is unlikely ever to represent girls and African Americans proportionately because of a reality about IQ tests: more boys score at the high end of the IQ scale (and, it should be said, more score at the low end; girls' IQ variance is smaller). And for reasons that no one understands, African Americans' IQ scores have tended to cluster about a standard deviation below the average—evidence for some that the tests themselves are biased.

Not everyone at the academy embraces a strict IQ-based definition of giftedness. Its curriculum director, Robert Schultz, emphasizes the importance of interpersonal skills, passion and tenacity in long-term success. Still, the Davidsons point out, correctly, that they are serving an underserved population, kids whose high IQs can make them outcasts. The academy provides a home for them and also functions to check their self-regard since they finally compete day to day with kids who are just as bright. Because everyone at Davidson performs so well, says Claire Evans, 12, "other kids can't say, 'Well, I'm better than you because I did this good.' I did that good too!" (Of course, being labeled prodigies in stories like this one probably inflates them, but researchers have found that outside labeling has less effect on your self-concept than where you fit in with peers you see every day.) Going to Davidson has been an adjustment for kids used to "being on the top of the pile," in the words of Colleen Harsin, 36, the academy's director. Harsin has heard Davidsonians arrive at difficult realizations: "I'm not as smart as I thought I was." "Somebody's better at math than I am. That's never happened."

A New Isolation?

No matter their IQs, these are still kids on the rocky promontory of adolescence. Hormones crackle; tempers rise. The boys shove; the girls gossip; a kid hits another kid during volleyball. "They are O.K. with the team sports, but this is a group that really loves the individual sports—the rock climbing was a big hit," says Kathy Dohr, the gym teacher. You do get the sense sometimes that the Davidson students are alone together. An older boy who says he was beaten up at other schools told me, "I can't say I have many friends here, but I'm not hated . . . The school does tend to be pretty much sort of cliquish."

The academy has been good for Annalisee Brasil, even though dividing into two households has been expensive and stressful for the Brasils. She has made friends at the academy and at the university, where this summer she completed a precalculus course so that she can take college calculus in the fall. She has also developed an interest in biochemistry. Socially, Annalisee is finally learning to get along with others in a close-knit setting. "It's been interesting having to deal with that and getting used to, you know, the judgments of other kids," she told me in February. "We get into arguments a lot, because we're all really smart people with opinions, and it doesn't always turn out that great. Sometimes I take things a little too personally. You know, I'm the typical sensitive artist, unfortunately."

The Davidson kids feel less isolated, but have the Davidsons simply created another kind of isolation for their students? When I asked curriculum director Schultz this question, he replied in an e-mail that schools can nurture traits like "civic virtue and community development." And he warned of the alternative: "Essentially these individuals are left to their own devices [in regular schools] and really struggle to find a space for themselves. . . . Some successfully traverse society's pitfalls (for instance, Albert Einstein); others are less successful (for instance, Theodore Kaczynski). In either case, unless performance was noted as deficient (in Einstein's case, he was believed to be a mute) via school personnel, schools did nothing to provide services. This continues today."

But there is something to be said for being left to one's own devices and learning to cope in difficult surroundings. Einstein is a good example: it's a myth that Einstein failed math, but he hated his Munich school, the Luitpold Gymnasium. Like many other gifted kids, he chafed at authority. "The teachers at the elementary school seemed to me like drill sergeants, and the teachers at the gymnasium are like lieutenants," he later said. Einstein was encouraged to leave the school, and he did so at 15. He didn't need a coddling academy to do O.K. later on.

That's not to say the best approach is a cold Dickensian bed. But Einstein's experience does suggest a middle course between moving to

Reno for an élite new school and striking out alone at age 15. Currently, gifted programs too often admit marginal, hardworking kids and then mostly assign field trips and extra essays, not truly accelerated course work pegged to a student's abilities. Ideally, school systems should strive to keep their most talented students through a combination of grade skipping and other approaches (dual enrollment in community colleges, telescoping classwork without grade skipping) that ensure they won't drop out or feel driven away to Nevada. The best way to treat the Annalisee Brasils of the world is to let them grow up in their own communities—by allowing them to skip ahead at their own pace. We shouldn't be so wary of those who can move a lot faster than the rest of us.

**Susan Winebrenner
and Dina Brulles**

➡ **NO**

The Cluster Grouping Handbook

Within the current politics of education, the focus of most educators is on the learning needs of students who score below grade-level standards. There is a general assumption that students who can score well on standardized tests must be learning. When we speak of children being "left behind," we are usually referring to those students who are scoring below desired levels. The need for students performing below grade level to be supported so they can meet and even exceed standards is not in dispute. Equally indisputable are the consequences faced by students, teachers, parents, administrators, and schools when students do not reach these standards. But in our efforts to reach and teach struggling students in order to bring all students to grade-level performance standards, are some students being overlooked or underserved? What attention is focused on learners who readily master the content and are ready to move forward even though many of their classmates are not? Or on those exceptional students who walk in the classroom on the first day of school already able to pass state grade-level tests with exemplary scores? If learning can be described as forward progress from the entry point at the beginning of a school year, then the students who are most likely to be "left behind" when it comes to individual academic growth may be the students with exceptionally high ability—those we call gifted learners.

The field of gifted education is currently experiencing its lowest level of political support since the early 1960s. The launching of *Sputnik I* by the Soviet Union had created intense interest in nurturing America's most capable students so they could help the United States compete with the Soviets in the space race. Now, decades later, attention to No Child Left Behind (NCLB) has significantly reduced political interest in challenging gifted students in our school. Budget cuts have led to the reduction or elimination of gifted-education positions in many school districts. This affects not only gifted students, but also high-performing students not necessarily categorized as gifted. Fewer students in the United States are majoring in science and mathematics than in past years. At the present time, more than 90 percent of the scientists in the world are being educated in Asia.

The United States' position as a world leader may be at greater risk from the challenges to its educational system than from any other factor. Egalitarian issues and budget concerns have led to the elimination of ability grouping in favor of heterogeneous grouping practices. The absence of ability grouping practices has led to the loss of attention to the differentiated learning needs of gifted and high-achieving students. As a consequence, many highly able students are leaving their established public schools in favor of charter schools and homeschooling, taking away from their school districts valuable talent along with considerable tax dollars.

Without visible and continuous support for gifted students, forces now present in the field of gifted education are being impacted. Some state legislatures have abandoned the practice of earmarking funds specifically for gifted education, which leaves the decision of funding gifted services to the discretion of each school or district. Fewer jobs are available for educators who want to specialize in teaching gifted students. Little state or national attention is directed toward the fact that gifted students may be consistently denied regular opportunities to experience at least one year's academic growth for each year they are in school. Most importantly, many parents are being told that their gifted children will experience differentiation in the regular classroom, while the reality is that very little of classroom teachers' efforts at differentiation are being addressed to gifted learners. It takes specialized training for classroom teachers to know how to challenge gifted students. Effective differentiation for the gifted will generally not take place until teachers have noticeable numbers of those students in their classes and until they have received training in how to effectively motivate and challenge them.

Why Meet the Learning Needs of High-Ability Students?

On a day-to-day basis, the highest-ability students usually receive the least amount of the teacher's time. Based on their high test scores and grades, these students are expected to make it on their own or with a minimal amount of guidance.

Looking at students on a bell curve provides a striking illustration of the inequity of this situation, and of what can be lost as a result. While the bell curve has the potential to create unease among some educators, we use it for one purpose only: to demonstrate that the learning needs of students at both ends of the learning continuum are identical.

. . . To teach a class of students, effective teachers usually plan the content, pacing, and quantity of instruction based on what is known about typical students of the age and grade for that class. In a mixed-ability classroom, these are the students in the middle of a heterogeneous group—those students of average abilities on the bell curve. In this same classroom, there will be a number of students who come to the grade level missing many of the basic understandings that typically would have been acquired in earlier grades. These are the students to the left on the bell curve. A third group of students will also be part of this classroom: those who are ahead of their grade-level peers in what they know and can do. These are the students to the right on the bell curve.

When teachers discover struggling students in their class—those below or left of average on the bell curve—they make instant adjustments to their methods of teaching. They may change the pace by moving a bit slower. They may lessen the amount of work for some students. They may change the methods they use to accommodate the learning styles of struggling students. They may change the way in which they interact with the students and try to pair them up with partners who can work well with them. They may adjust the content to reinforce prerequisite concepts that were not learned in earlier grades.

Teachers make these necessary adjustments because the students' learning needs *differ from the average*. Now imagine folding that bell curve in half, left to right. You will clearly see that gifted students are *as far removed from average* on the right side of the curve as are struggling students on the left side. While there are myriad reasons for supporting gifted children's educational growth, this fact alone provides a clear justification for exactly the same intervention to accommodate their needs—an adjustment of pacing, content, workload, and approach to teaching and learning. Gifted students need a faster pace, a smaller amount of practice with grade-level standards, an understanding of their independent work style, a teacher who is comfortable acting as a guide and coach, and opportunities to work with partners who are similar in learning ability, style, and preferences. They need this not because they are gifted, but because they are *not average*.

Gifted students are no more "special" than any others. However, grade-level standards describe what typical students should be able to learn at a certain age. When we accept the fact that gifted children are able to learn at levels that exceed their chronological age expectations, we immediately understand why grade-level standards must be adjusted for them. We do this because, like those students who struggle to meet the standards, gifted students are equally divergent from the "norm."

Meeting the Needs of All Students: The Schoolwide Cluster Grouping Model (SCGM)

We present a unique approach to help schools meet the needs of all students, including those who are gifted. It is called the Schoolwide Cluster Grouping Model (SCGM). The practice of cluster grouping students is gaining popularity in many states, since the method can provide full-time academic services to gifted students without major budget implications and it has the potential to raise achievement for all students in the grade levels that are clustered. With the SCGM, gifted students are grouped into classrooms based on their abilities, while all other students are placed according to their achievement levels. Cluster grouping with the SCGM is different from other cluster grouping methods because the classroom compositions are carefully structured with two main goals: (1) to ensure a balance of abilities throughout the grade level *without returning to the practice of tracking* and (2) to reduce the learning range found in every classroom.

. . . These two goals can be accomplished by dividing the students at a given grade level into five groups. Group 1 represents the identified gifted students who will be in the gifted cluster. Group 2 represents high-achieving students who are not gifted but are very capable learners. These students will be clustered and placed in the classes that do not have the gifted-cluster group. (Clustering gifted students and high-achieving students not identified as gifted in separate classrooms is a key component of the SCGM, which has been shown to expand academic growth for both groups.) Group 3 represents students with average academic performance. Group 4 represents students whose performance is below average, and Group 5 represents students who produce work that falls considerably below grade-level expectations, or those with significant learning challenges. Students who are identified as "twice-exceptional"—those who are gifted and also have a learning challenge—are placed in Group 1, as are identified gifted students who are not fluent in English. . . . Typical gifted-cluster classrooms will include students from Groups 1, 3, and 4; the other classrooms at the grade level will include students from Groups 2, 3, 4, and 5. Ideally, no classroom will include both gifted students *and* students who perform far below average, so the achievement range in all classrooms will be narrower than that of a randomly heterogeneous classroom.

How does this type of clustering differ from tracking? The two main differences are that, in the SCGM, all classes are heterogeneous and all students are provided a varied curriculum. Opportunities for moving faster or going deeper into the curriculum are consistently offered to the entire class, which means there are times when some students in the gifted-cluster group (Group 1) will be experiencing differentiation and times when they won't. There are also times when students not identified as gifted can benefit from available differentiated learning opportunities.

This is different from a tracking system, in which all students are grouped by ability for much of the school day and are rarely exposed to learning experiences that extend their expected achievement ranges. In a tracking system, students are assigned a set curriculum based on their ability level, and they generally do not veer from that curriculum. With schoolwide cluster grouping, every class in the grade level has students with a range of learning abilities and levels. In order to reach that range, the teachers naturally have to modify or extend the grade-level standards.

In the SCGM . . ., all classes have high-performing students. While one or two classes have a cluster of gifted students, all other classes have a cluster of high-achieving students who, while not identified as gifted, can easily serve as positive academic role models. In a cluster model, learning opportunities are open to all students in the class, and teachers use their students' entry points, or readiness, to determine levels and pace of curriculum. Teachers are trained in differentiation and curriculum compacting, students receive ongoing assessment, and the results of schoolwide cluster grouping are continually evaluated.

What the Research Says About Cluster Grouping

Research documenting the benefits of keeping gifted students together in their areas of greatest strength for at least part of the school day supports the philosophy behind schoolwide cluster grouping. Moreover, the research suggests that all students, including those categorized as average and below-average students, thrive when gifted students are placed in their own cluster groups within heterogeneous classes.

The SCGM is an inclusion model in which students with exceptional learning needs are integrated into mixed-ability classrooms and teachers are expected to provide appropriate differentiation opportunities for any students who need them. An inclusion model has already been in use for many years as a method for providing special education services to students who have been identified as having exceptional educational needs. However, it is only when a class has a noticeable group of gifted students—a cluster—that teachers will be most likely to accommodate *their* exceptional educational needs. When there are only one or two gifted students in a class, teachers often tend to assume the students are learning as long as they are getting high grades and, as a result, minimize or overlook their need for expanded learning opportunities. Teachers are also likely to count on these students to help other students with their learning, a practice that robs the gifted students of opportunities to move forward in academic areas.

Clustering requires that teachers differentiate instruction. Differentiation occurs when teachers modify the curriculum and their instructional methods in response to the needs, strengths, learning styles, and interests of individual students so that *all* students have an opportunity to learn at their full potential. To be successful, the gifted-cluster teacher must have ongoing training in how to teach high-ability students in the cluster model. The SCGM creates a setting for providing appropriate instruction that is feasible for teachers and for enhancing the likelihood that differentiation will take place.

The SCGM: Who Benefits, and How?

The SCGM offers a win-win educational approach that benefits all stakeholders in the school community—students, teachers, administrators, and parents. Grouping gifted children in a regular classroom can provide academic, social, and emotional advantages to the students and make teaching gifted students more manageable for teachers. Gifted students feel more comfortable when there are other students like them in the class. They are more likely to choose challenging tasks when they can do that work in the company of other students. Teachers attuned to differentiating instruction are more likely to provide appropriate learning opportunities for gifted students and for other students as well. The school is able to provide a full-time, cost-effective program for gifted students, since their learning needs are being met every day. Parents who are satisfied that their children are experiencing consistent challenge at school are more ready to work cooperatively with the school and the teachers and less likely to remove their children from public education.

Impact of the SCGM on Gifted Students

Gifted students who are clustered demonstrate high achievement because they experience more consistent challenge in their learning activities. Their scores on achievement tests show forward progress—rather than lost ground, as has been the case in some schools where gifted students are not placed in clusters or are not consistently challenged in other ways.

When gifted students are purposefully clustered in otherwise heterogeneous classes, rather than split up so that each class has one or two gifted students, their learning needs are much more likely to be noticed by the teacher. They also enjoy more attention to their social and emotional needs because of the specialized training the teacher receives.

Cluster grouping also makes it more likely that gifted kids will work to their full potential and take advantage of available differentiated learning opportunities, because they will have other students to work with on these advanced learning tasks. Having serious competition from other students like themselves, they begin to develop more realistic perceptions of their abilities and to better understand and accept their learning differences. With so many opportunities to work and learn together, gifted students become more comfortable working at extended levels of complexity and depth in a given subject or topic. Their willingness to take risks in learning experiences increases when they spend time with others who share the same interests, have similar abilities, and can also benefit from the available differentiation opportunities.

Impact of the SCGM on English Language Learners

Cluster grouping offers exciting opportunities for schools to meet the needs of gifted English language learners (ELL students). When gifted students are served only in a pull-out model, gifted students who are not proficient in English are frequently kept out of services because of their inability to work at the same pace and level as the gifted students already proficient in English. With cluster grouping, extended learning opportunities are available in the regular classroom. When ELL students with high learning potential are present in classes where consistent challenge is available, they make faster progress in attaining English fluency and academic achievement.

A significant increase in achievement in students of different ethnic groups can also be expected from using cluster grouping. These findings result from classes in which teachers can be more focused and effective in their teaching. Another reason for the achievement gains is that gifted-education training required for cluster teachers helps the teachers set high expectations for *all* students—expectations to which students respond positively.

Impact of the SCGM on All Students

It has already been noted that students at all ability levels benefit from this model because teachers have more training in how to differentiate the curriculum and the pacing for all types of students, ensuring that learning success can be within the reach of all. A further benefit results from the fact that gifted and high-achieving students are motivated, work more independently and are allowed to spend more learning time on activities that interest and challenge them, opening up more time for teachers to spend with those who need additional assistance.

As teachers become more adept at recognizing giftedness in their students, the number of students they nominate for gifted testing increases yearly in schools that use the SCGM. This is especially noticeable in classes that do *not* have the gifted cluster, demonstrating the benefit of clustering high-achieving children who are *not* identified as gifted in separate classrooms. These classroom structures provide opportunities for the high-achieving students to thrive and emerge as new academic leaders.

Impact of the SCGM on Teachers

Student achievement is positively correlated with effective teaching. The SCGM allows teachers to be more effective because they are teaching a class with a smaller range of learning levels. The system provides opportunities for teachers to more readily respond to the needs of all their students, to challenge gifted students clustered together in mixed-ability classes, and to engage in practices that lead to improved academic achievement for students not identified as gifted, working at or above grade level. As a result, over time with the SCGM, more students in a school are identified as high achievers and fewer as low achievers.

For a school that already has a pull-out program for gifted students, the cluster model makes scheduling out-of-class activities easier. The resource (pull-out) teacher has to work with only one classroom teacher's schedule per grade level instead of the schedules of all the teachers at a particular grade level. The gifted-cluster teacher, whose gifted students venture to another classroom for pull-out services, understands that while they are gone, students who remain should be experiencing activities that reinforce standards the gifted students have already mastered. Therefore, when the students return from the pull-out program, they do not have any "missed" classroom work to "make up," and the teacher does not have the added layer of planning and record keeping that typically comes with makeup work.

When the SCGM is implemented with the goal that all teachers will eventually receive the related staff development, over time it is possible to ensure that all teachers who wish to teach a classroom with a gifted cluster will have the opportunity. At the same time, teachers students in all classrooms benefit from the teachers' facility with differentiating the curriculum to meet student's varied learning needs.

Impact of the SCGM on Administrators

Schools that use the SCGM find that they can still offer valuable services for their gifted students even in the presence of reduced budgets or lack of political support. This helps administrators assure parents of gifted students that their children's learning needs will be served. Cluster grouping actually provides full-time placement and service for gifted students in the schools *without* the cost of creating and maintaining a separate gifted-education program. Gifted students are retained in the public school system and, moreover, gifted education becomes part of the school culture.

When schools take the time to implement the SCGM strategically, carefully planning the groups for cluster classrooms, training as many teachers as possible to implement gifted-education strategies, educating parents about how their children's school experience will be affected, and conducting ongoing student assessments and program evaluations, the result can be a cohesive and budget-friendly schoolwide approach to gifted education that brings the school community together as it raises student achievement levels.

Impact of the SCGM on Parents

Providing a cluster grouping model announces to the community that the school is committed to recognizing and serving its gifted students and enhancing achievement opportunities for all students. As parents of gifted students come to understand how clustering impacts their children's learning opportunities, they see that the schools are providing full-time gifted services, that teachers are responding to their children's needs, and that their gifted children spend time learning with other students of similar ability. Parents of students *not* identified as gifted are also likely to appreciate the opportunities the clustering arrangements and differentiation strategies afford their children. When these parents become familiar with the research that shows how the SCGM facilitates the emergence of new leaders in classes that do not have a gifted cluster, they may realize that, for the first time, their children have more opportunities to demonstrate academic leadership roles. Many students have had this very positive experience as a result of schoolwide cluster grouping.

POSTSCRIPT

Do Gifted and Talented Students Need Special Schools?

The authors describe two very different worlds. The students at Davidson Academy learn how to use the full range of their abilities, stretching each day. Ruf (*Losing Our Minds,* Great Potential Press, Scottsdale, AZ, 2005) identifies five levels of giftedness, emphasizing the critical need for specialized programming. Without this, students become frustrated with the boredom of everyday work and can appear to have behavior problems.

Winebrenner and Brulles present a model that provides the benefits of ability grouping without the isolation of tracking. Educators maintain high levels of professional skill, which benefits all learners. Carol Ann Tomlinson, who writes extensively about differentiated instruction, underscores the need to support teachers through the hard work of continuous differentiation.

Efficacy research is not conclusive, partially due to the inability to use control groups, but Schroth (P&K, 2008) finds one absolute: any service is better than none. As described, cluster models benefit a range of students, and more students are identified as high-achievers. They are, indeed, "financially friendly." On the other hand, students in public special schools with a disciplinary focus outperform gifted peers in all other learning environments. The logistics of residential schools, however, are frequently impractical.

Two other aspects of gifted education demand consideration: underrepresentation of minorities and of those who are twice-exceptional. Both must be considered.

The underrepresentation of ethnically diverse students in gifted programs is a long-acknowledged fact (Gentry, Hu, & Thomas, P&K, 2008). This is especially the case with African American boys and Latino children. Although Asians are frequently described as "overrepresented" in gifted education, a finer breakdown reveals that this is not uniformly so of all Asian groups. Ford (*Journal for the Education of the Gifted,* 2003) is concerned that the effects of poverty can mask the strengths of a gifted child. She advises a move away from traditional, normed IQ tests to alternative measures which take into consideration the complex contexts of student lives.

Context is also critical for twice-exceptional children—those who are both gifted and have a disability. An illuminating study by the National Education Association (http://www.nea.org.epooialod, 2006) found three basic categories of twice-exceptional children. First are those who have been formally identified as gifted, but not as having a disability: their giftedness masks the disability (think of a very bright child with a learning disability). Second are those formally identified as having a disability, but not as gifted: the disability masks the giftedness (consider someone's first impression of Helen Keller). The third group of children may not have been formally identified under either category: the characteristics combine to present the appearance of an average student.

Concern for gifted education has another dimension given NCLB's target of universal proficiency by 2013–14. Especially in working class schools, Carnevale (*Education Week*, 2007) warns that gifted students are left behind as the majority struggle to get to "average." In more affluent districts, parents may focus more on college entrance standards, raising the standards beyond the basic.

Each of these issues becomes more compelling when funds are in short supply. Cloud challenges us to explain why society's commitment to the gifted should not be at least as large its commitment to athletes, or to those with disabilities. And yet, according to the Javits Web site (http://www.ed.gov/programs/javits/awards.html), "In 2007, the Javits appropriation was cut substantially. As a result, a new competition . . . will not be held. Future competitions are contingent upon future appropriations." What is the future for our gifted children? Can we afford to wait to find out? Can they?

Contributors to This Volume

EDITOR

DR. MARYANN BYRNES is an associated professor in the Graduate School of Education at the University of Massachusetts–Boston. Dr. Byrnes consults with schools and districts on issues of policy, the implementation of IDEA, program evaluation, and professional development. Dr. Byrnes served as a special education administrator for 18 years, having taught at elementary, middle, and high school levels. She is immediate past president of the Massachusetts Federation of the Council for Exceptional Children and past president of the Massachusetts Association of Administrators of Special Education (ASE). Dr. Byrnes earned her undergraduate degree at the University of Chicago, her masters degree at Northwestern University, and her doctorate at Rutgers University. Dr. Byrnes' current research focuses on the use of explicit, unambiguous accommodations for students with disabilities.

AUTHORS

JAMES B. ADAMS is the father of a young girl with autism, diagnosed in 1994, and that is what led him to shift much of his research emphasis to autism, focusing on biological causes and treatments. He is currently a full professor in the department of chemical and materials engineering at Arizona State University. He created and teaches a course on heavy metal toxicity, focused on lead and mercury toxicity.

HOWARD S. ADELMAN is professor of psychology and co-director of the School Mental Health Project and the National Center for Mental Health in Schools at UCLA. He began his professional career as a remedial classroom teacher in 1960 and received his PhD in psychology from UCLA in 1966. He directed the Fernald School and Laboratory at UCLA from 1973 to 1986 and has co-directed the School Mental Health Project since 1986.

STEVEN ADELSHEIM is the director of New Mexico School Mental Health Programs.

ARTHUR ALLEN is a Washington-area writer whose work appears in *The Washington Post* magazine, the *New Republic,* and *Salon.com.*

LEWIS M. ANDREWS is executive director of the Yankee Institute for Public Policy at Trinity College, a Connecticut research and educational institute.

DR. RUSSELL A. BARKLEY is the director of psychology and professor of psychiatry and neurology at the University of Massachusetts Medical Center, and has written 14 books and more than 150 scientific articles related to the nature, assessment, and treatment of ADHD. As the leading expert on the subject, he speaks eloquently and passionately about the need to recognize the complexities of the disorder and to treat it properly.

JENNIFER BOOHER-JENNINGS is a doctoral candidate in the Department of Sociology at Columbia University in New York City. Her research focuses on accountability, school organization, and school choice.

ELLEN BRANTLINGER is a professor emeritus of the School of Education at Indiana University. She earned her B.S. at Antioch College in 1963 and her Ed.D. at Indiana University in 1977. She is an expert on how parents, educators, and caregivers view the sexuality of the mentally handicapped and on the sterilization of people with mental disabilities. She is the author of *Fighting for Darla* (1994) and *The Politics of Social Class in Secondary School* (1993).

RACHEL BROWN-CHIDSEY is an associate professor of school psychology at the University of Southern Maine. Her research areas include curriculum-based measurement, response to intervention, and scientifically based reading instruction methods.

MICHELE ST. PETER BRIGHAM is the choral music director and special education instructor at Western Albemarle High School and adjunct faculty in the School of Continuing Education and Professional Studies at the University of Virginia.

DINA BRULLES is director of the Gifted Education Department in the Paradise Valley Unified School District in Arizona and a faculty associate of the College of Education at Arizona State University, where she teaches graduate courses in gifted education. Dina currently serves as president of the Arizona Association for Gifted and Talented (AAGT), and vice president of the national gifted organization, Supporting Emotional Needs of the Gifted (SENG).

JOHN CLOUD is a staff writer for *Time Magazine,* where he has worked since 1997.

GERALD COLES is an educational psychologist and full-time researcher, writer, and lecturer on literacy, learning, and psychology. He is the author of numerous articles in education, psychology, and psychiatry journals, and his 1978 *Harvard Educational Review* paper on learning disabilities was identified by the Institute of Scientific Information as a "Citation Classic" because of the number of times it has been cited and because of its influence on other authors in the field.

CHRISTOPHER T. CROSS is a senior fellow at the Center for Education Policy and a distinguished senior fellow at the Education Commission of the States. During his 32 years in Washington, DC, he served in both the executive and the legislative branches, as an assistant secretary at the U.S. Department of Education, the Republican staff director of the House Committee on Education and Labor, and as deputy assistant secretary in the old Department of Health, Education and Welfare.

DONALD D. DESHLER is a professor of special education and the director of the Center for Research on Learning at the University of Kansas. He also serves as the co-director of the National Research Center on Learning Disabilities, funded by the Office of Special Education Programs in the U.S. Department of Education.

M. SUZANNE DONOVAN is a senior program officer at the National Research Council's Commission on Behavioral and Social Sciences and Education and study director for the Committee on Minority Representation in Special Education. Her interests span issues of education and public policy. She has a Ph.D. from the University of California, Berkeley, School of Public Policy, and was previously on the faculty of Columbia University's School of Public and International Affairs.

STEPHEN M. EDELSON has practiced medicine for more than 20 years. As an autoimmune specialist and founder of the Edelson Center for Environmental and Preventative Medicine in Atlanta, he has successfully treated thousands of patients using innovative and effective alternative therapies. Dr. Edelson lives and works in Atlanta, Georgia.

JEFFREY EVANS does research with the Institute for Applied Psychometrics (IAP) and the Woodcock-Johnson development team. He has published in the area of reading achievement. Jeff is currently working on educational test development and writing projects with IAP. He also serves on the volunteer board of directors of United Cerebral Palsy (UCP) of Central Minnesota. Jeff holds a master's in communications disorders from St. Cloud State University.

SUSAN C. FAIRCLOTH is an assistant professor at Pennsylvania State University. Dr. Faircloth's publications and research interests center on leadership, special education, higher education, cultural diversity, and the education of American Indians and Alaska Natives.

GREG FORSTER is a senior research associate at the Manhattan Institute's Education Research Office. He is the co-author of several education studies and op-ed articles. He received a Ph.D. with distinction in political science from Yale University in May 2002, and his B.A. from the University of Virginia, where he double-majored in political and social thought and rhetoric and communications studies, in 1995.

WILLIAM C. FRICK is an assistant professor at the University of Oklahoma.

DOUGLAS FUCHS is a professor of special education at Peabody College of Vanderbilt University. He also serves as the co-director of the National Research Center on Learning Disabilities, funded by the Office of Special Education Programs in the U.S. Department of Education.

LYNN S. FUCHS is the Nicholas Hobbs Professor of Special Education and Human Development at Vanderbilt University, where she also co-directs the Kennedy Center Reading Clinic. She has conducted research on assessment methods for enhancing instructional planning and on instructional methods for improving reading and math outcomes for students with learning disabilities.

PAUL J. GERBER is a professor in the Department of Foundations of Education and the Department of Special Education and Disability Policy, as well as a clinical professor of psychiatry, at Virginia Commonwealth University.

RUSSELL GERSTEN is the executive director of Instructional Research Group. Currently, he directs the mathematics component of the Center of Instruction, a comprehensive technical assistance center for No Child Left Behind. He is also a professor emeritus in the College for Education at the University of Oregon. He received his Ph.D. in special education from the University of Oregon in 1978.

TEMPLE GRANDIN is a designer of livestock handling facilities and a professor of animal science at Colorado State University. Facilities she has designed are located in the United States, Canada, Europe, Mexico, Australia, New Zealand, and other countries. In North America, almost half of the cattle are handled in a center track restrainer system that she designed for meat plants. She obtained her B.A. at Frankin Pierce College and her M.S. in animal science at Arizona State University. Dr. Grandin received her Ph.D. in animal science from the University of Illinois in 1989.

JAY P. GREENE is a senior fellow at the Manhattan Institute for Policy Research, where he conducts research and writes about education policy. He has conducted evaluations of school choice and accountability programs in Florida, Charlotte, Milwaukee, Cleveland, and San Antonio. He has also investigated the effects of school choice on civic values and integration.

WILLIAM E. GUSTASHAW III is an assistant professor in the College of Education, Special Education and Rehabilitation Counseling at the University of Virginia. His research interests include effective instructional practices for students with disabilities, teacher education, and special education policy.

KAREN R. HARRIS is the Currey-Ingram Professor of Special Education and Literacy at Vanderbilt University, Nashville, Tennessee. Dr. Harris' research focuses on the theoretical and intervention issues in the development of academic and self-regulation strategies among students who are at risk and those with severe learning challenges such as learning disabilities and attention deficit hyperactivity disorder.

J. AMOS HATCH is a professor of early childhood education at the University of Tennessee-Knoxville. Dr. Hatch has written/edited three books on qualitative methods and served a four-year term as editor of the International Journal of Qualitative Studies of Education.

JOHN HOCKENBERY is an award-winning television commentator, a radio host and a foreign correspondent, who became a paraplegic in an auto accident when he was 19. He lives in Brooklyn, New York, with his wife, Alison, and their two sets of twins—Zoe and Olivia, and Zachary and Regan.

ROBERT H. HORNER is a professor in the department of special education at the University of Oregon, Eugene. Dr. Horner has published over 150 professional papers and six texts. He currently co-directs the OSEP Technical Assistance Center on Positive Behavior Interventions and Supports and the OSEP Research and Demonstration Center on School-wide Behavior Support. Dr. Horner also co-directs the Positive Behavior Research and Support research unit at the University of Oregon.

JAMES M. KAUFFMAN is the Charles S. Robb Professor of Education at the University of Virginia in Charlottesville, Virginia, where he also serves as director of the doctoral program in special education. His primary areas of interest in special education are emotional and behavioral disorders and learning disabilities. He is co-editor of *Behavioral Disorders*, the journal of the Council for Children with Behavioral

Disorders, and he is co-principal investigator of the Center of Minority Research in Special Education (COMRISE). Among his many publications are *Characteristics of Emotional and Behavioral Disorders of Children and Youth*, 7th ed. (Prentice Hall PTR, 2000) and *The Least Restrictive Environment: Its Origins and Interpretations in Special Education*, co-authored with Jean B. Crockett (Lawrence Erlbaum, 1999). He received his M.Ed. in teaching in the elementary school from Washburn University in 1966 and his Ed.D. in special education from the University of Kansas in 1969.

NATHANIEL S. LEHRMAN is Clinical Director (retired) at the Kingsboro Psychiatric Center in Brooklyn, New York.

CATHY G. LITTY is an associate professor in the Department of Special Education/Human Services at Western Carolina University.

DANIEL J. LOSEN is a research associate with The Civil Rights Project at Harvard University and the principal investigator for the Conference on Minority Issues in Special Education in Public Schools. He is presently developing research and policy fact sheets for members of Congress on the topics of dropouts and Title I of the Elementary and Secondary School Act. Before becoming an attorney, he taught in public schools for nearly ten years and founded an alternative public school.

KANYA MAHITIVANICHCHA is a research analyst at the American Institutes for Research.

AMY DOCKSER MARCUS is a Boston-based staff reporter for the New York bureau of the *Wall Street Journal*. Born in Boston, Massachusetts, Marcus earned a bachelor's degree from Harvard University.

KEVIN S. McGREW is the director of the Institute on Applied Psychometrics (IAP) and is currently a visiting professor in the Department of Educational Psychology at the University of Minnesota. Dr. McGrew has extensive experience in both clinical (1:1) and large-scale assessment, and in data management and analysis. Dr. McGrew has published over sixty journal articles, books, or book chapters covering many areas of special education.

JAMES McLESKEY is a professor and chair of the Department of Special Education, University of Florida. His state and federal grants have addressed school reform and school improvement, preparation of teachers to meet the needs of a diverse range of students in general education classrooms, and preparation of leadership personnel in general and special education.

BARBARA MINER is a former managing editor of the Milwaukee-based newspaper *Rethinking Schools* and has two children in the Milwaukee public schools. She recently co-edited the book *Failing Our Kids: Why the Testing Craze Won't Fix Our Schools*.

ELIZABETH MOORE is research coordinator at the Center for School Mental Health Analysis and Action, University of Maryland School of Medicine.

ROBERT MULLIGAN is the director of special education and counseling in the Point Pleasant Beach (New Jersey) Public Schools.

NATIONAL COUNCIL ON DISABILITY (NCD) is an independent federal agency that makes recommendations to the president and Congress on issues affecting 54 million Americans with disabilities. The NCD is composed of 15 members appointed by the president and confirmed by the Senate. The NCD's overall purpose is to promote policies, programs, practices, and procedures that guarantee equal opportunity for all individuals with disabilities, regardless of the nature or severity of the disability, and to empower individuals with disabilities to achieve economic self-sufficiency, independent living, and inclusion and integration into all aspects of society.

SAMUEL L. ODOM is an assistant professor of education and Otting Professor of Special Education in the School of Education, Indiana University, Bloomington.

GARY ORFIELD is a professor at the Harvard Graduate School of Education and director of its Project on School Desegregation. His report, "The Growth of Segregation in American Schools: Changing Patterns of Separation and Poverty since 1968," was recently issued to the National School Board Association.

ROD PAIGE is the seventh U.S. Secretary of Education. Paige rallied the department to create the Blueprint for Management Excellence in order to build an organization worthy of the taxpayer's trust and the president's vision—a vision grounded in the belief that good government is not only closer to the people, but also more accountable to the people. Dr. Paige earned a bachelor's degree from Jackson State University in his home state. He then earned both a master's and a doctoral degree from Indiana University.

THOMAS PARRISH is the managing director of the Education and Human Development Program at the American Institutes for Research (AIR) and is a consulting professor in the School of Education at Stanford University.

LYNDA A. PRICE is an associate professor of special education at Temple University. She received her M.A. from the University of Minnesota in 1979 and her Ph.D. in 1995. Her professional interests include qualitative research methods and design in special education.

BERNARD RIMLAND is a research psychologist (Ph.D.) and a director of the Autism Research Institute, which he founded in 1967. He is also the founder of the Autism Society of America (1965) and the editor of the *Autism Research Review International*. His book, *Infantile Autism: The Syndrome and Its Implication for a Neural Theory of Behavior* (1964), is widely credited with changing the view that autism is an emotional illness, caused by destructive mothers, to the current recognition in the field of psychiatry that autism is a biological disorder.

BLAIR ROGER is an educational consultant based in Oakland, California.

DORENE D. ROSS is a professor in the School of Teaching and Learning, University of Florida. She also consults with school districts involved in restructuring and the establishment of collaborative professional learning environments in schools serving children of poverty. Dorene helped to design and implement the Unified Elementary ProTeach program.

MARCIA RUBIN is the director of Research & Sponsored Programs at the American School Health Association.

WAYNE SAILOR is a clinical psychologist, a professor of special education, and an associate director of the Beach Center on Disability at the University of Kansas, Lawrence.

BENNETT A. SHAYWITZ is professor of pediatrics and neurology and chief of pediatric neurology at the Yale University School of Medicine. Dr. Shaywitz was a pioneer in recognizing the great potential of functional brain imaging and led a national effort to apply this technology—especially functional magnetic resonance imaging (fMRI)—to the study of reading and dyslexia in children and adults. The author of over 300 scientific papers, Dr. Shaywitz has received many honors for his contributions to the understanding of the basic neurobiology of reading and dyslexia.

SALLY E. SHAYWITZ is professor of pediatrics at the Yale University School of Medicine. She has devoted her career to helping children and adults who are dyslexic; her research has provided the basis for understanding this disorder. Dr. Shaywitz is the author of over 200 scientific articles, chapters, and books, including *Overcoming Dyslexia: A New and Complete Science-Based Program for Reading Problems at Any Level* (Vintage, 2005).

TOM E.C. SMITH is professor of special education and department head of the department of curriculum and instruction at the University of Arkansas. His research interests include disability law and inclusion.

MARK W. STEEGE is a professor and clinical coordinator in the School Psychology Program at the University of Southern Maine. Dr. Steege earned his doctorate at the University of Iowa and completed postdoctoral work as a pediatric psychologist at the University of Iowa College of Medicine.

LINDA TAYLOR is co-director of the School Mental Health Project and the National Center for Mental Health in Schools at UCLA. Throughout her career, she has been concerned with a wide range of psychosocial and educational problems experienced by children and adolescents. Her early experiences included community agency work.

BRUCE THOMPSON is a professor and a distinguished research fellow in the department of educational psychology at Texas A&M University, College Station.

H. RUTHERFORD TURNBULL III is the co-founder and co-director of the Beach Center on Disability at the University of Kansas. He is a professor of special education and former courtesy professor of law there, and his research interests include special education law and policy, disability policy generally, and, most recently, the effects of federal policy on treatment issues raised by the Schiavo cases.

U.S. DEPARTMENT OF EDUCATION promotes educational excellence for all Americans. Created in 1980 by combining offices from several federal agencies, the USDE remains true to its original directive to ensure equal access to education and to promote educational excellence throughout the nation.

ROSALIND AND JOE VARGO, mother and father of Ro Vargo, use their voices to tell a powerful story of their daughter's success in fully inclusive educational programs, from kindergarten through college.

MARK D. WEIST is professor and director of the Division of Child and Adolescent Psychiatry in the Center for School Mental Health Analysis and Action, University of Maryland School of Medicine.

ANDREW L. WILEY joined the Center for Social Development and Education (CSDE) in 2005. Mr. Wiley has completed his doctoral coursework in special education at the University of Virginia and is currently completing his dissertation. Mr. Wiley has a bachelor's degree and a master of teaching degree from the University of Virginia. He has worked as a behavior resource teacher in an intensive center program for elementary students with emotional/behavioral disorders, as an autism resource teacher, and as a behavior specialist in Fairfax County, Virginia. Mr. Wiley has taught graduate courses in behavior management and methods for teaching exceptional children.

SUSAN WINEBRENNER is a full-time consultant who works with school districts to help them translate current educational research into classroom practice. She received her B.S. in education and her master's degree in curriculum and instruction from the University of Wisconsin.

MARCUS A. WINTERS is a senior fellow at the Manhattan Institute for Policy Research, where he conducts research and writes about education policy.

GORDON WROBEL has worked as a psychologist for Minneapolis Public Schools and the state of Minnesota.

NAOMI ZIGMOND is a professor in the School of Education, University of Pittsburgh. He earned his Ph.D. in learning disabilities from Northwestern University in 1966, his M.A. from Northwestern University in 1963, and his B.S. from McGill University in 1962. In 1997, Dr. Zigmond received the Research Award from the Council for Exceptional Children in recognition of research that has contributed significantly to the body of knowledge about the education of exceptional children and youth.